Camel in Action

Camel in Action

CLAUS IBSEN
JONATHAN ANSTEY

MANNING

Greenwich
(74° w. long.)

For online information and ordering of this and other Manning books, please visit
www.manning.com. The publisher offers discounts on this book when ordered in quantity.
For more information, please contact

    Special Sales Department
    Manning Publications Co.
    180 Broad Street, Suite 1323
    Stamford, CT 06901
    Email: orders@manning.com

Manning Publications Co.	Development editor:	Cynthia Kane
180 Broad Street, Suite 1323	Copyeditor:	Andy Carroll
Stamford, CT 06901	Cover designer:	Marija Tudor
	Typesetter:	Gordan Salinovic

ISBN 978-1-935182-36-8
Printed in the United States of America
1 2 3 4 5 6 7 8 9 10 – MAL – 15 14 13 12 11 10

To the Apache Camel community
May this book be a helpful companion on your journeys with Camel

brief contents

contents

foreword

Languages are a critical aspect of software development. They give us the vocabulary to express what a program should do. They force us to encode our requirements in precise and non-ambiguous terms. Lastly, they enable the sharing of knowledge between developers. No, I'm not talking about Java, Haskell, or PL/1. I'm talking about the languages we use to communicate from human to human, from developer to developer, or from end user to product manager. For a long time, the world of enterprise integration (or *EAI*, as it was commonly known in the "dark ages of integration") lacked such a vocabulary. Each vendor offered a proprietary solution, which not only failed to integrate at a technical level with other vendors' offerings, but also used a different language to describe the main components and their functions. This not only caused confusion, but was also a key inhibitor to creating a community of developers that could span the vast space of enterprise integration. Each "tribe" was essentially held hostage by the language bestowed upon them. Ironically, integration developers were faced with the same "tower of Babel" problem that their software was designed to solve!

Establishing a common vocabulary that enables knowledge sharing and collaboration was the key motivator for us to write Enterprise Integration Patterns (EIPs). Each of the 65 patterns has a descriptive name, which represents the solution to a design challenge in the integration space. Besides supporting effective communication, this vocabulary also raises the level of abstraction at which we can describe integration problems and solutions.

A shared vocabulary is a big step forward, but a giant step we could not imagine at the time was that our language would spur the development of a whole family of open source messaging and enterprise service bus (ESB) products. These tools embrace the EIP vocabulary by implementing many patterns directly in the platform. With Apache Camel, a Splitter pattern translates directly into a "split" element in the Camel DSL. We couldn't have wished for a more direct translation of the pattern language into an implementation platform.

Claus and Jon bring the saga to a grand finale by showing us how to use the Camel pattern language to compose real-life messaging solutions. In doing so, they not only cover fundamental concepts like routing and transformation, but also dig into often-neglected parts of the development process, including testing, monitoring, and deploying. They find the right balance of the pattern language, Camel core concepts, and running code to help you build easy-to-understand and robust messaging solutions.

GREGOR HOHPE
COAUTHOR OF *ENTERPRISE INTEGRATION PATTERNS*
WWW.EAIPATTERNS.COM

foreword

I was one of the original founders of both Apache ActiveMQ (an open source high-performance message broker) and ServiceMix (an open source ESB based on JBI and OSGi). I found that Enterprise Integration Patterns were becoming increasingly central to what we were doing on these projects and how we were using them; the only difference was the context and technologies with which we were using the patterns.

There have been many libraries and frameworks over the years to help with integration. But frequently the concepts behind the Enterprise Integration Patterns get transformed into some complex class hierarchies or objects that need to be wired together just so, and the original intentions and patterns are often lost. The developer is forced from then on to focus on the low-level detail and some complex class library API, losing the bigger picture and patterns.

Integration is hard and once you start down the path of integrating things together the code can very easily mushroom; being able to easily comprehend, communicate, adapt, and maintain integration solutions is vital to be able to solve integration problems efficiently in an agile way.

So we decided it was time for a new integration framework that put the EIPs at its core and tried to raise the abstraction level so that developers could describe declaratively in very concise terms what Enterprise Integration Patterns they wanted to use in a simple domain-specific language. Using a convention over configuration approach, developers would declaratively describe what they wanted to do, using the Enterprise Integration Pattern language; it would be both quick and easy to get things done and also very easy for any developer on a team (including the developer himself months after writing the code!) to understand and adapt the code.

There are many different places we wanted to use the EIPs; whether in a stand-alone application, a web services stack, an enterprise message broker like Apache ActiveMQ, or inside a full-blown ESB like Apache ServiceMix, so we wanted a light-weight framework that was middleware agnostic that users could embed anywhere they wanted it. We also wanted developers to focus on the Enterprise Integration Patterns first and foremost and not to get lost in the weeds of different middleware APIs and technologies.

We also wanted developers to be able to use whatever DSL flavor they wished (whether Java, XML, Groovy, Ruby, Scala, or whatever) and yet, at runtime, still be able to introspect the framework and understand all of the EIPs that were being used. They would be able to visualize the core patterns to the team at any point in the project life-cycle, auto-document the patterns, or even support things like graphical editing of the Enterprise Integration Patterns at design time or runtime.

So Apache Camel was born, and since then we've seen the codebase, community, and number of components, technologies, and data formats grow massively as more and more developers have found Apache Camel an ideal way to design, implement, and maintain the Enterprise Integration Patterns.

In this book Claus and Jon describe the Enterprise Integration Patterns and the concepts which underlie Apache Camel. Then they walk you through how to take the concepts and apply them to many real-life scenarios to provide scalable and efficient solutions that are easy to understand and quick to adapt to your integration needs. I hope you'll enjoy reading this book as much as I did!

JAMES STRACHAN
CO-FOUNDER OF APACHE ACTIVEMQ
CAMEL, AND SERVICEMIX
TECHNICAL DIRECTOR FUSESOURCE.COM
HTTP://MACSTRAC.BLOGSPOT.COM

preface

Developers who have done integration work know what a difficult task it can be. IT systems may not have been designed to be accessible from other systems, and if they were designed for interoperability, they may not speak the protocol you need. As a developer, you end up spending a considerable amount of time working with the plumbing of the integration protocols to open up the IT systems to the outside world.

In *Enterprise Integration Patterns*, Gregor Hohpe and Bobby Woolf gave us a standard way to describe, document, and implement complex integration problems. Developers and architects alike can use this common language and catalog of solutions to tackle their integration problems. But although Hohpe and Woolf gave us the theory, the industry still needed an open source implementation of the book.

James Strachan, Rob Davies, Guillaume Nodet, and Hiram Chirino, within the open source communities of Apache ActiveMQ and Apache ServiceMix, brought the idea of Camel to life. Apache Camel is essentially an implementation of the EIP book, and in the summer of 2007 version 1.0 was released.

Apache Camel is an integration framework whose main goal is to make integration easier. It implements many of the EIP patterns and allows you to focus on solving business problems, freeing you from the burden of plumbing. Using connectivity components has never been easier, because you don't have to implement JMS message listeners or FTP clients, deal with converting data between protocols, or mess with the raw details of HTTP requests. All of this is taken care of by Camel, which makes mediation and routing as easy as writing a few lines of Java code or XML in a Spring XML file.

Apache Camel has since become very popular and today has an ever-growing community. As with many open source projects that become popular, a logical next step is for someone to write a book about the project. Hadrian Zbarcea, the Project Management Committee chair of the Apache Camel project, realized this, and in early 2009 he contacted Manning to discuss the need for such a book. Hadrian got in touch with me (Claus Ibsen), inviting me in as a coauthor. It was perfect timing, as I was taking over from James Strachan as the lead on Apache Camel. Later that year, Hadrian had to step down as an author, but he invited Jonathan Anstey in as his replacement, to ensure the project could continue.

Jonathan and I are both integration specialists working for FuseSource, which is the professional company that offers enterprise services around various Apache projects. This book is written by the people who wrote the Camel code, which ensures you have the most updated Camel book on the market.

Writing this book has been a very intense journey, proven by the fact that we were able to complete the manuscript in a year. It took a long time to implement the examples and to ensure that the accompanying source code is of the highest standard. But the result is a great source of examples that should inspire you to get the best out of Camel, and it should be a good starting point for your Camel projects. While we were writing this book, we were also implementing new features in Camel, which often meant we had to go back and revise the material along the way. But we have kept up, and this book uses the latest Camel release at the time of writing (Camel 2.5).

We hope this book brings great value to you and helps you prosper in the Camel community.

Claus Ibsen

acknowledgments

We first want to thank Cynthia Kane, our development editor at Manning, who put up with our many missed deadlines and gave great feedback during the writing process. We'd also like to thank our awesome copy editor, Andy Carroll, for catching an amazing number of grammatical errors in the early revisions of the book. The greater Manning team deserves kudos as well; they've made for a very pleasant writing experience over the past year and a half.

Big thanks to our team of reviewers, who provided invaluable feedback during various stages of the book's development: Bruce Snyder, Charles Moulliard, Christophe Avare, Christopher Hunt, Domingo Suarez Torres, Doug Tillman, Fintan Bolton, Gordon Dickens, Gregor Hohpe, Jeroen Benckhuijsen, John S. Griffon, Kevin Jackson, Marco Ughetti, Martin Gilday, Martin Krasser, Michael Nash, Mick Knutson, Roman Kalukiewicz, Tijs Rademakers, and Willem Jiang.

Special thanks to Willem Jiang for being our technical proofreader, catching those bugs we missed, and helping improve the source code for the book.

Thanks to Martin Krasser for contributing appendix E, which is all about using Camel from the Akka project. We couldn't think of a better person to write about Camel and Akka.

We'd also like to thank Hadrian Zbarcea for getting this book project started—who knows when this book would have been written or by whom if he hadn't gotten us together!

We'd like to thank Gregor Hohpe and James Strachan for writing the forewords to our book. Gregor's book, *Enterprise Integration Patterns*, has been one of our favorite tech books for years now, so it's an honor to have Gregor on board to write the fore-word. Without the EIP book, Apache Camel would look a lot different than it does today, if it existed at all.

In our opinion, James is an inspiration to many developers out there—including us. He has co-founded tons of successful open source projects; Camel is just one of them. If James and the other Apache Camel co-founders had not decided to create Camel, we wouldn't be writing this book. So, again, thanks!

Finally, we'd like to give a big warm thank you to the community. Without the community, the Apache Camel project wouldn't be as successful as it is today. In fact, without the success, both of us would have different kinds of jobs today, which wouldn't involve hacking on Camel all day along.

CLAUS

I would like to thank my beautiful wife, Christina, for her understanding of the long hours I needed to spend during evenings and weekends working on the book. Knowing that you would never let my hand go, that the family life is safe and secure, is exactly the support any writer needs in taking up such a big challenge as writing a book.

A warm thank you goes to our dog, Bambi, who patiently sleeps in my office, and occasionally wakes up and politely "asks" me for a break and a walk. I must admit many of the ideas and thoughts behind this book came to me during my walks with Bambi.

JON

I would like to thank my amazing wife, Lisa, for the patience, support, and encouragement I needed throughout the writing of this book. It simply would not have happened if it wasn't for you. To Georgia, my beautiful daughter: thank you for cheering me up when the writing got the better of me. I love you both!

about this book

Apache Camel exists because integration is hard and Camel's creators wanted to make things easier for users. Camel's online documentation serves as a reference for its many features and components. In contrast, this book aims to guide readers through these features, starting with the simple points and building up to advanced Camel usage by the end of the book. Throughout the book, Camel's features are put into action in real-life scenarios.

Roadmap

The book is divided into three parts:

- Part 1—First steps
- Part 2—Core Camel
- Part 3—Out in the wild

Part 1 starts off simple by introducing you to Camel's core functionality and concepts, and it presents some basic examples.

- Chapter 1 introduces you to Camel and explains what Camel is and where it fits into the bigger enterprise software picture. You'll also learn the concepts and terminology of Camel.
- Chapter 2 covers Camel's main feature, which is message routing. The Java DSL and Spring DSL are covered as are several enterprise integration patterns (EIPs). EIPs are basically canned solutions to integration problems.

Building on part 1's foundation, part 2 covers the core features of Camel. You'll need many of these features when using Camel.

- Chapter 3 explains how Camel can help you transform your data to different formats while it's being routed.
- In chapter 4 we take a look at how you can use Java beans in Camel.
- Chapter 5 covers all of Camel's error-handling features.
- In chapter 6 we look at the testing facilities shipped with Camel. You can use these features for testing your own Camel applications or applications based on other stacks.
- Chapter 7 covers the most heavily used components among Camel's large selection of components.
- Chapter 8 looks in depth at five of the most complex EIPs.

In part 3 we cover the topics that are useful when you've gained a better understanding of Camel from the earlier chapters.

- Chapter 9 explains how you can use transactions in your Camel applications.
- In chapter 10 we discuss how to deal with concurrency and scalability in your Camel applications.
- Chapter 11 explains how to create new Camel projects, which could be Camel applications, custom components, or interceptors. This chapter doesn't require much additional Camel knowledge, so you could read this right after part 1. The Scala DSL is also touched on here.
- In chapter 12 we cover how to manage and monitor Camel applications. Among other things, how to read the Camel logs and how to control Camel with JMX are covered.
- In chapter 13 we discuss the many ways to start and stop Camel. Deployment to several of the most popular containers is also discussed.
- Chapter 14 covers what we consider extra features of Camel: routing with beans and using remoting to hide Camel APIs. We consider this extra because these features do routing without using any of Camel's DSLs and in some cases with no Camel APIs. They take a different approach than what was discussed throughout the book.

The appendixes at the end of the book contain useful reference material on the Simple expression language, expressions and predicates, the producer and consumer templates, and the Camel community. Appendix E is written by Martin Krasser and shows how to use Akka with Camel.

Who should read this book

We wrote this book primarily for developers who have found the online Camel documentation lacking and needed a guidebook that explained things in a more detailed and organized way. Although we mainly targeted existing Camel users, *Camel in Action* is a great way to start learning about Camel. Experienced engineers and architects are also encouraged to read this book, as it explains advanced Camel concepts that you just can't find elsewhere. Test and Q&A engineers will find Camel and this book useful as a means of driving tests that require communication with various transports and APIs. System administrators, too, may find the management, monitoring, and deployment topics of great value.

Camel's features are focused on the enterprise business community and its needs, but it's also a generic and very useful integration toolkit. Any Java developer who needs to send a message somewhere will probably find Camel and this book useful.

Code conventions

The code examples in this book are abbreviated in the interest of space. In particular, some of the namespace declarations in the XML configurations and package imports in Java classes have been omitted. We encourage you to use the source code when working with the examples. The line lengths of some of the examples exceed the page width, and in cases like these, the ➥ marker is used to indicate that a line has been wrapped for formatting.

All source code in listings or in text is in a `fixed-width font like this` to separate it from ordinary text. Code annotations accompany many of the listings, highlighting important concepts. In some cases, numbered bullets link to explanations that follow the listing.

Source code downloads

The source code for the examples in this book is available online from the publisher's website at http://www.manning.com/CamelinAction, as well as from this site: http://code.google.com/p/camelinaction.

Software requirements

The following software is required to run the examples:

- JDK 5 or better
- Maven 2.2.1 or better
- Apache Camel 2.5 or better

Apache Camel can be downloaded from its official website: http://camel.apache.org/download.html.

All the examples can be run using Maven. Chapter 1 shows you how to get started with Maven and run the examples.

Author Online

The purchase of *Camel in Action* includes free access to a private web forum run by Manning Publications, where you can make comments about the book, ask technical questions, and receive help from the authors and from other users. To access the forum and subscribe to it, point your web browser to http://www.manning.com/CamelinAction. This page provides information on how to get on the forum once you're registered, what kind of help is available, and the rules of conduct on the forum.

Manning's commitment to our readers is to provide a venue where a meaningful dialogue between individual readers and between readers and the authors can take place. It is not a commitment to any specific amount of participation on the part of the authors, whose contribution to the forum remains voluntary (and unpaid). We suggest you try asking the authors some challenging questions, lest their interest stray!

The Author Online forum and the archives of previous discussions will be accessible from the publisher's website as long as the book is in print.

about the cover illustration

The illustration on the cover of *Camel in Action* bears the caption "A Bedouin," and is taken from a collection of costumes of the Ottoman Empire published on January 1, 1802, by William Miller of Old Bond Street, London. The title page is missing from the collection and we have been unable to track it down to date. The book's table of contents identifies the figures in both English and French, and each illustration also bears the names of two artists who worked on it, both of whom would no doubt be surprised to find their art gracing the front cover of a computer programming book…200 years later.

The collection was purchased by a Manning editor at an antiquarian flea market in the "Garage" on West 26th Street in Manhattan. The seller was an American based in Ankara, Turkey, and the transaction took place just as he was packing up his stand for the day. The Manning editor did not have on his person the substantial amount of cash that was required for the purchase and a credit card and check were both politely turned down. With the seller flying back to Ankara that evening, the situation was getting hopeless. What was the solution? It turned out to be nothing more than an old-fashioned verbal agreement sealed with a handshake. The seller simply proposed that the money be transferred to him by wire and the editor walked out with the bank information on a piece of paper and the portfolio of images under his arm. Needless to say, we transferred the funds the next day, and we remain grateful and impressed by this unknown person's trust in one of us. It recalls something that might have happened a long time ago.

The pictures from the Ottoman collection, like the other illustrations that appear on our covers, bring to life the richness and variety of dress customs of two centuries ago. They recall the sense of isolation and distance of that period—and of every other historic period except our own hyperkinetic present. Dress codes have changed since then and the diversity by region, so rich at the time, has faded away. It is now often hard to tell the inhabitant of one continent from another. Perhaps, trying to view it optimistically, we have traded a cultural and visual diversity for a more varied personal life. Or a more varied and interesting intellectual and technical life.

We at Manning celebrate the inventiveness, the initiative, and, yes, the fun of the computer business with book covers based on the rich diversity of regional life of two centuries ago, brought back to life by the pictures from this collection.

about the authors

CLAUS IBSEN has worked as a software engineer and architect for more than 13 years. He has often worked with integration in various forms, from integrating with legacy systems on AS/400s to building custom in-house integration frameworks. Claus has designed and architected a large solution for custom clearance for the district of Shanghai, China. He tracks the trends in the open source integration space and it led him to Camel in late 2007. He became a committer in March 2008.

He currently holds a position as principal software engineer at FuseSource, as project lead on Apache Camel. Claus has ambitions to pick up speaking engagements, so you will likely be able to catch up with him at various conferences.

Claus lives in Sweden near Malmo with his wife and dog, which is spoiled as the only child in the family. He is Danish by nationality.

JONATHAN ANSTEY is a software engineer with varied experience in manufacturing control systems, build infrastructure, and enterprise integration. He got involved in the Apache Camel project in early 2008 and hasn't looked back since. Most recently, Jon has been working on Apache Camel and other Apache open source projects at FuseSource.

When Jon is not hacking on Camel, he likes to spend time with his wife and daughter in St. John's, Newfoundland.

Part 1

First steps

Apache Camel is an open source integration framework that aims to make integrating systems easier. In the first chapter of this book we'll introduce you to Camel and show you how it fits into the bigger enterprise software picture. You'll also learn the concepts and terminology of Camel.

Chapter 2 focuses on one of Camel's most important features: message routing. Camel has two main ways of defining routing rules: the Java-based domain-specific language (DSL) and the Spring XML configuration format. In addition to these route-creation techniques, we'll show you how to design and implement solutions to enterprise integration problems using enterprise integration patterns (EIPs) and Camel.

Meeting Camel

This chapter covers

- An introduction to Camel
- Camel's main features
- Your first Camel ride
- Camel's architecture and concepts

Building complex systems from scratch is a very costly endeavor, and one that's almost never successful. An effective and less risky alternative is to assemble a system like a jigsaw puzzle from existing, proven components. We depend daily on a multitude of such integrated systems, making possible everything from phone communications, financial transactions, and healthcare to travel planning and entertainment.

You can't finalize a jigsaw puzzle until you have a complete set of pieces that plug into each other simply, seamlessly, and robustly. That holds true for system integration projects as well. But whereas jigsaw puzzle pieces are made to plug into each other, the systems we integrate rarely are. Integration frameworks aim to fill this gap. As an integrator, you're less concerned about how the system you integrate works and more focused on how to interoperate with it from the outside. A good integration framework provides simple, manageable abstractions for the complex systems you're integrating and the "glue" for plugging them together seamlessly.

Apache Camel is such an integration framework. In this book, we'll help you understand what Camel is, how to use it, and why we think it's one of the best integration frameworks out there.

3

This chapter will start off by introducing Camel and highlighting some of its core features. We'll then take a look at the Camel distribution and explain how you can run the Camel examples in the book. We'll round off the chapter by bringing core Camel concepts to the table so you can understand Camel's architecture.

Are you ready? Let's meet Camel.

1.1   *Introducing Camel*

Camel is an integration framework that aims to make your integration projects productive and fun. The Camel project was started in early 2007, but although it's relatively young, Camel is already a mature open source project, available under the liberal Apache 2 license, and it has a strong community.

Camel's focus is on simplifying integration. We're confident that by the time you finish reading these pages, you'll appreciate Camel and add it to your "must have" list of tools.

The Apache Camel project was named Camel simply because the name is short and easy to remember. Rumor has it the name may be inspired by the fact that one of the founders once smoked Camel cigarettes. At the Camel website a FAQ entry (http://camel.apache.org/why-the-name-camel.html) lists other lighthearted reasons for the name.

1.1.1   *What is Camel?*

At the core of the Camel framework is a routing engine, or more precisely a routing-engine builder. It allows you to define your own routing rules, decide from which sources to accept messages, and determine how to process and send those messages to other destinations. Camel uses an integration language that allows you to define complex routing rules, akin to business processes.

One of the fundamental principles of Camel is that it makes no assumptions about the type of data you need to process. This is an important point, because it gives you, the developer, an opportunity to integrate any kind of system, without the need to convert your data to a canonical format.

Camel offers higher-level abstractions that allow you to interact with various systems using the same API regardless of the protocol or data type the systems are using. Components in Camel provide specific implementations of the API that target different protocols and data types. Out of the box, Camel comes with support for over 80 protocols and data types. Its extensible and modular architecture allows you to implement and seamlessly plug in support for your own protocols, proprietary or not. These architectural choices eliminate the need for unnecessary conversions and make Camel not only faster but also very lean. As a result, it's suitable for embedding into other projects that require Camel's rich processing capabilities. Other open source projects, such as Apache ServiceMix and ActiveMQ, already use Camel as a way to carry out enterprise integration.

We should also mention what Camel isn't. Camel isn't an enterprise service bus (ESB), although some call Camel a lightweight ESB because of its support for routing, transformation, monitoring, orchestration, and so forth. Camel doesn't have a container or a reliable message bus, but it can be deployed in one, such as Open-ESB or the previously mentioned ServiceMix. For that reason, we prefer to call Camel an *integration framework* rather than an *ESB*.

To understand what Camel is, it helps to look at its main features. So let's take a look at them.

1.1.2 Why use Camel?

Camel introduces a few novel ideas into the integration space, which is why its authors decided to create Camel in the first place, instead of using an existing framework. We'll explore the rich set of Camel features throughout the book, but these are the main ideas behind Camel:

- Routing and mediation engine
- Domain-specific language (DSL)
- Payload-agnostic router
- POJO model
- Automatic type converters
- Test kit
- Enterprise integration patterns (EIPs)
- Extensive component library
- Modular and pluggable architecture
- Easy configuration
- Lightweight core
- Vibrant community

Let's dive into the details of each of these features.

ROUTING AND MEDIATION ENGINE

The core feature of Camel is its routing and mediation engine. A routing engine will selectively move a message around, based on the route's configuration. In Camel's case, routes are configured with a combination of enterprise integration patterns and a domain-specific language, both of which we'll describe next.

ENTERPRISE INTEGRATION PATTERNS (EIPS)

Although integration problems are diverse, Gregor Hohpe and Bobby Woolf noticed that many problems and their solutions are quite similar. They cataloged them in their book *Enterprise Integration Patterns*, a must-read for any integration professional (http://www. enterpriseintegrationpatterns.com). If you haven't read it, we encourage you to do so. At the very least, it will help you understand Camel concepts faster and easier.

The enterprise integration patterns, or EIPs, are helpful not only because they provide a proven solution for a given problem, but also because they help define and communicate the problem itself. Patterns have known semantics, which makes communicating problems much easier. The difference between using a pattern language and describing the problem at hand is similar to using spoken language rather than sign language. If you've ever visited a foreign country, you've probably experienced the difference.

Camel is heavily based on EIPs. Although EIPs describe integration problems and solutions and also provide a common vocabulary, the vocabulary isn't formalized. Camel tries to close this gap by providing a language to describe the integration solutions. There's almost a one-to-one relationship between the patterns described in *Enterprise Integration Patterns* and the Camel DSL.

DOMAIN-SPECIFIC LANGUAGE (DSL)

Camel's domain-specific language (DSL) is a major contribution to the integration space. A few other integration frameworks currently feature a DSL (and some allow you to use XML to describe routing rules), but unlike Camel their DSLs are based on custom languages. Camel is unique because it offers multiple DSLs in regular programming languages such as Java, Scala, Groovy, and it also allows routing rules to be specified in XML.

The purpose of the DSL is to allow the developer to focus on the integration problem rather than on the tool—the programming language. Although Camel is written mostly in Java, it does support mixing multiple programming languages. Each language has its own strengths, and you may want to use different languages for different tasks. You have the freedom to build a solution your own way with as few constraints as possible.

Here are some examples of the DSL using different languages and staying functionally equivalent:

- Java DSL
  ```
  from("file:data/inbox").to("jms:queue:order");
  ```
- Spring DSL
  ```
  <route>
    <from uri="file:data/inbox"/>
    <to uri="jms:queue:order"/>
  </route>
  ```
- Scala DSL
  ```
  from "file:data/inbox" -> "jms:queue:order"
  ```

These examples are real code, and they show how easily you can route files from a folder to a JMS queue. Because there's a real programming language underneath, you can use the existing tooling support, such as code completion and compiler error detection, as illustrated in figure 1.1.

```java
public static void main(String args[]) throws Exception {
    CamelContext context = new DefaultCamelContext();

    context.addRoutes(new RouteBuilder() {
        public void configure() {
            from("file:data/inbox?noop=true").t
        }
    });

    context.start();
    Thread.sleep(10000);

    context.stop();
}
```

```
● threads() : ThreadsDefinition - ProcessorDefinition
● threads(int poolSize) : ThreadsDefinition - Processor[
● throttle(long maximumRequestCount) : ThrottleDefin
● throwException(Exception exception) : ProcessorDe
● to(Endpoint endpoint) : ProcessorDefinition - Process
● to(Endpoint... arg0) : ProcessorDefinition - Processor
● to(Iterable<Endpoint> arg0) : ProcessorDefinition - F
◉ to(String uri) : ProcessorDefinition - ProcessorDefiniti
● to(String... arg0) : ProcessorDefinition - ProcessorDe
● to(ExchangePattern pattern, Endpoint endpoint) : Pr
● to(ExchangePattern arg0, Endpoint... arg1) : Process
                    Press 'Ctrl+Space' to show Template Proposals
```

Figure 1.1   Camel DSLs use real programming languages like Java, so you can use existing tooling support.

Here you can see how the Eclipse IDE's autocomplete feature can give us a list of DSL terms that are valid to use.

EXTENSIVE COMPONENT LIBRARY

Camel provides an extensive library of more than 80 components. These components enable Camel to connect over transports, use APIs, and understand data formats.

PAYLOAD-AGNOSTIC ROUTER

Camel can route any kind of payload—you aren't restricted to carrying XML payloads. This freedom means that you don't have to transform your payload into a canonical format to facilitate routing.

MODULAR AND PLUGGABLE ARCHITECTURE

Camel has a modular architecture, which allows any component to be loaded into Camel, regardless of whether the component ships with Camel, is from a third party, or is your own custom creation.

POJO MODEL

Beans (or POJOs) are considered first-class citizens in Camel, and Camel strives to let you use beans anywhere and anytime in your integration projects. This means that in many places you can extend Camel's built-in functionality with your own custom code. Chapter 4 has a complete discussion of using beans within Camel.

EASY CONFIGURATION

The *convention over configuration* paradigm is followed whenever possible, which minimizes configuration requirements. In order to configure endpoints directly in routes, Camel uses an easy and intuitive URI configuration.

For example, you could configure a file consumer to scan recursively in a subfolder and include only a .txt file, as follows:

```
from("file:data/inbox?recursive=true&include=*.txt")...
```

AUTOMATIC TYPE CONVERTERS

Camel has a built-in type-converter mechanism that ships with more than 150 converters. You no longer need to configure type-converter rules to go from byte arrays to strings, for example. And if you find a need to convert to types that Camel doesn't support, you can create your own type converter. The best part is that it works under the hood, so you don't have to worry about it.

The Camel components also leverage this feature; they can accept data in most types and convert the data to a type they're capable of using. This feature is one of the top favorites in the Camel community. You may even start wondering why it wasn't provided in Java itself! Chapter 3 covers more about type converters.

LIGHTWEIGHT CORE

Camel's core can be considered pretty lightweight, with the total library coming in at about 1.6 MB and only having a dependency on Apache Commons Logging and Fuse-Source Commons Management. This makes Camel easy to embed or deploy anywhere you like, such as in a standalone application, web application, Spring application, Java

EE application, JBI container, OSGi bundle, Java Web Start, or on the Google App engine. Camel was designed not to be a server or ESB but instead to be embedded in whatever platform you choose.

TEST KIT

Camel provides a Test Kit that makes it easier for you to test your own Camel applications. The same Test Kit is used extensively to test Camel itself, and it includes more than 6,000 unit tests. The Test Kit contains test-specific components that, for example, can help you mock real endpoints. It also contains setup expectations that Camel can use to determine whether an application satisfied the requirements or failed. Chapter 6 covers testing with Camel.

VIBRANT COMMUNITY

Camel has an active community. This is essential if you intend to use any open source project in your application. Inactive projects have little community support, so if you run into issues, you're on your own. With Camel, if you're having any trouble, users and developers alike will come to your aid promptly. For more information on Camel's community, see appendix D.

Now that you've seen the main features that make up Camel, we'll get a bit more hands on by looking at the Camel distribution and trying out an example.

1.2   *Getting started*

In this section, we'll show you how to get your hands on a Camel distribution, explain what's inside, and then run an example using Apache Maven. After this, you'll know how to run any of the examples from the book's source code.

Let's first get the Camel distribution.

1.2.1   *Getting Camel*

Camel is available from the official Apache Camel website at http://camel.apache.org/download.html. On that page you'll see a list of all the Camel releases and also the downloads for the latest release.

For the purposes of this book, we'll be using Camel 2.5.0. To get this version, click on the Camel 2.5.0 Release link and near the bottom of the page you'll find two binary distributions: the zip distribution is for Windows users, and the tar.gz distribution is for Unix/Linux/Cygwin users. When you've downloaded one of the distributions, extract it to a location on your hard drive.

Open up a command prompt, and go to the location where you extracted the Camel distribution. Issuing a directory listing here will give you something like this:

```
janstey@mojo:~/apache-camel-2.5.0$ ls
doc  examples  lib  LICENSE.txt  NOTICE.txt  README.txt
```

As you can see, the distribution is pretty small, and you can probably guess what each directory contains already. Here are the details:

- doc—Contains the Camel Manual in PDF and HTML formats. This user guide is a download of a large portion of the Apache Camel wiki at the time of release. As such, it's a great reference for those not able to browse to the Camel website.
- examples—Includes 27 Camel examples. You'll see an example shortly.
- lib—Contains all Camel libraries and third-party dependencies needed for the core of Camel to run. You'll see later in the chapter how Maven can be used to easily grab dependencies for the components outside the core.
- LICENSE.txt—Contains the license of the Camel distribution. Because this is an Apache project, the license is the Apache License, version 2.0.
- NOTICE.txt—Contains copyright information about the third-party dependencies included in the Camel distribution.
- README.txt—Contains a short intro to what Camel is and a list of helpful links to get new users up and running fast.

Now let's try out one of the Camel examples.

1.2.2 Your first Camel ride

So far, we've shown you how to get a Camel distribution and we've explored what's inside. At this point, feel free to explore the distribution; all examples have instructions to help you figure them out.

From this point on, though, we won't be using the distribution at all. The examples in the book's source all use Apache Maven, which means that Camel libraries will be downloaded automatically for you—there's no need to make sure the Camel distribution's libraries are on the path, for example.

You can get the book's source code from either the book's website, at http://manning.com/ibsen or from the Google Code project that's hosting the source: http://code.google.com/p/camelinaction.

The first example we'll look at can be considered the "hello world" of integrations: routing files. Suppose you need to read files from one directory (data/inbox), process them in some way, and write the result to another directory (data/outbox). For simplicity, you'll skip the processing, so your

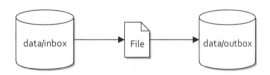

Figure 1.2   Files are routed from the data/inbox directory to the data/outbox directory.

output will be merely a copy of the original file. Figure 1.2 illustrates this process.

It looks pretty simple, right? Here's a possible solution using pure Java (with no Camel).

Listing 1.1   Routing files from one folder to another in plain Java

```
public class FileCopier {
    public static void main(String args[]) throws Exception {
        File inboxDirectory = new File("data/inbox");
        File outboxDirectory = new File("data/outbox");
```

```
            outboxDirectory.mkdir();

            File[] files = inboxDirectory.listFiles();

            for (File source : files) {
                if (source.isFile()) {
                    File dest = new File(
                        outboxDirectory.getPath()
                        + File.separator
                        + source.getName());
                    copyFIle(source, dest);
                }
            }
        }

        private static void copyFile(File source, File dest)
            throws IOException {
            OutputStream out = new FileOutputStream(dest);
            byte[] buffer = new byte[(int) source.length()];
            FileInputStream in = new FileInputStream(source);
            in.read(buffer);
            try {
                out.write(buffer);
            } finally {
                out.close();
                in.close();
            }
        }
    }
}
```

The `FileCopier` example in listing 1.1 is a pretty simple use case, but it still results in 34 lines of code. You have to use low-level file APIs and ensure that resources get closed properly, a task that can easily go wrong. Also, if you wanted to poll the data/inbox directory for new files, you'd need to set up a timer and also keep track of which files you've already copied. This simple example is getting more complex.

Integration tasks like these have been done thousands of times before—you shouldn't ever need to code something like this by hand. Let's not reinvent the wheel here. Let's see what a polling solution looks like if you use an integration framework like Apache Camel.

Listing 1.2   Routing files from one folder to another with Apache Camel

```
public class FileCopierWithCamel {
    public static void main(String args[]) throws Exception {
        CamelContext context = new DefaultCamelContext();
        context.addRoutes(new RouteBuilder() {
            public void configure() {
                from("file:data/inbox?noop=true")          ❶ Routes files from
                    .to("file:data/outbox");                     inbox to outbox
            }
        });
        context.start();

        Thread.sleep(10000);

        context.stop();
    }
}
```

Most of this code is boilerplate stuff when using Camel. Every Camel application uses a `CamelContext` that's subsequently started and then stopped. You also add a sleep method to allow your simple Camel application time to copy the files. What you should really focus on in listing 1.2 is the *route* ❶.

Routes in Camel are defined in such a way that they flow when read. This route can be read like this: consume messages `from` `file` location `data/inbox` with the `noop` option set, and send `to` `file` location `data/outbox`. The `noop` option tells Camel to leave the source file as is. If you didn't use this option, the file would be moved. Most people who have never seen Camel before will be able to understand what this route does. You may also want to note that, excluding the boilerplate code, you created a file-polling route in just one line of Java code ❶.

To run this example, you'll need to download and install Apache Maven from the Maven site at http://maven.apache.org/download.html. Once you have Maven up and working, open a terminal and browse to the chapter1/file-copy directory of the book's source. If you take a directory listing here, you'll see several things:

- data—Contains the inbox directory, which itself contains a single file named message1.xml.
- src—Contains the source code for the listings shown in this chapter.
- pom.xml—Contains information necessary to build the examples. This is the Maven Project Object Model (POM) XML file.

NOTE We used Maven 2.2.1 during the development of the book. Newer versions of Maven may not work or appear exactly as we've shown.

The POM is shown here.

Listing 1.3 The Maven POM required to use Camel's core library

```
<project xmlns="http://maven.apache.org/POM/4.0.0"
  xmlns:xsi="http://www.w3.org/2001/XMLSchema-instance"
  xsi:schemaLocation="http://maven.apache.org/POM/4.0.0
                      http://maven.apache.org/xsd/maven-4.0.0.xsd">
  <modelVersion>4.0.0</modelVersion>
  <parent>                                        ◁——❶ Parent POM
    <groupId>com.camelinaction</groupId>
    <artifactId>chapter1</artifactId>
    <version>1.0</version>
  </parent>

  <artifactId>file-copy</artifactId>

  <name>Camel in Action :: Chapter 1 :: File Copy Example</name>

  <dependencies>
    <dependency>
      <groupId>org.apache.camel</groupId>           ❷ Camel's
      <artifactId>camel-core</artifactId>          ◁—┘ core library
      <version>${camel-version}</version>
    </dependency>
  </dependencies>
</project>
```

Maven itself is a complex topic, and we won't go into great detail here. We'll give you enough information to be productive with the examples in this book. For an in-depth look at Maven, we recommend reading *Maven by Example* and *Maven: The Complete Reference*, both of which are freely available from http://www.sonatype.com/book. We'll also discuss using Maven to develop Camel applications in chapter 11, so there's a good deal of information there too.

The Maven POM in listing 1.3 is probably one of the shortest POMs you'll ever see—almost everything uses the defaults provided by Maven. Besides those defaults, there are also some settings configured in the parent POM ❶. Probably the most important section to point out here is the dependency on the Camel library ❷. This dependency element tells Maven to do the following:

1   Create a search path based on the `groupId`, `artifactId`, and `version`. The `version` element is set to the `camel-version` property, which is defined in the POM referenced in the parent element ❶, and will resolve to 2.5.0. The type of dependency was not specified, so the JAR file type will be assumed. The search path will be org/apache/camel/camel-core/2.5.0/camel-core-2.5.0.jar.

2   Because listing 1.3 defined no special places for Maven to look for the Camel dependencies, it will look in Maven's central repository, located at http://repo1.maven.org/maven2.

3   Combining the search path and the repository URL, Maven will try to download http://repo1.maven.org/maven2/org/apache/camel/camel-core/2.5.0/camel-core-2.5.0.jar.

4   This JAR will be saved to Maven's local download cache, which is typically located in the home directory under .m2/repository. This would be ~/.m2/repository on Linux/Unix and C:\Documents and Settings\<Username>\.m2\ repository on Windows XP, and C:\Users\<Username>\.m2\repository on Windows Vista/7.

5   When the application code in listing 1.2 is started, the Camel JAR will be added to the classpath.

To run the example in listing 1.2, use the following command:

```
mvn compile exec:java -Dexec.mainClass=camelinaction.FileCopierWithCamel
```

This instructs Maven to compile the source in the src directory and to execute the `FileCopierWithCamel` class with the camel-core JAR on the classpath.

> **NOTE** In order to run any of the examples in this book you'll need an Internet connection. A broadband speed connection is preferable because Apache Maven will download many JAR dependencies of the examples, some of which are large. The whole set of examples will download about 140 MB of libraries.

Run the Maven command from the chapter1/file-copy directory, and after it completes, browse to the data/outbox folder to see the file copy that has just been made. Congratulations, you've just run your first Camel example! It was a simple example, but knowing how it's set up will enable you to run pretty much any of the book's examples.

We now need to cover some Camel basics and the integration space in general to ensure that you're well prepared for using Camel. We'll turn our attention to the message model, the architecture, and a few other Camel concepts. Most of the abstractions are based on known service-oriented architecture (SOA) and EIP concepts and retain their names and semantics. We'll start with Camel's message model.

1.3 Camel's message model

In Camel, there are two abstractions for modeling messages, both of which we'll cover in this section.

- `org.apache.camel.Message`—The fundamental entity containing the data being carried and routed in Camel
- `org.apache.camel.Exchange`—The Camel abstraction for an exchange of messages. This exchange of messages has an "in" message and as a reply, an "out" message

We'll start by looking at Message to understand how data is modeled and carried in Camel. Then we'll look at how a "conversation" is modeled in Camel by the Exchange.

1.3.1 Message

Messages are the entities used by systems to communicate with each other when using messaging channels. Messages flow in one direction from a sender to a receiver, as illustrated in figure 1.3.

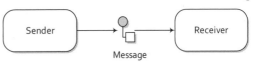

Messages have a body (a payload), headers, and optional attachments, as illustrated in figure 1.4.

Figure 1.3 Messages are entities used to send data from one system to another.

Messages are uniquely identified with an identifier of type `java.lang.String`. The identifier's uniqueness is enforced and guaranteed by the message creator, it's protocol dependent, and it doesn't have a guaranteed format. For protocols that don't define a unique message identification scheme, Camel uses its own UID generator.

HEADERS AND ATTACHMENTS

Headers are values associated with the message, such as sender identifiers, hints about content encoding, authentication information, and so on. Headers are name-value pairs; the name is a unique, case-insensitive string, and the value is of type `java.lang.Object`. This means that Camel imposes no constraints on the type of the headers. Headers are stored as a map within the message. A message can also have optional attachments, which are typically used for the web service and email components.

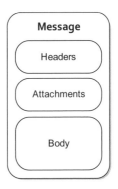

Figure 1.4
A message can contain headers, attachments, and a body.

BODY

The body is of type `java.lang.Object`. That means that a message can store any kind of content. It also means that it's up to the application designer to make sure that the receiver can understand the content of the message. When the sender and receiver use different body formats, Camel provides a number of mechanisms to transform the data into an acceptable format, and in many cases the conversion happens automatically with type converters, behind the scenes.

FAULT FLAG

Messages also have a fault flag. Some protocols and specifications, such as WSDL and JBI, distinguish between *output* and *fault* messages. They're both valid responses to invoking an operation, but the latter indicates an unsuccessful outcome. In general, faults aren't handled by the integration infrastructure. They're part of the contract between the client and the server and are handled at the application level.

During routing, messages are contained in an exchange.

1.3.2   *Exchange*

An *exchange* in Camel is the message's container during routing. An exchange also provides support for the various types of interactions between systems, also known as message exchange patterns (MEPs). MEPs are used to differentiate between one-way and request-response messaging styles. The Camel exchange holds a pattern property that can be either

- `InOnly`—A one-way message (also known as an `Event` message). For example, JMS messaging is often one-way messaging.
- `InOut`—A request-response message. For example, HTTP-based transports are often request reply, where a client requests to retrieve a web page, waiting for the reply from the server.

Figure 1.5 illustrates the contents of an exchange in Camel.

Let's look at the elements of figure 1.5 in more detail:

- *Exchange ID*—A unique ID that identifies the exchange. Camel will generate a default unique ID, if you don't explicitly set one.
- *MEP*—A pattern that denotes whether you're using the `InOnly` or `InOut` messaging style. When the pattern is `InOnly`, the exchange contains an in message. For `InOut`, an out message also exists that contains the reply message for the caller.

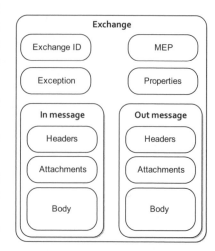

Figure 1.5   A Camel exchange has an ID, MEP, exception, and properties. It also has an *in* message to store the incoming message and an *out* message to store the result.

- *Exception*—If an error occurs at any time during routing, an `Exception` will be set in the exception field.
- *Properties*—Similar to message headers, but they last for the duration of the entire exchange. Properties are used to contain global-level information, whereas message headers are specific to a particular message. Camel itself will add various properties to the exchange during routing. You, as a developer, can store and retrieve properties at any point during the lifetime of an exchange.
- *In message*—This is the input message, which is mandatory. The in message contains the request message.
- *Out message*—This is an optional message that only exists if the MEP is `InOut`. The out message contains the reply message.

We discussed Camel's message model before the architecture because we wanted you to have a solid understanding of what a message is in Camel. After all, the most important aspect of Camel is routing messages. You're now well prepared to learn more about Camel and its architecture.

1.4 Camel's architecture

Let's now turn our attention to Camel's architecture. We'll first take a look at the high-level architecture and then drill down into the specific concepts. After you've read this section, you should be caught up on the integration lingo and be ready for chapter 2, where we'll explore Camel's routing capabilities.

1.4.1 Architecture from 10,000 feet

We think that architectures are best viewed first from high above. Figure 1.6 shows a high-level view of the main concepts that make up Camel's architecture.

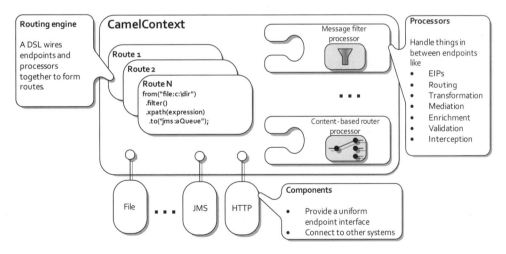

Figure 1.6 At a high level, Camel is composed of processors, components, and routes. All of these are contained within the `CamelContext`.

The routing engine uses routes as specifications for where messages are routed. Routes are defined using one of Camel's domain-specific languages (DSLs). Processors are used to transform and manipulate messages during routing and also to implement all the EIP patterns, which have corresponding keywords in the DSL languages. Components are the extension points in Camel for adding connectivity to other systems. To expose these systems to the rest of Camel, components provide an endpoint interface.

With that high-level view out of the way, let's take a closer look at the individual concepts in figure 1.6.

1.4.2 Camel concepts

Figure 1.6 revealed many new concepts, so let's take some time to go over them one by one. We'll start with the CamelContext, which is Camel's runtime.

CAMELCONTEXT

You may have guessed that the Camel-Context is a container of sorts, judging from figure 1.6. You can think of it as Camel's runtime system, which keeps all the pieces together.

Figure 1.7 shows the most notable services that the CamelContext keeps together.

As you can see from figure 1.7, there are a lot of services for the Camel-Context to keep track of. These are described in table 1.1.

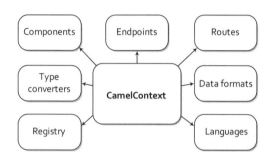

Figure 1.7 The CamelContext provides access to many useful services, the most notable being components, type converters, a registry, endpoints, routes, data formats, and languages.

The details of each of these services will be discussed throughout the book. Let's now take a look at routes and Camel's routing engine.

Table 1.1 The services that the CamelContext provides

Service	Description
Components	Contains the components used. Camel is capable of loading components on the fly either by autodiscovery on the classpath or when a new bundle is activated in an OSGi container. In chapter 7 we'll discuss components in more detail.
Endpoints	Contains the endpoints that have been created.
Routes	Contains the routes that have been added. We'll cover routes in chapter 2.
Type converters	Contains the loaded type converters. Camel has a mechanism that allows you to manually or automatically convert from one type to another. Type converters are covered in chapter 3.
Data formats	Contains the loaded data formats. Data formats are covered in chapter 3.

Table 1.1 The services that the `CamelContext` provides *(continued)*

Service	Description
Registry	Contains a registry that allows you to look up beans. By default, this will be a JNDI registry. If you're using Camel from Spring, this will be the Spring `ApplicationContext`. It can also be an OSGi registry if you use Camel in an OSGi container. We'll cover registries in chapter 4.
Languages	Contains the loaded languages. Camel allows you to use many different languages to create expressions. You'll get a glimpse of the XPath language in action when we cover the DSL. A complete reference to Camel's own Simple expression language is available in appendix A.

ROUTING ENGINE

Camel's routing engine is what actually moves messages under the hood. This engine isn't exposed to the developer, but you should be aware that it's there and that it does all the heavy lifting, ensuring that messages are routed properly.

ROUTES

Routes are obviously a core abstraction for Camel. The simplest way to define a route is as a chain of processors. There are many reasons for using routers in messaging applications. By decoupling clients from servers, and producers from consumers, routes can

- Decide dynamically what server a client will invoke
- Provide a flexible way to add extra processing
- Allow for clients and servers to be developed independently
- Allow for clients of servers to be stubbed out (using mocks) for testing purposes
- Foster better design practices by connecting disparate systems that do one thing well
- Enhance features and functionality of some systems (such as message brokers and ESBs)

Each route in Camel has a unique identifier that's used for logging, debugging, monitoring, and starting and stopping routes. Routes also have exactly one input source for messages, so they're effectively tied to an input endpoint.

To define a route, a DSL is used.

DOMAIN-SPECIFIC LANGUAGE (DSL)

To wire processors and endpoints together to form routes, Camel defines a DSL. The term *DSL* is used a bit loosely here. In Camel, DSL means a fluent Java API that contains methods named for EIP terms.

Consider this example:

```
from("file:data/inbox")
    .filter().xpath("/order[not(@test)]")
    .to("jms:queue:order")
```

Here, in a single Java statement, you define a route that consumes files from a file endpoint. Messages are then routed to the filter EIP, which will use an XPath predicate to test whether the message is a test order or not. If a message passes the test, it's forwarded to the JMS endpoint. Messages failing the filter test will be dropped.

Camel provides multiple DSL languages, so you could define the same route using the Spring DSL, like this:

```
<route>
  <from uri="file:data/inbox"/>
  <filter>
    <xpath>/order[not(@test)]</xpath>
    <to uri="jms:queue:order"/>
  </filter>
</route>
```

The DSLs provide a nice abstraction for Camel users to build applications with. Under the hood, though, a route is actually composed of a graph of processors. Let's take a moment to see what a processor really is.

PROCESSOR

The processor is a core Camel concept that represents a node capable of using, creating, or modifying an incoming exchange. During routing, exchanges flow from one processor to another; as such, you can think of a route as a graph having specialized processors as the nodes, and lines that connect the output of one processor to the input of another. Many of the processors are implementations of EIPs, but one could easily implement their own custom processor and insert it into a route.

So how do exchanges get in or out of this processor graph? To find out, we'll need to look at both components and endpoints.

COMPONENT

Components are the main extension point in Camel. To date, there are over 80 components in the Camel ecosystem that range in function from data transports, to DSLs, data formats, and so on. You can even create your own components for Camel—we'll discuss this in chapter 11.

From a programming point of view, components are fairly simple: they're associated with a name that's used in a URI, and they act as a factory of endpoints. For example, a `FileComponent` is referred to by `file` in a URI, and it creates `FileEndpoints`. The endpoint is perhaps an even more fundamental concept in Camel.

ENDPOINT

An endpoint is the Camel abstraction that models the end of a channel through which a system can send or receive messages. This is illustrated in figure 1.8.

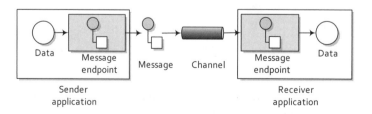

Data   Message   Message   Channel   Message   Data
        endpoint   endpoint

Sender   Receiver
application   application

Figure 1.8
An endpoint acts as a neutral interface allowing systems to integrate.

In Camel, you configure endpoints using URIs, such as `file:data/inbox?delay=5000`, and you also refer to endpoints this way. At runtime, Camel will look up an endpoint based on the URI notation. Figure 1.9 shows how this works.

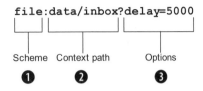

Figure 1.9 Endpoint URIs are divided into three parts: a scheme, a context path, and options.

The scheme ❶ denotes which Camel component handles that type of endpoint. In this case, the scheme of `file` selects the `FileComponent`. The `FileComponent` then works as a factory creating the `FileEndpoint` based on the remaining parts of the URI. The context path `data/inbox` ❷ tells the `FileComponent` that the starting folder is data/inbox. The option, `delay=5000` ❸ indicates that files should be polled at a 5 second interval.

There's more to an endpoint than meets the eye. Figure 1.10 shows how an endpoint works together with an exchange, producers, and consumers.

At first glance, figure 1.10 may seem a bit overwhelming, but it will all make sense in a few minutes. In a nutshell, an endpoint acts as a factory for creating consumers and producers that are capable of receiving and sending messages to a particular endpoint. We didn't mention producers or consumers in the high-level view of Camel in figure 1.6, but they're important concepts. We'll go over them next.

PRODUCER

A producer is the Camel abstraction that refers to an entity capable of creating and sending a message to an endpoint. Figure 1.10 illustrates where the producer fits in with other Camel concepts.

When a message needs to be sent to an endpoint, the producer will create an exchange and populate it with data compatible with that particular endpoint. For example, a `FileProducer` will write the message body to a file. A `JmsProducer`, on the other hand, will map the Camel message to a `javax.jms.Message` before sending it to a JMS destination. This is an important feature in Camel, because it hides the complexity of interacting with particular transports. All you need to do is route a message to an endpoint, and the producer does the heavy lifting.

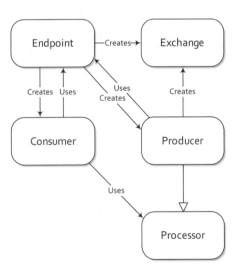

Figure 1.10 How endpoints work with producers, consumers, and an exchange

CONSUMER

A consumer is the service that receives messages produced by a producer, wraps them in an exchange, and sends them to be processed. Consumers are the source of the exchanges being routed in Camel.

Looking back at figure 1.10, we can see where the consumer fits in with other Camel concepts. To create a new exchange, a consumer will use the endpoint that wraps the payload being consumed. A processor is then used to initiate the routing of the exchange in Camel using the routing engine.

In Camel there are two kinds of consumers: event-driven consumers and polling consumers. The differences between these consumers are important, because they help solve different problems.

EVENT-DRIVEN CONSUMER

The most familiar consumer is probably the event-driven consumer, which is illustrated in figure 1.11.

This kind of consumer is mostly associated with client-server architectures and web services. It's also referred to as an *asynchronous receiver* in the EIP world. An event-driven consumer listens on a particular messaging channel, usu-

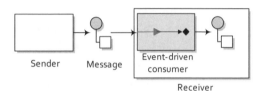

Figure 1.11   An event-driven consumer waits idle until a message arrives, at which point it wakes up and consumes the message.

ally a TCP/IP port or a JMS queue, and waits for a client to send messages to it. When a message arrives, the consumer wakes up and takes the message for processing.

POLLING CONSUMER

The other kind of consumer is the polling consumer illustrated in figure 1.12.

In contrast to the event-driven consumer, the polling consumer actively goes and fetches messages from a particular source, such as an FTP server. The polling consumer is also known as a *synchronous receiver* in EIP lingo, because it

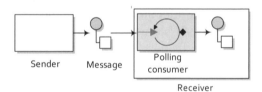

Figure 1.12   A polling consumer actively checks for new messages.

won't poll for more messages until it has finished processing the current message. A common flavor of the polling consumer is the scheduled polling consumer, which polls at scheduled intervals. File, FTP, and email transports all use scheduled polling consumers.

We've now covered all of Camel's core concepts. With this new knowledge, you can revisit your first Camel ride and see what's really happening.

1.5   *Your first Camel ride, revisited*

Recall that in your first Camel ride (section 1.2.2), you read files from one directory (data/inbox) and wrote the results to another directory (data/outbox). Now that you know the core Camel concepts, you can put this example in perspective.

Take another look at the Camel application.

Listing 1.4   Routing files from one folder to another with Apache Camel

```
public class FileCopierWithCamel {
    public static void main(String args[]) throws Exception {
        CamelContext context = new DefaultCamelContext();
        context.addRoutes(new RouteBuilder() {
            public void configure() {
                from("file:data/inbox?noop=true")          ❶ Java DSL
                    .to("file:data/outbox");                   route
            }
        });
        context.start();

        Thread.sleep(10000);

        context.stop();
    }
}
```

In this example, you first create a `CamelContext`, which is the Camel runtime. You then add the routing logic using a `RouteBuilder` and the Java DSL ❶. By using the DSL, you can cleanly and concisely let Camel instantiate components, endpoints, consumers, producers, and so on. All you have to focus on is defining the routes that matter for your integration projects. Under the hood, though, Camel is accessing the `FileComponent`, and using it as a factory to create the endpoint and its producer. The same `FileComponent` is used to create the consumer side as well.

1.6   *Summary*

In this chapter you met Camel. You saw how Camel simplifies integration by relying on known EIPs. You also saw Camel's DSL, which aims to make Camel code self documenting and keeps developers focused on what the glue code does, not how it does it.

We covered Camel's main features, what Camel is and isn't, and where it can be used. We looked at how Camel provides abstractions and an API that work over a large range of protocols and data formats.

At this point, you should have a good understanding of what Camel does and what the concepts behind Camel are. Soon you'll be able to confidently browse Camel applications and get a good idea of what they do.

In the rest of the book, we'll explore Camel's features and give you practical solutions you can apply in everyday integration scenarios. We'll also explain what's going on under Camel's tough skin. To make sure that you get the main concepts from each chapter, from now on we'll present you with a number of best practices and key points in the summary.

In the next chapter, we'll investigate routing, which is an essential feature and a fun one to learn.

Routing with Camel

This chapter covers

- An overview of routing
- Introducing the Rider Auto Parts scenario
- The basics of FTP and JMS endpoints
- Creating routes using the Java DSL
- Configuring routes from Spring
- Routing using enterprise integration patterns (EIPs)

One of the most important features of Camel is routing; without it, Camel would essentially be a library of transport connectors. In this chapter, we'll dive into routing with Camel.

Routing happens in many aspects of everyday life. When you mail a letter, for instance, it may be routed through several cities before reaching its final address. An email you send will be routed through many different computer network systems before reaching its final destination. In all cases, the router's function is to selectively move the message forward.

In the context of enterprise messaging systems, routing is the process by which a message is taken from an input queue and, based on a set of conditions, sent to one of several output queues, as shown in figure 2.1. This effectively means that the

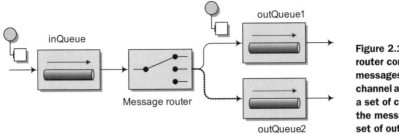

Figure 2.1 A message
router consumes
messages from an input
channel and, depending on
a set of conditions, sends
the message to one of a
set of output channels.

input and output queues are unaware of the conditions in between them. The conditional logic is decoupled from the message consumer and producer.

In Apache Camel, routing is a more general concept. It's defined as a step-by-step movement of the message, which originates from an endpoint in the role of a consumer. The consumer could be receiving the message from an external service, polling for the message on some system, or even creating the message itself. This message then flows through a processing component, which could be an enterprise integration pattern (EIP), a processor, an interceptor, or some other custom creation. The message is finally sent to a target endpoint that's in the role of a producer. A route may have many processing components that modify the message or send it to another location, or it may have none, in which case it would be a simple pipeline.

In this chapter, we'll first introduce the fictional company that we'll use as the running example throughout the book. To support this company's use case, you'll learn how to communicate over FTP and Java Message Service (JMS) using Camel's endpoints. Following this, we'll look in depth at the Java-based domain-specific language (DSL) and the Spring-based configuration format for creating routes. We'll also give you a glimpse of how to design and implement solutions to enterprise integration problems using EIPs and Camel. By the end of the chapter, you'll be proficient enough to create useful routing applications with Camel.

To start, let's look at the example company that we'll use to demonstrate the concepts throughout the book.

2.1   *Introducing Rider Auto Parts*

Our fictional motorcycle parts business, Rider Auto Parts, supplies parts to motorcycle manufacturers. Over the years, they've changed the way they receive orders several times. Initially, orders were placed by uploading comma-separated value (CSV) files to an FTP server. The message format was later changed to XML. Currently they provide a website through which orders are submitted as XML messages over HTTP.

Rider Auto Parts asks new customers to use the web interface to place orders, but because of service level agreements (SLAs) with existing customers, they must keep all the old message formats and interfaces up and running. All of these messages are converted to an internal Plain Old Java Object (POJO) format before processing. A high-level view of the order processing system is shown in figure 2.2.

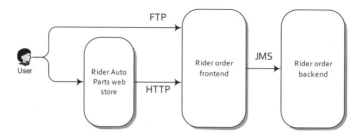

Figure 2.2 A customer has two ways of submitting orders to the Rider Auto Parts order-handling system: either by uploading the raw order file to an FTP server or by submitting an order through the Rider Auto Parts web store. All orders are eventually sent via JMS for processing at Rider Auto Parts.

Rider Auto Parts faces a pretty common problem: over years of operation, they have acquired software baggage in the form of transports and data formats that were popular at the time. This is no problem for an integration framework like Camel, though. In this chapter, and throughout the book, you'll help Rider Auto Parts implement their current requirements and new functionality using Camel.

As a first assignment, you'll need to implement the FTP module in the Rider order frontend system. Later in the chapter, you'll see how backend services are implemented too. Implementing the FTP module will involve the following steps:

1 Polling the FTP server and downloading new orders
2 Converting the order files to JMS messages
3 Sending the messages to the JMS `incomingOrders` queue

To complete steps 1 and 3, you'll need to understand how to communicate over FTP and JMS using Camel's endpoints. To complete the entire assignment, you'll need to understand routing with the Java DSL. Let's first take a look at how you can use Camel's endpoints.

2.2   *Understanding endpoints*

As you read in chapter 1, an endpoint is an abstraction that models the end of a message channel through which a system can send or receive messages. In this section, we're going to explain how you can use URIs to configure Camel to communicate over FTP and JMS. Let's first look at FTP.

2.2.1   *Working with files over FTP*

One of the things that make Camel easy to use is the endpoint URI. By specifying a URI, you can identify the component you want to use and how that component is configured. You can then decide to either send messages to the component configured by this URI, or to consume messages from it.

Take your first Rider Auto Parts assignment, for example. To download new orders from the FTP server, you need to do the following:

1 Connect to the rider.com FTP server on the default FTP port of 21

2 Provide a username of "rider" and password of "secret"

3 Change the directory to "orders"

4 Download any new order files

As shown in figure 2.3, you can easily configure Camel to do this by using URI notation.

Camel will first look up the `ftp` scheme in the component registry, which will resolve to the `FtpComponent`. The `FtpComponent` then works as a factory, creating the `FtpEndpoint` based on the remaining context path and options.

The context path of `rider.com/orders` tells the `FtpComponent` that it should log into the FTP server at rider.com on the default FTP port and change the directory to "orders". Finally, the only options specified are `username` and `password`, which are used to log in to the FTP server.

> **TIP** For the FTP component, you can also specify the username and password in the context path of the URI. So the following URI is equivalent to the one in figure 2.3: ftp://rider:secret@rider.com/orders.

The `FtpComponent` isn't part of the camel-core module, so you have to add an additional dependency to your project. Using Maven you just have to add the following dependency to the POM:

```xml
<dependency>
    <groupId>org.apache.camel</groupId>
    <artifactId>camel-ftp</artifactId>
    <version>2.5.0</version>
</dependency>
```

Although this endpoint URI would work equally well in a consumer or producer scenario, you'll be using it to download orders from the FTP server. To do so, you need to use it in a `from` node of Camel's DSL:

```
from("ftp://rider.com/orders?username=rider&password=secret")
```

That's all you need to do to consume files from an FTP server.

The next thing you need to do, as you may recall from figure 2.2, is send the orders you downloaded from the FTP server to a JMS queue. This process requires a little more setup, but it's still easy.

Figure 2.3 A Camel endpoint URI consists of three parts: a scheme, a context path, and a list of options.

2.2.2 Sending to a JMS queue

Camel provides extensive support for connecting to JMS-enabled providers, and we'll cover all the details in chapter 7. For now, though, we're just going to cover enough so that you can complete your first task for Rider Auto Parts. Recall that you need to download orders from an FTP server and send them to a JMS queue.

WHAT IS JMS?

JMS (Java Message Service) is a Java API that allows you to create, send, receive, and read messages. It also mandates that messaging is asynchronous and has specific elements of reliability, like guaranteed and once-and-only-once delivery. JMS is the de facto messaging solution in the Java community.

In JMS, message consumers and producers talk to one another through an intermediary—a JMS destination. As shown in figure 2.4, a destination can be either a queue or a topic. *Queues* are strictly point-to-point, where each message has only one consumer. *Topics* operate on a publish/subscribe scheme; a single message may be delivered to many consumers if they have subscribed to the topic.

JMS also provides a `ConnectionFactory` that clients (like Camel) can use to create a connection with a JMS provider. JMS providers are usually referred to as *brokers* because they manage the communication between a message producer and a message consumer.

HOW TO CONFIGURE CAMEL TO USE A JMS PROVIDER

To connect Camel to a specific JMS provider, you need to configure Camel's JMS component with an appropriate `ConnectionFactory`.

Apache ActiveMQ is one of the most popular open source JMS providers, and it's the primary JMS broker that the Camel team uses to test the JMS component. As such, we'll be using it to demonstrate JMS concepts within the book. For more information on Apache ActiveMQ, we recommend *ActiveMQ in Action* by Bruce Snyder, Dejan Bosanac, and Rob Davies, available from Manning Publications.

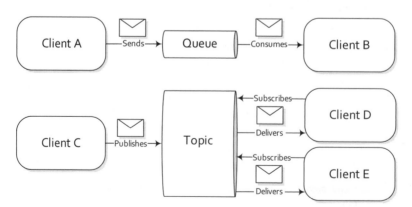

Figure 2.4 There are two types of JMS destinations: queues and topics. The queue is a point-to-point channel, where each message has only one recipient. A topic delivers a copy of the message to all clients who have subscribed to receive it.

So in the case of Apache ActiveMQ, you can create an `ActiveMQConnectionFactory` that points to the location of the running ActiveMQ broker:

```
ConnectionFactory connectionFactory =
  new ActiveMQConnectionFactory("vm://localhost");
```

The `vm://localhost` URI means that you should connect to an embedded broker named "localhost" running inside the current JVM. The `vm` transport connector in ActiveMQ creates a broker on demand if one isn't running already, so it's very handy for quickly testing JMS applications; for production scenarios, it's recommended that you connect to a broker that's already running. Furthermore, in production scenarios we recommend that connection pooling be used when connecting to a JMS broker. See chapter 7 for details on these alternate configurations.

Next, when you create your `CamelContext`, you can add the JMS component as follows:

```
CamelContext context = new DefaultCamelContext();
context.addComponent("jms",
    JmsComponent.jmsComponentAutoAcknowledge(connectionFactory));
```

The JMS component and the ActiveMQ-specific connection factory aren't part of the camel-core module. In order to use these, you'll need to add some dependencies to your Maven-based project. For the plain JMS component, all you have to add is this:

```
<dependency>
  <groupId>org.apache.camel</groupId>
  <artifactId>camel-jms</artifactId>
  <version>2.5.0</version>
</dependency>
```

The connection factory comes directly from ActiveMQ, so you'll need the following dependency:

```
<dependency>
  <groupId>org.apache.activemq</groupId>
  <artifactId>activemq-core</artifactId>
  <version>5.3.2</version>
</dependency>
```

Now that you've configured the JMS component to connect to an actual JMS broker, it's time to look at how URIs can be used to specify the destination.

USING URIS TO SPECIFY THE DESTINATION

Once the JMS component is configured, you can start sending and receiving JMS messages at your leisure. Because you're using URIs, this is a real breeze to configure.

Let's say you want to send a JMS message to the queue named `incomingOrders`. The URI in this case would be

```
jms:queue:incomingOrders
```

This is pretty self-explanatory. The "jms" prefix indicates that you're using the JMS component you configured before. By specifying "queue", the JMS component knows to send to a queue named incomingOrders. You could even have omitted the queue qualifier, because the default behavior is to send to a queue rather than a topic.

> **NOTE**   Some endpoints can have an intimidating list of endpoint URI properties. For instance, the JMS component has about 60 options, many of which are only used in specific JMS scenarios. Camel always tries to provide built-in defaults that fit most cases, and you can always find out what the default values are by browsing to the component's page in the online Camel documentation. The JMS component is discussed here: http://camel.apache.org/jms.html.

Using Camel's Java DSL, you can send a message to the incomingOrders queue by using the to keyword like this:

```
...to("jms:queue:incomingOrders")
```

This can be read as sending to the JMS queue named incomingOrders.

Now that you know the basics of communicating over FTP and JMS with Camel, you can get back to the routing theme of this chapter and start routing some messages!

2.3   *Creating routes in Java*

In chapter 1, you saw how each CamelContext can contain multiple routes and also how a RouteBuilder could be used to create a route. It may not have been obvious, though, that the RouteBuilder isn't the final route that the CamelContext will use at runtime; it's a builder of one or more routes, which are then added to the CamelContext. This is illustrated in figure 2.5.

The addRoutes method of the CamelContext accepts a RoutesBuilder, not just a RouteBuilder. The RoutesBuilder interface has a single method defined:

```
void addRoutesToCamelContext(CamelContext context) throws Exception;
```

This means that you could use your own custom class to build Camel routes. The most common way to build routes, though, is to use the RouteBuilder class, which implements RoutesBuilder. The RouteBuilder class also gives you access to Camel's Java DSL for route creation.

In the next sections, you'll learn how to use a RouteBuilder and the Java DSL to create simple routes. Once you know that, you'll be well prepared to take on the Spring DSL in section 2.4 and routing using EIPs in section 2.5.

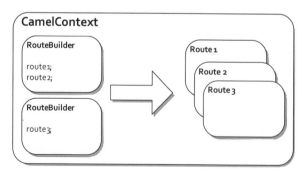

Figure 2.5 `RouteBuilders` are used to create routes in Camel. Each `RouteBuilder` can create multiple routes.

2.3.1 *Using the RouteBuilder*

The abstract `org.apache.camel.builder.RouteBuilder` class in Camel is one that you'll see frequently. You'll need to use it any time you create a route in Java.

To use the `RouteBuilder` class, you extend a class from it and implement the `configure` method, like this:

```
class MyRouteBuilder extends RouteBuilder {
    public void configure() throws Exception {
        ...
    }
}
```

You then need to add the class to the `CamelContext` with the `addRoutes` method:

```
CamelContext context = new DefaultCamelContext();
context.addRoutes(new MyRouteBuilder());
```

Alternatively, you can combine the `RouteBuilder` and `CamelContext` configuration by adding an anonymous `RouteBuilder` class directly into the `CamelContext`, like this:

```
CamelContext context = new DefaultCamelContext();
context.addRoutes(new RouteBuilder() {
    public void configure() throws Exception {
        ...
    }
});
```

Within the `configure` method, you define your routes using the Java DSL. We'll discuss the Java DSL in detail in the next section, but you can start a route now to get an idea of how it works.

In chapter 1, you should have downloaded the source code from the book's website and set up Apache Maven. If you didn't do this, please do so now. Change to the chapter2/ftp-jms directory in your terminal, and type this command:

```
mvn eclipse:eclipse
```

This will generate an Eclipse project file.

> **NOTE** Eclipse is a popular open source IDE that you can find at http://eclipse.org. During the book's development, we used Eclipse 3.5.2.

When the command has completed, you can import this project by selecting File > Import > Existing Projects into Workspace in the Eclipse menus and selecting the chapter2/ftp-jms directory. For more information on developing Camel projects in Eclipse, see chapter 11.

> **NOTE** You don't need an IDE to use Camel, but it does make it a lot easier! Feel free to skip to the next section if you don't want to see the IDE-related setup.

When the ftp-jms project is loaded in Eclipse, open the src/main/java/camelinaction/ RouteBuilderExample.java file. As shown in figure 2.6, when you try autocomplete

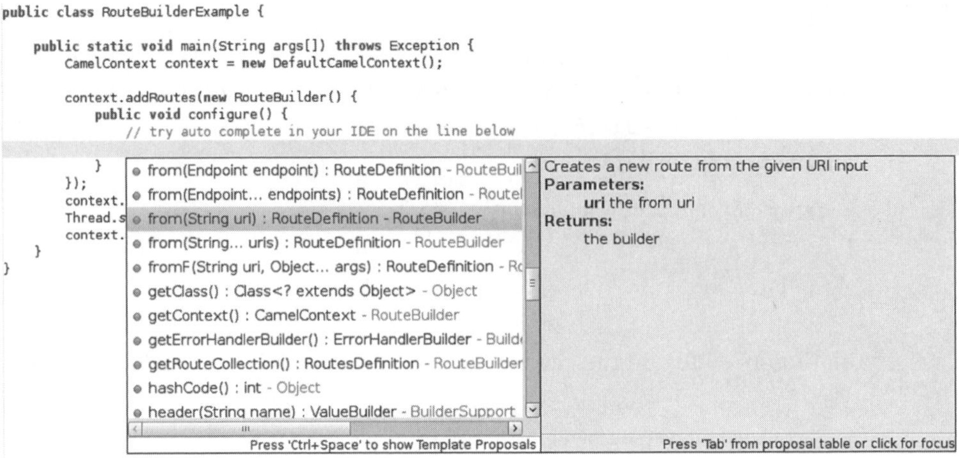

```
public class RouteBuilderExample {

    public static void main(String args[]) throws Exception {
        CamelContext context = new DefaultCamelContext();

        context.addRoutes(new RouteBuilder() {
            public void configure() {
                // try auto complete in your IDE on the line below
```

}
});
context.
Thread.s
context.
}
	○ from(Endpoint endpoint) : RouteDefinition - RouteBuil
	○ from(Endpoint... endpoints) : RouteDefinition - Routel
	○ from(String uri) : RouteDefinition - RouteBuilder
	○ from(String... uris) : RouteDefinition - RouteBuilder
	○ fromF(String uri, Object... args) : RouteDefinition - Rc
	○ getClass() : Class<? extends Object> - Object
	○ getContext() : CamelContext - RouteBuilder
	○ getErrorHandlerBuilder() : ErrorHandlerBuilder - Build
	○ getRouteCollection() : RoutesDefinition - RouteBuilder
	○ hashCode() : int - Object
	○ header(String name) : ValueBuilder - BuilderSupport
		Creates a new route from the given URI input
		Parameters:
		    uri the from uri
		Returns:
		    the builder

	Press 'Ctrl+Space' to show Template Proposals	Press 'Tab' from proposal table or click for focus

Figure 2.6   Use autocomplete to start your route. All routes start with a `from` method.

(Ctrl-space in Eclipse) in the `configure` method, you'll be presented with a number of methods. To start a route, you should use the `from` method.

The `from` method accepts an endpoint URI as an argument. You can add a FTP endpoint URI to connect to Rider Auto Parts' order server as follows:

```
from("ftp://rider.com/orders?username=rider&password=secret")
```

The `from` method returns a `RouteDefinition` object, on which you can invoke a number of different methods that implement EIPs and other messaging concepts.

Congratulations, you're now using Camel's Java DSL! Let's take a closer look at what's going on here.

2.3.2   *The Java DSL*

Domain-specific languages (DSLs) are computer languages that target a specific problem domain, rather than a general purpose domain like most programming languages.

For example, you have probably used the regular expression DSL to match strings of text and found it to be a clear and concise way of matching strings. Doing the same string matching in Java wouldn't be so easy. The regular expression DSL is an *external DSL*—it has a custom syntax and so requires a separate compiler or interpreter to execute.

Internal DSLs, in contrast, use an existing general purpose language, such as Java, in such a way that the DSL feels like a language from a particular domain. The most obvious way of doing this is by naming methods and arguments to match concepts from the domain in question.

Another popular way of implementing internal DSLs is by using *fluent interfaces (aka fluent builders)*. When using a fluent interface, you build up objects with methods that perform an operation and then return the current object instance; another method is then invoked on this object instance, and so on.

NOTE For more information on internal DSLs, see Martin Fowler's "Domain Specific Language" entry on his bliki (blog plus wiki) at http://www.martin-fowler.com/bliki/DomainSpecificLanguage.html. He also has an entry on "Fluent Interfaces" at http://www.martinfowler.com/bliki/FluentInterface.html. For more information on DSLs in general, we recommend *DSLs in Action* by Debasish Ghosh, available from Manning Publications.

Camel's domain is enterprise integration, so the Java DSL is essentially a set of fluent interfaces that contain methods named after terms from the EIP book. In the Eclipse editor, take a look at what is available using autocomplete after a `from` method in the `RouteBuilder`. You should see something like what's shown in figure 2.7. The screenshot shows several EIPs—Pipeline, Enricher, and Recipient List—and there are many others that we'll discuss later.

For now, select the `to` method and finish the route with a semicolon. Each Java statement that starts with a `from` method in the `RouteBuilder` creates a new route. This new route now completes your first task at Rider Auto Parts—consuming orders from an FTP server and sending them to the `incomingOrders` JMS queue.

If you want, you can load up the completed example from the book's source code, in chapter2/ftp-jms and open src/main/java/camelinaction/FtpToJMSExample.java. The code is shown in listing 2.1.

```java
public class RouteBuilderExample {

    public static void main(String args[]) throws Exception {
        CamelContext context = new DefaultCamelContext();

        context.addRoutes(new RouteBuilder() {
            @Override
            public void configure() {
                // try auto complete in your IDE on the line below
                from("ftp://rider.com/orders?username=rider&password=secret").
            }
        });
        context.start();
        Thread.sleep(10000);
        context.stop();
    }
}
```

```
● pipeline(String... uris) : RouteDefinition - ProcessorDefiniti ▲
● policy(Policy policy) : PolicyDefinition - ProcessorDefinitio
● policy(String ref) : PolicyDefinition - ProcessorDefinition
● pollEnrich(String resourceUri) : RouteDefinition - Processo
● pollEnrich(String resourceUri, AggregationStrategy aggreg
● pollEnrich(String resourceUri, long timeout) : RouteDefinit
● pollEnrich(String resourceUri, long timeout, AggregationS
● pollEnrichRef(String resourceRef, long timeout, String agg
● process(Processor processor) : RouteDefinition - Processo
● processRef(String ref) : RouteDefinition - ProcessorDefinit
● recipientList() : ExpressionClause<RecipientListDefinition ▼
                    Press 'Ctrl+Space' to show Template Proposals
```

Figure 2.7 After the `from` method, use your IDE's autocomplete feature to get a list of EIPs (such as Pipeline, Enricher, and Recipient List) and other useful integration functions.

Listing 2.1   Polling for FTP messages and sending them to the `incomingOrders` queue

```
import javax.jms.ConnectionFactory;

import org.apache.activemq.ActiveMQConnectionFactory;
import org.apache.camel.CamelContext;
import org.apache.camel.builder.RouteBuilder;
import org.apache.camel.component.jms.JmsComponent;
import org.apache.camel.impl.DefaultCamelContext;

public class FtpToJMSExample {

    public static void main(String args[]) throws Exception {
        CamelContext context = new DefaultCamelContext();

        ConnectionFactory connectionFactory =
            new ActiveMQConnectionFactory("vm://localhost");
        context.addComponent("jms",
            JmsComponent.jmsComponentAutoAcknowledge(connectionFactory));

        context.addRoutes(new RouteBuilder() {
            public void configure() {
                from("ftp://rider.com/orders"
                    + "?username=rider&password=secret")      ❶ Java statement
                    .to("jms:incomingOrders");                   that forms a
            }                                                     route
        });

        context.start();
        Thread.sleep(10000);

        context.stop();
    }
}
```

NOTE Because you're consuming from ftp://rider.com, which doesn't exist, you can't run this example. It's only useful for demonstrating the Java DSL constructs. For runnable FTP examples, please see chapter 7.

As you can see, this listing includes a bit of boilerplate setup and configuration, but the actual solution to the problem is concisely defined within the `configure` method as a single Java statement ❶. The `from` method tells Camel to consume messages from an FTP endpoint, and the `to` method instructs Camel to send messages to a JMS endpoint.

The flow of messages in this simple route can be viewed as a basic pipeline, where the output of the consumer is fed into the producer as input. This is depicted in figure 2.8.

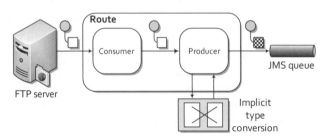

Figure 2.8   The route shown in listing 2.1 forms a simple pipeline. The output of the FTP consumer is fed into the input of the JMS producer. The payload conversion from file to JMS message is done automatically.

One thing you may have noticed is that we didn't do any conversion from the FTP file type to the JMS message type—this was done automatically by Camel's TypeConverter facility. You can force type conversions to occur at any time during a route, but often you don't have to worry about them at all. Data transformation and type conversion is covered in detail in chapter 3.

You may be thinking now that although this route is nice and simple, it would be really nice to see what's going on in the middle of the route. Fortunately, Camel always lets the developer stay in control by providing ways to hook into flows or inject behavior into features. There is a pretty simple way of getting access to the message by using a processor, and we'll discuss that next.

ADDING A PROCESSOR

The Processor interface in Camel is an important building block of complex routes. It's a simple interface, having a single method:

```
public void process(Exchange exchange) throws Exception;
```

This gives you full access to the message exchange, letting you do pretty much whatever you want with the payload or headers.

All EIPs in Camel are implemented as processors. You can even add a simple processor to your route inline, like so:

```
from("ftp://rider.com/orders?username=rider&password=secret").
process(new Processor() {
    public void process(Exchange exchange) throws Exception {
        System.out.println("We just downloaded: "
            + exchange.getIn().getHeader("CamelFileName"));
    }
}).
to("jms:incomingOrders");
```

This route will now print out the filename of the order that was downloaded before sending it to the JMS queue.

By adding this processor into the middle of the route, you've effectively added it to the conceptual pipeline we mentioned earlier, as illustrated in figure 2.9. The output of the FTP consumer is fed into the processor as input; the processor doesn't modify the message payload or headers, so the exchange moves on to the JMS producer as input.

> **NOTE** Many components, like the FileComponent and the FtpComponent, set useful headers describing the payload on the incoming message. In the previous example, you used the CamelFileName header to retrieve the filename of the file that was downloaded via FTP. The component pages of the online documentation contain information about the headers set for each individual component. You'll find information about the FTP component at http://camel.apache.org/ftp2.html.

Camel's main method for creating routes is through the Java DSL. It is, after all, built into the camel-core module. There are other ways of creating routes though, some of which may better suit your situation. For instance, Camel provides extensions for writing routes in Groovy, Scala, and, as we'll discuss next, Spring XML.

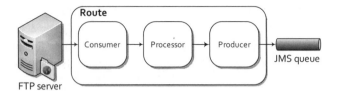

Figure 2.9   **With a processor in the mix, the output of the FTP consumer is now fed into the processor, and then the output of the processor is fed into the JMS producer.**

2.4   Creating routes with Spring

Spring is the most popular Inversion of Control (IoC) Java container out there. The core framework allows to you "wire" beans together to form applications. This wiring is done through an XML configuration file.

In this section, we'll give you a quick introduction to creating applications with Spring. For a more comprehensive view of Spring, we recommend *Spring in Action*, by Craig Walls (http://www.manning.com/walls4/).

We'll then go on to show you how Camel uses Spring to form a replacement or complementary solution to the Java DSL.

2.4.1   Bean injection and Spring

Creating an application from beans using Spring is pretty simple. All you need are a few Java beans (classes), a Spring XML configuration file, and an ApplicationContext. The ApplicationContext is similar to the CamelContext, in that it's the runtime container for Spring. Let's look at a simple example.

Consider an application that prints out a greeting followed by your username. In this application you don't want the greeting to be hardcoded, so you can use an interface to break this dependency. Consider the following interface:

```
public interface Greeter {
    public String sayHello();
}
```

This interface is implemented by the following classes:

```
public class EnglishGreeter implements Greeter {
    public String sayHello() {
        return "Hello " + System.getProperty("user.name");
    }
}
public class DanishGreeter implements Greeter {
    public String sayHello() {
        return "Davs " + System.getProperty("user.name");
    }
}
```

You can now create a greeter application as follows:

```
public class GreetMeBean {
    private Greeter greeter;

    public void setGreeter(Greeter greeter) {
        this.greeter = greeter;
    }
```

```
    public void execute() {
        System.out.println(greeter.sayHello());
    }
}
```

This application will output a different greeting depending on how you configure it. To configure this application using Spring, you could do something like this:

```xml
<beans xmlns="http://www.springframework.org/schema/beans"
       xmlns:xsi="http://www.w3.org/2001/XMLSchema-instance"
       xsi:schemaLocation="
       http://www.springframework.org/schema/beans
       http://www.springframework.org/schema/beans/spring-beans-3.0.xsd">

  <bean id="myGreeter" class="camelinaction.EnglishGreeter"/>

  <bean id="greetMeBean" class="camelinaction.GreetMeBean">
    <property name="greeter" ref="myGreeter"/>
  </bean>

</beans>
```

This XML file instructs Spring to do the following:

1 Create an instance of EnglishGreeter and names the bean myGreeter
2 Create an instance of GreetMeBean and names the bean greetMeBean
3 Set the reference of the greeter property of the GreetMeBean to the bean named myGreeter

This configuring of beans is called *wiring*.

In order to load this XML file into Spring, you can use the ClassPathXmlApplicationContext, which is a concrete implementation of the ApplicationContext that's provided with the Spring framework. This class loads Spring XML files from a location specified on the classpath.

Here is the final version of GreetMeBean:

```java
public class GreetMeBean {
    ...

    public static void main(String[] args) {
        ApplicationContext context =
            new ClassPathXmlApplicationContext("beans.xml");
        GreetMeBean bean = (GreetMeBean) context.getBean("greetMeBean");
        bean.execute();
    }
}
```

The ClassPathXmlApplicationContext you instantiate here loads up the bean definitions you saw previously in the beans.xml file. You then call getBean on the context to look up the bean with the greetMeBean ID in the Spring registry. All beans defined in this file are accessible in this way.

To run this example, go to the chapter2/spring directory in the book's source code and run this Maven command:

```
mvn compile exec:java -Dexec.mainClass=camelinaction.GreetMeBean
```

This will output something like the following on the command line:

```
Hello janstey
```

If you had wired the `DanishGreeter` in instead, you'd have seen something like this on the console:

```
Davs janstey
```

This example may seem pretty simple, but it should give you an understanding of what Spring and, more generally, an IoC container, really is.

So how does Camel fit into this? Essentially, Camel can be configured as if it were another bean. For instance, you configured the JMS component to connect to an ActiveMQ broker in section 2.2.2, but you could have done this in Spring by using the bean terminology, as follows:

```
<bean id="jms" class="org.apache.camel.component.jms.JmsComponent">
  <property name="connectionFactory">
    <bean class="org.apache.activemq.ActiveMQConnectionFactory">
      <property name="brokerURL" value="vm://localhost" />
    </bean>
  </property>
</bean>
```

In this case, Camel will know to look for beans of type `org.apache.camel.Component` and add them to the `CamelContext` automatically—a task you did manually in section 2.2.2.

But where is the `CamelContext` defined in Spring? Well, to make things easier on the eyes, Camel utilizes Spring extension mechanisms to provide custom XML syntax for Camel concepts within the Spring XML file. To load up a `CamelContext` in Spring, you can do the following:

```
<beans xmlns="http://www.springframework.org/schema/beans"
       xmlns:xsi="http://www.w3.org/2001/XMLSchema-instance"
       xsi:schemaLocation="
       http://www.springframework.org/schema/beans
       http://www.springframework.org/schema/beans/spring-beans-3.0.xsd
       http://camel.apache.org/schema/spring
       http://camel.apache.org/schema/spring/camel-spring.xsd">

  ...

  <camelContext xmlns="http://camel.apache.org/schema/spring"/>

</beans>
```

This will automatically start a `SpringCamelContext`, which is a subclass of the `DefaultCamelContext` you used for the Java DSL. Also notice that you had to include the http://camel.apache.org/schema/spring/camel-spring.xsd XML schema definition in the XML file—this is needed to import the custom XML elements.

This snippet alone isn't going to do much for you. You need to tell Camel what routes to use, as you did when using the Java DSL. The following code uses Spring to produce the same results as the code in listing 2.1.

> **Listing 2.2   A Spring configuration that produces the same results as listing 2.1**

```
<beans xmlns="http://www.springframework.org/schema/beans"
       xmlns:xsi="http://www.w3.org/2001/XMLSchema-instance"
       xsi:schemaLocation="
       http://www.springframework.org/schema/beans
       http://www.springframework.org/schema/beans/spring-beans-3.0.xsd
       http://camel.apache.org/schema/spring
       http://camel.apache.org/schema/spring/camel-spring.xsd">

  <bean id="jms" class="org.apache.camel.component.jms.JmsComponent">
    <property name="connectionFactory">
      <bean class="org.apache.activemq.ActiveMQConnectionFactory">
        <property name="brokerURL" value="vm://localhost" />
      </bean>
    </property>
  </bean>

  <bean id="ftpToJmsRoute" class="camelinaction.FtpToJMSRoute"/>

  <camelContext xmlns="http://camel.apache.org/schema/spring">
    <routeBuilder ref="ftpToJmsRoute"/>
  </camelContext>

</beans>
```

You may have noticed that we're referring to the `camelinaction.FtpToJMSRoute` class as a `RouteBuilder`. In order to reproduce the Java DSL example in listing 2.1, you have to factor out the anonymous `RouteBuilder` into its own named class. The `FtpToJMS-Route` class looks like this:

```
public class FtpToJMSRoute extends RouteBuilder {
  public void configure() {
    from("ftp://rider.com" +
      "/orders?username=rider&password=secret")
      .to("jms:incomingOrders");
  }
}
```

Now that you know the basics of Spring and how to load Camel inside it, we can go further by looking at how to write Camel routing rules purely in XML—no Java DSL required.

2.4.2   *The Spring DSL*

What we've seen of Camel's integration with Spring is adequate, but it isn't taking full advantage of Spring's methodology of configuring applications using no code. To completely invert the control of creating applications using Spring XML, Camel provides custom XML extensions that we call the *Spring DSL*. The Spring DSL allows you to do almost everything you can do in the Java DSL.

Let's continue with the Rider Auto Parts example shown in listing 2.2, but this time you'll specify the routing rules defined in the `RouteBuilder` purely in XML. The following Spring XML does this.

Listing 2.3   A Spring DSL example that produces the same results as listing 2.1

```
<beans xmlns="http://www.springframework.org/schema/beans"
       xmlns:xsi="http://www.w3.org/2001/XMLSchema-instance"
       xsi:schemaLocation="
       http://www.springframework.org/schema/beans
       http://www.springframework.org/schema/beans/spring-beans-3.0.xsd
       http://camel.apache.org/schema/spring
       http://camel.apache.org/schema/spring/camel-spring.xsd">

  <bean id="jms" class="org.apache.camel.component.jms.JmsComponent">
    <property name="connectionFactory">
      <bean class="org.apache.activemq.ActiveMQConnectionFactory">
        <property name="brokerURL" value="vm://localhost" />
      </bean>
    </property>
  </bean>

  <camelContext xmlns="http://camel.apache.org/schema/spring">
    <route>
      <from
uri="ftp://rider.com/orders?username=rider&password=secret"/>
      <to uri="jms:incomingOrders"/>
    </route>
  </camelContext>

</beans>
```

In this listing, under the `camelContext` element you replace `routeBuilder` with the route element. Within the `route` element, you specify the route using elements with names similar to ones used inside the Java DSL `RouteBuilder`. This listing is function-ally equivalent to the Java DSL version in listing 2.1 and the Spring plus Java DSL combo in listing 2.2.

In the book's source code, we changed the `from` method to consume messages from a local file directory instead. The new route looks like this:

```
<route>
  <from uri="file:src/data?noop=true"/>
  <to uri="jms:incomingOrders"/>
</route>
```

The file endpoint will load order files from the relative src/data directory. The `noop` property configures the endpoint to leave the file as is after processing; this option is very useful for testing. In chapter 7, you'll also see how Camel allows you to delete or move the files after processing.

This route won't display anything interesting yet. You need to add an additional processing step for testing.

ADDING A PROCESSOR

Adding additional processing steps is simple, as in the Java DSL. Here you'll add a cus-tom processor like you did in section 2.3.2.

Because you can't refer to an anonymous class in Spring XML, you need to factor out the anonymous processor into the following class:

```java
public class DownloadLogger implements Processor {
    public void process(Exchange exchange) throws Exception {
        System.out.println("We just downloaded: "
                + exchange.getIn().getHeader("CamelFileName"));
    }
}
```

You can now use it in your Spring DSL route as follows:

```xml
<bean id="downloadLogger" class="camelinaction.DownloadLogger"/>

<camelContext xmlns="http://camel.apache.org/schema/spring">
  <route>
    <from uri="file:src/data?noop=true"/>
    <process ref="downloadLogger"/>
    <to uri="jms:incomingOrders"/>
  </route>
</camelContext>
```

Now you're ready to run the example. Go to the chapter2/spring directory in the book's source code and run this Maven command:

```
mvn clean compile camel:run
```

Because there is only one message file named message1.xml in the src/data directory, this will output something like the following on the command line:

```
We just downloaded: message1.xml
```

What if you wanted to print this message after consuming it from the incomingOrders queue? To do this, you'll need to create another route.

USING MULTIPLE ROUTES

You may recall that in the Java DSL each Java statement starting with a from creates a new route. You can also create multiple routes with the Spring DSL. To do this, simply add an additional route element within the camelContext element.

For example, move the DownloadLogger bean into a second route, after the order gets sent to the incomingOrders queue:

```xml
<camelContext xmlns="http://camel.apache.org/schema/spring">
  <route>
    <from uri="file:src/data?noop=true"/>
    <to uri="jms:incomingOrders"/>
  </route>
  <route>
    <from uri="jms:incomingOrders"/>
    <process ref="downloadLogger"/>
  </route>
</camelContext>
```

Now you are consuming the message from the incomingOrders queue in the second route. So, the downloaded message will be printed after the order is sent to the queue.

CHOOSING WHICH DSL TO USE

Which DSL is best to use in a particular scenario is a common question for Camel users, but it mostly comes down to personal preference. If you like working with

Spring or like defining things in XML, you may prefer a pure Spring approach. If you want to be hands-on with Java, maybe a pure Java DSL approach is better for you.

In either case, you'll be able to access nearly all of Camel's functionality. The Java DSL is a slightly richer language to work with because you have the full power of the Java language at your fingertips. Also, some Java DSL features, like value builders (for building expressions and predicates[1]), aren't available in the Spring DSL. On the other hand, using Spring gives you access to the wonderful object construction capabilities as well as commonly used Spring abstractions for things like database connections and JMS integration.

A common compromise (and our favorite usage) is to use both Spring and the Java DSL, which is one of the topics we'll cover next.

2.4.3 *Using Camel and Spring*

Whether you write your routes in the Java or Spring DSL, running Camel in a Spring container gives you many other benefits. For one, if you're using the Spring DSL, you don't have to recompile any code when you want to change your routing rules. Also, you gain access to Spring's portfolio of database connectors, transaction support, and more.

Let's take a closer look at what other Spring integrations Camel provides.

FINDING ROUTE BUILDERS

Using the Spring `CamelContext` as a runtime and the Java DSL for route development is a great way of using Camel. In fact, it's the most frequent usage of Camel.

You saw before that you can explicitly tell the Spring `CamelContext` what route builders to load. You can do this by using the `routerBuilder` element:

```
<camelContext xmlns="http://camel.apache.org/schema/spring">
  <routeBuilder ref="ftpToJmsRoute"/>
</camelContext>
```

Being this explicit results in a clean and concise definition of what is being loaded into Camel.

Sometimes, though, you may need to be a bit more dynamic. This is where the `packageScan` and `contextScan` elements come in:

```
<camelContext xmlns="http://camel.apache.org/schema/spring">
  <packageScan>
    <package>camelinaction.routes</package>
  </packageScan>
</camelContext>
```

This `packageScan` element will load all `RouteBuilder` classes found in the camelinaction.routes package, including all subpackages.

You can even be a bit more picky about what route builders are included:

```
<camelContext xmlns="http://camel.apache.org/schema/spring">
  <packageScan>
    <package>camelinaction.routes</package>
```

---

[1] See appendix B for more information on expressions and predicates.

```
        <excludes>**.*Test*</excludes>
        <includes>**.*</includes>
    </packageScan>
</camelContext>
```

In this case, you're loading all route builders in the camelinaction.routes package, except for ones with "Test" in the class name. The matching syntax is similar to what is used in Apache Ant's file pattern matchers.

The `contextScan` element takes advantage of Spring's component-scan feature to load any Camel route builders that are marked with the `@org.springframework.stereotype.Component` annotation. Let's modify the `FtpToJMSRoute` class to use this annotation:

```
@Component
public class FtpToJMSRoute extends SpringRouteBuilder {

    public void configure() {
    from("ftp://rider.com" +
        "/orders?username=rider&password=secret")
        .to("jms:incomingOrders");
    }
}
```

Notice that this version uses the `org.apache.camel.spring.SpringRouteBuilder` class, which is an extension of `RouteBuilder` that contains extra Spring utility functions. You can now enable the component scanning by using the following configuration in your Spring XML file:

```
<context:component-scan base-package="camelinaction.routes"/>

<camelContext xmlns="http://camel.apache.org/schema/spring">
    <contextScan/>
</camelContext>
```

This will load up any Spring route builders within the camelinaction.routes package that have the `@Component` annotation.

Under the hood, some of Camel's components, like the JMS component, are built on top of abstraction libraries from Spring. It makes sense that configuring those components is easy in Spring.

CONFIGURING COMPONENTS AND ENDPOINTS

You saw in section 2.4.1 that components could be defined in Spring XML and would be picked up automatically by Camel. For instance, look at the JMS component again:

```
<bean id="jms" class="org.apache.camel.component.jms.JmsComponent">
    <property name="connectionFactory">
        <bean class="org.apache.activemq.ActiveMQConnectionFactory">
            <property name="brokerURL" value="vm://localhost" />
        </bean>
    </property>
</bean>
```

The bean `id` defines what this component will be called. This gives you the flexibility to give the component a more meaningful name based on the use case. Your application may require the integration of two JMS brokers, for instance. One could be for Apache ActiveMQ and another could be for SonicMQ:

```
<bean id="activemq" class="org.apache.camel.component.jms.JmsComponent">
  ...
</bean>
<bean id="sonicmq" class="org.apache.camel.component.jms.JmsComponent">
  ...
</bean>
```

You could then use URIs like activemq:myActiveMQQueue or sonicmq:mySonicQueue.

Endpoints can also be defined using Camel's Spring XML extensions. For example, you can break out the FTP endpoint for connecting to Rider Auto Parts' legacy order server and see what the route looks like:

```
<camelContext xmlns="http://camel.apache.org/schema/spring">
  <endpoint id="ridersFtp"
uri="ftp://rider.com/orders?username=rider&password=secret"/>
  <route>
    <from ref="ridersFtp"/>
    <to uri="jms:incomingOrders"/>
  </route>
</camelContext>
```

> **NOTE** You may notice that credentials have been added directly into the endpoint URI, which isn't always the best solution. A better way would be to refer to credentials that are defined and sufficiently protected elsewhere. In section 6.1.6 of chapter 6, you can see how the Camel Properties component or Spring property placeholders are used to do this.

IMPORTING CONFIGURATION AND ROUTES

A common practice in Spring development is to separate out an application's wiring into several XML files. This is mainly done to make the XML more readable; you probably wouldn't want to wade through thousands of lines of XML in a single file without some separation.

Another reason to separate an application into several XML files is the potential for reuse. For instance, some other application may require a similar JMS setup, so you can define a second Spring XML file called jms-setup.xml with these contents:

```
<beans xmlns="http://www.springframework.org/schema/beans"
       xmlns:xsi="http://www.w3.org/2001/XMLSchema-instance"
       xsi:schemaLocation="
       http://www.springframework.org/schema/beans
       http://www.springframework.org/schema/beans/spring-beans-3.0.xsd">

  <bean id="jms" class="org.apache.camel.component.jms.JmsComponent">
    <property name="connectionFactory">
      <bean class="org.apache.activemq.ActiveMQConnectionFactory">
        <property name="brokerURL" value="vm://localhost" />
      </bean>
    </property>
  </bean>
</beans>
```

This file could then be imported into the XML file containing the `CamelContext` by using the following line:

```
<import resource="jms-setup.xml"/>
```

Now the `CamelContext` can use the JMS component configuration even though it's defined in a separate file.

Other useful things to define in separate files are the Spring DSL routes themselves. Because route elements need to be defined within a `camelContext` element, an additional concept is introduced to define routes. You can define routes within a `routeContext` element, as shown here:

```
<routeContext id="ftpToJms" xmlns="http://camel.apache.org/schema/spring">
  <route>
    <from uri="ftp://rider.com/orders?username=rider&password=secret"/>
    <to uri="jms:incomingOrders"/>
  </route>
</routeContext>
```

This `routeContext` element could be in another file or in the same file. You can then import the routes defined in this `routeContext` with the `routeContextRef` element. You use the `routeContextRef` element inside a `camelContext` as follows:

```
<camelContext xmlns="http://camel.apache.org/schema/spring">
  <routeContextRef ref="ftpToJms"/>
</camelContext>
```

If you import the `routeContext` into multiple `CamelContexts`, a new instance of the route is created in each. In the preceding case, two identical routes, with the same endpoint URIs, will lead to them competing for the same resource. In this case, only one route at a time will receive a particular file from FTP. In general, you should take care when reusing routes in multiple `CamelContexts`.

ADVANCED CONFIGURATION OPTIONS

There are many other configuration options available when using the Spring `Camel-Context`:

- Pluggable bean registries are discussed in chapter 4.
- The Tracer and Delay mechanisms are covered in chapter 12.
- Custom class resolvers, tracing, fault handling and startup are mentioned in chapter 13.
- The configuration of interceptors is covered in chapter 6.

With these route configuration techniques behind us, you're ready to tackle more advanced routing topics using Camel's implementation of the EIPs.

2.5 Routing and EIPs

So far we haven't touched much on the EIPs that Camel was built to implement. This was intentional. We wanted to make sure you had a good understanding of what Camel is doing in the simplest cases before moving on to more complex examples.

As far as EIPs go, we'll be looking at the Content-Based Router, Message Filter, Multicast, Recipient List, and Wire Tap right away. Other patterns will be introduced throughout the book, and in chapter 8 we'll be covering the most complex EIPs. The complete list of EIPs supported by Camel is available from the Camel website (http://camel.apache.org/enterprise-integration-patterns.html).

For now, let's start by looking at the most well known EIP, the Content-Based Router.

2.5.1   Using a content-based router

As the name implies, a Content-Based Router (CBR) is a message router that routes a message to a destination based on its content. The content could be a message header, the payload data type, part of the payload itself—pretty much anything in the message exchange.

To demonstrate, let's go back to Rider Auto Parts. Some customers have started uploading orders to the FTP server in the newer XML format rather than CSV. That means you have two types of messages coming in to the incomingOrders queue. We didn't touch on this before, but you need to convert the incoming orders into an internal POJO format. You obviously need to do different conversions for the different types of incoming orders.

As a possible solution, you could use the filename extension to determine whether a particular order message should be sent to a queue for CSV orders or a queue for XML orders. This is depicted in figure 2.10.

As you saw earlier, you can use the CamelFileName header set by the FTP consumer to get the filename.

To do the conditional routing required by the CBR, Camel introduces a few keywords in the DSL. The choice method creates a CBR processor, and conditions are added by following choice with a combination of a when method and a predicate.

Camel's creators could have chosen contentBasedRouter for the method name, to match the EIP, but they stuck with choice because it reads more naturally. It looks like this:

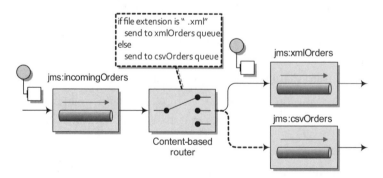

Figure 2.10   The CBR routes messages based on their content. In this case, the filename extension (as a message header) is used to determine which queue to route to.

```
from("jms:incomingOrders")
.choice()
    .when(predicate)
        .to("jms:xmlOrders")
    .when(predicate)
        .to("jms:csvOrders");
```

You may have noticed that we didn't fill in the predicates required for each when method. A predicate in Camel is a simple interface that only has a matches method:

```
public interface Predicate {
    boolean matches(Exchange exchange);
}
```

For example, you can think of a predicate as a Boolean condition in a Java if statement.

You probably don't want to look inside the exchange yourself and do a comparison. Fortunately, predicates are often built up from expressions, and expressions are used to extract a result from an exchange based on the expression content. There are many different expression languages to choose from in Camel, some of which include Simple, EL, JXPath, Mvel, OGNL, PHP, BeanShell, JavaScript, Groovy, Python, Ruby, XPath, and XQuery. As you'll see in chapter 4, you can even use a method call to a bean as an expression in Camel. In this case, you'll be using the expression builder methods that are part of the Java DSL.

Within the RouteBuilder, you can start by using the header method, which returns an expression that will evaluate to the header value. For example, header("CamelFileName") will create an expression that will resolve to the value of the CamelFileName header on the incoming exchange. On this expression you can invoke a number of methods to create a predicate. So, to check whether the filename extension is equal to .xml, you can use the following predicate:

```
header("CamelFileName").endsWith(".xml")
```

The completed CBR is shown here.

Listing 2.4 A complete content-based router

```
context.addRoutes(new RouteBuilder() {
    public void configure() {
        from("file:src/data?noop=true").to("jms:incomingOrders");

        from("jms:incomingOrders")
        .choice()
            .when(header("CamelFileName")
            .endsWith(".xml"))                              ❶ Content-based
                .to("jms:xmlOrders")                            router
            .when(header("CamelFileName")
            .endsWith(".csv"))                              ❷ Test routes
                .to("jms:csvOrders");                          that print
                                                               message
        from("jms:xmlOrders").process(new Processor() {        content
            public void process(Exchange exchange) throws Exception {
```

```
                    System.out.println("Received XML order: "
                        + exchange.getIn().getHeader("CamelFileName"));
            }
        });
```

Test routes that print ❷
message content

```
        from("jms:csvOrders").process(new Processor() {
            public void process(Exchange exchange) throws Exception {
                System.out.println("Received CSV order: "
                    + exchange.getIn().getHeader("CamelFileName"));
            }
        });
    }
});
```

To run this example, go to the chapter2/cbr directory in the book's source code and run this Maven command:

```
mvn clean compile exec:java -Dexec.mainClass=camelinaction.OrderRouter
```

This will consume two order files in the chapter2/cbr/src/data directory and output the following:

```
Received CSV order: message2.csv
Received XML order: message1.xml
```

The output comes from the two routes at the end of the `configure` method ❷. These routes consume messages from the xmlOrders and csvOrders queues and then print out messages. You use these routes to test that the router ❶ is working as expected. More advanced route-testing techniques will be discussed in chapter 6.

USING THE OTHERWISE CLAUSE

One of Rider Auto Parts' customers sends CSV orders with the .csl extension. Your current route only handles .csv and .xml files and will drop all orders with other extensions. This isn't a good solution, so you need to improve things a bit.

One way to handle the extra extension is to use a regular expression as a predicate instead of the simple `endsWith` call. The following route can handle the extra file extension:

```
from("jms:incomingOrders")
.choice()
    .when(header("CamelFileName").endsWith(".xml"))
        .to("jms:xmlOrders")
    .when(header("CamelFileName").regex("^.*(csv|csl)$"))
        .to("jms:csvOrders");
```

This solution still suffers from the same problem, though. Any orders not conforming to the file extension scheme will be dropped. Really, you should be handling bad orders that come in so someone can fix the problem. For this you can use the otherwise clause:

```
from("jms:incomingOrders")
.choice()
    .when(header("CamelFileName").endsWith(".xml"))
```

```
        .to("jms:xmlOrders")
    .when(header("CamelFileName").regex("^.*(csv|csl)$"))
        .to("jms:csvOrders")
    .otherwise()
        .to("jms:badOrders");
```

Now, all orders not having an extension of .csv, .csl, or .xml are sent to the badOrders queue for handling.

To run this example, go to the chapter2/cbr directory in the book's source and run this command:

```
mvn clean compile exec:java
➥ -Dexec.mainClass=camelinaction.OrderRouterOtherwise
```

This will consume four order files in the chapter2/cbr/src/data directory and output the following:

```
Received CSV order: message2.csv
Received XML order: message1.xml
Received bad order: message4.bad
Received CSV order: message3.csl
```

You can now see that a bad order has been received.

ROUTING AFTER A CBR

The CBR may seem like it's the end of the route; messages are routed to one of several destinations, and that's it. Continuing the flow means you need another route, right?

Well, there are several ways you can continue routing after a CBR. One is by using another route, like you did in listing 2.4 for printing a test message to the console. Another way of continuing the flow is by closing the choice block and adding another processor to the pipeline after that.

You can close the choice block by using the end method:

```
from("jms:incomingOrders")
.choice()
    .when(header("CamelFileName").endsWith(".xml"))
        .to("jms:xmlOrders")
    .when(header("CamelFileName").regex("^.*(csv|csl)$"))
        .to("jms:csvOrders")
    .otherwise()
        .to("jms:badOrders")
.end()
.to("jms:continuedProcessing");
```

Here, the choice has been closed and another to has been added to the route. Now, after each destination with the choice, the message will be routed to the continued-Processing queue as well. This is illustrated in figure 2.11.

You can also control what destinations are final in the choice block. For instance, you may not want bad orders continuing through the rest of the route. You'd like them to be routed to the badOrders queue and stop there. In this case, you can use the stop method in the DSL:

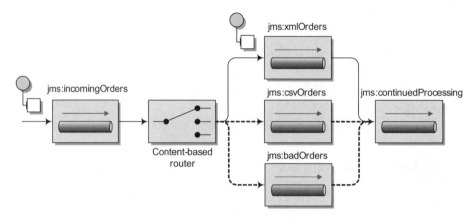

Figure 2.11   By using the end method, you can route messages to a destination after the CBR.

```
from("jms:incomingOrders")
.choice()
    .when(header("CamelFileName").endsWith(".xml"))
        .to("jms:xmlOrders")
    .when(header("CamelFileName").regex("^.*(csv|csl)$"))
        .to("jms:csvOrders")
    .otherwise()
        .to("jms:badOrders").stop()
.end()
.to("jms:continuedProcessing");
```

Now, any orders entering into the otherwise block will only be sent to the badOrders queue—not to the continuedProcessing queue.

Using the Spring DSL, this route looks a bit different:

```
<route>
  <from uri="jms:incomingOrders"/>
  <choice>
    <when>
      <simple>${header.CamelFileName} regex '^.*xml$'</simple>
      <to uri="jms:xmlOrders"/>
    </when>
    <when>
      <simple>${header.CamelFileName} regex '^.*(csv|csl)$'</simple>
      <to uri="jms:csvOrders"/>
    </when>
    <otherwise>
      <to uri="jms:badOrders"/>
      <stop/>
    </otherwise>
  </choice>
  <to uri="jms:continuedProcessing"/>
</route>
```

Other than being in XML rather than Java, there are two main differences to note here, compared to the Java DSL version:

- You use a Simple expression instead of the Java-based predicate. The Simple expression language is typically used as a replacement for predicates from the Java DSL. A complete guide on the Simple expression language can be found in appendix A.
- You don't have to use an `end()` call to end the choice block because XML requires an explicit end block in the form of the closing element `</choice>`.

2.5.2 Using message filters

Rider Auto Parts now has a new issue—their QA department has expressed the need to be able to send test orders into the live web frontend of the order system. Your current solution would accept these orders as real and send them to the internal systems for processing. You've suggested that QA should be testing on a development clone of the real system, but management has shot down this idea, citing a limited budget. What you need is a solution that will discard these test messages while still operating on the real orders.

The Message Filter EIP, shown in figure 2.12, provides a nice way of dealing with this kind of problem. Incoming messages only pass through the filter if a certain condition is met. Messages failing the condition will be dropped.

Let's see how you can implement this using Camel. Recall that the web frontend that Rider Auto Parts uses only sends orders in the XML format, so you can place this filter after the `xmlOrders` queue, where all orders are XML. Test messages have an extra `test` attribute set, so you can use this to do the filtering. A test message looks like this:

```
<?xml version="1.0" encoding="UTF-8"?>
<order name="motor" amount="1" customer="foo" test="true"/>
```

The entire solution is implemented in OrderRouterWithFilter.java, which is included with the chapter2/filter project in the book's source distribution. The filter looks like this:

```
from("jms:xmlOrders").filter(xpath("/order[not(@test)]"))
.process(new Processor() {
    public void process(Exchange exchange) throws Exception {
        System.out.println("Received XML order: "
                + exchange.getIn().getHeader("CamelFileName"));
    }
});
```

To run this example, execute the following Maven command on the command line:

```
mvn clean compile exec:java
    -Dexec.mainClass=camelinaction.OrderRouterWithFilter
```

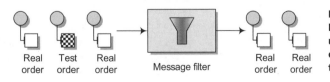

Figure 2.12 A Message Filter allows you to filter out uninteresting messages based on some condition. In this case, test messages are filtered out.

Real order   Test order   Real order   Message filter   Real order   Real order

This will output the following on the command line:

```
Received XML order: message1.xml
```

You'll only receive one message after the filter because the test message was filtered out.

You may have noticed that this example filters out the test message with an XPath expression. XPath expressions are useful for creating conditions based on XML payloads. In this case, the expression will evaluate `true` for orders that don't have the `test` attribute.

As you saw back in section 2.4.2, when the Spring DSL is used, you cannot use an anonymous inner class for a processor. You must name the `Processor` class and add a bean entry in the Spring XML file. So a message filter route in the Spring DSL looks like this:

```
<route>
  <from uri="jms:xmlOrders"/>
  <filter>
    <xpath>/order[not(@test)]</xpath>
    <process ref="orderLogger"/>
  </filter>
</route>
```

The flow remains the same as in the Java DSL version of this route, but here you reference the processor as `orderLogger`, which is defined as a bean entry in the Spring XML file.

So far, the EIPs we've looked at only sent messages to a single destination. Next we'll take a look at how you can send to multiple destinations.

2.5.3   *Using multicasting*

Often in enterprise applications you'll need to send a copy of a message to several different destinations for processing. When the list of destinations is known ahead of time and is static, you can add an element to the route that will consume messages from a source endpoint and then send the message out to a list of destinations. Borrowing terminology from computer networking, we call this the Multicast EIP.

Currently at Rider Auto Parts, orders are processed in a step-by-step manner. They're first sent to accounting for validation of customer standing and then to production for manufacture. A bright new manager has suggested that they could improve the speed of operations by sending orders to accounting and production at the same time. This would cut out the delay involved when production waits for the OK from accounting. You've been asked to implement this change to the system.

Using a multicast, you could envision the solution shown in figure 2.13.

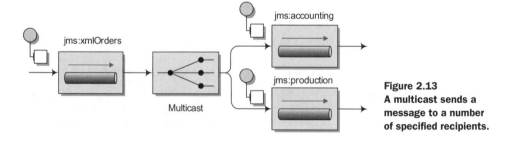

**Figure 2.13
A multicast sends a
message to a number
of specified recipients.**

With Camel, you can use the `multicast` method in the Java DSL to implement this solution:

```
from("jms:xmlOrders").multicast().to("jms:accounting", "jms:production");
```

To run this example, go to the chapter2/multicast directory in the book's source code and run this command:

```
mvn clean compile exec:java
-Dexec.mainClass=camelinaction.OrderRouterWithMulticast
```

You should see the following output on the command line:

```
Accounting received order: message1.xml
Production received order: message1.xml
```

These two lines of output are coming from two test routes that consume from the accounting and production queues and then output text to the console that qualifies the message.

> **TIP** For dealing with responses from services invoked in a multicast, an aggregator is used. See more about aggregation in chapter 8.

By default, the multicast sends message copies sequentially. In the preceding example, a message is sent to the accounting queue and then to the production queue. But what if you wanted to send them in parallel?

PARALLEL MULTICASTING

Sending messages in parallel using the multicast involves only one extra DSL method: `parallelProcessing`. Extending the previous multicast example, you can add the `parallelProcessing` method as follows:

```
from("jms:xmlOrders")
    .multicast().parallelProcessing()
    .to("jms:accounting", "jms:production");
```

This will set up the multicast to distribute messages to the destinations in parallel.

A default thread pool size of 10 is used if you don't specify anything else. If you want to change this default, you can set the underlying `java.util.concurrent.ExecutorService` that's used to launch new asynchronous message sends by using the `executorService` DSL method. Here's an example:

```
ExecutorService executor = Executors.newFixedThreadPool(16);

from("jms:xmlOrders")
    .multicast().parallelProcessing().executorService(executor)
    .to("jms:accounting", "jms:production");
```

This code increases the maximum number of threads to 16, in order to handle a larger number of incoming requests. For more information on the Camel threading model and thread pools, please see chapter 10.

By default, the multicast will continue sending messages to destinations even if one fails. In your application, though, you may consider the whole process as failed if one destination fails. What do you do in this case?

STOPPING THE MULTICAST ON EXCEPTION

Our multicast solution at Rider Auto Parts suffers from a problem: if the order failed to send to the accounting queue, it might take longer to track down the order from production and bill the customer. To solve this problem, you can take advantage of the `stopOnException` feature of the multicast. When enabled, this feature will stop the multicast on the first exception caught, so you can take any necessary action.

To enable this feature, use the `stopOnException` method as follows:

```
from("jms:xmlOrders")
    .multicast().stopOnException()
    .parallelProcessing().executorService(executor)
    .to("jms:accounting", "jms:production");
```

To handle the exception coming back from this route, you'll need to use Camel's error-handling facilities, which are described in detail in chapter 5.

When using the Spring DSL, this route looks a little bit different:

```
<route>
  <from uri="jms:xmlOrders"/>
  <multicast stopOnException="true" parallelProcessing="true"
➥ executorServiceRef="executor">
    <to uri="jms:accounting"/>
    <to uri="jms:production"/>
  </multicast>
</route>
```

The main difference is that the methods used to set flags such as `stopOnException` in the Java DSL are now attributes on the `multicast` element. Also, the executor service is now specified as a reference to a Spring bean defined as follows:

```
<bean id="executor" class="java.util.concurrent.Executors"
➥ factory-method="newFixedThreadPool">
  <constructor-arg index="0" value="16"/>
</bean>
```

Now you know how to multicast messages in Camel, but you may be thinking that this seems like a pretty static solution, because changing the destinations means changing the route. Let's see how you can make sending to multiple recipients more dynamic.

2.5.4   *Using recipient lists*

In the previous section, you implemented a new manager's suggestion to parallelize the accounting and production queues so orders could be processed more quickly. Rider Auto Parts' top-tier customers first noticed the problem with this approach: now that all orders are going directly into production, top-tier customers are not getting priority over the smaller customers. Their orders are taking longer, and they're losing business opportunities. Management suggested immediately going back to the old scheme, but you suggested a simple solution to the problem: by parallelizing only top-tier customers' orders, all other orders would have to go to accounting first, thereby not bogging down production.

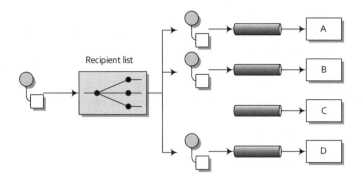

Figure 2.14 A recipient list inspects the incoming message and determines a list of recipients based on the content of the message. In this case, the message is only sent to the A, B, and D destinations.

This solution can be realized by using the Recipient List EIP. As shown in figure 2.14, a recipient list first inspects the incoming message, then generates a list of desired recipients based on the message content, and sends the message to those recipients. A recipient is specified by an endpoint URI. Note that the recipient list is different from the multicast because the list of recipients is dynamic.

Camel provides a `recipientList` method for implementing the Recipient List EIP. For example, the following route will take the list of recipients from a header named `recipients`, where each recipient is separated from the next by a comma:

```
from("jms:xmlOrders")
.recipientList(header("recipients"));
```

This is useful if you already have some information in the message that can be used to construct the destination names—you could use an expression to create the list. In order for the recipient list to extract meaningful endpoint URIs, the expression result must be iterable. Values that will work are `java.util.Collection`, `java.util.Iterator`, Java arrays, `org.w3c.dom.NodeList`, and, as shown in the example, a `String` with comma-separated values.

In the Rider Auto Parts situation, the message doesn't contain that list. You need some way of determining whether the message is from a top-tier customer or not. A simple solution could be to add a custom processor to do this:

```
from("jms:xmlOrders")
.setHeader("customer", xpath("/order/@customer"))
.process(new Processor() {
    public void process(Exchange exchange) throws Exception {
        String recipients = "jms:accounting";
        String customer =
            exchange.getIn().getHeader("customer", String.class);
        if (customer.equals("honda")) {
            recipients += ",jms:production";
        }
        exchange.getIn().setHeader("recipients", recipients);
    }
})
.recipientList(header("recipients"));
```

The processor now sets the `recipients` header to `"jms:accounting, jms:produc-tion"` only if the customer is at the gold level of support. The check for gold-level support here is greatly simplified—ideally you'd query a database for this check. Any other orders will be routed only to accounting, which will send them to production after the checks are complete.

The Spring DSL version of this route follows a very similar layout:

```
<route>
  <from uri="jms:xmlOrders" />
  <setHeader headerName="customer">
    <xpath>/order/@customer</xpath>
  </setHeader>
  <process ref="calculateRecipients" />
  <recipientList>
    <header>recipients</header>
  </recipientList>
</route>
```

As you may have expected, the anonymous processor specified in the Java DSL route had to be separated out into a named processor. This processor was then loaded as a Spring bean and given the name `calculateRecipients`, which is then referenced in the `process` element by using the `ref` attribute.

It's common for recipients to not be embedded in the message as headers or parts of the body, and using a custom processor for this case is perfectly functional, but not very nice. In using a custom processor, you have to manipulate the exchange and message APIs directly. Fortunately, Camel supports a better way of implementing a recipient list.

RECIPIENT LIST ANNOTATION

Rather than using the `recipientList` method in the DSL, you can add a `@Recipient-List` annotation to a method in a plain Java class (a Java bean). This annotation tells Camel that the annotated method should be used to generate the list of recipients from the exchange. This behavior only gets invoked, however, if the class is used with Camel's bean integration.

For example, replacing the custom processor you used in the previous section with an annotated bean results in a greatly simplified route:

```
from("jms:xmlOrders").bean(RecipientListBean.class);
```

Now all the logic for calculating the recipients and sending out messages is captured in the `RecipientListBean` class, which looks like this:

```
public class RecipientListBean {
    @RecipientList
    public String[] route(@XPath("/order/@customer") String customer) {
        if (isGoldCustomer(customer)) {
            return new String[] {"jms:accounting", "jms:production"};
        } else {
            return new String[] {"jms:accounting"};
        }
    }
```

```
    private boolean isGoldCustomer(String customer) {
        return customer.equals("honda");
    }
}
```

Notice that the return type of the bean is a list of the desired recipients. Camel will take this list and send a copy of the message to each destination in the list.

One nice thing about implementing the recipient list this way is that it's entirely separated from the route, which makes it a bit easier to read. You also have access to Camel's bean-binding annotations, which allow you to extract data from the message using expressions, so you don't have to manually explore the exchange. This example uses the @XPath bean-binding annotation to grab the customer attribute of the order element in the body. We'll cover these annotations in chapter 4, which is all about using beans.

To run this example, go to the chapter2/recipientlist directory in the book's source code and run this command:

```
mvn clean compile exec:java
-Dexec.mainClass=camelinaction.OrderRouterWithRecipientListBean
```

This will output the following on the command line:

```
Accounting received order: message1.xml
Production received order: message1.xml
Accounting received order: message2.xml
```

Why do you get this output? Well, you had the following two orders in the src/data directory:

- message1.xml
  ```
  <?xml version="1.0" encoding="UTF-8"?>
  <order name="motor" amount="1000" customer="honda"/>
  ```
- message2.xml
  ```
  <?xml version="1.0" encoding="UTF-8"?>
  <order name="motor" amount="2" customer="joe's bikes"/>
  ```

The first message is from a gold customer, according to the Rider Auto Parts rules, so it was routed to both accounting and production. The second order is from a smaller customer, so it went to accounting for verification of the customer's credit standing.

What this system lacks now is a way to inspect these messages as they're flowing through the route, rather than waiting until they reach the end. Let's see how a wire tap can help.

2.5.5   *Using the wireTap method*

Often in enterprise applications it's useful and necessary to inspect messages as they flow through a system. For instance, when an order fails, you need a way to look at which messages were received to determine the cause of the failure.

You could use a simple processor, as you've done before, to output information about a incoming message to the console or append it to a file. Here is a processor that outputs the message body to the console:

```
from("jms:incomingOrders")
.process(new Processor() {
    public void process(Exchange exchange) throws Exception {
        System.out.println("Received order: " +
            exchange.getIn().getBody());
    }
})
...
```

This is fine for debugging purposes, but it's a pretty poor solution for production use. What if you wanted the message headers, exchange properties, or other data in the message exchange? Ideally you could copy the whole incoming exchange and send that to another channel for auditing. As shown in figure 2.15, the Wire Tap EIP defines such a solution.

By using the `wireTap` method in the Java DSL, you can send a copy of the exchange to a secondary destination without affecting the behavior of the rest of the route:

```
from("jms:incomingOrders")
.wireTap("jms:orderAudit")
.choice()
    .when(header("CamelFileName").endsWith(".xml"))
        .to("jms:xmlOrders")
    .when(header("CamelFileName").regex("^.*(csv|csl)$"))
        .to("jms:csvOrders")
    .otherwise()
        .to("jms:badOrders");
```

The preceding code sends a copy of the exchange to the `orderAudit` queue, and the original exchange continues on through the route, as if you hadn't used a wire tap at all. Camel doesn't wait for a response from the wire tap because the wire tap sets the message exchange pattern (MEP) to `InOnly`. This means that the message will be sent to the `orderAudit` queue in a fire-and-forget fashion—it won't wait for a reply.

In the Spring DSL, you can configure a wire tap just as easily:

```
<route>
  <from uri="jms:incomingOrders"/>
  <wireTap uri="jms:orderAudit"/>
  ..
```

What can you do with a tapped message? A number of things could be done at this point:

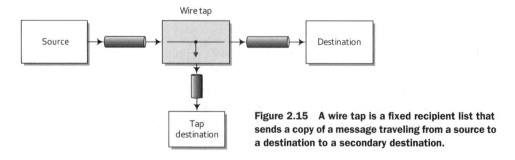

Figure 2.15   A wire tap is a fixed recipient list that sends a copy of a message traveling from a source to a destination to a secondary destination.

- You could print the information to the console like you did before. This is useful for simple debugging purposes.
- You could save the message in a persistent store (in a file or database) for retrieval later.

The wire tap is a pretty useful monitoring tool, but it leaves most of the work up to you. We'll discuss some of Camel's more powerful tracing and auditing tools in chapter 12.

2.6 Summary and best practices

In this chapter, we've covered one of the core abilities of Camel: routing messages. By now you should know how to create routes in either the Java or Spring DSL and know the differences in their configuration. You should also have a good grasp of when to apply several EIP implementations in Camel and how to use them. With this knowledge, you can create Camel applications that do useful tasks.

Here are some of the key concepts you should take away from this chapter:

- *Routing occurs in many aspects of everyday life.* Whether you're surfing the Internet, doing online banking, booking a flight or hotel room, messages are being routed behind the scenes using some sort of router.
- *Use Apache Camel for routing messages.* Camel is primarily a message router that allows to you route messages from and to a variety of transports and APIs.
- *Camel's DSLs are used to define routing rules.* The Java DSL allows you to write in the popular Java language, which gives you autocompletion of terms in most IDEs. It also allows you to use the full power of the Java language when writing routes. It's considered the main DSL in Camel. The Spring DSL allows you to write routing rules without any Java code at all.
- *The Java DSL and Spring* `CamelContext` *are a powerful combination.* In section 2.4.3 we described our favorite way to write Camel applications, which is to boot up the `CamelContext` in Spring and write routing rules in Java DSL `RouteBuilders`. This gives you the best of both: the most expressive DSL that Camel has in the Java DSL, and a more feature-rich and standard container in the Spring `CamelContext`.
- *Use enterprise integration patterns (EIPs) to solve integration and routing problems.* EIPs are like design patterns from object oriented programming, but for the enterprise integration world.
- *Use Camel's built-in EIP implementations rather than creating your own.* Camel implements most EIPs as easy-to-use DSL terms, which allows you to focus on the actual business problem rather than the integration architecture.

In the coming chapters we'll build on this foundation to show you things like data transformation, error handling, testing, sending data over other transports, and more. In the next chapter, we'll look at how Camel makes data transformation a breeze.

Part 2

Core Camel

In part 1, we guided you through what we consider introductory topics in Camel. They were topics you absolutely needed to know to use Camel. In this next part, we'll cover in depth the core features of Camel. You'll need many of these features when using Camel in real-world applications.

In chapter 3 we'll take a look at the data in the messages being routed by Camel. In particular, we'll look at how you can transform this data to other formats using Camel.

Camel has great support for integrating beans into your routing applications. In chapter 4 we'll look at the many ways beans can be used in Camel applications.

In complex enterprise systems, lots of things can go wrong. This is why Camel features an extensive set of error-handling abilities. In chapter 5 we'll discuss these in detail.

In chapter 6 we'll take a look at another important topic in application development: testing. We'll look at the testing facilities shipped with Camel. You can use these features for testing your own Camel applications or applications based on other stacks.

Components are the main extension mechanism in Camel. As such, they include functionality to connect to many different transports, APIs, and other extensions to Camel's core. Chapter 7 covers the most heavily used components that ship with Camel.

The last chapter of this part revisits the important topic of enterprise integration patterns (EIPs) in Camel. Back in chapter 2, we covered some of the simpler EIPs; in chapter 8, we'll look at several of the more complex EIPs.

Transforming
data with Camel

This chapter covers

- Transforming data using EIPs and Java
- Transforming XML data
- Transforming using well-known data formats
- Writing your own data formats for transformations
- Understanding the Camel type-converter mechanism

In the previous chapter, we covered routing, which is the single most important feature any integration kit must provide. In this chapter, we'll take a look at the second most important feature: data or message transformation.

Just as in the real world, where people speak different languages, the IT world speaks different protocols. Software engineers regularly need to act as mediators between various protocols when IT systems must be integrated. To address this, the data models used by the protocols must be transformed from one form to another, adapting to whatever protocol the receiver understands. Mediation and data transformation is a key feature in any integration kit, including Camel.

In this chapter, you'll learn all about how Camel can help you with your data transformation challenges. We'll start with a brief overview of data transformation in Camel and then look at how you can transform data into any custom format you may have. Then we'll look at some Camel components that are specialized for transforming XML data and other well-known data formats. We'll end the chapter by looking into Camel's type-converter mechanism, which supports implicitly and explicitly type coercing.

After reading this chapter, you'll know how to tackle any data transformation you're faced with and which Camel solution to leverage.

3.1   *Data transformation overview*

Camel provides many techniques for data transformation, and we'll cover them shortly. But first we'll start with an overview of data transformation in Camel.

Data transformation is a broad term that covers two types of transformation:

- *Data format transformation*—The data format of the message body is transformed from one form to another. For example, a CSV record is formatted as XML.
- *Data type transformation*—The data type of the message body is transformed from one type to another. For example a `java.lang.String` is transformed into a `javax.jms.TextMessage`.

Figure 3.1 illustrates the principle of transforming a message body from one form into another. This transformation can involve any combination of format and type transformations. In most cases, the data transformation you'll face with Camel is format transformation, where you have to mediate between two protocols. Camel has a built-in type-converter mechanism that can automatically convert between types, which greatly reduces the need for end users to deal with type transformations.

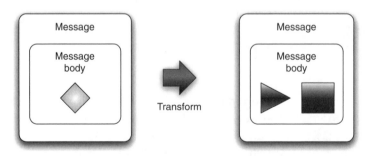

Figure 3.1   Camel offers many features for transforming data from one form to another.

Camel has many data-transformation features. We'll introduce them in the following section, and then look at them one by one. After reading this chapter, you'll have a solid understanding of how to use Camel to transform your data.

3.1.1   *Data transformation with Camel*

In Camel, data transformation typically takes places in the six ways listed in table 3.1.

Table 3.1   Six ways data transformation typically takes place in Camel

Transformation	Description
Data transformation in routes	You can explicitly enforce transformation in the route using the Message Translator or the Content Enricher EIPs. This gives you the power to do data mapping using regular Java code. We'll cover this in section 3.2.
Data transformation using components	Camel provides a range of components for transformation, such as the XSLT component for XML transformation. We'll dive into this in section 3.3.
Data transformation using data formats	Data formats are Camel transformers that come in pairs to transform data back and forth between well-known formats.
Data transformation using templates	Camel provides a range of components for transforming using templates, such as Apache Velocity. We'll look at this in section 3.5.
Data type transformation using Camel's type-converter mechanism	Camel has an elaborate type-converter mechanism that activates on demand. This is convenient when you need to convert from common types such as `java.lang.Integer` to `java.lang.String` or even from `java.io.File` to `java.lang.String`. Type converters are covered in section 3.6.
Message transformation in component adapters	Camel's many components adapt to various commonly used protocols and, as such, need to be able to transform messages as they travel to and from those protocols. Often these components use a combination of custom data transformations and type converters. This happens seamlessly, and only component writers need to worry about it. We'll cover writing custom components in chapter 11.

In this chapter, we'll cover the first five of the data transformation methods listed in table 3.1. We'll leave the last one for chapter 11.

3.2   *Transforming data using EIPs and Java*

Data mapping is the process of mapping between two distinct data models, and it's a key factor in data integration. There are many existing standards for data models, governed by various organizations or committees. As such, you'll often find yourself needing to map from a company's custom data model to a standard data model.

Camel provides great freedom in data mapping because it allows you to use Java code—you aren't limited to using a particular data mapping tool that at first might seem elegant but that turns out to make things impossible.

In this section, we'll look at how you can map data using a `Processor`, which is a Camel API. Camel can also use beans for mapping, which is a good practice, because it allows your mapping logic to be independent of the Camel API.

3.2.1   *Using the Message Translator EIP*

The Message Translator EIP is illustrated in figure 3.2.

This pattern covers translating a message from one format to another. It's the equivalent of the Adapter pattern from the Gang of Four book.

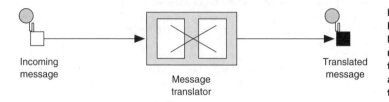

Figure 3.2   In the Message Translator EIP, an incoming message goes through a translator and comes out as a translated message.

Incoming message

Message translator

Translated message

NOTE   The Gang of Four book is *Design Patterns: Elements of Reusable Object-Oriented Software* by Erich Gamma, Richard Helm, Ralph Johnson, and John Vlissides. See the "Design Patterns" Wikipedia article for more information: http://en.wikipedia.org/wiki/Design_Patterns_(book).

Camel provides three ways of using this pattern:

- Using a `Processor`
- Using beans
- Using `<transform>`

We'll look at them each in turn.

TRANSFORMING USING A PROCESSOR

The Camel `Processor` is an interface defined in `org.apache.camel.Processor` with a single method:

```
public void process(Exchange exchange) throws Exception;
```

The `Processor` is a low-level API where you work directly on the Camel `Exchange` instance. It gives you full access to all Camel's moving parts from the `CamelContext`, which you can obtain `Exchange` using the `getCamelContext` method.

Let's look at an example. At Rider Auto Parts you've been asked to generate daily reports of newly received orders to be outputted to a CSV file. The company uses a custom format for order entries, but to make things easy, they already have an HTTP service that returns a list of orders for whatever date you input. The challenge you face is mapping the returned data from the HTTP service to a CSV format and writing the report to a file.

Because you want to get started on a prototype quickly, you decide to use the Camel `Processor`.

Listing 3.1   Using a `Processor` to translate from a custom format to CSV format

```
import org.apache.camel.Exchange;
import org.apache.camel.Processor;

public class OrderToCsvProcessor implements Processor {

    public void process(Exchange exchange) throws Exception {
        String custom = exchange.getIn()
                    .getBody(String.class);
```

① Gets custom payload

```
        String id = custom.substring(0, 9);
        String customerId = custom.substring(10, 19);
        String date = custom.substring(20, 29);
        String items = custom.substring(30);
        String[] itemIds = items.split("@");

        StringBuilder csv = new StringBuilder();
        csv.append(id.trim());
        csv.append(",").append(date.trim());
        csv.append(",").append(customerId.trim());
        for (String item : itemIds) {
            csv.append(",").append(item.trim());
        }
        exchange.getIn().setBody(csv.toString());
    }

}
```

2 Extracts data to local variables

3 Maps to CSV format

4 Replaces payload with CSV payload

First you grab the custom format payload from the exchange **1**. It's a `String` type, so you pass `String` in as the parameter to have the payload returned as a `String`. Then you extract data from the custom format to the local variables **2**. The custom format could be anything, but in this example it's a fixed-length custom format. Then you map the CSV format by building a string with comma-separated values **3**. Finally, you replace the custom payload with your new CSV payload **4**.

You can use the `OrderToCsvProcessor` from listing 3.1 in a Camel route as follows:

```
from("quartz://report?cron=0+0+6+*+*+?")
    .to("http://riders.com/orders/cmd=received&date=yesterday")
    .process(new OrderToCsvProcessor())
    .to("file://riders/orders?fileName=report-${header.Date}.csv");
```

The preceding route uses Quartz to schedule a job to run once a day at 6 a.m. It then invokes the HTTP service to retrieve the orders received yesterday, which are returned in the custom format. Next, it uses `OrderToCSVProcessor` to map from the custom format to CSV format before writing the result to a file.

The equivalent route in Spring XML is as follows:

```
<bean id="csvProcessor" class="camelinaction.OrderToCsvProcessor"/>

<camelContext xmlns="http://camel.apache.org/schema/spring">
  <route>
    <from uri="quartz://report?cron=0+0+6+*+*+?"/>
    <to uri="http://riders.com/orders/cmd=received&amp;date=yesterday"/>
    <process ref="csvProcessor"/>
    <to uri="file://riders/orders?fileName=report-${header.Date}.csv"/>
  </route>
</camelContext>
```

You can try this example yourself—we've provided a little unit test with the book's source code. Go to the chapter3/transform directory, and run these Maven goals:

```
mvn test -Dtest=OrderToCsvProcessorTest
mvn test -Dtest=SpringOrderToCsvProcessorTest
```

After the test runs, a report file is written in the target/orders/received directory.

Using the `getIn` and `getOut` methods on exchanges

The Camel `Exchange` defines two methods for retrieving messages: `getIn` and `getOut`. The `getIn` method returns the incoming message, and the `getOut` method accesses the outbound message.

There are two scenarios where the Camel end user will have to decide among using these methods:

- A read-only scenario, such as when you're logging the incoming message
- A write scenario, such as when you're transforming the message

In the second scenario, you'd assume `getOut` should be used. That's correct according to theory, but in practice there's a common pitfall when using `getOut`: the incoming message headers and attachments will be lost. This is often not what you want, so you must copy the headers and attachments from the incoming message to the outgoing message, which can be tedious. The alternative is to set the changes directly on the incoming message using `getIn`, and not to use `getOut` at all. This is the practice we use in this book.

Using a processor has one disadvantage: you're required to use the Camel API. In the next section, we'll look at how to avoid this by using a bean.

TRANSFORMING USING BEANS

Using beans is a great practice because it allows you to use any Java code and library you wish. Camel imposes no restrictions whatsoever. Camel can invoke any bean you choose, so you can use existing beans without having to rewrite or recompile them.

Let's try using a bean instead of a `Processor`.

Listing 3.2   Using a bean to translate from a custom format to CSV format

```
public class OrderToCsvBean {

    public static String map(String custom) {
        String id = custom.substring(0, 9);
        String customerId = custom.substring(10, 19);
        String date = custom.substring(20, 29);            ❶ Extracts data to
        String items = custom.substring(30);                  local variables
        String[] itemIds = items.split("@");

        StringBuilder csv = new StringBuilder();
        csv.append(id.trim());
        csv.append(",").append(date.trim());
        csv.append(",").append(customerId.trim());
        for (String item : itemIds) {
            csv.append(",").append(item.trim());
        }
                                                            ❷ Returns CSV
        return csv.toString();                                 payload
    }
}
```

The first noticeable difference between listings 3.1 and 3.2 is that listing 3.2 doesn't use any Camel imports. This means your bean is totally independent of the Camel API. The next difference is that you can name the method signature in listing 3.2—in this case it's a static method named `map`.

The method signature defines the contract, which means that the first parameter, (`String custom`), is the message body you're going to use for translation. The method returns a `String`, which means the translated data will be a `String` type. At runtime, Camel binds to this method signature. We won't go into any more details here; we'll cover much more about using beans in chapter 4.

The actual mapping ❶ is the same as with the processor. At the end, you return the mapping output ❷.

You can use `OrderToCsvBean` in a Camel route as shown here:

```
from("quartz://report?cron=0+0+6+*+*+?")
    .to("http://riders.com/orders/cmd=received&date=yesterday")
    .bean(new OrderToCsvBean())
    .to("file://riders/orders?fileName=report-${header.Date}.csv");
```

The equivalent route in Spring XML is as follows:

```
<bean id="csvBean" class="camelinaction.OrderToCsvBean"/>

<camelContext xmlns="http://camel.apache.org/schema/spring">
  <route>
    <from uri="quartz://report?cron=0+0+6+*+*+?"/>
    <to uri="http://riders.com/orders/cmd=received&amp;date=yesterday"/>
    <bean ref="csvBean"/>
    <to uri="file://riders/orders?fileName=report-${header.Date}.csv"/>
  </route>
</camelContext>
```

You can try this example from the chapter3/transform directory by using the following Maven goals:

```
mvn test -Dtest=OrderToCsvBeanTest
mvn test -Dtest=SpringOrderToCsvBeanTest
```

It will generate a test report file in the target/orders/received directory.

Another advantage of using beans over processors for mappings is that unit testing is much easier. For example, listing 3.2 doesn't require the use of Camel at all, as opposed to listing 3.1 where you need to create and pass in an `Exchange` instance.

We'll leave the beans for now, because they're covered extensively in the next chapter. But you should keep in mind that beans are very useful for doing message transformation.

TRANSFORMING USING THE TRANSFORM() METHOD FROM THE JAVA DSL

`Transform()` is a method in the Java DSL that can be used in Camel routes to transform messages. By allowing the use of expressions, `transform()` permits great flexibility, and using expressions directly within the DSL can sometimes save time. Let's look at a little example.

Suppose you need to prepare some text for HTML formatting by replacing all line breaks with a `<br/>` tag. This can be done with a built-in Camel expression that searches and replaces using regular expressions:

```
from("direct:start")
    .transform(body().regexReplaceAll("\n", "<br/>"))
    .to("mock:result");
```

What this route does is use the `transform()` method to tell Camel that the message should be transformed using an expression. Camel provides what is know as the Builder pattern to build expressions from individual expressions. This is done by chaining together method calls, which is the essence of the Builder pattern.

NOTE   For more information on the Builder pattern, see the Wikipedia article: http://en.wikipedia.org/wiki/Builder_pattern.

In this example, you combine `body()` and `regexReplaceAll()`. The expression should be read as follows: take the `body` and perform a regular expression that replaces all new lines (`\n`) with `<br/>` tags. Now you've combined two methods that conform to a compound Camel expression.

You can run this example from chapter3/transform directly by using the following Maven goal:

```
mvn test -Dtest=TransformTest
```

> **The Direct component**
>
> The example here uses the Direct component (http://camel.apache.org/direct) as the input source for the route (`from("direct:start")`). The Direct component provides direct invocation between a producer and a consumer. It only allows connectivity from within Camel, so external systems can't send messages directly to it. This component is used within Camel to do things such as link routes together or for testing.

Camel also allows you to use custom expressions. This is useful when you need to be in full control and have Java code at your fingertips. For example, the previous example could have been implemented as follows:

```
from("direct:start")
    .transform(new Expression() {
        public <T> T evaluate(Exchange exchange, Class<T> type) {
            String body = exchange.getIn().getBody(String.class);
            body = body.replaceAll("\n", "<br/>");
            body = "<body>" + body + "</body>";
            return (T) body;
        }
    })
    .to("mock:result");
```

As you can see, this code uses an inlined Camel `Expression` that allows you to use Java code in its `evaluate` method. This follows the same principle as the Camel `Processor` you saw before.

Now let's see how you can transform data using Spring XML.

TRANSFORMING USING <TRANSFORM> FROM SPRING XML

Using <transform> from Spring XML is a bit different than from Java DSL because the XML DSL isn't as powerful. In Spring XML, the Builder pattern expressions aren't available because with XML you don't have a real programming language underneath. What you can do instead is invoke a method on a bean or use scripting languages.

Let's see how this works. The following route uses a method call on a bean as the expression:

```
<bean id="htmlBean" class="camelinaction.HtmlBean"/>

<camelContext id="camel" xmlns="http://camel.apache.org/schema/spring">
    <route>
        <from uri="direct:start"/>
        <transform>
            <method bean="htmlBean" method="toHtml"/>
        </transform>
        <to uri="mock:result"/>
    </route>
</camelContext>
```

1 Does the transformation

2 Invokes toHtml method on bean

First, you declare a regular spring bean to be used to transform the message **1**. Then, in the route, you use <transform> with a <method> call expression to invoke the bean **2**.

The implementation of the htmlBean is very straightforward:

```
public class HtmlBean {
    public static String toHtml(String body) {
        body = body.replaceAll("\n", "<br/>");
        body = "<body>" + body + "</body>";
        return body;
    }
}
```

You can also use scripting languages as expressions in Camel. For example, you can use Groovy, MVEL, JavaScript, or Camel's own scripting language, called Simple (explained in some detail in appendix A). We won't go in detail on how to use the other scripting languages at this point, but the Simple language can be used to build strings using placeholders. It pretty much speaks for itself—I'm sure you'll understand what the following transformation does:

```
<transform>
    <simple>Hello ${body} how are you?</simple>
</transform>
```

You can try the Spring transformation examples provided in the book's source code by running the following Maven goals from the chapter3/transform directory:

```
mvn test -Dtest= SpringTransformMethodTest
mvn test -Dtest= SpringTransformScriptTest
```

They're located in the chapter3/transform directory and are named SpringTransformMethodTest and SpringTransformScriptTest.

We're done covering the Message Translator EIP, so let's look at the related Content Enricher EIP.

3.2.2 *Using the Content Enricher EIP*

The Content Enricher EIP is illustrated in figure 3.3. This pattern documents the scenario where a message is enriched with data obtained from another resource.

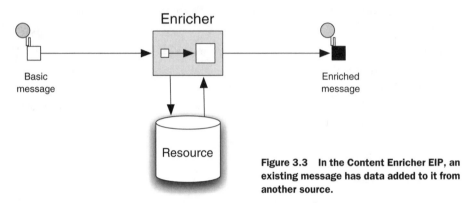

Figure 3.3   In the Content Enricher EIP, an existing message has data added to it from another source.

To help understand this pattern, we'll turn back to Rider Auto Parts. It turns out that the data mapping you did in listing 3.1 wasn't sufficient. Orders are also piled up on an FTP server, and your job is to somehow merge this information into the existing report. Figure 3.4 illustrates the scenario.

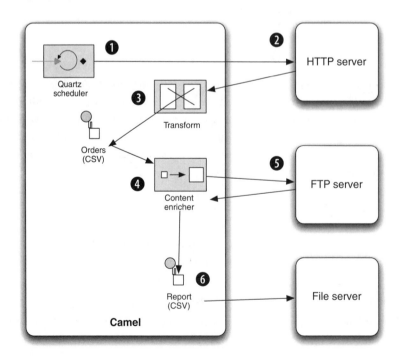

Figure 3.4
An overview of the route that generates the orders report, now with the content enricher pulling in data from an FTP server

In figure 3.4, a scheduled consumer using Quartz starts the route every day at 6 a.m. ❶. It then pulls data from an HTTP server, which returns orders in a custom format ❷, which is then transformed into CSV format ❸. At this point, you have to perform the additional content enrichment step ❹ with the data obtained from the FTP server ❺. After this, the final report is written to the file server ❻.

Before we dig into the code and see how to implement this, we need to take a step back and look at how the Content Enricher EIP is implemented in Camel. Camel provides two operations in the DSL for implementing the pattern:

- `pollEnrich`—This operation merges data retrieved from another source using a consumer.
- `enrich`—This operation merges data retrieved from another source using a producer.

The difference between `pollEnrich` and `enrich`

The difference between `pollEnrich` and `enrich` is that the former uses a consumer and the latter a producer to retrieve data from the source. Knowing the difference is important: the file component can be used with both, but using `enrich` will write the message content as a file; using `pollEnrich` will read the file as the source, which is most likely the scenario you'll be facing when enriching with files. The HTTP component only works with `enrich`; it allows you to invoke an external HTTP service and use its reply as the source.

Camel uses the `org.apache.camel.processor.AggregationStrategy` interface to merge the result from the source with the original message, as follows:

```
Exchange aggregate(Exchange oldExchange, Exchange newExchange);
```

This `aggregate` method is a callback that you must implement. The method has two parameters: the first, named `oldExchange`, contains the original exchange; the second, `newExchange`, is the enriched source. Your task is to enrich the message using Java code and return the merged result. This may sound a bit confusing, so let's see it in action.

To solve the problem at Rider Auto Parts, you need to use `pollEnrich` because it's capable of polling a file from an FTP server.

ENRICHING USING POLLENRICH

Listing 3.3 shows how you can use `pollEnrich` to retrieve the additional orders from the remote FTP server and aggregate this data with the existing message using Camel's `AggregationStrategy`.

Listing 3.3 Using `pollEnrich` to merge additional data with an existing message

```
from("quartz://report?cron=0+0+6+*+*+?")
    .to("http://riders.com/orders/cmd=received")
    .process(new OrderToCSVProcessor())
    .pollEnrich("ftp://riders.com/orders/?username=rider&password=secret",
```

```
            new AggregationStrategy() {
    public Exchange aggregate(Exchange oldExchange,
                              Exchange newExchange) {
        if (newExchange == null) {
            return oldExchange;
        }
        String http = oldExchange.getIn()
                        .getBody(String.class);
        String ftp = newExchange.getIn()
                        .getBody(String.class);
        String body = http + "\n" + ftp;
        oldExchange.getIn().setBody(body);

        return oldExchange;
    }
})
.to("file://riders/orders");
```

1 Uses pollEnrich to read FTP file

2 Merges data using AggregationStrategy

3 Writes output to file

The route is triggered by Quartz to run at 6 a.m. every day. You invoke the HTTP service to retrieve the orders and transform them to CSV format using a processor.

At this point, you need to enrich the existing data with the orders from the remote FTP server. This is done by using pollEnrich **1**, which consumes the remote file.

To merge the data, you use AggregationStrategy **2**. First, you check whether any data was consumed or not. If newExchange is null, there is no remote file to consume, and you just return the existing data. If there is a remote file, you merge the data by concatenating the existing data with the new data and setting it back on the old-Exchange. Then, you return the merged data by returning the oldExchange. To write the CSV report file, you use the file component **3**.

PollEnrich uses a polling consumer to retrieve messages, and it offers three time-out modes:

- pollEnrich(timeout = -1)—Polls the message and waits until a message arrives. This mode will block until a message exists.
- pollEnrich(timeout = 0)—Immediately polls the message if any exists; otherwise null is returned. It will never wait for messages to arrive, so this mode will never block. This is the default mode.
- pollEnrich(timeout > 0)—Polls the message, and if no message exists, it will wait for one, waiting at most until the timeout triggers. This mode will potentially block.

It's a best practice to either use timeout = 0 or to assign a timeout value when using pollEnrich to avoid waiting indefinitely if no message arrives.

Enrich and pollEnrich can't access information in the current exchange

Neither enrich nor pollEnrich can leverage any information from the current exchange. This means, for example, that you can't store a filename header on the exchange for pollEnrich to use to select a particular file. This may change in the future if the Camel team can find a solution.

Now let's take a quick look at how to use `enrich` with Spring XML; it's a bit different than when using the Java DSL.

ENRICHING USING ENRICH

`Enrich` is used when you need to enrich the current message with data from another source using request-response messaging. A prime example would be to enrich the current message with the reply from a web service call. But we'll look at another example, using Spring XML to enrich the current message using the TCP transport:

```
<bean id="quoteStrategy"                              ❶ Bean implementing
    class="camelinaction.QuoteStrategy"/>                AggregationStrategy

<route>
    <from uri="activemq:queue:quotes"/>
    <enrich url="mina:tcp://riders.com:9876?textline=true&sync=true"
            strategyRef="quoteStrategy"/>
    <to uri="log:quotes"/>
</route>
```

Here you use the Camel `mina` component for TCP transport, configured to use request-response messaging by using `sync=true` option. To merge the original message with data from the remote server, `<enrich>` must refer to an `AggregationStrategy`. This is done using the `strategyRef` attribute. As you can see in the example, the `quoteStrategy` being referred to is a bean id ❶, which contains the actual implementation of the `AggregationStrategy`, where the merging takes place.

You've seen a lot about how to transform data in Camel, using Java code for the actual transformations. Now let's take a peek into the XML world and look at the XSLT component, which is used for transforming XML messages using XSLT stylesheets.

3.3 *Transforming XML*

Camel provides two ways to perform XML transformations:

- *XSLT component*—For transforming an XML payload into another format using XSLT stylesheets
- *XML marshaling*—For marshaling and unmarshaling objects to and from XML

Both of these will be covered in following sections.

3.3.1 *Transforming XML with XSLT*

XSL Transformations (XSLT) is a declarative XML-based language used to transform XML documents into other documents. For example, XSLT can be used to transform XML into HTML for web pages or to transform an XML document into another XML document with a different structure. XSLT is powerful and versatile, but it's also a complex language that takes time and effort to fully understand and master. Think twice before deciding to pick up and use XSLT.

Camel provides XSLT as a component in camel-spring.jar because it leverages Spring's resource loading. This means greater flexibility in loading stylesheets because Spring enables them to be loaded from various locations, such as the classpath, file paths, and over HTTP.

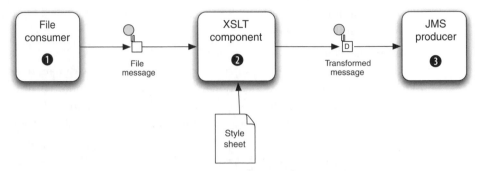

Figure 3.5   A Camel route using an XSLT component to transform an XML document before it's sent to a JMS queue

Using the XSLT component is straightforward because it's just another Camel component. The following route shows an example of how you could use it; this route is also illustrated in figure 3.5.

```
from("file://rider/inbox")
    .to("xslt://camelinaction/transform.xsl")
    .to("activemq:queue:transformed")
```

The file consumer picks up new files and routes them to the XSLT component, which transforms the payload using the stylesheet. After the transformation, the message is routed to a JMS producer, which sends the message to the JMS queue. Notice in the preceding code how the URL for the XSLT component is defined: `xslt://camelinaction/transform.xsl`. The part after the scheme is the URI location of the stylesheet to use. Camel will look in the classpath by default.

As mentioned before, the Camel XSLT component leverages Spring to load the stylesheet. You can prefix the resource name with any of the three prefixes listed in table 3.2.

Table 3.2   Prefixes supported by the XSLT component for loading stylesheets

Prefix	Example	Description
`<none>`	`xslt://camelinaction/transform.xsl`	If no prefix is provided, Camel loads the resource from the classpath
`classpath:`	`xslt://classpath:com/mycompany/transform.xml`	Loads the resource from the classpath
`file:`	`xslt://file:/rider/config/transform.xml`	Loads the resource from the filesystem
`http:`	`xslt://http://rider.com/styles/transform.xsl`	Loads the resource from an URL

Let's leave the XSLT world now and take a look at how you can do XML-to-object marshaling with Camel.

3.3.2   *Transforming XML with object marshaling*

Any software engineer who has worked with XML knows that it's a challenge to use the low-level XML API that Java offers. Instead, people often prefer to work with regular Java objects and use marshaling to transform between Java objects and XML representations.

In Camel, this marshaling process is provided in ready-to-use components known as *data formats*. We'll cover data formats in full detail in section 3.4, but we'll take a quick look at the XStream and JAXB data formats here as we cover XML transformations using marshaling.

TRANSFORMING USING XSTREAM

XStream is a simple library for serializing objects to XML and back again. To use it, you need camel-xstream.jar on the classpath and the XStream library itself.

Suppose you need to send messages in XML format to a shared JMS queue, which is then used to integrate two systems. Let's look at how this can be done.

Listing 3.4   Using XStream to transform a message into XML

```
<camelContext id="camel" xmlns="http://camel.apache.org/schema/spring">
    <dataFormats>
        <xstream id="myXstream"/>                     ◁──┐  Specifies XStream
    </dataFormats>                                        ❶  data format

    <route>
        <from uri="direct:foo"/>                         ❷  Transforms
        <marshal ref="myXstream"/>                   ◁──┘     to XML
        <to uri="activemq:queue:foo"/>
    </route>
</camelContext>
```

When using the XML DSL, you can declare the data formats used at the top ❶ of the `<camelContext>`. By doing this, you can share the data formats in multiple routes. In the first route, where you send messages to a JMS queue, you use `marshal` ❷, which refers to the `id` from ❶, so Camel knows that the XStream data format is being used.

You can also use the XStream data format directly in the route, which can shorten the syntax a bit, like this:

```
<route>
    <from uri="direct:foo"/>
    <marshal><xstream/></marshal>
    <to uri="activemq:queue:foo"/>
</route>
```

The same route is a bit shorter to write in the Java DSL, because you can do it with one line per route:

```
from("direct:foo").marshal().xstream().to("uri:activemq:queue:foo");
```

Yes, using XStream is that simple. And the reverse operation, unmarshaling from XML to an object, is just as simple:

```
<route>
    <from uri="activemq:queue:foo"/>
    <unmarshal ref="myXstream"/>
    <to uri="direct:handleFoo"/>
</route>
```

You've now seen how easy it is to use XStream with Camel. Let's take a look at using JAXB with Camel.

TRANSFORMING USING JAXB

JAXB (Java Architecture for XML Binding) is a standard specification for XML binding, and it's provided out of the box in the Java runtime. Like XStream, it allows you to serialize objects to XML and back again. It's not as simple, but it does offer more bells and whistles for controlling the XML output. And because it's distributed in Java, you don't need any special JAR files on the classpath.

Unlike XStream, JAXB requires that you do a bit of work to declare the binding between Java objects and the XML form. This is often done using annotations. Suppose you define a model bean to represent an order, as shown in listing 3.5, and you want to transform this into XML before sending it to a JMS queue. Then you want to transform it back to the order bean again when consuming from the JMS queue. This can be done as shown in listings 3.5 and 3.6.

> **Listing 3.5   Annotating a bean with JAXB so it can be transformed to and from XML**

```
package com.acme.order;

import javax.xml.bind.annotation.XmlAccessType;
import javax.xml.bind.annotation.XmlAccessorType;
import javax.xml.bind.annotation.XmlAttribute;
import javax.xml.bind.annotation.XmlRootElement;

@XmlRootElement                                          ❶ PurchaseOrder class
@XmlAccessorType(XmlAccessType.FIELD)                       is JAXB annotated
public class PurchaseOrder {
    @XmlAttribute
    private String name;
    @XmlAttribute
    private double price;
    @XmlAttribute
    private double amount;
}
```

Listing 3.5 shows how to use JAXB annotations to decorate your model object (omitting the usual getters and setters). First you define @XmlRootElement ❶ as a class-level annotation to indicate that this class is an XML element. Then you define the @Xml-AccessorType to let JAXB access fields directly. To expose the fields of this model object as XML attributes, you mark them with the @XmlAttribute annotation.

Using JAXB, you should be able to marshal a model object into an XML representation like this:

```
<purchaseOrder name="Camel in Action" price="4995" amount="1"/>
```

Listing 3.6 shows how you can use JAXB in routes to transform the `PurchaseOrder` object to XML before it's sent to a JMS queue, and then back again from XML to the `PurchaseOrder` object when consuming from the same JMS queue.

Listing 3.6   Using JAXB to serialize objects to and from XML

```
<camelContext id="camel" xmlns="http://camel.apache.org/schema/spring">
    <dataFormats>
        <jaxb id="jaxb" contextPath="camelinaction"/>        Declares JAXB
    </dataFormats>                                        ① data format

    <route>
        <from uri="direct:order"/>              ② Transforms from
        <marshal ref="jaxb"/>                     model to XML
        <to uri="activemq:queue:order"/>
    </route>

    <route>
        <from uri="activemq:queue:order"/>      ③ Transforms from
        <unmarshal ref="jaxb"/>                   XML to model
        <to uri="direct:doSomething"/>
    </route>
</camelContext>
```

First you need to declare the JAXB data format ①. Note that a `contextPath` attribute is also defined on the JAXB data format—this is a package name that instructs JAXB to look in this package for classes that are JAXB-annotated.

The first route then marshals to XML ② and the second route unmarshals to transform the XML back into the `PurchaseOrder` object ③.

You can try this example by running the following Maven goal from the chapter3/order directory:

```
mvn test -Dtest=PurchaseOrderJaxbTest
```

> **NOTE**   To tell JAXB which classes are JAXB-annotated, you need to drop a special `jaxb.index` file into the context path. It's a plain text file in which each line lists the class name. In the preceding example, the file contains a single line with the text `PurchaseOrder`.

That's the basis of using XML object marshaling with XStream and JAXB. Both of them are implemented in Camel via data formats that are capable of transforming back and forth between various well-known formats.

3.4   *Transforming with data formats*

In Camel, data formats are pluggable transformers that can transform messages from one form to another and vice versa. Each data format is represented in Camel as an interface in `org.apace.camel.spi.DataFormat` containing two methods:

- `marshal`—For marshaling a message into another form, such as marshaling Java objects to XML, CSV, EDI, HL7, or other well-known data models
- `unmarshal`—For performing the reverse operation, which turns data from well-known formats back into a message

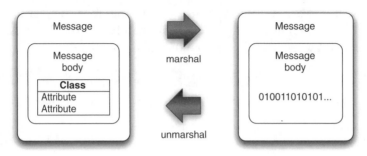

Figure 3.6   An object is marshaled to a binary representation; `unmarshal` can be used to get the object back.

You may already have realized that these two functions are opposites, meaning that one is capable of reversing what the other has done, as illustrated in figure 3.6.

We touched on data formats in section 3.3, where we covered XML transformations. This section will cover data formats in more depth and using other data types than XML, such as CSV and JSON. We'll even look at how you can create your own data formats.

We'll start our journey by briefly looking at the data formats Camel provides out of the box.

3.4.1   Data formats provided with Camel

Camel provides data formats for a range of well-known data models, as listed in table 3.3.

Table 3.3   Data formats provided out of the box with Camel

Data format	Data model	Artifact	Description
Bindy	CSV, FIX, fixed length	camel-bindy	Binds various data models to model objects using annotations
Castor	XML	camel-castor	Uses Castor for XML binding to and from Java objects
Crypto	Any	camel-crypto	Encrypts and decrypts data using the Java Cryptography Extension
CSV	CSV	camel-csv	Transforms to and from CSV using the Apache Commons CSV library
Flatpack	CSV	camel-flatpack	Transforms to and from CSV using the FlatPack library
GZip	Any	camel-gzip	Compresses and decompresses files (compatible with the popular gzip/gunzip tools)
HL7	HL7	camel-hl7	Transforms to and from HL7, which is a well-known data format in the health care industry
JAXB	XML	camel-jaxb	Uses the JAXB 2.x standard for XML binding to and from Java objects
Jackson	JSON	camel-jackson	Transforms to and from JSON using the ultra-fast Jackson library
Protobuf	XML	camel-protobuf	Transforms to and from XML using the Google Protocol Buffers library
SOAP	XML	camel-soap	Transforms to and from SOAP

Table 3.3   Data formats provided out of the box with Camel (continued)

Data format	Data model	Artifact	Description
Serialization	Object	camel-core	Uses Java Object Serialization to transform objects to and from a serialized stream
TidyMarkup	HTML	camel-tagsoup	Tidies up HTML by parsing ugly HTML and returning it as pretty well-formed HTML
XmlBeans	XML	camel-xmlbeans	Uses XmlBeans for XML binding to and from Java objects
XMLSecurity	XML	camel-xmlsecurity	Facilitates encryption and decryption of XML documents
XStream	XML	camel-xstream	Uses XStream for XML binding to and from Java objects
XStream	JSON	camel-xstream	Transforms to and from JSON using the XStream library
Zip	Any	camel-core	Compresses and decompresses messages; it's most effective when dealing with large XML- or text-based payloads

As you can see, Camel provides 18 data formats out of the box. We've picked 3 to cover in the following section. They're among the most commonly used, and what you learn about those will also apply for the remainder of the data formats. You can read more about all these data formats at the Camel website (http://camel.apache.org/data-format.html).

3.4.2 Using Camel's CSV data format

The camel-csv data format is capable of transforming to and from CSV format. It leverages Apache Commons CSV to do the actual work.

Suppose you need to consume CSV files, split out each row, and send it to a JMS queue. Sounds hard to do, but it's possible with little effort in a Camel route:

```
from("file://rider/csvfiles")
    .unmarshal().csv()
    .split(body()).to("activemq:queue.csv.record");
```

All you have to do is unmarshal the CSV files, which will read the file line by line and store all lines in the message body as a java.util.List<List> type. Then you use the splitter to split up the body, which will break the java.util.List<List<String>> into rows (each row represented as another List<String> containing the fields) and send each row to the JMS queue. You may not want to send each row as a List type to the JMS queue, so you can transform the row before sending, perhaps using a processor.

The same example in Spring XML is a bit different, as shown here:

```
<camelContext id="camel" xmlns="http://camel.apache.org/schema/spring">
    <route>
        <from uri="file://rider/csvfiles"/>
        <unmarshal><csv/></unmarshal>
```

```
        <split>
            <simple>body</simple>
            <to uri="activemq:queue.csv.record"/>
        </split>
    </route>
</camelContext>
```

The noticeable difference is how you tell `<split>` that it should split up the message body. To do this you need to provide `<split>` with an `Expression`, which is what the splitter should iterate when it performs the splitting. To do so, you can use Camel's built-in expression language called Simple (see appendix A), which knows how to do that.

NOTE   The Splitter EIP is fully covered in section 8.1 of this book.

This example is in the source code for the book in the chapter3/order directory. You can try the examples by running the following Maven goals:

```
mvn test -Dtest=PurchaseOrderCsvTest
mvn test -Dtest=PurchaseOrderCsvSpringTest
```

At first, the data types that the CSV data format uses may seem a bit confusing. They're listed in table 3.4.

Table 3.4   Data types that camel-csv uses when transforming to and from CSV format

Operation	From type	To type	Description
marshal	Map<String, Object>	OutputStream	Contains a single row in CSV format
marshal	List<Map<String, Object>>	OutputStream	Contains multiple rows in CSV format where each row is separated by \n (newline)
unmarshal	InputStream	List<List<String>>	Contains a List of rows where each row is another List of fields

One problem with camel-csv is that it uses generic data types, such as `Maps` or `Lists`, to represent CSV records. Often you'll already have model objects to represent your data in memory. Let's look at how you can use model objects with the camel-bindy component.

3.4.3   *Using Camel's Bindy data format*

The two existing CSV-related data formats (camel-csv and camel-flatpack) are older libraries that don't take advantage of the new features in Java 1.5, such as annotations and generics. In light of this deficiency, Charles Moulliard stepped up and wrote the camel-bindy component to take advantage of these new possibilities. It's capable of binding CSV, FIX, and fixed-length formats to existing model objects using annotations. This is similar to what JAXB does for XML.

Suppose you have a model object that represents a purchase order. By annotating the model object with camel-bindy annotations, you can easily transform messages between CSV and Java model objects.

Listing 3.7   Model object annotated for CSV transformation

```
package camelinaction.bindy;

import java.math.BigDecimal;
import org.apache.camel.dataformat.bindy.annotation.CsvRecord;
import org.apache.camel.dataformat.bindy.annotation.DataField;

@CsvRecord(separator = ",", crlf = "UNIX")          ◁┐   Maps to
public class PurchaseOrder {                          ❶  CSV record

    @DataField(pos = 1)                             ◁┐
    private String name;

    @DataField(pos = 2, precision = 2)              ◁ ❷  Maps to column
    private BigDecimal price;                            in CSV record

    @DataField(pos = 3)                             ◁┘
    private int amount;
}
```

First you mark the class with the `@CsvRecord` annotation ❶ to indicate that it represents a record in CSV format. Then you annotate the fields with `@DataField` according to the layout of the CSV record ❷. Using the `pos` attribute, you can dictate the order in which they're outputted in CSV; `pos` starts with a value of `1`. For numeric fields, you can additionally declare precision, which in this example is set to `2`, indicating that the price should use two digits for cents. Bindy also has attributes for fine-grained layout of the fields, such as `pattern`, `trim`, and `length`. You can use `pattern` to indicate a data pattern, `trim` to trim the input, and `length` to restrict a text description to a certain number of characters.

Before we look at how to use Bindy in Camel routes, we need to take a step back and look at the data types Bindy expects to use. They're listed in table 3.5.

Table 3.5   Data types that Bindy uses when transforming to and from CSV format

Operation	From type	To type	Output description
marshal	List<Map<String, Object>>	OutputStream	Contains multiple rows in CSV format where each row is separated by a \n (newline)
unmarshal	InputStream	List<Map<String, Object>>	Contains a List of rows where each row contains 1..n data models contained in a Map

The important thing to notice in table 3.5 is that Bindy uses a `Map<String, Object>` to represent a CSV row. At first, this may seem odd. Why doesn't it just use a single model object for that? The answer is that you can have multiple model objects with the CSV record being scattered across those objects. For example, you could have fields 1 to 3 in one model object, fields 4 to 9 in another, and fields 10 to 12 in a third.

The map entry <String, Object> is distilled as follows:

- Map key (String)—Must contain the fully qualified class name of the model object
- Map value (Object)—Must contain the model object

If this seems a bit confusing, don't worry. The following example should make it clearer.

Listing 3.8 Using Bindy to transform a model object to CSV format

```
public class PurchaseOrderBindyTest extends TestCase {

public void testBindy() throws Exception {
    CamelContext context = new DefaultCamelContext();
    context.addRoutes(createRoute());
    context.start();

    MockEndpoint mock = context.getEndpoint("mock:result",
                                    MockEndpoint.class);
    mock.expectedBodiesReceived("Camel in Action,49.95,1\n");

    PurchaseOrder order = new PurchaseOrder();          ◁─    ❶ Creates model
    order.setAmount(1);                                         object as usual
    order.setPrice(new BigDecimal("49.95"));
    order.setName("Camel in Action");

    ProducerTemplate template = context.createProducerTemplate();
    template.sendBody("direct:toCsv", order);           ◁─
                                                          ❷ Starts test
    mock.assertIsSatisfied();
}
public RouteBuilder createRoute() {
    return new RouteBuilder() {
        public void configure() throws Exception {            ❸ Transforms
            from("direct:toCsv")                                model object
                .marshal().bindy(BindyType.Csv,                 to CSV
                        "camelinaction.bindy")          ◁─
                .to("mock:result");
        }
    };
}
```

In this listing, you first create and populate the order model using regular Java setters ❶. Then you send the order model to the route by sending it to the direct:toCsv endpoint ❷ that is used in the route. The route will then marshal the order model to CSV using Bindy ❸. Notice how Bindy is configured to use CSV mode via BindyType.Csv. To let Bindy know how to map to order model object, you need to provide a package name that will be scanned for classes annotated with Bindy annotations. This is the same solution JAXB offers.

> **NOTE** Listing 3.8 uses MockEndpoint to easily test that the CSV record is as expected. Chapter 6 will covered testing with Camel, and you'll learn all about using MockEndpoints.

You can try this example from the chapter3/order directory using the following Maven goal:

```
mvn test –Dtest=PurchaseOrderBindyTest
```

The source code for the book also contains a *reverse* example of how to use Bindy to transform a CSV record into a Java object. You can try it by using the following Maven goal:

```
mvn test –Dtest=PurchaseOrderUnmarshalBindyTest
```

CSV is only one of the well-known data formats that Bindy supports. Bindy is equally capable of working with fixed-length and FIX data formats, both of which follow the same principles as CSV.

It's now time to leave CSV and look at a more modern format: JSON.

3.4.4 *Using Camel's JSON data format*

JSON (JavaScript Object Notation) is a data-interchange format, and Camel provides two components that support the JSON data format: camel-xstream and camel-jackson. In this section, we'll focus on camel-jackson because Jackson is a very popular JSON library.

Back at Rider Auto Parts, you now have to implement a new service that returns order summaries rendered in JSON format. Doing this with Camel is fairly easy, because Camel has all the ingredients needed to brew this service. Listing 3.9 shows how you could ramp up a prototype.

Listing 3.9 An HTTP service that returns order summaries rendered in JSON format

```
<bean id="orderService" class="camelinaction.OrderServiceBean"/>

<camelContext id="camel" xmlns="http://camel.apache.org/schema/spring">
    <dataFormats>
        <json id="json" library="Jackson"/>           Sets up JSON
    </dataFormats>                                  ❶ data format

    <route>
        <from uri="jetty://http://0.0.0.0:8080/order"/>
        <bean ref="orderService" method="lookup"/>       Invokes bean to
        <marshal ref="json"/>                          ❷ retrieve data for reply
    </route>
</camelContext>
```

First you need to set up the JSON data format and specify that the Jackson library should be used ❶. Then you define a route that exposes the HTTP service using the Jetty endpoint. This example exposes the Jetty endpoint directly in the URI. By using http://0.0.0.0:8080/order, you tell Jetty that any client can reach this service on port 8080. Whenever a request hits this HTTP service, it's routed to the orderService bean ❷ and the lookup method is invoked on that bean. The result of this bean invocation is then marshaled to JSON format and returned back to the HTTP client.

The order service bean could have a method signature such as this:

```
public PurchaseOrder lookup(@Header(name = "id") String id)
```

This signature allows you to implement the lookup logic as you wish. You'll learn more about the @Header annotation in section 4.5.3, when we cover how bean parameter binding works in Camel.

Notice that the service bean can return a POJO that the JSON library is capable of marshaling. For example, suppose you used the PurchaseOrder from listing 3.7, and had JSON output as follows:

```
{"name":"Camel in Action","amount":1.0,"price":49.95}
```

The HTTP service itself can be invoked by an HTTP Get request with the id of the order as a parameter: http://0.0.0.0:8080/order/service?id=123.

Notice how easy it is with Camel to bind the HTTP id parameter as the String id parameter with the help of the @Header annotation.

You can try this example yourself from chapter3/order directory by using the following Maven goal.

```
mvn test -Dtest=PurchaseOrderJSONTest
```

So far we've used data formats with their default settings. But what if you need to configure the data format, such as to use another splitter character with the CSV data format? That's the topic of the next section.

3.4.5 *Configuring Camel data formats*

In section 3.4.2, you used the CSV data format, but this data format offers many additional settings. This listing shows how you can configure the CSV data format.

Listing 3.10 Configuring the CSV data format

```
public void configure() {
    CSVConfig custom = new CSVConfig();
    custom.setDelimiter(';');
    custom.setEndTrimmed(true);
    custom.addField(new CSVField("id"));
    custom.addField(new CSVField("customerId"));       ❶ Configures custom
    custom.addField(new CSVField("date"));                CSV data format
    custom.addField(new CSVField("item"));
    custom.addField(new CSVField("amount"));
    custom.addField(new CSVField("description"));

    CsvDataFormat myCsv = new CsvDataFormat();         ❷ Creates custom
    myCsv.setConfig(custom);                              CSV data format
    myCsv.setAutogenColumns(false);
                                         ❸ Uses CSV
    from("direct:toCsv")                    data format
        .marshal(myCsv)
        .to("file://acme/outbox/csv");
}
```

Configuring data formats in Camel is done using regular Java code; you use the API that the data format provides. In listing 3.10, the CSV data format offers a CSVConfig object ❶ that is used to set the semicolon as a delimiter and to specify the order of the fields. The data format itself is then created ❷ and set to use the configuration. The use of the data format stays the same, so all you need to do is refer to it from the marshal ❸ or unmarshal methods. This same principle applies to all data formats in Camel. You can configure them using the APIs they provide.

Now that you know how to use data formats, let's look at how you can write your own data format.

3.4.6 *Writing your own data format*

You may find yourself needing to transform data to and from a custom data format. In this section, we'll look at how you can develop a data format that can reverse strings.

Developing your own data format is fairly easy, because Camel provides a single API you must implement: org.apache.camel.spi.DataFormat. Let's look at how you could implement a string-reversing data format.

Listing 3.11 Developing a custom data format that can reverse strings

```
package camelinaction;

import java.io.InputStream;
import java.io.OutputStream;

import org.apache.camel.Exchange;
import org.apache.camel.spi.DataFormat;

public class ReverseDataFormat implements DataFormat {        ❶ Marshals to
                                                                reverse string
    public void marshal(Exchange exchange,
                Object graph, OutputStream stream) throws Exception {
        byte[] bytes = exchange.getContext().getTypeConverter()
                            .mandatoryConvertTo(byte[].class, graph);
        String body = reverseBytes(bytes);
        stream.write(body.getBytes());
    }
                                                              ❷ Unmarshals to
    public Object unmarshal(Exchange exchange,                  unreverse string
                InputStream stream) throws Exception {
        byte[] bytes = exchange.getContext().getTypeConverter()
                            .mandatoryConvertTo(byte[].class, stream);
        String body = reverseBytes(bytes);
        return body;
    }

    private static String reverseBytes(byte[] data) {
        StringBuilder sb = new StringBuilder(data.length);
        for (int i = data.length - 1; i >= 0; i--) {
            char ch = (char) data[i];
            sb.append(ch);
        }
        return sb.toString();
    }
}
```

The custom data format must implement the DataFormat interface, which forces you to develop two methods: marshal ❶ and unmarshal ❷. That's no surprise, as they're the same methods you use in the route. The `marshal` method ❶ needs to output the result to the `OutputStream`. To do this, you need to get the message payload as a `byte[]`, and then reverse it with a helper method. Then you write that data to the `OutputStream`. Note that you use the Camel type converters to return the message payload as a `byte[]`. This is very powerful and saves you from doing a manual typecast in Java or trying to convert the payload yourself.

The `unmarshal` method ❷ is nearly the same. You use the Camel type-converter mechanism again to provide the message payload as a `byte[]`. `unmarshal` also reverses the bytes to get the data back in its original order. Note that in this method you return the data instead of writing it to a stream.

> **TIP**   As a best practice, use the Camel type converters instead of typecasting or converting between types yourself. We'll cover Camel's type converters in section 3.6.

To use this new data format in a route, all you have to do is define it as a Spring bean and refer to it from `<marshal>` and `<unmarshal>` as follows:

```
<bean id="reverse" class="camelinaction.ReverseDataFormat"/>

<camelContext id="camel" xmlns="http://camel.apache.org/schema/spring">
    <route>
        <from uri="direct:marshal"/>
        <marshal ref="reverse"/>
        <to uri="log:marshal"/>
    </route>

    <route>
        <from uri="direct:unmarshal"/>
        <unmarshal ref="reverse"/>
        <to uri="log:unmarshal"/>
    </route>
</camelContext>
```

You'll find this example in the chapter3/order directory, and you can try it by using the following Maven goal:

```
mvn test -Dtest=ReverseDataFormatTest
```

You've now learned all about data formats and even how to develop your own. It's time to say goodbye to data formats and take a look at how you can use templating with Camel for data transformation. Templating is extremely useful when you need to generate automatic reply emails.

3.5   *Transforming with templates*

Camel provides slick integration with two different template languages:

- *Apache Velocity*—Probably the best known templating language (http://camel. apache.org/velocity.html)
- *FreeMarker*—Another popular templating language that may be a bit more advanced than Velocity (http://camel.apache.org/freemarker.html)

These two templating languages are fairly similar to use, so we'll only discuss Velocity here.

3.5.1 Using Apache Velocity

Rider Auto Parts has implemented a new order system that must send an email reply when a customer has submitted an order. Your job is to implement this feature.

The reply email could look like this:

```
Dear customer

Thank you for ordering X piece(s) of XXX at a cost of XXX.

This is an automated email, please do not reply.
```

There are three pieces of information in the email that must be replaced at runtime with real values. What you need to do is adjust the email to use the Velocity template language, and then place it into the source repository as src/test/resources/email.vm:

```
Dear customer

Thank you for ordering ${body.amount} piece(s) of ${body.name} at a cost of
    ${body.price}.

This is an automated email, please do not reply.
```

Notice that we've inserted ${ } placeholders in the template, which instructs Velocity to evaluate and replace them at runtime. Camel prepopulates the Velocity context with a number of entities that are then available to Velocity. Those entities are listed in table 3.6.

NOTE The entities in table 3.6 also apply for other templating languages, such as FreeMarker.

Table 3.6 Entities prepopulated in the Velocity context and that are available at runtime

Entity	Type	Description
camelContext	org.apache.camel.CamelContext	The CamelContext.
exchange	org.apache.camel.Exchange	The current exchange.
in	org.apache.camel.Message	The input message. This can clash with a reserved word in some languages; use request instead.
request	org.apache.camel.Message	The input message.
body	java.lang.Object	The input message body.
headers	java.util.Map	The input message headers.
response	org.apache.camel.Message	The output message.
out	org.apache.camel.Message	The output message. This can clash with a reserved word in some languages; use response instead.

Using Velocity in a Camel route is as simple as this:

```
from("direct:sendMail")
    .setHeader("Subject", constant("Thanks for ordering"))
    .setHeader("From", constant("donotreply@riders.com"))
    .to("velocity://rider/mail.vm")
    .to("smtp://mail.riders.com?user=camel&password=secret");
```

All you have to do is route the message to the Velocity endpoint that's configured with the template you want to use, which is the rider/mail.vm file that's loaded from the classpath by default. All the template components in Camel leverage the Spring resource loader, which allows you to load templates from the classpath, file paths, and other such locations. You can use the same prefixes listed in table 3.2.

You can try this example by going to the chapter3/order directory in the book's source code and running the following Maven goal:

```
mvn test -Dtest=PurchaseOrderVelocityTest
```

> **TIP**   For more details on the Camel Velocity component, consult the online documentation (http://camel.apache.org/velocity.html).

We'll now leave data transformation and look at type conversion. Camel has a powerful type-converter mechanism that removes all need for boilerplate type-converter code.

3.6   *About Camel type converters*

Camel provides a built-in type-converter system that automatically converts between well-known types. This system allows Camel components to easily work together without having type mismatches. And from the Camel user's perspective, type conversions are built into the API in many places without being invasive. For example, you used it in listing 3.1:

```
String custom = exchange.getIn().getBody(String.class);
```

The getBody method is passed the type you want to have returned. Under the covers, the type-converter system converts the returned type to a `String` if needed.

In this section, we'll take a look at the insides of the type-converter system. We'll explain how Camel scans the classpath on startup to register type converters dynamically. We'll also show how you can use it from a Camel route, and how to build your own type converters.

3.6.1   *How the Camel type-converter mechanism works*

To understand the type-converter system, you first need to know what a type converter in Camel is. Figure 3.7 illustrates the relationship between the `TypeConverterRegistry` and the `TypeConverters` it holds.

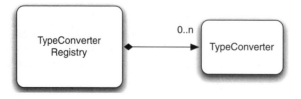

Figure 3.7
The `TypeConverterRegistry`
contains many `TypeConverters`

The `TypeConverterRegistry` is where all the type converters are registered when Camel is started. At runtime, Camel uses the `TypeConverterRegistry`'s lookup method to look up a suitable `TypeConverter`:

```
TypeConverter lookup(Class<?> toType, Class<?> fromType);
```

By using the `TypeConverter`, Camel can then convert one type to another using `TypeConverter`'s convertTo method, which is defined as follows:

```
<T> T convertTo(Class<T> type, Object value);
```

> **NOTE** Camel implements about 150 or more type converters out of the box, which are capable of converting to and from the most commonly used types.

LOADING TYPE CONVERTERS INTO THE REGISTRY

On startup, Camel loads all the type converters into the `TypeConverterRegistry` by using a classpath-scanning solution. This allows Camel to pick up not only type converters from camel-core but also from any of the other Camel components, including your Camel applications—you'll see this in section 3.6.3 when you build your own type converter.

To scan and load the type converters, Camel uses `org.apache.camel.impl.converter.AnnotationTypeConverterLoader`. To avoid scanning zillions of classes, it reads a service discovery file in the META-INF folder: META-INF/services/org/apache/camel/TypeConverter. This is a plain text file that has a list of packages that contain Camel type converters. The special file is needed to avoid scanning every possible JAR and all their packages, which would be time consuming. This special file tells Camel whether or not the JAR file contains type converters. For example, the file in camel-core contains the following three entries:

```
org.apache.camel.converter
org.apache.camel.component.bean
org.apache.camel.component.file
```

The `AnnotationTypeConverterLoader` will scan those packages and their subpackages for classes that have been annotated with `@Converter`, and it searches within them for public methods that are annotated with `@Converter`. Each of those methods is considered a type converter.

This is best illustrated with an example. The following code is a snippet from `IOConverter` class from camel-core JAR:

```
@Converter
public final class IOConverter {

    @Converter
    public static InputStream toInputStream(URL url) throws IOException {
        return url.openStream();
    }
}
```

Camel will go over each method annotated with `@Converter` and look at the method signature. The first parameter is the *from* type, and the return type is the *to* type—in this example you have a `TypeConverter` that can convert from a `URL` to an `InputStream`. By doing this, Camel loads all the built-in type converters, including those from the Camel components in use.

Now that you know how the Camel type converters are loaded, let's look at using them.

3.6.2 *Using Camel type converters*

As we mentioned, the Camel type converters are used throughout Camel, often automatically. But you might want to use them to force a specific type to be used in a route, such as before sending data back to a caller or a JMS destination. Let's look at how to do that.

Suppose you need to route files to a JMS queue using `javax.jmx.TextMessage`. To do so, you can convert each file to a `String`, which forces the JMS component to use `TextMessage`. This is easy to do in Camel—you use the `convertBodyTo` method, as shown here:

```
from("file://riders/inbox")
    .convertBodyTo(String.class)
    .to("activemq:queue:inbox");
```

If you're using Spring XML, you provide the type as an attribute instead, like this:

```
<route>
    <from uri="file://riders/inbox"/>
    <convertBodyTo type="java.lang.String"/>
    <to uri="activemq:queue:inbox"/>
</route>
```

You can omit the `java.lang.` prefix on the type, which can shorten the syntax a bit: `<convertBodyTo type="String"/>`.

Another reason for using `convertBodyTo` is to read files using a fixed encoding such as `UTF-8`. This is done by passing in the encoding as the second parameter:

```
from("file://riders/inbox")
    .convertBodyTo(String.class, "UTF-8")
    .to("activemq:queue:inbox");
```

> **TIP** If you have trouble with a route because of the payload or its type, try using `.convertBodyTo(String.class)` at the start of the route to convert to a `String` type, which is a well-supported type. If the payload cannot be converted to the desired type, a `NoTypeConversionAvailableException` exception is thrown.

That's all there is to using type converters in Camel routes. Before we wrap up this chapter, though, let's take a look at how you can write your own type converter.

3.6.3 *Writing your own type converter*

Writing your own type converter is easy in Camel. You already saw what a type converter looks like in section 3.6.1, when we looked at how type converters work.

Suppose you wanted to write a custom type converter that can convert a byte[] into a PurchaseOrder model object (an object you used in listing 3.7). As you saw earlier, you need to create a @Converter class containing the type-converter method.

Listing 3.12 A custom type converter to convert from byte[] to PurchaseOrder type

```
@Converter                                                            Grabs    ❶
public final class PurchaseOrderConverter                     TypeConverter
                                                                   to reuse

    @Converter
    public static PurchaseOrder toPurchaseOrder(byte[] data,
                                                Exchange exchange) {
        TypeConverter converter = exchange.getContext()
                            .getTypeConverter();
        String s = converter.convertTo(String.class, data);
        if (s == null || s.length() < 30) {
            throw new IllegalArgumentException("data is invalid");
        }
        s = s.replaceAll("##START##", "");
        s = s.replaceAll("##END##", "");

        String name = s.substring(0, 9).trim();

        String s2 = s.substring(10, 19).trim();
        BigDecimal price = new BigDecimal(s2);          ❷ Converts
        price.setScale(2);                                from String to
                                                          PurchaseOrder
        String s3 = s.substring(20).trim();
        Integer amount = converter
                        .convertTo(Integer.class, s3);

        return new PurchaseOrder(name, price, amount);
    }
}
```

In listing 3.12, the Exchange gives you access to the CamelContext and thus to the parent TypeConverter ❶, which you use in this method to convert between strings and numbers. The rest of the code is the logic for parsing the custom protocol and returning the PurchaseOrder ❷. Notice how you can use the converter to easily convert between well-known types.

All you need to do now is add the service discovery file, named TypeConverter, in the META-INF directory. As explained previously, this file contains one line identifying each package to be scanned for @Converter classes.

If you cat the magic file, you'll see this:

```
cat src/main/resources/META-INF/services/org/apache/camel/TypeConverter
camelinaction
```

This example can be found in the chapter3/converter directory of the book's source code, which you can try using the following Maven goal:

```
mvn test -Dtest=PurchaseOrderConverterTest
```

And that completes this chapter on transforming data with Camel.

3.7   *Summary and best practices*

Data transformation is the cornerstone of any integration kit; it bridges the gap between different data types and formats. It's also essential in today's industry because more and more disparate systems need to be integrated to support the ever-changing businesses and world we live in.

This chapter covered many of the possibilities Camel offers for data transformation. You learned how to format messages using EIPs and beans. You also learned that Camel provides special support for transforming XML documents using XSLT components and XML-capable data formats. Camel provides data formats for well-known data models, which you learned to use, and it even allows you to build your own data formats. We also took a look into the templating world, which can be used to format data in specialized cases, such as generating email bodies. Finally, we looked at how the Camel type-converter mechanism works and learned that it's used internally to help all the Camel components work together. You learned how to use it in routes and how to write your own converters.

Here are a few key tips you should take away from this chapter:

- *Data transformation is often required.* Integrating IT systems often requires you to use different data formats when exchanging data. Camel can act as the mediator and has strong support for transforming data in any way possible. Use the various features in Camel to aid with your transformation needs.
- *Java is powerful.* Using Java code isn't a worse solution than using a fancy mapping tool. Don't underestimate the power of the Java language. Even if it takes 50 lines of grunt boilerplate code to get the job done, you have a solution that can easily be maintained by fellow engineers.
- *Prefer to use beans over processors.* If you're using Java code for data transformation, you can use beans or processors. Processors are more dependent on the Camel API, whereas beans allow loose coupling. We'll cover how to use beans in chapter 4.

In the preceding two chapters, we've covered two crucial features of integration kits: routing and transformation. The next chapter dives into the world of beans, and you'll see how Camel can easily adapt to and leverage your existing beans. This allows a higher degree of reuse and loose coupling, so you can keep your business and integration logic clean and apart from Camel and other middleware APIs.

Using beans with Camel

This chapter covers

- Understanding the Service Activator EIP
- How Camel looks up beans using registries
- How Camel selects bean methods to invoke
- Bean parameter binding with single and multiple parameters

If you've been developing software for five years or longer, you've likely worked with different component models, such as CORBA, EJB, JBI, SCA, and lately OSGi. Some of these models, especially the earlier ones, imposed a great deal on the programming model, dictating what you could and couldn't do, and they often required complex packaging and deployment models. This left the everyday engineer with a lot of concepts to learn and master. In some cases, much more time was spent working around the restrictive programming and deployment models than on the business application itself.

Because of this growing complexity and the resulting frustrations, a simpler, more pragmatic programming model arose from the open source community: the POJO model. Later this was formalized as the Spring Framework.

The Spring Framework has opened the door to the enterprise, proving that the POJO programming model and a lightweight container indeed meet the expectations of today's businesses. In fact, the simple programming model and light-weight container concept proved superior to the heavyweight and over-complex enterprise application and integration servers that were used before.

So what does this have to do with Camel? Well, Camel doesn't mandate using a specific component or programming model. It doesn't mandate a heavy specification that you must learn and understand to be productive. Camel doesn't require you to repackage any of your existing libraries or require you to use the Camel API to fulfill your integration needs. Camel is on the same page as the Spring Framework, with both of them being lightweight containers favoring the POJO programming model.

In fact, Camel recognizes the power of the POJO programming model and goes great lengths to work with your beans. By using beans, you fulfill an important goal in the software industry, which is to reduce coupling. Camel not only offers reduced coupling with beans, but you get the same loose coupling with Camel routes. For example, three teams can work simultaneously on their own sets of routes, which can easily be combined into one system.

We'll start this chapter by showing you how *not* to use beans with Camel, which will make it clearer how you should use beans. After that, we'll take a look at the theory behind the Service Activator EIP and dive inside Camel to see how this pattern is implemented. Finally, we'll look at the bean-binding process, which gives you fine-grained control over binding information to the parameters on the invoked method from within Camel and the currently routed message. It may sound confusing at first, but don't worry—it will make sense shortly.

4.1　Using beans the hard way and the easy way

In this section, we'll walk through an example that shows how not to use beans with Camel—the hard way to use beans. Then we'll look at how to use beans the easy way.

Suppose you have an existing bean that offers an operation (a service) you need to use in your integration application. For example, `HelloBean` offers the `hello` method as its service:

```
public class HelloBean {

    public String hello(String name) {
        return "Hello " + name;
    }
}
```

Let's look at some different ways you could use this bean in your application.

4.1.1　Invoking a bean from pure Java

By using a Camel `Processor`, you can invoke a bean from Java code.

> **Listing 4.1　Using a `Processor` to invoke the `hello` method on the `HelloBean`**

```
public class InvokeWithProcessorRoute extends RouteBuilder {

public void configure() throws Exception {
    from("direct:hello")
        .process(new Processor() {
```

❶ Uses a processor

```
        public void process(Exchange exchange) throws Exception {
            String name = exchange.getIn().getBody(String.class);

            HelloBean hello = new HelloBean();                    ❷ Invokes
            String answer = hello.hello(name);                       HelloBean

            exchange.getOut().setBody(answer);
        }
    });
}
```

Listing 4.1 shows a RouteBuilder, which defines the route. You use an inlined Camel Processor ❶, which gives you the process method, in which you can work on the message with Java code. First, you must extract the message body from the input message, which is the parameter you'll use when you invoke the bean later. Then you need to instantiate the bean and invoke it ❷. Finally you must set the output from the bean on the output message.

Now that you've done it the hard way using the Java DSL, let's take a look at using Spring XML.

4.1.2 Invoking a bean defined in Spring

You'll often use Spring as a bean container and define beans using its XML files. Listings 4.2 and 4.3 show how to revise listing 4.1 to work with a Spring bean this way.

Listing 4.2 Setting up Spring to use a Camel route that uses the HelloBean

```
<bean id="helloBean" class="camelinaction.HelloBean"/>    ◁──❶ Defines HelloBean

<bean id="route" class="camelinaction.InvokeWithProcessorSpringRoute"/>

<camelContext id="camel" xmlns="http://camel.apache.org/schema/spring">
    <routeBuilder ref="route"/>
</camelContext>
```

First you define HelloBean in the Spring XML file with the id helloBean ❶. You still want to use the Java DSL to build the route, so you need to declare a bean that contains the route. Finally, you define a CamelContext, which is the way you get Spring and Camel to work together.

Now let's take a closer look at the route.

Listing 4.3 A Camel route using a Processor to invoke HelloBean

```
public class InvokeWithProcessorSpringRoute extends RouteBuilder {

    @Autowired                                           ◁──  Injects
    private HelloBean hello;                                ❶ HelloBean

    public void configure() throws Exception {
        from("direct:hello")
            .process(new Processor() {
                public void process(Exchange exchange) throws Exception {
                    String name = exchange.getIn().getBody(String.class);
                    String answer = hello.hello(name);     ◁──
                    exchange.getOut().setBody(answer);        Invokes
                                                           ❷ HelloBean
```

```
                    }
            });
        }
    }
```

The route in listing 4.3 is nearly identical to the route in listing 4.1. The difference is that now the bean is injected using the Spring @Autowired annotation ❶, and instead of instantiating the bean, you use the injected bean directly ❷.

You can try these examples on your own; they're in the chapter4/bean directory of the book's source code. Run Maven with these goals to try the last two examples:

```
mvn test -Dtest=InvokeWithProcessorTest
mvn test -Dtest=InvokeWithProcessorSpringTest
```

So far you've seen two examples of using beans with a Camel route, and there's a bit of plumbing to get it all to work. Here are some reasons why it's hard to work with beans:

- You must use Java code to invoke the bean.
- You must use the Camel Processor, which clutters the route, making it harder to understand what happens (route logic is mixed in with implementation logic).
- You must extract data from the Camel message and pass it to the bean, and you must move any response from the bean back into the Camel message.
- You must instantiate the bean yourself, or have it dependency-injected.

Now let's look at the easy way of doing it.

4.1.3   *Using beans the easy way*

Suppose you were to define the Camel route in the Spring XML file instead of using a RouteBuilder class. The following snippet shows how this might be done:

```
<bean id="helloBean" class="camelinaction.HelloBean"/>

<camelContext id="camel" xmlns="http://camel.apache.org/schema/spring">
    <route>
        <from uri="direct:start"/>                    ❶ Insert something
        < What goes here >                               here to use beans
    </route>
</camelContext>
```

First you define the bean as a Spring bean, and then you define the Camel route with the direct:start input. At ❶ you want to invoke HelloBean, but you're in trouble—this is XML, and you can't add Java code in the XML file.

In Camel, the easy way to use beans is to use the <bean> tag at ❶:

```
<bean ref="helloBean" method="hello"/>
```

That gives you the following route:

```
<camelContext id="camel" xmlns="http://camel.apache.org/schema/spring">
    <route>
        <from uri="direct:start"/>
```

```
        <bean ref="helloBean" method="hello"/>
    </route>
</camelContext>
```

Camel offers the same solution when using the Java DSL. You can simplify the route in listing 4.3 like this:

```
public void configure() throws Exception {
    from("direct:hello").beanRef("helloBean", "hello");
}
```

That's a staggering reduction from eight lines of code to one. And on top of that, the one code line is much easier to understand. It's all high-level abstraction, containing no low-level code details, which were required when using inlined `Processors`.

You could even omit the `hello` method, because the bean only has a single method:

```
public void configure() throws Exception {
    from("direct:hello").beanRef("helloBean");
}
```

Using the `<bean>` tag is an elegant solution for working with beans. Without using that tag, you had to use a Camel `Processor` to invoke the bean, which is a tedious solution.

> **TIP** In the Java DSL, you don't have to preregister the bean in the registry. Instead, you can provide the class name of the bean, and Camel will instantiate the bean on startup. The previous example could be written simply as `from("direct:hello").bean(HelloBean.class);`.

Now let's look at how you can work with beans in Camel from the EIP perspective.

4.2 The Service Activator pattern

The Service Activator pattern is an enterprise pattern described in Hohpe and Woolf's *Enterprise Integration Patterns* book (http://www.enterpriseintegrationpatterns.com/). It describes a service that can be invoked easily from both messaging and non-messaging services. Figure 4.1 illustrates this principle.

Figure 4.1 shows a service activator component that invokes a service based on an incoming request and returns an outbound reply. The service activator acts as a mediator between the requester and the POJO service. The requester sends a request to the service activator ❶, which is responsible for adapting the request to a format the POJO service understands (mediating) and passing the request on to the service ❷.

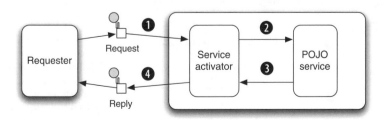

Figure 4.1 The service activator mediates between the requestor and the POJO service.

The POJO service then returns a reply to the service activator ❸, which passes it back (requiring no translation on the way back) to the waiting requester ❹.

As you can see in figure 4.1, the service is the POJO and the service activator is *something* in Camel that can adapt the request and invoke the service. That *something* is the Camel Bean component, which eventually uses the `org.apache.camel.compo-nent.bean.BeanProcessor` to do the work. We'll look at how this `BeanProcessor` works in section 4.4. You should regard the Camel Bean component as the Camel implementation of the Service Activator pattern.

Compare the Service Activator pattern in figure 4.1 to the Camel route example we looked at in section 4.1.3, as illustrated in figure 4.2.

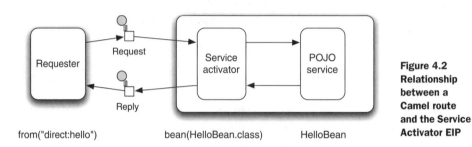

Figure 4.2 Relationship between a Camel route and the Service Activator EIP

Figure 4.2 shows how the Camel route maps to the Service Activator EIP. The requester is the node that comes before the bean—it's the `from("direct:hello")` in our example. The service activator itself is the bean node, which is represented by the `BeanProcessor` in Camel. And the POJO service is the `HelloBean` bean itself.

You now know the theory behind how Camel works with beans—the Service Activator pattern. But before you can use a bean, you need to know where to look for it. This is where the registry comes into the picture. Let's look at how Camel works with different registries.

4.3   Camel's bean registries

When Camel works with beans, it looks them up in a registry to locate them. Camel's philosophy is to leverage the best of the available frameworks, so it uses a pluggable registry architecture to integrate them. Spring is one such framework, and figure 4.3 illustrates how the registry works.

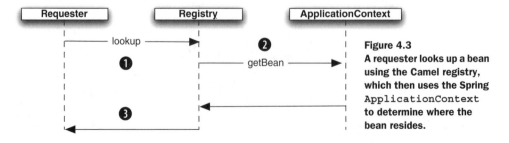

Figure 4.3 A requester looks up a bean using the Camel registry, which then uses the Spring `ApplicationContext` to determine where the bean resides.

Figure 4.3 shows that the Camel registry is an abstraction that sits between the caller and the real registry. When a requester needs to look up a bean ❶, it uses the Camel `Registry`. The Camel `Registry` then does the lookup via the real registry ❷. The bean is then returned to the requester ❸. This structure allows loose coupling but also a pluggable architecture that integrates with multiple registries. All the requester needs to know is how to interact with the Camel `Registry`.

The registry in Camel is merely a Service Provider Interface (SPI) defined in the `org.apache.camel.spi.Registry` interface, as follows:

```
Object lookup(String name);

<T> T lookup(String name, Class<T> type)

<T> Map<String, T> lookupByType(Class<T> type)
```

You'll most often use one of the first two methods to look up a bean by its name. For example, to look up the `HelloBean`, you would do this:

```
HelloBean hello = (HelloBean) context.getRegistry().lookup("helloBean");
```

To get rid of that ugly typecast, you can use the second method instead:

```
HelloBean hello = context.getRegistry()
                    .lookup("helloBean", HelloBean.class);
```

> **NOTE** The second method offers typesafe lookups because you provide the expected class as the second parameter. Under the hood, Camel uses its type-converter mechanism to convert the bean to the desired type, if necessary.

The last method, `lookupByType`, is mostly used internally by Camel to support convention over configuration—it allows Camel to look up beans by type without knowing the bean name.

The registry itself is an abstraction and thus an interface. Table 4.1 lists the four implementations shipped with Camel.

Table 4.1 Registry implementations shipped with Camel

Registry	Description
SimpleRegistry	A simple implementation to be used when unit testing or running Camel in the Google App engine, where only a limited number of JDK classes are available.
JndiRegistry	An implementation that uses an existing Java Naming and Directory Interface (JNDI) registry to look up beans.
ApplicationContextRegistry	An implementation that works with Spring to look up beans in the Spring `ApplicationContext`. This implementation is automatically used when you're using Camel in a Spring environment.
OsgiServiceRegistry	An implementation capable of looking up beans in the OSGi service reference registry. This implementation is automatically used when using Camel in an OSGi environment.

In the following sections, we'll go over each of these four registries.

4.3.1 SimpleRegistry

The SimpleRegistry is a Map-based registry that's used for testing or when running Camel standalone.

For example, if you wanted to unit test the HelloBean example, you could use the SimpleRegistry to enlist the HelloBean and refer to it from the route.

Listing 4.4 Using `SimpleRegistry` to unit test a Camel route

```
public class SimpleRegistryTest extends TestCase {
    private CamelContext context;
    private ProducerTemplate template;

    protected void setUp() throws Exception {
        SimpleRegistry registry = new SimpleRegistry();          ❶ Registers
        registry.put("helloBean", new HelloBean());                 HelloBean in
                                                                    SimpleRegistry
        context = new DefaultCamelContext(registry);    ← Uses SimpleRegistry
        template = context.createProducerTemplate();    ❷ with Camel

        context.addRoutes(new RouteBuilder() {
            public void configure() throws Exception {
                from("direct:hello").beanRef("helloBean");
            }
        });
        context.start();
    }

    protected void tearDown() throws Exception {        ❸ Cleans up resources
        template.stop();                                    after test
        context.stop();
    }

    public void testHello() throws Exception {
        Object reply = template.requestBody("direct:hello", "World");
        assertEquals("Hello World", reply);
    }
}
```

First you create an instance of SimpleRegistry and populate it with HelloBean under the helloBean name ❶. Then, to use this registry with Camel, you pass the registry as a parameter to the DefaultCamelContext constructor ❷. To aid when testing, you create a ProducerTemplate, which makes it simple to send messages to Camel, as can be seen in the test method. Finally, when the test is done, you clean up the resources by stopping Camel ❸. In the route, you use the beanRef method to invoke HelloBean by the helloBean name you gave it when it was enlisted in the registry ❶.

You can try this test by going to the chapter4/bean directory and running this Maven goal:

```
mvn test -Dtest=SimpleRegistryTest
```

Now let's look at the next registry: JndiRegistry.

4.3.2 *JndiRegistry*

The `JndiRegistry`, as its name implies, integrates with a JNDI-based registry. It was the first registry that Camel integrated, so it's also the default registry if you create a Camel instance without supplying a specific registry, as this code shows:

```
CamelContext context = new DefaultCamelContext();
```

The `JndiRegistry` (like the `SimpleRegistry`) is often used for testing or when running Camel standalone. Many of the unit tests in Camel use the `JndiRegistry` because they were created before the `SimpleRegistry` was added to Camel.

The `JndiRegistry` is useful when you use Camel together with a Java EE application server that provides a JNDI-based registry out of the box. Suppose you need to leverage the JNDI registry of a WebSphere Application Server—you would have to set up the pieces as follows:

Creates Hashtable containing ❶ JNDI configuration

```
protected CamelContext createCamelContext() throws Exception {
    Hashtable env = new Hashtable();              ◁────
    env.put(Context.INITIAL_CONTEXT_FACTORY,
            "com.ibm.websphere.naming.WsnInitialContextFactory");
    env.put(Context.PROVIDER_URL,
            "corbaloc:iiop:myhost.mycompany.com:2809");
    env.put(Context.SECURITY_PRINCIPAL, "username");
    env.put(Context.SECURITY_CREDENTIALS, "password");

    Context ctx = new InitialContext(env);        ❷ Creates
    JndiRegistry jndi = new JndiRegistry(ctx);      JndiRegistry

    return new DefaultCamelContext(jndi);
}
```

You need to use a `Hashtable` ❶ to store information about the JNDI registry you wish to use. After this, it's a matter of creating the `javax.naming.Context` that the `JndiRegistry` should use ❷.

Camel also allows you to use the `JndiRegistry` with Spring XML. All you have to do is define it as a Spring bean and Camel will automatically pick it up:

```
<bean id="registry" class="org.apache.camel.impl.JndiRegistry"/>
```

You can use the usual Spring lingo to pass the `Hashtable` parameter in the `JndiRegistry` constructor.

The next registry is for when you use Spring together with Camel.

4.3.3 *ApplicationContextRegistry*

The `ApplicationContextRegistry` is the default registry when Camel is used with Spring. More precisely, it's the default when you set up Camel in the Spring XML, as this snippet illustrates:

```
<camelContext id="camel" xmlns="http://camel.apache.org/schema/spring">
    <route>
        <from uri="direct:start"/>
```

```
        <bean ref="helloBean" method="hello"/>
    </route>
</camelContext>
```

Defining Camel using the `<camelContext>` tag will automatically let Camel use the `ApplicationContextRegistry`. This registry allows you to define beans in Spring XML files as you would normally do when using Spring. For example, you could define the `helloBean` bean as follows:

```
<bean id="helloBean" class="camelinaction.HelloBean"/>
```

It can hardly be simpler than that. When you use Camel with Spring, you can keep on using Spring beans as you would normally, and Camel will use those beans seamlessly without any configuration.

The final registry applies when you use Camel with OSGi.

4.3.4 *OsgiServiceRegistry*

When Camel is used in an OSGi environment, Camel uses a two-step lookup process. First, it will look up whether a service with the name exists in the OSGi service registry. If not, Camel will fall back and look up the name in the regular registry, such as the Spring `ApplicationContextRegistry`.

Suppose you want to expose `HelloBean` as an OSGi service. You could do it as follows:

```
<osgi:service id="helloService" interface="camelinaction.HelloBean"
              ref="helloBean"/>

  <bean id="helloBean" class="camelinaction.HelloBean"/>
```

With help from the `osgi:service` namespace provided by Spring Dynamic Modules (Spring DM; http://www.springsource.org/osgi), you export the `HelloBean` into the OSGi registry under the name `helloService`. You can use the `HelloBean` from a Camel route the same way you've already learned, by referring to its OSG service name:

```
<camelContext id="camel" xmlns="http://camel.apache.org/schema/spring">
    <route>
        <from uri="direct:start"/>
        <bean ref="helloService" method="hello"/>
    </route>
</camelContext>
```

It's that simple. All you have to remember is the name with which the bean was exported. Camel will look it up in the OSGi service registry and the Spring bean container for you. This is convention over configuration.

NOTE   We'll look at OSGi again when we cover Camel deployment in chapter 13.

This concludes our tour of registries. Next we'll focus on how Camel selects which method to invoke on a given bean.

4.4 *Selecting bean methods*

You've seen how Camel works with beans from the route perspective. Now it's time to dig down and see the moving parts in action. You first need to understand the mechanism Camel uses to selects the method to invoke.

Remember, Camel acts as a service activator using the `BeanProcessor`, which sits between the caller and the actual bean. At compile time there are no direct bindings, and the JVM can't link the caller to the bean—Camel must resolve this at runtime.

Figure 4.4 illustrates how the `BeanProcessor` leverages the registry to look up the bean to invoke.

At runtime, a Camel exchange is routed, and at a given point in the route, it reaches the `BeanProcessor`. The `BeanProcessor` then processes the exchange, performing these general steps:

1 Looks up the bean in the registry
2 Selects the method to invoke on the bean
3 Binds to the parameters of the selected method (for example, using the body of the input message as a parameter; this is covered in detail in section 4.5)
4 Invokes the method
5 Handles any invocation errors that occur (any exceptions thrown from the bean will be set on the Camel exchange for further error handling)
6 Sets the method's reply (if there is one) as the body on the output message on the Camel exchange

We've covered how registry lookups are done in section 4.3. The next two steps (steps 2 and 3 in the preceding list) are more complex, and we'll cover them in the remainder of this chapter. The reason why this is more complex in Camel is because Camel has to compute which bean and method to invoke at runtime, whereas Java code is linked at compile time.

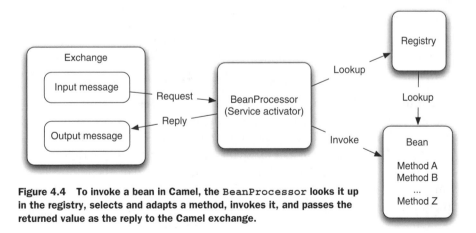

Figure 4.4   To invoke a bean in Camel, the `BeanProcessor` looks it up in the registry, selects and adapts a method, invokes it, and passes the returned value as the reply to the Camel exchange.

> ### Why does Camel need to select a method?
>
> Why is there more than one possible method name when you invoke a method? The answer is that beans can have overloaded methods, and in some cases the method name isn't specified either, which means Camel has to pick among all methods on the bean.
>
> Suppose you have the following methods:
>
> ```
> String echo(String s);
> int echo(int number);
> void doSomething(String something);
> ```
>
> There are a total of three methods for Camel to select among. If you explicitly tell Camel to use the echo method, you're still left with two methods to choose from. We'll look at how Camel resolves this dilemma.

We'll first take a look at the algorithm Camel uses to select the method. Then we'll look at a couple of examples and see what could go wrong and how to avoid problems.

4.4.1   How Camel selects bean methods

Unlike at compile time, when the Java compiler can link method invocations together, the Camel BeanProcessor has to select the method to invoke at runtime.

Suppose you have the following class:

```
public class EchoBean {
    String echo(String name) {
        return name + " " + name;
    }
}
```

At compile time, you can express your code to invoke the echo method like this:

```
EchoBean echo = new EchoBean();
String reply = echo.echo("Camel");
```

This will ensure that the echo method is invoked at runtime.

On the other hand, suppose you use the EchoBean in Camel in a route as follows:

```
from("direct:start").bean(EchoBean.class, "echo").to("log:reply");
```

When the compiler compiles this code, it can't see that you want to invoke the echo method on the EchoBean. From the compiler's point of view, EchoBean.class and "echo" are parameters to the bean method. All the compiler can check is that the EchoBean class exists; if you had misspelled the method name, perhaps typing "ekko", the compiler could not catch this mistake. The mistake would end up being caught at runtime, when the BeanProcessor would throw a MethodNotFoundException stating that the method named ekko does not exists.

Camel also allows you not to explicitly name a method. For example, you could write the previous route as follows:

```
from("direct:start").bean(EchoBean.class).to("log:reply");
```

Regardless of whether the method name is explicitly given or not, Camel has to compute which method to invoke. Let's look at how Camel chooses.

4.4.2 Camel's method-selection algorithm

The BeanProcessor uses a complex algorithm to select which method to invoke on a bean. You won't need to understand or remember every step in this algorithm—we simply want to outline what goes on inside Camel to make working with beans as simple as possible for you.

Figure 4.5 shows the first part of this algorithm, and it's continued in figure 4.6. Here's how the algorithm selects the method to invoke:

1 If the Camel message contains a header with the key CamelBeanMethodName, its value is used as the explicit method name. Go to step 5.

2 If a method is explicitly defined, Camel uses it, as we mentioned at the start of this section. Go to step 5.

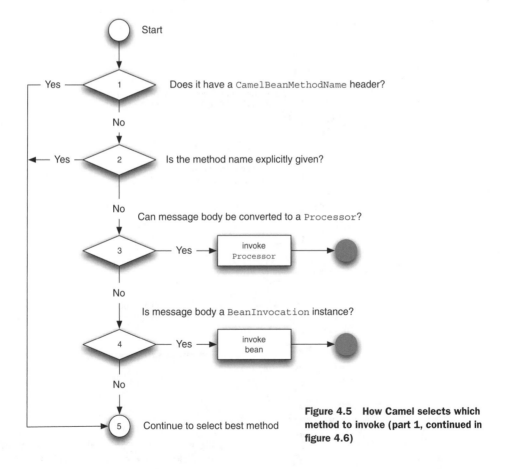

Figure 4.5   How Camel selects which method to invoke (part 1, continued in figure 4.6)

3 If the bean can be converted to a `Processor` using the Camel type-converter mechanism, the `Processor` is used to process the message. This may seem a bit odd, but it allows Camel to turn any bean into a message-driven bean equivalent. For example, with this technique Camel allows any `javax.jms.Message-Listener` bean to be invoked directly by Camel without any integration glue. This method is rarely used by end users of Camel, but it can be a useful trick.

4 If the body of the Camel message can be converted into an `org.apache.camel.component.bean.BeanInvocation`, that's used to invoke the method and pass the arguments to the bean. This is also rarely used by end users of Camel.

5 Continued in the second part of the algorithm, shown in figure 4.6.

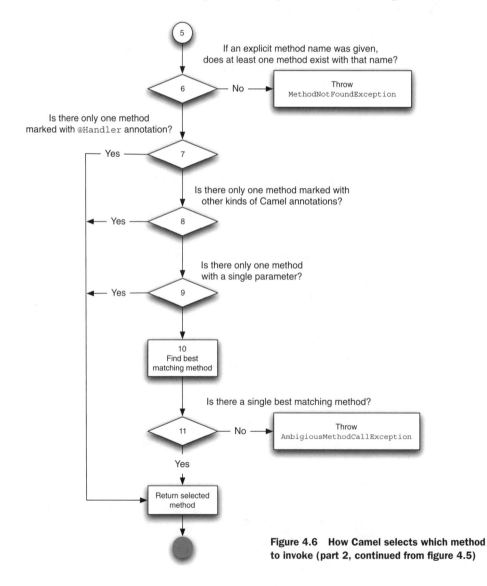

Figure 4.6   How Camel selects which method to invoke (part 2, continued from figure 4.5)

Figure 4.6 is a bit more complex, but its main goal is to narrow down the number of possible methods and select a method if one stands out. Don't worry if you don't entirely understand the algorithm; we'll look at a couple of examples shortly that should make it much clearer.

Let's continue with the algorithm and cover the last steps:

6 If a method name was given and no methods exist with that name, a `Method-NotFoundException` exception is thrown.

7 If only a single method has been marked with the `@Handler` annotation, it's selected.

8 If only a single method uses any of the other Camel bean parameter-binding annotations, such as `@Body`, `@Header`, and so on, it's selected. (We'll look at how Camel binds to method parameters using annotations in section 4.5.3.)

9 If, among all the methods on the bean, there's only one method with exactly one parameter, that method is selected. For example, this would be the situation for the `EchoBean` bean we looked at in section 4.4.1, which has only the `echo` method with exactly one parameter. Single parameter methods are preferred because they map easily with the payload from the Camel exchange.

10 Now the computation gets a bit complex. There are multiple candidate methods, and Camel must determine whether there's a single method that stands out as the best fit. The strategy is to go over the candidate methods and filters out methods that don't fit. Camel does this by trying to match the first parameter of the candidate method; if the parameter isn't the same type and it's not possible to coerce the types, the method is filtered out. In the end, if there is only a single method left, that method is selected.

11 If Camel can't select a method, an `AmbigiousMethodCallException` exception is thrown with a list of ambiguous methods.

Clearly Camel goes through a lot to select the method to invoke on your bean. Over time you'll learn to appreciate all this—it's convention over configuration to the fullest.

NOTE The algorithm laid out in this book is based on Apache Camel version 2.5. This method-selection algorithm may change in the future to accommodate new features.

Now it's time to take a look at how this algorithm applies in practice.

4.4.3 *Some method-selection examples*

To see how this algorithm works, we'll use the `EchoBean` from section 4.4.1 as an example, but we'll add another method to it—the `bar` method—to better explain what happens when there are multiple candidate methods.

```
public class EchoBean {

    public String echo(String echo) {
        return echo + " " + eco;
    }
```

```
    public String bar() {
        return "bar";
    }
}
```

And we'll start with this route:

```
from("direct:start").bean(EchoBean.class).to("log:reply");
```

If you send the `String` message `"Camel"` to the Camel route, the reply logger will surely output `"Camel Camel"` as expected. Despite the fact that `EchoBean` has two methods, `echo` and `bar`, only the `echo` method has a single parameter. This is what step 9 in figure 4.6 ensures—Camel will pick the method with a single parameter if there is only one of them.

To make the example a bit more challenging, let's change the `bar` method as follows:

```
public String bar(String name) {
    return "bar " + name;
}
```

What do you expect will happen now? You now have two identical method signatures with a single method parameter. In this case, Camel can't pick one over the other, so it throws an `AmbigiousMethodCallException` exception, according to step 11 in figure 4.6.

How can you resolve this? One solution would be to provide the method name in the route, such as specifying the `bar` method:

```
from("direct:start").bean(EchoBean.class, "bar").to("log:reply");
```

But there's another solution that doesn't involve specifying the method name in the route. You can use the `@Handler` annotation to select the method. This solution is dealt with in step 7 of figure 4.6. The `@Handler` is a Camel-specific annotation that you can add to a method. It simply tells Camel to use this method by default.

```
@Handler
public String bar(String name) {
    return "bar " + name;
}
```

Now the `AmbigiousMethodCallException` won't be thrown because the `@Handler` annotation tells Camel to select the `bar` method.

> **TIP** It's a good idea either to declare the method name in the route or to use the `@Handler` annotation. This ensures that Camel picks the method you want, and you won't be surprised if Camel chooses another method.

Suppose you change `EchoBean` to include two methods with different parameter types:

```
public class EchoBean {

    public String echo(String echo) {
        return echo + " " + echo;
    }
```

```
public Integer double(Integer num) {
    return num.intValue() * num.intValue();
}
}
```

The echo method works with a String, and the double method with an Integer. If you don't specify the method name, the BeanProcessor will have to choose between these two methods at runtime.

Step 10 in figure 4.6 allows Camel to be smart about deciding which method stands out. It does so by inspecting the message payloads of two or more candidate methods and comparing those with the message body type, checking whether there is an exact type match in any of the methods.

Suppose you send in a message to the route that contains a String body with the word "Camel". It's not hard to guess that Camel will pick the echo method, because it works with a String. On the other hand, if you send in a message with the Integer value of 5, Camel will select the double method, because it uses the Integer type.

Despite this, things can still go wrong, so let's go over a couple of common situations.

4.4.4 *Potential method-selection problems*

There are a few things that can go wrong when invoking beans at runtime:

- *Specified method not found*—If Camel can't find any method with the specified name, a MethodNotFoundException exception is thrown. This only happens when you have explicitly specified the method name.

- *Ambiguous method*—If Camel can't single out a method to call, an Ambigious-MethodCallException exception is thrown with a list of the ambiguous methods. This can happen even when an explicit method name was defined because the method could potentially be overloaded, which means the bean would have multiple methods with the same name; only the number of parameters would vary.

- *Type conversion failure*—Before Camel invokes the selected method, it must convert the message payload to the parameter type required by the method. If this fails, a NoTypeConversionAvailableException exception is thrown.

Let's take a look at examples of each of these three situations using the following EchoBean:

```
public class EchoBean {

    public String echo(String name) {
        return name + name;
    }

    public String hello(String name) {
        return "Hello " + name;
    }
}
```

First, you could specify a method that doesn't exist by doing this:

```
<bean ref="echoBean" method="foo"/>
```

Here you try to invoke the foo method, but there is no such method, so Camel throws a MethodNotFoundException exception.

On the other hand, you could omit specifying the method name:

```
<bean ref="echoBean"/>
```

In this case, Camel can't single out a method to use because both the echo and hello methods are ambiguous. When this happens, Camel throws an AmbigiousMethod-CallException exception containing a list of the ambiguous methods.

The last situation that could happen is when the message contains a body that can't be converted to the type required by the method. Suppose you have the following OrderServiceBean:

```
public class OrderServiceBean {

    public String handleXML(Document xml) {
        ...
    }
}
```

And suppose you need to use that bean in this route:

```
from("jms:queue:orders")
    .beanRef("orderService", "handleXML")
    .to("jms:queue:handledOrders");
```

The handleXML method requires a parameter to be of type org.w3c.dom.Document, which is an XML type, but what if the JMS queue contains a javax.jms.TextMessage not containing any XML data, but just a plain text message, such as "Camel rocks". At runtime you'll get the following stracktrace:

```
Caused by: org.apache.camel.NoTypeConversionAvailableException: No type
converter available to convert from type: java.lang.byte[] to the
required type: org.w3c.dom.Document with value [B@b3e1c9
    at
org.apache.camel.impl.converter.DefaultTypeConverter.mandatoryConvertTo
(DefaultTypeConverter.java:115)
    at
org.apache.camel.impl.MessageSupport.getMandatoryBody(MessageSupport.java
:101)
    ... 53 more
Caused by: org.apache.camel.RuntimeCamelException:
org.xml.sax.SAXParseException: Content is not allowed in prolog.
    at
org.apache.camel.util.ObjectHelper.invokeMethod(ObjectHelper.java:724)
    at
org.apache.camel.impl.converter.InstanceMethodTypeConverter.convertTo
(InstanceMethodTypeConverter.java:58)
    at
org.apache.camel.impl.converter.DefaultTypeConverter.doConvertTo
```

```
(DefaultTypeConverter.java:158)
    at
org.apache.camel.impl.converter.DefaultTypeConverter.mandatoryConvertTo
(DefaultTypeConverter.java:113)
    ... 54 more
```

What happened is that Camel tried to convert the `javax.jms.TextMessage` to a `org.w3c.dom.Document` type, but it failed. In this situation, Camel wraps the error and throws it as a `NoTypeConverterException` exception.

By further looking into this stacktrace, you may notice that the cause of this problem is that the XML parser couldn't parse the data to XML. It reports, "Content is not allowed in prolog," which is a common error indicating that the XML declaration (`<?xml version="1.0"?>`) is missing.

You may wonder what would happen if such a situation occurred at runtime. In this case, the Camel error-handling system would kick in and handle it. Error handling is covered thoroughly in chapter 5.

That's all you need to know about how Camel selects methods at runtime. Now we need to look at the bean parameter-binding process, which happens after Camel has selected the method.

4.5 *Bean parameter binding*

In the last section, we covered the process that selects which method to invoke on a bean. This section covers what happens next—how Camel adapts to the parameters on the method signature. Any bean method can have multiple parameters and Camel must somehow pass in meaningful values. This process is known as *bean parameter binding*.

We've already seen parameter binding in action in the many examples so far in this chapter. What those examples had in common was using a single parameter to which Camel bound the input message body. Figure 4.7 illustrates this using Echo-Bean as an example.

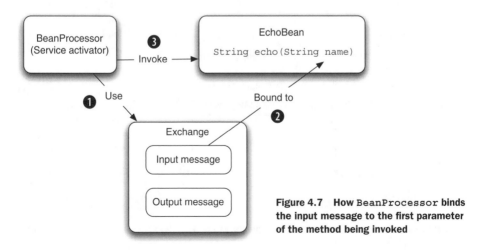

Figure 4.7 How `BeanProcessor` binds the input message to the first parameter of the method being invoked

The `BeanProcessor` uses the input message ❶ to bind its body to the first parameter of the method ❷, which happens to be the `String name` parameter. Camel does this by creating an expression that type-converts the input message body to the `String` type. This ensures that when Camel invokes the `echo` method ❸, the parameter matches the expected type.

This is important to understand, because most beans have methods with a single parameter. The first parameter is expected to be the input message body, and Camel will automatically convert the body to the same type as the parameter.

So what happens when a method has multiple parameters? That's what we'll look at in the remainder of the chapter.

4.5.1   *Binding with multiple parameters*

Figure 4.8 illustrates the principle of bean parameter binding when multiple parameters are used.

At first, figure 4.8 may seem a bit overwhelming. Many new types come into play when you deal with multiple parameters. The big box entitled "Bean parameter bindings" contains the following four boxes:

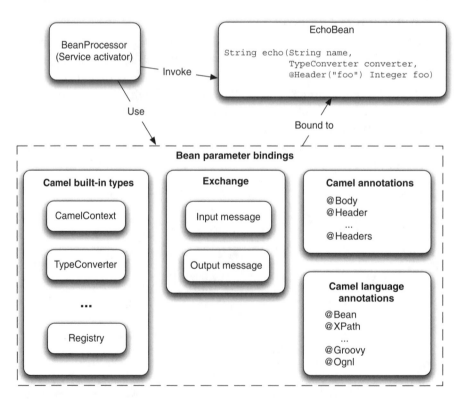

Figure 4.8   Parameter binding with multiple parameters involves a lot more options than with single parameters.

- *Camel built-in types*—Camel provides special bindings for a series of Camel concepts. We'll cover them in section 4.5.2.
- *Exchange*—This is the Camel exchange, which allows binding to the input message, such as its body and headers. The Camel exchange is the source of the values that must be bound to the method parameters. It will be covered in the sections to come.
- *Camel annotations*—When dealing with multiple parameters, you use annotations to distinguish them. This is covered in section 4.5.3.
- *Camel language annotations*—This is a less commonly used feature that allows you to bind parameters to languages. It's ideal when working with XML messages that allow you to bind parameters to XPath expressions. This is covered in section 4.5.4.

Working with multiple parameters

Using multiple parameters is more complex than using single parameters. It's generally a good idea to follow these rules of thumb:

- Use the first parameter as the message body, which may or may not use the @Body annotation.
- Use either a built-in type or add Camel annotations for subsequent parameters.

In our experience, it becomes complicated when multiple parameters don't follow these guidelines, but Camel will make its best attempt to adapt the parameters to the method signature.

Let's start by looking at using the Camel built-in types.

4.5.2 Binding using built-in types

Camel provides a set of fixed types that are always bound. All you have to do is declare a parameter of one of the types listed in table 4.2.

Table 4.2 Parameter types that Camel automatically binds

Type	Description
Exchange	The Camel exchange. This contains the values that will be bound to the method parameters.
Message	The Camel input message. It contains the body that is often bound to the first method parameter.
CamelContext	The CamelContext. This can be used in special circumstances when you need access to all Camel's moving parts.
TypeConverter	The Camel type-converter mechanism. This can be used when you need to convert types. We covered the type-converter mechanism in section 3.6.

Table 4.2 Parameter types that Camel automatically binds *(continued)*

Type	Description
Registry	The bean registry. This allows you to look up beans in the registry.
Exception	An exception, if one was thrown. Camel will only bind to this if the exchange has failed and contains an exception. This allows you to use beans to handle errors.

Let's look at a couple of examples using the types from table 4.2. First, suppose you add a second parameter that's one of the built-in types to the echo method:

```
public string echo(String echo, CamelContext context)
```

In this example, you bind the CamelContext, which gives you access to all the moving parts of Camel.

Or you could bind the registry, in case you need to look up some beans:

```
public string echo(String echo, Registry registry) {
    OtherBean other = registry.lookup("other", OtherBean.class);
    ...
}
```

You aren't restricted to having only one additional parameter; you can have as many as you like. For example, you could bind both the CamelContext and the registry:

```
public string echo(String echo, CamelContext context, Registry registry)
```

So far, you've always bound to the message body; how would you bind to a message header? The next section will explain that.

4.5.3 *Binding using Camel annotations*

Camel provides a range of annotations to help bind from the exchange to bean parameters. You should use these annotations when you want more control over the bindings. For example, without these annotations, Camel will always try to bind the method body to the first parameter, but with the @Body annotation you can bind the body to any parameter in the method.

Suppose you have the following bean method:

```
public String orderStatus(Integer customerId, Integer orderId)
```

And you have a Camel message that contains the following data:

- Body, with the order ID, as a String type
- Header with the customer ID as an Integer type

With the help of Camel annotations, you can bind the Exchange to the method signature as follows:

```
public String orderStatus(@Header("customerId") Integer customerId,
                          @Body Integer orderId)
```

Notice how you can use the @Header annotation to bind the message header to the first parameter and @Body to bind the message body to the second parameter.

Table 4.3 lists all the Camel parameter-binding annotations.

Table 4.3 Parameter-binding annotations provided by Camel

Annotation	Description
`@Attachments`	Binds the parameter to the message attachments. The parameter must be a `java.util.Map` type.
`@Body`	Binds the parameter to the message body.
`@Header(name)`	Binds the parameter to the given message header.
`@Headers`	Binds the parameter to all the input headers. The parameter must be a `java.util.Map` type.
`@OutHeaders`	Binds the parameter to the output headers. The parameter must be a `java.util.Map` type. This allows you to add headers to the output message.
`@Property(name)`	Binds the parameter to the given exchange property.
`@Properties`	Binds the parameter to all the exchange properties. The parameter must be a `java.util.Map` type.

You've already seen the first two types in action, so let's try a couple of examples with the other annotations. For example, you could use `@Headers` to bind the input headers to a Map type:

```
public String orderStatus(@Body Integer orderId, @Headers Map headers) {
    Integer customerId = (Integer) headers.get("customerId");
    String customerType = (String) headers.get("customerType");
    ...
}
```

You would use this when you have many headers, so you don't have to add a parameter for every single header.

The `@OutHeaders` annotation is used when you're working with request-response messaging (also identified as the InOut Message Exchange pattern). `@OutHeaders` provides direct access to the output message headers, which means you can manipulate these headers directly from the bean. Here's an example:

```
public String orderStatus(@Body Integer orderId, @OutHeaders Map headers) {
    ...
    headers.put("status", "APPROVED");
    headers.put("confirmId", "444556");
    return "OK";
}
```

Notice that you use `@OutHeaders` as the second parameter. Unlike `@Headers`, `@OutHeaders` is empty when the method is invoked. The idea is that you put the headers that you want to preserve in the output message into this map.

Finally, let's look at Camel's language annotations, which bind parameters to a language.

4.5.4 *Binding using Camel language annotations*

Camel provides additional annotations that allow you to use other languages as parameters. This may sound a bit strange, but it will become clearer with an example.

The most common language to use is XPath, which allows you to evaluate XPath expressions on the message body. For example, suppose the message contains the following XML document:

```
<order customerId="123">
  <status>in progress</status>
</order>
```

By using XPath expressions, you can extract parts of the document and bind them to parameters, like this:

```
public void updateStatus(@XPath("/order/@customerId") Integer customerId,
                         @XPath("/order/status/text()") String status)
```

You can bind as many parameters as you like—the preceding example binds two parameters using the @XPath annotations. You can also mix and match annotations, so you can use @XPath for one parameter and @Header for another.

Table 4.4 lists the language annotations provided in Camel 2.5. In the future, we may add additional languages to Camel, which often also means that a corresponding annotation for bean parameter binding is added as well.

Table 4.4 Camel's language-based bean binding annotations

Annotation	Description	Dependency
@Bean	Invokes a method on a bean	camel-core
@BeanShell	Evaluates a bean shell script	camel-script
@EL	Evaluates an EL script (unified JSP and JSF scripts)	camel-juel
@Groovy	Evaluates a Groovy script	camel-script
@JavaScript	Evaluates a JavaScript script	camel-script
@MVEL	Evaluates a MVEL script	camel-mvel
@OGNL	Evaluates an OGNL script	camel-ognl
@PHP	Evaluates a PHP script	camel-script
@Python	Evaluates a Python script	camel-script
@Ruby	Evaluates a Ruby script	camel-script
@Simple	Evaluates a Simple expression (Simple is a built-in language provided with Camel; see appendix A for more details)	camel-core
@XPath	Evaluates an XPath expression	camel-core
@XQuery	Evaluates an XQuery expression	camel-saxon

It may seem a bit magical that you can use a @Bean annotation when invoking a method, because the @Bean annotation itself also invokes a method. Let's try out an example.

Suppose you already have a service that must be used to stamp unique order IDs on incoming orders. The service is implemented as follows.

Listing 4.5 A service that stamps an order ID on an XML document

```
public Document handleIncomingOrder(Document xml, int customerId,
                                    int orderId) {
    Attr attr = xml.createAttribute("orderId");          Creates orderId
    attr.setValue("" + orderId);                       ❶ attribute

    Node node = xml.getElementsByTagName("order").item(0);
    node.getAttributes().setNamedItem(attr);             Adds orderId attribute
                                                       ❷ to order node
    return xml;
}
```

As you can see, the service creates a new XML attribute with the value of the given order ID ❶. Then it inserts this attribute in the XML document ❷ using the rather clumsy XML API from Java ❷.

To generate the unique order ID, you have the following class:

```
public final class GuidGenerator {
    public static int generate() {
        Random ran = new Random();
        return ran.nextInt(10000000);
    }
}
```

(In a real system, you'd generate unique order IDs based on another scheme.)

In Camel, you have the following route that listens for new order files and invokes the service before sending the orders to a JMS destination for further processing:

```
<bean id="xmlOrderService" class="camelinaction.XmlOrderService"/>

<camelContext id="camel" xmlns="http://camel.apache.org/schema/spring">
    <route>
        <from uri="file://riderautoparts/order/inbox"/>
        <bean ref="xmlOrderService"/>
        <to uri="jms:queue:order"/>
    </route>
</camelContext>
```

What is missing is the step that generates a unique ID and provides that ID in the handle-IncomingOrder method (shown in listing 4.5). To do this, you need to declare a bean in the spring XML file with the ID generator, as follows:

```
<bean id="guid" class="camelinaction.GuidGenerator"/>
```

Now you're ready to connect the last pieces of the puzzle. You need to tell Camel that it should invoke the generate method on the guid bean when it invokes the handleIncomingOrder method from listing 4.5. To do this, you use the @Bean annotation and change the method signature to the following:

```
public Document handleIncomingOrder(@Body Document xml,
                @XPath("/order/@customerId") int customerId,
                @Bean(ref = "guid", method="generate") int orderId);
```

We've prepared a unit test you can use to run this example. Use the following Maven goal from the chapter4/bean directory:

```
mvn test -Dtest=XmlOrderTest
```

When it's running, you should see two log lines that output the XML order before and after the service has stamped the order ID. Here's an example:

```
2009-10-28 16:18:58,485 [: FileComponent] INFO  before
Exchange[BodyType:org.apache.camel.component.file.GenericFile,
Body:<order customerId="4444"><item>Camel in action</item></order>]
2009-10-28 16:18:58,564 [: FileComponent] INFO  after
Exchange[BodyType:com.sun.org.apache.xerces.internal.dom.
DeferredDocumentImpl, Body:<order customerId="4444"
orderId="7303381"><item>Camel in action</item></order>]
```

Here you can see that the second log line has an `orderId` attribute with the value of 7303381, whereas the first doesn't. If you run it again, you'll see a different order ID because it's a random value. You can experiment with this example, perhaps changing how the order ID is generated.

USING NAMESPACES WITH @XPATH

In the preceding example the XML order did not include a namespace. When using namespaces the bean parameter binding must include the namespace(s) in the method signature as highlighted:

```
public Document handleIncomingOrder(
    @Body Document xml,
    @XPath(
        value = "/c:order/@customerId",
        namespaces = @NamespacePrefix(
            prefix = "c",
            uri = "http://camelinaction.com/order")) int customerId,
    @Bean(ref = "guid", method = "generate") int orderId);
```

The namespace is defined using the **@NamespacePrefix** annotation embedded in the @XPath annotation. Notice the XPath expression value must use the prefix, which means the expression is changed from /order/@customerId to /**c**:order/@customerId.

The prefix value isn't required to be a certain value; instead of c you can use any value you like.

The source code for the book contains this example in the chapter4/bean directory; you can try using the following Maven goal:

```
mvn test -Dtest=XmlOrderNamespaceTest
```

If your XML document includes multiple namespaces, you can define those as well in the @XPath annotation as it accepts an array of **@NamespacePrefix**.

Bean binding summary

Camel's rules for bean parameter binding can be summarized as follows:

- All parameters having a Camel annotation will be bound (table 4.3 and 4.4)
- All parameters of a Camel built-in type will be bound (table 4.2)
- The first parameter is assumed to be the message IN body (if not already bound)
- All remaining parameters will be unbound, and Camel will pass in empty values

You've seen all there is to bean binding. Camel has a flexible mechanism that adapts to your existing beans, and when you have multiple parameters, Camel provides annotations to bind the parameters properly.

4.6 Summary and best practices

We've now covered another cornerstone of using beans with Camel. It's important that end users of Camel can use the POJO programming model and have Camel easily leverage those beans (POJOs). Beans are just Java code, which is a language you're likely to feel comfortable using. If you hit a problem that you can't work around or figure out how to resolve using Camel and EIPs, you can always resort to using a bean and letting Camel invoke it.

We unlocked the algorithm used by Camel to select which method to invoke on a bean. You learned why this is needed—Camel must resolve method selection at runtime, whereas regular Java code can link method invocations at compile time.

We also covered what bean parameter binding is and how you can bind a Camel exchange to any bean method and its parameters. You learned how to use annotations to provide fine-grained control over the bindings, and even how Camel can help bind XPath expressions to parameters, which is a great feature when working with XML messages.

Let's pull out some of the key practices you should take away from this chapter:

- *Use beans.* Beans are Java code and they give you all the horsepower of Java.
- *Use loose coupling.* Prefer using beans that don't have a strong dependency on the Camel API. Camel is capable of adapting to existing bean method signatures, so you can leverage any existing API you may have, even if it has no dependency on the Camel API. Unit testing is also easier because your beans don't depend on any Camel API. You can even have developers with no Camel experience develop the beans, and then have developers with Camel experience use those beans.
- *Prefer simple method signatures.* Camel bean binding is much simpler when method signatures have as few parameters as possible.
- *Specify method names.* Tell Camel which method you intend to invoke, so Camel doesn't have to figure this out itself. You can also use `@Handler` in the bean to tell Camel which method it should pick and use.
- *Use bean parameter annotations.* Use the powers that the various Camel bean parameter annotations offer.

We've now covered three crucial features of integration kits: routing, transformations, and using beans. We'll now take a leap into another world, one that's often tackled as an afterthought in integration projects: how to handle situations when things go wrong. We've devoted an entire chapter to Camel's extensive support for error handling.

Error handling

In the last three chapters, we've covered three key functions that any integration kit should provide: routing, transformation, and mediation. In this chapter, we turn our focus to what happens when things go wrong. We want to introduce you to error handling early in this book, because we firmly believe that error handling should not be an afterthought but a key piece in your design from the start.

Writing applications that integrate disparate systems are a challenge when it comes to handling unexpected events. In a single system that you fully control, you can handle these events and recover. But systems that are integrated over the network have additional risks: the network connection could be broken, a remote system might not respond in a timely manner, or it might even fail for no apparent reason. Even on your local server, unexpected events can occur, such as the server's disk filling up or the server running out of memory. Regardless of which errors occur, your application should be prepared to handle them.

In these situations, log files are often the only evidence of the unexpected event, so logging is important. Camel has extensive support for logging and for handling errors to ensure your application can continue to operate.

In this chapter, you'll discover how flexible, deep, and comprehensive Camel's error handling is and how to tailor it to deal with most situations. We'll cover all the error handlers Camel provides out of the box, and when they're best used, so you can pick the ones best suited to your applications. You'll also learn how to configure and master redelivery, so Camel can try to recover from particular errors. We'll also look at exception policies, which allow you to differentiate among errors and handle specific ones, and at how scopes can help you define general rules for implementing route-scoped error handling. Finally, we'll look at what Camel offers when you need fine-grained control over error handling, so that it only reacts under certain conditions.

5.1 Understanding error handling

Before jumping into the world of error handling with Camel, we need to take a step back and look at errors more generally. There are two main categories of errors, recoverable and irrecoverable, and we need to look at where and when error handling starts, because there are some prerequisites that must happen beforehand.

5.1.1 Recoverable and irrecoverable errors

When it comes to errors, we can divide them into *recoverable* and *irrecoverable* errors, as illustrated in figure 5.1.

An *irrecoverable error* is an error that remains an error now matter how many times you try to perform the same action again. In the integration space, that could mean trying to access a database table that doesn't exist, which would cause the JDBC driver to throw an SQLException.

A *recoverable error,* on the other hand, is a temporary error that might not cause a problem on the next attempt. A good example of such an error is a problem with the network connection resulting in a java.io.IOException. On a subsequent attempt, the network issue could be resolved and your application could continue to operate.

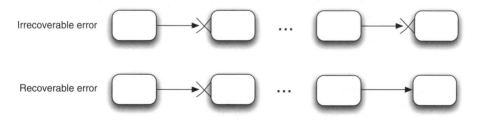

Figure 5.1 Errors can be categorized as either recoverable or irrecoverable. Irrecoverable errors continue to be errors on subsequent attempts; recoverable errors may be quickly resolved on their own.

In your daily life as a Java developer, you won't encounter this division of errors into recoverable and irrecoverable often. Generally, exception handling code uses one of the two patterns illustrated in the following two code snippets.

The first snippet illustrates a common error-handling idiom, where all kinds of exceptions are considered irrecoverable and you give up immediately, throwing the exception back to the caller, often wrapped:

```java
public void handleOrder(Order order) throws OrderFailedException {
    try {
        service.sendOrder(order);
    } catch (Exception e) {
        throw new OrderFailedException(e);
    }
}
```

The next snippet improves on this situation by adding a bit of logic to handle redelivery attempts before eventually giving up:

```java
public void handleOrder(Order order) throws OrderFailedException {
    boolean done = false;
    int retries = 5;                          ❶ Attempts
    while (!done) {                              redelivery
        try {
            service.sendOrder(order);
            done = true;
        } catch (Exception e) {
            if (--retries == 0) {
                throw new OrderFailedException(e);
            }
        }
    }
}
```

Around the invocation of the service is the logic that attempts redelivery, in case an error occurs. After five attempts, it gives up and throws the exception.

What the preceding example lacks is logic to determine whether the error is recoverable or irrecoverable, and to react accordingly. In the recoverable case, you could try again, and in the irrecoverable case, you could give up immediately and rethrow the exception.

In Camel, a recoverable error is represented as a plain `Throwable` or `Exception` that can be set or accessed from `org.apache.camel.Exchange` using one of the following two methods:

```java
void setException(Throwable cause);
```

or

```java
Exception getException();
```

> **NOTE** The `setException` method on `Exchange` accepts a `Throwable` type, whereas the `getException` method returns an `Exception` type. `getException` also doesn't return a `Throwable` type because of API compatibility.

An irrecoverable error is represented as a message with a fault flag that can be set or accessed from `org.apache.camel.Exchange`. For example, to set `"Unknown customer"` as a fault message, you would do the following:

```
Message msg = Exchange.getOut();
msg.setFault(true);
msg.setBody("Unknown customer");
```

The fault flag must be set using the `setFault(true)` method.

So why are the two types of errors represented differently? There are two reasons: First, the Camel API was designed around the Java Business Integration (JBI) specification, which includes a fault message concept. Second, Camel has error handling built into its core, so whenever an exception is thrown back to Camel, it catches it and sets the thrown exception on the `Exchange` as a recoverable error, as illustrated here:

```
try {
    processor.process(exchange);
} catch (Throwable e) {
    exchange.setException(e);
}
```

Using this pattern allows Camel to catch and handle all exceptions that are thrown. Camel's error handling can then determine how to deal with the errors—retry, propagate the error back to the caller, or do something else. End users of Camel can set irrecoverable errors as fault messages, and Camel can react accordingly and stop routing the message.

Now that you've seen recoverable and irrecoverable errors in action, let's summarize how they're represented in Camel:

- Exceptions are represented as recoverable errors.
- Fault messages are represented as irrecoverable errors.

Now let's look at when and where Camel's error handling applies.

5.1.2 *Where Camel's error handling applies*

Camel's error handling doesn't apply everywhere. To understand why, take a look at figure 5.2.

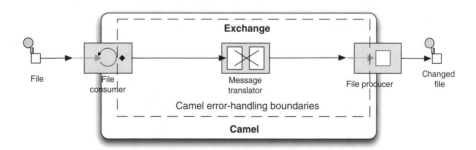

Figure 5.2 Camel's error handling only applies within the lifecycle of an exchange.

Figure 5.2 shows a simple route that translates files. You have a file consumer and producer as the input and output facilities, and in between is the Camel routing engine, which routes messages encompassed in an exchange. It's during the lifecycle of this exchange that the Camel error handling applies. That leaves a little room on the input side where this error handling can't operate—the file consumer must be able to successfully read the file, instantiate the `Exchange`, and start the routing before the error handling can function. This applies to any kind of Camel consumer.

So what happens if the file consumer can't read the file? The answer is component-specific, and each Camel component must deal with this in its own way. Some components will ignore and skip the message, others will retry a number of times, and others will gracefully recover.

> **NOTE**   There are a number of Camel components that provide minor error-handling features: File, FTP, Mail, iBATIS, RSS, Atom, JPA, and SNMP. These components are based on the `ScheduledPollConsumer` class, which offers a pluggable `PollingConsumerPollStrategy` that you can use to create your own error-handling strategy. You can learn more about this on the Camel website, at http://camel.apache.org/polling-consumer.html.

That's enough background information—let's dig into how error handling in Camel works. In the next section, we'll start by looking at the different error handlers Camel provides.

5.2   *Error handlers in Camel*

In the previous section you learned that Camel regards all exceptions as recoverable and stores them on the exchange using the `setException(Throwable cause)` method. This means error handlers in Camel will only react to exceptions set on the exchange. By default, they won't react if an irrecoverable error has been set as a fault message. The rule of thumb is that error handlers in Camel only trigger when `exchange.getException() != null`.

> **NOTE**   In section 5.3.4, you'll learn how you can instruct Camel error handlers to react to fault messages as well.

Camel provides a range of error handlers. They're listed in table 5.1.

Table 5.1   The error handlers provided in Camel

Error handler	Description
`DefaultErrorHandler`	This is the default error handler that's automatically enabled, in case no other has been configured.
`DeadLetterChannel`	This error handler implements the Dead Letter Channel EIP.
`TransactionErrorHandler`	This is a transaction-aware error handler extending the default error handler. Transactions are covered in chapter 9 and are only briefly touched on in this chapter. We'll revisit this error handler in chapter 9.

Table 5.1 The error handlers provided in Camel *(continued)*

Error handler	Description
NoErrorHandler	This handler is used to disable error handling altogether.
LoggingErrorHandler	This error handler just logs the exception.

At first glance, having five error handlers may seem overwhelming, but you'll learn that the default error handler is used in most cases.

The first three error handlers in table 5.1 all extend the RedeliveryErrorHandler class. That class contains the majority of the error-handling logic that the first three error handlers all leverage. The latter two error handlers have limited functionality and don't extend RedeliveryErrorHandler.

We'll look at each of these error handlers in turn.

5.2.1 The default error handler

Camel is preconfigured to use the DefaultErrorHandler, which covers most use cases. To understand it, consider the following route:

```
from("direct:newOrder")
    .beanRef("orderService, "validate")
    .beanRef("orderService, "store");
```

The default error handler is preconfigured and doesn't need to be explicitly declared in the route. So what happens if an exception is thrown from the validate method on the order service bean?

To answer this, we need to dive into Camel's inner processing, where the error handler lives. In every Camel route, there is a Channel that sits between each node in the route graph, as illustrated in figure 5.3.

The Channel is in between each node of the route path, which ensures it can act as a controller that monitors and controls the routing at runtime. This is the feature that allows Camel to enrich the route with error handling, message tracing, interceptors, and much more. For now, you just need to know that this is where the error handler lives.

Turning back to the example route, imagine that an exception was thrown from the order service bean during invocation of the validate method. In figure 5.3, the processor ❸ would throw an exception, which would be propagated back to the previous channel ❷, where the error handler would catch it. This gives Camel the chance to react accordingly. For example, Camel could try again (redeliver), or it could route

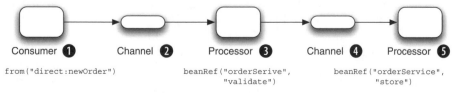

Figure 5.3 A detailed view of a route path, where channels act as controllers between the processors

the message to another route path (detour using exception policies), or it could give up and propagate the exception back to the caller. With the default settings, Camel will propagate the exception back to the caller.

The default error handler is configured with these settings:

- No redelivery
- Exceptions are propagated back to the caller

These settings match what happens when you're working with exceptions in Java, so Camel's behavior won't surprise Camel end users.

Let's continue with the next error handler, the dead letter channel.

5.2.2   *The dead letter channel error handler*

The `DeadLetterChannel` error handler is similar to the default error handler except for the following differences:

- The dead letter channel is the only error handler that supports moving failed messages to a dedicated error queue, which is known as the dead letter queue.
- Unlike the default error handler, the dead letter channel will, by default, handle exceptions and move the failed messages to the dead letter queue.
- The dead letter channel supports using the original input message when a message is moved to the dead letter queue.

Let's look at each of these in a bit more detail.

THE DEAD LETTER CHANNEL

The `DeadLetterChannel` is an error handler that implements the principles of the Dead Letter Channel EIP. This pattern states that if a message can't be processed or delivered, it should be moved to a dead letter queue. Figure 5.4 illustrates this pattern.

As you can see, the consumer ❶ consumes a new message that is supposed to be routed to the processor ❸. The channel ❷ controls the routing between ❶ and ❸, and if the message can't be delivered to ❸, the channel invokes the deal letter channel error handler, which moves the message to the dead letter queue ❹. This keeps the message safe and allows the application to continue operating.

This pattern is often used with messaging. Instead of allowing a failed message to block new messages from being picked up, the message is moved to a dead letter queue to get it out of the way.

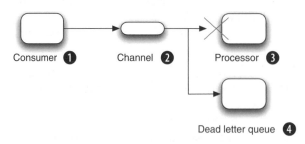

Figure 5.4   The Dead Letter Channel EIP moves failed messages to a dead letter queue.

The same idea applies to the dead letter channel error handler in Camel. This error handler has an associated dead letter queue, which is based on an endpoint, allowing you to use any Camel endpoint you choose. For example, you can use a database, a file, or just log the failed messages.

When you choose to use the dead letter channel error handler, you must configure the dead letter queue as an endpoint so the handler knows where to move the failed messages. This is done a bit differently in the Java DSL and Spring XML. For example, here is how you'd log the message at ERROR level in Java DSL:

```
errorHandler(deadLetterChannel("log:dead?level=ERROR"));
```

And here is how you'd do it in Spring XML:

```
<errorHandler id="myErrorHandler" type="DeadLetterChannel"
              deadLetterUri="log:dead?level=ERROR"/>
```

Now, let's look at how the dead letter channel error handler handles exceptions when it moves the message to the dead letter queue.

HANDLING EXCEPTIONS BY DEFAULT

By default, Camel handles exceptions by suppressing them; it removes the exceptions from the exchange and stores them as properties on the exchange. After a message has been moved to the dead letter queue, Camel stops routing the message and the caller regards it as processed.

When a message is moved to the dead letter queue, you can obtain the exception from the exchange using the `Exchange.CAUSED_EXCEPTION` property.

```
Exception e = exchange.getProperty(Exchange.CAUSED_EXCEPTION,
                                   Exception.class);
```

Now let's look at using the original message.

USING THE ORIGINAL MESSAGE WITH THE DEAD LETTER CHANNEL

Suppose you have a route in which the message goes through a series of processing steps, each altering a bit of the message before it reaches its final destination, as in the following code:

```
errorHandler(deadLetterChannel("jms:queue:dead"));

from("jms:queue:inbox")
    .beanRef("orderService", "decrypt")
    .beanRef("orderService", "validate")
    .beanRef("orderService", "enrich")
    .to("jms:queue:order");
```

Now imagine that an exception occurs at the `validate` method, and the dead letter channel error handler moves the message to the dead letter queue. Suppose a new message arrives and an exception occurs at the `enrich` method, and this message is also moved to the same dead letter queue. If you want to retry those messages, can you just drop them into the inbox queue?

In theory, you could do this, but the messages that were moved to the dead letter queue no longer match the messages that originally arrived at the inbox queue—they were altered as the messages were routed. What you want instead is for the original message content to have been moved to the dead letter queue, so that you have the original message to retry.

The `useOriginalMessage` option instructs Camel to use the original message when it moves messages to the dead letter queue. You configure the error handler to use the `useOriginalMessage` option as follows:

```
errorHandler(deadLetterChannel("jms:queue:dead").useOriginalMessage());
```

In Spring XML, you would do this:

```
<errorHandler id="myErrorHandler" type="DeadLetterChannel"
              deadLetterUri="jms:queue:dead" useOriginalMessage="true"/>
```

Let's move on to the transaction error handler.

5.2.3   *The transaction error handler*

The `TransactionErrorHandler` is built on top of the default error handler and offers the same functionality, but it's tailored to support transacted routes. Chapter 9 focuses on transactions and discusses this error handler in detail, so we won't say much about it here. For now, you just need to know that it exists and it's a core part of Camel.

The remaining two error handlers are seldom used and are much simpler.

5.2.4   *The no error handler*

The `NoErrorHandler` is used to disable error handling. The current architecture of Camel mandates that an error handler must be configured, so if you want to disable error handling, you need to provide an error handler that's basically an empty shell with no real logic. That's the `NoErrorHandler`.

5.2.5   *The logging error handler*

The `LoggingErrorHandler` logs the failed message along with the exception. The logger uses standard log format from log kits such as log4j, commons logging, or the Java Util Logger.

Camel will, by default, log the failed message and the exception using the log name `org.apache.camel.processor.LoggingErrorHandler` at `ERROR` level. You can, of course, customize this.

That covers the five error handlers provided with Camel. Let's now look at the major features these error handlers provide.

5.2.6   *Features of the error handlers*

The default, dead letter channel, and transaction error handlers are all built on the same base, `org.apache.camel.processor.RedeliveryErrorHandler`, so they all have several major features in common. These features are listed in table 5.2.

At this point, you may be eager to see the error handlers in action. In section 5.4.6 we'll build a use case that introduces error handling, so there will be

Table 5.2 Noteworthy features provided by the error handlers

Feature	Description
Redelivery policies	Redelivery policies allow you to define policies for whether or not redelivery should be attempted. The policies also define settings such as the maximum number of redelivery attempts, delays between attempts, and so on.
Scope	Camel error handlers have two possible scopes: context (high level) and route (low level). The context scope allows you to reuse the same error handler for multiple routes, whereas the route scope is used for a single route only.
Exception policies	Exception policies allow you to define special policies for specific exceptions.
Error handling	This option allows you to specify whether or not the error handler should handle the error. You can let the error handler deal with the error or leave it for the caller to handle.

plenty of opportunities to try this on your own. But first, let's look at the major features. We'll look at redelivery and scope in section 5.3. Exception policies and error handling will be covered in section 5.4.

5.3 *Using error handlers with redelivery*

Communicating with remote servers relies on network connectivity that can be unreliable and have outages. Luckily these disruptions cause recoverable errors—the network connection could be reestablished in a matter of seconds or minutes. Remote services can also be the source of temporary problems, such as when the service is restarted by an administrator. To help address these problems, Camel supports a redelivery mechanism that allows you to control how recoverable errors are dealt with.

In this section, we'll take a look at a real-life error-handling scenario, and then focus on how Camel controls redelivery and how you can configure and use it. We'll also take a look at how you can use error handlers with fault messages. We'll end this section by looking at error-handling scope and how it can be used to support multiple error handlers scoped at different levels.

5.3.1 *An error-handling use case*

Suppose you have developed an integration application at Rider Auto Parts that once every hour should upload files from a local directory to an HTTP server, and your boss asks why the files haven't been updated in the last few days. You're surprised, because the application has been running for the last month without a problem. This could well be a situation where neither error handling nor monitoring was in place.

Here's the Java file that contains the integration route:

```
from("file:/riders/files/upload?delay=1h")
    .to("http://riders.com?user=gear&password=secret");
```

This route will periodically scan for files in the /riders/files/upload folder, and if any files exist, it will upload them to the receiver's HTTP server using the HTTP endpoint.

But there is no explicit error handling configured, so if an error occurs, the default error handler is triggered. That handler doesn't handle the exception but instead propagates it back to the caller. Because the caller is the file consumer, it will log the exception and do a file rollback, meaning that any picked-up files will be left on the file system, ready to be picked up in the next scheduled poll.

At this point, you need to reconsider how errors should be handled in the application. You aren't in major trouble, because you haven't lost any files—Camel will only move successfully processed files out of the upload folder—failed files will just stack up.

The error occurs when sending the files to the HTTP server, so you look into the log files and quickly determine that Camel can't connect to the remote HTTP server due to network issues. Your boss decides that the application should retry uploading the files if there's an error, so the files won't have to wait for the next hourly upload.

To implement this, you can configure the error handler to redeliver up to 5 times with 10-second delays:

```
errorHandler(defaultErrorHandler()
    .maximumRedeliveries(5).redeliveryDelay(10000));
```

Configuring redelivery can hardly get any simpler than that. But let's take a closer look at how to use redelivery with Camel.

5.3.2   *Using redelivery*

The first three error handlers in table 5.1 all support redelivery. This is implemented in the `RedeliveryErrorHandler` class, which they extend. The `RedeliveryError-Handler` must then know whether or not to attempt redelivery; this is what the redelivery policy is for.

A redelivery policy defines how and whether redelivery should be attempted. Table 5.3 outlines the options supported by the redelivery policy and what the default settings are.

Table 5.3   Options provided in Camel for configuring redelivery

Option	Type	Default	Description
MaximumRedeliveries	int	0	Maximum number of redelivery attempts allowed. 0 is used to disable redelivery, and -1 will attempt redelivery forever until it succeeds.
RedeliveryDelay	long	1000	Fixed delay in milliseconds between each redelivery attempt.
MaximumRedeliveryDelay	long	60000	An upper bound in milliseconds for redelivery delay. This is used when you specify non-fixed delays, such as exponential backoff, to avoid the delay growing too large.

Table 5.3 Options provided in Camel for configuring redelivery *(continued)*

Option	Type	Default	Description
AsyncDelayedRedelivery	boolean	false	Dictates whether or not Camel should use asynchronous delayed redelivery. When a redelivery is scheduled to be redelivered in the future, Camel would normally have to block the current thread until it's time for redelivery. By enabling this option, you let Camel use a scheduler so that an asynchronous thread will perform the redelivery. This ensures that no thread is blocked while waiting for redelivery.
BackOffMultiplier	double	2.0	Exponential backoff multiplier used to multiply each consequent delay. RedeliveryDelay is the starting delay. Exponential backoff is disabled by default.
CollisionAvoidanceFactor	double	0.15	A percentage to use when calculating a random delay offset (to avoid using the same delay at the next attempt). Will start with the RedeliveryDelay as the starting delay. Collision avoidance is disabled by default.
DelayPattern	String	–	A pattern to use for calculating the delay. The pattern allows you to specify fixed delays for interval groups. For example, the pattern "0:1000; 5:5000;10:30000" will use a 1 second delay for attempts 0 to 4, 5 seconds for attempts 5 to 9, and 30 seconds for subsequent attempts.
RetryAttemptedLogLevel	LoggingLevel	DEBUG	Log level used when a redelivery attempt is performed.
RetriesExhaustedLogLevel	LoggingLevel	ERROR	Log level used when all redelivery attempts have failed.
LogStackTrace	boolean	true	Specifies whether or not stacktraces should be logged when all redelivery attempts have failed.
LogRetryStackTrace	boolean	false	Specifies whether or not stacktraces should be logged when a delivery has failed.
LogRetryAttempted	boolean	true	Specifies whether or not redelivery attempts should be logged.
LogExhausted	boolean	true	Specifies whether or not the exhaustion of redelivery attempts (when all redelivery attempts have failed) should be logged.
LogHandled	boolean	false	Specifies whether or not handled exceptions should be logged.

In the Java DSL, Camel has fluent builder methods for configuring the redelivery policy on the error handler. For instance, if you want to redeliver up to five times, use exponential backoff, and have Camel log at WARN level when it attempts a redelivery, you could use this code:

```
errorHandler(defaultErrorHandler()
    .maximumRedeliveries(5)
    .backOffMultiplier(2)
    .retryAttemptedLogLevel(LoggingLevel.WARN));
```

Configuring this in Spring XML is done as follows:

```
<errorHandler id="myErrorHandler" type="DefaultErrorHandler"
    <redeliveryPolicy maximumRedeliveries="5"
                      retryAttemptedLogLevel="WARN"
                      backOffMultiplier="2"
                      useExponentialBackOff="true"/>
</errorHandler>
```

There are two things to notice in this Spring XML configuration. By using the type option on the <errorHandler> tag, you select which type of error handler to use. In this example, it's the default error handler. You also have to enable exponential back-off explicitly by setting the useExponentialBackOff option to true.

We've now established that Camel uses the information from the redelivery policy to determine whether and how to do redeliveries. But what happens inside Camel? As you'll recall from figure 5.3, Camel includes a Channel between every processing step in a route path, and there is functionality in these Channels, such as error handlers. The error handler detects every exception that occurs and acts on it, deciding what to do, such as redeliver or give up.

Now that you know a lot about the DefaultErrorHandler, it's time to try a little example.

USING THE DEFAULTERRORHANDLER WITH REDELIVERY

In the source code for the book, you'll see an example in the chapter5/errorhandler directory. The example uses the following route configuration:

```
errorHandler(defaultErrorHandler()              ◁──┐  Configures
    .maximumRedeliveries(2)                      ❶  error handler
    .redeliveryDelay(1000)
    .retryAttemptedLogLevel(LoggingLevel.WARN));

from("seda:queue.inbox")
    .beanRef("orderService", "validate")
    .beanRef("orderService", "enrich")          ❷  Invokes enrich
    .log("Received order ${body}")              ◁──   method
    .to("mock:queue.order");
```

This configuration first defines a context-scoped error handler ❶ that will attempt at most two redeliveries using a 1-second delay. When it attempts the redelivery, it will log this at the WARN level (as you'll see in a few seconds). The example is constructed to fail when the message reaches the enrich method ❷.

You can run this example using the following Maven goal from the chapter5/ errorhandler directory:

```
mvn test -Dtest=DefaultErrorHandlerTest
```

When running the example, you'll see the following log entries outputted on the console. Notice how Camel logs the redelivery attempts:

```
2009-12-16 14:28:16,959 [a://queue.inbox] WARN  DefaultErrorHandler
     - Failed delivery for exchangeId: 64bc46c0-5cb0-4a78-a4a8-9159f5273601.
     On delivery attempt: 0 caught: camelinaction.OrderException: ActiveMQ in
     Action is out of stock
2009-12-16 14:28:17,960 [a://queue.inbox] WARN  DefaultErrorHandler
     - Failed delivery for exchangeId: 64bc46c0-5cb0-4a78-a4a8-9159f5273601.
     On delivery attempt: 1 caught: camelinaction.OrderException: ActiveMQ in
     Action is out of stock
```

These log entries show that Camel failed to deliver a message, which means the entry is logged *after* the attempt is made. On delivery attempt: 0 identifies the first attempt; attempt 1 is the first *redelivery* attempt. Camel also logs the exchangeId (which you can use to correlate messages) and the exception that caused the problem (without the stacktrace, by default).

When Camel performs a redelivery attempt it does this at the point of *origin*. In the preceding example the error occurred when invoking the enrich method ❷, which means Camel will redeliver by retrying the .beanRef("orderService", "enrich") step in the route.

After all redelivery attempts have failed, we say it's *exhausted*, and Camel logs this at the ERROR level by default. (You can customize this with the options listed in table 5.3.) When the redelivery attempts are exhausted, the log entry is similar to the previous ones, but Camel explains that it's exhausted after three attempts:

```
2009-12-16 14:28:18,961 [a://queue.inbox] ERROR DefaultErrorHandler
     - Failed delivery for exchangeId: 64bc46c0-5cb0-4a78-a4a8-9159f5273601.
     Exhausted after delivery attempt: 3 caught:
     camelinaction.OrderException: ActiveMQ in Action is out of stock
```

TIP The default error handler has many options, which are listed in table 5.3. We encourage you to try loading this example into your IDE and playing with it. Change the settings on the error handler and see what happens.

The preceding log output identifies the number of redelivery attempts, but how does Camel know this? Camel stores this information on the Exchange. Table 5.4 reveals where this information is stored.

Table 5.4 Headers on the Exchange related to error handling

Header	Type	Description
Exchange.REDELIVERY_COUNTER	int	The current redelivery attempt.
Exchange.REDELIVERED	boolean	Whether this Exchange is being redelivered.
Exchange.REDELIVERY_EXHAUSTED	boolean	Whether this Exchange has attempted (exhausted) all redeliveries and has still failed.

The information in table 5.4 is only available when Camel performs a redelivery; these headers are absent on the regular first attempt. It's only when a redelivery is triggered that these headers are set on the exchange.

USING ASYNCHRONOUS DELAYED REDELIVERY

In the previous example, the error handler was configured to use delayed redelivery with a 1-second delay between attempts. When a redelivery is to be conducted, Camel will wait for 1 second before carrying out the redelivery.

If you look at the console output, you can see the redelivery log entries are 1 second apart, and it's the same thread processing the attempts; this can be identified by the [a://queue.inbox] being logged. This is known as *synchronous delayed redelivery*. There will also be situations where you want to use *asynchronous delayed redelivery*. So what does that mean?

Suppose two orders are sent to the seda:queue:inbox endpoint. The consumer will pick up the first order from the queue and process it. If it fails, it's scheduled for redelivery. In the synchronous case, the consumer thread is blocked while waiting to carry out the redelivery. This means the second order on the queue can only be processed when the first order has been completed.

This isn't the case in asynchronous mode. Instead of the consumer thread being blocked, it will break out and be able to pick up the second order from the queue and continue processing it. This helps achieve higher scalability because threads aren't blocked and doing nothing. Instead the threads are being put to use servicing new requests.

> **TIP** We'll cover the threading model in chapter 10, which will explain how Camel can schedule redeliveries for the future to be processed by other threads. The Delayer and Throttler EIPs have similar asynchronous delayed modes, which you can leverage by enabling the asyncDelayed option.

The source code for the book contains an example that illustrates the difference between synchronous and asynchronous delayed redelivery, in the chapter5/ errorhandler directory. You can try it using the following Maven goal:

```
mvn test -Dtest=SyncVSAsyncDelayedRedeliveryTest
```

The example contains two methods: one for the synchronous mode and another for the asynchronous.

The console output for the synchronous mode should be displayed in the following order:

```
[a://queue.inbox] INFO - Received input amount=1,name=ActiveMQ in Action
[a://queue.inbox] WARN - Failed delivery for exchangeId: xxxx
[a://queue.inbox] WARN - Failed delivery for exchangeId: xxxx
[a://queue.inbox] WARN - Failed delivery for exchangeId: xxxx
[a://queue.inbox] INFO - Received input amount=1,name=Camel in Action
[a://queue.inbox] INFO - Received order amount=1,name=Camel in
    Action,id=123,status=OK
```

Compare that with the following output from the asynchronous mode:

```
[a://queue.inbox] INFO - Received input amount=1,name=ActiveMQ in Action
[a://queue.inbox] WARN - Failed delivery for exchangeId: xxxx
[a://queue.inbox] INFO - Received input amount=1,name=Camel in Action
[a://queue.inbox] INFO - Received order amount=1,name=Camel in
    Action,id=123,status=OK
[rRedeliveryTask] WARN - Failed delivery for exchangeId: xxxx
[rRedeliveryTask] WARN - Failed delivery for exchangeId: xxxx
```

Notice how the *Camel in Action* order is processed immediately when the first order fails and is scheduled for redelivery. Also pay attention to the thread name that executes the redelivery, identified by [rRedeliveryTask] being logged. As you can see, it's not the consumer anymore; its a redelivery task.

5.3.3 Error handlers and scopes

Scopes can be used to define error handlers at different levels. Camel supports two scopes: a context scope and a route scope.

Camel allows you to define a global context-scoped error handler that's used by default, and, if needed, you can also configure a route-scoped error handler that applies only for a particular route. This is illustrated in listing 5.1.

Listing 5.1   Using two error handlers at different scopes

```
errorHandler(defaultErrorHandler()                          ← ❶ Defines context-scoped
    .maximumRedeliveries(2)                                       error handler
    .redeliveryDelay(1000)
    .retryAttemptedLogLevel(LoggingLevel.WARN));

from("file://target/orders?delay=10000")
    .beanRef("orderService", "toCsv")
    .to("mock:file")
    .to("seda:queue.inbox");

from("seda:queue.inbox")                                     ❷ Defines route-scoped
    .errorHandler(deadLetterChannel("log:DLC")              ←    error handler
        .maximumRedeliveries(5).retryAttemptedLogLevel(LoggingLevel.INFO)
        .redeliveryDelay(250).backOffMultiplier(2))         ❸ Invokes enrich
    .beanRef("orderService", "validate")                   ←    method
    .beanRef("orderService", "enrich")
    .to("mock:queue.order");
```

Listing 5.1 is an improvement over the previous error-handling example. The default error handler is configured as in the previous example ❶, but you have a new route that picks up files, processes them, and sends them to the second route. This first route will use the default error handler ❶ because it doesn't have a route-scoped error handler configured, but the second route has a route-scoped error handler ❷. It's a Dead Letter Channel that will send failed messages to a log. Notice that it has different options configured than the former error handler.

The source code for the book includes this example, which you can run using the following Maven goal from the chapter5/errorhandler directory:

```
mvn test -Dtest=RouteScopeTest
```

This example should fail for some messages when the enrich ❸ method is invoked. This demonstrates how the route-scoped error handler is used as error handler.

The most interesting part of this test class is the testOrderActiveMQ method, which will fail in the second route and therefore show the Dead Letter Channel in action. There are a couple of things to notice about this, such as the exponential backoff, which causes Camel to double the delay between redelivery attempts, starting with 250 milliseconds and ending with 4 seconds.

The following snippets show what happens at the end when the error handler is exhausted.

```
2009-12-16 17:03:44,534 [a://queue.inbox] INFO  DeadLetterChannel
    - Failed delivery for exchangeId: e80ed4ba-12b3-472c-9b35-31beed4ff51b.
    On delivery attempt: 5 caught: camelinaction.OrderException: ActiveMQ in
    Action is out of stock
2009-12-16 17:03:44,541 [a://queue.inbox] INFO  DLC
    - Exchange[BodyType:String, Body:amount=1,name=ActiveMQ in
    Action,id=123]
2009-12-16 17:03:44,542 [a://queue.inbox] ERROR DeadLetterChannel
    - Failed delivery for exchangeId: e80ed4ba-12b3-472c-9b35-31beed4ff51b.
    Exhausted after delivery attempt: 6 caught:
    camelinaction.OrderException: ActiveMQ in Action is out of stock.
    Processed by failure processor: sendTo(Endpoint[log://DLC])
```

As you can see, the Dead Letter Channel moves the message to its dead letter queue, which is the log://DLC endpoint. After this, Camel also logs an ERROR line indicating that this move was performed.

We encourage you to try this example and adjust the configuration settings on the error handlers to see what happens.

So far, the error-handling examples we've looked at have used the Java DSL. Let's take a look at configuring error handling with Spring XML.

USING ERROR HANDLING WITH SPRING XML

Let's revise the example in listing 5.1 to use Spring XML. Here's how that's done.

Listing 5.2 Using error handling with Spring XML

```
<bean id="orderService" class="camelinaction.OrderService"/>          ❶ Specifies
                                                                         context-scoped
<camelContext id="camel" errorHandlerRef="defaultEH"                     error handler
             xmlns="http://camel.apache.org/schema/spring">

<errorHandler id="defaultEH">
   <redeliveryPolicy maximumRedeliveries="2" redeliveryDelay="1000"
                  retryAttemptedLogLevel="WARN"/>
</errorHandler>                    ❸ Sets up route-scoped        Sets up context-
                                      error handler               scoped error
<errorHandler id="dlc"                                            handler ❷
             type="DeadLetterChannel" deadLetterUri="log:DLC">
   <redeliveryPolicy maximumRedeliveries="5" redeliveryDelay="250"
                  retryAttemptedLogLevel="INFO"
                  backOffMultiplier="2" useExponentialBackOff="true"/>
</errorHandler>
```

```
<route>
    <from uri="file://target/orders?delay=10000"/>
    <bean ref="orderService" method="toCsv"/>
    <to uri="mock:file"/>
    <to uri="seda:queue.inbox"/>
</route>

<route errorHandlerRef="dlc">
    <from uri="seda:queue.inbox"/>
    <bean ref="orderService" method="validate"/>
    <bean ref="orderService" method="enrich"/>
    <to uri="mock:queue.order"/>
</route>

</camelContext>
```

4 Specifies route-scoped error handler

To use a context-scoped error handler in Spring XML, you must configure it using an errorHandlerRef attribute **1** on the camelContext tag. The errorHandlerRef refers to an <errorHandler>, which in this case is the default error handler with id "defaultEH" **2**. There's another error handler, a DeadLetterChannel error handler **3**, that is used at route scope in the second route **4**.

As you can see, the differences between the Java DSL and Spring XML mostly result from using the errorHandlerRef attribute to reference the error handlers in Spring XML, whereas Java DSL can have route-scoped error handlers within the routes.

You can try this example by running the following Maven goal from the chapter5/errorhandler directory:

```
mvn test -Dtest=SpringRouteScopeTest
```

The Spring XML file is located in the src/test/resources/camelinaction directory.

This concludes our discussion of scopes and redelivery. We'll now look at how you can use Camel error handlers to handle faults.

5.3.4 Handling faults

In the introduction to section 5.2, we mentioned that by default the Camel error handlers will only react to exceptions. Because a fault isn't represented as an exception but as a message that has the fault flag enabled, faults will not be recognized and handled by Camel error handlers.

There may be times when you want the Camel error handlers handle faults as well. Suppose a Camel route invokes a remote web service that returns a fault message, and you want this fault message to be treated like an exception and moved to a dead letter queue.

We've implemented this scenario as a unit test, simulating the remote web service using a bean:

```
errorHandler(deadLetterChannel("mock:dead"));

from("seda:queue.inbox")
    .beanRef("orderService", "toSoap")
    .to("mock:queue.order");
```

Now, imagine that the `orderService` bean returns the following SOAP fault:

```
<?xml version="1.0" encoding="UTF-8" standalone="yes"?>
<ns2:Envelope xmlns:ns2="http://schemas.xmlsoap.org/soap/envelope/"
              xmlns:ns3="http://www.w3.org/2003/05/soap-envelope">
    <ns2:Body>
        <ns2:Fault>
            <faultcode>ns3:Receiver</faultcode>
            <faultstring>ActiveMQ in Action is out of stock</faultstring>
        </ns2:Fault>
    </ns2:Body>
</ns2:Envelope>
```

Under normal situations, the Camel error handler won't react when the SOAP fault occurs. To make it do so, you have to instruct Camel by enabling fault handling.

To enable fault handling on the `CamelContext` (context scope), you simply do this:

```
getContext().setHandleFault(true);
```

To enable it on a per route basis (route scope), do this:

```
from("seda:queue.inbox").handleFault()
    .beanRef("orderService", "toSoap")
    .to("mock:queue.order");
```

Once fault handling is enabled, the Camel errors handlers will recognize the SOAP faults and react. Under the hood, the SOAP fault is converted into an `Exception` with the help of an interceptor.

You can enable fault handling in Spring XML as follows:

```
<route handleFault="true">
    <from uri="seda:queue.inbox"/>
    <bean ref="orderService" method="toSoap"/>
    <to uri="mock:queue.order"/>
</route>
```

The source code for the book contains this example in the chapter5/errorhandler directory, which you can try using the following Maven goals:

```
mvn test -Dtest=HandleFaultTest
mvn test -Dtest=SpringHandleFaultTest
```

> **TIP** You can enable fault handling to let Camel error handlers react to faults returned from components such as CXF, SOAP, JBI, or NMR.

We'll continue in the next section to look at the other two major features that error handlers provide, as listed in table 5.2: exception policies and error handling.

5.4   *Using exception policies*

Exception policies are used to intercept and handle specific exceptions in particular ways. For example, exception policies can influence, at runtime, the redelivery policies the error handler is using. They can also handle an exception or even detour a message.

NOTE In Camel, exception policies are specified with the `onException` method in the route, so we'll use the term `onException` interchangeably with "exception policy."

We'll cover exception policies piece by piece, looking at how they catch exceptions, how they works with redelivery, and how they handle exceptions. Then we'll take a look at custom error handling and put it all to work in an example.

5.4.1 Understanding how onException catches exceptions

We'll start by looking at how Camel inspects the exception hierarchy to determine how to handle the error. This will give you a better understanding of how you can use `onException` to your advantage.

Imagine you have this exception hierarchy being thrown:

```
org.apache.camel.RuntimeCamelException (wrapper by Camel)
+ com.mycompany.OrderFailedException
  + java.net.ConnectException
```

The real cause is a `ConnectException`, but it's wrapped in an `OrderFailedException` and yet again in a `RuntimeCamelException`.

Camel will traverse the hierarchy from the bottom up to the root searching for an `onException` that matches the exception. In this case, Camel will start with `java.net.ConnectException`, move on to `com.mycompany.OrderFailedException`, and finally reach `RuntimeCamelException`. For each of those three exceptions, Camel will compare the exception to the defined `onExceptions` to select the best matching `onException` policy. If no suitable policy can be found, Camel relies on the configured error handler settings. We'll drill down and look at how the matching works, but for now you can think of this as Camel doing a big `instanceof` check against the exceptions in the hierarchies, following the order in which the `onExceptions` were defined.

Suppose you have a route with the following `onException`:

```
onException(OrderFailedException.class).maximumRedeliveries(3);
```

The aforementioned `ConnectException` is being thrown, and the Camel error handler is trying to handle this exception. Because you have an exception policy defined, it will check whether the policy matches the thrown exception or not. The matching is done as follows:

1. Camel starts with the `java.net.ConnectException` and compares it to `onException(OrderFailedException.class)`. Camel checks whether the two exceptions are exactly the same type, and in this case they're not—`ConnectionException` and `OrderFailedException` aren't the same type.

2. Camel checks whether `ConnectException` is a subclass of `OrderFailedException`, and this isn't true either. So far, Camel has not found a match.

3. Camel moves up the exception hierarchy and compares again with `OrderFailedException`. This time there is an exact match, because they're both of the type `OrderFailedException`.

No more matching takes place—Camel got an exact match, and the exception policy will be used.

When an exception policy has been selected, its configured policy will be used by the error handler. In this example, the policy defines the maximum redeliveries to be 3, so the error handler will attempt at most 3 redeliveries when this kind of exception is thrown.

Any value configured on the exception policy will override options configured on the error handler. For example, suppose the error handler had the `maximumRedeliveries` option configured as 5. Because the `onException` has the same option configured, its value of 3 will be used instead.

> **NOTE**   The book's source code has an example that demonstrates what you've just learned. Take a look at the `OnExceptionTest` class in chapter5/onexception. It has multiple test methods, each showing a scenario of how `onException` works.

Let's make the example a bit more interesting and add a second `onException` definition:

```
onException(OrderFailedException.class).maximumRedeliveries(3);
onException(ConnectException.class).maximumRedeliveries(10);
```

If the same exception hierarchy is thrown as in the previous example, Camel would select the second `onException` because it directly matches the `ConnectionException`. This allows you to define different strategies for different kinds of exceptions. In this example, it is configured to use more redelivery attempts for connection exceptions than for order failures.

> **TIP**   This example demonstrates how `onException` can influence the redelivery polices the error handler uses. If an error handler was configured to perform only 2 redelivery attempts, the preceding `onException` would overload this with 10 redelivery attempts in the case of connection exceptions.

But what if there are no direct matches? Let's look at another example. This time, imagine that a `java.io.IOException` exception was thrown. Camel will do its matching, and because `OrderFailedException` isn't a direct match, and `IOException` isn't a subclass of it, it's out of the game. The same applies for the `ConnectException`. In this case, there are no `onException` definitions that match, and Camel will fall back to using the configuration of the current error handler.

You can see this in action by running the following Maven goal from chapter 5/onexception directory:

```
mvn test -Dtest=OnExceptionFallbackTest
```

ONEXCEPTION AND GAP DETECTION

Can Camel do better if there isn't a direct hit? Yes, it can, because Camel uses a gap-detection mechanism that calculates the gaps between a thrown exception and the `onExceptions` and then selects the `onException` with the lowest gap as the winner. This may sound confusing, so let's look at an example.

Suppose you have these three onException definitions, each having a different redelivery policy:

```
onException(ConnectException.class)
    .maximumRedeliveries(5);
onException(IOException.class)
    .maximumRedeliveries(3).redeliveryDelay(1000);
onException(Exception.class)
    .maximumRedeliveries(1).redeliveryDelay(5000);
```

And imagine this exception is thrown:

```
org.apache.camel.OrderFailedException
+ java.io.FileNotFoundException
```

Which of those three onExceptions would be selected?

Camel starts with the java.io.FileNotFoundException and compares it to the onException definitions. Because there are no direct matches, Camel uses gap detection. In this example, only onException(IOException.class) and onException(Exception.class) partly match, because java.io.FileNotFoundException is a subclass of java.io.IOException and java.lang.Exception.

Here's the exception hierarchy for FileNotFoundException:

```
java.lang.Exception
+ java.io.IOException
  + java.io.FileNotFoundException
```

Looking at this exception hierarchy, you can see that java.io.FileNotFoundException is a direct subclass of java.io.Exception, so the gap is computed as 1. The gap between java.lang.Exception and java.io.FileNotFoundException is 2. At this point, the best candidate has a gap of 1.

Camel will then go the same process with the next exception from the thrown exception hierarchy, which is OrderFailedException. This time, it's only the onException(Exception.class) that partly matches, and the gap between OrderFailedException and Exception is also 1:

```
java.lang.Exception
+ OrderNotFoundException
```

So what now? You have two gaps, both calculated as 1. In the case of a tie, Camel will always pick the first match, because the cause exception is most likely the last in the hierarchy. In this case, it's a FileNotFoundException, so the winner will be onException(IOException.class).

This example is provided in the source code for the book in the chapter5/onexception directory. You can try it using the following Maven goal:

```
mvn test -Dtest=OnExceptionGapTest
```

Gap detection allows you to define coarse-grained policies and also to have a few fine-grained policies that overrule the coarse-grained ones. Does this sound familiar? Yes, it's related to the scoping that we covered in section 5.3.

MULTIPLE EXCEPTIONS PER ONEXCEPTION

So far, you've only seen examples with one exception per onException, but you can define multiple exceptions in the same onException:

```
onException(XPathException.class, TransformerException.class)
    .to("log:xml?level=WARN");

onException(IOException.class, SQLException.class, JMSException.class)
    .maximumRedeliveries(5).redeliveryDelay(3000);
```

Here's the same example using Spring XML:

```xml
<camelContext xmlns="http://camel.apache.org/schema/spring">
    <onException>
        <exception>javax.xml.xpath.XPathException</exception>
        <exception>javax.xml.transform.TransformerException</exception>
        <to uri="log:xml?level=WARN"/>
    </onException>

    <onException>
        <exception>java.io.IOException</exception>
        <exception>java.sql.SQLException</exception>
        <exception>javax.jms.JmsException</exception>
        <redeliverPolicy maximumRedeliveries="5" redeliveryDelay="3000"/>
    </onException>
</camelContext>
```

Our next topic is how onException works with redelivery. Even though we've touched on this already in our examples, we'll go into the details in the next section.

5.4.2 *Understanding how onException works with redelivery*

onException works with redeliveries, but there are a couple of things you need to be aware of that might not be immediately obvious.

Suppose you have the following route:

```
from("jetty:http://0.0.0.0/orderservice")
    .to("mina:tcp://erp.rider.com:4444?textline=true")
    .beanRef("orderBean", "prepareReply");
```

You use the Camel Jetty component to expose an HTTP service where statuses of pending orders can be queried. The order status information is retrieved from a remote ERP system by the MINA component using low-level socket communication. You've learned how to configure this on the error handler itself, but it's also possible to configure this on the onException.

Suppose you want Camel to retry invoking the external TCP service, in case there has been an IO-related error, such as a lost network connection. To do this, you can simply add the onException and configure the redelivery policy as you like. In the following example, the redelivery tries at most 5 times:

```
onException(IOException.class).maximumRedeliveries(5);
```

You've already learned that onException(IOException.class) will catch those IO-related exceptions and act accordingly. But what about the delay between redeliveries?

In this example, the delay will be 1 second. Camel will use the default redelivery policy settings outlined in table 5.3 and then override those values with values defined in the onException. Because the delay was not overridden in the onException, the default value of 1 second is used.

> **TIP** When you configure redelivery policies, they override the existing redelivery policies set in the current error handler. This is convention over configuration, because you only need to configure the differences, which is often just the number of redelivery attempts or a different redelivery delay.

Now let's make it a bit more complicated:

```
errorHandler(defaultErrorHandler().maximumRedeliveries(3).delay(3000));

onException(IOException.class).maximumRedeliveries(5);

from("jetty:http://0.0.0.0/orderservice")
    .to("mina:tcp://erp.rider.com:4444?textline=true")
    .beanRef("orderBean", "prepareReply");
```

What would the redelivery delay be if an IOException were thrown? Yes, it's 3 seconds, because onException will fall back and use the redelivery policies defined by the error handler, and its value is configured as delay(3000).

Now let's remove the maximumRedeliveries(5) option from the onException, so it's defined as onException(IOException.class):

```
errorHandler(defaultErrorHandler().maximumRedeliveries(3).delay(3000));

onException(IOException.class);

from("jetty:http://0.0.0.0/orderservice")
    .to("mina:tcp://erp.rider.com:4444?textline=true")
    .beanRef("orderBean", "prepareReply");
```

What would the redelivery delay be now, if an IOException were thrown? I am sure you'll say the answer is 3—the value defined on the error handler. In this case, though, the answer is 0. Camel won't attempt to do any redelivery because any onException will override the maximumRedeliveries to 0 by default (redelivery is disabled by default) unless you explicitly set the maximumRedeliveries option.

The reason why Camel implements this behavior is our next topic: using onException to handle exceptions.

5.4.3 Understanding how onException can handle exceptions

Suppose you have a complex route that processes a message in multiple steps. Each step does some work on the message, but any step can throw an exception to indicate that the message can't be processed and that it should be discarded. This is where handling exceptions with onException comes into the game.

Handling an exception with onException is similar to exception handling in Java itself. You can think of it as being like using a try ... catch block.

This is best illustrated with an example. Imagine you need to implement an ERP server-side service that serves order statuses. This is the ERP service you called from the previous section:

```
public void configure() {
    try {
        from("mina:tcp://0.0.0.0:4444?textline=true")
            .process(new ValidateOrderId())
            .to("jms:queue:order.status")
            .process(new GenerateResponse());
    } catch (JmsException e) {
        .process(new GenerateFailureResponse());
    }
}
```

❶ Rethrows caught exception

This snippet of pseudocode involves multiple steps in generating the response. If something goes wrong, you catch the exception and return a failure response ❶.

We call this pseudocode because it shows your intention but the code won't compile. This is because the Java DSL uses the fluent builder syntax, where method calls are stacked together to define the route. The regular try ... catch mechanism in Java works at runtime to catch exceptions that are thrown when the configure() method is executed, but in this case the configure() method is only invoked once, when Camel is started (when it initializes and builds up the route path to use at runtime).

Don't despair. Camel has a counterpart to the classic try ... catch ... finally block in its DSL: doTry ... doCatch ... doFinally.

USING DOTRY, DOCATCH, AND DOFINALLY

Listing 5.3 shows how you can make the code compile and work at runtime as you would expect with a try ... catch block.

Listing 5.3 Using doTry ... doCatch with Camel routing

```
public void configure() {
    from("mina:tcp://0.0.0.0:4444?textline=true")
        .doTry()
            .process(new ValidateOrderId())
            .to("jms:queue:order.status")
            .process(new GenerateResponse());
        .doCatch(JmsException.class)
            .process(new GenerateFailureResponse())
        .end();
}
```

The doTry ... doCatch block was a bit of a sidetrack, but it's useful because it helps bridge the gap between thinking in regular Java code and thinking in EIPs.

USING ONEXCEPTION TO HANDLE EXCEPTIONS

The doTry ... doCatch block has one limitation—it's only route scoped. The blocks only work in the route in which they're defined. OnException, on the other hand, works in both context and route scopes, so you can try revising listing 5.3 using onException. This is illustrated in listing 5.4.

Listing 5.4   Using `onException` in context scope

```
onException(JmsException.class)
    .handled(true)
    .process(new GenerateFailureResponse());

from("mina:tcp://0.0.0.0:4444?textline=true")
    .process(new ValidateOrderId())
    .to("jms:queue:order.status")
    .process(new GenerateResponse());
```

**Handles all
JmsExceptions** ❶

A difference between `doCatch` and `onException` is that `doCatch` will handle the exception, whereas `onException` will, by default, not handle it. That's why you use `handled(true)` ❶ to instruct Camel to handle this exception. As a result, when a `JmsException` is thrown, the application acts as if the exception were caught in a `catch` block using the regular Java `try ... catch` mechanism.

In listing 5.4, you should also notice how the concerns are separated and the normal route path is laid out nicely and simply; it isn't mixed up with the exception handling.

Imagine that a message arrives on the TCP endpoint, and the Camel application routes the message. The message passes the validate processor and is about to be sent to the JMS queue, but this operation fails and a `JmsException` is thrown. Figure 5.5 is a sequence diagram showing the steps that take place inside Camel in such a situation. It shows how `onException` is triggered to handle the exception.

Figure 5.5 shows how the `JmsProducer` throws the `JmsException` to the `Channel`, which is where the error handler lives. The route has an `OnException` defined that reacts when a `JmsException` is thrown, and it processes the message. The `GenerateFailure-Response` processor generates a custom failure message that is supposed to be returned

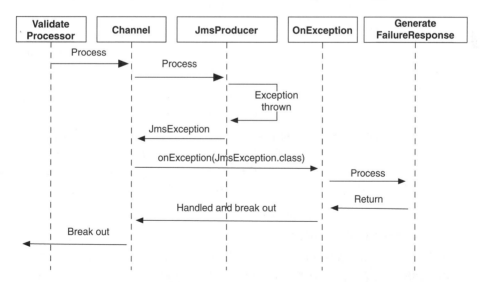

Figure 5.5   Sequence diagram of a message being routed and a `JmsException` being thrown from the `JmsProducer`, which is handled by the `onException`. `OnException` generates a failure that is to be returned to the caller.

to the caller. Because the OnException was configured to handle exceptions—handled(true)—Camel will *break out* from continuing the routing and will return the failure message to the initial consumer, which in turn returns the custom reply message.

> **NOTE** OnException doesn't handle exceptions by default, so listing 5.4 uses handled(true) to indicate that onException should handle the exception. This is important to remember, because it must be specified when you want to handle the exception. Handling an exception will *not* continue routing from the point where the exception was thrown. Camel will *break out* of the route and continue routing on the onException. If you want to ignore the exception and continue routing, you must use continued(true), which will be discussed in section 5.4.5.

Before we move on, let's take a minute to look at the example from listing 5.4 revised to use Spring XML. The syntax is a bit different, as you can see:

Listing 5.5   Spring XML revision of listing 5.4

```
<camelContext xmlns="http://camel.apache.org/schemas/spring">

    <onException>
        <exception>javax.jms.JmsException</exception>
        <handled><constant>true</constant></handled>          Handles all
        <process ref="failureResponse"/>                   ❶ JmsExceptions
    </onException>

    <route>
        <from uri="mina:tcp://0.0.0.0:4444?textline=true"/>
        <process ref="validateOrder"/>
        <to uri="jms:queue:order.status"/>
        <process ref="generateResponse"/>
    </route>

</camelContext>
                                                        ❷ Processor generates
<bean id="failureResponse"                                 failure response
      class="camelinaction.FailureResponseProcessor"/>

<bean id="validateOrder" class="camelinaction.ValidateProcessor"/>

<bean id="generateResponse" class="camelinaction.ResponseProcessor"/>
```

Notice how onException is set up—you must define the exceptions in the exception tag. Also, handled(true) ❶ is a bit longer because you must enclose it in the <constant> expression. There are no other noteworthy differences in the rest of the route.

Listing 5.5 uses a custom processor to generate a failure response ❷. Let's take a closer look at that.

5.4.4   *Custom exception handling*

Suppose you want to return a custom failure message, as in listing 5.5, that indicates not only what the problem was but that also includes details from the current Camel Message. How can you do that?

Listing 5.5 laid out how to do this using onException. Listing 5.6 shows how the failure Processor could be implemented.

Listing 5.6 Using a processor to create a failure response to be returned to the caller

```
public class FailureResponseProcessor implements Processor {

    public void process(Exchange exchange) throws Exception {
        String body = exchange.getIn().getBody(String.class);
        Exception e = exchange.getProperty(Exchange.EXCEPTION_CAUGHT,
                            Exception.class);

        StringBuilder sb = new StringBuilder();
        sb.append("ERROR: ");
        sb.append(e.getMessage());
        sb.append("\nBODY: ");
        sb.append(body);

        exchange.getIn().setBody(sb.toString());
    }
}
```

❶ **Gets the exception**

First, you grab the information you need: the message body and the exception ❶. It may seem a bit odd that you get the exception as a property and not using `exchange.getException()`. You do that because you've marked `onException` to handle the exception; this was done at ❶ in listing 5.5. When you do that, Camel moves the exception from the Exchange to the `Exchange.EXCEPTION_CAUGHT` property. The rest of the processor builds the custom failure message that's to be returned to the caller.

You may wonder whether there are other properties Camel sets during error handling, and there are. They're listed in table 5.5. But from an end-user perspective, it's only the first two properties in table 5.5 that matter. The other two properties are used internally by Camel in its error-handling and routing engine.

One example of when the `FAILURE_ENDPOINT` property comes in handy is when you route messages through the Recipient List EIP, which sends a copy of the message to a dynamic number of endpoints. Without this information, you wouldn't know precisely which of those endpoints failed.

Table 5.5 Properties on the `Exchange` related to error handling

Property	Type	Description
Exchange.EXCEPTION_ CAUGHT	Exception	The exception that was caught.
Exchange.FAILURE_ ENDPOINT	String	The URL of the endpoint that failed if a failure occurred when sending to an endpoint. If the failure did not occur while sending to an endpoint, this property is null.
Exchange.ERRORHANDLER_ HANDLED	Boolean	Whether or not the error handler handled the exception.
Exchange.FAILURE_ HANDLED	Boolean	Whether or not onException handled the exception. Or true if the Exchange was moved to a dead letter queue.

It's worth noting that in listing 5.6 you use a Camel Processor, which forces you to depend on the Camel API. You can use a bean instead, as follows:

```
public class FailureResponseBean {

    public String failMessage(String body, Exception e) {         ◁    Exception
        StringBuilder sb = new StringBuilder();                          provided as
        sb.append("ERROR: ");                                      ❶    parameter
        sb.append(e.getMessage());
        sb.append("\nBODY: ");
        sb.append(body);
        return sb.toString();
    }
}
```

As you can see, you can use Camel's parameter binding ❶ to declare the parameter
types you want to use. The first parameter is the message body, and the second is the
exception.

There will be situations where you'll want to simply ignore the exception and continue routing.

5.4.5 Ignoring exceptions

In section 5.4.3 we learned about how `onException` can handle exceptions. Handling an exception means that Camel will break out of the route. But there are times
when all you want is to catch the exception and continue routing. This is possible to
do in Camel using `continued`. All you have to do is to use `continued(true)` instead
of `handled(true)`.

Suppose we want to ignore any `ValidationException` which may be thrown in the
route, laid out in listing 5.4. Listing 5.7 shows how we can do this.

Listing 5.7 Using `continued` to ignore `ValidationExceptions`

```
onException(JmsException.class)
    .handled(true)
    .process(new GenerateFailueResponse());

onException(ValidationException.class)                      ❶    Ignores all
    .continued(true);                                     ◁          ValidationExceptions

from("mina:tcp://0.0.0.0:4444?textline=true")
    .process(new ValidateOrderId())
    .to("jms:queue:order.status")
    .process(new GenerateResponse());
```

As you can see, all you have to do is add another `onException` that leverages `contin-
ued(true)` ❶.

> **NOTE** You can't use both `handled` and `continued` on the same `onException`;
> `continued` automatically implies `handled`.

Now imagine that a message once again arrives on the TCP endpoint, and the Camel
application routes the message. But this time the validate processor throws a `Valida-
tionException`. This situation is illustrated in figure 5.6.

When the `ValidateProcessor` throws the `ValidationException`, it's propagated
back to the `Channel`, which lets the error handler kick in. The route has an `onException`
defined that instructs the `Channel` to continue routing the message—`continued(true)`.

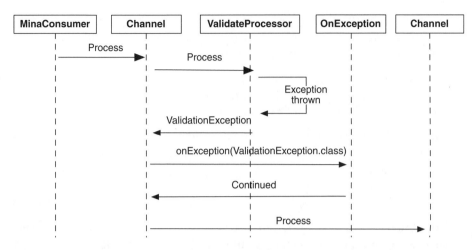

Figure 5.6 Sequence diagram of a message being routed and a `ValidationException` being thrown from the `ValidateProcessor`. The exception is handled and continued by the `onException` policy, causing the message to continue being routed as if the exception were not thrown.

When the message arrives at the next `Channel`, it's as if the exception were not thrown. This is much different from what you saw in section 5.4.3 when using `handled(true)`, which causes the processing to break out and *not* continue routing.

You've learned a bunch of new stuff, so let's continue with the error handler example and put your knowledge into practice.

5.4.6 Implementing an error handler solution

Suppose your boss brings you a new problem. This time, the remote HTTP server used for uploading files is unreliable, and he wants you to implement a secondary failover to transfer the files by FTP to a remote FTP server.

You have been studying *Camel in Action*, and you've learned that Camel has extensive support for error handling and that you could leverage `onException` to provide this kind of feature. With great confidence, you fire up the editor and alter the route as shown in listing 5.8.

Listing 5.8 Route using error handling with failover to FTP

```
errorHandler(defaultErrorHandler()
    .maximumRedeliveries(5).redeliveryDelay(10000));

onException(IOException.class).maximumRedeliveries(3)
    .handled(true)
    .to("ftp://gear@ftp.rider.com?password=secret");

from("file:/rider/files/upload?delay=3600000")
    .to("http://rider.com?user=gear&password=secret");
```

❶ Exception policy

This listing adds an `onException` ❶ to the route, telling Camel that in the case of an `IOException`, it should try redelivering up to 3 times using a 10-second delay. If there is still an error after the redelivery attempts, Camel will handle the exception and reroute the message to the FTP endpoint instead. The power and flexibility of the Camel routing engine shines here. The onException is just another route, and Camel will continue on this route instead of the original route.

> **NOTE** In listing 5.8, it's only when onException is exhausted that it will reroute the message to the FTP endpoint ❶. The onException has been configured to redeliver up till 3 times before giving up and being exhausted.

The book's source code contains this example in the chapter5/usecase directory, and you can try it out yourself. The example contains a server and a client that you can start using Maven:

```
mvn exec:java -PServer
mvn exec:java -PClient
```

Both the server and client output instructions on the console about what to do next, such as copying a file to the target/rider folder to get the ball rolling.

Before we finish up this chapter, we must take a look at a few more error-handling features. They're used rarely, but they provide power in situations where you need more fine-grained control.

5.5   *Other error-handling features*

We'll end this chapter by looking at some of the other features Camel provides for error handling:

- onWhen—Allows you to dictate when an exception policy is in use
- onRedeliver—Allows you to execute some code before the message is redelivered
- retryWhile—Allows you, at runtime, to determine whether or not to continue redelivery or to give up

We'll look at each in turn.

5.5.1   *Using onWhen*

The onWhen predicate filter allows more fine-grained control over when an onException should be triggered.

Suppose a new problem has emerged with your application in listing 5.8. This time the HTTP service rejects the data and returns an HTTP 500 response with the constant text "ILLEGAL DATA". Your boss wants you to handle this by moving the file to a special folder where it can be manually inspected to see why it was rejected.

First, you need to determine when an HTTP error 500 occurs and whether it contains the text "ILLEGAL DATA". You decide to create a Java method that can test this, as shown in listing 5.9.

Listing 5.9   A helper to determine whether an HTTP error 500 occurred

```
public final class MyHttpUtil {

    public static boolean isIllegalDataError(
                        HttpOperationFailedException cause) {
```

```
        int code = cause.getStatusCode();
        if (code != 500) {
            return false;
        }
        return "ILLEGAL DATA".equals(cause.getResponseBody().toString());
    }
}
```

Gets HTTP
❶ status code

When the HTTP operation isn't successful, the Camel HTTP component will throw an `org.apache.camel.component.http.HttpOperationFailedException` exception, containing information why it failed. The `getStatusCode()` method on `HttpOperationFailedException` ❶, returns the HTTP status code. This allows you to determine if it's an HTTP error code 500 with the "ILLEGAL DATA" body text.

Next, you need to use the utility class from listing 5.9 in your existing route from listing 5.8. But first you add the `onException` to handle the `HttpOperationFailedException` and detour the message to the illegal folder:

```
onException(HttpOperationFailedException.class)
    .handled(true)
    .to("file:/rider/files/illegal");
```

Now, whenever an `HttpOperationFailedException` is thrown, Camel moves the message to the illegal folder.

It would be better if you had more fine-grained control over when this `onException` triggers. How could you incorporate your code from listing 5.9 with the `onException`?

I am sure you have guessed where we're going—yes, you can use the `onWhen` predicate. All you need to do is insert the `onWhen` into the `onException`, as shown here:

```
onException(HttpOperationFailedException.class)
    .onWhen(bean(MyHttpUtil.class, "isIllegalData"))
    .handled(true)
    .to("file:/acme/files/illegal");
```

Camel adapts to your POJO classes and uses them as is, thanks to the power of Camel's parameter binding, which we covered in the previous chapter. This is a powerful way to develop your application without being tied to the Camel API. `onWhen` is a general function that also exists in other Camel features, such as interceptors and `onCompletion`, so you can use this technique in various situations.

Next, let's look at `onRedeliver`, which allows fine-grained control when a redelivery is about to occur.

5.5.2 *Using onRedeliver*

The purpose of `onRedeliver` is to allow some code to be executed before a redelivery is performed. This gives you the power to do custom processing on the `Exchange` before Camel makes a redelivery attempt. You can, for instance, use it to add custom headers to indicate to the receiver that this is a redelivery attempt. `OnRedeliver` uses an `org.apache.camel.Processor`, in which you implement the code to be executed.

`OnRedeliver` can be configured on the error handler, on `onException`, or on both, as follows:

```
errorHandler(defaultErrorHandler()
    .maximumRedeliveries(3)
    .onRedeliver(new MyOnRedeliveryProcessor());

onException(IOException.class)
    .maximumRedeliveries(5)
    .onRedeliver(new MyOtherOnRedeliveryProcessor());
```

OnRedeliver is also scoped, so if an onRedeliver is set on an onException, it over-rules any onRedeliver set on the error handler.

In Spring DSL, onRedeliver is configured as a reference to a spring bean, as follows:

```
<onException onRedeliveryRef="myOtherRedelivery">
    <exception>java.io.IOException</exception>
</onException>

<bean id="myOtherRedelivery"
      class="com.mycompany.MyOtherOnRedeliveryProceossor"/>
```

Finally, let's look at one last feature: RetryWhile.

5.5.3   *Using retryWhile*

RetryWhile is used when you want fine-grained control over the number of redelivery attempts. It's also a predicate that's scoped, so you can define it on the error handler or on onException.

You can use retryWhile to implement your own generic retry ruleset that determines how long it should retry. Listing 5.10 shows some skeleton code demonstrating how this can be done.

Listing 5.10   Skeleton code to illustrate principle of using `retryWhile`

```
public class MyRetryRuleset {

public boolean shouldRetry(
                  @Header(Exchange.REDELIVERY_COUNTER) Integer counter,
                  Exception causedBy) {
    ...
}
```

Using your own MyRetryRuleset class, you can implement your own logic determining whether it should continue retrying or not. If the method returns true, a redelivery attempt is conducted; if it returns false, it give up.

To use your ruleset, you configure retryWhile on the onException as follows:

```
onException(IOException.class).retryWhile(bean(MyRetryRuletset.class));
```

In Spring XML you configure retryWhile as shown:

```
<onException>
  <exception>java.io.IOException</exception>
  <retryWhile><method ref="myRetryRuleset"/></retryWhile>
</onException>

<bean id="myRetryRuleset" class="com.mycompany.MyRetryRuleset"/>
```

That gives you fine-grained control over the number of redelivery attempts performed by Camel.

That's it! We've now covered all the features Camel provides for fine-grained control over error handling.

5.6   *Summary and best practices*

In this chapter, you saw how recoverable and irrecoverable errors are represented in Camel. We also looked at all the provided error handlers, focusing on the most important of them. You saw how Camel can control how exceptions are dealt with, using redelivery policies to set the scene and exception policies to handle specific exceptions differently. Finally, we looked at what Camel has to offer when it comes to fine-grained control over error handling, putting you in control of error handling in Camel.

Let's revisit some of the key ideas from this chapter, which you can take away and apply to your own Camel applications:

- *Error handling is hard.* Realize from the beginning that the unexpected can happen and that dealing with errors is hard. The challenge keeps rising when businesses have more and more of their IT portfolio integrated and operate it 24/7/365.
- *Error handling isn't an afterthought.* When IT systems are being integrated, they exchange data according to agreed-upon protocols. Those protocols should also specify how errors will be dealt with.
- *Separate routing logic from error handling.* Camel allows you to separate routing logic from error-handling logic. This avoids cluttering up your logic, which otherwise could become harder to maintain. Use Camel features such as error handlers, onException, and doTry ... doCatch.
- *Try to recover.* Some errors are recoverable, such as connection errors. You should apply strategies to recover from these errors.
- *Use asynchronous delayed redelivery.* If the order of messages processed from consumers doesn't matter, leverage asynchronous redelivery to achieve higher scalability.
- *Handle fault messages.* If you use components such as JBI, CXF, or SOAP, which may return fault messages, you can enable fault handling in Camel to let the error handlers react to those faults.
- *Use monitoring tooling.* Use tooling to monitor your Camel applications so it can react and alert personnel if severe errors occur. Chapter 12 covers such strategies.
- *Build unit tests.* Build unit tests that simulate errors to see if your error-handling strategies are up to the task. Section 6.3 shows how to do this.

In the next chapter, we'll look at a topic that can help make you a successful integration specialist, and without it, you'll almost certainly be in trouble: testing with Camel. We'll also look at how you can simulate errors to test whether your error handling strategies work as expected.

Testing with Camel

In the last chapter, we covered error handling and learned that it's hard to handle and cater for all difficulties that can possibly arise. To help address this problem, you can test as many situations as possible. In this chapter, we'll look at how to test with Camel—not only testing your projects when everything goes well, but also simulating errors and testing whether your error handling strategies are up to the job.

Testing is vital to ensuring that your integration projects are successful. JUnit has become the standard API for unit testing, and the Camel Test Kit builds on top of JUnit, leveraging the existing JUnit tooling. If you aren't familiar with JUnit, you can read about it in *JUnit in Action*, second edition (http://www.manning.com/tahchiev).

A good way to perform unit testing on a Camel application is to start the application, send messages to the application, and verify that the messages are routed as expected. This is illustrated in figure 6.1. You send a message to the application, which transforms the message to another format and returns the

Figure 6.1   Testing a Camel application by sending a message to the application and then verifying the returned output

output. You can then verify that the output is as expected.

This is how the Camel Test Kit is used for testing. You'll learn to set up expectations as preconditions for your unit tests, start the tests by sending in messages, and verify the results to determine whether the tests passed. The Mock component is based on this principle, and we'll cover it thoroughly. Then we'll look at several techniques for simulating errors, so you can test your error handling as well.

Let's get started.

6.1   Introducing the Camel Test Kit

Camel provides rich facilities for testing your projects, and it includes a test kit that gets you writing unit tests quickly in familiar waters using the regular JUnit API. In fact, it's the same test kit that Camel uses for testing itself. Figure 6.2 gives a high-level overview of the Camel Test Kit.

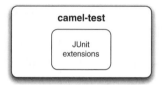   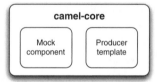

Figure 6.2   The Camel Test Kit is provided in two JAR files containing the JUnit extensions, Mock component, and producer template.

Figure 6.2 boils down to three parts. The JUnit extensions are a number of classes on top of JUnit that make unit testing with Camel much easier. We'll cover them in the next section. The Mock component is covered in section 6.2. And you're already familiar with the `ProducerTemplate`—it's a convenient feature that allows you to easily send messages to Camel when testing.

Let's now look at the Camel JUnit extensions and see how to use them to write Camel unit tests.

6.1.1   The Camel JUnit extensions

So what are the Camel JUnit extensions? They are six classes in a small JAR file, camel-test.jar, that ships with Camel. The classes are listed in table 6.1.

Of the six classes listed in table 6.1, you'll often only use the ones suited for unit testing either the older JUnit 3.x or the newer JUnit 4.x version. Let's get started using the Camel Test Kit.

Table 6.1   Classes in the Camel Test Kit, provided in camel-test.jar

Class	Description
`org.apache.camel.test.TestSupport`	JUnit 3.x abstract base test class with additional assertion methods.
`org.apache.camel.test.CamelTestSupport`	JUnit 3.x base test class prepared for testing Camel routes. This is the test class you should use when using JUnit 3.x.
`org.apache.camel.test.CamelSpringTestSupport`	JUnit 3.x base test class prepared for testing Camel routes defined using Spring DSL. This class extends `CamelTestSupport` and has additional Spring-related methods.
`org.apache.camel.test.junit4.TestSupport`	JUnit 4.x abstract base test class with additional assertion methods.
`org.apache.camel.test.junit4.CamelTestSupport`	JUnit 4.x base test class prepared for testing Camel routes. This is the test class you should use when using JUnit 4.x.
`org.apache.camel.test.junit4.CamelSpringTestSupport`	JUnit 4.x base test class prepared for testing Camel routes defined using Spring DSL. This class extends `CamelTestSupport` and has additional Spring-related methods.

6.1.2   Using the Camel Test Kit

We'll start simply and use the following route for testing:

```
from("file:inbox").to("file:outbox");
```

This is the "Hello World" example for integration kits that moves files from one folder to another. So how do you go about unit testing this route?

You could do it the traditional way and write unit test code with the plain JUnit API. This would require at least 30 lines of code, because the API for file handling in Java is very low level, and you need a fair amount of code when working with files.

An easier solution is to use the Camel Test Kit. In the next couple of sections, you'll work with the `CamelTestSupport` class—it's the easiest to get started with. Then in section 6.1.5 you'll try the `CamelSpringTestSupport` class and see how you can do unit testing based on Spring routes.

6.1.3   Unit testing with the CamelTestSupport class

In this chapter, we've kept the dependencies low when using the Camel Test Kit. All you need to include is the following dependency in the Maven pom.xml file:

```xml
<dependency>
    <groupId>org.apache.camel</groupId>
    <artifactId>camel-test</artifactId>
    <version>2.5.0</version>
    <scope>test</scope>
</dependency>

<dependency>
    <groupId>junit</groupId>
    <artifactId>junit</artifactId>
```

```
    <version>4.8.1</version>
    <scope>test</scope>
</dependency>
```

WARNING Spring 2.5 only works with JUnit 4.4 or lower. Spring 3.0 works
with higher versions of JUnit such as 4.8.1, used in the preceding code.

We won't go into detail here on how to set up your Java editor for developing with
Camel; chapter 11 will cover this in detail. For now, you just need to know that the
Camel Test Kit lives in the camel-test-2.5.jar file and that the other JARs needed are
JUnit and camel-core, which are implied.

Let's try it. You want to build a unit test to test a Camel route that copies files from
one directory to another. The unit test is shown in listing 6.1.

Listing 6.1 A first unit test using the Camel Test Kit

```
package camelinaction;

import java.io.File;
import org.apache.camel.Exchange;
import org.apache.camel.builder.RouteBuilder;
import org.apache.camel.test.junit4.CamelTestSupport;
import org.junit.Test;

public class FirstTest extends CamelTestSupport {

@Override
protected RouteBuilder createRouteBuilder() throws Exception {
    return new RouteBuilder() {
        @Override                                               ❶ Defines
        public void configure() throws Exception {                 route to test
            from("file://target/inbox").to("file://target/outbox");
        }
    };
}

@Test
public void testMoveFile() throws Exception {
    template.sendBodyAndHeader("file://target/inbox", "Hello World",
                Exchange.FILE_NAME, "hello.txt");
                                                           ❷ Creates
    Thread.sleep(1000);                                       hello.txt file

    File target = new File("target/outbox/hello.txt");
    assertTrue("File not moved", target.exists());         ❸ Verifies file
}                                                              is moved
}
```

The FirstTest class must extend the org.apache.camel.junit4.CamelTestSupport
class to conveniently leverage the Camel Test Kit. By overriding the createRoute-
Builder method, you can provide any route builder you wish. You use an inlined
route builder, which allows you to write the route directly within the unit test class. All
you need to do is override the configure method ❶ and include your route.

The test methods are regular JUnit methods, so the method must be annotated
with @Test to be included when testing. You'll notice that the code in this method is

fairly short. Instead of using the low-level Java File API, this example leverages Camel as a client by using `ProducerTemplate` to send a message to a file endpoint ❷, which writes the message as a file.

In the test, you sleep one second after dropping the file in the inbox folder; this gives Camel a bit of time to react and route the file. By default, Camel scans twice per second for incoming files, so you wait one second to be on the safe side. Finally you assert that the file was moved to the outbox folder ❸.

The book's source code includes this example. You can try it on your own by running the following Maven goal from the chapter6/firsttest directory:

```
mvn test -Dtest=FirstTest
```

When you run this example, it should output the result of the test as shown here:

```
Tests run: 1, Failures: 0, Errors: 0, Skipped: 0
```

This indicates that the test completed successfully; there are no failures or errors.

> **TIP**   From Camel 2.6 onward it's now even easier to debug Camel routes from within the IDE. See more details at http://camel.apache.org/debugger.

IMPROVING THE UNIT TEST

The unit test in listing 6.1 could be improved in a few areas, such as ensuring that the starting directory is empty and that the written file's content is what you expect.

The former is easy, because the `CamelTestSupport` class has a method to delete a directory. You can do this in the `setUp` method:

```
public void setUp() throws Exception {
    deleteDirectory("target/inbox");
    deleteDirectory("target/outbox");
    super.setUp();
}
```

Camel can also test the written file's content to ensure it's what you expect. You may remember that Camel provides a very elaborate type converter system, and that this system goes beyond converting between simple types and literals. The Camel type system includes file-based converters, so there is no need to fiddle with the various cumbersome Java IO file streams. All you need to do is ask the type converter system to grab the file and return it to you as a `String`.

Just as you had access to the template in listing 6.1, the Camel Test Kit also gives you direct access to the `CamelContext`. The `testMoveFile` method in listing 6.1 could have been written as follows:

```
@Test
public void testMoveFile() throws Exception {
    template.sendBodyAndHeader("file://target/inbox", "Hello World",
                Exchange.FILE_NAME, "hello.txt");

    File target = new File("target/outbox/hello.txt");
    assertTrue("File not moved", target.exists());

    String content = context.getTypeConverter()
```

```
                              .convertTo(String.class, target);
        assertEquals("Hello World", content);
}
```

The preceding examples cover the case where the route is defined in the unit test class as an anonymous inner class. But what if you have a route defined in another class? How do you go about unit testing that route instead? Let's look at that next.

6.1.4 Unit testing an existing RouteBuilder class

It's common to define Camel routes in separate RouteBuilder classes, as in the File-MoveRoute class here:

```
package camelinaction;

import org.apache.camel.builder.RouteBuilder;

public class FileMoveRoute extends RouteBuilder {

    @Override
    public void configure() throws Exception {
        from("file://target/inbox").to("file://target/outbox");
    }
}
```

How could you unit test this route from the FileMoveRoute class? You don't want to copy the code from the configure method into a JUnit class. Fortunately, it's quite easy to set up unit tests that use the FileMoveRoute, as you can see here:

```
protected RouteBuilder createRouteBuilder() throws Exception {
    return new FileMoveRoute();
}
```

Yes, it's that simple! Just return a new instance of your route class.

Now you have learned how to use CamelTestSupport for unit testing routes based on the Java DSL. But there is also a Spring-based CamelSpringTestSupport class to be used for Spring XML routes. The next section shows how to test using Spring XML–based routes.

6.1.5 Unit testing with the SpringCamelTestSupport class

SpringCamelTestSupport is a base test class that's used to unit test routes based on Spring XML.

We'll look at unit testing the route in listing 6.2, which is a Spring version of the route in listing 6.1.

Listing 6.2   A Spring-based version of the route in listing 6.1 (firststep.xml)

```
<beans xmlns="http://www.springframework.org/schema/beans"
       xmlns:xsi="http://www.w3.org/2001/XMLSchema-instance"
       xsi:schemaLocation="
          http://www.springframework.org/schema/beans
          http://www.springframework.org/schema/beans/spring-beans-2.5.xsd
          http://camel.apache.org/schema/spring
```

```
                http://camel.apache.org/schema/spring/camel-spring.xsd">

    <camelContext id="camel" xmlns="http://camel.apache.org/schema/spring">
        <route>
            <from uri="file://target/inbox"/>
            <to uri="file://target/outbox"/>
        </route>
    </camelContext>

</beans>
```

Notice that the route is the same route defined in listing 6.1. So how can you unit test this route? Ideally you should be able to use unit tests regardless of the language used to define the route.

Camel is able to handle this; the difference between using SpringCamelTestSupport and CamelTestSupport is just a matter of how the route is loaded. The unit test in listing 6.3 illustrates this point.

Listing 6.3 A first unit test using Spring XML routes

```
package camelinaction;

import java.io.File;

import org.apache.camel.Exchange;
import org.apache.camel.test.junit4.CamelSpringTestSupport;
import org.junit.Test;
import org.springframework.context.support.AbstractXmlApplicationContext;
import org.springframework.context.support.ClassPathXmlApplicationContext;

public class SpringFirstTest extends CamelSpringTestSupport {

    protected AbstractXmlApplicationContext createApplicationContext() {
        return new ClassPathXmlApplicationContext(
                    "camelinaction/firststep.xml");      ◁  Loads Spring
    }                                                     ❶ XML file

    @Test
    public void testMoveFile() throws Exception {
        template.sendBodyAndHeader("file://target/inbox",
                "Hello World", Exchange.FILE_NAME, "hello.txt");

        Thread.sleep(1000);

        File target = new File("target/outbox/hello.txt");
        assertTrue("File not moved", target.exists());

        String content = context.getTypeConverter()
                            .convertTo(String.class, target);
        assertEquals("Hello World", content);
    }
}
```

You extend the CamelSpringTestSupport class so you can unit test with Spring XML–based routes. And unlike listing 6.1, you need to use a Spring-based mechanism to load the routes ❶; you use the ClassPathXmlApplicationContext, which loads your route from the classpath. This mechanism is entirely Spring-based, so you can also use the `FileSystemXmlApplicationContext`, include multiple XML files, and so on—Camel doesn't impose any restrictions. The `testMoveFile` method is exactly the same as it was in listing 6.1, which means you can use the same unit testing code regardless of how the route is defined.

In real life projects, you'll have different deployment environments, such as local, test, preproduction, and production. In the next section, we'll look at how you can test the same project in those different environments with minimal effort.

6.1.6 *Unit testing in multiple environments*

A Camel route is often tested in different environments—you may want to test it locally on your laptop, then later on a dedicated test platform, and so forth. But you don't want to rewrite tests every time you move to a new environment. That's why you externalize dynamic parts.

We'll cover two solutions for externalizing dynamic parts using property files. The first solution is based on the Camel Properties component and the second leverages Spring property placeholders.

USING THE CAMEL PROPERTIES COMPONENT

Camel has a Properties component to support externalizing properties defined in the routes. The Properties component works in much the same way as Spring property placeholders, but it has a few noteworthy improvements:

- It is built in the camel-core JAR, which means it can be leveraged without the need for Spring or any third-party framework.
- It can be used in all the DSLs, such as the Java DSL, and is not limited to Spring XML files.
- It supports using placeholders in property files.

NOTE For more details on the Properties component, see the Camel documentation: http://camel.apache.org/properties.html.

Suppose you wanted to test the file-move unit test in two environments: production and test. To use the Camel Properties component in Spring XML, you have to declare it as a Spring bean with the id `properties`, as shown:

```
<bean id="properties"
    class="org.apache.camel.component.properties.PropertiesComponent">
  <property name="location" value="classpath:rider-prod.properties"/>
</bean>
```

In the rider-prod.properties file, you define the externalized properties as key/value pairs:

```
file.inbox=rider/files/inbox
file.outbox=rider/files/outbox
```

The `camelContext` element can then take advantage of the externalized properties directly in the endpoint URI, as shown in bold in this route:

```
<camelContext id="camel" xmlns="http://camel.apache.org/schema/spring">
    <route>
        <from uri="{{file.inbox}}"/>
        <to uri="{{file.outbox}}"/>
    </route>
</camelContext>
```

You should notice that the Camel syntax for property placeholders is a bit different than for Spring property placeholders. The Camel Properties component uses the {{key}} syntax, whereas Spring uses ${key}.

Instead of using a Spring bean to define the Camel Properties component, you can use a specialized <propertyPlaceholder> within the camelContext, as follows:

```
<camelContext id="camel" xmlns="http://camel.apache.org/schema/spring">
    <propertyPlaceholder id="properties"
                        location="classpath:rider-prod.properties"/>
    <route>
        <from uri="{{file.inbox}}"/>
        <to uri="{{file.outbox}}"/>
    </route>
</camelContext>
```

Your next goal is to create a reusable unit test that, with minimal effort, can be configured to test in either environment. Listing 6.4 shows how this can be done.

Listing 6.4   A reusable unit test for the test and production environments

```
public class CamelRiderTest extends CamelSpringTestSupport {

private String inboxDir;
private String outboxDir;

@EndpointInject(uri = "file:{{file.inbox}}")          ①  Injects
private ProducerTemplate inbox;                            ProducerTemplate

public void setUp() throws Exception {
    super.setUp();

    inboxDir = context.resolvePropertyPlaceholders(
                "{{file.inbox}}");
    outboxDir = context.resolvePropertyPlaceholders(      ②  Looks up
                "{{file.outbox}}");                            properties used

    deleteDirectory(inboxDir);
    deleteDirectory(outboxDir);
}

@Override
protected AbstractXmlApplicationContext createApplicationContext() {
    return new ClassPathXmlApplicationContext(new String[]
        {"camelinaction/rider-camel-prod.xml",
         "camelinaction/rider-came-test.xml"});           ③  Loads Spring
}                                                             XML files

@Test
public void testMoveFile() throws Exception {
    inbox.sendBodyAndHeader("Hello World",
```

```
                    Exchange.FILE_NAME, "hello.txt");

    Thread.sleep(1000);

    File target = new File(outboxDir + "/hello.txt");
    assertTrue("File not moved", target.exists());

    String content = context.getTypeConverter()
                        .convertTo(String.class, target);
    assertEquals("Hello World", content);
}
}
```

In the `testMoveFile` method, you start the unit test by creating a file in the inbox directory, and to help with that you retrieve the `ProducerTemplate`. Note that you use the
`@EndpointInject` annotation and refer to the inbox endpoint by the placeholder ❶.

In the `setUp` method, you use the `CamelContext` to resolve the placeholders ❷,
because you'll later need to know the actual values for `file.inbox` and `file.outbox`.

The `createApplicationContext` method loads the Spring XML files. You load two
files ❸ to minimize effort. Spring allows you to load multiple files and have the next
file override the previous file—the idea is to define the `CamelContext` once, in the
rider-camel-prod.xml file. Because rider-camel-test.xml is defined as the second file, it
will override identical beans from the former files. You leverage this to override the
properties bean and instruct it to load a different properties file, the rider-test.proper-
ties file.

The rider-camel-test.xml file is short and simple:

```
<bean id="properties"
      class="org.apache.camel.component.properties.PropertiesComponent">
    <property name="location" value="classpath:rider-test.properties"/>
</bean>
```

This way, `CamelContext` is only defined once. If you had the route defined in multiple files targeted for specific environments, you'd put the burden on yourself to syn-
chronize those routes if you change something in the route.

By using this approach, you can unit test the route in different environments with
minimal effort. All you have to do is specify the files in the `createApplicationCon-
text` method targeted for the environment you're testing.

This example is included in the book's source code in the chapter6/firsttest directory. You can try it using the following Maven goal:

```
mvn test -Dtest=CamelRiderTest
```

TIP If you're not using Spring XML, you can still reuse Camel routes and
unit tests for multiple environments. You can use `@EndpointInject` in your
`RouteBuilder` class to dynamically inject endpoints for the environment you
wish to test.

The Camel Properties component can also be used without Spring. The following listing
sets up the Camel Properties component and uses it in a Java DSL–based route. The
`setUp` and `testMoveFile` methods are omitted because they're the same as in listing 6.4.

Listing 6.5   Using the Camel Properties component with the Java DSL

```
public class CamelRiderJavaDSLProdTest extends CamelTestSupport {

    protected CamelContext createCamelContext() throws Exception {
        CamelContext context = super.createCamelContext();

        PropertiesComponent prop = context.getComponent("properties",
                                        PropertiesComponent.class);
        prop.setLocation("classpath:rider-prod.properties");

        return context;
    }

    protected RouteBuilder createRouteBuilder() throws Exception {
        return new RouteBuilder() {
            public void configure() throws Exception {
                from("file:{{file.inbox}}").to("file:{{file.outbox}}");
            }
        };
    }
}
```

To ensure that the property placeholder is loaded and in use as early as possible, you have to configure the `PropertiesComponent` when the `CamelContext` is created. You can do this by overriding the `createCamelContext` method, which ensures the Properties component is available to the `RouteBuilder` when it encounters the property placeholders in the endpoints used in the route.

You can run try this example using the following Maven goals from the chapter6/firsttest directory:

```
mvn test -Dtest=CamelRiderJavaDSLTest
mvn test -Dtest=CamelRiderJavaDSLProdTest
```

> **TIP** You can use the Jasypt component to encrypt sensitive information in the properties file. For example, you may not want to have passwords in clear text in the properties file. You can read about the Jasypt component at the Camel website: http://camel.apache.org/jasypt.

We'll now cover the same example but using Spring property placeholders instead of the Camel Properties component.

USING SPRING PROPERTY PLACEHOLDERS

The Spring Framework supports externalizing properties defined in the Spring XML files using a feature known as Spring *property placeholders*. We'll review the example from the previous section using Spring property placeholders instead of the Camel Properties component.

The first thing you need to do is set up the route having the endpoint URIs externalized. This could be done as follows. Notice that Spring uses the ${key} syntax.

```
<context:property-placeholder properties-ref="properties"/>

<util:properties id="properties"
                location="classpath:rider-prod.properties"/>

<camelContext id="camel" xmlns="http://camel.apache.org/schema/spring">
    <route>
```

```
        <from uri="${file.inbox}"/>
        <to uri="${file.outbox}"/>
    </route>
```

Unfortunately the Spring Framework doesn't support using placeholders directly in endpoint URIs in the route, so you must define endpoints that include those placeholders by using the `<endpoint>` tag. The following code snippet shows how this is done:

```
<context:property-placeholder properties-ref="properties"/>          ❶ Loads prop-
                                                                        erties from
<util:properties id="properties"                                        external file
                 location="classpath:rider-prod.properties"/>
<camelContext id="camel" xmlns="http://camel.apache.org/schema/spring">
    <endpoint id="inbox" uri="file:${file.inbox}"/>
    <endpoint id="outbox" uri="file:${file.outbox}"/>
                                                                 Defines endpoints
    <route>                                                      using property
        <from ref="inbox"/>        ◁─┐  Refers to            ❷ placeholders
        <to ref="outbox"/>            endpoints
    </route>                       ❸ in route
</camelContext>
```

To use Spring property placeholders, you must declare the `<context:property-place-holder>` tag where you refer to a `properties` bean ❶ that will load the properties file from the classpath. Note that this XML file is based on the production environment.

In the `camelContext` element, you define two endpoints ❷ that use placeholders for dynamic file paths. The `${file.inbox}` is a Spring property placeholder that refers to a property with the key `file.inbox`. The same goes for `${file.outbox}`, which refers to the `file.outbox` property.

In the route, you must refer to these endpoints ❸ instead of using the regular URI notations. Notice the use of the `ref` attribute in the `<from>` and `<to>` tags.

The rider-prod.properties properties file contains the following two lines:

```
file.inbox=rider/files/inbox
file.outbox=rider/files/outbox
```

This example is included in the book's source code in the chapter6/firsttest directory. You can try it using the following Maven goal:

```
mvn test -Dtest=SpringRiderTest
```

The Camel Properties component versus Spring property placeholders

The Camel Properties component is more powerful than the Spring property placeholder mechanism. The latter only works when defining routes using Spring XML, and you have to declare the endpoints in dedicated `<endpoint>` tags for the property placeholders to work.

The Camel Properties component is provided out of the box, which means you can use it without using Spring at all. And it supports the various DSL languages you can use to define routes, such as Java, Spring XML, Groovy, and Scala. On top of that, you can declare the placeholders anywhere in the route definitions.

You have now seen the Camel Test Kit and learned to use its JUnit extension to write your first unit tests. Camel helps a lot when working with files, but things get more complex when you use more protocols—especially complex ones such as Java Message Service (JMS) messaging. Testing an application that leverages many protocols has always been challenging.

This is why mocks were invented. By using mocks, you can simulate real components and reduce the number of variables in your tests. Mock components are the topic of the next section.

6.2   *Using the Mock component*

The Mock component is a cornerstone when testing with Camel—it makes testing much easier. In much the same way as a car designer uses a crash test dummy to simulate vehicle impact on humans, the Mock component is used to simulate real components in a controlled way.

Mock components are useful in several situations:

- When the real component doesn't yet exist or isn't reachable in the development and test phases. For example, if you only have access to the component in preproduction and production phases.
- When the real component is slow or requires much effort to set up and initialize, such as a database.
- When you would have to incorporate special logic into the real component for testing purposes, which isn't practical or possible.
- When the component returns nondeterministic results, such as the current time, which would make it difficult to unit test at any given time of day.
- When you need to simulate errors caused by network problems or faults from the real component.

Without the Mock component, your only option would be to test using the real component, which is usually much harder. You may already have used mocking before; there are many frameworks out there that blend in well with testing frameworks like JUnit.

Camel takes testing very seriously, and the Mock component was included in the first release of Camel. The fact that it resides in camel-core JAR indicates its importance—the Mock component is used rigorously in unit testing Camel itself.

In this section, we'll look at how to use the Mock component in unit tests and how to add mocking to existing unit tests. Then we'll spend some time on how you can use mocks to set expectations to verify test results, as this is where the Mock component excels.

Let's get started.

6.2.1 Introducing the Mock component

The three basic steps of testing are illustrated in figure 6.3.

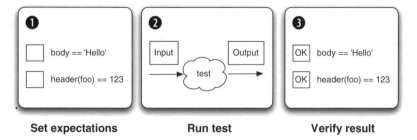

Figure 6.3   Three steps for testing: set expectations, run the test, and verify the result.

Before the test is started, you set the expectations of what should happen ❶. Then you run the test ❷. Finally, you verify the outcome of the test against the expectations ❸. The Camel Mock component allows you to easily implement these steps when testing Camel applications. On the mock endpoints, you can set expectations that are used to verify the test results when the test completes.

Mock components can verify a rich variety of expectations, such as the following:

- That the correct number of messages are received on each endpoint
- That the messages arrive in the correct order
- That the correct payloads are received
- That the test ran within the expected time period

Mock components allow you to configure coarse- and fine-grained expectations and to simulate errors such as network failures.

Let's get started and try using the Mock component.

6.2.2 Unit testing with the Mock component

As we look at how to use the Mock component, we'll use the following basic route to keep things simple:

```
from("jms:topic:quote").to("mock:quote");
```

This route will consume messages from a JMS topic, named `quote`, and route the messages to a mock endpoint with the name `quote`.

The mock endpoint is implemented in Camel as the `org.apache.camel.component.mock.MockEndpoint` class; it provides a large number of methods for setting expectations. Table 6.2 lists the most commonly used methods on the mock endpoint. The `expectedMessageCount` method is exactly what you need to set the expectation that one message should arrive at the `mock:quote` endpoint. You can do this as shown in listing 6.6.

Table 6.2   Commonly used methods in the `MockEndpoint` class

Method	Description
`expectedMessageCount(int count)`	Specifies the expected number of messages arriving at the endpoint
`expectedMinimumMessageCount` `(int count)`	Specifies the expected minimum number of messages arriving on the endpoint
`expectedBodiesReceived` `(Object... bodies)`	Specifies the expected message bodies and their order arriving at the endpoint
`expectedBodiesReceivedInAnyOrder` `(Object... bodies)`	Specifies the expected message bodies arriving at the endpoint; ordering doesn't matter
`assertIsSatisfied()`	Validates that all expectations set on the endpoint are satisfied

Listing 6.6   Using `MockEndpoint` in unit testing

```
package camelinaction;

import org.apache.camel.builder.RouteBuilder;
import org.apache.camel.component.mock.MockEndpoint;
import org.apache.camel.test.junit4.CamelTestSupport;

public class FirstMockTest extends CamelTestSupport {

    @Override
    protected RouteBuilder createRouteBuilder() throws Exception {
        return new RouteBuilder() {
            @Override
            public void configure() throws Exception {
                from("jms:topic:quote").to("mock:quote");
            }
        };
    }

    @Test
    public void testQuote() throws Exception {
        MockEndpoint quote = getMockEndpoint("mock:quote");
        quote.expectedMessageCount(1);

        template.sendBody("jms:topic:quote", "Camel rocks");

        quote.assertIsSatisfied();
    }
}
```

❶ Expects one message

❷ Verifies expectations

To obtain the `MockEndpoint`, you use the `getMockEndpoint` method from the `Camel-TestSupport` class. Then you set your expectations—in this case, you expect one message to arrive ❶. You start the test by sending a message to the JMS topic, and the mock endpoint verifies whether the expectations were met or not by using the `assertIsSatisfied` method ❷. If a single expectation fails, Camel throws a `java.lang.AssertionError` stating the failure.

You can compare what happens in listing 6.6 to what you saw in figure 6.3: you set expectations, ran the test, and verified the results. It can't get any simpler than that.

NOTE By default, the `assertIsSatisfied` method runs for 10 seconds before timing out. You can change the wait time with the `setResultWait-Time(long timeInMillis)` method if you have unit tests that run for a long time.

REPLACING JMS WITH SEDA

Listing 6.6 uses JMS, but, for now, let's keep things simple by simulating JMS using the SEDA component. (We'll look at testing JMS with ActiveMQ in section 6.4.)

NOTE For details about the SEDA component, see the Camel documentation: http://camel.apache.org/seda.html.

You can simulate JMS by registering the SEDA component as the JMS component, like this:

```
@Override
protected CamelContext createCamelContext() throws Exception {
    CamelContext context = super.createCamelContext();
    context.addComponent("jms", context.getComponent("seda"));
    return context;
}
```

You override the `createCamelContext` method and add the SEDA component as the JMS component. By doing this, you fool Camel into using the SEDA component when you refer to the JMS component.

The book's source code contains this test. You can try it by running the following Maven goal from the chapter6/firsttest directory:

```
mvn test -Dtest=FirstMockTest
```

You may have noticed in listing 6.5 that the expectation was coarse-grained in the sense that you just expected a message to arrive. You did not specify anything about the message's content or other characteristics, so you don't know whether the message that arrived was the same "Camel rocks" message that was sent. The next section covers how to test this.

6.2.3   *Verifying that the correct message arrived*

The `expectedMessageCount` method can only be used to verify that a certain number of messages arrived. It doesn't dictate anything about the content of the message. Let's improve the unit test in listing 6.6 so that it expects the message being sent to match the message that arrives at the mock endpoint.

You can do this using the `expectedBodiesReceived` method, as follows:

```
@Test
public void testQuote() throws Exception {
    MockEndpoint mock = getMockEndpoint("mock:quote");
```

```
mock.expectedBodiesReceived("Camel rocks");

template.sendBody("jms:topic:quote", "Camel rocks");

mock.assertIsSatisfied();
}
```

This is intuitive and easy to understand, but the method states bodies in plural as if there could be more bodies. Camel does support expectations of multiple messages, so you could send in two messages. Here's a revised version of the test:

```
@Test
public void testQuotes() throws Exception {
    MockEndpoint mock = getMockEndpoint("mock:quote");
    mock.expectedBodiesReceived("Camel rocks", "Hello Camel");

    template.sendBody("jms:topic:quote", "Camel rocks");
    template.sendBody("jms:topic:quote", "Hello Camel");

    mock.assertIsSatisfied();
}
```

Camel now expects two messages to arrive in the specified order. Camel will fail the test if the "Hello Camel" message arrives before the "Camel rocks" message.

In cases where the order doesn't matter, you can use the expectedBodiesReceived-InAnyOrder method instead, like this:

```
mock.expectedBodiesReceivedInAnyOrder("Camel rocks", "Hello Camel");
```

It could hardly be any easier than that.

But if you expect a much larger number of messages to arrive, the bodies you pass in as an argument will be very large. How can you do that? The answer is to use a List containing the expected bodies as a parameter:

```
List bodies = ...
mock.expectedBodiesReceived(bodies);
```

The Mock component has many other features we need to cover, so let's continue and see how you can use expressions to set fine-grained expectations.

6.2.4   *Using expressions with mocks*

Suppose you want to set an expectation that a message should contain the word "Camel" in its content. One way of doing this is shown in listing 6.7.

Listing 6.7   Using expressions with MockEndpoint to set expectations

```
@Test
public void testIsCamelMessage() throws Exception {
    MockEndpoint mock = getMockEndpoint("mock:quote");
    mock.expectedMessageCount(2);                              ◁─── ❶ Expects 2
                                                                        messages
    template.sendBody("jms:topic:quote", "Hello Camel");
    template.sendBody("jms:topic:quote", "Camel rocks");
```

```
assertMockEndpointsSatisfied();

List<Exchange> list = mock.getReceivedExchanges();
String body1 = list.get(0).getIn()
                  .getBody(String.class);
String body2 = list.get(1).getIn()
                  .getBody(String.class);

assertTrue(body1.contains("Camel"));
assertTrue(body2.contains("Camel"));
}
```

Verifies 2 messages ② received

③ Verifies "Camel" is in received messages

First you set up your expectation that the mock:quote endpoint will receive two messages ①. You then send in two messages to the JMS topic to start the test. Then you assert that the mock received the two messages by using the assertMockEndpoints-Satisfied method ②, which is a one-stop method for asserting all mocks. This method is more convenient to use than having to invoke the assertIsSatisfied method on *every* mock endpoint you may have in use.

At this point, you can use the getReceivedExchanges method to access all the exchanges the mock:quote endpoint has received ③. You use this method to get hold of the two received message bodies so you can assert that they contain the word "Camel".

At first you may think it a bit odd to define expectations in two places—before and after the test has run. Is it not possible to define the expectations in one place, such as before you run the test? Yes, of course it is, and this is where Camel expressions come into the game.

NOTE The getReceivedExchanges method still has its merits. It allows you to work with the exchanges directly, giving you the ability to do whatever you want with them.

Table 6.3 lists some additional MockEndpoint methods that let you use expressions to set expectations.

Table 6.3 Expression-based methods commonly used on MockEndpoint

Method	Description
message(int index)	Defines an expectation on the *n*'th message received
allMessages()	Defines an expectation on all messages received
expectsAscending(Expression expression)	Expects messages to arrive in ascending order
expectsDescending(Expression expression)	Expects messages to arrive in descending order
expectsDuplicates(Expression expression)	Expects duplicate messages

Table 6.3   Expression-based methods commonly used on `MockEndpoint` *(continued)*

Method	Description
`expectsNoDuplicates(Expression expression)`	Expects no duplicate messages
`expects(Runable runable)`	Defines a custom expectation

You can use the `message` method to improve the unit test in listing 6.7 and group all your expectations together, as shown here:

```
@Test
public void testIsCamelMessage() throws Exception {
    MockEndpoint mock = getMockEndpoint("mock:quote");
    mock.expectedMessageCount(2);
    mock.message(0).body().contains("Camel");
    mock.message(1).body().contains("Camel");

    template.sendBody("jms:topic:quote", "Hello Camel");
    template.sendBody("jms:topic:quote", "Camel rocks");

    assertMockEndpointsSatisfied();
}
```

Notice that you can use the `message(int index)` method to set an expectation that the body of the message should contain the word "Camel". Instead of doing this for each message based on its index, you can use the `allMessages()` method to set the same expectation for all messages:

```
mock.allMessages().body().contains("Camel");
```

So far you've only seen expectations based on the message body, but what if you want to set an expectation based on a header? That's easy—you use `header(name)`, as follows:

```
mock.message(0).header("JMSPriority").isEqualTo(4);
```

You probably noticed the `contains` and `isEqualTo` methods we used in the preceding couple of code snippets. They're builder methods used to create predicates for expectations. Table 6.4 lists all the builder methods available.

Table 6.4   Builder methods for creating predicates to be used as expectations

Method	Description
`contains(Object value)`	Sets an expectation that the message body contains the given value
`isInstanceOf(Class type)`	Sets an expectation that the message body is an instance of the given type
`startsWith(Object value)`	Sets an expectation that the message body starts with the given value

Table 6.4   Builder methods for creating predicates to be used as expectations *(continued)*

Method	Description
`endsWith(Object value)`	Sets an expectation that the message body ends with the given value
`in(Object... values)`	Sets an expectation that the message body is equal to any of the given values
`isEqualTo(Object value)`	Sets an expectation that the message body is equal to the given value
`isNotEqualTo(Object value)`	Sets an expectation that the message body isn't equal to the given value
`isGreaterThan(Object value)`	Sets an expectation that the message body is greater than the given value
`isGreaterThanOrEqual(Object value)`	Sets an expectation that the message body is greater than or equal to the given value
`isLessThan(Object value)`	Sets an expectation that the message body is less than the given value
`isLessThanOrEqual(Object value)`	Sets an expectation that the message body is less than or equal to the given value
`isNull(Object value)`	Sets an expectation that the message body is `null`
`isNotNull(Object value)`	Sets an expectation that the message body isn't `null`
`regex(String pattern)`	Sets an expectation that the message body matches the given regular expression

At first it may seem odd that the methods in table 6.4 often use `Object` as the parameter type—why not a specialized type such as `String`? This is because of Camel's strong type-converter mechanism, which allows you to compare apples to oranges—Camel can regard both of them as fruit and evaluate them accordingly. You can compare strings with numeric values without having to worry about type mismatches, as illustrated by the following two code lines:

```
mock.message(0).header("JMSPriority").isEqualTo(4);
mock.message(0).header("JMSPriority").isEqualTo("4");
```

Now suppose you want to create an expectation that all messages contain the word "Camel" and end with a period. You could use a regular expression to set this in a single expectation:

```
mock.allMessages().body().regex("^.*Camel.*\\.$");
```

This will work, but Camel allows you to enter multiple expectations, so instead of using the regex method, you can create a more readable solution:

```
mock.allMessages().body().contains("Camel");
mock.allMessages().body().endsWith(".");
```

You have learned a lot about how to set expectations, including fine-grained ones using the builder methods listed in table 6.4. Now it's time to move on and test the ordering of the messages received.

6.2.5 *Testing the ordering of messages*

Suppose you need to test that messages arrive in sequence-number order. For example, messages arriving in the order 1, 2, 3 are accepted, whereas the order 1, 3, 2 is invalid and the test should fail.

The Mock component provides features to test ascending and descending orders. For example, you can use the `expectsAscending` method like this:

```
mock.expectsAscending(header("Counter"));
```

The preceding expectation will test that the received messages are in ascending order, judged by the `Counter` value in the message header, but it doesn't dictate what the starting value must be. If the first message that arrives has a value of 5, the expectation tests whether or not the next message has a value greater than 5, and so on.

What if you must test that the first message has a value of 1? In that case, you can add another expectation that tests the first message, using `message(0)`, as follows:

```
mock.message(0).header("Counter").isEqualTo(1);
mock.expectsAscending(header("Counter"));
```

Together these expectations test that messages arrive in the order 1, 2, 3, ..., but orders such as 1, 2, 4, 5, 6, 8, 10, ... also pass the test. That's because the `expectsAscending` and `expectsDescending` methods don't detect whether there are *gaps* between messages. These methods use generic comparison functions that work on any types, not only numbers.

To detect gaps in the sequence, you need to use a custom expression that implements gap-detection logic.

USING A CUSTOM EXPRESSION

When the provided expressions and predicates don't cut it, you can use a custom expression. By using a custom expression, you have the full power of Java code at your fingertips to implement your assertions.

Let's look at the problem of gap detection. Camel doesn't provide any expressions for that, so you must do it with a custom expression. Listing 6.8 shows how this can be done.

Listing 6.8 Using a custom expression to detect gaps in message ordering

```
@Test
public void testGap() throws Exception {
    final MockEndpoint mock = getMockEndpoint("mock:quote");
    mock.expectedMessageCount(3);
    mock.expects(new Runnable() {              ◁──┐   Custom expression
        public void run() {                       ❶  to detect gaps
            int last = 0;
```

```
            for (Exchange exchange : mock.getExchanges()) {
                int current = exchange.getIn()
                                .getHeader("Counter", Integer.class);
                if (current <= last) {
                    fail("Counter is not greater than last counter");
                } else if (current - last != 1) {
                    fail("Gap detected: last: " + last
                        + " current: " + current);
                }
                last = current;
            }
        }
    });

    template.sendBodyAndHeader("jms:topic:quote", "A", "Counter", 1);
    template.sendBodyAndHeader("jms:topic:quote", "B", "Counter", 2);
    template.sendBodyAndHeader("jms:topic:quote", "C", "Counter", 4);

    mock.assertIsNotSatisfied();
}
```

To set up a custom expression, you use the expects method, which allows you to provide your own logic as a Runnable ❶. In the Runnable, you can loop through the exchanges received and extract the current counter header. Then you can verify whether all the counters are incremented by one and don't have any gaps. You can use the JUnit fail method to fail when a gap is detected.

To test whether this works, you send in three messages, each of which contains a Counter. Notice that there is a gap in the sequence: 1, 2, 4. You expect this unit test to fail, so you instruct the mock to *not* be satisfied using the assertIsNotSatisfied method.

Next, you test a positive situation where no gaps exist. To do so, you use the assert-IsSatisfied method and send in three messages in sequence, as follows:

```
template.sendBodyAndHeader("seda:topic:quote", "A", "Counter", 1);
template.sendBodyAndHeader("seda:topic:quote", "B", "Counter", 2);
template.sendBodyAndHeader("seda:topic:quote", "C", "Counter", 3);

mock.assertIsSatisfied();
```

That's all there is to developing and using a custom expression.

Now let's get back to the mock components and learn about using mocks to simulate real components. This is useful when the real component isn't available or isn't reachable from a local or test environment.

6.2.6 *Using mocks to simulate real components*

Suppose you have a route like the following one, in which you expose an HTTP service using Jetty so clients can obtain an order status:

```
from("jetty:http://web.rider.com/service/order")
    .process(new OrderQueryProcessor())
    .to("mina:tcp://miranda.rider.com:8123?textline=true")
    .process(new OrderResponseProcessor());
```

Clients send an HTTP GET, with the order ID as a query parameter, to the http://web.rider.com/service/order URL. Camel will use the `OrderQueryProcessor` to transform the message into a format that Rider Auto Parts' mainframe (named Miranda) understands. The message is then sent to Miranda using TCP, and Camel waits for the reply to come back. The reply message is then processed using the `OrderResponse-Processor` before it's returned to the HTTP client.

Now suppose you have been asked to write a unit test to verify that clients can obtain the order status. The challenge is that you don't have access to Miranda, which contains the actual order status. You have been asked to simulate this server by replying with a canned response.

Camel provides the two methods listed in table 6.5 to help simulate a real component.

Table 6.5   Methods to control responses when simulating a real component

Method	Description
`whenAnyExchangeReceived` `(Processor processor)`	Uses a custom processor to set a canned reply
`whenExchangeReceived` `(int index, Processor processor)`	Uses a custom processor to set a canned reply when the *n*'th message is received

You can simulate a real endpoint by mocking it with the Mock component and controlling the reply using the methods in table 6.5. To do this, you need to replace the actual endpoint in the route with the mocked endpoint, which is done by replacing it with `mock:miranda`. Because you want to run the unit test locally, you also need to change the HTTP hostname to `localhost`, allowing you to run the test locally on your own laptop.

```
from("jetty:http://localhost:9080/service/order")
    .process(new OrderQueryProcessor())
    .to("mock:miranda")
    .process(new OrderResponseProcessor());
```

The unit test that leverages the preceding route follows.

Listing 6.9   Simulating a real component by using a mock endpoint

```
public class MirandaTest extends CamelTestSupport {
    private String url = "http://localhost:9080/service/order?id=123";

    @Override
    protected RouteBuilder createRouteBuilder() throws Exception {
        return new RouteBuilder() {
            @Override
            public void configure() throws Exception {
                from("jetty:http://localhost:9080/service/order")
                    .process(new OrderQueryProcessor())
                    .to("mock:miranda")
                    .process(new OrderResponseProcessor());
```

```
            }
        };
    }

    @Test
    public void testMiranda() throws Exception {
        MockEndpoint mock = getMockEndpoint("mock:miranda");        ❶ Returns
        mock.expectedBodiesReceived("ID=123");                        canned
        mock.whenAnyExchangeReceived(new Processor() {      ◁─┘       response
            public void process(Exchange exchange) throws Exception {
                exchange.getIn().setBody("ID=123,STATUS=IN PROGRESS");
            }
        });

        String out = template.requestBody(url, null, String.class);
        assertEquals("IN PROGRESS", out);    ◁──┐
                                                 Verifies
        assertMockEndpointsSatisfied();         expected   ❸ Transforms
    }                                        ❷  reply         to format
    private class OrderQueryProcessor                         understood
                    implements Processor {        ◁─┘         by Miranda
        public void process(Exchange exchange) throws Exception {
            String id = exchange.getIn().getHeader("id", String.class);
            exchange.getIn().setBody("ID=" + id);
        }
    }                                                       ❹ Transforms
    private class OrderResponseProcessor                       to response
                    implements Processor {        ◁─          format
        public void process(Exchange exchange) throws Exception {
            String body = exchange.getIn().getBody(String.class);
            String reply = ObjectHelper.after(body, "STATUS=");
            exchange.getIn().setBody(reply);
        }
    }
  }
}
```

In the testMiranda method, you obtain the mock:miranda endpoint, which is the mock that simulates the Miranda server, and you set an expectation that the input message contains the body "ID=123". To return a canned reply, you use the whenAnyExchangeReceived method ❶, which allows you to use a custom processor to set the canned response. This response is set to be "ID=123,STATUS=IN PROGRESS".

Then you start the unit test by sending a message to the http://localhost:9080/service/order?id=123 endpoint; the message is an HTTP GET using the requestBody method from the template instance. You then assert that the reply is "IN PROGRESS" using the regular JUnit assertEquals method ❷. You use two processors (❸ and ❹) to transform the data to and from the format that the Miranda server understands.

You can find the code for this example in the chapter6/miranda folder of the book's source code, which you can try using the following Maven goal:

```
mvn test -Dtest=MirandaTest
```

You've now learned all about the Camel Test Kit and how to use it for unit testing with Camel. We looked at using the Mock component to easily write tests with expectations, run tests, and have Camel verify whether the expectations were satisfied. You also saw how to use the Mock component to simulate a real component. You may wonder whether there is a more cunning way to simulate a real component than by using a mock, and there is. We're going to look at how to simulate errors next, but the techniques involved could also be applied to simulating a real component.

6.3   Simulating errors

In the previous chapter, you learned how to use error handling to act upon errors. Now the question is how to test that your code works when errors happen.

You could test for errors by unplugging network cables and swinging an axe at the servers, but that's a bit extreme. Instead we'll look at how to simulate errors in unit tests using the three different techniques listed in table 6.6.

Table 6.6   Three techniques for simulating errors

Technique	Summary
Processor	Using processors is easy, and they give you full control, as a developer. This technique is covered in section 6.3.1.
Mock	Using mocks is a good overall solution. Mocks are fairly easy to apply, and they provide a wealth of other features for testing, as you saw in section 6.2. This technique is covered in section 6.3.2.
Interceptor	This is the most sophisticated technique because it allows you to use an existing route without modifying it. Interceptors aren't tied solely to testing; they can be used anywhere and anytime. We'll cover interceptors in section 6.3.3.

The following three sections cover these three techniques.

6.3.1   Simulating errors using a processor

Errors are simulated in Camel by throwing exceptions, which is exactly how errors occur in real life. For example, Java will throw an exception if it can't connect to a remote server. Throwing such an exception is easy—you can do that from any Java code, such as from a `Processor`. That's the topic of this section.

To illustrate this, we'll take the use case from the previous chapter—you're uploading reports to a remote server using HTTP, and you're using FTP as a fallback method. This allows you to simulate errors with HTTP connectivity.

The route from listing 5.8 is repeated here.

Listing 6.10   Route using error handling with a failover to FTP

```
errorHandler(defaultErrorHandler()
    .maximumRedeliveries(5).redeliveryDelay(10000));

onException(IOException.class).maximumRedeliveries(3)
```

```
    .handled(true)
    .to("ftp://gear@ftp.rider.com?password=secret");

from("file:/rider/files/upload?delay=1h")
    .to("http://rider.com?user=gear&password=secret");
```

What you want to do now is simulate an error when sending a file to the HTTP service, and you'll expect that it will be handled by onException and uploaded using FTP instead. This will ensure that the route is working correctly.

Because you want to concentrate the unit test on the error-handling aspect and not on the actual components used, you can just mock the HTTP and FTP endpoints. This frees you from the burden of setting up HTTP and FTP servers, and leaves you with a simpler route for testing:

```
errorHandler(defaultErrorHandler()
    .maximumRedeliveries(5).redeliveryDelay(1000));

onException(IOException.class).maximumRedeliveries(3)
    .handled(true)
    .to("mock:ftp");

from("direct:file")
        .to("mock:http");
```

This route also reduces the redelivery delay from 10 seconds to 1 second, to speed up unit testing. Notice that the file endpoint is stubbed with a direct endpoint that allows you to start the test by sending a message to the direct endpoint; this is much easier than writing an actual file.

To simulate a communication error when trying to send the file to the HTTP endpoint, you add a processor to the route that forces an error by throwing a Connect-Exception exception:

```
from("direct:file")
    .process(new Processor()) {
        public void process(Exchange exchange) throws Exception {
            throw new ConnectException("Simulated connection error");
        }
    })
    .to("mock:http");
```

You then write a test method to simulate this connection error, as follows:

```
@Test
public void testSimulateConnectionError() throws Exception {
    getMockEndpoint("mock:http").expectedMessageCount(0);

    MockEndpoint ftp = getMockEndpoint("mock:ftp");
    ftp.expectedBodiesReceived("Camel rocks");

    template.sendBody("direct:file", "Camel rocks");

    assertMockEndpointsIsSatisfied();
}
```

You expect no messages to arrive at the HTTP endpoint because you predicted the error would be handled and the message would be routed to the FTP endpoint instead.

The book's source code contains this example. You can try it by running the following Maven goal from the chapter6/error directory:

```
mvn test -Dtest=SimulateErrorUsingProcessorTest
```

Using the `Processor` is easy, but you have to alter the route to insert the `Processor`. When testing your routes, you might prefer to test them *as is* without changes that could introduce unnecessary risks. What if you could test the route without changing it at all? The next two techniques do this.

6.3.2   *Simulating errors using mocks*

You saw in section 6.2.6 that the Mock component could be used to simulate a real component. But instead of simulating a real component, you can use what you learned there to simulate errors. If you use mocks, we don't need to alter the route; you write the code to simulate the error directly into the test method, instead of mixing it in with the route. Listing 6.11 shows this.

> **Listing 6.11   Simulating an error by throwing an exception from the mock endpoint**

```
@Test
public void testSimulateConnectionErrorUsingMock() throws Exception {
    getMockEndpoint("mock:ftp").expectedMessageCount(1);

    MockEndpoint http = getMockEndpoint("mock:http");
    http.whenAnyExchangeReceived(new Processor() {
        public void process(Exchange exchange) throws Exception {
            throw new ConnectException("Simulated connection error");
        }
    });

    template.sendBody("direct:file", "Camel rocks");

    assertMockEndpointsSatisfied();
}
```

To simulate the connection error, you need to get hold of the HTTP mock endpoint, where you use the `whenAnyExchangeReceived` method to set a custom `Processor`. That `Processor` can simulate the error by throwing the connection exception.

By using mocks, you put the code that simulates the error into the unit test method, instead of in the route, as is required by the processor technique.

Now let's look at the last technique for simulating errors.

6.3.3   *Simulating errors using interceptors*

Suppose your boss wants you to write integration tests for listing 6.10 that should, among other things, test what happens when communication with the remote HTTP server fails. How can you do that? This is tricky because you don't have control over the remote HTTP server, and you can't easily force communication errors in the network layer. Luckily, Camel provides features to address this problem. We'll get to that in a moment, but first we need to look at interceptors, which provide the means to simulate errors.

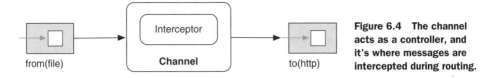

Figure 6.4 The channel acts as a controller, and it's where messages are intercepted during routing.

In a nutshell, an interceptor allows you to intercept any given message and act upon it. Figure 6.4 illustrates where the interception takes place in a route.

Figure 6.4 shows a low-level view of a Camel route, where you route messages from a file consumer to an HTTP producer. In between sits the channel, which acts as a controller, and this is where the interceptors (among others) live.

Channels play a key role

This may look familiar—we looked at channels in figure 5.3. It's the same channel that sits between every node in the route path and acts as a controller. Channels play a key role in the Camel routing engine, handling such things as routing the message to the next designated target, error handling, interception, tracing messages and gathering metrics.

The three types of interceptors that Camel provides out of the box are listed in table 6.7.

Table 6.7 The three flavors of interceptors provided out of the box in Camel

Interceptor	Description
intercept	Intercepts every single step a message takes. This interceptor is invoked continuously as the message is routed.
interceptFromEndpoint	Intercepts incoming messages arriving on a particular endpoint. This interceptor is only invoked once.
interceptSendToEndpoint	Intercepts messages that are about to be sent to a particular endpoint. This interceptor is only invoked once.

To write integration tests, you can use interceptSendToEndpoint to intercept messages sent to the remote HTTP server and redirect them to a processor that simulates the error, as shown here:

```
interceptSendToEndpoint("http://rider.com/rider")
    .skipSendToOriginalEndpoint();
    .process(new SimulateHttpErrorProcessor());
```

When a message is about to be sent to the HTTP endpoint, it's intercepted by Camel and the message is routed to your custom processor, where you simulate an error. When this detour is complete, the message would normally be sent to the originally intended endpoint, but you instruct Camel to skip this step using the skipSendToOriginalEndpoint method.

TIP　The last two interceptors in table 6.7 support using wildcards (*) and regular expressions in the endpoint URL. You can use these techniques to intercept multiple endpoints or to be lazy and just match all HTTP endpoints. We'll look at this in a moment.

Because you're doing an integration test, you want to keep the original route *untouched*, which means you can't add interceptors or mocks directly in the route. Because you still want to use interceptors in the route, you need another way to somehow add the interceptors. Camel provides the adviceWith method to address this.

USING ADVICEWITH TO ADD INTERCEPTORS TO AN EXISTING ROUTE

The adviceWith method is available during unit testing, and it allows you to add such things as interceptors and error handling to an existing route.

To see how this works, let's look at an example. The following code snippet shows how you can use adviceWith in a unit test method:

```
@Test
public void testSimulateErrorUsingInterceptors() throws Exception {
    RouteDefinition route = context.getRouteDefinitions().get(0);

    route.adviceWith(context, new RouteBuilder() {          Uses adviceWith
        public void configure() throws Exception {          to add interceptor
            interceptSendToEndpoint("http://*")          ❶ to route
                .skipSendToOriginalEndpoint()
                .process(new SimulateHttpErrorProcessor());
        }
    });
```

The key issue when using adviceWith is to know which route to use. Because you only have one route in this case, you can refer to the first route enlisted in the route definitions list. The route definitions list contains the definitions of all routes registered in the current CamelContext.

When you've got the route, it's just a matter of using the adviceWith method ❶, which leverages a RouteBuilder—this means that in the configure method you can use the Java DSL to define the interceptors. Notice that the interceptor uses a wildcard to match all HTTP endpoints.

TIP　If you have multiple routes, you'll need to select the correct route to be used. To help select the route, you can assign unique IDs to the routes, which you then can use to look up the route, such as context.getRouteDefinition("myCoolRoute").

We've included this integration test in the book's source code in the chapter6/error directory. You can try it using the following Maven goal:

```
mvn test -Dtest=SimulateErrorUsingInterceptorTest
```

TIP　Interceptors aren't only for simulating errors—they're a general purpose feature that can also be used for other types of testing. For example, when you're testing production routes, you can use interceptors to detour messages to mock endpoints.

The last section of this chapter covers how to do integration testing without mocks.

6.4   *Testing without mocks*

So far in this chapter, you've learned that mocks play a central role when testing Camel applications. For example, integration testing often involves real live components, and substituting mocks isn't an option, as the point of the integration test is to test with live components. In this section, we'll look at how to test such situations without using mocks.

Rider Auto Parts has a client application that business partners can use to submit orders. The client dispatches orders over JMS to an incoming order queue at the Rider Auto Parts message broker. A Camel application is then used to further process these incoming orders. Figure 6.5 illustrates this.

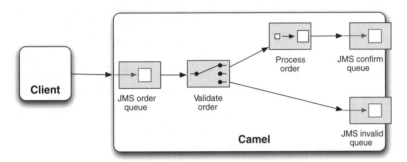

Figure 6.5   The client sends orders to an order queue, which is routed by a Camel application. The order is either accepted and routed to a confirm queue, or it's not accepted and is routed to an invalid queue.

The client application is written in Java, but it doesn't use Camel at all. The challenge you're facing is how to test that the client and the Camel application work as expected? How can you do integration testing?

6.4.1   *Integration testing*

Integration testing the scenario outlined in figure 6.5 requires you to use live components, which means you must start the test by using the client to send a message to the order queue. Then you let the Camel application process the message. When this is complete, you'll have to inspect whether the message ended up in the right queue—the confirm or the invalid queue.

You have to perform these three tasks:

1 Use the client to send an order message
2 Wait for the Camel application to process the message
3 Inspect the confirm and invalid queues to see if the message arrived as expected

So let's tackle each step.

USE THE CLIENT TO SEND AN ORDER MESSAGE

The client is easy to use. All you're required to do is provide an IP address to the remote Rider Auto Parts message broker, and then use its `sendOrder` method to send the order.

The following code has been simplified in terms of the information required for order details:

```
OrderClient client = new OrderClient("localhost:61616");
client.sendOrder(123, date, "4444", "5555");
```

WAIT FOR THE CAMEL APPLICATION TO PROCESS THE MESSAGE

The client has sent an order to the order queue on the message broker. The Camel application will now react and process the message according to the route outlined in figure 6.5.

The problem you're facing now is that the client doesn't provide any API you can use to wait until the process is complete. What you need is an API that provides insight into the Camel application. All you need to know is when the message has been processed, and optionally whether it completed successfully or failed.

Camel provides the `NotifyBuilder`, which provides such insight. We'll cover the `NotifyBuilder` in more detail in section 6.4.2, but the following code shows how to have `NotifyBuilder` notify you when Camel is finished processing the message:

```
NotifyBuilder notify = new NotifyBuilder(context).whenDone(1).create();

OrderClient client = new OrderClient("tcp://localhost:61616");
client.sendOrder(123, date, "4444", "5555");

boolean matches = notify.matches(5, TimeUnit.SECONDS);
assertTrue(matches);
```

First, you configure `NotifyBuilder` to notify you when one message is done. Then you use the client to send the message. Invoking the `matches` method on the `notify` instance will cause the test to wait until the condition applies, or the 5-second timeout occurs.

The last task tests whether the message was processed correctly.

INSPECT THE QUEUES TO SEE IF THE MESSAGE ARRIVED AS EXPECTED

After the message has been processed, you need to investigate whether the message arrived at the correct message queue. If you want to test that a valid order arrived in the confirm queue, you can use the `BrowsableEndpoint` to browse the messages on the JMS queue. By using the `BrowsableEndpoint`, you only peek inside the message queue, which means the messages will still be present on the queue.

Doing this requires a little bit of code, as shown in here:

```
BrowsableEndpoint be = context.getEndpoint("activemq:queue:confirm",
                                    BrowsableEndpoint.class);
List<Exchange> list = be.getExchanges();
assertEquals(1, list.size());
String body = list.get(0).getIn().getBody(String.class);
assertEquals("OK,123,2010-04-20T15:47:58,4444,5555", body);
```

By using `BrowsableEndpoint`, you can retrieve the exchanges on the JMS queue using the `getExchanges` method. You can then use the exchanges to assert that the message arrived as expected.

The source code for the book contains this example in the chapter6/notify directory, which you can try using the following Maven goal:

```
mvn test -Dtest=OrderTest
```

We've now covered an example of how to do integration testing without mocks. Along the road, we introduced the `NotifiyBuilder`, which has many more nifty features. We'll review it in the next section.

6.4.2 Using NotifyBuilder

`NotifyBuilder` is located in the `org.apache.camel.builder` package. It uses the Builder pattern, which means you stack methods on it to build an expression. You use it to define conditions for messages being routed in Camel. Then it offers methods to test whether the conditions have been meet. We already used it in the previous section, but this time we'll raise the bar and show how you can build more complex conditions.

In the previous example, you used a simple condition:

```
NotifyBuilder notify = new NotifyBuilder(context).whenDone(1).create();
```

This condition will match when one or more messages have been processed in the entire Camel application. This is a very coarse-grained condition. Suppose you have multiple routes, and another message was processed as well. That would cause the condition to match even if the message you wanted to test was still in progress.

To remedy this, you can pinpoint the condition so it applies only to messages originating from a specific endpoint, as shown in bold:

```
NotifyBuilder notify = new NotifyBuilder(context)
    .from("activemq:queue:order").whenDone(1).create();
```

Now you've told the notifier that the condition only applies for messages that originate from the order queue.

Suppose you send multiple messages to the order queue, and you want to test whether a specific message was processed. You can do this using a predicate to indicate when the desired message was completed. This is done using the `whenAnyDone-Matches` method, as shown here in bold:

```
NotifyBuilder notify = new NotifyBuilder(context)
    .from("activemq:queue:order").whenAnyDoneMatches(
    body().isEqualTo("OK,123,2010-04-20'T'15:48:00,2222,3333"))
    .create();
```

In this example we want the predicate to determine if the body is equal to the expected result which is the string starting with `"OK,123,..."`.

We've now covered some examples using `NotifyBuilder`, but the builder has many methods that allow you to build even more complex expressions. Table 6.8 lists the most commonly used methods.

The `NotifyBuilder` has over 30 methods, and we've only listed the most commonly used ones in table 6.8. Consult the online Camel documentation to see all the supported methods: http://camel.apache.org/notifybuilder.html.

Table 6.8 Noteworthy methods on `NotifyBuilder`

Method	Description
`from(uri)`	Specifies that the message must originate from the given endpoint. You can use wildcards and regular expressions in the given URI to match multiple endpoints. For example, you could use `from ("activemq:queue:*")` to match any JMS queues.
`filter(predicate)`	Filters unwanted messages.
`whenDone(number)`	Matches when a minimum number of messages are done.
`whenCompleted(number)`	Matches when a minimum number of messages are completed.
`whenFailed(number)`	Matches when a minimum number of messages have failed.
`whenBodiesDone(bodies...)`	Matches when messages are done with the specified `bodies` in the given order.
`whenAnyDoneMatches (predicate)`	Matches when any message is done and matches the `predicate`.
`create`	Creates the notifier.
`matches`	Tests whether the notifier currently matches. This operation returns immediately.
`matches(timeout)`	Waits until the notifier matches or times out. Returns `true` if it matched, or `false` if a timeout occurred.

NOTE The `NotifyBuilder` works in principle by adding an `EventNotifier` to the given `CamelContext`. The `EventNotifier` then invokes callbacks during the routing of exchanges. This allows the `NotifyBuilder` to listen for those events and react accordingly. The `EventNotifier` is covered in section 12.3.5.

The `NotifyBuilder` identifies three ways a message can complete:

- *Done*—This means the message is done, regardless of whether it completed or failed.
- *Completed*—This means the message completed with success (no failure).
- *Failed*—This means the message failed (for example, an exception was thrown and not handled).

The names of these three ways are also incorporated in the names of the builder methods: `whenDone`, `whenCompleted`, and `whenFailed` (listed in table 6.8).

TIP You can create multiple instances of `NotifyBuilder` if you want to be notified of different conditions. The `NotifyBuilder` also supports using binary operations (and, or, not) to stack together multiple conditions.

The source code for the book contains some example of using `NotifyBuilder` in the chapter6/notify directory. You can run them using the following Maven goal:

```
mvn test -Dtest=NotifyTest
```

We encourage you to take a look at this source code and also the online documentation.

That's it for testing without mocks, and that marks the end of this chapter.

6.5   Summary and best practices

Testing is a challenge for every project. It's generally considered bad practice to only do testing at the end of a project, so testing often begins when development starts and continues through the remainder of the project lifecycle.

Testing isn't something you only do once, either. Testing is involved in most phases in a project. You should do unit testing while you develop the application. And you should also implement integration testing to ensure that the different components and systems work together. You also have the challenge of ensuring you have the right environments for testing.

Camel can't eliminate these challenges, but it does provide a great Test Kit that makes writing tests with Camel applications easier and less time consuming. We looked at this Test Kit, and we also looked at how to externalize dynamic parts using property place-holders, so you can reuse and test the same test cases in different environments.

We also reviewed how you can simulate real components using mocks in the earlier phases of a project, allowing you to test against systems you may not currently have access to. In chapter 5 you learned about error handling, and in this chapter you saw how you can use the Camel Test Kit to test error handling by simulating errors.

We reviewed techniques for integration testing that don't involve using mocks. Doing integration testing, using live components and systems, is often harder than unit testing, where mocks are a real advantage. In integration testing, mocks aren't available to use, and you have to use other techniques such as setting up a notification scheme that can notify you when certain messages have been processed. This allows you to inspect the various systems to see whether the messages were processed as expected (such as by peeking into a JMS queue or looking at a database table).

Here are a few best practices to take away from the chapter:

- *Use unit tests.* Use the Camel Test Kit from the beginning, and write unit tests in your projects.
- *Use the Mock component.* The Mock component is a powerful component for unit testing. Use it rigorously in your unit tests.
- *Test error handling.* Integration is difficult, and unexpected errors can occur. Use the techniques you've learned in this chapter to simulate errors and test that your application is capable of dealing with these failures.
- *Use integration tests.* Build and use integration tests to test that your application works when integrated with real and live systems.

The next chapter will cover the use of components with Camel. You've already used components, such as the file and SEDA components. But there is much more to components, so we've devoted an entire chapter to cover them in detail.

Understanding
components

This chapter covers

- An overview of Camel components
- Working with files and databases
- Messaging with JMS
- Web services using Apache CXF
- Networking with Apache MINA
- In-memory messaging
- Automating tasks with the Quartz and Timer components

So far, we've only touched on a handful of ways that Camel can communicate with external applications, and we haven't gone into much detail on most components. It's time to take your use of the components you've already seen to the next level, and to introduce new components that will enable your Camel applications to communicate with the outside world.

First, we'll discuss exactly what it means to be a component in Camel. We'll also see how components are added to Camel. Then, although we can't describe every component in Camel—that would at least triple the length of this book—we'll look at the most commonly used components.

Table 7.1 lists the components we'll cover in this chapter and lists the URLs for their official documentation.

Table 7.1   Components discussed in this chapter

Component function	Component	Camel documentation reference
File I/O	File	http://camel.apache.org/file2.html
	FTP	http://camel.apache.org/ftp2.html
Asynchronous messaging	JMS	http://camel.apache.org/jms.html
Using web services	CXF	http://camel.apache.org/cxf.html
Networking	MINA	http://camel.apache.org/mina.html
Working with databases	JDBC	http://camel.apache.org/jdbc.html
	JPA	http://camel.apache.org/jpa.html
In-memory messaging	Direct	http://camel.apache.org/direct.html
	SEDA	http://camel.apache.org/seda.html
	VM	http://camel.apache.org/vm.html
Automating tasks	Timer	http://camel.apache.org/timer.html
	Quartz	http://camel.apache.org/quartz.html

Let's start off with an overview of Camel components.

7.1   Overview of Camel components

Components are the primary extension point in Camel. Over the years since Camel's inception, the list of components has really grown. As of version 2.5.0, Camel ships with more than 80 components, and there are dozens more available separately from other community sites.[1] These components allow you to bridge to many different APIs, protocols, data formats, and so on. Camel saves you from having to code these integrations yourself, thus it achieves its primary goal of making integration easier.

What does a Camel component look like? Well, if you think of Camel routes as highways, components are roughly analogous to on and off ramps. A message traveling down a route will need to take an off ramp to get to another route or external service. If the message is headed for another route, it will need to take an on ramp to get onto that route.

---

[1]   See appendix D for information on some of these community sites.

Figure 7.1 A component creates endpoints and may use the `CamelContext`'s facilities to accomplish this.

From an API point of view, a Camel component is simple, consisting of a class implementing the `Component` interface, shown here:

```
public interface Component {
    Endpoint createEndpoint(String uri) throws Exception;
    CamelContext getCamelContext();
    void setCamelContext(CamelContext context);
}
```

The main responsibility of a component is to be a factory for endpoints. To do this, a component also holds on to a reference of the `CamelContext`. The `CamelContext` provides access to Camel's common facilities, like the registry, class loader, and type converters. This relationship is shown in figure 7.1.

There are two main ways in which components are added to a Camel runtime: by manually adding them to the `CamelContext` and through autodiscovery.

7.1.1 *Manually adding components*

You've seen the manual addition of a component already. In chapter 2, you had to add a configured JMS component to the `CamelContext` to utilize a `Connection-Factory`. This was done using the `addComponent` method of the `CamelContext` interface, as follows:

```
CamelContext context = new DefaultCamelContext();
context.addComponent("jms",
    JmsComponent.jmsComponentAutoAcknowledge(connectionFactory));
```

In this example, you add a component created by the `JmsComponent.jmsComponent-AutoAcknowledge` method and assign it a name of "jms". This component can be selected in a URI by using the "jms" scheme.

7.1.2 *Autodiscovering components*

The other way components can be added to Camel is through autodiscovery. The autodiscovery process is illustrated in figure 7.2.

Autodiscovery is the way the components that ship with Camel are registered. In order to discover new components, Camel looks in the META-INF/services/org/apache/camel/component directory on the classpath for files. Files in this directory determine what the name of a component is and what the fully qualified class name is.

As an example, let's look at the Bean component. It has a file named "bean" in the META-INF/services/org/apache/camel/component directory that contains a single line:

```
class=org.apache.camel.component.bean.BeanComponent
```

This class property tells Camel to load up the org.apache.camel.component.bean.BeanComponent class as a new component, and the filename gives the component the name of "bean".

TIP We'll discuss how to create your own Camel component in section 11.3 in chapter 11.

Most of the components in Camel are in separate Java modules from the camel-core module, because they usually depend on third-party dependencies that would bloat the core. For example, the Atom component depends on Apache Abdera to communicate over Atom. We wouldn't want to make every Camel application depend on Abdera, so the Atom component is included in a separate camel-atom module.

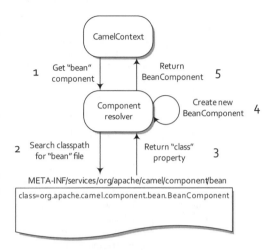

Figure 7.2   To autodiscover a component named "bean", the component resolver searches for a file named "bean" in a specific directory on the classpath. This file specifies that the component class that will be created is BeanComponent.

The camel-core module has 13 useful components built in, though. These are listed in table 7.2.

Table 7.2   Components in the camel-core module

Component	Description	Camel documentation reference
Bean	Invokes a Java bean in the registry. You saw this used extensively in chapter 4.	http://camel.apache.org/bean.html
Browse	Allows you to browse the list of exchanges that passed through a browse endpoint. This can be useful for testing, visualization tools, or debugging.	http://camel.apache.org/browse.html
DataSet	Allows you to create large numbers of messages for soak or load testing.	http://camel.apache.org/dataset.html
Direct	Allows you to synchronously call another endpoint with little overhead. We'll look at this component in section 7.7.1.	http://camel.apache.org/direct.html
File	Reads or writes to files. We'll discuss this component in section 7.2.	http://camel.apache.org/file2.html
Language	Executes a script against the incoming exchange using one of the languages supported by Camel.	http://camel.apache.org/language-component.html
Log	Logs messages to a number of different logging providers.	http://camel.apache.org/log.html

Table 7.2   Components in the camel-core module *(continued)*

Component	Description	Camel documentation reference
Mock	Tests that messages flow through a route as expected. You saw the Mock component in action in chapter 6.	http://camel.apache.org/mock.html
Properties	Allows you to use property placeholders in endpoint URIs. We talked about this in chapter 6.	http://camel.apache.org/properties.html
Ref	Looks up endpoints in the registry.	http://camel.apache.org/ref.html
SEDA	Allows you to asynchronously call another endpoint in the same `CamelContext`. We'll look at this component in section 7.7.2.	http://camel.apache.org/seda.html
Timer	Sends out messages at regular intervals. You'll learn more about the Timer component and a more powerful scheduling endpoint based on Quartz in section 7.8 of this chapter.	http://camel.apache.org/timer.html
VM	Allows you to asynchronously call another endpoint in the same JVM. We'll discuss this component in section 7.7.2.	http://camel.apache.org/vm.html

Now let's look at each component in detail. We'll start by looking at the File component.

7.2   *Working with files (File and FTP components)*

It seems that in integration projects, you always end up needing to interface with a filesystem somewhere. You may find this strange, as new systems often provide nice web services and other remoting APIs to serve as integration points. The problem is that in integration, we often have to deal with older legacy systems, and file-based integrations are common.

For example, you might need to read a file that was written by another application—it could be sending a command, an order to be processed, data to be logged, or anything else. This kind of information exchange, illustrated in figure 7.3, is called a *file transfer* in EIP terms.

Another reason why file-based integrations are so common is that they're easy to understand. Even novice computer users know something about filesystems.

Even though they're easy to understand, file-based integrations are difficult to get right. Developers commonly have to battle with complex IO APIs, platform-specific filesystem issues, concurrent access, and the like.

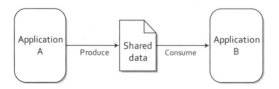

Figure 7.3   A file transfer between two applications is a common way to integrate with legacy systems.

Camel has extensive support for interacting with filesystems. In this section, we'll look at how to use the File component to read files from and write them to the local filesystem. We'll also cover some advanced options for file processing and discuss how to access remote files with the FTP component.

7.2.1 *Reading and writing files with the File component*

As you saw before, the File component is configured through URI options. Some common options are shown in table 7.3; for a complete listing, see the online documentation (http://camel.apache.org/file2.html).

Table 7.3 Common URI options used to configure the File component

Option	Default value	Description
delay	500	Specifies the number of milliseconds between polls of the directory.
recursive	false	Specifies whether or not to recursively process files in all subdirectories of this directory.
noop	false	Specifies file-moving behavior. By default, Camel will move files to the .camel directory after processing them. To stop this behavior and keep the original files in place, set the noop option to true.
fileName	null	Uses an expression to set the filename used. For consumers, this acts as a filename filter; in producers, it's used to set the name of the file being written.
fileExist	Override	Specifies what a file producer will do if the same filename already exists. Valid options are Override, Append, Fail, and Ignore. Override will cause the file to be replaced. Append adds content to the file. Fail causes an exception to be thrown. If Ignore is set, an exception won't be thrown and the file won't be written.
delete	false	Specifies whether Camel will delete the file after processing. By default, Camel will not delete the file.
move	.camel	Specifies the directory to which Camel moves files after it's done processing them.
include	null	Specifies a regular expression. Camel will process only those files that match this expression.
exclude	null	Specifies a regular expression. Camel will exclude files based on this expression.

Let's first see how Camel can be used to read files.

READING FILES

As you've seen in previous chapters, reading files with Camel is pretty straightforward. Here's a simple example:

```
public void configure() {
    from("file:data/inbox?noop=true").to("stream:out");
}
```

This route will read files from the data/inbox directory and print the contents of each to the console. The printing is done by sending the message to the System.out stream, accessible by using the Stream component. As stated in table 7.3, the noop flag tells Camel to leave the original files as is. This is a convenience option for testing, because it means that you can run the route many times without having to repopulate a directory of test files.

To run this yourself, change to the chapter7/file directory in the book's source code, and run this command:

```
mvn compile exec:java -Dexec.mainClass=camelinaction.FilePrinter
```

What if you removed the noop flag and changed the route to the following:

```
public void configure() {
    from("file:data/inbox").to("stream:out");
}
```

This would use Camel's default behavior, which is to move the consumed files to a special .camel directory (though the directory can be changed with the move option); the files are moved after the routing has completed. This behavior was designed so that files would not be processed over and over, but it also keeps the original files around in case something goes wrong. If you don't mind losing the original files, you can use the delete option listed in table 7.2.

By default, Camel will also lock any files that are being processed. The locks are released after routing is complete.

Both of the two preceding routes will consume any file not beginning with a period, so they will ignore files like .camel, .m2, and so on. You can customize which files are included by using the include and exclude options.

WRITING FILES

You just saw how to read files created by other applications or users. Now let's see how Camel can be used to write files. Here's a simple example:

```
public void configure() {
    from("stream:in?promptMessage=Enter something:").to("file:data/outbox");
}
```

This example uses the Stream component to accept input from the console. The stream:in URI will instruct Camel to read any input from System.in on the console and create a message from that. The promptMessage option displays a prompt, so you know when to enter text. The file:data/outbox URI instructs Camel to write out the message body to the data/outbox directory.

To see what happens firsthand, you can try the example by changing to the chapter7/file directory in the book's source code and executing the following command:

```
mvn compile exec:java -Dexec.mainClass=camelinaction.FileSaver
```

When this runs, you'll see an "Enter something:" prompt. Enter some text into the console, and press Enter, like this:

```
INFO: Apache Camel 2.5.0 (CamelContext: camel-1) started
Enter something:Hello
```

This text (in this case, "Hello") will be read in by the Stream component and added as the body of a new message. This message's body (the text you entered) will then be written out to a file in the data/outbox directory (which will be created if it doesn't exist).

If you run a directory listing on the data/outbox directory now, you'll see a single file that has a rather strange name:

```
f6a3a5ee-536b-43c3-8307-1b96e1ae7778
```

Because you did not specify a filename to use, Camel chose a unique filename based on the message ID.

To set the filename that should be used, you can add a `fileName` option to your URI. For example, you could change the route so it looks like this:

```
public void configure() {
    from("stream:in?promptMessage=Enter something:")
        .to("file:data/outbox?fileName=prompt.txt");
}
```

Now, any text entered into the console will be saved into the prompt.txt file in the data/outbox directory.

Camel will by default overwrite prompt.txt, so you now have a problem with this route. If text is frequently entered into the console, you may want new files created each time, so they don't overwrite the old ones. To implement this in Camel, you can use an expression for the filename. You can use the Simple expression language to put the current time and date information into your filename:

```
public void configure() {
    from("stream:in?promptMessage=Enter something:")
        .to("file:data/outbox?fileName=${date:now:yyyyMMdd-hh:mm:ss}.txt");
}
```

The `date:now` expression returns the current date, and you can also use any formatting options permitted by `java.text.SimpleDataFormat`.

Now if you enter text into the console at 2:00 p.m. on January 31, 2010, the file in the data/outbox directory will be named something like this:

```
20100131-02:00:53.txt
```

The simple techniques for reading from and writing to files discussed here will be adequate for most of the cases you'll encounter in the real world. For the trickier cases, there are a plethora of configuration possibilities listed in the online documentation.

We've started slowly with the File component, to get you comfortable with using components in Camel. Next we'll look at the FTP component, which builds on the File component but introduces messaging across a network. After that, we'll be getting into more complex topics.

7.2.2   *Accessing remote files with the FTP component*

Probably the most common way to access remote files is by using FTP, and Camel supports three flavors of FTP:

- Plain FTP mode transfer
- SFTP for secure transfer
- FTPS (FTP Secure) for transfer with the Transport Layer Security (TLS) and Secure Sockets Layer (SSL) cryptographic protocols enabled

The FTP component inherits all the features and options of the File component, and it adds a few more options, as shown in table 7.4. For a complete listing of options for the FTP component, see the online documentation (http://camel.apache.org/ftp2.html).

Table 7.4   Common URI options used to configure the FTP component

Option	Default value	Description
username	null	Provides a username to the remote host for authentication. If no username is provided, anonymous login is attempted. You can also specify the username by prefixing username@ to the hostname in the URI.
password	null	Provides a password to the remote host to authenticate the user. You can also specify the password by prefixing the hostname in the URI with username:password@.
binary	false	Specifies the transfer mode. By default, Camel will transfer in ASCII mode; set this option to true to enable binary transfer.
disconnect	false	Specifies whether Camel will disconnect from the remote host right after use. The default is to remain connected.
maximumReconnectAttempts	3	Specifies the maximum number of attempts Camel will make to connect to the remote host. If all these attempts are unsuccessful, Camel will throw an exception. A value of 0 disables this feature.
reconnectDelay	1000	Specifies the delay in milliseconds between reconnection attempts.

Because the FTP component isn't part of the camel-core module, you need to add an additional dependency to your project. If you use Maven, you just have to add the following dependency to your POM:

```
<dependency>
  <groupId>org.apache.camel</groupId>
  <artifactId>camel-ftp</artifactId>
  <version>2.5.0</version>
</dependency>
```

To demonstrate accessing remotes files, let's use the Stream component as in the previous section to interactively generate and send files over FTP. A route that accepts text on the console and then sends it over FTP would look like this:

```
<route>
  <from uri="stream:in?promptMessage=Enter something:" />
  <to uri="ftp://rider:secret@localhost:21000/data/outbox"/>
</route>
```

This is a Spring-based route—Spring makes it easy to hook start and stop methods to an embedded FTP server. This FTP endpoint URI specifies that Camel should send the message to an FTP server on the `localhost` listening on port `21000`, using `rider` as the username and `secret` as the password. It also specifies that messages are to be stored in the data/outbox directory of the FTP server.

To run this example for yourself, change to the chapter7/ftp directory and run this command:

```
mvn camel:run
```

After Camel has started, you'll need to enter something into the console:

```
INFO  Apache Camel 2.5.0 (CamelContext: camelContext) started
Enter something:Hello
```

The example will keep running until you press Ctrl-C.

You can now check to see if the message made it into the FTP server. The FTP server's root directory was set up to be the current directory of the application, so you can check data/outbox for a message:

```
cat data/outbox/8ff0787f-1eab-4d11-9a60-5c3f5a05e498
Hello
```

As you can see, using the FTP component is similar to using the File component. Now that you know how to do the most basic of integrations with files and FTP, let's move on to more advanced topics, like JMS and web services.

7.3 *Asynchronous messaging (JMS component)*

JMS messaging is an incredibly useful integration technology. It promotes loose coupling in application design, has built-in support for reliable messaging, and is by nature asynchronous. As you saw in chapter 2, when we looked at JMS, it's also easy to use from Camel. In this section, we'll expand on what we covered in chapter 2 by going over some of the more commonly used configurations of the JMS component.

Camel doesn't ship with a JMS provider; you need to configure it to use a specific JMS provider by passing in a `ConnectionFactory` instance. For example, to connect to an Apache ActiveMQ broker listening on port 61616 of the local host, you could configure the JMS component like this:

```
<bean id="jms" class="org.apache.camel.component.jms.JmsComponent">
  <property name="connectionFactory">
    <bean class="org.apache.activemq.ActiveMQConnectionFactory">
```

```
        <property name="brokerURL" value="tcp://localhost:61616" />
      </bean>
    </property>
</bean>
```

The tcp://localhost:61616 URI passed in to the ConnectionFactory is JMS provider-specific. In this example, you're using the ActiveMQConnectionFactory so the URI is parsed by ActiveMQ. The URI tells ActiveMQ to connect to a broker using TCP on port 61616 of the local host.

If you wanted to connect to a broker over some other protocol, ActiveMQ supports connections over VM, SSL, UDP, multicast, and so on. Throughout this section, we'll be demonstrating JMS concepts using ActiveMQ as the JMS provider, but any provider could have been used here.

The ActiveMQ component

By default, a JMS ConnectionFactory doesn't pool connections to the broker, so it will spin up new connections for every message. The way to avoid this is to use connection factories that use connection pooling.

For convenience to Camel users, ActiveMQ ships with the ActiveMQ component, which configures connection pooling automatically for improved performance. The ActiveMQ component is used as follows:

```
<bean id="activemq"
    class="org.apache.activemq.camel.component.ActiveMQComponent">
    <property name="brokerURL" value="tcp://localhost:61616" />
</bean>
```

When using this component, you'll also need to depend on the activemq-camel module from ActiveMQ:

```
<dependency>
    <groupId>org.apache.activemq</groupId>
    <artifactId>activemq-camel</artifactId>
    <version>5.4.1</version>
</dependency>
```

This module contains the ActiveMQ component and type converters for ActiveMQ data types.

Camel's JMS component has a daunting list of configuration options—over 60 to date. Many of these will only be seen in very specific JMS usage scenarios. The common ones are listed in table 7.5.

To use the JMS component in your project, you'll need to include the camel-jms module on your classpath as well as any JMS provider JARs. If you're using Maven, the JMS component can be added with the following dependency:

```
<dependency>
    <groupId>org.apache.camel</groupId>
```

```
    <artifactId>camel-jms</artifactId>
    <version>2.5.0</version>
</dependency>
```

Table 7.5 Common URI options used to configure the JMS component

Option	Default value	Description
autoStartup	true	Controls whether consumers start listening right after creation. If set to `false`, you'll need to invoke the `start()` method on the consumer manually at a later time.
clientId	null	Sets the JMS client ID, which must be unique among all connections to the JMS broker. The client ID set in the `ConnectionFactory` overrides this one if set.
concurrentConsumers	1	Sets the number of consumer threads to use. It's a good idea to increase this for high-volume queues, but it's not advisable to use more than one concurrent consumer for JMS topics, because this will result in multiple copies of the same message.
disableReplyTo	false	Specifies whether Camel should ignore the `JMSReplyTo` header in any messages or not. Set this if you don't want Camel to send a reply back to the destination specified in the `JMSReplyTo` header.
durableSubscriptionName	null	Specifies the name of the durable topic subscription. If `clientId` is also set, the topic subscription is made durable automatically.
maxConcurrentConsumers	1	Sets the maximum number of consumer threads to use. If this value is higher than `concurrentConsumers`, new consumers are started dynamically as load demands. If load drops down, these extra consumers will be freed and the number of consumers will be equal to `concurrentConsumers` again. Increasing this value isn't advisable when using topics.
replyTo	null	Sets the destination that the reply is sent to. This overrides the `JMSReplyTo` header in the message. By setting this, Camel will use a fixed reply queue. By default, Camel will use a temporary reply queue.
requestTimeout	20000	Specifies the time in milliseconds before Camel will time-out sending a message.
selector	null	Sets the JMS message selector expression. Only messages passing this predicate will be consumed.
timeToLive	null	When sending messages, sets the amount of time the message should live. After this time expires, the JMS provider may discard the message.
transacted	false	Enables transacted sending and receiving of messages in `InOnly` mode.

The best way to show that Camel is a great tool for JMS messaging is with an example. Let's look at how to send and receive messages over JMS.

7.3.1 Sending and receiving messages

In chapter 2, you saw how orders are processed at Rider Auto Parts. It started out as a step-by-step process: they were first sent to accounting to validate the customer standing and then to production for manufacture. This process was improved by sending orders to accounting and production at the same time, cutting out the delay involved when production waited for the OK from accounting. A multicast EIP was used to implement this scenario.

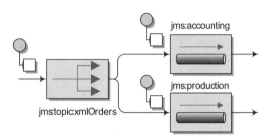

Figure 7.4 illustrates another possible solution, which is to use a JMS topic following a publish-subscribe model. In that model, listeners such as accounting and production could subscribe to the topic, and new orders would be published to the topic. In this way, both accounting and production would receive a copy of the order message.

Figure 7.4   Orders are published to the xmlOrders topic, and the two subscribers (the accounting and production queues) get a copy of the order.

To implement this in Camel, you'd set up two consumers, which means there will be two routes needed:

```
from("jms:topic:xmlOrders").to("jms:accounting");
from("jms:topic:xmlOrders").to("jms:production");
```

When a message is sent (published) to the xmlOrders topic, both the accounting and production queues will receive a copy.

As you saw in chapter 2, an incoming order could originate from another route (or set of routes), like one that receives orders via a file, as shown in listing 7.1.

Listing 7.1   Topics allow multiple receivers to get a copy of the message

```
from("file:src/data?noop=true").to("jms:incomingOrders");

from("jms:incomingOrders")
    .choice()
    .when(header("CamelFileName").endsWith(".xml"))         XML orders
        .to("jms:topic:xmlOrders")                          are routed to
    .when(header("CamelFileName").regex("^.*(csv|csl)$"))   xmlOrders topic
        .to("jms:topic:csvOrders");

from("jms:topic:xmlOrders").to("jms:accounting");    Both listening
from("jms:topic:xmlOrders").to("jms:production");    queues get copies
```

To run this example, go to the chapter7/jms directory in the book's source, and run this command:

```
mvn clean compile camel:run
```

This will output the following on the command line:

```
Accounting received order: message1.xml
Production received order: message1.xml
```

Why did you get this output? Well, you had a single order file named message1.xml, and it was published to the xmlOrders topic. Both the accounting and production queues were subscribed to the topic, so each received a copy. Testing routes consumed the messages on those queues and output the messages.

Messages can also be sent "by hand" to a JMS destination using a `ProducerTemplate`. A template class, in general, is a utility class that simplifies access to an API; in this case, the `Producer` interface. For example, to send an order to the topic using a `ProducerTemplate`, you could use the following snippet:

```
ProducerTemplate template = camelContext.createProducerTemplate();
template.sendBody("jms:topic:xmlOrders", "<?xml ...");
```

This is a useful feature for getting direct access to any endpoint in Camel. For more on the `ProducerTemplate`, see appendix C.

All of the JMS examples so far have been one-way only. Let's look at how you can deliver a reply to the sent message.

7.3.2 Request-reply messaging

JMS messaging with Camel (and in general) is asynchronous by default. Messages are sent to a destination, and the client doesn't wait for a reply. But there are times when it's useful to be able to wait and get a reply after sending to a destination. One obvious application is when the JMS destination is a frontend to a service—in this case, a client sending to the destination would be expecting a reply from the service.

JMS supports this type of messaging by providing a `JMSReplyTo` header, so that the receiver knows where to send the reply, and a `JMSCorrelationID`, used to match replies to requests if there are multiple replies awaiting. This flow of messages is illustrated in figure 7.5.

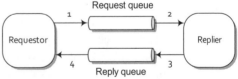

Camel takes care of this style of messaging, so you don't have to create special reply queues, correlate reply messages, and the like. By changing the message exchange pattern (MEP) to `InOut`, Camel will enable request-reply mode for JMS.

Figure 7.5 In request-reply messaging, a requestor sends a message to a request queue and then waits for a reply in the reply queue. The replier waits for a new message in the request queue, inspects the `JMSReplyTo` address, and then sends a reply back to that destination.

To demonstrate, let's take a look at an order validation service within Rider Auto Parts' backend systems that checks orders against the company database to make sure the parts listed are actual products. This service is exposed via a queue named validate. The route exposing this service over JMS could be as simple as this:

```
from("jms:validate").bean(ValidatorBean.class);
```

When calling this service, you just need to tell Camel to use request-reply messaging by setting the MEP to InOut. You can use the exchangePattern option to set this as follows:

```
from("jms:incomingOrders").to("jms:validate?exchangePattern=InOut")...
```

You can also specify the MEP using the inOut DSL method:

```
from("jms:incomingOrders").inOut().to("jms:validate")...
```

With the inOut method, you can even pass in an endpoint URI as an argument, which shortens your route:

```
from("jms:incomingOrders").inOut("jms:validate")...
```

By specifying an InOut MEP, Camel will send the message to the validate queue and wait for a reply on a temporary queue that it creates automatically. When the Valida-torBean returns a result that message is propagated back to the temporary reply queue, and the route continues on from there.

Rather than using temporary queues, you can also explicitly specify a reply queue. This can be done by setting the JMSReplyTo header on the message or by using the replyTo URI option described in table 7.5.

A handy way of calling an endpoint that can return a response is by using the request methods of the ProducerTemplate. For example, you can send a message into the incomingOrders queue and get a response back with the following call:

```
Object result = template.requestBody("jms:incomingOrders",
    "<order name=\"motor\" amount=\"1\" customer=\"honda\"/>");
```

This will return the result of the ValidatorBean.

To try this out for yourself, go to the chapter7/jms directory in the book's source, and run this command:

```
mvn test -Dtest=RequestReplyJmsTest
```

The command will run a unit test demonstrating request-reply messaging as we've discussed in this section.

In the JMS examples we've looked at so far, several data mappings have been happening behind the scenes—mappings that are necessary to conform to the JMS specification. Camel could be transporting any type of data, so that data needs to be converted to a type that JMS supports. We'll look into this next.

7.3.3 *Message mappings*

Camel hides a lot of the details when doing JMS messaging, so you don't have to worry about them. But one detail you should be aware of is that Camel maps both bodies and headers from the arbitrary types and names allowed in Camel to JMS-specific types.

BODY MAPPING

Although Camel poses no restrictions on what a message's body contains, JMS specifies different message types based on what the body type is. Figure 7.6 shows the five concrete JMS message implementations.

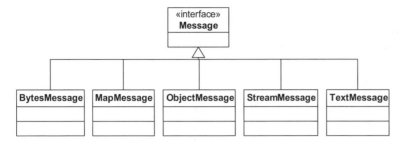

Figure 7.6
The `javax.`
`jms.Message`
interface has five
implementations,
each of which is
built for a different
body type.

The conversion to one of these five JMS message types occurs when the exchange reaches a JMS producer; said another way, it happens when the exchange reaches a route node like this:

```
to("jms:jmsDestinationName")
```

At this point, Camel will examine the body type and determine which JMS message to create. This newly created JMS message is then sent to the JMS destination specified.

Table 7.6 shows what body types are mapped to JMS messages.

Table 7.6   When sending messages to a JMS destination, Camel body types are mapped to specific JMS message types.

Camel body type	JMS message type
`String, org.w3c.dom.Node`	`TextMessage`
`byte[], java.io.File, java.io.Reader,` `java.io.InputStream, java.nio.ByteBuffer`	`BytesMessage`
`java.util.Map`	`MapMessage`
`java.io.Serializable`	`ObjectMessage`

Another conversion happens when consuming a message from a JMS destination. Table 7.7 shows the mappings in this case.

JMS message type	Camel body type
`TextMessage`	`String`
`BytesMessage`	`byte[]`
`MapMessage`	`java.util.Map`
`ObjectMessage`	`Object`
`StreamMessage`	No mapping occurs

Table 7.7   When receiving messages from a JMS destination, JMS message types are mapped to Camel body types

Although this automatic message mapping allows you to utilize Camel's transformation and mediation abilities fully, you may sometimes need to keep the JMS message intact. An obvious reason would be to increase performance; not mapping every message means it will take less time for each message to be processed. Another reason could be that you're storing an object type that doesn't exist on Camel's classpath. In this case, if Camel tried to deserialize it, it would fail when finding the class.

> **TIP** You can also implement your own custom Spring `org.springframework.jms.support.converter.MessageConverter` by using the `messageConverter` option.

To disable message mapping for body types, set the `mapJmsMessage` URI option to `false`.

HEADER MAPPING

Headers in JMS are even more restrictive than body types. In Camel, a header can be named anything that will fit in a Java `String` and its value can be any Java object. This presents a few problems when sending to and receiving from JMS destinations.

These are the restrictions in JMS:

- Header names that start with "JMS" are reserved; you can't use these header names.
- Header names must be valid Java identifiers.
- Header values can be any primitive type and their corresponding object types. These include `boolean`, `byte`, `short`, `int`, `long`, `float`, and `double`. Valid object types include `Boolean`, `Byte`, `Short`, `Integer`, `Long`, `Float`, `Double`, and `String`.

To handle these restrictions, Camel does a number of things. First, any headers that you set starting with "JMS" will be dropped before sending to a JMS destination. Camel also attempts to convert the header names to be JMS-compliant. Any period (.) characters are replaced by "_DOT_" and any hyphens (-) are replaced with "_HYPHEN_". For example, a header named `org.apache.camel.Test-Header` would be converted to `org_DOT_apache_DOT_camel_DOT_Test_HYPHEN_Header` before being sent to a JMS destination. If this message is consumed by a Camel route at some point down the line, the header name will be converted back.

To conform to the JMS specification, Camel will drop any header that has a value not listed in the list of primitives or their corresponding object types. Camel also allows `CharSequence`, `Date`, `BigDecimal`, and `BigInteger` header values, all of which are converted to their `String` representations to conform to the JMS specification.

You should now have a good grasp of what Camel can do for your JMS messaging applications.

JMS messaging applications are typically used within an organization—users outside the corporate firewall rarely send JMS messages to internal systems. For messaging with the external world, web services can be used. We'll look at how Camel uses Apache CXF to access and serve up web services next.

7.4   *Web services (CXF component)*

You would be hard pressed to find any modern enterprise project that doesn't use web services of some sort. They're an extremely useful integration technology for distributed applications. Web services are often associated with service-oriented architecture (SOA), where each service is defined as a web service.

You can think of a web service as an API on the network. The API itself is defined using the Web Services Description Language (WSDL), specifying what operations you can call on a web service and what the input and output types are, among other things. Messages are typically XML, formatted to comply with the Simple Object Access Protocol (SOAP) schema. In addition, these messages are typically sent over HTTP. As illustrated in figure 7.7, web services allow you to write Java code and make that Java code callable over the Internet, which is pretty neat!

For accessing and publishing web services, Camel uses Apache CXF (http://cxf.apache.org). CXF is a popular web services framework that supports many web services standards, most of which we won't discuss here. We'll mainly be focusing on developing web services using the Java API for XML Web Services (JAX-WS) specification. JAX-WS defines annotations that allow you to tell a tool like CXF how your POJO should be represented on the web.

We'll be covering two types of web services development with CXF in this section:

- *Contract-first development*—Recall that WSDLs define what operations and types a web service provides. This is often referred to as a web services contract, and in order to communicate with a web service, you must satisfy the contract. Contract-first development means that you start out by writing a WSDL file (either by hand or with the help of tooling), and then generating stub Java class implementations from the WSDL file by using a tool like CXF.
- *Code-first development*—The other way to develop web services is by starting out with a Java class and then letting the web service framework handle the job of generating a WSDL contract for you. This is by far the easiest mode of development, but it also means that the tool (CXF in this case) is in control of what the contract will be. When you want to fine-tune your WSDL file, it may be better to go the contract-first route.

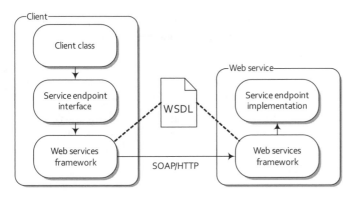

Figure 7.7   A client invokes a remote web service over HTTP. To the client, it looks as if it's calling a Java method on the service endpoint interface (SEI). Under the hood, this method invocation passes through the web services framework, across a network, and finally calls into the service endpoint implementation on the remote server.

To show these concepts in action, let's going back to Rider Auto Parts, where they need a new piece of functionality implemented. In chapter 2 (figure 2.2) you saw how customers could place orders in two ways:

- Uploading the order file to an FTP server
- Submitting the order from the Rider Auto Parts web store via HTTP

What we didn't say then was that this HTTP link to the backend order processing systems needed to be a web service.

Before you jump into creating this web service, let's take a moment to go over how CXF can be configured within Camel.

7.4.1 Configuring CXF

There are two main ways to configure a CXF component URI: by referencing a bean containing the configuration or by configuring it within the URI.

CONFIGURING USING URI OPTIONS

When configuring CXF using only URI options, a CXF endpoint URI looks like this,

```
cxf://anAddress[?options]
```

where `anAddress` is a URL like http://rider.com:9999/order, and `options` are appended as usual from the possible options in table 7.8.

These options can also be used to configure a reusable CXF endpoint bean in Spring.

Table 7.8   Common URI options used to configure the CXF component

Option	Default value	Description
`wsdlURL`	Retrieved from the end-point address	Specifies the location of the WSDL contract file.
`serviceClass`	`null`	Specifies the name of the service endpoint interface (SEI). Typically this interface will have JAX-WS annotations. The SEI is required if the CXF data format mode is POJO. If you already have an instance of a concrete class, you can reference it using the #beanName style.
`serviceName`	Obtained from the WSDL	Specifies the service to use. The format is a qualified name (QName) that has a namespace and name like `{http://order.camelinaction}OrderEndpointService`.
		Note that if there is only one service in a WSDL, Camel will choose this as the default service. If there is more than one service defined, you need to set the `serviceName` property.
`portName`	Obtained from the WSDL	Specifies the port to use. The format is a qualified name (QName) that has a namespace and name like `{http://order.camelinaction}OrderService`.

Table 7.8 Common URI options used to configure the CXF component *(continued)*

Option	Default value	Description
		Note that if there is only one port in a WSDL, Camel will choose this as the default port. If there is more than one port defined per service, you need to set the `portName` property.
`dataFormat`	`POJO`	Sets the data format type that CXF uses for its messages. The possible values are `POJO`, `PAYLOAD`, and `MESSAGE`. We'll only be covering `POJO` mode in this chapter; you can find more information on the other two modes on the CXF component page in the Camel online documentation: http://camel.apache.org/cxf.html.

CONFIGURING USING A CXF ENDPOINT BEAN

When using a CXF endpoint bean in Spring, you have much more power than by configuring CXF via URI options. In the CXF endpoint bean, you can configure things like CXF interceptors, JAX-WS handlers, and the CXF bus. The URI for configuring the CXF component looks like this:

```
cxf:bean:beanName
```

The beanName name specifies the ID of the CXF endpoint bean defined in your Spring XML file. This bean supports the URI options listed in table 7.8 as well as an `address` attribute that tells Camel what address to use for the web service.

Listing 7.2 shows how a CXF endpoint bean is configured.

Listing 7.2 The CXF endpoint bean format

```xml
<beans xmlns="http://www.springframework.org/schema/beans"
       xmlns:xsi="http://www.w3.org/2001/XMLSchema-instance"
       xmlns:cxf="http://camel.apache.org/schema/cxf"
       xsi:schemaLocation="
         http://www.springframework.org/schema/beans
         http://www.springframework.org/schema/beans/spring-beans-3.0.xsd
         http://camel.apache.org/schema/cxf
         http://camel.apache.org/schema/cxf/camel-cxf.xsd">

  <import resource="classpath:META-INF/cxf/cxf.xml"/>
  <import resource="classpath:META-INF/cxf/
    cxf-extension-soap.xml"/>
  <import resource="classpath:META-INF/cxf/
    cxf-extension-http-jetty.xml"/>

  <cxf:cxfEndpoint
    id="orderEndpoint"
    address="http://localhost:9000/order/"
    serviceClass="camelinaction.order.OrderEndpoint"/>
</beans>
```

➥ *Configures CXF to use HTTP transport and SOAP binding*

Sets bean ID, address, and SEI

After configuring an endpoint as shown in listing 7.2, you can use it in a producer or consumer using the following URI:

```
cxf:bean:orderEndpoint
```

There is a notable difference when using producers versus consumers.

PRODUCERS VERSUS CONSUMERS

In the context of a web service, a *producer* in Camel calls a remote web service. This web service could be defined by Camel or by some other web framework.

To invoke a web service in Camel, you use the familiar `to` Java DSL method:

```
...to("cxf:bean:orderEndpoint");
```

Consumers are a little more interesting, as they expose an entire route to the world as a web service. This is a powerful concept. A Camel route could be a complex process, with many branches and processing nodes, but the caller will only see it as a web service with input parameters and a reply.

Say you start out with a route that consists of several steps, like this:

```
from("jms:myQueue").
to("complex step 1").
...
to("complex step N");
```

To expose this route to the web, you can add a CXF endpoint to the beginning:

```
from("cxf:bean:myCXFEndpointBean").
to("complex step 1").
...
to("complex step N");
```

Now, when the web service configured by `myCXFEndpointBean` is called, the whole route will be invoked.

> **TIP** If you're coming from a background in SOA or have used web services before, you may be scratching your head about consumers in Camel. In the web services world, a consumer is typically a client that calls a remote service. In Camel, a consumer is a server, so the definition is reversed!

MAVEN DEPENDENCIES

In order to use the CXF component, you'll have to add some dependencies. First, you need to depend on the camel-cxf module:

```
<dependency>
  <groupId>org.apache.camel</groupId>
  <artifactId>camel-cxf</artifactId>
  <version>2.5.0</version>
</dependency>
```

That will get you most of the way to a usable CXF component, but you also need to add a module for the CXF transport you're using. In most cases, this will be HTTP, so you'll need to add another dependency to your POM:

```
<dependency>
  <groupId>org.apache.cxf</groupId>
  <artifactId>cxf-rt-transports-http-jetty</artifactId>
  <version>2.2.10</version>
</dependency>
```

CXF supports several other transports as well, and you can find more information about them on the CXF website at http://cxf.apache.org/docs/transports.html.

Now that you have a sense of the configuration details, let's take a hands-on look at how to develop web services with Camel.

7.4.2 Using a contract-first approach

In contract-first development, you start by creating a WSDL document and then getting a web service tool to generate the necessary Java code. This process is illustrated in figure 7.8.

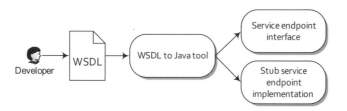

Figure 7.8 In contract-first web service development, you start out by creating a WSDL document and letting a tool generate the required source interfaces and stubs.

Creating the WSDL contract for a particular web service is a non-trivial task. It's often best to think about what methods, types, and parameters you'll need before starting.

In this case, to place an order at Rider Auto Parts with a web service, you need a single method call named order. This method will accept part name, amount, and customer name parameters. When the method is complete, it will return a result code to the client. The web service should be exposed on the server's http://local-host:9000/order address.

The WSDL for this web service is shown in listing 7.3.

Listing 7.3 The WSDL for an order service

```
<wsdl:definitions xmlns:soap="http://schemas.xmlsoap.org/wsdl/soap/"
    xmlns:tns="http://order.camelinaction"
    xmlns:xs="http://www.w3.org/2001/XMLSchema"
    xmlns:http="http://schemas.xmlsoap.org/wsdl/http/"
    xmlns:wsdl="http://schemas.xmlsoap.org/wsdl/"
    targetNamespace="http://order.camelinaction">     ❶ Defines input and
                                                          output parameters
  <wsdl:types>
    <xs:schema targetNamespace="http://order.camelinaction">
      <xs:element type="xs:string" name="partName" />
      <xs:element type="xs:int" name="amount" />
      <xs:element type="xs:string" name="customerName" />
      <xs:element type="xs:string" name="resultCode" />
    </xs:schema>
  </wsdl:types>
                                                       ❷ Defines
  <wsdl:message name="purchaseOrder">                     messages
    <wsdl:part name="partName" element="tns:partName" />
    <wsdl:part name="amount" element="tns:amount"/>
    <wsdl:part name="customerName" element="tns:customerName"/>
  </wsdl:message>
```

```
<wsdl:message name="orderResult">
  <wsdl:part name="resultCode" element="tns:resultCode" />
</wsdl:message>

<wsdl:portType name="OrderEndpoint">                    ⟵┐  ❸ Defines
  <wsdl:operation name="Order">                             interface to call
    <wsdl:input message="tns:purchaseOrder" />
    <wsdl:output message="tns:orderResult" />
  </wsdl:operation>
</wsdl:portType>                                        ❹ Uses SOAP encoding
                                                   ⟵┐    over HTTP transport
<wsdl:binding name="OrderBinding"
  type="tns:OrderEndpoint">
  <soap:binding transport="http://schemas.xmlsoap.org/soap/http" />
  <wsdl:operation name="order">
    <soap:operation
soapAction="http://order.camelinaction/Order" style="document" />
    <wsdl:input>
      <soap:body parts="in" use="literal" />
    </wsdl:input>
    <wsdl:output>
      <soap:body parts="out" use="literal" />
    </wsdl:output>
  </wsdl:operation>
</wsdl:binding>                                         ❺ Exposes service
                                                   ⟵┐    using interface
<wsdl:service name="OrderEndpointService">
  <wsdl:port name="OrderService" binding="tns:OrderBinding">
    <soap:address location="http://localhost:9000/order" />
  </wsdl:port>
</wsdl:service>

</wsdl:definitions>
```

As you can see in listing 7.3, a WSDL contract is quite a mouthful! Writing this kind of document from scratch would be pretty hard to get right. Typically, a good way to start one of these is to use a wizard or GUI tooling. For instance, in Eclipse you can use the File > New > Other > Web Services > WSDL wizard to generate a skeleton WSDL file based on several options. Tweaking this skeleton file is much easier than starting from scratch.

CXF also has command-line tools to help you create a WSDL contract properly. Once you have a portType element defined, you can pass the WSDL fragment through CXF's wsdl2xml tool (http://cxf.apache.org/docs/wsdl-to-xml.html), which will add a binding element for you. When the binding element is defined, the wsdl2service tool (http://cxf.apache.org/docs/wsdl-to-service.html) can then generate a service element for you.

> ### WSDL 1.1 versus 2.0
> If you've used WSDL documents before, you may have picked up on the version of the WSDL specification we used in listing 7.3. We used WSDL version 1.1 because the current version of CXF only supports 1.1. This is also the most common WSDL version you'll see in use. WSDL 2.0 changes things substantially, and to date few web services tools (like CXF) support it.

There are five main elements specified in the WSDL file shown in listing 7.3, and all WSDL files follow this same basic structure:

- `types`—Data types used by the web service
- `message`—Messages used by the web service
- `portType`—Interface name and operation performed by the web service
- `binding`—Transport type and message encoding used by the web service
- `service`—Web service definition, which specifies the binding to use as well as the network address to use

You first define what parameters the web service will be passing around ❶. This configuration is done using the XML schema, which may make it a bit more familiar to you. You specify a name and a type for each parameter.

The next section of listing 7.3 defines the messages used by the web service ❷. These messages allow you to assign parameters to use as input versus output.

You then define the `portType` ❸, which is the interface that you'll be exposing over the web. On this interface, you define a single operation (method) that takes a `purchaseOrder` message as input and returns an `orderResult` message.

The `binding` section ❹ then specifies the use of the HTTP transport for the messages and that the messages should be encoded over the wire using *document literal* style. Document literal means that the SOAP message body will be an XML document. The format of this XML document is specified using the XML schema.

> **NOTE** There are more options to choose from for WSDL binding and encoding. An excellent introduction is available from the IBM developerWorks website: http://www.ibm.com/developerworks/webservices/library/ws-whichwsdl.

Finally, the `service` section ❺ exposes a port using a specific binding on an address. There can be more than one port listed here. In this example, you use the port and binding definitions from before and set the web service address to http://localhost:9000/order.

The next step in contract-first web service development is taking the WSDL and generating Java code that implements it. CXF provides the wsdl2java tool (http://cxf.apache.org/docs/wsdl-to-java.html) to do this for you. Listing 7.4 shows how this tool can be used from a Maven POM file.

Listing 7.4 Using CXF's wsdl2java tool

```
<plugin>
  <groupId>org.apache.cxf</groupId>
  <artifactId>cxf-codegen-plugin</artifactId>
  <version>2.2.10</version>
  <executions>
    <execution>
      <id>generate-sources</id>
      <phase>generate-sources</phase>
      <configuration>
```

```
      <sourceRoot>
        ${basedir}/target/generated/src/main/java          ◁──  Location of
      </sourceRoot>                                          ❶  generated source
      <wsdlOptions>
        <wsdlOption>
          <wsdl>
        ${basedir}/src/main/resources/wsdl/order.wsdl     ◁──  Location of
          </wsdl>                                            ❷  input WSDL
          <extraargs>
            <extraarg>-impl</extraarg>
          </extraargs>
        </wsdlOption>
      </wsdlOptions>
    </configuration>
    <goals>
      <goal>wsdl2java</goal>
    </goals>
  </execution>
  </executions>
</plugin>
```

The tool accepts your WSDL file ❷ and an output location for the generated source ❶. To run this tool for yourself, change to the chapter7/cxf/contract_first directory and run the following command:

```
mvn generate-sources
```

After this completes, you can look in the output directory and see that there are four files generated:

```
ObjectFactory.java
OrderEndpointImpl.java
OrderEndpoint.java
OrderEndpointService.java
```

These files implement a stubbed-out version of the order web service. If you were not using Camel, you would write your business logic in the `OrderEndpointImpl` file that was generated.

To use this web service in Camel, you need to define a CXF endpoint. Listing 7.5 shows how to do this in Spring.

Listing 7.5 CXF endpoint configuration in camel-cxf.xml

```
<beans xmlns="http://www.springframework.org/schema/beans"
       xmlns:xsi="http://www.w3.org/2001/XMLSchema-instance"
       xmlns:cxf="http://camel.apache.org/schema/cxf"
       xsi:schemaLocation="
         http://www.springframework.org/schema/beans
         http://www.springframework.org/schema/beans/spring-beans-3.0.xsd
         http://camel.apache.org/schema/cxf
         http://camel.apache.org/schema/cxf/camel-cxf.xsd">

  <import resource="classpath:META-INF/cxf/cxf.xml"/>
  <import resource="classpath:META-INF/cxf/cxf-extension-soap.xml"/>
```

```
<import resource="classpath:META-INF/cxf/cxf-extension-http-jetty.xml"/>

<cxf:cxfEndpoint id="orderEndpoint"                                          ◁┐
                 address="http://localhost:9000/order/"
                 serviceClass="camelinaction.order.OrderEndpoint"
                 wsdlURL="wsdl/order.wsdl"/>
</beans>                                                            Defines endpoint to
                                                                   be used from Camel
```

This endpoint configures CXF under the hood to use the web service located at http: //localhost:9000/order and using the `camelinaction.order.OrderEndpoint` interface. Because there is only one service defined in order.wsdl, CXF will choose that automatically. If there were more than one service, you would need to set the `serviceName` and `endpointName` attributes on the endpoint bean. The `serviceName` is the name of the WSDL service element, and `endpointName` is the name of the port element.

You can browse a web service's WSDL yourself by appending `?wsdl` to any web service URL in your browser. For this address, that would be http://localhost:9000/ order?wsdl. This WSDL is the same as the file provided in the `wsdlURL` attribute of the endpoint bean.

ADDING A WEB SERVICE TO YOUR ROUTE

With all that set up, you're ready to start using the order web service within a Camel route. Listing 7.6 shows a route using the web service.

Listing 7.6   Web-enabled route configuration

```
<import                                                        ◁┐  Imports CXF
  resource="classpath:META-INF/spring/camel-cxf.xml" />        ❶  endpoint bean

<camelContext xmlns="http://camel.apache.org/schema/spring">
  <route>
    <from uri="cxf:bean:orderEndpoint" />               ◁┐  Exposes route
    <to uri="seda:incomingOrders" />                     ❷  as web service
    <transform>
      <constant>OK</constant>                        ◁┐  Returns OK
    </transform>                                       ❸  reply to caller
  </route>
</camelContext>
```

Because you defined your CXF web service as an endpoint bean in listing 7.5, you just had to import the bean configuration ❶ and refer to the bean ID to set up the consumer ❷. Recall that setting up a CXF consumer effectively turns the entire route into a web service, so once the order data is sent to an internal queue for processing, the output produced by the route ❸ is returned to the caller of the web service ❷.

How does one call this web service? Well, you could use pure CXF or another web services framework compatible with CXF. In this case, you'll use Camel. You used an endpoint bean to configure CXF earlier, so you can use that to send to the web service as well.

You first need to prepare the parameters to be passed into the web service:

```
List<Object> params = new ArrayList<Object>();
params.add("motor");
params.add(1);
params.add("honda");
```

Recall that, in the WSDL, you specified that the web service accepted parameters for part name, number of parts, and customer name.

Next, you can use a `ProducerTemplate` to send a message to the web service:

```
String reply = template
  .requestBody("cxf:bean:orderEndpoint", params, String.class);
assertEquals("OK", reply);
```

To try this out for yourself, change to the chapter7/cxf/contract_first directory, and run the following Maven command:

```
mvn test
```

This will run the wsdl2java tool to generate the code from the WSDL, and then run a test that loads up the web-enabled route and calls it using a `ProducerTemplate`.

SELECTING THE OPERATION WHEN INVOKING WEB SERVICES

If you call a web service with multiple operations, you need to specify which operation Camel should invoke. You can do this by setting the `operationName` header on the message before sending it to a CXF endpoint. Here is an example:

```
<route>
  <from uri="direct:startOrder" />
  <setHeader headerName="operationName">
    <constant>order</constant>
  </setHeader>
  <to uri="cxf:bean:orderEndpoint"/>
</route>
```

In this case, you're invoking the `orderEndpoint`, which only has one operation, but this demonstrates how you can use this header. The header is set to the operation name `order`, which you can find in the WSDL under the `wsdl:operation` element.

Other ways of communicating over HTTP

The CXF component provides extensive support for many web services standards. In some cases, you may not need to or won't be able to use those standards and you'll just need to communicate over HTTP. For example, you may be interfacing with an HTTP-based service that has been up since before the WS-* specifications were created. You could also need a barebones web service where you manually handle things like parsing the messages. Or maybe you want to download a remote file over HTTP—there are lots of reasons you might need HTTP support.

Camel provides two main ways of doing raw communications over HTTP: the Jetty component and the HTTP component. The HTTP component can only be used for sending (producing) to a remote service, whereas the Jetty component can handle consuming and producing.

(continued)

For the special case where you can't start up an embedded Jetty server and need to hook in to the existing servlet container (like Apache Tomcat), you can use the Servlet component.

You can find more information on these components on the Camel website:

- HTTP component—http://camel.apache.org/http.html
- Jetty component—http://camel.apache.org/jetty.html
- Servlet component—http://camel.apache.org/servlet.html

Think contract-first development is hard? Well, some developers do, even though it gives you complete control over your web service contract—an important detail. Next we'll look at how to develop web services using a code-first approach.

7.4.3 Using a code-first approach

Code-first web services development is often touted as a much easier alternative to contract-first development. In code-first development, you start out with Java that's annotated with JAX-WS annotations, and then you get the web services framework to generate the underlying WSDL contract for you. This process is illustrated in figure 7.9.

To see how this is possible with Camel, let's try implementing the solution presented in the previous section in a code-first manner.

You start much as you do with contract-first development—you need to think about what methods, types, and parameters you need. Because you're starting with Java, you'll need an interface to represent the web service:

```
@WebService
public interface OrderEndpoint {
    String order(String partName, int amount, String customerName);
}
```

The JAX-WS `javax.jws.WebService` annotation will tell CXF that this interface is a web service. There are many annotations that allow you to fine-tune the generated WSDL, but for many cases the defaults work quite well.

In order to use this interface as a web service, you don't have to change any of your Camel configuration from the previous section. Yes, you read that correctly. Your CXF endpoint bean is still defined as follows:

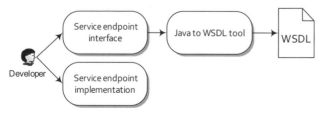

Figure 7.9 In code-first web services development, you start out by coding the service interface and implementation and then using a tool to generate the required WSDL.

```
<cxf:cxfEndpoint id="orderEndpoint"
                 address="http://localhost:9000/order/"
                 serviceClass="camelinaction.order.OrderEndpoint"/>
```

To use this bean in a Camel route, you can reference it as before:

```
<from uri="cxf:bean:orderEndpoint" />
```

To try this out for yourself, change to the chapter7/cxf/code_first directory and run the following Maven command:

```
mvn test
```

This will run a test that loads up the web-enabled route and calls it using a Producer-Template. The Java to WSDL process happens automatically in the background.

Certainly, the code-first approach allows you to implement web services quickly. But it's good to understand what is happening under the hood of a web service, because it's a complex technology.

Speaking of under the hood, several types of messaging that we've looked at before, like FTP, JMS, and now web services, all run on top of other protocols. Let's look at how you can use Camel for these kinds of low-level communications.

7.5   *Networking (MINA component)*

So far in this chapter, you've seen a mixture of old integration techniques, such as file-based integration, and newer technologies like JMS and web services. All of these can be considered essential in any integration framework. Another essential mode of integration is using low-level networking protocols, such as the Transmission Control Protocol (TCP) and the User Datagram Protocol (UDP). Even if you haven't heard of these protocols before, you've definitely used them—protocols like email, FTP, and HTTP run on top of TCP.

To communicate over these and other protocols, Camel uses Apache MINA and Netty. Both MINA and Netty are networking frameworks that provide asynchronous event-driven APIs and communicate over various protocols like TCP and UDP. In this section, we'll be using MINA to demonstrate low-level network communication with Camel. For more information on using Netty with Camel, see the camel-netty component's documentation (http://camel.apache.org/netty.html).

The MINA component is located in the camel-mina module of the Camel distribution. You can access this by adding it as a dependency to your Maven POM like this:

```
<dependency>
  <groupId>org.apache.camel</groupId>
  <artifactId>camel-mina</artifactId>
  <version>2.5.0</version>
</dependency>
```

The most common configuration options are listed in table 7.9.

Table 7.9   Common URI options used to configure the MINA component

Option	Default value	Description
codec	null	Specifies the codec used to marshal the message body. Codecs need to be loaded into the registry and referenced using the #beanName style.
textline	false	Enables the textline codec when you're using TCP and no other codec is specified. The textline codec understands bodies that have string content and end with a line delimiter.
textlineDelimiter	DEFAULT	Sets the delimiter used for the textline codec. Possible values include: DEFAULT, AUTO, WINDOWS, UNIX, or MAC.
sync	true	Sets the synchronous mode of communication. This means that clients will be able to get a response back from the server.
timeout	30000	Sets the time in milliseconds to wait for a response from a remote server.
encoding	JVM default	Specifies the java.nio.charset.Charset used to encode the data.
transferExchange	false	Specifies whether only the message body is transferred. Enable this property to serialize the entire exchange for transmission.
filters	null	Specifies what MINA org.apache.mina.common.IoFilter beans to use. It should be specified as a comma-separated list of bean references, like "#filter1,#filter2".

In addition to the URI options, you also have to specify the transport type and port you want to use. In general, a MINA component URI will look like this,

```
mina:transport://hostname[:port][?options]
```

where transport is one of tcp, udp, multicast/mcast, or vm.

Let's now see how you can use the MINA component to solve a problem at Rider Auto Parts.

7.5.1   Using MINA for network programming

Back at Rider Auto Parts, the production group has been using automated manufacturing robots for years to assist in producing parts. What they've been lacking, though, is a way of tracking the whole plant's health from a single location. They currently have floor personnel monitoring the machines manually. What they'd like to have is an operations center with a single-screen view of the entire plant.

To accomplish this, they've purchased sensors that communicate machine status over TCP. The new operations center needs to consume these messages over JMS. Figure 7.10 illustrates this setup.

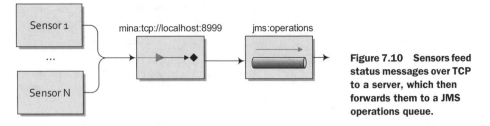

Figure 7.10   Sensors feed status messages over TCP to a server, which then forwards them to a JMS operations queue.

Hand-coding a TCP server such as this wouldn't be a trivial exercise. You'd need to spin up new threads for each incoming socket connection, as well as transform the body to a format suitable for JMS. Not to mention the pain involved in managing the low-level networking protocols.

In Camel, a possible solution is accomplished with a single line:

```
from("mina:tcp://localhost:8999?textline=true&sync=false")
    .to("jms:operations");
```

Here you set up a TCP server on port 8999 using MINA, and it parses messages using the `textline` codec. The `sync` property is set to `false` to make this route InOnly—any clients sending a message won't get a reply back.

You may be wondering what a `textline` codec is, and maybe even what a codec is! In TCP communications, a single message payload going out may not reach its destination in one piece. All will get there, but it may be broken up or fragmented into smaller packets. It's up to the receiver (in this case, the server) to wait for all the pieces and assemble them back into one payload.

A *codec* decodes or encodes the message data into something that the applications on either end of the communications link can understand. As figure 7.11 illustrates, the `textline` codec is responsible for grabbing packets as they come in and trying to piece together a message that's terminated by a specified character.

This example is provided in the book's source in the chapter7/mina directory. Try it out using the following command:

```
mvn test -Dtest=MinaTcpTest
```

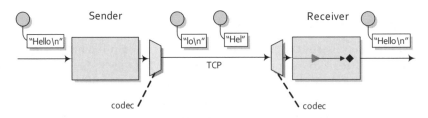

Figure 7.11   During TCP communications, a payload may be broken up into multiple packets. A MINA `textline` codec can assemble the TCP packets into a full payload by appending text until it encounters a delimiter character.

OBJECT SERIALIZATION CODEC

If you had not specified the `textline` URI option in the previous example, the MINA component would have defaulted to using the object serialization codec. This codec will take any `Serializable` Java object and send its bytes over TCP. This is a pretty handy codec if you aren't sure what payload format to use. If you're using this codec, you'll also need to ensure that the classes are on the classpath of both the sender and the receiver.

There are times when your payload will have a custom format that neither `textline` or object serialization accommodates. In this case, you'll need to create a custom codec.

7.5.2 Using custom codecs

The TCP server you set up for Rider Auto Parts in the previous section has worked out well. Sensors have been sending back status messages in plain text, and you used the MINA `textline` codec to successfully decode them. But one type of sensor has been causing an issue: the sensor connected to the welding machine sends its status back in a custom binary format. You need to interpret this custom format and send a status message formatted like the ones from the other sensors. We can do this with a custom MINA codec.

In MINA, a codec consists of three parts:

- `ProtocolEncoder`—The `ProtocolEncoder` has the job of taking an input payload and putting bytes onto the TCP channel. In this example, the sensor will be transmitting the message over TCP, so you don't have to worry about this too much, except for testing that the server works.

- `ProtocolDecoder`—The `ProtocolDecoder` interprets the custom binary message from the sensor and returns a message that your application can understand.

- `ProtocolCodecFactory`—As implied by the name, the `ProtocolCodecFactory` creates the encoder and decoder.

You can specify a custom codec in a Camel URI by using the `codec` property and specifying a reference to a `ProtocolCodecFactory` instance in the registry.

The custom binary payload that you have to interpret with your codec is 8 bytes in total; the first 7 bytes are the machine ID and the last byte is a value indicating the status. You need to convert this to the plain text format used by the other sensors, as illustrated in figure 7.12.

Machine ID   Status   WelderDecoder

Figure 7.12   The custom welder sensor decoder is used to interpret an 8-byte binary payload and construct a plain text message body. The first 7 bytes are the machine ID and the last byte represents a status. In this case, a value of 1 means "Good".

Your route looks similar to the previous example:

```
from("mina:tcp://localhost:8998?codec=#welderCodec&sync=false")
    .to("jms:operations");
```

Note that you need to change the port that it listens on, so as not to conflict with your other TCP server. You also add a reference to the custom codec loaded into the registry. In this case, the codec is loaded into a JndiRegistry like this:

```
JndiRegistry jndi = ...
jndi.bind("welderCodec", new WelderSensorCodec());
```

The WelderSensorCodec is defined as a MINA ProtocolCodecFactory object. It merely creates the encoder and decoder, as shown here:

```
public class WelderSensorCodec implements ProtocolCodecFactory {
    public ProtocolEncoder getEncoder() throws Exception {
        return new WelderEncoder();
    }

    public ProtocolDecoder getDecoder() throws Exception {
        return new WelderDecoder();
    }
}
```

Now that the setup is complete, you can get to the real meat of the custom codec. If you recall, decoding the custom binary format into a plain text message was the most important task for this particular application. This decoder is shown in listing 7.7.

Listing 7.7   The decoder for the welder sensor

```
class WelderDecoder extends CumulativeProtocolDecoder {
    static final int PAYLOAD_SIZE = 8;

    protected boolean doDecode(IoSession session,
ByteBuffer in, ProtocolDecoderOutput out) throws Exception {
        if (in.remaining() >= PAYLOAD_SIZE) {               ◁─┐  Waits for
            byte[] buf = new byte[in.remaining()];            │  all 8 bytes
            in.get(buf);                                    ❶  of payload

            StringBuilder sb = new StringBuilder();
            sb.append("MachineID=")
            .append(
              new String(buf, 0, PAYLOAD_SIZE - 1))         ◁─┐  Gets first 7 bytes
            .append(";")                                    ❷  as machine ID
            .append("Status=");
            if (buf[PAYLOAD_SIZE - 1] == '1') {             ◁─┐  Gets last byte
                sb.append("Good");                          ❸  as status
            } else {
                sb.append("Failure");
            }
            out.write(sb.toString());
            return true;
        } else {
            return false;
        }
    }
}
```

The decoder shown in listing 7.7 may look a bit complex, but it's only doing three main things: waiting for 8 bytes of payload to arrive on the TCP channel ❶, extracting the first 7 bytes and using that as the machine ID string ❷, and checking the last byte for a status of 1, which means "Good" ❸.

To try this example yourself, go to the chapter7/mina directory of the book's source and run the following unit test:

```
mvn test -Dtest=MinaCustomCodecTest
```

Now that you've tried out low-level network communications, its time to interact with one of the most common applications in the enterprise. That's the database.

7.6   *Working with databases (JDBC and JPA components)*

In pretty much every enterprise-level application, you'll need to integrate with a database at some point. So it makes sense that Camel has first-class support for accessing databases. Camel has five components that let you access databases in a number of ways:

- *JDBC component*—Allows you to access JDBC APIs from a Camel route.
- *SQL component*—Allows you to write SQL statements directly into the URI of the component for utilizing simple queries.
- *JPA component*—Persists Java objects to a relational database using the Java Persistence Architecture.
- *Hibernate component*—Persists Java objects using the Hibernate framework. This component isn't distributed with Apache Camel due to licensing incompatibilities. You can find it at the camel-extra project (http://code.google.com/p/camel-extra).
- *iBATIS component*—Allows you to map Java objects to relational databases.

In this section, we'll be covering both the JDBC and JPA components. These are the most-used database-related components in Camel. You can do pretty much any database-related task with them that you can do with the others. For more information on the other components, see the relevant pages on the Camel website's components list (http://camel.apache.org/components.html).

Let's look first at the JDBC component.

7.6.1   *Accessing data with the JDBC component*

The Java Database Connectivity (JDBC) API defines how Java clients can interact with a particular database. It tries to abstract away details about the actual database being used. To use this component, you need to add the camel-jdbc module to your project:

```
<dependency>
  <groupId>org.apache.camel</groupId>
  <artifactId>camel-jdbc</artifactId>
  <version>2.5.0</version>
</dependency>
```

The most common URI options are shown in table 7.10.

Table 7.10   Common URI options used to configure the JDBC component

Option	Default value	Description
readSize	0	Sets the maximum number of rows that can be returned. The default of 0 causes the readSize to be unbounded.
statement.propertyName	null	Sets the property with name propertyName on the underlying java.sql.Statement.
useJDBC4ColumnNameAndLabelSemantics	true	Sets the column and label semantics to use. Default is to use the newer JDBC 4 style, but you can set this property to false to enable JDBC 3 style.

The endpoint URI for the JDBC component points Camel to a javax.sql.DataSource loaded into the registry, and, like other components, it allows for configuration options to be set. The URI syntax is as follows:

```
jdbc:dataSourceName[?options]
```

After this is specified, the component is ready for action. But you may be wondering where the actual SQL statement is specified.

The JDBC component is a dynamic component in that it doesn't merely deliver a message to a destination but takes the body of the message as a command. In this case, the command is specified using SQL. In EIP terms, this kind of message is called a command message. Because a JDBC endpoint accepts a command, it doesn't make sense to use it as a consumer, so, you can't use it in a from DSL statement. Of course, you can still retrieve data using a select SQL statement as the command message. In this case, the query result will be added as the outgoing message on the exchange.

To demonstrate the SQL command-message concept, let's revisit the order router at Rider Auto Parts. In the accounting department, when an order comes in on a JMS queue, the accountant's business applications can't use this data. They can only import data from a database. So any incoming orders need to be put into the corporate database. Using Camel, a possible solution is illustrated in figure 7.13.

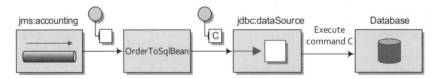

Figure 7.13   A message from the JMS accounting queue is transformed into an SQL command message by the OrderToSqlBean bean. The JDBC component then executes this command against its configured data source.

The main takeaway from figure 7.13 is that you're using a bean to create the SQL statement from the incoming message body. This is the most common way to prepare a command message for the JDBC component. You could use the DSL directly to create the SQL statement (by setting the body with an expression), but you have much more control when you use a custom bean.

The route for the implementation of figure 7.13 is simple on the surface:

```
from("jms:accounting")
    .to("bean:orderToSql")
    .to("jdbc:dataSource");
```

There are two things that require further explanation here. First, the JDBC endpoint is configured to load the javax.sql.DataSource with the name dataSource in the registry. The bean endpoint here is using the bean with the name orderToSql to convert the incoming message to an SQL statement.

The orderToSql bean is shown in listing 7.8.

Listing 7.8 A bean that converts an incoming order to an SQL statement

```
public class OrderToSqlBean {

    public String toSql(@XPath("order/@name") String name,
                        @XPath("order/@amount") int amount,
                        @XPath("order/@customer") String customer) {

        StringBuilder sb = new StringBuilder();
        sb.append("insert into incoming_orders ");
        sb.append("(part_name, quantity, customer) values (");
        sb.append("'").append(name).append("', ");
        sb.append("'").append(amount).append("', ");
        sb.append("'").append(customer).append("') ");

        return sb.toString();
    }
}
```

The orderToSql bean uses XPath to parse an incoming order message with a body something like this:

```
<?xml version="1.0" encoding="UTF-8"?>
<order name="motor" amount="1" customer="honda"/>
```

The data in this order is then converted to an SQL statement like this:

```
insert into incoming_orders (part_name, quantity, customer)
values ('motor', '1', 'honda')
```

This SQL statement then becomes the body of a message that will be passed into the JDBC endpoint. In this case, you're updating the database by inserting a new row. So you won't be expecting any result back. But Camel will set the CamelJdbcUpdateCount header to the number of rows updated. If there were any problems running the SQL command, an SQLException would be thrown.

If you were running a query against the database (an SQL select command), Camel would return the rows as an ArrayList<HashMap<String, Object>>. Each entry in the `ArrayList` is a `HashMap` that maps the column name to a column value. Camel would also set the `CamelJdbcRowCount` header to the number of rows returned from the query.

To run this example for yourself, change to the chapter7/jdbc directory of the book's source, and run the following command:

```
mvn test -Dtest=JdbcTest
```

Having raw access to the database through JDBC is a must-have ability in any integration framework. There are times, though, that you need to persist more than raw data—sometimes you need to persist whole Java objects. You can do this with the JPA component, which we'll look at next.

7.6.2 *Persisting objects with the JPA component*

There is a new requirement at Rider Auto Parts: instead of passing around XML order messages, management would like to adopt a POJO model for orders.

A first step would be to transform the incoming XML message into an equivalent POJO form. In addition, the order persistence route in the accounting department would need to be updated to handle the new POJO body type. You could manually extract the necessary information as you did for the XML message in listing 7.8, but there is a better solution for persisting objects.

The Java Persistence Architecture (JPA) is a wrapper layer on top of object-relational mapping (ORM) products such as Hibernate, OpenJPA, TopLink, and the like. These products map Java objects to relational data in a database, which means you can save a Java object in your database of choice, and load it up later when you need it. This is a pretty powerful ability, and it hides many details. Because this adds quite a bit of complexity to your application, plain JDBC should be considered first to see if it meets your requirements.

To use the JPA component, you need to add the camel-jpa module to your project:

```
<dependency>
  <groupId>org.apache.camel</groupId>
  <artifactId>camel-jpa</artifactId>
  <version>2.5.0</version>
</dependency>
```

You'll also need to add JARs for the ORM product and database you're using. The examples in this section will use OpenJPA and the HyperSQL database, so you need the following dependencies as well:

```
<dependency>
  <groupId>org.apache.openjpa</groupId>
  <artifactId>openjpa-persistence-jdbc</artifactId>
  <version>1.2.2</version>
</dependency>
<dependency>
  <groupId>hsqldb</groupId>
  <artifactId>hsqldb</artifactId>
  <version>1.8.0.7</version>
</dependency>
```

The JPA component has a number of URI options, many of which can only be applied to either a consumer or producer endpoint. The possible URI options are shown in table 7.11.

Table 7.11 Common URI options used to configure the JPA component

Option	Consumer/ producer mode	Default value	Description
persistenceUnit	Both	camel	Specifies the JPA persistence unit name used.
transactionManager	Both	null	Sets the transaction manager to be used. If transactions are enabled and this property isn't specified, Camel will use a JpaTransactionManager. For more on transactions, see chapter 9.
maximumResults	Consumer	-1	Specifies the maximum number of objects to be returned from a query. The default of -1 means an unlimited number of results.
maxMessagesPerPoll	Consumer	0	Sets the maximum number of objects to be returned during a single poll. The default of 0 means an unlimited number of results.
consumeLockEntity	Consumer	true	Specifies whether the entities in the database will lock while they're being consumed by Camel. By default, they will lock.
consumeDelete	Consumer	true	Specifies whether the entity should be deleted in the database after it's consumed.
consumer.delay	Consumer	500	Sets the delay in milliseconds between each poll.
consumer.initialDelay	Consumer	1000	Sets the initial delay in milliseconds before the first poll.
consumer.query	Consumer		Sets the custom SQL query to use when consuming objects.
consumer.namedQuery	Consumer		References a named query to consume objects.
consumer.nativeQuery	Consumer		Specifies a query in the native SQL dialect of the database you're using. This isn't very portable, but it allows you to take advantage of features specific to a particular database.
flushOnSend	Producer		Causes objects that are sent to a JPA producer to be persisted to the underlying database immediately. Otherwise, they may stay in memory with the ORM tool until it decides to persist.

A requirement in JPA is to annotate any POJOs that need to be persisted with the javax.persistence.Entity annotation. The term *entity* is borrowed from relational database terminology and roughly translates to an object in object-oriented programming. This means that your new POJO order class needs to have this annotation if you wish to persist it with JPA. The new order POJO is shown in listing 7.9.

Listing 7.9 An annotated POJO representing an incoming order

```
@Entity                                                    ◁─┐  Required annotation
public class PurchaseOrder implements Serializable {         │  for objects to be
    private String name;                                     │  persisted
    private double amount;
    private String customer;

    public PurchaseOrder() {
    }

    public double getAmount() {
        return amount;
    }

    public void setAmount(double amount) {
        this.amount = amount;
    }

    public String getName() {
        return name;
    }

    public void setName(String name) {
        this.name = name;
    }

    public void setCustomer(String customer) {
        this.customer = customer;
    }

    public String getCustomer() {
        return customer;
    }
}
```

This POJO can be created from the incoming XML order message easily with a message translator, as shown in chapter 3. For testing purposes, you can use a producer template to send a new PurchaseOrder to the accounting JMS queue, like so:

```
PurchaseOrder purchaseOrder = new PurchaseOrder();
purchaseOrder.setName("motor");
purchaseOrder.setAmount(1);
purchaseOrder.setCustomer("honda");
template.sendBody("jms:accounting", purchaseOrder);
```

Your route from section 7.6.1 is now a bit simpler. You send directly to the JPA endpoint after an order is received on the queue:

```
from("jms:accounting").to("jpa:camelinaction.PurchaseOrder");
```

Now that your route is in place, you have to configure the ORM tool. This is by far the most configuration you'll have to do when using JPA with Camel. As we've mentioned, ORM tools can be complex.

There are two main bits of configuration: hooking the ORM tool's entity manager up to Camel's JPA component, and configuring the ORM tool to connect to your database. For demonstration purposes here, we'll be using Apache OpenJPA, but you could use any other JPA-compliant ORM tool.

The beans required to set up the OpenJPA entity manager are shown in listing 7.10.

Listing 7.10   Hooking up the Camel JPA component to OpenJPA

```
<beans xmlns="http://www.springframework.org/schema/beans"          Hooks JPA  ❶
    xmlns:xsi="http://www.w3.org/2001/XMLSchema-instance"           component up
    xsi:schemaLocation="                                            to entity manager
        http://www.springframework.org/schema/beans
        http://www.springframework.org/schema/beans/spring-beans-3.0.xsd">

  <bean id="jpa"
  class="org.apache.camel.component.jpa.JpaComponent">
    <property name="entityManagerFactory" ref="entityManagerFactory" />
  </bean>
                                                      ❷ Creates entity manager
  <bean id="entityManagerFactory"
  class="org.springframework.orm.jpa.LocalEntityManagerFactoryBean">
    <property name="persistenceUnitName" value="camel" />
    <property name="jpaVendorAdapter" ref="jpaAdapter" />           ❸ Uses OpenJPA
  </bean>                                                              and HyperSQL
                                                                      database
  <bean id="jpaAdapter"
  class="org.springframework.orm.jpa.vendor.OpenJpaVendorAdapter">
    <property name="databasePlatform"
    value="org.apache.openjpa.jdbc.sql.HSQLDictionary" />          ❹ Allows JPA
    <property name="database" value="HSQL" />                        component to
  </bean>                                                            participate in
                                                                     transactions
  <bean id="transactionTemplate"
  class="org.springframework.transaction.support.TransactionTemplate">
    <property name="transactionManager">
      <bean class="org.springframework.orm.jpa.JpaTransactionManager">
        <property name="entityManagerFactory" ref="entityManagerFactory" />
      </bean>
    </property>
  </bean>

</beans>
```

The Spring beans file shown in listing 7.10 does a number of things to set up JPA. First off, it creates a Camel `JpaComponent` and specifies the entity manager to be used ❶. This entity manager ❷ is then hooked up to OpenJPA and the HyperSQL order database ❸. It also sets up the entity manager so it can participate in transactions ❹.

There is one more thing left to configure before JPA is up and running. When the entity manager was created in listing 7.10 ❷, you set the `persistenceUnitName` to `"camel"`. This persistence unit defines what entity classes will be persisted, as well as the connection information for the underlying database. In JPA, this configuration is stored in the persistence.xml file in the META-INF directory on the classpath. Listing 7.11 shows the configuration required for your application.

Listing 7.11   Configuring the ORM tool with the persistence.xml file

```
<persistence xmlns="http://java.sun.com/xml/ns/persistence"
  xmlns:xsi="http://www.w3.org/2001/XMLSchema-instance" version="1.0">

  <persistence-unit name="camel" transaction-type="RESOURCE_LOCAL">
    <class>camelinaction.PurchaseOrder</class>          ❶ Lists entity classes
                                                            to be persisted
    <properties>
      <property name="openjpa.ConnectionDriverName"     ❷ Provides database
value="org.hsqldb.jdbcDriver" />                          connection
      <property name="openjpa.ConnectionURL"             information
value="jdbc:hsqldb:mem:order" />
      <property name="openjpa.ConnectionUserName" value="sa" />
      <property name="openjpa.ConnectionPassword" value="" />
      <property name="openjpa.jdbc.SynchronizeMappings"
value="buildSchema" />
    </properties>

  </persistence-unit>
</persistence>
```

There are two main things in listing 7.11 to be aware of. First, classes that you need persisted need to be defined here ❶, and there can be more than one class element. Also, if you need to connect to another database or otherwise change the connection information to the database, you'll need to do so here ❷.

Now that all of the setup is complete, your JPA route is complete. To try out this example, browse to the chapter7/jpa directory and run the JpaTest test case with this Maven command:

```
mvn test -Dtest=JpaTest
```

This example sends a PurchaseOrder to the accounting queue and then queries the database to make sure the entity class was persisted.

Manually querying the database via JPA is a useful ability, especially in testing. In JpaTest, the query was performed like so:

```
JpaEndpoint endpoint =
  (JpaEndpoint) context.getEndpoint("jpa:camelinaction.PurchaseOrder");
jpaTemplate = endpoint.getTemplate();

List list =
  jpaTemplate.find("select x from camelinaction.PurchaseOrder x");

assertEquals(1, list.size());
assertIsInstanceOf(PurchaseOrder.class, list.get(0));
```

First off, you grab the instance of the JpaTemplate on the JpaEndpoint. You then search for instances of your entity class in the database using JPQL, which is similar to SQL but deals with JPA entity objects instead of tables. A simple check is then performed to make sure the object is the right type and that there is only one result.

Now that we've covered accessing databases, and messaging that can span the entire web, we're going to shift our attention to communication within the JVM.

7.7   *In-memory messaging (Direct, SEDA, and VM components)*

Having braved so many of Camel's different messaging abilities in this chapter, you might think there couldn't be more. Yet there is still another important messaging topic to cover: in-memory messaging.

Camel provides three main components in the core to handle in-memory messaging. For synchronous messaging, there is the Direct component. For asynchronous messaging, there are the SEDA and VM components. The only difference between SEDA and VM is that the SEDA component can be used for communication within a single `CamelContext`, whereas the VM component is a bit broader and can be used for communication within a JVM. If you have two `CamelContexts` loaded into an application server, you can send messages between them using the VM component.

> **NOTE**   For more information on staged event-driven architecture (SEDA) in general, see Matt Welsh's SEDA page at http://www.eecs.harvard.edu/~mdw/proj/seda/.

Let's look first at the Direct component.

7.7.1   *Synchronous messaging with the Direct component*

The Direct component is about as simple as a component can get, but it's extremely useful. It's probably the most common Camel endpoint you'll see in a route.

A direct endpoint URI looks like this:

```
direct:endpointName
```

There are no options that you can specify or backends to configure; there is just an endpoint name.

So what does this give you? The Direct component lets you make a synchronous call to a route or, conversely, expose a route as a synchronous service.

To demonstrate, say you have a route that's exposed by a direct endpoint as follows:

```
from("direct:startOrder")
  .to("cxf:bean:orderEndpoint");
```

Sending a message to the `direct:startOrder` endpoint will invoke a web service defined by the `orderEndpoint` CXF endpoint bean. Let's also say that you send a message to this endpoint using a `ProducerTemplate`, as you saw in section 7.4.2:

```
String reply =
  template.requestBody("direct:startOrder", params, String.class);
```

The `ProducerTemplate` will create a `Producer` under the hood that sends to the `direct:startOrder` endpoint. In most other components, some processing happens in between the producer and the consumer. For instance, in a JMS component, the message could be sent to a queue on a JMS broker. With the Direct component, the producer *directly* calls the consumer. And by *directly*, we mean that in the producer there is a method invocation on the consumer. The only overhead of using the Direct component is a method call!

This simplicity and minimal overhead make the Direct component a great way of starting routes and synchronously breaking up routes into multiple pieces. But even though there is little overhead to using the Direct component, its synchronous nature doesn't fit well with all applications. If you need to operate asynchronously, you need the SEDA or VM components, which we'll look at next.

7.7.2 Asynchronous messaging with SEDA and VM

As you saw in the discussion of JMS earlier in the chapter (section 7.3), there are many benefits to using message queuing as a means of sending messages. You also saw how a routing application can be broken up into many logical pieces (routes) and connected by using JMS queues as bridges. But using JMS for this purpose in an application on a single host adds unnecessary complexity for some use cases.

If you want to reap the benefits of asynchronous messaging but aren't concerned with JMS specification conformance or the built-in reliability that JMS provides, you may want to consider an in-memory solution. By ditching the specification conformance and any communications with a message broker (which can be costly), an in-memory solution can be much faster. Note that there is no message persistence to the disk, like in JMS, so you run the risk of losing messages in the event of a crash—your application should be tolerant of losing messages.

Camel provides two in-memory queuing components: SEDA and VM. They both share the options listed in table 7.12.

Table 7.12 Common URI options used to configure the SEDA and VM components

Option	Default value	Description
size	Unbounded	Sets the maximum number of messages the queue can hold.
concurrentConsumers	1	Sets the number of threads servicing incoming exchanges. Increase this number to process more exchanges concurrently.
waitForTaskToComplete	IfReplyExpected	Specifies whether or not the client should wait for an asynchronous task to complete. The default is to only wait if its an InOut MEP. Other values include Always and Never.
timeout	30000	Sets the time in milliseconds to wait for an asynchronous send to complete. A value less than or equal to 0 will disable the timeout.
multipleConsumers	false	Specifies whether to allow the SEDA queue to have behavior like a JMS topic (a publish-subscribe style of messaging).

One of the most common uses for SEDA queues in Camel is to connect routes together to form a routing application. For example, recall the example presented in 7.3.1 where you used a JMS topic to send copies of an incoming order to the accounting and production departments. In that case, you used JMS queues to connect your routes together. Because the only parts that are hosted on separate hosts are the accounting and production queues, you can use SEDA queues for everything else. This new faster solution is illustrated in figure 7.14.

Any JMS messaging that you were doing within a `CamelContext` could be switched over to SEDA. You still need to use JMS for the accounting and production queues, because they're located in physically separate departments.

You may have noticed that the JMS `xmlOrders` topic has been replaced with a SEDA queue in figure 7.14. In order for this SEDA queue to behave like a JMS topic (using a publish-subscribe messaging model), you need to set the `multipleConsumers` URI option to `true`, as shown in listing 7.12.

Listing 7.12 A topic allows multiple receivers to get a copy of the message

```
from("file:src/data?noop=true")
    .to("seda:incomingOrders");                    ◁──┐  Orders enter
                                                       │  set of routes
from("seda:incomingOrders")
    .choice()                                                       XML orders
    .when(header("CamelFileName").endsWith(".xml"))                 are routed to
        .to("seda:xmlOrders?multipleConsumers=true")       ◁──┘    xmlOrders topic
    .when(header("CamelFileName").regex("^.*(csv|csl)$"))
        .to("seda:csvOrders?multipleConsumers=true");

from("seda:xmlOrders?multipleConsumers=true")
    .to("jms:accounting");                                 Both listening
from("seda:xmlOrders?multipleConsumers=true")              queues get copies
    .to("jms:production");
```

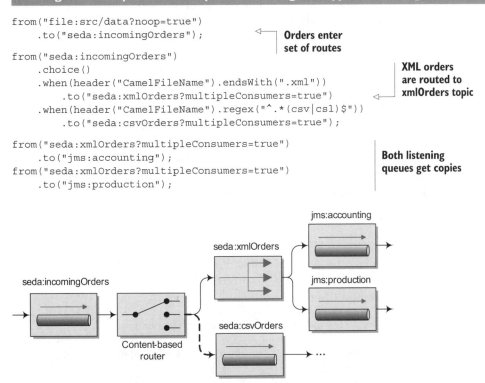

Figure 7.14   SEDA queues can be used as a low-overhead replacement for JMS when messaging is within a `CamelContext`. For messages being sent to other hosts, JMS can be used. In this case, all order routing is done via SEDA until the order needs to go to the accounting and production departments.

This example behaves in the same way as the example in section 7.3.1, except that it uses SEDA endpoints instead of JMS. Another important detail in this listing is that SEDA endpoint URIs that are reused in consumer and producer scenarios need to be exactly the same as each other. It's not enough to specify the correct SEDA queue name; you need to use the queue name and all options.

To run this example, go to the chapter7/seda directory in the book's source, and run this command:

```
mvn compile exec:java -Dexec.mainClass=camelinaction.OrderRouter
```

This will output the following on the command line:

```
Accounting received order: message1.xml
Production received order: message1.xml
```

Why did you get this output? Well, you had a single order file named message1.xml, and it was published to the xmlOrders topic. Both the accounting and production queues were subscribed to the topic, so each received a copy. The testing routes consumed the messages on those queues and output the messages.

So far you've been kicking off routes either by hand or by consuming from a filesystem directory. How can you kick off routes automatically? Or better yet, how can you schedule a route's execution to occur?

7.8   *Automating tasks (Timer and Quartz components)*

Often in enterprise projects you'll need to schedule tasks to occur either at a specified time or at regular intervals. Camel supports this kind of service with the Timer and Quartz components. The Timer component is useful for simple recurring tasks, but when you need more control of when things get started, the Quartz component is a must.

In this section, we're first going to look at the Timer component and then move on to the more advanced Quartz component.

7.8.1   *Using the Timer component*

The Timer component comes with Camel's core library and uses the JRE's built-in timer mechanism to generate message exchanges at regular intervals. This component only supports consuming, because sending to a timer doesn't really make sense.

Some common URI options are listed in table 7.13.

Table 7.13   Common URI options used to configure the Timer component

Option	Default value	Description
period	1000	Specifies the time in milliseconds between generated events.
delay	0	Specifies the time in milliseconds before the first event is generated.
fixedRate	false	Specifies whether to create events at a fixed rate based on the period.
daemon	true	Sets the timer thread to run as a daemon.

As an example, let's print a message stating the time to the console every 2 seconds. The route looks like this:

```
from("timer://myTimer?period=2000")
.setBody().simple("Current time is ${header.firedTime}")
.to("stream:out");
```

The timer URI is configuring the underlying `java.util.Timer` to have the name `myTimer` and an execution interval of 2000 milliseconds.

> **TIP** When the value of milliseconds gets large, you can opt for a shorter notation using the `s`, `m`, and `h` keywords. For example, 2000 milliseconds can be written as `2s`, meaning 2 seconds. 90000 milliseconds can be written as `1m30s`, and so on.

When this timer fires an event, Camel creates an exchange with an empty body and sends it along the route. In this case, you're setting the body of the message using a Simple language expression. The `firedTime` header was set by the Timer component; for a full list of headers set, see the online documentation (http://camel.apache.org/timer.html).

> **NOTE** The `Timer` object and corresponding thread can be shared. If you use the same timer name in another route, it will reuse the same `Timer` object.

You can run this simple example by changing to the chapter7/timer directory of the book's source and running this command:

```
mvn compile exec:java -Dexec.mainClass=camelinaction.TimerExample
```

You'll see output similar to the following:

```
Current time is Wed Feb 10 00:43:31 NST 2010
Current time is Wed Feb 10 00:43:33 NST 2010
Current time is Wed Feb 10 00:43:35 NST 2010
```

As you can see, an event was fired every 2 seconds. But suppose you wanted to schedule a route to execute on the first day of each month? You couldn't do this easily with the Timer component. You now have a need for Quartz.

7.8.2 Enterprise scheduling with Quartz

Like the Timer component, the Quartz component allows you to schedule the generation of message exchanges. But the Quartz component gives you much more control over how this scheduling happens. You can also take advantage of Quartz's many other enterprise features.

We won't be covering all of Quartz's features here—only ones exposed directly in Camel. For a complete look at how to use Quartz, please see the Quartz website: http://www.quartz-scheduler.org.

The common URI options for the Quartz component are listed in table 7.14.

Table 7.14 Common URI options used to configure the Quartz component

Option	Default value	Description
cron	none	Specifies a cron expression used to determine when the timer fires.
trigger.repeatCount	0	Specifies the number of times to repeat the trigger. A value of -1 causes the timer to repeat indefinitely.
trigger.repeatInterval	0	Specifies the interval in milliseconds at which to generate events.
job.propertyName	null	Sets the property with name propertyName on the underlying Quartz JobDetail.
trigger.propertyName	null	Sets the property with name propertyName on the underlying Quartz Trigger.

Before you can use the Quartz component, you'll need to add the following dependency to your Maven POM file:

```
<dependency>
  <groupId>org.apache.camel</groupId>
  <artifactId>camel-quartz</artifactId>
  <version>2.5.0</version>
</dependency>
```

Let's now reproduce the timer example from the previous section with Quartz. To do this, you can use the trigger.repeatInterval option, which is similar to the period option for the Timer component. The route looks like this:

```
from("quartz://myTimer?trigger.repeatInterval=2000&trigger.repeatCount=-1")
.setBody().simple("Current time is ${header.firedTime}")
.to("stream:out");
```

Although this behaves in the same way as the Timer example, there are a few different things going on under the covers.

First off, myTimer sets the underlying Trigger object's name. Timers in Quartz are made up of a Trigger and a JobDetail. Triggers can also have a group name associated with them, which you can specify by adding the group name to your URI, as follows:

```
quartz://myGroupName/myTimer?options...
```

If the group name is omitted, as in the previous route, "Camel" is used as the group name. By default, a SimpleTrigger is created to schedule events.

The trigger.repeatInterval and trigger.repeatCount properties configured this trigger to fire every 2000 milliseconds for as long as the application is running (a repeat count of -1 causes the trigger to repeat indefinitely). You may be thinking that the option names are a bit long, but there is a reason for this. As stated in table 7.14, options starting with trigger allow you to set properties on the Trigger object. In the case of the `trigger.repeatInterval` URI option, this will call the `setRepeatInterval` method on the `SimpleTrigger` object.

You can similarly set options on the `JobDetail` by using properties that start with `job`, followed by a valid property name. For instance, you can set the job name by using the `job.name` URI option.

USING CRON TRIGGERS

So far, you've replaced the Timer component example with a functionally equivalent Quartz-based example. How would you schedule something more complex, like kicking off a route on the first day of each month? The answer is by using *cron* expressions. Readers familiar with Linux or Unix will probably have heard of the cron scheduling application. Quartz allows you to use scheduling syntax similar to the venerable cron application.

A cron expression is a string consisting of 6–7 fields separated by white space. Each field denotes a date or range of dates. The structure of a cron expression is as follows:

```
<Seconds> <Minutes> <Hours> <Day of Month> <Month> <Day of week> <Year>
```

These accept numeric values (and optional textual ones) for the times you want a trigger to fire. More information on cron expressions can be found on the Quartz website (http://www.quartz-scheduler.org/docs/tutorials/crontrigger.html).

The cron expression for occurring on the first day of each month at 6:00 a.m. is the following:

```
0 0 6 1 * ?
```

In this expression, the third digit denotes the hour at which to execute, and the fourth digit is the day of the month. You can also see that a star was placed in the month column so that every month would be triggered.

Setting up Quartz to use cron triggers in Camel is easy. You just need to use the `cron` option and make sure to replace all white space with plus characters (+). Your URI becomes the following:

```
quartz://firstDayOfTheMonth?cron=0+0+6+1+*+?
```

Using this URI in a route will cause a message exchange to be generated (running the route) on the first day of each month.

You should be able to see now how the scheduling components in Camel can allow you to execute routes at specified times. This is an important ability in time-sensitive enterprise applications.

7.9 *Summary and best practices*

Congratulations on making it through the barrage of components we covered in this chapter. By now, you should have a good understanding of how to use them in your own applications.

Here are some of the key ideas you should take away from this chapter:

- *There are tons of Camel components.* One of the great things about Camel is its extensive component library. You can rest easy knowing that most things you'll ever need to connect to are covered by Camel.

- *The Camel website has documentation on all components available.* We could only cover the most widely used and important components in this book, so you should be aware that if you need to use one of the many other components, documentation is available at http://camel.apache.org/components.html.

- *Camel's component model allows for your own extensions.* We briefly touched on how components are resolved at runtime in Camel. Camel imposes no restrictions on where your components come from, so you can easily write your own (as described in chapter 11) and include it in your Camel application.

- *Don't write to files manually; use the File and FTP components.* Camel's File and FTP components have many options that will suit most file-processing scenarios. Don't reinvent the wheel—use what Camel has to offer.

- *Use the JMS component for asynchronous messaging with JMS.* Camel makes it easy to send messages to and receive them from JMS providers. You will no longer have to write dozens of lines of JMS API calls to send or receive a simple message.

- *Use the CXF component for all your web services needs.* The CXF component allows you to make calls to a variety of web service types or to expose your Camel route to the world as a web service.

- *Use the MINA component for network communications.* Network programming can be difficult, given the low-level concepts you need to deal with. The MINA component handles these details for you, making it easy to communicate over network protocols such as TCP and UDP.

- *Hook your routes into databases using the JDBC and JPA components.* The JDBC component allows you to access databases using tried-and-true SQL, whereas the JPA component is all about persisting Java objects into databases.

- *Use in-memory messaging when reliability isn't a concern but speed is.* Camel provides three choices for in-memory messaging: the Direct, SEDA, and VM components.

- *Kick off routes at specified intervals using the Quartz or Timer components.* Camel routes can do useful things. Some tasks need to be executed at specified intervals, and the Quartz and Timer components come into play here.

Components in Camel fill the role of bridging out to other transports, APIs, and data formats. They're also the on and off ramps to Camel's routing abilities.

Back in chapter 2, you were exposed to some of Camel's routing capabilities by using some standard EIPs. In the next chapter, we'll look at some of the more complex EIPs available in Camel. Unlike when you read chapter 2, you're now armed with the knowledge of how to connect to many different services with Camel. Keep your knowledge of components handy—you can think up some interesting integration scenarios!

Enterprise
integration patterns

Today's businesses aren't run on a single monolithic system, and most businesses have a full range of disparate systems. There is an ever-increasing demand for those systems to integrate with each other and with external business partners and government systems.

Let's face it, integration is hard. To help deal with the complexity of integration problems, enterprise integration patterns (EIPs) have become the standard way to describe, document, and implement complex integration problems. We explain the patterns we discuss in this book, but to learn more about them and others, see the Enterprise Integration Patterns website and the associated book: http://www.enterpriseintegrationpatterns.com/.

8.1   *Introducing enterprise integration patterns*

Apache Camel implements EIPs, and because the EIPs are essential building blocks in the Camel routes, you'll bump into EIPs throughout this book, starting in chapter 2. It would be impossible for this book to cover all the EIPs Camel supports, which currently total around 60 patterns. This chapter is devoted to covering five of the most powerful and feature-rich patterns. The patterns discussed in this chapter are listed in table 8.1.

Table 8.1   EIPs covered in this chapter

Pattern	Summary
Aggregator	Used to combine results of individual but related messages into a single outgoing message. You can view this as the *reverse* of the Splitter pattern. This pattern is covered in section 8.2.
Splitter	Used to split a message into pieces that are routed separately. This pattern is covered in section 8.3.
Routing Slip	Used to route a message in a series of steps, where the sequence of steps isn't known at design time and may vary for each message. This pattern is covered in section 8.4.
Dynamic Router	Used to route messages with a dynamic router dictating where the message goes. This pattern is covered in section 8.5.
Load Balancer	Used to balance the load to a given endpoint using a variety of different balancing policies. This pattern is covered in section 8.6.

Let's look at these patterns in a bit more detail.

8.1.1   *The Aggregator and Splitter EIPs*

The first two patterns listed in table 8.1 are related. The Splitter can split out a single message into multiple submessages, and the Aggregator can combine those submessages back into a single message. They're opposite patterns.

The EIPs allow you to build patterns *LEGO style*, which means that patterns can be combined together to form new patterns. For example, you can combine the Splitter and the Aggregator into what is known as the Composed Message Processor EIP, as illustrated in figure 8.1.

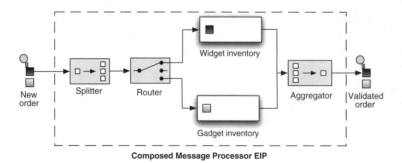

Composed Message Processor EIP

Figure 8.1
The Composed Message Processor EIP splits up the message, routes the submessages to the appropriate destinations, and re-aggregates the response back into a single message.

The Aggregator EIP is likely the most sophisticated and most advanced EIP implemented in Camel. It has many use cases, such as aggregating incoming bids for auctions or throttling stock quotes.

8.1.2 The Routing Slip and Dynamic Router EIPs

A question that is often asked on the Camel mailing list is how to route messages dynamically. The answer is to use EIPs such as Recipient List, Routing Slip, and Dynamic Router. We covered Recipient List in chapter 2, and in this chapter we'll show you how to use the Routing Slip and Dynamic Router patterns.

8.1.3 The Load Balancer EIP

The EIP book doesn't list the Load Balancer, which is a pattern implemented in Camel. Suppose you route PDF messages to network printers, and those printers come and go online. You can use the Load Balancer to send the PDF messages to another printer if one printer is unresponsive.

That covers the five EIPs we'll cover in this chapter. It's now time to look at the first one in detail, the Aggregator EIP.

8.2 The Aggregator EIP

The Aggregator EIP is important and complex, so we'll cover it well. Don't despair if you don't understand the pattern in the first few pages.

The Aggregator combines many related incoming messages into a single aggregated message, as illustrated in figure 8.2.

The Aggregator receives a stream of messages and identifies messages that are related, which are then aggregated into a single combined message. Once a completion

> ### Example uses of Aggregator
> The Aggregator EIP supports many use cases, such as the loan broker example from the EIP book, where brokers send loan requests to multiple banks and aggregate the replies to determine the *best deal*.
>
> You could also use the Aggregator in an auction system to aggregate current bids. Also imagine a stock market system that continuously receives a stream of stock quotes, and you want to throttle this to publish the latest quote every 5 seconds. This can be done using the Aggregator to choose the latest message and thus trigger a completion every 5 seconds.

Figure 8.2 The Aggregator stores incoming messages until it receives a complete set of related messages. Then the Aggregator publishes a single message distilled from the individual messages.

condition occurs, the aggregated message is sent to the output channel for further processing. We'll cover how this process works in detail in the next section.

When using the Aggregator, you have to pay attention to the following three configuration settings, which must be configured. Failure to do so will cause Camel to fail on startup and to report an error regarding the missing configuration.

- *Correlation identifier*—An `Expression` that determines which incoming messages belong together
- *Completion condition*—A `Predicate` or time-based condition that determines when the result message should be sent
- *Aggregation strategy*—An `AggregationStrategy` that specifies how to combine the messages into a single message

In this section, we'll look at a simple example that will aggregate messages containing alphabetic characters, such as *A*, *B*, and *C*. This will keep things simple, making it easier to follow what's going on. The Aggregator is equally equipped to work with big loads, but that can wait until we've covered the basic principles.

8.2.1   Introducing the Aggregator EIP

Suppose you want to collect any three messages together and combine them together. Given three messages containing *A*, *B*, and *C*, you want the aggregator to output a single message containing "ABC".

Figure 8.3 shows how this would work. When the first message with correlation identifier 1 arrives, the aggregator initializes a new aggregate and stores the message inside the aggregate. In this example, the completion condition is when three messages have been aggregated, so the aggregate isn't yet complete. When the second message with correlation identifier 1 arrives, the EIP adds it to the already existing aggregate. The third message specifies a different correlation identifier value of 2, so the aggregator starts a new aggregate for that value. The fourth message relates to the first aggregate (identifier 1), so the aggregate has now aggregated three messages and the completion condition is fulfilled. As a result, the aggregator marks the aggregate as complete and publishes the resulting message:

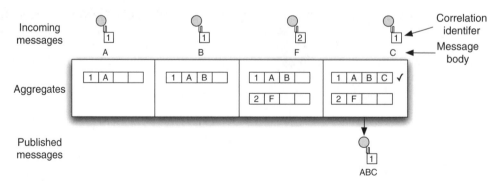

Figure 8.3   Illustrates the Aggregator EIP in action, with partial aggregated messages updated with arriving messages.

As mentioned before, there are three configurations in play when using the Aggregator EIP: correlation identifier, completion condition, and aggregation strategy. To understand how these three are specified and how they work, let's start with the example of a Camel route in the Java DSL (with the configurations in bold):

```
public void configure() throws Exception {
    from("direct:start")
        .log("Sending ${body} with correlation key ${header.myId}")
        .aggregate(header("myId"), new MyAggregationStrategy())
            .completionSize(3)
            .log("Sending out ${body}")
            .to("mock:result");
```

The correlation identifier is header("myId"), and it's a Camel Expression. It returns the header with the key "myId". The second configuration element is the AggregationStrategy, which is a class. We'll cover this class in more detail in a moment. Finally, the completion condition is based on size (there are five kinds of completion conditions, listed in table 8.3). It simply states that when three messages have been aggregated, the completion should trigger.

The same example in Spring XML is as follows:

```
<bean id="myAggregationStrategy"
      class="camelinaction.MyAggregationStrategy"/>

<camelContext xmlns="http://camel.apache.org/schema/spring">
    <route>
        <from uri="direct:start"/>
        <log message="Sending ${body} with key ${header.myId}"/>
        <aggregate strategyRef="myAggregationStrategy" completionSize="3">
            <correlationExpression>
                <header>myId</header>
            </correlationExpression>
            <log message="Sending out ${body}"/>
            <to uri="mock:result"/>
        </aggregate>
    </route>
</camelContext>
```

The Spring XML is a little different than the Java DSL because you define the AggregationStrategy using the strategyRef attribute on the <aggregate> tag. This refers to a Spring <bean>, which is listed in the top of the Spring XML file. The completion condition is also defined as a completionSize attribute. The most noticeable difference is how the correlation identifier is defined. In Spring XML, it is defined using the <correlationExpression> tag, which has a child tag that includes the Expression.

The source code for the book contains this example in the chapter8/aggregator directory. You can run the examples using the following Maven goals:

```
mvn test -Dtest=AggregateABCTest
mvn test -Dtest=SpringAggregateABCTest
```

The examples use the following unit test method:

```
public void testABC() throws Exception {
    MockEndpoint mock = getMockEndpoint("mock:result");
    mock.expectedBodiesReceived("ABC");

    template.sendBodyAndHeader("direct:start", "A", "myId", 1);
    template.sendBodyAndHeader("direct:start", "B", "myId", 1);
    template.sendBodyAndHeader("direct:start", "F", "myId", 2);
    template.sendBodyAndHeader("direct:start", "C", "myId", 1);

    assertMockEndpointsSatisfied();
}
```

This unit test sends the same messages as shown in figure 8.3—four messages in total. When you run the test, you will see the output on the console:

```
INFO route1 - Sending A with correlation key 1
INFO route1 - Sending B with correlation key 1
INFO route1 - Sending F with correlation key 2
INFO route1 - Sending C with correlation key 1
INFO route1 - Sending out ABC
```

Notice how the console output matches the sequence in which the messages were aggregated in the example from figure 8.3. As you can see from the console output, the messages with correlation key 1 were completed, because they met the completion condition, which was size based on three messages. The last line of the output shows the published message, which contains the letters "ABC."

So what happens with the *F* message? Well, its completion condition has not been met, so it waits in the aggregator. You could modify the test method to send in additional two messages to complete that second group as well:

```
template.sendBodyAndHeader("direct:start", "G", "myId", 2);
template.sendBodyAndHeader("direct:start", "H", "myId", 2);
```

Let's now turn our focus to how the Aggregator EIP combines the messages, which causes the *A*, *B*, and *C* messages to be published as a single message. This is where the AggregationStrategy comes into the picture, because it orchestrates this.

USING AGGREGATIONSTRATEGY

The AggregationStrategy class is located in the org.apache.camel.processor.aggregation package, and it defines a single method:

```
public interface AggregationStrategy {
    Exchange aggregate(Exchange oldExchange, Exchange newExchange);
}
```

If you are having a déjà vu moment, its most likely because AggregationStrategy is also used by the Content Enricher EIP, which we covered in chapter 3.

Listing 8.1 shows the strategy used in the previous example.

Listing 8.1 AggregationStrategy for merging messages together

```
import org.apache.camel.Exchange;
import org.apache.camel.processor.aggregate.AggregationStrategy;

public class MyAggregationStrategy implements AggregationStrategy {

    public Exchange aggregate(Exchange oldExchange, Exchange newExchange) {
        if (oldExchange == null) {
```

```
        return newExchange;
    }
    String oldBody = oldExchange.getIn()
                        .getBody(String.class);
    String newBody = newExchange.getIn()
                        .getBody(String.class);
    String body = oldBody + newBody;

    oldExchange.getIn().setBody(body);
    return oldExchange;
    }
}
```

❶ Occurs for a new group

❷ Combines message bodies

At runtime, the `aggregate` method is invoked every time a new message arrives. In this example, it will be invoked four times: one for each arriving message *A*, *B*, *F*, and *C*. To show how this works, we've listed the invocations as they would happen, in table 8.2.

Table 8.2   Sequence of invocations of `aggregate` method occurring at runtime

Arrived	oldExchange	newExchange	Description
A	null	A	The first message arrives for the first group
B	A	B	The second messages arrives for the first group
F	null	F	The first message arrives for the second group
C	AB	C	The third message arrives for the first group

Notice in table 8.2 that the `oldExchange` parameter is `null` on two occasions. This occurs when a new correlation group is formed (no preexisting messages have arrived with the same correlation identifier). In this situation, you simply want to return the message as is, because there are no other messages to combine it with ❶.

On the subsequent aggregations, neither parameter is `null` so you need to merge the data into one `Exchange`. In this example, you grab the message bodies and add them together ❷. Then you replace the existing body in the `oldExchange` with the updated body.

> **NOTE**   The Aggregator EIP uses synchronization, which ensures that the `AggregationStrategy` is thread safe—only one thread is invoking the `aggregate` method at any time. The Aggregator also ensures ordering, which means the messages are aggregated in the same order as they are sent into the Aggregator.

You should now understand the principles of how the Aggregator works. For a message to be published from the Aggregator, a completion condition must have been met. In the next section, we'll discuss this and review the different conditions Camel provides out of the box.

8.2.2   Completion conditions for the Aggregator

Completion conditions play a bigger role in the Aggregator than you might think. Imagine a situation where a condition never occurs, causing aggregated messages never to be published. For example, suppose the *C* message never arrived in the example in section 8.2.1. To remedy this, you could add a timeout condition that would react if all messages aren't received within a certain time period.

To cater for that situation and others, Camel provides five different completion conditions, which are listed in table 8.3. You can mix and match them according to your needs.

Table 8.3 **Different kinds of completion conditions provided by the Aggregator EIP**

Condition	Description
completionSize	Defines a completion condition based on the number of messages aggregated together. You can either use a fixed value (int) or use an Expression to dynamically decide a size at runtime.
completionTimeout	Defines a completion condition based on an inactivity timeout. This condition triggers if a correlation group has been inactive longer than the specified period. Timeouts are scheduled for each correlation group, so the timeout is individual to each group.
	You can either use a fixed value (long) or use an Expression to dynamically decide a timeout at runtime. The period is defined in milliseconds. You can't use this condition together with the completionInterval.
completionInterval	Defines a completion condition based on a scheduled interval. This condition triggers periodically. There is a single scheduled timeout for *all* correlation groups, which causes all groups to complete at the same time.
	The period (long) is defined in milliseconds. You can't use this condition together with the completionTimeout.
completionPredicate	Defines a completion condition based on whether the Predicate matched. See also the eagerCheckCompletion option in table 8.5.
completionFromBatchConsumer	Defines a completion condition that is only applicable when the arriving Exchanges are coming from a BatchConsumer (http://camel.apache.org/batch-consumer.html). At the time of writing, the following components support this condition: File, FTP, Mail, iBatis, and JPA.

The Aggregator supports using multiple completion conditions, such as using both the completionSize and completionTimeout conditions. When using multiple conditions, though, the winner takes all—the completion condition that completes first will result in the message being published.

> **NOTE** The source code for the book contains examples in the chapter8/ aggregator directory for all conditions; you can refer to them for further details. Also the Aggregator documentation on the Camel website has more details: http://camel.apache.org/aggregator2.

We'll now look at how you can use multiple completion conditions.

USING MULTIPLE COMPLETION CONDITIONS

The source code for this book contains an example in the chapter8/aggregator directory showing how to use multiple completion conditions. You can run the example using the following Maven goals:

```
mvn test -Dtest=AggregateXMLTest
mvn test -Dtest=SpringAggregateXMLTest
```

The route in the Java DSL is as follows:

```
import static org.apache.camel.builder.xml.XPathBuilder.xpath;

public void configure() throws Exception {
    from("direct:start")
        .log("Sending ${body}")
        .aggregate(xpath("/order/@customer"), new MyAggregationStrategy())
            .completionSize(2).completionTimeout(5000)
            .log("Sending out ${body}")
            .to("mock:result");
}
```

As you can see from the bold code in the route, using a second condition is just a matter of adding an additional completion condition.

The same example in Spring XML is shown here:

```
<bean id="myAggregationStrategy"
      class="camelinaction.MyAggregationStrategy"/>

<camelContext xmlns="http://camel.apache.org/schema/spring">
    <route>
        <from uri="direct:start"/>
        <log message="Sending ${body}"/>
        <aggregate strategyRef="myAggregationStrategy"
                    completionSize="2" completionTimeout="5000">
            <correlationExpression>
                <xpath>/order/@customer</xpath>
            </correlationExpression>
            <log message="Sending out ${body}"/>
            <to uri="mock:result"/>
        </aggregate>
    </route>
</camelContext>
```

If you run this example, it will use the following test method:

```
public void testXML() throws Exception {
    MockEndpoint mock = getMockEndpoint("mock:result");
    mock.expectedMessageCount(2);
    template.sendBody("direct:start",
        "<order name=\"motor\" amount=\"1000\" customer=\"honda\"/>");
    template.sendBody("direct:start",
        "<order name=\"motor\" amount=\"500\" customer=\"toyota\"/>");
    template.sendBody("direct:start",
```

```
            "<order name=\"gearbox\" amount=\"200\" customer=\"toyota\"/>");
    assertMockEndpointsSatisfied();
}
```

This example should cause the aggregator to publish two outgoing messages, as shown in the following console output; one for Honda and one for Toyota.

```
09:37:35 - Sending <order name="motor" amount="1000" customer="honda"/>
09:37:35 - Sending <order name="motor" amount="500" customer="toyota"/>
09:37:35 - Sending <order name="gearbox" amount="200" customer="toyota"/>
09:37:35 - Sending out
          <order name="motor" amount="500" customer="toyota"/>
          <order name="gearbox" amount="200" customer="toyota"/>
09:37:41 - Sending out
          <order name="motor" amount="1000" customer="honda"/>
```

If you look closely at the test method and the output from the console, you should notice that the Honda order arrived first, but it was the last to be published. This is because its completion was triggered by the timeout, which was set to 5 seconds. In the meantime, the Toyota order had its completion triggered by the size of two messages, so it was published first.

TIP The Aggregator EIP allows you to use up to four completion conditions; the `completionTimeout` and `completionInterval` conditions can't be used at the same time.

Using multiple completion conditions makes good sense if you want to ensure that aggregated messages eventually get published. For example, the timeout condition ensures that after a period of inactivity the message will be published. In that regard, you can use the timeout condition as a fallback condition, with the price being that the published message will only be partly aggregated. Suppose you expected two messages to be aggregated into one, but you only received one message; the next section reveals how you can tell which condition triggered the completion.

AGGREGATED EXCHANGE PROPERTIES

Camel enriches the published `Exchange` with the completion details listed in table 8.4.

Table 8.4 Properties on the `Exchange` related to aggregation

Property	Type	Description
Exchange.AGGREGATED SIZE	Integer	The total number of arrived messages aggregated.
Exchange.AGGREGATED COMPLETED BY	String	The condition that triggered the completion. Possible values are "size", "timeout", "interval", "predicate", and "consumer".
		The "consumer" value represents the completion from batch consumer.
Exchange.AGGREGATED CORRELATION KEY	String	The correlation identifier as a String.

The information listed in table 8.4 allows you to know how a published aggregated Exchange was completed, and how many messages were combined. For example, you could log to the console which condition completed, simply by adding this to the Camel route:

```
.log("Completed by ${property.CamelAggregatedCompletedBy}")
```

This information might come in handy in your business logic, when you need to know whether or not all messages were aggregated. You can tell this by checking the AGGREGATED_COMPLETED_BY property, which could contain either the value "size" or "timeout". If the value is "size", all the messages were aggregated; if the value is "timeout", a timeout occurred, and not all expected message were aggregated.

The Aggregator has additional configuration options that you may need to use. For example, you can specify how it should react when an arrived message contains an invalid correlation identifier.

ADDITIONAL CONFIGURATION OPTIONS

The Aggregator is the most sophisticated EIP implemented in Camel, and table 8.5 lists the additional configuration options you can use to tweak it to fit your needs.

Table 8.5   Additional configuration options available for the Aggregator EIP

Configuration option	Default	Description
eagerCheckCompletion	false	This option specifies whether or not to eager-check for completion. Eager checking means Camel will check for completion conditions before aggregating. By default, Camel will check for completion after aggregation.
		This option is used to control how the completion-Predicate condition behaves. If the option is false, the completion predicate will use the aggregated Exchange for evaluation. If true, the incoming Exchange is used for evaluation.
closeCorrelationKey-OnCompletion	null	This option determines whether a given correlation group should be marked as closed when it's completed. If a correlation group is closed, any subsequent arriving Exchanges are rejected and a ClosedCorrelationKeyException is thrown.
		This option uses an Integer parameter that represents a maximum bound for a least recently used (LRU) cache, which keeps track of closed correlation keys. Note that this cache is in-memory only and will be reset if Camel is restarted.

Table 8.5 Additional configuration options available for the Aggregator EIP *(continued)*

Configuration option	Default	Description
ignoreInvalid-CorrelationKeys	false	This option specifies whether or not to ignore invalid correlation keys. By default, Camel throws a CamelExchange-Exception for invalid keys. You can suppress this by setting this option to true, in which case Camel skips the invalid message.
groupExchanges	false	This option is used for grouping arriving Exchanges into a single combined Exchange holder that contains the Exchanges. If it's enabled, you should *not* configure an AggregationStrategy.

If you want to learn more about the configuration options listed in table 8.5, there are examples for each option in the source code for the book in the chapter8/aggregator directory. You can run test examples using the following Maven goals:

```
mvn test -Dtest=AggregateABCEagerTest
mvn test -Dtest=SpringAggregateABCEagerTest
mvn test -Dtest=AggregateABCCloseTest
mvn test -Dtest=SpringAggregateABCCloseTest
mvn test -Dtest=AggregateABCInvalidTest
mvn test -Dtest=SpringAggregateABCInvalidTest
mvn test -Dtest=AggregateABCGroupTest
mvn test -Dtest=SpringAggregateABCGroupTest
```

In the next section, we'll look at solving the problems with persistence. The Aggregator, by default, uses an in-memory repository to hold the current in-progress aggregated messages, and those messages will be lost if the application is stopped or the server crashes. To remedy this, you need to use a persisted repository.

8.2.3 Using persistence with the Aggregator

The Aggregator is a stateful EIP because it needs to store the in-progress aggregates until completion conditions occur and the aggregated message can be published. By default, the Aggregator will keep state in memory only. If the application is shut down or the host container crashes, the state will be lost.

To remedy this problem, you need to store the state in a persistent repository. Camel provides a pluggable feature so you can use a repository of your choice. This comes in two flavors:

- AggregationRepository—An interface that defines the general operations for working with a repository, such as adding data to and removing data from it. By default, Camel uses MemoryAggregationRepository, which is a memory-only repository.

- RecoverableAggregationRepository—An interface that defines additional operations supporting recovery. Camel provides such a repository out of the box in the camel-hawtdb component. We'll cover recovery in section 8.2.4.

About HawtDB

HawtDB is a lightweight and embeddable file-based key/value database. It allows Camel to provide persistence for various Camel features, such as the Aggregator. In the future, other Camel features will leverage HawtDB.

You can find more information about HawtDB at its website: http://hawtdb.fusesource.org.

We'll look at how you can use HawtDB as a persistent repository.

USING CAMEL-HAWTDB

To demonstrate how to use HawtDB with the Aggregator, we'll return to the ABC example. In essence, all you need to do is instruct the Aggregator to use `HawtDB-AggregationRepository` as its repository.

First, though, you must set up HawtDB, which is done as follows:

```
AggregationRepository myRepo = new
    HawtDBAggregationRepository("myrepo", "data/myrepo.dat");
```

Or, in Spring XML you would do this:

```
<bean id="myRepo
    class="org.apache.camel.component.hawtdb.HawtDBAggregationRepository">
    <property name="repositoryName" value="myrepo"/>
    <property name="persistentFileName" value="data/myrepo.dat"/>
</bean>
```

As you can see, this creates a new instance of `HawtDBAggregationRepository` and provides two parameters: the repository name, which is a symbolic name, and the physical filename to use as persistent storage. The repository name must be specified because you can have multiple repositories in the same file.

TIP You can find information about the additional supported options for the HawtDB component at the Camel website: http://camel.apache.org/hawtdb

To use `HawtDBAggregationRepository` in the Camel route, you can instruct the Aggregator to use it as shown here.

Listing 8.2 Using HawtDB with Aggregator in Java DSL

```
AggregationRepository myRepo = new
    HawtDBAggregationRepository("myrepo", "data/myrepo.dat");

from("file://target/inbox")
    .log("Consuming ${file:name}")
```

```
.aggregate(constant(true), new MyAggregationStrategy())
  .aggregationRepository(myRepo)
  .completionSize(3)
  .log("Sending out ${body}")
  .to("mock:result");
```

Here's the same example in Spring XML.

Listing 8.3 Using HawtDB with Aggregator in Spring XML

```
<bean id="myAggregationStrategy"
    class="camelinaction.MyAggregationStrategy"/>            ❶ HawtDB persistent
                                                                repository
<bean id="myRepo
    class="org.apache.camel.component.hawtdb.HawtDBAggregationRepository">
    <property name="repositoryName" value="myrepo"/>
    <property name="persistentFileName" value="data/myrepo.dat"/>
</bean>

<camelContext xmlns="http://camel.apache.org/schema/spring">
    <route>
        <from uri="file://target/inbox"/>
        <log message="Consuming ${file:name}"/>
        <aggregate strategyRef="myAggregationStrategy" completionSize="3"
                    aggregationRepositoryRef="myRepo">
            <correlationExpression>
                <constant>true</constant>
            </correlationExpression>
            <log message="Sending out ${body}"/>
        </aggregate>
    </route>
</camelContext>
```

As you can see from listing 8.3, a Spring bean tag is defined with the ID "myRepo" ❶,
which sets up the persistent AggregationRepository. The name for the repository
and the filename are configured as properties on the bean tag. In the Camel route,
you then refer to this repository using the aggregationRepositoryRef attribute on
the aggregate tag.

RUNNING THE EXAMPLE

The source code for the book contains this example in the chapter8/aggregator
directory. You can run it using the following Maven goals:

```
mvn test -Dtest=AggregateABCHawtDBTest
mvn test -Dtest=SpringAggregateABCHawtDBTest
```

To demonstrate how the persistence store works, the example will start up and run
for 20 seconds. In that time, you can copy files in the target/inbox directory and
have those files consumed and aggregated. On every third file, the Aggregator will
complete and publish a message.

The example will display instructions on the console about how to do this:

```
Copy 3 files to target/inbox to trigger the completion
Files to copy:
  copy src/test/resources/a.txt target/inbox
```

```
copy src/test/resources/b.txt target/inbox
copy src/test/resources/c.txt target/inbox
```

```
Sleeping for 20 seconds
You can let the test terminate (or press ctrl + c) and then start it again
Which should let you be able to resume.
```

For example, if you copy the first two files and then let the example terminate, you'll see the following:

```
cd chapter8/aggregator
chapter8/aggregator$ cp src/test/resources/a.txt target/inbox
chapter8/aggregator$ cp src/test/resources/b.txt target/inbox
```

The console should indicate that it consumed two files and was shut down:

```
2010-04-25 INFO route1 - Consuming file a.txt
2010-04-25 INFO route1 - Consuming file b.txt
...
2010-04-25 INFO DefaultCamelContext - Apache Camel 2.5.0 is shutdown
```

The next time you start the example, you can resume where you left off, and copy the last file:

```
chapter8/aggregator$ cp src/test/resources/c.txt target/inbox
```

Then the Aggregator should complete and publish the message:

```
2010-04-25 INFO HawtDBAggregationRepository - On startup there are 1
    aggregate exchanges (not completed) in repository: myrepo
2010-04-25 INFO DefaultCamelContext - Apache Camel 2.5.0 is started
...
2010-04-25 INFO route1 - Consuming file c.txt
2010-04-25 INFO route1 - Sending out ABC
```

Notice how it logs on startup how many exchanges are in the persistent repository. In this example there is one existing Exchange on startup.

Now you've seen the persistent Aggregator in action. Let's move on to look at using recovery with the Aggregator, which ensures that published messages can be safely recovered and be routed in a transactional way.

8.2.4 *Using recovery with the Aggregator*

The examples covered in the previous section focused on ensuring that messages are persisted during aggregation. But there's another place where messages may be lost: messages that have been published (send out) from the Aggregator, could potentially fail during routing as well.

To remedy this problem you could use one of these two approaches:

- *Camel error handlers (covered in chapter 5)*—these provide redelivery and dead letter channel capabilities.
- *The HawtDB component*—the HawtDBAggregationRepository provides recovery, redelivery, dead letter channel, and transactional capabilities.

Camel error handlers aren't tightly coupled with the Aggregator, so message handling is in the hands of the error handler. If a message repeatedly fails, the error handler can only deal with this by retrying or eventually giving up and moving the message to a dead letter channel.

> **NOTE** `RecoverableAggregationRepository` is an interface extending `AggregationRepository`, which offers the recovery, redelivery, and dead letter channel features. The `HawtDBAggregationRepository` implements this interface.

The `HawtDBAggregationRepository` on the other hand, is tightly integrated into the Aggregator, which allows additional benefits such as leveraging the persistence store for recovery and offering transactional capabilities. It ensures published messages that fail will be recovered and redelivered. You can think of this as what a JMS broker, such as Apache ActiveMQ, can do by bumping failed messages back up on the JMS queue for redelivery.

UNDERSTANDING RECOVERY

To better understand how recovery works, we've provided the following two figures.

Figure 8.4 shows what happens when an aggregated message is being published for the first time, and the message fails during processing. This could also be the situation when a server crashes while processing the message.

An aggregated message is complete, so the Aggregator signals ❶ this to the `RecoverableAggregationRepository`, which fetches the aggregated message to be

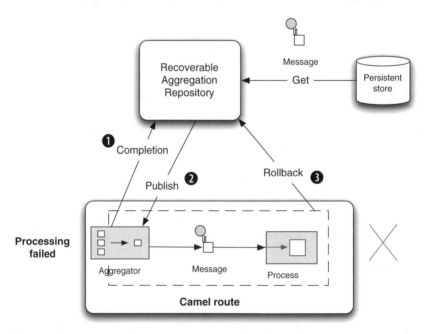

Figure 8.4   An aggregated message is completed ❶, it's published from the Aggregator ❷, and processing fails ❸, so the message is rolled back.

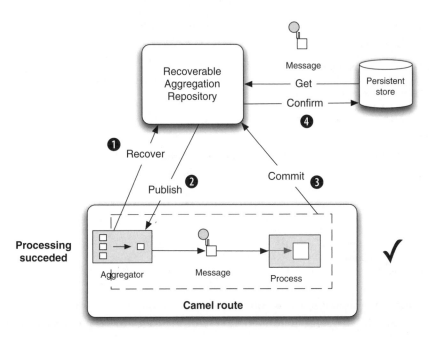

Figure 8.5 The Aggregator recovers ❶ failed messages, which are published again ❷, and this time the messages completed ❸ successfully ❹.

published ❷. The message is then routed in Camel—but suppose it fails during routing ❸. A signal is sent from the Aggregator to the RecoverableAggregationRepository, which can act accordingly.

Now imagine the same message is recovered and redelivered, as shown in figure 8.5.

The Aggregator uses a background task, which runs every 5 seconds, to scan for previously published messages to be recovered ❶. Any such messages will be republished ❷, and the message will be routed again. This time, the message could be processed successfully, which lets the Aggregator issue a commit ❸. The repository confirms ❹ the message, ensuring it won't be recovered on subsequent scans.

NOTE   The transactional behavior provided by RecoverableAggregationRepository isn't based on Spring's TransactionManager (which we'll cover in chapter 9). The transactional behavior is based on HawtDB's own transaction mechanism.

RUNNING THE EXAMPLE

The source code for the book contains this example in the chapter8/aggregator directory. You can run it using the following Maven goals:

```
mvn test -Dtest=AggregateABCRecoverTest
mvn test -Dtest=SpringAggregateABCRecoverTest
```

The example is constructed to fail when processing the published messages, no matter what. This means that eventually you'll have to move the message to a dead letter channel.

To use recovery with routes in the Java DSL, you have to set up `HawtDBAggrega-tionRepository` as shown here:

```
HawtDBAggregationRepository hawtDB = new
    HawtDBAggregationRepository("myrepo", "data/myrepo.dat");
hawtDB.setUseRecovery(true);
hawtDB.setMaximumRedeliveries(4);
hawtDB.setDeadLetterUri("mock:dead");
hawtDB.setRecoveryInterval(3000);
```

In Spring XML, you can set this up as a spring <bean> tag, as follows:

```
<bean id="myRepo"
    class="org.apache.camel.component.hawtdb.HawtDBAggregationRepository">
    <property name="repositoryName" value="myrepo"/>
    <property name="persistentFileName" value="data/myrepo.dat"/>
    <property name="useRecovery" value="true"/>
    <property name="recoveryInterval" value="3000"/>
    <property name="maximumRedeliveries" value="4"/>
    <property name="deadLetterUri" value="mock:dead"/>
</bean>
```

The options may make sense as you read them now, but we'll revisit them in table 8.7. In this example, the Aggregator will check for messages to be recovered every 3 seconds. To avoid a message being repeatedly recovered, the maximum redeliveries are set to 4. This means that after 4 failed recovery attempts, the message is exhausted and is moved to the dead letter channel. If you omit the maximum redeliveries option, Camel will keep recovering failed messages forever until they can be processed successfully.

If you run the example, you'll notice that the console outputs the failures as stack traces, and at the end you'll see a WARN entry that indicates the message has been moved to the dead letter channel:

```
2010-04-26 [AggregateRecoverChecker] WARN - The recovered exchange is
exhausted after 4 attempts, will now be moved to dead letter channel:
mock:dead
```

We encourage you to try this example and read the code comments in the source code to better understand how this works.

The preceding log output identifies the number of redelivery attempts, but how does Camel know this? Obviously Camel stores this information on the Exchange. Table 8.6 reveals where this information is stored.

Table 8.6   Headers on Exchange related to redelivery

Header	Type	Description
Exchange.REDELIVERY_COUNTER	int	The current redelivery attempt. The counter starts with the value of 1.
Exchange.REDELIVERED	boolean	Whether this Exchange is being redelivered.
Exchange.REDELIVERY_EXHAUSTED	boolean	Whether this Exchange has attempted all redeliveries and still failed (also known as being exhausted).

The information in table 8.6 is only available when Camel performs a recovery. These headers are absent on the regular first attempt. It's only when a recovery is triggered that these headers are set on the `Exchange`.

Table 8.7 lists the options for the `RecoverableAggregationRepository` that are related to recovery.

Table 8.7 `RecoverableAggregationRepository` **configuration options related to recovery**

Option	Default	Description
`useRecovery`	`true`	Whether or not recovery is enabled.
`recoveryInterval`	`5000`	How often the recovery background tasks are executed. The value is in milliseconds.
`deadLetterUri`	`null`	An optional dead letter channel, where published messages that are exhausted should be sent. This is similar to the `DeadLetterChannel` error handler, which we covered in chapter 5. This option is disabled by default. When in use, the `maximumRedeliveries` option must be configured as well.
`maximumRedeliveries`	`null`	A limit that defines when published messages that repeatedly fail are considered exhausted and should be moved to the dead letter URI. This option is disabled by default.

We won't go into more detail regarding the options in table 8.7, as we've already covered an example using them.

This concludes our extensive coverage of the sophisticated and probably most complex EIP implemented in Camel—the Aggregator. In the next section, we'll look at the Splitter pattern.

8.3 *The Splitter EIP*

Messages passing through an integration solution may consist of multiple elements, such as an order, which typically consists of more than a single line item. Each line in the order may need to be handled differently, so you need an approach that processes the complete order, treating each line item individually. The solution to this problem is the Splitter EIP, illustrated in figure 8.6.

In this section, we'll teach you all you need to know about the Splitter. We'll start with a simple example and move on from there.

Figure 8.6   The Splitter breaks out the incoming message into a series of individual messages.

8.3.1 *Using the Splitter*

Using the Splitter in Camel is straightforward, so let's try a basic example that will split one message into three messages, each containing one of the letters *A*, *B*, and *C*. Listing 8.4 shows the example using a Java DSL–based Camel route and a unit test.

Listing 8.4   A basic example of the Splitter EIP

```
public class SplitterABCTest extends CamelTestSupport {

    public void testSplitABC() throws Exception {
        MockEndpoint mock = getMockEndpoint("mock:split");
        mock.expectedBodiesReceived("A", "B", "C");

        List<String> body = new ArrayList<String>();
        body.add("A");
        body.add("B");
        body.add("C");
        template.sendBody("direct:start", body);

        assertMockEndpointsSatisfied();
    }

    protected RouteBuilder createRouteBuilder() throws Exception {
        return new RouteBuilder() {
            public void configure() throws Exception {
                from("direct:start")
                    .split(body())                       ◁⎯┐  Splits incoming
                        .log("Split line ${body}")        ❶  message body
                        .to("mock:split");
            }
        };
    }
}
```

The test method sets up a mock endpoint that expects three messages to arrive, in the order *A*, *B*, and *C*. Then you construct a single combined message body that consists of a List of Strings containing the three letters. The Camel route will use the Splitter EIP to split up the message body ❶.

   If you run this test, the console should log the three messages, as follows:

```
INFO  route1 - Split line A
INFO  route1 - Split line B
INFO  route1 - Split line C
```

When using the Splitter EIP in Spring XML, you have to do this a bit differently because the Splitter uses an Expression to return what is to be split.

   In the Java DSL we defined the Expression shown in bold:

```
.split(body())
```

Here, body() is a method available on the RouteBuilder, which returns an org.apache.camel.Expression instance. In Spring XML you need to do this as shown in bold:

```
<camelContext xmlns="http://camel.apache.org/schema/spring">
    <route>
        <from uri="direct:start"/>
```

```
    <split>
        <simple>${body}</simple>
        <log message="Split line ${body}"/>
        <to uri="mock:split"/>
    </split>
  </route>
</camelContext>
```

In Spring XML, you use the Camel's expression language, known as Simple (discussed in appendix A), to tell the Splitter that it should split the message body.

The source code for the book contains this example in the chapter8/splitter directory. You can run it using the following Maven goals:

```
mvn test -Dtest=SplitterABCTest
mvn test -Dtest=SpringSplitterABCTest
```

Now you've seen the Splitter in action. To better understand how you can tell Camel what it should split, you need to understand how it works.

HOW THE SPLITTER WORKS

The Splitter works something like a big iterator that iterates through something and processes each entry. The sequence diagram in figure 8.7 shows more details about how this *big iterator* works.

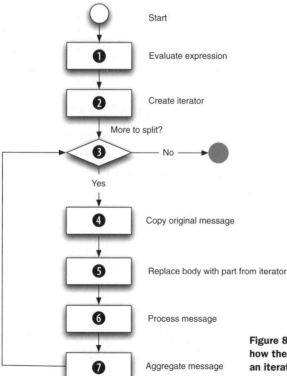

Start

1 Evaluate expression

2 Create iterator

More to split?

3 — No ⟶ ●

Yes

4 Copy original message

5 Replace body with part from iterator

6 Process message

7 Aggregate message

Figure 8.7 A sequence diagram showing how the Splitter works internally, by using an iterator to iterate through the message and process each entry.

When working with the Splitter, you have to configure an `Expression`, which is evaluated ❶ when a message arrives. In listing 8.4, the evaluation returned the message body. The result from the evaluation is used to create a `java.util.Itetator` ❷.

> **What can be iterated?**
>
> When Camel creates the iterator ❷, it supports a range of types. Camel knows how to iterate through the following types: `Collection`, `Iterator`, `Array`, `org.w3c.dom.NodeList`, `String` (with entries separated by commas). Any other type will be iterated once.

Then the Splitter uses the iterator ❸ until there is no more data. Each message to be sent out of the iterator is a copy of the message ❹, which has had its message body replaced with the part from the iterator ❺. In listing 8.4, there would be three parts: each of the letters *A*, *B*, and *C*. The message to be sent out is then processed ❻, and when the processing is done, the message may be aggregated ❼ (more about this in section 8.3.4).

The Splitter will decorate each message it sends out with properties on the `Exchange`, which are listed in table 8.8.

Table 8.8   Properties on the `Exchange` related to the Splitter EIP

Property	Type	Description
`Exchange.SPLIT_INDEX`	`Integer`	The index for the current message being processed. The index is zero-based.
`Exchange.SPLIT_SIZE`	`Integer`	The total number of messages the original message has been split into. Note that this information isn't available in streaming mode (see section 8.3.3 for more details about streaming).
`Exchange.SPLIT_COMPLETE`	`Boolean`	Whether or not this is the last message being processed.

You may find yourself in a situation where you need more power to do the splitting, such as to dictate exactly how a message should be split. And what better power is there than Java? By using Java code, you have the ultimate control and can tackle any situation.

8.3.2   *Using beans for splitting*

Suppose you need to split messages that contain complex payloads. Suppose the message payload is a `Customer` object containing a list of `Departments`, and you want to split by `Department`, as illustrated in figure 8.8:

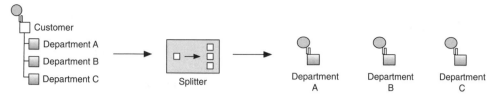

Figure 8.8   Splitting a complex message into submessages by department

The `Customer` object is a simple bean containing the following information (getter and setter methods omitted):

```
public class Customer {
    private int id;
    private String name;
    private List<Department> departments;
}
```

The `Department` object is simple as well:

```
public class Department {
    private int id;
    private String address;
    private String zip;
    private String country;
}
```

You may wonder why you can't split the message as in the previous example, using `split(body())`? The reason is that the message payload (the message body) isn't a `List`, but a `Customer` object. Therefore you need to tell Camel how to split, which you do as follows:

```
public class CustomerService {
    public List<Department> splitDepartments(Customer customer) {
        return customer.getDepartments();
    }
}
```

The `splitDepartments` method returns a `List` of `Department` objects, which is what you want to split by.

In the Java DSL, you can use the `CustomerService` bean for splitting by telling Camel to invoke the `splitDepartments` method. This is done by using the `method` call expression as shown in bold:

```
public void configure() throws Exception {
    from("direct:start")
        .split().method(CustomerService.class, "splitDepartments")
            .to("log:split")
            .to("mock:split");
}
```

In Spring XML, you'd have to declare the `CustomerService` in a Spring bean tag, as follows:

```
<bean id="customerService" class="camelinaction.CustomerService"/>

<camelContext xmlns="http://camel.apache.org/schema/spring">
    <route>
        <from uri="direct:start"/>
        <split>
            <method bean="customerService" method="splitDepartments"/>
            <to uri="log:split"/>
            <to uri="mock:split"/>
        </split>
    </route>
</camelContext>
```

The source code for the book contains this example in the chapter8/splitter directory. You can run it using the following Maven goals:

```
mvn test -Dtest=SplitterBeanTest
mvn test -Dtest=SpringSplitterBeanTest
```

The logic in the `splitDepartments` method is simple, but it shows how you can use a method on a bean to do the splitting. In your use cases, you may need more complex logic.

> **TIP** The logic in the `splitDepartments` method seems trivial, and it's possible to use Camel's expression language (Simple) to invoke methods on the message body. In Java DSL you could define the route as follows: `.split().simple ("${body.departments}")`. In Spring XML you would use the `<simple>` tag instead of the `<method>` tag: `<simple>${body.departments}</simple>`.

The Splitter will usually operate on messages that are loaded into memory. But there are situations where the messages are so big that it's not feasible to have the entire message in memory at once.

8.3.3 *Splitting big messages*

Rider Auto Parts has an ERP system that contains inventory information from all its suppliers. To keep the inventory updated, each supplier must submit updates to Rider Auto Parts. Some suppliers do this once a day using good old-fashioned files as a means of transport. Those files could potentially be very large, so you have to split those files without loading the entire file into memory.

This can be done by using streams, which allow you to read on demand from a stream of data. This resolves the memory issue, because you can read in a chunk of data, process the data, read in another chunk, process the data, and so on.

Figure 8.9 shows the flow of the application used by Auto Rider Parts to pick up the files from the suppliers and update the inventory.

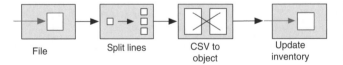

File   Split lines   CSV to object   Update inventory

Figure 8.9 A route that picks up incoming files, splits them, and transforms them so they're ready for updating the inventory in the ERP system

We'll revisit this example again in chapter 10, and cover it in much greater detail when we cover concurrency.

Implementing the route outlined in figure 8.9 is easy to do in Camel, as follows.

Listing 8.5   Splitting big files using streaming mode

```
public void configure() throws Exception {
    from("file:target/inventory")
        .log("Starting to process big file: ${header.CamelFileName}")
        .split(body().tokenize("\n")).streaming()          ❶ Splits file using
            .bean(InventoryService.class, "csvToObject")       streaming mode
            .to("direct:update")
        .end()
        .log("Done processing big file: ${header.CamelFileName}");

    from("direct:update")                                  Denotes where
        .bean(InventoryService.class, "updateInventory");  the splitting
}                                                          route ends ❷
```

As you can see in listing 8.5, all you have to do is enable streaming mode using .streaming() ❶. This tells Camel to not load the entire payload into memory, but instead to iterate the payload in a streaming fashion. Also notice the use of end() ❷ to indicate the end of the splitting route. The end() in the Java DSL is the equivalent of the end tag </split> when using Spring XML.

In Spring XML, you enable streaming using the streaming attribute on the <split> tag, as follows.

Listing 8.6   Splitting big files using streaming mode in Spring XML

```
<camelContext xmlns="http://camel.apache.org/schema/spring">
    <route>
        <from uri="file:target/inventory"/>
        <log message="Processing big file: ${header.CamelFileName}"/>
        <split streaming="true">
            <tokenize token="\n"/>
            <bean beanType="camelinaction.InventoryService"
                method="csvToObject"/>
            <to uri="direct:update"/>
        </split>
        <log message="Done processing big file: ${header.CamelFileName}"/>
    </route>

    <route>
        <from uri="direct:update"/>
        <bean beanType="camelinaction.InventoryService"
            method="updateInventory"/>
    </route>
</camelContext>
```

You may have noticed in listings 8.5 and 8.6 that the files are split using a tokenizer. The tokenizer is a powerful feature that works well with streaming. The tokenizer leverages java.util.Scanner, which supports streaming. The Scanner is capable of iterating, which means that it only reads chunks of data into memory. A token must be provided to indicate the boundaries of the chunks. In the preceding code, you use a newline (\n) as the token. So, in this example, the Scanner will only read the file into memory on a line-by-line basis, resulting in low memory consumption.

NOTE When using streaming mode, be sure the message you're splitting can be split into well-known chunks that can be iterated. You can use the tokenizer or convert the message body to a type that can be iterated, such as an Iterator.

The Splitter EIP in Camel includes an aggregation feature that lets you recombine split messages into single outbound messages, while they are being routed.

8.3.4   *Aggregating split messages*

Being able to split and aggregate messages again is a powerful mechanism. You could use this to split an order into individual order lines, process them, and then recombine them into a single outgoing message. This pattern is known as the Composed Message Processor, which we briefly touched on in section 8.1. It's shown in figure 8.1.

The Camel Splitter provides a built-in aggregator, which makes it even easier to aggregate split messages back into single outgoing messages. Figure 8.10 illustrates this principle, with the help of the "ABC" message example.

Suppose you want to translate each of the *A*, *B*, and *C* messages into a phrase, and have all the phrases combined into a single message again. This can easily be done with the Splitter—all you need to provide is the logic that combines the messages. This logic is created using an AggregationStrategy implementation.

Implementing the Camel route outlined in figure 8.10 can be done as follows in the Java DSL. The configuration of the AggregationStrategy is shown in bold:

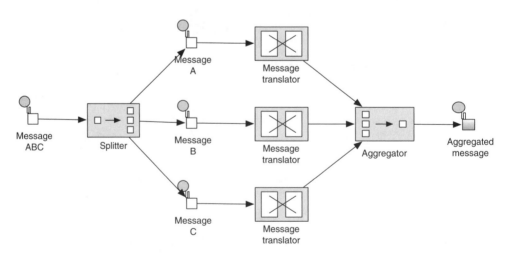

Figure 8.10   The Splitter has a built-in aggregator that can recombine split messages into a combined outgoing message.

```
from("direct:start")
    .split(body(), new MyAggregationStrategy())
        .log("Split line ${body}")
        .bean(WordTranslateBean.class)
        .to("mock:split")
    .end()
    .log("Aggregated ${body}")
    .to("mock:result");
```

In Spring XML, you have to declare the AggregationStrategy as a Spring bean tag, as shown in bold:

```
<bean id="translate" class="camelinaction.WordTranslateBean"/>

<bean id="myAggregationStrategy"
      class="camelinaction.MyAggregationStrategy"/>

<camelContext xmlns="http://camel.apache.org/schema/spring">
    <route>
        <from uri="direct:start"/>
        <split strategyRef="myAggregationStrategy">
            <simple>body</simple>
            <log message="Split line ${body}"/>
            <bean ref="translate"/>
            <to uri="mock:split"/>
        </split>
        <log message="Aggregated ${body}"/>
        <to uri="mock:result"/>
    </route>
</camelContext>
```

To combine the split messages back into a single combined message, you use the AggregationStrategy.

Listing 8.7 Combining split messages back into a single outgoing message

```
public class MyAggregationStrategy implements AggregationStrategy {

    public Exchange aggregate(Exchange oldExchange, Exchange newExchange) {
        if (oldExchange == null) {
            return newExchange;
        }

        String body = newExchange.getIn().getBody(String.class);
        String existing = oldExchange.getIn().getBody(String.class);

        oldExchange.getIn().setBody(existing + "+" + body);
        return oldExchange;
    }
}
```

As you can see from listing 8.7, you combine the messages into a single String body, with individual phrases (from the message bodies) being separated with + signs.

The source code for the book contains this example in the chapter8/splitter directory. You can run it using the following Maven goals:

```
mvn test -Dtest=SplitterAggregateABCTest
mvn test -Dtest=SpringSplitterAggregateABCTest
```

The example uses the three phrases: "Aggregated Camel rocks", "Hi mom", and "Yes it works". When you run the example, you'll see the console output the aggregated message at the end.

```
INFO   route1 - Split line A
INFO   route1 - Split line B
INFO   route1 - Split line C
INFO   route1 - Aggregated Camel rocks+Hi mom+Yes it works
```

Before we wrap up our coverage of the Splitter, let's take a look at what happens if one of the split messages fails with an exception.

8.3.5 *When errors occur during splitting*

The Splitter processes messages and those messages can fail when some business logic throws an exception. Camel's error handling is active during the splitting, so the errors you have to deal with in the Splitter are errors that Camel's error handling couldn't handle.

You have two choices for handling errors with the Splitter:

- *Stop*—The Splitter will split and process each message in sequence. Suppose the second message failed. In this situation, you could either immediately stop and let the exception propagate back, or you could continue splitting the remainder of the messages, and let the exception propagate back at the end (default behavior).
- *Aggregate*—You could handle the exception in the AggregationStrategy and decide whether or not the exception should be propagated back.

Let's look into the choices.

USING STOPONEXCEPTION

The first solution requires you to configure the stopOnException option on the Splitter as follows:

```
from("direct:start")
    .split(body(), new MyAggregationStrategy())
        .stopOnException()
        .log("Split line ${body}")
        .bean(WordTranslateBean.class)
        .to("mock:split")
    .end()
    .log("Aggregated ${body}")
    .to("mock:result");
```

In Spring XML, you use the stopOnException attribute on the <split> tag, as follows:

```
<split strategyRef="myAggregationStrategy" stopOnException="true">
```

The source code for the book contains this example in the chapter8/splitter directory. You can run it using the following Maven goals:

```
mvn test -Dtest=SplitterStopOnExceptionABCTest
mvn test -Dtest=SpringSplitterStopOnExceptionABCTest
```

The second option is to handle exceptions from the split messages in the AggregationStrategy.

HANDLING EXCEPTIONS USING AGGREGATIONSTRATEGY

The AggregationStrategy allows you to handle the exception by either ignoring it or letting it be propagated back. Here's how you could ignore the exception.

Listing 8.8   Handling an exception by ignoring it

```
public class MyIgnoreFailureAggregationStrategy
            implements AggregationStrategy {

    public Exchange aggregate(Exchange oldExchange, Exchange newExchange) {
        if (newExchange.getException() != null) {
            return oldExchange;                             ◁──┐  Ignores the
        }                                                   ❶  exception

        if (oldExchange == null) {
            return newExchange;
        }

        String body = newExchange.getIn().getBody(String.class);
        String existing = oldExchange.getIn().getBody(String.class);
        oldExchange.getIn().setBody(existing + "+" + body);
        return oldExchange;
    }
}
```

When handling exceptions in the AggregationStrategy, you can detect whether an exception occurred or not by checking the getException method from the new-Exchange parameter. The preceding example ignores the exception by returning the oldExchange ❶.

If you want to propagate back the exception, you need to keep it stored on the aggregated exception, which can be done as follows.

Listing 8.9   Propagating back an exception

```
public class MyPropagateFailureAggregationStrategy
            implements AggregationStrategy {

    public Exchange aggregate(Exchange oldExchange, Exchange newExchange) {
        if (newExchange.getException() != null) {
            if (oldExchange == null) {
                return newExchange;
            } else {
                oldExchange.setException(                    ❶  Propagates
                    newExchange.getException());           ◁──┘  exception
                return oldExchange;
            }
        }

        if (oldExchange == null) {
            return newExchange;
        }

        String body = newExchange.getIn().getBody(String.class);
        String existing = oldExchange.getIn().getBody(String.class);
        oldExchange.getIn().setBody(existing + "+" + body);
```

```
            return oldExchange;
        }
    }
}
```

As you can see, it requires a bit more work to keep the exception. On the first invocation of the `aggregate` method, the `oldExchange` parameter is `null` and you simply return the `newExchange` (which has the exception). Otherwise you must transfer the exception to the `oldExchange` ❶.

> **WARNING**   When using a custom `AggregationStrategy` with the Splitter, it's important to know that you're responsible for handling exceptions. If you don't propagate the exception back, the Splitter will assume you have handled the exception and will ignore it.

The source code for the book contains this example in the chapter8/splitter directory. You can run it using the following Maven goals:

```
mvn test -Dtest=SplitterAggregateExceptionABCTest
mvn test -Dtest=SpringSplitterAggregateExceptionABCTest
```

Now you've learned all there is to know about the Splitter. Well, almost all. We'll revisit the Splitter in chapter 10 when we look at concurrency. In the next two sections, we'll look at EIPs that support dynamic routing, starting with the Routing Slip pattern.

8.4   *The Routing Slip EIP*

There are times when you need to route messages dynamically. For example, you may have an architecture that requires incoming messages to undergo a sequence of processing steps and business rule validations. Because the steps and validations vary widely, you can implement each step as a separate filter. The filter acts as a dynamic model to apply the business rule and validations.

This architecture could be implemented using the Pipes and Filters EIP together with the Filter EIP. But as often happens with EIPs, there's a better way, known as the Routing Slip EIP. The Routing Slip acts as a dynamic router that dictates the next step a message should undergo. Figure 8.11 shows this principle.

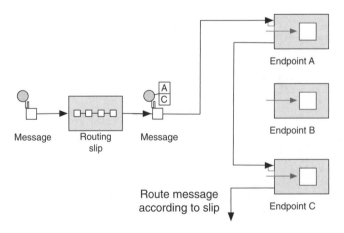

Figure 8.11   **The incoming message has a slip attached that specifies the sequence of the processing steps. The Routing Slip EIP reads the slip and routes the message to the next endpoint in the list.**

The Camel Routing Slip EIP requires a preexisting header or Expression as the attached slip. Either way, the initial slip must be prepared before the message is sent to the Routing Slip EIP.

8.4.1 Using the Routing Slip EIP

We'll start with a simple example that shows how to use the Routing Slip EIP to perform the sequence outlined in figure 8.11.

In the Java DSL, the route is as simple as this:

```
from("direct:start").routingSlip("mySlip");
```

It's also easy in Spring XML:

```
<route>
    <from uri="direct:start"/>
    <routingSlip>
        <header>mySlip</header>
    </routingSlip>
</route>
```

This example assumes the incoming message contains the slip in the header with the key "mySlip". The following test method shows how you should fill out the key:

```
public void testRoutingSlip() throws Exception {
    getMockEndpoint("mock:a").expectedMessageCount(1);
    getMockEndpoint("mock:b").expectedMessageCount(0);
    getMockEndpoint("mock:c").expectedMessageCount(1);

    template.sendBodyAndHeader("direct:start", "Hello World",
                               "mySlip", "mock:a,mock:c");
    assertMockEndpointsSatisfied();
}
```

As you can see, the value of the key is the endpoint URIs separated by commas. The comma is the default delimiter, but the routing slip supports using custom delimiters. For example, to use a semicolon, you could do this:

```
from("direct:start").routingSlip("mySlip", ";");
```

And in Spring XML, you'd do this:

```
<routingSlip uriDelimiter=";">
    <header>mySlip</header>
</routingSlip>
```

This example expects a preexisting header containing the routing slip. But what if the message doesn't contain such a header? In those situations, you have to compute the header in any way you like. In the next example, we look at how to compute the header using a bean.

8.4.2 Using a bean to compute the routing slip header

To keep things simple, the logic to compute a header that contains two or three steps has been kept in a single method, as follows:

```
public class ComputeSlip {
    public String compute(String body) {
        String answer = "mock:a";
        if (body.contains("Cool")) {
            answer += ",mock:b";
        }
        answer += ",mock:c";
        return answer;
    }
}
```

All you how to do now is leverage this bean to compute the header to be used as routing slip.

In the Java DSL, you can use the method call expression to invoke the bean and set the header:

```
from("direct:start")
    .setHeader("mySlip").method(ComputeSlip.class)
    .routingSlip("mySlip");
```

In Spring XML, you can do it as follows:

```
<route>
    <from uri="direct:start"/>
    <setHeader headerName="mySlip">
        <method beanType="camelinaction.ComputeSlip"/>
    </setHeader>
    <routingSlip>
        <header>mySlip</header>
    </routingSlip>
</route>
```

In this example, you use a method call expression to set a header that is then used by the routing slip. But you might want to skip the step of setting the header and instead use the expression directly.

8.4.3 *Using an Expression as the routing slip*

Instead of setting a header, you can use an `Expression`, such as the method call expression we covered in the previous section. Here's how you'd do so with the Java DSL:

```
from("direct:start")
    .routingSlip("mySlip").method(ComputeSlip.class);
```

The equivalent Spring XML is as follows:

```
<route>
    <from uri="direct:start"/>
    <routingSlip>
        <method beanType="camelinaction.ComputeSlip"/>
    </routingSlip>
</route>
```

Another way of using the Routing Slip EIP in Camel is to use beans and annotations.

8.4.4   *Using @RoutingSlip annotation*

The `@RoutingSlip` annotation allows you to turn a regular bean method into the Routing Slip EIP. Let's go over an example.

Suppose you have the following `SlipBean`:

```
public class SlipBean {

    @RoutingSlip
    public String slip(String body) {
        String answer = "mock:a";
        if (body.contains("Cool")) {
            answer += ",mock:b";
        }
        answer += ",mock:c";
        return answer;
    }
}
```

As you can see, all this does is annotate the `slip` method with `@RoutingSlip`. When Camel invokes the `slip` method, it detects the `@RoutingSlip` annotation and continues routing according to the Routing Slip EIP.

> **WARNING**   When using `@RecipientList` it's important to not use `recipientList` in the DSL at the same time. By doing this, Camel will double up using Recipient List EIP, which is not the intention. Instead, do as shown in the example below.

Notice that there's no mention of the routing slip in the DSL. The route is just invoking a bean.

```
from("direct:start").bean(SlipBean.class);
```

Here it is in the Spring DSL:

```
<bean id="myBean" class="camelinaction.SlipBean"/>

<route>
    <from uri="direct:start"/>
    <bean ref="myBean"/>
</route>
```

Why might you want to use this? Well, by using `@RoutingSlip` on a bean, it becomes more flexible in the sense that the bean is accessible using a endpoint URI. Any Camel client or route could easily send a message to the bean and have it continued being routed as a routing slip.

For example, using a `ProducerTemplate` you could send a message to the bean:

```
ProducerTemplate template = ...
template.sendBody("bean:myBean", "Camel rocks");
```

That `"Camel rocks"` message would then be routed as a routing slip with the slip generated as the result of the `myBean` method invocation.

The source code for the book contains the examples we've covered in the chapter8/routingslip directory. You can try them using the following Maven goals:

```
mvn test -Dtest=RoutingSlipSimpleTest
mvn test -Dtest=SpringRoutingSlipSimpleTest
mvn test -Dtest=RoutingSlipHeaderTest
mvn test -Dtest=SpringRoutingSlipHeaderTest
mvn test -Dtest=RoutingSlipTest
mvn test -Dtest=SpringRoutingSlipTest
mvn test -Dtest=RoutingSlipBeanTest
mvn test -Dtest=SpringRoutingSlipBeanTest
```

You've now seen the Routing Slip EIP in action.

8.5   *The Dynamic Router EIP*

In the previous section, you learned that the Routing Slip pattern acts as a dynamic router. So what's the difference between the Routing Slip and Dynamic Router EIPs? The difference is minimal: the Routing Slip needs to compute the slip up front, whereas the Dynamic Router will evaluate on-the-fly where the message should go next.

8.5.1   *Using the Dynamic Router*

Just like the Routing Slip, the Dynamic Router requires you to provide *logic*, which determines where the message should be routed. Such logic is easily implemented using Java code, and in this code you have total freedom to determine where the message should go next. For example, you might query a database or a rules engine to compute where the message should go.

Listing 8.10 shows the Java bean used in the example.

Listing 8.10   Java bean deciding where the message should be routed next

```
public class DynamicRouterBean {

public String route(String body,
    @Header(Exchange.SLIP_ENDPOINT) String previous) {        ◁──┐  Previous
    return whereToGo(body, previous);                          ❶  endpoint URI
}

private String whereToGo(String body, String previous) {
    if (previous == null) {
        return "mock://a";
    } else if ("mock://a".equals(previous)) {
        return "language://simple:Bye ${body}";
    } else {
        return null;                            ◁──┐  Ends
    }                                           ❷  router
}
}
```

The idea with the Dynamic Router is to let Camel keep invoking the route method until it indicates the end. The first time the route method is invoked, the previous parameter will be null ❶. On every subsequent invocation, the previous parameter contains the endpoint URI of the last step.

As you can see in the `whereToGo` method, you use this fact and return different URIs depending on the previous step. When the dynamic router is to end, you return `null` ❷.

Using the Dynamic Router from the Java DSL is easy to do:

```
from("direct:start")
    .dynamicRouter(bean(DynamicRouterBean.class, "route"))
    .to("mock:result");
```

The same route in Spring XML is just as easy as shown:

```
<bean id="myDynamicRouter" class="camelinaction.DynamicRouterBean"/>

<camelContext xmlns="http://camel.apache.org/schema/spring">
    <route>
        <from uri="direct:start"/>
        <dynamicRouter>
            <method ref="myDynamicRouter" method="route"/>
        </dynamicRouter>
        <to uri="mock:result"/>
    </route>
</camelContext>
```

The source code for the book contains this example in the chapter8/dynamicrouter directory. You can try it using the following Maven goals:

```
mvn test -Dtest=DynamicRouterTest
mvn test -Dtest=SpringDynamicRouterTest
```

There is also a Dynamic Router annotation you can use.

8.5.2 *Using the @DynamicRouter annotation*

To demonstrate how to use the `@DynamicRouter` annotation let's change the previous example to use the annotation instead. To do that, just annotate the Java code from listing 8.10 as follows:

```
@DynamicRouter
public String route(String body,
                    @Header(Exchange.SLIP_ENDPOINT) String previous) {
    ...
}
```

The next step is to invoke the `route` method on the bean, as if it were a regular bean. That means you should not use the Routing Slip EIP in the route, but use a bean instead.

In the Java DSL, this is done as follows:

```
from("direct:start")
    .bean(DynamicRouterBean.class, "route")
    .to("mock:result");
```

In Spring XML, you likewise change the `<dynamicRouter>` to a `<bean>` tag:

```
<camelContext xmlns="http://camel.apache.org/schema/spring">
    <route>
        <from uri="direct:start"/>
```

```
        <bean ref="myDynamicRouter" method="route"/>
        <to uri="mock:result"/>
    </route>
</camelContext>
```

> **WARNING**   When using `@DynamicRouter` its important to not use `dynamic-Router` in the DSL at the same time. Instead do as shown above.

The source code for the book contains this example in the chapter8/dynamicrouter directory. You can try it using the following Maven goals:

```
mvn test -Dtest=DynamicRouterAnnotationTest
mvn test -Dtest=SpringDynamicRouterAnnotationTest
```

This concludes the coverage of the dynamic routing patterns. In the next section, you'll learn about Camel's built-in Load Balancer EIP, which is useful when an existing load-balancing solution isn't in place.

8.6   *The Load Balancer EIP*

You may already be familiar with the load balancing concept in computing. Load balancing is a technique to distribute workload across computers or other resources, "in order to get optimal resource utilization, maximize throughput, minimize response time, and avoid overload" (http://en.wikipedia.org/wiki/Load_balancer). This service can be provided either in the form of a hardware device or as a piece of software, such as the Load Balancer EIP in Camel.

> **NOTE**   The Load Balancer was not distilled in the EIP book, but it will likely be added if there is a second edition of the book.

In this section, we'll introduce the Load Balancer EIP by walking through an example. Then, in section 8.6.2, we'll look at the various types of load balancers Camel offers out of the box. We'll focus on the failover type in section 8.6.3 and finally show how you can build your own load balancer in section 8.6.4.

8.6.1   *Introducing the Load Balancer EIP*

The Camel Load Balancer EIP is a `Processor` that implements the `org.apache.camel.processor.loadbalancer.LoadBalancer` interface. The `LoadBalancer` offers methods to add and remove `Processors` that should participate in the load balancing.

By using `Processors` instead of `Endpoints`, the load balancer is capable of balancing anything you can define in your Camel routes. But, that said, you'll most often balance across a number of remote services. Such an example is illustrated in figure 8.12, where a Camel application needs to load balance across two services.

When using the Load Balancer EIP, you have to select a balancing strategy. A common and understandable strategy is to take turns among the services—this is known as the round robin strategy. In section 8.6.2, we'll take a look at all the strategies Camel provides out of the box.

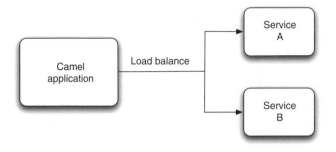

Figure 8.12 A Camel application load balances across two services.

Let's look at how you can use the Load Balancer with the round robin strategy. Here's the Java DSL with the Load Balancer:

```
from("direct:start")
    .loadBalance().roundRobin()
        .to("seda:a").to("seda:b")
    .end();

from("seda:a")
    .log("A received: ${body}")
    .to("mock:a");

from("seda:b")
    .log("B received: ${body}")
    .to("mock:b");
```

The equivalent route in Spring XML is as follows:

```
<route>
    <from uri="direct:start"/>
    <loadBalance>
        <roundRobin/>
        <to uri="seda:a"/>
        <to uri="seda:b"/>
    </loadBalance>
</route>

<route>
    <from uri="seda:a"/>
    <log message="A received: ${body}"/>
    <to uri="mock:a"/>
</route>

<route>
    <from uri="seda:b"/>
    <log message="B received: ${body}"/>
    <to uri="mock:b"/>
</route>
```

In this example, you use the SEDA component to simulate the remote services. In a real-life situation, the remote services could be a web service.

Suppose you start sending messages to the route. The first message would be sent to the `"seda:a"` endpoint, and the next would go to `"seda:b"`. The third message would start over and be sent to `"seda:a"`, and so forth.

The source code for the book contains this example in the chapter8/loadbalancer directory. You can try it by using the following Maven goals:

```
mvn test -Dtest=LoadBalancerTest
mvn test -Dtest=SpringLoadBalancerTest
```

If you run the example, the console will output something like this:

```
[Camel Thread 0 - seda://a] INFO route2 - A received: Hello
[Camel Thread 1 - seda://b] INFO route3 - B received: Camel rocks
[Camel Thread 0 - seda://a] INFO route2 - A received: Cool
[Camel Thread 1 - seda://b] INFO route3 - B received: Bye
```

In the next section, we'll review the various load-balancing strategies you can use with the Load Balancer EIP.

8.6.2 Load-balancing strategies

A load-balancing strategy dictates which Processor should process an incoming message—it's up to each strategy how the Processor is chosen. Camel allows the six different strategies listed in table 8.9.

Table 8.9 Load-balancing strategies provided by Camel

Strategy	Description
Random	Chooses a processor randomly.
Round robin	Chooses a processor in a round robin fashion, which spreads the load evenly. This is a classic and well-known strategy. We covered this in section 8.6.1.
Sticky	Uses an expression to calculate a correlation key that dictates the processor chosen. You can think of this as the session ID used in HTTP requests.
Topic	Sends the message to all processors. This is like sending to a JMS topic.
Failover	Retries using another processor. We'll cover this in section 8.6.3.
Custom	Uses your own custom strategy. This is covered in section 8.6.4.

The first four strategies in table 8.9 are easy to set up and use in Camel. For example, using the random strategy is just a matter of specifying it in the Java DSL:

```
from("direct:start")
    .loadBalance().random()
        .to("seda:a").to("seda:b")
    .end();
```

It's similar in Spring XML:

```
<route>
    <from uri="direct:start"/>
    <loadBalance>
        <random/>
        <to uri="seda:a"/>
        <to uri="seda:b"/>
    </loadBalance>
</route>
```

The sticky strategy requires you provide a correlation expression, which is used to calculate a hashed value to indicate which processor should be used. Suppose your messages contain a header indicating different levels. By using the sticky strategy, you can have messages with the same level chose the same processor over and over again.

In the Java DSL, you would provide the expression using a header expression as shown here:

```
from("direct:start")
    .loadBalance().sticky(header("type"))
        .to("seda:a").to("seda:b")
    .end();
```

In Spring XML, you'd do the following:

```
<route>
    <from uri="direct:start"/>
    <loadBalance>
        <sticky>
            <correlationExpression>
                <header>type</header>
            </correlationExpression>
        </sticky>
        <to uri="seda:a"/>
        <to uri="seda:b"/>
    </loadBalance>
</route>
```

The source code for the book contains examples of using the strategies listed in table 8.9 in the chapter8/loadbalancer directory. To try the random, sticky, or topic strategies, use the following Maven goals:

```
mvn test -Dtest=RandomLoadBalancerTest
mvn test -Dtest=SpringRandomLoadBalancerTest
mvn test -Dtest=StickyLoadBalancerTest
mvn test -Dtest=SpringStickyLoadBalancerTest
mvn test -Dtest=TopicLoadBalancerTest
mvn test -Dtest=SpringTopicLoadBalancerTest
```

The failover strategy is a more elaborate strategy, which we'll cover next.

8.6.3 *Using the failover load balancer*

Load balancing is often used to implement failover—the continuation of a service after a failure. The Camel failover load balancer detects the failure when an exception occurs and reacts by letting the next processor take over processing the message.

Given the following route snippet, the failover will always start by sending the messages to the first processor (`"direct:a"`) and only in the case of a failure will it let the next processor (`"direct:b"`) take over.

```
from("direct:start")
    .loadBalance().failover()
        .to("direct:a").to("direct:b")
    .end();
```

The equivalent snippet in Spring XML is as follows:

```
<route>
    <from uri="direct:start"/>
    <loadBalance>
        <failover/>
        <to uri="direct:a"/>
        <to uri="direct:b"/>
    </loadBalance>
</route>
```

The source code for the book contains this example in the chapter8/loadbalancer directory. You can try it using the following Maven goals:

```
mvn test -Dtest=FailoverLoadBalancerTest
mvn test -Dtest=SpringFailoverLoadBalancerTest
```

If you run the example, it will send in four messages. The second message will failover and be processed by the "direct:b" processor. The other three messages will be processed successfully by "direct:a".

In this example, the failover load balancer will react to any kind of exception being thrown, but you can provide it with a number of exceptions to react to.

Suppose you only want to failover if an IOException is thrown (which indicates communication errors with remote services, such as no connection). This is easy to configure, as shown in the Java DSL:

```
from("direct:start")
    .loadBalance().failover(IOException.class)
        .to("direct:a").to("direct:b")
    .end();
```

Here it is configured in Spring XML:

```
<route>
    <from uri="direct:start"/>
    <loadBalance>
        <failover>
            <exception>java.io.IOException</exception>
        </failover>
        <to uri="direct:a"/>
        <to uri="direct:b"/>
    </loadBalance>
</route>
```

In this example, only one exception is specified, but you can specify multiple exceptions, as follows:

```
from("direct:start")
    .loadBalance().failover(IOException.class, SQLException.class)
        .to("direct:a").to("direct:b")
    .end();
```

In Spring XML, you do as follows:

```
<route>
    <from uri="direct:start"/>
    <loadBalance>
        <failover>
```

```
        <exception>java.io.IOException</exception>
        <exception>java.sql.SQLException</exception>
    </failover>
    <to uri="direct:a"/>
    <to uri="direct:b"/>
  </loadBalance>
</route>
```

You may have noticed in the failover examples that it always chooses the first processor, and sends the failover to subsequent processors. You can think of this as the first processor being the master, and the others slaves. But the failover load balancer also offers a strategy that combines round robin with failure support.

USING FAILOVER WITH ROUND ROBIN

The Camel failover load balancer in round robin mode gives you the best of both worlds; it distributes the load evenly between the services, and it provides automatic failover.

In this scenario, you have three configuration options on the load balancer to dictate how it operates, as listed in table 8.10.

Table 8.10   Failover load balancer configuration options

Configuration option	Default	Description
maximumFailover-Attempts	-1	Specifies how many failover attempts to try before exhausting (giving up): ■ Use -1 to attempt forever (never give up). ■ Use 0 to never failover (give up immediately). ■ Use a positive value to specify a number of attempts. For example, a value of 3 will try up to 3 failover attempts before giving up.
inheritError-Handler	true	Specifies whether or not Camel error handling is being used. When enabled, the load balancer will let the error handler be involved. If disabled, the load balancer will failover immediately if an exception is thrown.
roundRobin	false	Specifies whether or not the load balancer operates in round robin mode.

To better understand the options in table 8.10 and how the round robin mode works, we'll start with a fairly simple example.

In the Java DSL, you have to configure failover with all the options in bold:

```
from("direct:start")
    .loadBalance().failover(1, false, true)
        .to("direct:a").to("direct:b")
    .end();
```

In this example, the maximumFailoverAttempts option is set to 1, which means it will at most try to failover once (it will make one attempt for the initial request and one more for the failover attempt). If both attempts fail, Camel will propagate the exception back to the caller.

The second parameter is set to `false`, which means it isn't inheriting Camel's error handling. This allows the failover load balancer to failover immediately when an exception occurs, instead of having to wait for the Camel error handler to give up first.

The last parameter indicates that it's using the round robin mode.

In Spring XML, you configure the options as attributes on the `failover` tag:

```
<route>
    <from uri="direct:start"/>
    <loadBalance>
        <failover roundRobin="true" maximumFailoverAttempts="1"/>
        <to uri="direct:a"/>
        <to uri="direct:b"/>
    </loadBalance>
</route>
```

The source code for the book contains this example in the chapter8/loadbalancer directory. You can try it using the following Maven goals:

```
mvn test -Dtest=FailoverLoadBalancerTest
mvn test -Dtest=SpringFailoverLoadBalancerTest
```

If you're curious about the `inheritErrorHandler` configuration option, take a look at the following examples in the source code for the book:

```
mvn test -Dtest=FailoverInheritErrorHandlerLoadBalancerTest
mvn test -Dtest=SpringFailoverInheritErrorHandlerLoadBalancerTest
```

This concludes our tour of the failover load balancer. The next section explains how to implement and use your own custom strategy, which you may want to do when you need to use special load-balancing logic.

8.6.4 *Using a custom load balancer*

Custom load balancers allow you to be in full control of the balancing strategy in use. For example, you could build a strategy that acquires load statistics from various services and picks the service with the lowest load.

Let's look at an example. Suppose you want to implement a priority-based strategy that sends gold messages to a certain processor and the remainder to a secondary destination. Figure 8.13 illustrates this principle.

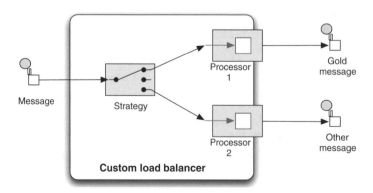

Figure 8.13 Using a custom load balancer to route gold messages to processor 1 and other messages to processor 2

When implementing a custom load balancer, you will often extend the SimpleLoad-BalancerSupport class, which provides a good starting point. Listing 8.11 shows how you can implement a custom load balancer.

Listing 8.11   Custom load balancer

```
import org.apache.camel.Exchange;
import org.apache.camel.Processor;
import org.apache.camel.processor.loadbalancer.SimpleLoadBalancerSupport;

public class MyCustomLoadBalancer extends SimpleLoadBalancerSupport {

    public boolean process(Exchange exchange) throws Exception {
        Processor target = chooseProcessor(exchange);
        target.process(exchange);
    }

    @Override
    protected Processor chooseProcessor(Exchange exchange) {
        String type = exchange.getIn().getHeader("type", String.class);
        if ("gold".equals(type)) {
            return getProcessors().get(0);
        } else {
            return getProcessors().get(1);
        }
    }
}
```

As you can see, it doesn't take much code. In the process() method, you invoke the chooseProcessor() method, which is the strategy that picks the processor to process the message. In this example, it will pick the first processor if the message is a gold type, and the second processor if not.

In the Java DSL, you use a custom load balancer as shown in bold:

```
from("direct:start")
    .loadBalance(new MyCustomLoadBalancer())
        .to("seda:a").to("seda:b")
    .end();
```

In Spring XML, you need to declare a Spring bean tag:

```
<bean id="myCustom" class="camelinaction.MyCustomLoadBalancer"/>
```

Which you then refer to from the <loadBalance> tag:

```
<route>
    <from uri="direct:start"/>
    <loadBalance ref="myCustom">
        <to uri="seda:a"/>
        <to uri="seda:b"/>
    </loadBalance>
</route>
```

The source code for the book contains this example in the chapter8/loadbalancer directory. You can try it using the following Maven goals:

```
mvn test -Dtest=CustomLoadBalancerTest
mvn test -Dtest=SpringCustomLoadBalancerTest
```

We've now covered the Load Balancer EIP in Camel, which brings us to the end of our long journey to visit five great EIPs implemented in Camel.

8.7   Summary and best practices

Since the arrival of the *Enterprise Integration Patterns* book on the scene, we have had a common vocabulary, graphical notation, and concepts for designing applications to tackle today's integration challenges. You have encountered these EIPs throughout this book. In chapter 2 we reviewed the most common patterns, and this chapter reviews five of the most complex and sophisticated patterns in great detail. You may view the EIP book as the theory and Camel as the software implementation of the book.

Here are some EIP best practices to take away from this chapter:

- *Learn the patterns.* Take the time to study the EIPs, especially the common patterns we covered in chapter 2 and those we presented in this chapter. Consider getting the EIP book to read more about the patterns—there's great advice given in the book. The patterns are universal and the knowledge you gain when using EIPs with Camel is something you can take with you.
- *Use the patterns.* If you have a problem you don't know how to resolve, there's a good chance others have scratched that itch before. Consult the EIP book and the online Camel patterns catalog: http://camel.apache.org/enterprise-integration-patterns.html.
- *Start simply.* When learning to use an EIP, you should create a simple test to try out the pattern and learn how to use it. Having too many new moving parts in a Camel route can clutter your view and make it difficult to understand what's happening and maybe why it doesn't do what you expected.
- *Come back to this chapter.* If you're going to use any of the five EIPs covered in this chapter, we recommend you reread the relevant parts of the chapter. These patterns are very sophisticated and have many features and options to tweak.

The Transactional Client EIP is useful for controlling transactions, and it's the topic of the next chapter.

Part 3

Out in the wild

With Camel's core concepts under your belt, you may feel like you can tackle any integration problem with Camel. There is still more to cover, though. In this final part of the book, we'll cover the topics that are useful when you know the core concepts and want to build something for the real world.

One concept you'll encounter in many real-world applications is transactions. In chapter 9, we'll explain how to use Spring's transaction framework to let Camel routes participate in transactions.

In chapter 10, we'll discuss the important, and sometimes complex, topic of concurrency. Understanding how to configure and tune threading in Camel is a must-read for performance-centric projects. We'll also cover how you can improve the scalability of your Camel applications.

In chapter 11, we'll discuss a topic you could really read right after part 1: how to develop new Camel projects. In this chapter, we'll show you how to create new Camel projects, which could be Camel applications, custom components, or interceptors. The Scala DSL is also touched on here.

Once your application is running in the wild, you'll need to know how to manage it and monitor its operations. Chapter 12 discusses topics in this category ranging from viewing the Camel logs to controlling Camel with JMX, to extending the notification mechanism in Camel so it works with your own custom monitoring application.

A topic you'll need to read about before your Camel application is in production is deployment. Camel was designed as a framework, and, as such, it has virtually unlimited deployment possibilities. In chapter 13, we'll discuss some of the most popular deployment options for Camel. We'll also cover the various ways you can start and stop Camel.

In the last chapter of the book, chapter 14, we cover what we consider "extra features" of Camel: routing with beans and using remoting to hide Camel APIs. We think of these as extra features because they perform routing without using any of Camel's DSLs and, in some cases, without any Camel APIs at all. They use a quite different approach than what has been discussed throughout the book.

Using transactions

9

This chapter covers

- Why you need transactions
- How to use and configure transactions
- The differences between local and global transactions
- How to return custom reply messages on rollback
- How to compensate when transactions aren't supported

To help explain what transactions are, let's look at an example from real life. You may well have ordered this book from Manning's online bookstore, and if you did, you likely followed these steps:

1 Find the book *Camel in Action*
2 Put the book into the basket
3 Maybe continue shopping and look for other books
4 Go to the checkout
5 Enter shipping and credit card details
6 Confirm the purchase
7 Wait for the confirmation
8 Leave the web store

What seems like an everyday scenario is actually a fairly complex series of events. You have to put books in the basket before you can check out; you must fill in the shipping and credit card details before you can confirm the purchase; if your credit card is declined, the purchase won't be confirmed; and so on. The ultimate resolution of this transaction is either of two states: either the purchase was accepted and confirmed, or the purchase was declined, leaving your credit card balance uncharged.

This particular story involves computer systems because it's about using an online bookstore, but the same main points happen when you shop in the supermarket. Either you leave the supermarket with your groceries or without.

In the software world, transactions are often explained in the context of SQL statements manipulating database tables—updating or inserting data. While the transaction is in progress, a system failure could occur, and that would leave the transaction's participants in an inconsistent state. That's why the series of events is described as *atomic*: either they all are completed or they all fail—it's all or nothing. In transactional terms, they either *commit* or *roll back*.

> **NOTE** I expect you know about the database ACID properties, so I won't explain what atomic, consistent, isolated, and durable mean in the context of transactions. If you aren't familiar with ACID, the Wikipedia page is a good place to start learning about it: http://en.wikipedia.org/wiki/ACID.

In this chapter, we'll first look at the reasons why you should use transactions (in the context of Rider Auto Parts). Then we'll look at transactions in more detail and at Spring's transaction management, which orchestrates the transactions. You'll learn about the difference between local and global transactions and how to configure and use transactions. Toward the end of the chapter, you'll see how to compensate for when you're using resources that don't support transactions.

9.1 Why use transactions?

There are many good reasons why using transactions makes sense. But before we focus on using transactions with Camel, let's look at what can go wrong when you don't use transactions.

In this section, we'll review an application Rider Auto Parts uses to collect metrics that will be published to an incident management system. We'll see what goes wrong when the application doesn't use transactions, and then we'll apply transactions to the application.

9.1.1 The Rider Auto Parts partner integration application

Lately Rider Auto Parts has had a dispute with a partner about whether or not their service meets the terms of the service level agreement (SLA). When such incidents occur, it's often a labor-intensive task to investigate and remedy the incident.

In light of this, Rider Auto Parts has developed an application to record what happens, as evidence for when a dispute comes up. The application periodically measures the communication between Rider Auto Parts and its external partner servers. The application records performance and uptime metrics, which are sent to a JMS queue, where the data awaits further processing.

Rider Auto Parts already has an existing incident management application with a web user interface for upper management. What's missing is an application to populate the collected metrics to the database used by the incident management application. Figure 9.1 illustrates the scenario.

It's a fairly simple task: a JMS consumer listens for new messages on the JMS queue ❶. Then the data is transformed from XML to SQL ❷ before it's written to the database ❸.

In no time, you can come up with a route that matches figure 9.1:

```
<camelContext id="camel" xmlns="http://camel.apache.org/schema/spring">
    <route id="partnerToDB">
        <from uri="activemq:queue:partners"/>
        <bean ref="partner" method="toSql"/>
        <to uri="jdbc:myDataSource"/>
    </route>
</camelContext>
```

The reports are sent to the JMS queue in a simple in-house XML format, like this:

```
<?xml version="1.0"?>
<partner id="123">
    <date>200911150815</date>
    <code>200</code>
    <time>4387</time>
</partner>
```

The database table that stores the data is also mapped easily because it has the following layout:

```
create table partner_metric
    ( partner_id varchar(10), time_occurred varchar(20),
      status_code varchar(3), perf_time varchar(10) )
```

That leaves you with the fairly simple task of mapping the XML to the database. Because you're pragmatic and want to make a simple and elegant solution that anybody should be capable of maintaining in the future, you decide not to bring in the

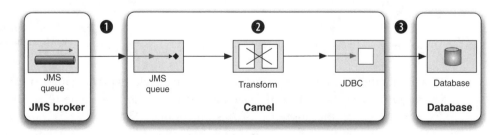

Figure 9.1 Partner reports are received from the JMS broker, transformed in Camel to SQL format, and then written to the database.

big guns with the Java Persistence API (JPA) or Hibernate. You put the following mapping code in a good old-fashioned bean.

Listing 9.1 Using a bean to map from XML to SQL

```
import org.apache.camel.language.XPath;

public class PartnerServiceBean {

    public String toSql(@XPath("partner/@id") int id,
                        @XPath("partner/date/text()") String date,
                        @XPath("partner/code/text()") int statusCode,
                        @XPath("partner/time/text()") long responseTime) {

        StringBuilder sb = new StringBuilder();

        sb.append("INSERT INTO PARTNER_METRIC (partner_id, time_occurred,
                status_code, perf_time) VALUES (");
        sb.append("'").append(id).append("', ");
        sb.append("'").append(date).append("', ");
        sb.append("'").append(statusCode).append("', ");
        sb.append("'").append(responseTime).append("')");

        return sb.toString();
    }
}
```

❶ Extracts data from XML payload

❷ Constructs SQL statement

Coding the 10 or so lines in listing 9.1 was faster than getting started on the JPA wagon or opening any heavyweight and proprietary mapping software. The code speaks for itself, but let's go over it anyway.

First you define the method to accept the four values to be mapped. Notice that you use the @XPath annotation to grab the data from the XML document ❶. Then you use a StringBuilder to construct the SQL INSERT statement with the input values ❷.

To test this, you can crank up a unit test as follows:

```
public void testSendPartnerReportIntoDatabase() throws Exception {
    String sql = "select count(*) from partner_metric";
    assertEquals(0, jdbc.queryForInt(sql));

    String xml = "<?xml version=\"1.0\"?>
                + <partner id=\"123\"><date>200911150815</date>
                + <code>200</code><time>4387</time></partner>";

    template.sendBody("activemq:queue:partners", xml);

    Thread.sleep(5000);

    assertEquals(1, jdbc.queryForInt(sql));
}
```

❶ Asserts there are no rows in database

❷ Asserts one row was inserted into database

This test method outlines the principle. First you check that the database is empty ❶. Then you construct sample XML data and send it to the JMS queue using the Camel ProducerTemplate. Because the processing of the JMS message is asynchronous, you must wait a bit to let it process. At the end, you check that the database contains one row ❷.

9.1.2 Setting up the JMS broker and the database

To run this unit test, you need to use a local JMS broker and a database. You can use Apache ActiveMQ as the JMS broker and HSQLDB (HyperSQL Database) as the database. HSQLDB can be used as an in-memory database without the need to run it separately. Apache ActiveMQ is an extremely versatile broker, and it's even embeddable in unit tests.

All you have to do is master a bit of Spring XML magic to set up the JMS broker and the database. This is shown in listing 9.2.

Listing 9.2 XML configuration for the Camel route, JMS broker, and database

```xml
<beans xmlns="http://www.springframework.org/schema/beans"
    xmlns:xsi="http://www.w3.org/2001/XMLSchema-instance"
    xmlns:broker="http://activemq.apache.org/schema/core"
    xsi:schemaLocation="
    http://www.springframework.org/schema/beans
    http://www.springframework.org/schema/beans/spring-beans-2.5.xsd
    http://camel.apache.org/schema/spring
    http://camel.apache.org/schema/spring/camel-spring.xsd
    http://activemq.apache.org/schema/core
    http://activemq.apache.org/schema/core/activemq-core.xsd">

<bean id="partner" class="camelinaction.PartnerServiceBean"/>

<camelContext id="camel" xmlns="http://camel.apache.org/schema/spring">
    <route id="partnerToDB">
        <from uri="activemq:queue:partners"/>
        <bean ref="partner" method="toSql"/>
        <to uri="jdbc:myDataSource"/>
    </route>
</camelContext>
```
❶ Configures ActiveMQ component

```xml
<bean id="activemq"
    class="org.apache.activemq.camel.component.ActiveMQComponent">
    <property name="brokerURL" value="tcp://localhost:61616"/>
</bean>

<broker:broker useJmx="false" persistent="false" brokerName="localhost">
    <broker:transportConnectors>
        <broker:transportConnector uri="tcp://localhost:61616"/>
    </broker:transportConnectors>
</broker:broker>
```
❸ Sets up database   **❷ Sets up embedded JMS broker**

```xml
<bean id="myDataSource"
    class="org.springframework.jdbc.datasource.DriverManagerDataSource">
    <property name="driverClassName" value="org.hsqldb.jdbcDriver"/>
    <property name="url" value="jdbc:hsqldb:mem:partner"/>
    <property name="username" value="sa"/>
    <property name="password" value=""/>
</bean>

</beans>
```

In listing 9.2, you first define the partner bean from listing 9.1 as a Spring bean that you'll use in the route. Then, to allow Camel to connect to ActiveMQ, you must define it as a Camel component ❶. The brokerURL property is configured with the URL for the remote ActiveMQ broker, which, in this example, happens to be running on the same machine. Then you set up a local embedded ActiveMQ broker ❷, which is configured to use TCP connectors. Finally, you set up the JDBC data source ❸.

> **Using VM instead of TCP with an embedded ActiveMQ broker**
>
> If you use an embedded ActiveMQ broker, you can use the VM protocol instead of TCP; doing so bypasses the entire TCP stack and is much faster. For example, in listing 9.2, you could use `vm://localhost` instead of `tcp://localhost:61616`.
>
> Actually, the `localhost` in `vm://localhost` is the broker name, not a network address. For example, you could use `vm://myCoolBroker` as the broker name and configure the name on the broker tag accordingly: `brokerName="myCoolBroker"`.
>
> A plausible reason why you're using `vm://localhost` in listing 9.2 is that the engineers are lazy, and they changed the protocol from TCP to VM but left the broker name as `localhost`.

The full source code for this example is located in the chapter9/riderautoparts-partner directory, and you can try out the example by running the following Maven goal:

```
mvn test -Dtest=RiderAutoPartsPartnerTest
```

In the source code, you'll also see how we prepared the database by creating the table and dropping it after testing.

9.1.3   *The story of the lost message*

The previous test is testing a positive situation, but what happens if the connection to the database fails. How can you test that?

Chapter 6 covered how to simulate a connection failure using Camel interceptors. Writing a unit test is just a matter of putting all that logic in a single method, as shown in listing 9.3.

Listing 9.3   Simulating a connection failure that causes lost messages

```
public void testNoConnectionToDatabase() throws Exception {
    RouteBuilder rb = new RouteBuilder() {                       Simulates no
        public void configure() throws Exception {            ❶ connection to database
            interceptSendToEndpoint("jdbc:*")
                .throwException(new ConnectException("Cannot connect"));
        }
    };

    RouteDefinition route = context.getRouteDefinition("partnerToDB");
    route.adviceWith(context, rb);                                  Advises
                                                                    simulation into
    String sql = "select count(*) from partner_metric";         ❷ existing route
    assertEquals(0, jdbc.queryForInt(sql));

    String xml = "<?xml version=\"1.0\"?>
                + <partner id=\"123\"><date>200911150815</date>
```

```
            + <code>200</code><time>4387</time></partner>";

template.sendBody("activemq:queue:partners", xml);

Thread.sleep(5000);

assertEquals(0, jdbc.queryForInt(sql));
}
```

❸ **Asserts no rows**
inserted into database

To test a failed connection to the database, you need to intercept the routing to the
database and simulate the error. You do this with the `RouteBuilder`, where you define
this scenario **❶**. Next you need to add the interceptor with the existing route **❷**,
which is done using the `adviceWith` method. The remainder of the code is almost
identical to the previous test, but you test that no rows are added to the database **❸**.

> **NOTE** You can read about simulating errors using interceptors in chapter 6,
> section 6.3.3.

The test runs successfully. But what happened to the message you sent to the JMS
queue? It was not stored in the database, so where did it go?

It turns out that the message is lost because you're not using transactions. By default,
the JMS consumer uses *auto-acknowledge mode*, which means the client acknowledges the
message when it's received, and the message is dequeued from the JMS broker.

What you must do instead is use *transacted acknowledge mode*. We'll look at how to do
this in section 9.3, but first we'll discuss how transactions work in Camel.

9.2 Transaction basics

A transaction is a series of events. The start of a transaction is often named *begin*, and
the end is *commit* (or *rollback* if the transaction isn't successfully completed). Figure 9.2
illustrates this.

Figure 9.2 A transaction is a series of events between begin and commit.

To demonstrate the sequence in figure 9.2, you could write what are known as locally
managed transactions, where the transaction is managed manually in the code. The
following code illustrates this; it's based on using JPA-managed transactions.

```
EntityManager em = emf.getEntityManager();
EntityTransaction tx = em.getTransaction();
try {
    tx.begin();
```

```
    tx.commit();
} catch (Exception e) {
    tx.rollback();
}
em.close();
```

You start the transaction using the begin method. Then you have a series of events to do whatever work needs to be done. At the end, you either commit or roll back the transaction, depending on whether an exception was thrown or not.

You may already be familiar with this principle, and transactions in Camel use the same principle at a higher level of abstraction. In Camel transactions, you don't invoke begin and commit methods from Java code—you use declarative transactions, which are configured in the Spring XML file. We'll look at the details of how this works in the next section, so don't worry if it's still a bit unclear.

What are the benefits of defining transactions declaratively? With Spring's approach, you configure all this in the Spring XML regardless of which runtime environment you're using. This removes the need for changing Java code to match the targeted environment. Spring also makes it easy to set up diverse environments using minimal configuration. Spring's transaction support is a great piece of technology, and that's why Camel leverages it instead of rolling out it's own transaction framework.

NOTE For more information on Spring's transaction management, see chapter 10, "Transaction Management," in the *Spring Framework Reference Documentation*: http://static.springsource.org/spring/docs/3.0.x/spring-framework-reference/html/transaction.html.

Now that we've established that Camel works with Spring's transaction support, let's look at how they work together.

9.2.1 *About Spring's transaction support*

To understand how Camel works together with Spring's transaction support, take a look at figure 9.3. This figure shows that Spring orchestrates the transaction while Camel takes care of the rest.

Figure 9.4 adds more details, to illustrate that the JMS broker also plays an active part in the transaction. In this figure you can see how the JMS broker, Camel, and the Spring JmsTransaction-Manager work together. The Jms-TransactionManager orchestrates the resources that participate in the transaction ❶, which in this example is the JMS broker.

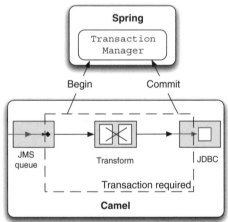

Figure 9.3 Spring's TransactionManager orchestrates the transaction by issuing begins and commits. The entire Camel route is transacted, and the transaction is handled by Spring.

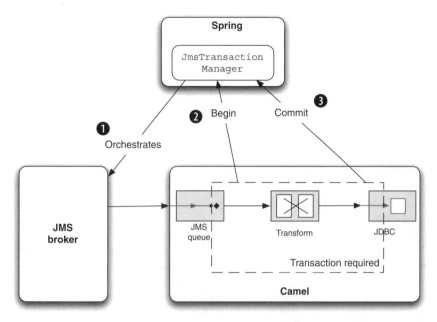

Figure 9.4 The Spring `JmsTransactionManager` orchestrates the transaction with the JMS broker. The Camel route completes successfully and signals the commit to the `JmsTransactionManager`.

When a message has been consumed from the queue and fed into the Camel application, Camel issues a begin ❷ to the `JmsTransactionManager`. Depending on whether the Camel route completes with success or failure ❸, the `JmsTransactionManager` will ensure the JMS broker commits or rolls back.

It's now time to see how this works in practice. In the next section, we'll fix the lost-message problem by adding transactions.

9.2.2 Adding transactions

At the end of section 9.1, you left Rider Auto Parts with the problem of losing messages because you did not use transactions. Your task now is to apply transactions, which should remedy the problem.

You'll start by introducing Spring transactions to the Spring XML file and adjusting the configuration accordingly. Listing 9.4 shows how this is done.

Listing 9.4 XML configuration using Spring transactions

```
<bean id="activemq"
    class="org.apache.activemq.camel.component.ActiveMQComponent">
    <property name="transacted" value="true"/>
    <property name="transactionManager" ref="txManager"/>
</bean>

<bean id="txManager"
    class="org.springframework.jms.connection.JmsTransactionManager">
```

❶ Enables transacted acknowledge mode

❷ Configures Spring JmsTransactionManager

```
        <property name="connectionFactory" ref="jmsConnectionFactory"/>
</bean>

<bean id="jmsConnectionFactory"
      class="org.apache.activemq.ActiveMQConnectionFactory">
    <property name="brokerURL" value="tcp://localhost:61616"/>
</bean>
```

The first thing you do is turn on `transacted` for the ActiveMQ component ❶, which instructs it to use transacted acknowledge mode. Then you need to refer to the transaction manager, which is a Spring `JmsTransactionManager` ❷ that manages transactions when using JMS messaging. The transaction manager needs to know how to connect to the JMS broker, which refers to the connection factory. In the `jmsConnectionFactory` definition, you configure the `brokerURL` to point at the JMS broker.

> **TIP**   The `JmsTransactionManager` has other options for configuring transaction behavior, such as timeouts, strategies for rollback on commit failure, and so on. Consult the Spring documentation for details: http://static.springsource.org/spring/docs/3.0.x/spring-framework-reference/html/transaction.html.

So far you've only reconfigured beans in the Spring XML file, which is mandatory when using Spring. In Camel, itself, you have not yet configured anything in relation to transactions. Camel offers great convention over configuration for transaction support, so all you have to do is to add `<transacted/>` to the route, right after `<from>`, as highlighted here:

```
<camelContext id="camel" xmlns="http://camel.apache.org/schema/spring">
    <route id="partnerToDB">
        <from uri="activemq:queue:partners"/>
        <transacted/>
        <bean ref="partner" method="toSql"/>
        <to uri="jdbc:myDataSource"/>
    </route>
</camelContext>
```

When you specify `<transacted/>` in a route, Camel uses transactions for that particular route. Under the hood, Camel looks up the Spring transaction manager and leverages it. This is the convention over configuration kicking in.

Using `transacted` in the Java DSL is just as easy, as shown here:

```
from("activemq:queue:partners")
    .transacted()
    .beanRef("partner", "toSql")
    .to("jdbc:myDataSource");
```

The convention over configuration only applies when you have a single Spring transaction manager configured. In more complex scenarios, with multiple transaction managers, you have to do additional configuration to set up transactions. We'll cover that in section 9.4.1.

NOTE When using transacted() in the Java DSL, you must add it right after from() to ensure that the route is properly configured to use transactions. This isn't enforced in the DSL because the DSL is loosely defined to make it easy to maintain and develop Camel. There are a few tradeoffs such as this.

In this example, all you had to do to configure Camel was to add <transacted/> in the route. You relied on the transactional default configurations, which greatly reduces the effort required to set up the various bits. In section 9.4, we'll go deeper into configuring transactions.

Let's see if this configuration is correct by testing it.

9.2.3 *Testing transactions*

When you test Camel routes using transactions, it's common to test with live resources, such as a real JMS broker and a database. For example, the source code for this book uses Apache ActiveMQ and HSQLDB as live resources. We picked these because they can be easily downloaded using Apache Maven and they're lightweight and embeddable, which makes them perfect for unit testing. There is no upfront work needed to install them. To demonstrate how this works, we'll return to the Rider Auto Parts example.

Last time you ran a unit test, you lost the message when there was no connection to the database. Let's try that unit test again, but this time with transactional support. You can do this by running the following Maven goal from the chapter9/rider-autoparts-partner directory:

```
mvn test -Dtest=RiderAutoPartsPartnerTXTest
```

When you run the unit test, you'll notice a lot of stacktraces printed on the console, and they'll contain the following snippet:

```
2009-11-22 12:47:22,158 [enerContainer-1] ERROR EndpointMessageListener
 - java.net.ConnectException: Cannot connect to the database
org.apache.camel.spring.spi.TransactedRuntimeCamelException:
java.net.ConnectException: Cannot connect to the database
        at
org.apache.camel.spring.spi.TransactionErrorHandler.wrapTransacted
RuntimeException(TransactionErrorHandler.java:173)
        at
org.apache.camel.spring.spi.TransactionErrorHandler$1.doInTransaction
WithoutResult(TransactionErrorHandler.java:123)
        at
org.springframework.transaction.support.TransactionCallbackWithout
Result.doInTransaction(TransactionCallbackWithoutResult.java:33)
        at
org.springframework.transaction.support.TransactionTemplate.execute
(TransactionTemplate.java:128)
        at
org.apache.camel.spring.spi.TransactionErrorHandler.process
(TransactionErrorHandler.java:86)
```

You can tell from the stacktrace that `EndpointMessageListener` (shown in bold) logged an exception at `ERROR` level, which indicates the transaction is being rolled back. This happens because `EndpointMessageListener` is a `javax.jms.Message-Listener`, which is invoked when a new message arrives on the JMS destination. It will roll back the transaction if an exception is thrown.

So where is the message now? It should be on the JMS queue, so let's add a little code to the unit test to check that. Add the following code at the end of the unit test method in listing 9.3.

```
Object body = consumer.receiveBodyNoWait("activemq:queue:partners");
assertNotNull("Should not lose message", body);
```

Now you can run the unit test to ensure that the message wasn't lost—and the unit test will fail with this assertion error:

```
java.lang.AssertionError: Should not lose message
    at org.junit.Assert.fail(Assert.java:74)
    at org.junit.Assert.assertTrue(Assert.java:37)
    at org.junit.Assert.assertNotNull(Assert.java:356)
    at
camelinaction.RiderAutoPartsPartnerTXTest.testNoConnectionToDatabase
(RiderAutoPartsPartnerTXTest.java:96)
```

We're using transactions, and they've been configured correctly, but the message is still being lost. What's wrong? If you dig into the stacktraces, you'll discover that the message is always redelivered six times, and then no further redelivery is conducted.

> **TIP**   If you're using Apache ActiveMQ, we recommend you pick up a copy of *ActiveMQ in Action*, by Bruce Snyder, Dejan Bosanac, and Rob Davies. Among other things, this book explains how to use transactions and redelivery in more detail.

What happens is that ActiveMQ performs the redelivery according to its default settings, which say it will redeliver at most six times before giving up and moving the message to a dead letter queue. This is, in fact, the Dead Letter Channel EIP. You may remember that we covered this in chapter 5 (look back to figure 5.4). ActiveMQ implements this pattern, which ensures that the broker won't be doomed by a poison message that can't be successfully processed and that would cause arriving messages to stack up on the queue.

Instead of looking for the message on the partner's queue, you should look for the message in the default ActiveMQ dead letter queue, which is named `ActiveMQ.DLQ`. If you change the code accordingly (as shown in bold), the test will pass:

```
Object body = consumer.receiveBodyNoWait("activemq:queue:ActiveMQ.DLQ");
assertNotNull("Should not lose message", body);

Tests run: 2, Failures: 0, Errors: 0, Skipped: 0
```

You need to do one additional test to cover the situation where the connection to the database only fails at first, but works on subsequent calls. Here's that test.

Listing 9.5   Testing a simulated rollback on the first try and a commit on the second try

```
public void testFailFirstTime() throws Exception {
    RouteBuilder rb = new RouteBuilder() {
        public void configure() throws Exception {
            interceptSendToEndpoint("jdbc:*")                    ❶ Causes failure
                .choice()                                              first time
                    .when(header("JMSRedelivered").isEqualTo("false"))
                        .throwException(new ConnectException(
                                "Cannot connect to the database"))
                .end();
        }
    };

    context.getRouteDefinition("partnerToDB").adviceWith(context, rb);

    String sql = "select count(*) from partner_metric";
    assertEquals(0, jdbc.queryForInt(sql));

    String xml = "<?xml version=\"1.0\"?>
                + <partner id=\"123\"><date>200911150815</date>
                + <code>200</code><time>4387</time></partner>";
    template.sendBody("activemq:queue:partners", xml);

    Thread.sleep(5000);                              Asserts message ❷
                                                          not in DLQ
    assertEquals(1, jdbc.queryForInt(sql));

    Object dlq = consumer.receiveBodyNoWait("activemq:queue:ActiveMQ.DLQ");
    assertNull("Should not be in the DLQ", dlq);
}
```

The idea is to throw a `ConnectionException` only the first time. You do this by relying on the fact that any message consumed from a JMS destination has a set of standard JMS headers, and the `JMSRedelivered` header is a `Boolean` type indicating whether the JMS message is being redelivered or not.

The interceptor logic is done in a Camel `RouteBuilder`, so you have the full DSL at your disposal. You use the Content-Based Router EIP ❶ to test the `JMSRedelivered` header and only throw the exception if it's `false`, which means it's the first delivery. The rest of the unit test should verify correct behavior, so you first check that the database is empty before sending the message to the JMS queue. Then you sleep a bit to let the routing complete. After completion, you check that the database has one row. Because you previously were tricked by the JMS broker's dead letter queue, you also check that it's empty ❷.

The example we've just covered uses what are called local transactions, because they're based on using only a single resource in the transaction—Spring was only orchestrating the JMS broker. But there was also the database resource, which, in the example, was not under transactional control. Leveraging both the JMS broker and the database as resources participating in the same transaction requires more work, and the next section explains about using single and multiple resources in a transaction. First, we'll look at this from the EIP perspective.

9.3   *The Transactional Client EIP*

The Transactional Client EIP distills the problem of how a client can control transactions when working with messaging. It's depicted in figure 9.5.

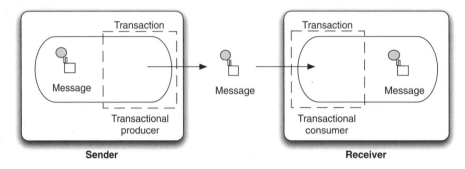

Figure 9.5   A transactional client handles the client's session with the receivers so the client can specify transaction boundaries that encompass the receiver.

Figure 9.5 shows how this pattern was portrayed in Gregor Hohpe and Bobby Woolf's *Enterprise Integration Patterns* book, so it may be a bit difficult to understand how it relates to using transactions with Camel. What the figure shows is that both a sender and a receiver can be transactional by working together. When a receiver initiates the transaction, the message is neither sent nor removed from the queue until the transaction is committed. When a sender initiates the transaction, the message isn't available to the consumer until the transaction has been committed. Figure 9.6 illustrates this principle.

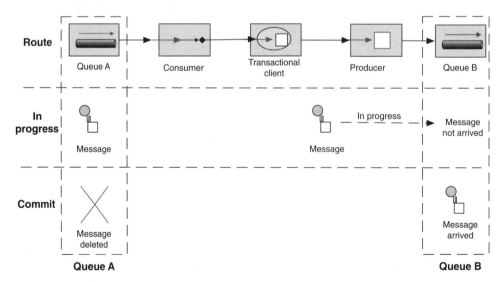

Figure 9.6   A message is being moved from queue A to queue B. Transactions ensure the message is moved in what appears to be an atomic operation.

The top section of figure 9.6 illustrates the route using EIP icons, with a message being moved from queue A to B using a transaction. The remainder of the figure shows a use case when one message is being moved.

The middle section shows a snapshot in time when the message is being moved. The message still resides in queue A and has not yet arrived in queue B. The message stays on queue A until a commit is issued, which ensures that the message isn't lost in case of a severe failure.

The bottom section shows the situation when a commit has been issued. The message is then deleted from queue A and inserted into queue B. Transactional clients make this whole process appear as an atomic, isolated, and consistent operation.

When talking about transactions, we need to distinguish between single- and multiple-resource transactions. The former are also known as *local* transactions and the latter as *global* transactions. In the next two sections, we'll look at these two flavors.

9.3.1 Using local transactions

Figure 9.7 depicts the situation of using a single resource, which is the JMS broker.

In this situation, the `JmsTransactionManager` orchestrates the transaction with the single participating resource, which is the JMS broker ❶. The `JmsTransaction-Manager` from Spring can only orchestrate JMS-based resources, so the database isn't orchestrated.

In the Rider Auto Parts example in section 9.1, the database didn't participate as a resource in the transaction, but the approach seemed to work anyway. That was

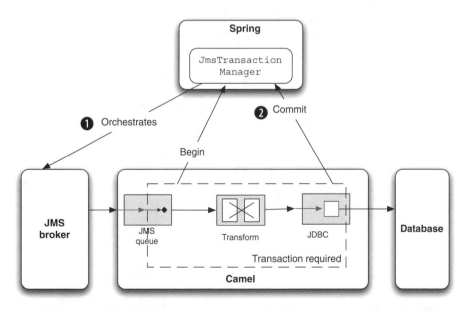

Figure 9.7 Using `JmsTransactionManager` as a single resource in a transaction. The database isn't a participant in the transaction.

because if the database decides to roll back the transaction, it will throw an exception that the Camel `TransactionErrorHandler` propagates back to the `JmsTransaction-Manager`, which reacts accordingly and issues a rollback ❷.

This scenario isn't exactly equivalent to enrolling the database in the transaction, because it still has failure scenarios that could leave the system in an inconsistent state. For example, the JMS broker could fail after the database is successfully updated, but before the JMS message is committed. To be absolutely sure that both the JMS broker and the database are in sync in terms of the transaction, you must use the much heavier global transactions. Let's take a look at that now.

9.3.2   *Using global transactions*

Using transactions with a single resource is appropriate when a single resource is involved. But the situation changes dramatically when you need to span multiple resources in the same transaction, such as JMS and JDBC resources, as depicted in figure 9.8.

In this figure, we've switched to using the `JtaTransactionManager`, which handles multiple resources. Camel consumes a message from the queue, and a begin is issued ❶. The message is processed, updating the database, and it completes successfully ❷.

So what is the `JtaTransactionManager`, and how is it different from the `JmsTransactionManager` used in the previous section (see figure 9.7)? To answer this, you first need to learn a bit about global transactions and where the Java Transaction API (JTA) fits in.

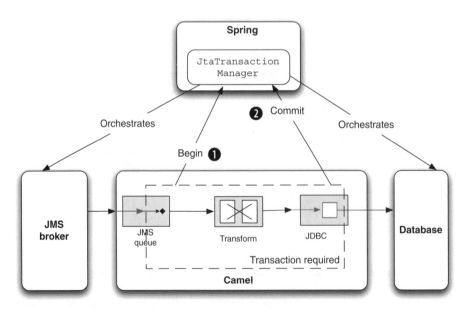

Figure 9.8 Using `JtaTransactionManager` with multiple resources in a transaction. Both the JMS broker and the database participate in the transaction.

In Java, JTA is an implementation of the XA standard protocol, which is a global transaction protocol. To be able to leverage XA, the resource drivers must be XA-compliant, which some JDBC and most JMS drivers are. JTA is part of the JAVA EE specification, which means that any JAVA EE-compliant application server must provide JTA support. This is one of the benefits of JAVA EE servers, which have JTA out of the box, unlike some lightweight alternatives, such as Apache Tomcat.

Using JTA outside a JAVA EE server takes some work to set up because you have to find and use a JTA transaction manager, such as one of these:

- JOTM—http://jotm.ow2.org/xwiki/bin/view/Main/WebHome
- Atomikos—http://www.atomikos.com
- Bitronix—http://www.bitronix.be

Then you need to figure out how to install and use it in your container and unit tests. The good news is that using JTA with Camel and Spring is just a matter of configuration.

NOTE For more information on JTA, see the Wikipedia page on the subject: http://en.wikipedia.org/wiki/Java_Transaction_API. XA is also briefly discussed: http://en.wikipedia.org/wiki/X/Open_XA.

When using JTA (XA), there are a couple of differences from using local transactions. First, you have to use XA-capable drivers, which means you have to use the `ActiveMQ-XAConnectionFactory` to let ActiveMQ participate in global transactions.

```
<bean id="jmsXaConnectionFactory"
      class="org.apache.activemq.ActiveMQXAConnectionFactory">
    <property name="brokerURL" value="tcp://localhost:61616"/>
</bean>
```

The same applies for the JDBC driver—you need to use an XA-capable driver. HSQLDB doesn't support XA, so you can fall back and use an Atomikos feature that's capable of simulating XA for non-XA JDBC drivers:

```
<bean id="myDataSource"
      class="com.atomikos.jdbc.nonxa.AtomikosNonXADataSourceBean">
    <property name="uniqueResourceName" value="hsqldb"/>
    <property name="driverClassName" value="org.hsqldb.jdbcDriver"/>
    <property name="url" value="jdbc:hsqldb:mem:partner"/>
    <property name="user" value="sa"/>
    <property name="password" value=""/>
    <property name="poolSize" value="3"/>
</bean>
```

In a real production system, you should prefer to use a JDBC driver that's XA-capable, because the simulation has a few drawbacks. You can find out more about this at the Atomikos website listed previously.

Having configured the XA drivers, you also need to use the Spring `JtaTransactionManager`. It should refer to the real XA transaction manager, which is Atomikos in this example:

```
<bean id="jtaTransactionManager"
     class="org.springframework.transaction.jta.JtaTransactionManager">
   <property name="transactionManager" ref="atomikosTransactionManager"/>
   <property name="userTransaction" ref="atomikosUserTransaction"/>
</bean>
```

The remainder of the configuration involves configuring Atomikos itself, which you can see in the book's source code, in the file chapter9/xa/src/test/resources/camel-spring.xml.

Suppose you want to add an additional step in the route shown in figure 9.8. You'll process the message *after* it has been inserted into the database. This additional step will influence the outcome of the transaction, whether or not it throws an exception.

Suppose it does indeed throw an exception, as portrayed in figure 9.9.

In figure 9.9, the message is being routed ❶ and, at the last step in the route (in the bottom-right corner with the X), it fails by throwing an exception. The JtaTransactionManager handles this by issuing rollbacks ❷ to both the JMS broker and the database. Because this scenario uses global transactions, both the database and the JMS broker will roll back, and the final result is as if the entire transaction hadn't taken place.

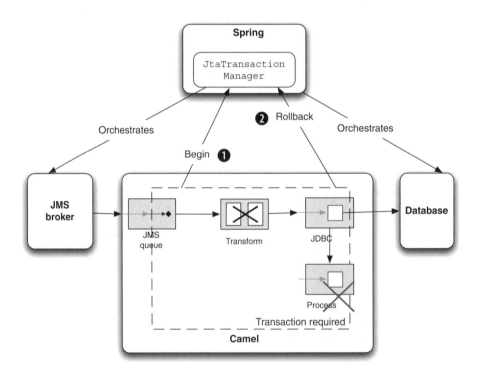

Figure 9.9 A failure to process a message at the last step in the route causes the JtaTransactionManager to issue rollbacks to both the JMS broker and the database.

The source code for the book contains this example in the chapter9/xa directory. You can test it using the following Maven goals:

```
mvn test -Dtest=AtomikosXACommitTest
mvn test -Dtest=AtomikosXARollbackBeforeDbTest
mvn test -Dtest=AtomikosXARollbackAfterDbTest
```

We'll leave the topic of global transactions here and move on to learn more about configuring and using transactions.

9.4 Configuring and using transactions

So far, we've used convention over configuration when configuring transactions in Camel, by just adding <transacted/> to the route. This is often all you'll need to use, but there can be situations where you need more fine-grained control, such as when specifying transaction propagation settings.

That's the first thing we'll look at in this section. Then we'll look at how transactions work when multiple routes are used. At the end of the section, we'll look at how you can return custom responses to the caller when a transaction fails.

9.4.1 Configuring transactions

When you configure transactions, you'll come across the term *transaction propagation*. In this section, you'll learn what that term means and why it's related to configuring transactions.

If you have ever worked with Enterprise JavaBeans (EJBs), you may be familiar with transaction propagation already. Transaction propagation options specify what will happen if a method is invoked and a transaction context already exists. For example, should it join the existing transaction? Should a new transaction be started? Or should it fail?

In most use cases, you end up using one of two options: joining the existing transaction (PROPAGATION_REQUIRED) or starting a new transaction (PROPAGATION_REQUIRES_NEW).

To use transaction propagation, you must configure it in the Spring XML file as shown in the following example. This example uses PROPAGATION_REQUIRED as indicated in bold:

```
<bean id="required"
      class="org.apache.camel.spring.spi.SpringTransactionPolicy">
   <property name="transactionManager" ref="txManager"/>
   <property name="propagationBehaviorName"
             value="PROPAGATION_REQUIRED"/>
</bean>

<camelContext id="camel" xmlns="http://camel.apache.org/schema/spring">
   <route id="partnerToDB">
       <from uri="activemq:queue:partners"/>
       <transacted ref="required"/>
       <bean ref="partner" method="toSql"/>
       <to uri="jdbc:myDataSource"/>
   </route>
</camelContext>
```

Defining policy with propagation required ❶

Using policy definition in Camel route ❷

First you define a bean with the id "required", which is a SpringTransactionPolicy type **1**. The bean must refer to both the transaction manager and the choice of transaction propagation to be used. In the Camel route, you then refer to the required bean from within the <transacted> tag, using the ref attribute **2**.

If you want to use PROPAGATION_REQUIRES_NEW, it's just a matter of changing the property on the bean as shown in bold:

```
<property name="propagationBehaviorName"
          value="PROPAGATION_REQUIRES_NEW"/
```

If you have ever used Spring transactions, you may have named beans with the transaction propagation type directly, like this:

```
<bean id="PROPAGATION_REQUIRED"
      class="org.apache.camel.spring.spi.SpringTransactionPolicy">
  <property name="transactionManager" ref="txManager"/>
</bean>
```

There is no practical difference between these two styles—it's a matter of taste as to which you prefer.

Notice that you don't have to specify the propagationBehaviorName property on the bean. This is because Camel uses convention over configuration to detect whether the bean id matches any of the known propagation behavior names. In this example, the bean id is "PROPAGATION_REQUIRED", which tells Camel to use this propagating behavior. All together, it allows you to avoid repeating yourself by specifying the propagationBehaviorName property as well.

Let's look at what else is specified by convention over configuration.

USING CONVENTION OVER CONFIGURATION FOR TRANSACTIONS IN CAMEL ROUTES

In section 9.2, you used the default transaction configuration, which relies on convention over configuration. This works well when you want to use the required transaction propagation, because it removes the need for some boilerplate configuration.

The first example from section 9.2.2 could be reduced to only the Camel route, as follows:

```
<camelContext id="camel" xmlns="http://camel.apache.org/schema/spring">
    <route id="partnerToDB">
        <from uri="activemq:queue:partners"/>
        <transacted/>
        <bean ref="partner" method="toSql"/>
        <to uri="jdbc:myDataSource"/>
    </route>
</camelContext>
```

All you do here is declare <transacted/> in the Camel route, and Camel takes it from there. Camel will use PROPAGATION_REQUIRED by convention, and will look up the Spring transaction manager for you.

> **NOTE** This is a common situation. Usually all you have to do is configure the Spring transaction manager and add <transacted/> in the Camel route.

You have now learned how to configure and use transactions with Camel. But there's more to learn. In the next section, we'll look at how transactions work when you have multiple routes and when you need different propagation behavior.

9.4.2 *Using transactions with multiple routes*

In Camel, it's common to have multiple routes and to let one route reuse another by sending messages to it. In this section, we'll look at how this works when one or all routes are transacted. Then we'll look at some of the implications of using transactions with request-response messaging style.

We'll start out simply and look at what happens when you use a non-transacted route from a transacted route.

USING TRANSACTIONS WITH A NON-TRANSACTED ROUTE

Listing 9.6 shows the parts of a unit test that you can use to see what happens when a transacted route calls a non-transacted route.

Listing 9.6 Unit test with a transacted route calling a non-transacted route

```
public class TXToNonTXTest extends CamelSpringTestSupport {

protected AbstractXmlApplicationContext createApplicationContext() {
    return new ClassPathXmlApplicationContext("spring-context.xml");
}

protected int getExpectedRouteCount() {
    return 0;
}

protected RouteBuilder createRouteBuilder() throws Exception {
    return new SpringRouteBuilder() {
        public void configure() throws Exception {         ❶ Transacted
            from("activemq:queue:a")                          route
                .transacted()
                .to("direct:quote")
                .to("activemq:queue:b");          ❷ Non-transacted
                                                      route
            from("direct:quote")
                .choice()
                    .when(body().contains("Camel"))
                        .transform(constant("Camel rocks"))
                    .when(body().contains("Donkey"))
                        .throwException(new IllegalArgumentException(
                                "Donkeys not allowed"))
                    .otherwise()
                        .transform(body().prepend("Hello "));
        }
    };
}
```

In listing 9.6, you first import the Spring XML file, which contains all the Spring configuration to set up the JMS broker, Spring, and the Camel ActiveMQ component. The content of the spring-context.xml file is the same as in listing 9.4.

The getExpectedRouteCount method may at first seem a bit odd, but it's needed to indicate to CamelSpringTestSupport that the Spring XML file doesn't contain any Camel routes—it does this by saying that there are 0 routes. Next, you have the two routes. First, the transacted route ❶ moves messages from queue A to B. During this move, the message is also processed by the non-transacted route ❷, which transforms the message using a content-based router. Notice that if the message contains the word "Donkey", the route will force a failure by throwing an exception.

You can run this unit test by running the following Maven goal from the chapter9/multuple-routes directory:

```
mvn test -Dtest=TXToNonTXTest
```

The unit test has three methods: two test situations that commit the transaction, and one rolls back the transaction because of the exception being thrown. Here are two tests showing the commit and rollback situations:

```
public void testWithCamel() throws Exception {
    template.sendBody("activemq:queue:a", "Hi Camel");
    Object reply = consumer.receiveBody("activemq:queue:b", 10000);
    assertEquals("Camel rocks", reply);
}

public void testWithDonkey() throws Exception {
    template.sendBody("activemq:queue:a", "Donkey");
    Object reply = consumer.receiveBody("activemq:queue:b", 10000);
    assertNull("There should be no reply", reply);

    reply = consumer.receiveBody("activemq:queue:ActiveMQ.DLQ", 10000);
    assertNotNull("It should have been moved to DLQ", reply);
}
```

What can you learn from this? The unit test proves that when a transacted route uses a non-transacted route, the transactional behavior works as if all routes are transacted, which is what you'd expect. The last unit test proves that when the non-transacted route fails by throwing an exception, the transacted route detected this and issued a rollback. You can see this because the message is moved to the JMS broker's dead letter queue.

This is great news, because there are no surprises. It's safe for transacted routes to reuse existing non-transacted routes.

> **NOTE** The transaction manager requires messages to be processed in the *same* thread context, to support the transaction. This means that when you use multiple routes, you must link them together in a way that ensures the message is processed in the same thread. Using the Direct component does this—the Direct component was used in listing 9.6 to link the two routes together. This won't work with the SEDA component, which routes messages using another thread.

Let's continue and see what happens when both routes are transacted.

USING TRANSACTIONS WITH ANOTHER TRANSACTED ROUTE

Now let's modify the unit test from listing 9.6 and create a new situation, where both routes are transacted, and see what happens. Here are the routes.

Listing 9.7 Two transacted routes

```java
public void configure() throws Exception {
    from("activemq:queue:a")
        .transacted()
        .to("direct:quote")
        .to("activemq:queue:b");

    from("direct:quote")
        .transacted()
        .choice()
            .when(body().contains("Camel"))
                .to("activemq:queue:camel")
            .otherwise()
                .throwException(new IllegalArgumentException
                    ("Unsupported animal"));
}
```

You can run this example by running the following Maven goal:

```
mvn test -Dtest=TXToTXTest
```

Once again, the unit test will prove that there are no surprises here. When the exception is thrown, the entire route is rolled back, which is what you'd expect. When the message hits the second route and the second `transacted`, it participates in the existing transaction. This is because `PROPAGATION_REQUIRED` is the default propagation behavior when using `transacted`.

Next, we'll make it more challenging by using two different transaction propagations.

USING MULTIPLE TRANSACTIONS WITH ONE EXCHANGE

In some situations, you may need to use multiple transactions with the same exchange, as illustrated in figure 9.10.

In figure 9.10 an exchange is being routed in Camel. It starts off using the required transaction, and then you need to use another transaction that's independent of the existing transaction. You can do this by using `PROPAGATION_REQUIRES_NEW`, which will start a new transaction regardless of whether an existing transaction exists

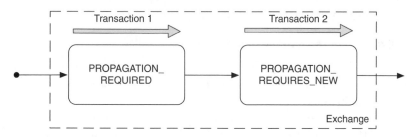

Figure 9.10 Using two independent transactions in a single exchange

or not. When the exchange completes, the transaction manager will issue commits to these two transactions, which ensures that they both commit at the same point.

> **NOTE** The example outlined in figure 9.10 requires the transaction manager to support the suspension and resumption of transactions. This isn't supported by all transaction manager implementations.

In Camel, a route can only be configured to use at most one transaction propagation, which means figure 9.10 must use two routes. The first route uses PROPAGATION_ REQUIRED and the second route uses PROPAGATION_REQUIRES_NEW.

Suppose you have an application that updates orders in a database. The application must store all incoming orders in an audit log, and then it either updates or inserts the order in the order database. The audit log should always insert a record, even if subsequent processing of the order fails. Implementing this in Camel should be done using two routes, as follows:

```
from("direct:orderToDB")
    .transacted("PROPAGATION_REQUIRED")
    .beanRef("orderDAO", "auditOrder")
    .to("direct:saveOrderInDB");

from("direct:saveOrderInDB")
    .onException(Exception.class).markRollbackOnlyLast().end()
    .transacted("PROPAGATION_REQUIRES_NEW")
    .beanRef("orderDAO", "updateOrInsertOrder");
```

The first route uses PROPAGATION_REQUIRED to make the route transactional. The second route, in contrast, uses PROPAGATION_REQUIRES_NEW to ensure that a new transaction is used within this route.

Now suppose an error occurs while processing the second route—you could either let both routes roll back, or only roll back the second route. Camel will, by default, roll back both routes, and because you only want the second route to roll back, you have to tell Camel this. This is done by declaring a route-level onException where you leverage markRollbackOnlyLast, to instruct Camel to only roll back the last (current) transaction. If you wanted to roll back both routes, you could either remove the onException declaration or use markRollbackOnly instead of markRollbackOnlyLast.

In the next section, we'll return to Rider Auto Parts and look at an example that covers a common use case: using web services together with transactions. How do you return a custom web service response if a transaction fails?

9.4.3   *Returning a custom response when a transaction fails*

Rider Auto Parts has a Camel application that exposes a web service to a selected number of business partners. The partners use this application to submit orders. Figure 9.11 illustrates the application.

As you can see in the figure, the business partners invoke a web service to submit an order **①**. The received order is stored in a database for audit purposes **②**. The

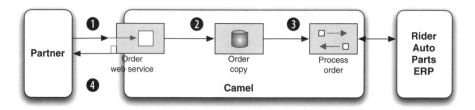

Figure 9.11 A web service used by business partners to submit orders. A copy of the order is stored in a database before it's processed by the ERP system.

order is then processed by the enterprise resource planning (ERP) system ③, and a reply is returned to the waiting business partner ④.

The web service is deliberately kept simple so partners can easily leverage it with their IT systems. There is a single return code that indicates whether or not the order succeeded or failed. The following code snippet is part of the WSDL definition for the reply (outputOrder):

```
<xs:element name="outputOrder">
    <xs:complexType>
        <xs:sequence>
            <xs:element type="xs:string" name="code"/>
        </xs:sequence>
    </xs:complexType>
</xs:element>
```

The code field should contain "OK" if the order was accepted; any other value is considered a failure. This means that the Camel application must deal with any thrown exceptions and return a custom failure message, instead of propagating the thrown exception back to the web service.

Your Camel application needs to do the following three things:

- Catch the exception and handle it to prevent it propagating back
- Mark the transaction to roll back
- Construct a reply message with a code value of "ERROR"

Camel can support such complex use cases because you can leverage onException, which you learned about in chapter 5. What you do is add an onException to the Camel-Context, as shown here:

```
<onException>
    <exception>java.lang.Exception</exception>
    <handled><constant>true</constant></handled>
    <transform><method bean="order" method="replyError"/></transform>
    <rollback markRollbackOnly="true"/>
</onException>
```

You first tell Camel that this onException should trigger for any kind of exception that's thrown. You then mark the exception as handled, which removes the exception from the exchange, because you want to use a custom reply message instead of the thrown exception.

> **NOTE** The `<rollback/>` definition must always be at the end of the onException because it stops the message from being further routed. That means you *must* have prepared the reply message before you issue the `<rollback/>`.

To construct the reply message, you use the order bean, invoking its replyError method:

```
public OutputOrder replyError(Exception cause) {
    OutputOrder error = new OutputOrder();
    error.setCode("ERROR: " + cause.getMessage());
    return error;
}
```

This is easy to do, as you can see. You first define the replyError method to have an Exception as a parameter—this will contain the thrown exception. You then create the OutputOrder object, which you populate with the "ERROR" text and the exception message.

The source code for the book contains this example in the chapter9/riderautoparts-order directory. You can start the application by using the following Maven goal:

```
mvn camel:run
```

Then you can send web service requests to http://localhost:9000/order. The WSDL is accessible at http://localhost:9000/order?wsdl.

To work with this example, you need to use web services. SoapUI (http://www.soapui.org/) is a popular application for testing with web services. It's also easy to set up and get started. You create a new project and import the WSDL file from http://localhost:9000/order?wsdl. Then you create a sample web service request and fill in the request parameters, as shown in figure 9.12. You then send the request by clicking the green play button, and it will display the reply in the pane on the right side.

Figure 9.12 shows an example where we caused a failure to occur. Our example behaves according to what you specify in the refNo field. You can force different behavior by specifying either FATAL or FAIL-ONCE in the refNo field. Entering any other value

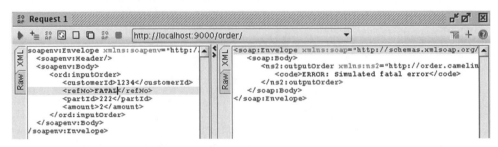

Figure 9.12 A web service message causes the transaction to roll back, and a custom reply message is returned.

will cause the request to succeed. As figure 9.12 shows, we entered FATAL, which causes an exception to occur and an ERROR reply to be returned.

So far we've been using resources that support transactions, such as JMS and JDBC, but the majority of components don't support transactions. So what can you do instead? In the next section, we'll look at compensating when transactions aren't supported.

9.5 Compensating for unsupported transactions

The number of resources that can participate in transactions is limited—they're mostly confined to JMS- and JDBC-based resources. This section covers what you can do to compensate for the absence of transactional support in other resources. Compensation, in Camel, involves the unit of work concept.

First, we'll look at how a unit of work is represented in Camel and how you can use this concept. Then we'll walk through an example demonstrating how the unit of work can help simulate the orchestration that a transaction manager does. We'll also discuss how you can use a unit of work to compensate for the lack of transactions by doing the work that a transaction manager's rollback would do in the case of failure.

9.5.1 Introducing UnitOfWork

The concept of the unit of work is to batch together a group of tasks as a single coherent unit. The idea is to use the unit of work as a way of mimicking transactional boundaries.

In Camel the unit of work is represented by the org.apache.camel.spi.UnitOf-Work interface offering a range of methods including the following:

```
void addSynchronization(Synchronization synchronization);
void removeSynchronization(Synchronization synchronization);
void done(Exchange exchange);
```

The addSynchronization and removeSynchronization methods are used to register and unregister a Synchronization (a callback), which we'll look at shortly. The done method is invoked when the unit of work is complete, and it invokes the registered callbacks.

The Synchronization callback is the interesting part for Camel end users because it's the interface you use to execute custom logic when an exchange is complete. It's represented by the org.apache.camel.spi.Synchronization interface and offers these two methods:

```
void onComplete(Exchange exchange);
void onFailure(Exchange exchange);
```

When the exchange is done, either the onComplete or onFailure method is invoked, depending on whether the exchange failed or not.

Figure 9.13 illustrates how these concepts are related to each other. As you can see from this figure, each Exchange has exactly one UnitOfWork, which you can access using the getUnitOfWork method from the Exchange. The UnitOfWork is private to the Exchange and is not shared with others.

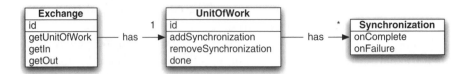

Figure 9.13   An `Exchange` **has one** `UnitOfWork`, **which in turn has from zero to many** `Synchronizations`.

> **How** `UnitOfWork` **is orchestrated**
>
> Camel will automatically inject a new `UnitOfWork` into an `Exchange` when it's routed. This is done by an internal processor, `UnitOfWorkProcessor`, which is involved in the start of every route. When the `Exchange` is done, this processor invokes the registered `Synchronization` callbacks. The `UnitOfWork` boundaries are always at the beginning and end of Camel routes.

When an `Exchange` is done being routed, you hit the end boundary of the `UnitOfWork`, and the registered `Synchronization` callbacks are invoked one by one. This is the same mechanism the Camel components leverage to add their custom `Synchronization` callbacks to the `Exchange`. For example, the File and FTP components use this mechanism to perform *after-processing* operations such as moving or deleting processed files.

> **TIP**   Use `Synchronization` callbacks to execute any after-processing you want done when the `Exchange` is complete. Don't worry about throwing exceptions from your custom `Synchronization`—Camel will catch those and log them at `WARN` level, and will then continue to invoke the next callback. This ensures that all callbacks are invoked even if one happens to fail.

A good way of understanding how this works is to review an example, which we'll do now.

9.5.2   *Using Synchronization callbacks*

Rider Auto Parts has a Camel application that sends email messages containing invoice details to customers. First, the email content is generated, and then, before the email is sent, a backup of the email is stored in a file for reference. Whenever an invoice is to be sent to a customer, the Camel application is involved. Figure 9.14 shows the principle of this application.

Imagine what would happen if there were a problem sending an email. You can't use transactions to roll back, because filesystem resources can't participate in transactions. Instead, you can perform custom logic, which *compensates* for the failure by deleting the file.

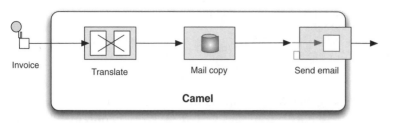

Figure 9.14
Emails are sent to customers listing their invoice details. Before the email is sent, a backup is stored in the file system.

The compensation logic is trivial to implement, as shown here:

```
public class FileRollback implements Synchronization {

    public void onComplete(Exchange exchange) {
    }

    public void onFailure(Exchange exchange) {
        String name = exchange.getIn().getHeader(
                            Exchange.FILE_NAME_PRODUCED, String.class);
        LOG.warn("Failure occurred so deleting backup file: " + name);
        FileUtil.deleteFile(new File(name));
    }
}
```

In the `onFailure` method, you delete the backup file, retrieving the filename used by the Camel File component from the `Exchange.FILE_NAME_PRODUCED` header.

What you must do next is instruct Camel to use the `FileRollback` class to perform this compensation. To do so, you can add it to the `UnitOfWork` by using the `add-Synchronization` method, which was depicted in figure 9.13. This can be done using the Java DSL as highlighted:

```
public void configure() throws Exception {
    from("direct:confirm")
        .process(new Processor() {
            public void process(Exchange exchange) throws Exception {
                exchange.getUnitOfWork()
                        .addSynchronization(new FileRollback());
            }
        })
        .bean(OrderService.class, "createMail")
        .log("Saving mail backup file")
        .to("file:target/mail/backup")
        .log("Trying to send mail to ${header.to}")
        .bean(OrderService.class, "sendMail")
        .log("Mail send to ${header.to}");
}
```

The source code for the book contains this example in the chapter9/uow directory. You can try it by using the following Maven goal:

```
mvn test -Dtest=FileRollbackTest
```

If you run the example, it will output something like the following to the console:

```
INFO  route1 - Saving mail backup file
INFO  route1 - Trying to send to FATAL
ERROR DefaultErrorHandler - Failed delivery for exchangeId:
  9edc1ecb-43be-43ee-9f32-7371452967bd.
WARN  FileRollback - Failure occurred so deleting backup file:
  target/mail/backup/02630ec4-724d-4e73-8eb6-c969720578c
```

One thing that may bother you is that you must use an inlined `Processor` to add the `FileRollback` class as a `Synchronization`. Camel offers a convenient method on the `Exchange`, so you could do it with less code:

```
exchange.addOnCompletion(new FileRollback());
```

But it still requires the inlined `Processor`. Isn't there a more convenient way? Yes there is, and that's where `onCompletion` comes into the picture.

9.5.3 *Using onCompletion*

`OnCompletion` takes the `Synchronization` into the world of routing, enabling you to easily add the `FileRollback` class as `Synchronization`.

So let's see how it's done. `OnCompletion` is available in both Java DSL and Spring XML variations. Here's how `onCompletion` is used with Spring XML.

Listing 9.8 Using `onCompletion` as a transactional rollback

```xml
<bean id="orderService" class="camelinaction.OrderService"/>

<bean id="fileRollback" class="camelinaction.FileRollback"/>

<camelContext xmlns="http://camel.apache.org/schema/spring">

    <onCompletion onFailureOnly="true">
        <bean ref="fileRollback" method="onFailure"/>
    </onCompletion>

    <route>
        <from uri="direct:confirm"/>
        <bean ref="orderService" method="createMail"/>
        <log message="Saving mail backup file"/>
        <to uri="file:target/mail/backup"/>
        <log message="Trying to send mail to ${header.to}"/>
        <bean ref="orderService" method="sendMail"/>
        <log message="Mail send to ${header.to}"/>
    </route>

</camelContext>
```

As you can see from the code, `<onCompletion>` is defined as a separate Camel route. It will be executed right after the regular route has completed. You're only interested in executing `onCompletion` when the exchange fails, so you can specify this by setting the `onFailureOnly` attribute to `true`.

The source code for the book contains this example, which you can run using the following Maven goal:

```
mvn test -Dtest=SpringFileRollbackTest
```

When you run it, you'll find that it acts just like the previous example. It will delete the backup file if the exchange fails.

> **The difference between onCompletion and Synchronization**
>
> There is one major difference between using `onCompletion` and using a `Synchronization`, and that's the thread model in use. Synchronization uses the same thread to perform the tasks, so it will block and wait until it completes. In contrast, `onCompletion` transfers the exchange to be executed by a separate thread.
>
> The reason for this design decision is that onCompletion should not affect the original exchange and its outcome. Suppose during `onCompletion` an exception was thrown—what should happen then? Or what if `onCompletion` unexpectedly or deliberately changed the content of the exchange, which would affect the reply being sent back to the caller?
>
> The bottom line is that onCompletion uses a separate route based on a copy of the completed exchange. It will not affect the outcome of the original route.

`OnCompletion` can also be used in situations where the exchange did not fail. Suppose you want to log activity about exchanges being processed. For example, in the Java DSL you could do it as follows:

```
onCompletion().beanRef("logService", "logExchange");
```

`OnCompletion` also supports scoping, exactly the same `onException` does at either context or route scope (as you saw in chapter 5). You could create a Java DSL–based version of listing 9.8 using route-scoped `onCompletion` as follows:

```
from("direct:confirm")
    .onCompletion().onFailureOnly()
        .bean(FileRollback.class, "onFailure")
    .end()
    .bean(OrderService.class, "createMail")
    .log("Saving mail backup file")
    .to("file:target/mail/backup")
    .log("Trying to send mail to ${header.to}")
    .bean(OrderService.class, "sendMail")
    .log("Mail send to ${header.to}");
```

Now you've learned all there is to know about `onCompletion`, which brings us to the end of this chapter.

9.6 Summary and best practices

Transactions play a crucial role when grouping distinct events together so that they act as a single, coherent, atomic event.

In this chapter, we looked at how transactions work in Camel and discovered that Camel lets Spring orchestrate and manage transactions. By leveraging Spring transactions, Camel lets you use an existing and proven transaction framework that works well with the most popular application servers, message brokers, and database systems.

Here are the best practices you should take away from this chapter:

- *Use transactions when appropriate.* Transactions can only be used by a limited number of resources, such as JMS and JDBC. Therefore, it only makes sense to use transactions when you can leverage these kinds of resources. If transactions aren't applicable, you can consider using your own code to compensate and to work as a rollback mechanism.
- *Local or global transactions.* If your route only involves one transactional resource, use local transactions. They're simpler and much less resource-intensive. Only use global transactions if multiple resources are involved.
- *Test your transactions.* Build unit and integration tests to ensure that your transactions work as expected.

We'll now turn our attention to using concurrency with Camel. You'll learn to how to improve performance, understand the threading model used in Camel, and more.

Concurrency
and scalability

This chapter covers

- Camel's threading model
- Configuring thread pools and thread profiles
- Using concurrency with EIPs
- Message synchronicity and concurrency
- Camel's client concurrency API
- Scalability with Camel

Concurrency is another word for multitasking, and we multitask all the time in our daily lives. We put the coffee on, start up the computer, and while it's booting grab the paper to glance at the news. Computers are also capable of doing multiple tasks—you may have multiple tabs open in your web browser while your mail application is fetching new email, for example.

Juggling multiple tasks is also very common in enterprise systems, such as when you're processing incoming orders, handling invoices, and doing inventory management, and these demands only grow over time. With concurrency, you can

315

achieve higher performance; by executing in parallel, you can get more work done in less time.

Camel processes multiple messages concurrently in Camel routes, and it leverages the concurrency features from Java, so we'll first discuss how concurrency works in Java before we can move on to how thread pools work and how you define and use them in Camel. The thread pool is the mechanism in Java that orchestrates multiple tasks. After we've discussed thread pools, we'll move on to how you can use concurrency with the EIPs, and we'll dive into how message synchronicity works. We'll then look at Camel's client concurrency API, which makes it easier for clients to work with concurrency. The last section of this chapter focuses on how you can achieve high scalability with Camel and how you can leverage this in your custom components.

10.1   *Introducing concurrency*

As we've mentioned, you can achieve higher performance with concurrency. When performance is limited by the availability of a resource, we say it's *bound* by that resource: CPU-bound, IO-bound, database-bound, and so on. Integration applications are often IO-bound, waiting for replies to come back from remote servers, or for files to load from a disk. This usually means you can achieve higher performance by utilizing resources more effectively, such as by keeping CPUs busy doing useful work.

Camel is often used to integrate disparate systems, where data is exchanged over the network. This means there's often a mix of resources, which are either CPU-bound or IO-bound. It's very likely you can achieve higher performance by using concurrency.

To help explain the world of concurrency, we'll look at an example. Rider Auto Parts has an inventory of all the parts its suppliers currently have in stock. It's vital for any business to have the most accurate and up-to-date information in their central ERP system. Having the information locally in the ERP system means the business can operate without depending on online integration with their suppliers. Figure 10.1 illustrates this business process.

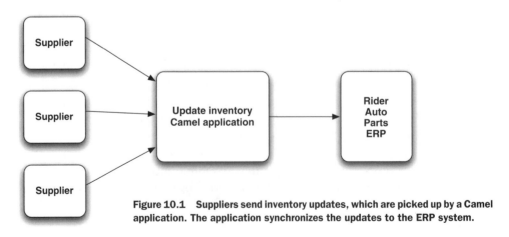

Figure 10.1   Suppliers send inventory updates, which are picked up by a Camel application. The application synchronizes the updates to the ERP system.

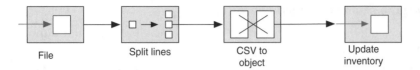

Figure 10.2 A route picks up incoming files, which are split and transformed to be ready for updating the inventory in the ERP system.

Figure 10.2 shows the route of the inventory-updating Camel application from figure 10.1. This application is responsible for loading the files and splitting the file content on a line-by-line basis using the Splitter EIP, which converts the line from CSV format to an internal object model. The model is then sent to another route that's responsible for updating the ERP system. Implementing this in Camel is straightforward.

Listing 10.1 Rider Auto Parts application for updating inventory

```
public void configure() throws Exception {
    from("file:rider/inventory")
        .log("Starting to process file: ${header.CamelFileName}")
        .split(body().tokenize("\n")).streaming()          Splits file
            .bean(InventoryService.class, "csvToObject")   ❶ line by line
            .to("direct:update")
        .end()
        .log("Done processing file: ${header.CamelFileName}");

    from("direct:update")                                   Updates
        .bean(InventoryService.class, "updateInventory");  ❷ ERP system
}
```

Listing 10.1 shows the `configure` method of the Camel `RouteBuilder` that contains the two routes for implementing the application. As you can see, the first route picks up the files and then splits the file content line by line ❶. This is done by using the Splitter EIP in *streaming mode*. The streaming mode ensures that the entire file isn't loaded into memory; instead it's loaded piece by piece on demand, which ensures low memory usage.

To convert each line from CSV to an object, you use a bean—the `InventoryService` class. To update the ERP system, you use the `updateInventory` method of the `InventoryService`, as shown in the second route ❷.

Now suppose you're testing the application by letting it process a big file with 100,000 lines. If each line takes a tenth of a second to process, processing the file would take 10,000 seconds, which is roughly 167 minutes. That's a long time. In fact, you might end up in a situation where you can't process all the files within the given timeframe.

In a moment, we'll look at different techniques for speeding things up by leveraging concurrency. But first we'll set up the example to run without concurrency to create a baseline to compare to the concurrent solutions.

10.1.1 *Running the example without concurrency*

The source code for the book contains this example (both with and without concurrency) in the chapter10/bigfile directory.

First, you need a big file to be used for testing. To create a file with 1000 lines, use the following Maven goal:

```
mvn compile exec:java -PCreateBigFile -Dlines=1000
```

A bigfile.csv file will be created in the target/inventory directory.

The next step is to start a test that processes the bigfile.csv without concurrency. This is done by using the following Maven goal:

```
mvn test -Dtest=BigFileTest
```

When the test runs, it will output its progress to the console.

BigFileTest simulates updating the inventory by sleeping for a tenth of a second, which means it should complete processing the bigfile.csv in approximately 100 seconds. When the test completes, it should log the total time taken:

```
[ad 0 - file://target/inventory] INFO - Inventory 997 updated
[ad 0 - file://target/inventory] INFO - Inventory 998 updated
[ad 0 - file://target/inventory] INFO - Inventory 999 updated
[ad 0 - file://target/inventory] INFO - Done processing big file
Took 102 seconds
```

In the following section, we'll see three different solutions to run this test more quickly using concurrency.

10.1.2 *Using concurrency*

The application can leverage concurrency by updating the inventory in parallel. Figure 10.3 shows this principle by using the Concurrent Consumers EIP.

As you can see in figure 10.3, the idea is to use concurrency ❸ after the lines have been split ❷. By doing this, you can parallelize steps ❹ and ❺ in the route. In this example, those two steps could process messages concurrently.

The last step ❺, which sends messages to the ERP system concurrently, is only possible if the system allows a client to send messages concurrently to it. There can be situations where a system does not permit concurrency, or it may only allow up to a

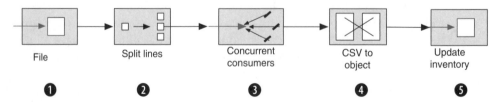

Figure 10.3   Using the Concurrent Consumers EIP to leverage concurrency and process inventory updates in parallel

certain number of concurrent messages. Check the SLA (service level agreement) for the system you integrate with. Another reason to disallow concurrency would be if the messages have to be processed in the exact order they are split.

Let's try out three different ways to run the application faster with concurrency:

- Using `parallelProcessing` options on the Splitter EIP
- Using a custom thread pool on the Splitter EIP
- Using staged event-driven architecture (SEDA)

The first two solutions are features that the Splitter EIP provides out of the box. The last solution is based on the SEDA principle, which uses queues between tasks.

USING PARALLELPROCESSING

The Splitter EIP offers an option to switch on parallel processing, as shown here:

```
.split(body().tokenize("\n")).streaming().parallelProcessing()
    .bean(InventoryService.class, "csvToObject")
    .to("direct:update")
.end()
```

Configuring this in Spring XML is very simple as well:

```
<split streaming="true" parallelProcessing="true">
    <tokenize token="\n"/>
    <bean beanType="camelinaction.InventoryService"
        method="csvToObject"/>
    <to uri="direct:update"/>
</split>
```

To run this example, use the following Maven goals:

```
mvn test -Dtest=BigFileParallelTest
mvn test -Dtest=SpringBigFileParallelTest
```

As you'll see, the test is now much faster and completes in about a tenth of the previous time.

```
[Camel Thread 1 - Split] INFO - Inventory 995 updated
[Camel Thread 4 - Split] INFO - Inventory 996 updated
[Camel Thread 9 - Split] INFO - Inventory 997 updated
[Camel Thread 3 - Split] INFO - Inventory 998 updated
[Camel Thread 2 - Split] INFO - Inventory 999 updated
[e://target/inventory?n] INFO - Done processing big file
Took 11 seconds
```

What happens is that when `parallelProcessing` is enabled, the Splitter EIP uses a thread pool to process the messages concurrently. The thread pool is, by default, configured to use 10 threads, which helps explain why it's about 10 times faster: the application is mostly IO-bound (reading files and remotely communicating with the ERP system involves a lot of IO activity). The test would not be 10 times faster if it were solely CPU-bound; for example, if all it did was "crunch numbers."

NOTE In the console output you'll see that the thread name is displayed, containing a unique thread number, such as `Camel Thread 4 - Split`. This thread number is a sequential, unique number assigned to each thread as it's created, in any thread pool. This means if you use a second Splitter EIP, the second splitter will most likely have numbers assigned from 11 upwards.

You may have noticed from the previous console output that the lines were processed in order; it ended by updating 995, 996, 997, 998, and 999. This is a coincidence, because the 10 concurrent threads are independent and they run at their own pace. The reason why they appear in order here is because we simulated the update by delaying the message for a tenth of a second, which means they'll all take approximately the same amount of time. But if you take a closer look in the console output, you'll probably see some interleaved lines, such as with order lines 954 and 953:

```
[Camel Thread 5 - Split] INFO - Inventory 951 updated
[Camel Thread 7 - Split] INFO - Inventory 952 updated
[Camel Thread 8 - Split] INFO - Inventory 954 updated
[Camel Thread 9 - Split] INFO - Inventory 953 updated
```

You now know that `parallelProcessing` will use a default thread pool to achieve concurrency. What if you want to have more control over which thread pool is being used?

USING A CUSTOM THREAD POOL

The Splitter EIP also allows you to use a custom thread pool for concurrency. You can create a thread pool using the `java.util.Executors` factory:

```
ExecutorService threadPool = Executors.newCachedThreadPool();
```

The `newCachedThreadPool` method will create a thread pool suitable for executing many small tasks. The pool will automatically grow and shrink on demand.

To use this pool with the Splitter EIP, you need to configure it as shown here:

```
.split(body().tokenize("\n")).streaming().executorService(threadPool)
    .bean(InventoryService.class, "csvToObject")
    .to("direct:update")
.end()
```

Creating the thread pool using Spring XML is done as follows:

```
<bean id="myPool" class="java.util.concurrent.Executors"
    factory-method="newCachedThreadPool"/>
```

The Splitter EIP uses the pool by referring to it, using the `executorServiceRef` attribute, as shown:

```
<split streaming="true" executorServiceRef="myPool">
    <tokenize token="\n"/>
    <bean beanType="camelinaction.InventoryService"
        method="csvToObject"/>
    <to uri="direct:update"/>
</split>
```

To run this example, use the following Maven goals:

```
mvn test -Dtest=BigFileCachedThreadPoolTest
mvn test -Dtest=SpringBigFileCachedThreadPoolTest
```

The test is now much faster and completes within a few seconds:

```
[pool-1-thread-442] INFO - Inventory 971 updated
[pool-1-thread-443] INFO - Inventory 972 updated
[pool-1-thread-449] INFO - Inventory 982 updated
[e://target/invene] INFO - Done processing big file
Took 2 seconds
```

You may wonder why it's now so fast. The reason is that the cached thread pool is designed to be very aggressive and to spawn new threads on demand. It has no upper bounds and no internal work queue, which means that when a new task is being handed over, it will create a new thread if there are no available threads in the thread pool.

You may also have noticed the thread name in the console output, which indicates that many threads were created; the output shows thread numbers 442, 443, and 449. Many threads have been created because the Splitter EIP splits the file lines more quickly than the tasks update the inventory. This means that the thread pool receives new tasks at a higher pace than it can execute them; new threads are created to keep up.

This can cause unpredicted side effects in an enterprise system—a high number of newly created threads may impact applications in other areas. That's why it's often desirable to use thread pools with an upper limit for the number of threads.

For example, instead of using the cached thread pool, you could use a fixed thread pool. You can use the same Executors factory to create such a pool:

```
ExecutorService threadPool = Executors.newFixedThreadPool(20);
```

Creating a fixed thread pool in Spring XML is done as follows:

```
<bean id="myPool" class="java.util.concurrent.Executors"
      factory-method="newFixedThreadPool">
   <constructor-arg index="0" value="20"/>
</bean>
```

To run this example, use the following Maven goals:

```
mvn test -Dtest=BigFileFixedThreadPoolTest
mvn test -Dtest=SpringBigFileFixedThreadPoolTest
```

The test is now limited to use 20 threads at most.

```
[pool-1-thread-13] INFO - Inventory 997 updated
[pool-1-thread-19] INFO - Inventory 998 updated
[ pool-1-thread-5] INFO - Inventory 999 updated
[ ntory?noop=true] INFO - Done processing big file
Took 6 seconds
```

As you can see by running this test, you can process the 1,000 lines in about 6 seconds using only 20 threads. The previous test was faster, as it completed in about 2 seconds, but it used nearly 500 threads (this number can vary on different systems). By increasing the fixed thread pool to a reasonable size, you should be able to reach the same time-frame as with the cached thread pool. For example, running with 50 threads completes in about 3 seconds. You can experiment with different pool sizes.

Now, on to the last concurrency solution, SEDA.

USING SEDA

SEDA (staged event-driven architecture) is an architecture design that breaks down a complex application into a set of stages connected by queues. In Camel lingo, that means using internal memory queues to hand over messages between routes.

> **NOTE**   The Direct component in Camel is the counterpart to SEDA. Direct is fully synchronized, and it works like a direct method call invocation.

Figure 10.4 shows how you can use SEDA to implement the example. The first route runs sequentially in a single thread. The second route uses concurrent consumers to process the messages that arrive on the SEDA endpoint, using multiple concurrent threads.

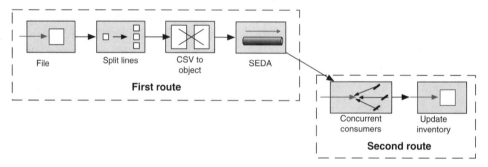

Figure 10.4   Messages pass from the first to the second route using SEDA. Concurrency is used in the second route.

Listing 10.2 shows how to implement this solution in Camel by using the `seda` endpoints, shown in bold.

Listing 10.2   Rider Auto Parts inventory-update application using SEDA

```
public void configure() throws Exception {
    from("file:rider/inventory")
        .log("Starting to process file: ${header.CamelFileName}")
        .split(body().tokenize("\n")).streaming()
            .bean(InventoryService.class, "csvToObject")
            .to("seda:update")
        .end()
        .log("Done processing file: ${header.CamelFileName}");

    from("seda:update?concurrentConsumers=20")          ◁─┐ SEDA
        .bean(InventoryService.class, "updateInventory");     consumers
}                                                             using
                                                          ① concurrency
```

By default, a `seda` consumer will only use one thread. To leverage concurrency, you use the `concurrentConsumers` option to increase the number of threads—to 20 in this listing ❶.

To run this example, use the following Maven goals:

```
mvn test -Dtest=BigFileSedaTest
mvn test -Dtest=SpringBigFileSedaTest
```

The test is fast and completes in about 6 seconds.

```
[ead 20 - seda://update] INFO - Inventory 997 updated
[ead 18 - seda://update] INFO - Inventory 998 updated
[read 9 - seda://update] INFO - Inventory 999 updated
Took 6 seconds
```

As you can see from the console output, you're now using 20 concurrent threads to process the inventory update. For example, the last three thread numbers from the output are 20, 18, and 9.

> **NOTE** When using `concurrentConsumers` with SEDA endpoints, the thread pool uses a fixed size, which means that a fixed number of active threads are waiting at all times to process incoming messages. That's why it's best to leverage the concurrency features provided by the EIPs, such as the `parallelProcessing` on the Splitter EIP. It will leverage a thread pool that can grow and shrink on demand, so it won't consume as many resources as a SEDA endpoint will.

We've now covered three different solutions for applying concurrency to an existing application, and they all greatly improve performance. We were able to reduce the 11-second processing time down to 3 to 7 seconds, using a reasonable size for the thread pool.

In the next section, we'll review thread pools in more detail and learn about the threading model used in Camel. With this knowledge, you can go even further with concurrency.

10.2 Using thread pools

Using thread pools is common when using concurrency. In fact, thread pools were used in the example in the previous section. It was a thread pool that allowed the Splitter EIP to work in parallel and speed up the performance of the application.

In this section, we'll start from the top and briefly recap what a thread pool is and how it's represented in Java. Then we'll look at the default thread pool profile used by Camel and how to create custom thread pools using Java DSL and Spring XML. We'll also look at how you can use a custom strategy to delegate the creation of thread pools to an external resource, such as a Java `WorkManager` on a JAVA EE server.

10.2.1 Understanding thread pools in Java

A thread pool is a group of threads that are created to execute a number of tasks in a task queue. Figure 10.5 shows this principle.

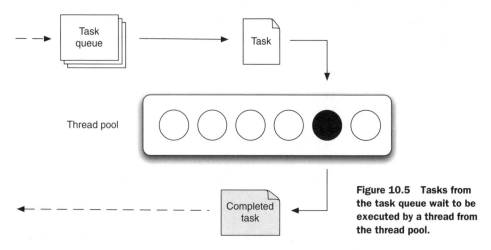

Figure 10.5   Tasks from the task queue wait to be executed by a thread from the thread pool.

NOTE For more info on the Thread Pool pattern, see the Wikipedia article on the subject: http://en.wikipedia.org/wiki/Thread_pool.

Thread pools were introduced into Java 1.5 by the new concurrency API residing in the `java.util.concurrent` package. In the concurrency API, the `ExecutorService` interface is the client API that you use to submit tasks for execution. Clients of this API are both Camel end users and Camel itself, because Camel fully leverages the concurrency API from Java.

NOTE Readers already familiar with Java's concurrency API may be in familiar waters as we go further in this chapter. If you want to learn in depth about the Java concurrency API, we highly recommend the book *Java Concurrency in Practice* by Brian Goetz.

In Java, the `ThreadPoolExecutor` class is the implementation of the `ExecutorService` interface, and it provides a thread pool with the options listed in table 10.1.

Table 10.1   Options provided by thread pools

Option	Type	Description
`corePoolSize`	`int`	Specifies the number of threads to keep in the pool, even if they're idle
`maximumPoolSize`	`int`	Specifies the maximum number of threads to keep in the pool
`keepAliveTime`	`long`	Sets the idle time for excess threads to wait before they're discarded
`unit`	`TimeUnit`	Specifies the time unit used for the `keepAliveTime` option
`rejected`	`RejectedExecutionHandler`	Identifies a handler to use when execution is blocked because the thread pool is exhausted

Table 10.1 Options provided by thread pools *(continued)*

Option	Type	Description
`workQueue`	`BlockingQueue`	Identifies the task queue for holding waiting tasks before they're executed
`threadFactory`	`ThreadFactory`	Specifies a factory to use when a new thread is created

As you can see from table 10.1, there are many options you can use when creating thread pools in Java. To make it easier to create commonly used types of pools, Java provides `Executors` as a factory, which you saw in section 10.1.2. In section 10.2.3, you'll see how Camel makes creating thread pools even easier.

When working with thread pools, there are often additional tasks you must deal with. For example, it's important to ensure the thread pool is shut down when your application is being shut down; otherwise it can lead to memory leaks. This is particularly important in server environments when running multiple applications in the same server container, such as a JAVA EE or OSGi container.

When using Camel to create thread pools, the activities listed in table 10.2 are taken care of out of the box.

Table 10.2 Activities for managing thread pools

Activity	Description
Shutdown	Ensures the thread pool will be properly shut down, which happens when Camel shuts down.
Management	Registers the thread pool in JMX, which allows you to manage the thread pool at runtime. We'll look at management in chapter 12.
Unique thread names	Ensures the created threads will use unique and human-readable names.
Activity logging	Logs lifecycle activity of the pool.

Another good practice that's often neglected is to use human-understandable thread names, because those names are logged in production logs. By allowing Camel to name the threads using a common naming standard, you can better understand what happens when looking at log files (particularly if your application is running together with other frameworks that create their own threads). For example, this log entry indicates it's a thread from the Camel File component:

```
[Camel Thread 7 - file://riders/inbox] DEBUG - Total 3 files to consume
```

If Camel didn't do this, the thread name would be generic and wouldn't give any hint that it's from Camel, nor that it's the file consumer.

```
[Thread 0] DEBUG - Total 3 files to consume
```

> **TIP** Camel uses a customizable pattern for naming threads. The default pattern is `"Camel Thread ${counter} - ${name}"`. A custom pattern can be configured using `ExecutorServiceStrategy`. In Camel 2.6 the default pattern has been improved to include the Camel id `"Camel (${camelId}) thread ${counter} - ${name}"`.

We'll cover the options listed in table 10.1 in more detail in the next section, when we review the default thread profile used by Camel.

10.2.2 Camel thread pool profiles

Thread pools aren't created and configured directly, but via the configuration of *thread pool profiles*. A thread pool profile is a profile that dictates how a thread pool should be created, based on a selection of the options listed earlier in table 10.1.

Thread pool profiles are organized in a simple two-layer hierarchy with custom and default profiles. There is always one default profile and you can optionally have multiple custom profiles.

The default profile is defined using the options listed in table 10.3.

Table 10.3 Settings for the default thread pool profile

Option	Default value	Description
poolSize	10	The thread pool will always contain at least 10 threads in the pool.
maxPoolSize	20	The thread pool can grow up to at most 20 threads.
keepAliveTime	60	Idle threads are kept alive for 60 seconds, after which they're terminated.
maxQueueSize	1000	The task queue can contain up to 1000 tasks before the pool is exhausted.
rejectedPolicy	CallerRuns	If the pool is exhausted, the caller thread will execute the task.

As you can see from the default values in table 10.3, the default thread pool can use from 10 to 20 threads to execute tasks concurrently. The `rejectedPolicy` option corresponds to the `rejected` option from table 10.1, and it's an enum type allowing four different values: `Abort`, `CallerRuns`, `DiscardOldest`, and `Discard`. The `Caller-Runs` option will use the caller thread to execute the task itself. The other three options will either abort by throwing an exception, or discard an existing task from the task queue.

There is no one-size-fits-all solution for every Camel application, so you may have to tweak the default profile values. But usually you're better off leaving the default values alone. Only by load testing your applications can you determine that tweaking the values will produce better results.

CONFIGURING THE DEFAULT THREAD POOL PROFILE

You can configure the default thread pool profile from either Java or Spring XML.

In Java, you access the `ThreadPoolProfile` starting from `CamelContext`. The following code shows how to change the maximum pool size to 50.

```
ExecutorServiceStrategy strategy = context.getExecutorServiceStrategy();
ThreadPoolProfile profile = strategy.getDefaultThreadPoolProfile();
profile.setMaxPoolSize(50);
```

The default `ThreadPoolProfile` is accessible from `ExecutorServiceStrategy`, which is an abstraction in Camel allowing you to plug in different thread pool providers. We'll cover `ExecutorServiceStrategy` in more detail in section 10.2.4.

In Spring XML, you configure the default thread pool profile using the `<thread-PoolProfile>` tag:

```
<camelContext id="camel" xmlns="http://camel.apache.org/schema/spring">
    <threadPoolProfile id="myDefaultProfile"
                       defaultProfile="true"
                       maxPoolSize="50"/>
    ...
</camelContext>
```

It's important to set the `defaultProfile` attribute to `true` to tell Camel that this is the default profile. You can add additional options if you want to override any of the other options from table 10.3.

There are situations where one profile isn't sufficient, so you can also define custom profiles.

CONFIGURING CUSTOM THREAD POOL PROFILES

Defining custom thread pool profiles is much like configuring the default profile.

In Java DSL, a custom profile is created using the `ThreadPoolProfileSupport` class:

```
ThreadPoolProfile custom = new ThreadPoolProfileSupport("bigPool");
custom.setMaxPoolSize(200);
context.getExecutorServiceStrategy().registerThreadPoolProfile(custom);
```

This example increases the maximum pool size to 200. All other options will be inherited from the default profile, which means it will use the default values listed in table 10.3; for example, `keepAliveTime` will be 60 seconds. Notice that this custom profile is given the name `bigPool`; you can refer to the profile in the Camel routes by using `executorServiceRef`:

```
.split(body().tokenize("\n")).streaming().executorServiceRef("bigPool")
    .bean(InventoryService.class, "csvToObject")
    .to("direct:update")
.end()
```

When Camel creates this route with the Splitter EIP, it refers to a thread pool with the name `bigPool`. Camel will now look in the registry for an `ExecutorService` type registered with the ID `bigPool`. If none is found, it will fall back and see if there is a known thread pool profile with the ID `bigPool`. And because such a profile has been registered, Camel will use the profile to create a new thread pool to be used by the Splitter EIP. All of which means that `executorServiceRef` supports using thread pool profiles to create the desired thread pools.

When using Spring XML, it's simpler to define custom thread pool profiles. All you have to do is use the `<threadPoolProfile>` tag:

```
<camelContext id="camel" xmlns="http://camel.apache.org/schema/spring">
    <threadPoolProfile id="bigPool" maxPoolSize="100"/>
</camelContext>
```

Besides using thread pool profiles, you can create thread pools in other ways. For example, you may need to create custom thread pools if you're using a third-party library that requires you to provide a thread pool. Or you may need to create one as we did in section 10.1 to leverage concurrency with the Splitter EIP.

10.2.3 *Creating custom thread pools*

Creating thread pools with the Java API is a bit cumbersome, so Camel provides a nice way of doing this in both Java DSL and Spring XML.

CREATING CUSTOM THREAD POOLS IN JAVA DSL

In Java DSL, you use `org.apache.camel.builder.ThreadPoolBuilder` to create thread pools, as follows:

```
ThreadPoolBuilder builder = new ThreadPoolBuilder(context);
ExecutorService myPool = builder.poolSize(5).maxPoolSize(25)
                          .maxQueueSize(200).build("MyPool");
```

The `ThreadPoolBuilder` requires `CamelContext` in its constructor, because it will use the default thread pool profile as the baseline when building custom thread pools. That means `myPool` will use the default value for `keepAliveTime`, which would be 60 seconds.

CREATING CUSTOM THREAD POOLS IN SPRING XML

In Spring XML, creating a thread pool is done using the `<threadPool>` tag:

```
<camelContext xmlns="http://camel.apache.org/schema/spring">

    <threadPool id="myPool" threadName="Cool"
             poolSize="5" maxPoolSize="15" maxQueueSize="250"/>

    <route>
        <from uri="direct:start"/>
        <to uri="log:start"/>
        <threads executorServiceRef="myPool">       ❶ Using thread pool
            <to uri="log:hello"/>                       in the route
        </threads>
    </route>
</camelContext>
```

As you can see, the `<threadPool>` is used inside a `<camelContext>` tag. This is because it needs access to the default thread profile, which is used as baseline (just as the `ThreadPoolBuilder` requires `CamelContext` in its constructor).

The preceding route uses a `<threads>` tag, that references the custom thread pool ❶. If a message is sent to the `direct:start` endpoint, it should be routed to `<threads>`, which will continue routing the message using the custom thread pool. This can be seen in the console output that logs the thread names:

```
[Camel Thread 0 - Cool] INFO hello - Exchange[Body:Hello Camel]
```

> **NOTE** When using `executorServiceRef` to look up a thread pool, Camel will first check for a custom thread pool. If none are found, Camel will fall back and see if a thread pool profile exists with the given name; if so, a new thread pool is created based on that profile.

All thread pool creation is done using `ExecutorServiceStrategy`, which defines a pluggable API for using thread pool providers.

10.2.4 *Using ExecutorServiceStrategy*

The `org.apache.camel.spi.ExecutorServiceStrategy` interface defines a pluggable API for thread pool providers. Camel will, by default, use the `DefaultExecutorServiceStrategy` class, which creates thread pools using the concurrency API in Java. When you need to use a different thread pool provider, for example, a provider from a JAVA EE server, you can create a custom `ExecutorServiceStrategy` to work with the provider.

In this section, we'll show you how to configure Camel to use a custom `ExecutorServiceStrategy`, leaving the implementation of the provider up to you.

CONFIGURING CAMEL TO USE A CUSTOM EXECUTORSERVICESTRATEGY

In Java, you configure Camel to use a custom `ExecutorServiceStrategy` via the `setExecutorServiceStrategy` method on `CamelContext`:

```
CamelContext context = ...
context.setExecutorServiceStrategy(myExecutorServiceStrategy);
```

In Spring XML, it's easy because all you have to do is define a Spring bean. Camel will automatically detect and use it:

```
<bean id="myExecutorService"
      class="camelinaction.MyExecutorServiceStrategy"/>
```

So far in this chapter, we've mostly used thread pools in Camel routes, but they're also used in other areas, such as in some Camel components.

USING EXECUTORSERVICESTRATEGY IN A CUSTOM COMPONENT

The `ExecutorServiceStrategy` defines methods for working with thread pools.

Suppose you're developing a custom Camel component and you need to run a scheduled background task. When running a background task, it's recommended that you use the `ScheduledExecutorService` as the thread pool, because it's capable of executing tasks in a scheduled manner.

Creating the thread pool is easy with the help of Camel's `ExecutorServiceStrategy`.

Listing 10.3 Using `ExecutorServiceStrategy` to create a thread pool

```
public class MyComponent extends DefaultComponent implements Runnable {
    private static final Log LOG = LogFactory.getLog(MyComponent.class);
    private ScheduledExecutorService executor;

    public void run() {                                    ❶ Runs
        LOG.info("I run now");                                 scheduled task
    }

    protected void doStart() throws Exception {
        super.doStart();
        executor = getCamelContext().getExecutorServiceStrategy()
            .newScheduledThreadPool(this,
```

```
                "MyBackgroundTask", 1);
        executor.scheduleWithFixedDelay(this, 1, 1, TimeUnit.SECONDS);
    }
```

Creates scheduled thread pool ❷

```
    protected void doStop() throws Exception {
        getCamelContext().getExecutorServiceStrategy().shutdown(executor);
        super.doStop();
    }
}
```

Listing 10.3 illustrates the principle of using a scheduled thread pool to repeatedly execute a background task. The custom component extends DefaultComponent, which allows you to override the doStart and doStop methods to create and shut down the thread pool. In the doStart method, you create the ScheduledExecutorService using ExecutorServiceStrategy ❷ and schedule it to run the task ❶ once every second using the scheduleWithFixedDelay method.

The source code for the book contains this example in the chapter10/pools directory. You can try it using the following Maven goal:

```
mvn test -Dtest=MyComponentTest
```

When it runs, you'll see the following output in the console:

```
Waiting for 10 seconds before we shutdown
[Camel Thread 0 - MyBackgroundTask] INFO  MyComponent - I run now
[Camel Thread 0 - MyBackgroundTask] INFO  MyComponent - I run now
```

You now know that thread pools are how Java achieves concurrency; they're used as executors to execute tasks concurrently. You also know how to leverage this to process messages concurrently in Camel routes, and you saw several ways of creating and defining thread pools in Camel.

When modeling routes in Camel, you'll often use EIPs to build the routes to support your business cases. In section 10.1, you used the Splitter EIP and learned to improve performance using concurrency. In the next section, we'll take a look at other EIPs you can use with concurrency.

10.3   *Using concurrency with EIPs*

Some of the EIPs in Camel support concurrency out of the box—they're listed in table 10.4. In this section, we'll take a look at them and the benefits they offer.

Table 10.4   EIPs in Camel that supports concurrency

EIP	Description
Aggregate	The Aggregator EIP allows concurrency when sending out completed and aggregated messages. We covered this pattern in chapter 8.
Multicast	The Multicast EIP allows concurrency when sending a copy of the same message to multiple recipients. We discussed this pattern in chapter 2, and we'll use it in an example in section 10.3.2.

Table 10.4   EIPs in Camel that supports concurrency *(continued)*

EIP	Description
Recipient List	The Recipient List EIP allows concurrency when sending copies of a single message to a dynamic list of recipients. This works in the same way as the Multicast EIP, so what you learned there also applies for this pattern. We covered this pattern in chapter 2.
Splitter	The Splitter EIP allows concurrency when each split message is being processed. You saw how to do this in section 10.1. This pattern was also covered in chapter 8.
Threads	The Threads EIP always uses concurrency to hand over messages to a thread pool that will continue processing the message. You saw an example of this in section 10.2.3, and we'll cover it a bit more in section 10.3.1.
Wire Tap	The Wire Tap EIP allows you to spawn a new message and let it be sent to an endpoint using a new thread, while the calling thread can continue to process the original message. The Wire Tap EIP always uses a thread pool to execute the spawned message. This is covered in section 10.3.3. We encountered the Wire Tap pattern in chapter 2.

All the EIPs from table 10.4 can be configured to enable concurrency in the same way. You can turn on `parallelProcessing` to use thread pool profiles to apply a matching thread pool; this is likely what you'll want to use in most cases. Or you can refer to a specific thread pool using the `executorService` option. You've already seen this in action in section 10.1.2, where you used the Splitter EIP.

In the following three sections, we'll look at how to use the Threads, Multicast, and Wire Tap EIPs in a concurrent way.

10.3.1   *Using concurrency with the Threads EIP*

The Threads EIP is the only EIP that has additional options in the DSL offering fine-grained definition of the thread pool to be used. These additional options are listed in table 10.3.

For example, the thread pool from section 10.2.3 could be written as follows:

```
<camelContext xmlns="http://camel.apache.org/schema/spring">
    <route>
        <from uri="direct:start"/>
        <to uri="log:start"/>
        <threads threadName="Cool" poolSize="5" maxPoolSize="15"
                maxQueueSize="250">
            <to uri="log:cool"/>
        </threads>
    </route>
</camelContext>
```

Figure 10.6 illustrates which threads are in use when a message is being routed using the Threads EIP.

There will be two threads active when a message is being routed. The caller thread will hand over the message to the thread pool. The thread pool will then find an available thread in its pool to continue routing the message.

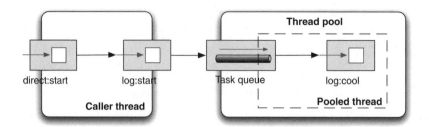

Figure 10.6   Caller and pooled threads are in use when a message is routed.

You can run this example from the chapter10/pools directory using the following Maven goal:

```
mvn test -Dtest=SpringInlinedThreadPoolTest
```

You'll see the following in the console:

```
[main]                  INFO start - Exchange[Body:Hello Camel]
[Camel Thread 0 - Cool]  INFO hello - Exchange[Body:Hello Camel]
```

The first set of brackets contains the thread name. You see, as expected, two threads in play: main is the caller thread, and Cool is from the thread pool.

> **TIP**   You can use the Threads EIP to achieve concurrency when using Camel components that don't offer concurrency. A good example is the Camel file component, which uses a single thread to scan and pick up files. By using the Threads EIP, you can allow the picked up files to be processed concurrently.

Let's look at how Rider Auto Parts improves performance by leveraging concurrency with the Multicast EIP.

10.3.2   *Using concurrency with the Multicast EIP*

Rider Auto Parts has a web portal where its employees can look up information, such as the current status of customer orders. When selecting a particular order, the portal needs to retrieve information from three different systems to gather an overview of the order. Figure 10.7 illustrates this.

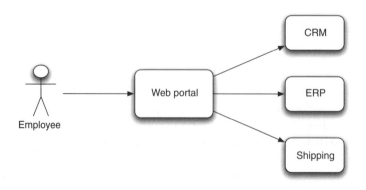

**Figure 10.7
The web portal gathers information from three systems to compile the overview that's presented to the employee.**

Your boss has summoned you to help with this portal. The employees have started to complain about poor performance, and it doesn't take you more than an hour to find out why; the portal retrieves the data from the three sources in sequence. This is obviously a good use case for leveraging concurrency to improve performance.

You also look in the production logs and see that a single overview takes 4.0 seconds (1.4 + 1.1 + 1.5 seconds) to complete. You tell your boss that you can improve the performance by gathering the data in parallel.

Back at your desk, you build a portal prototype in Camel that resembles the current implementation. The prototype uses the Multicast EIP to retrieve data from the three external systems as follows:

```
<route>
    <from uri="direct:portal"/>
    <multicast strategyRef="aggregatedData">
        <to uri="direct:crm"/>
        <to uri="direct:erp"/>
        <to uri="direct:shipping"/>
    </multicast>
    <bean ref="combineData"/>
</route>
```

The Multicast EIP will send copies of a message to the three endpoints and aggregate their replies using the `aggregatedData` bean. When all data has been aggregated, the `combineData` bean is used to create the reply that will be displayed in the portal.

You decide to test this route by simulating the three systems using the same response times as from the production logs. Running your test yields the following performance metrics:

```
TIMER - [Message: 123] sent to: direct://crm took: 1404 ms.
TIMER - [Message: 123] sent to: direct://erp took: 1101 ms.
TIMER - [Message: 123] sent to: direct://shipping took: 1501 ms.
TIMER - [Message: 123] sent to: direct://portal took: 4139 ms.
```

As you can see, the total time is 4.1 seconds when running in sequence. Now you enable concurrency with the `parallelProcessing` options:

```
<route>
    <from uri="direct:portal"/>
        <multicast strategyRef="aggregatedData"
                   parallelProcessing="true">
            <to uri="direct:crm"/>
            <to uri="direct:erp"/>
            <to uri="direct:shipping"/>
        </multicast>
    <bean ref="combineData"/>
</route>
```

This gives much better performance:

```
TIMER - [Message: 123] sent to: direct://erp took: 1105 ms.
TIMER - [Message: 123] sent to: direct://crm took: 1402 ms.
TIMER - [Message: 123] sent to: direct://shipping took: 1502 ms.
TIMER - [Message: 123] sent to: direct://portal took: 1623 ms.
```

The numbers show that response time went from 4.1 to 1.6 seconds, which is an improvement of roughly 250 percent. Note that the logged lines aren't in the same order as the sequential example. With concurrency enabled, the lines are logged in the order that the remote services' replies come in. Without concurrency, the order is always fixed in the sequential order defined by the Camel route.

The source code for the book contains this example in the chapter10/eip directory. You can try the two scenarios using the following Maven goals:

```
mvn test -Dtest=MulticastTest
mvn test -Dtest=MulticastParallelTest
```

You have now seen how the Multicast EIP can be used concurrently to improve performance. The Aggregate, Recipient List, and Splitter EIPs can be configured with concurrency in the same way as the Multicast EIP.

The next pattern we'll look at using with concurrency is the Wire Tap EIP. We encountered it the first time in chapter 2, section 2.5.5.

10.3.3 *Using concurrency with the Wire Tap EIP*

The Wire Tap EIP leverages a thread pool to process the tapped messages concurrently. You can configure which thread pool it should use, and if no pool has been configured, it will fall back and create a thread pool based on the default thread pool profile.

Suppose you want to use a custom thread pool when using the Wire Tap EIP. First you must create the thread pool to be used, and then you pass that in as a reference to the wire tap in the route, as highlighted in bold:

```
public void configure() throws Exception {
    ExecutorService lowPool = new ThreadPoolBuilder(context)
        .poolSize(1).maxPoolSize(5).build("LowPool");

    from("direct:start")
        .log("Incoming message ${body}")
        .wireTap("direct:tap", lowPool)
        .to("mock:result");

    from("direct:tap")
        .log("Tapped message ${body}")
        .to("mock:tap");
}
```

The equivalent route in Spring XML is as follows:

```
<camelContext xmlns="http://camel.apache.org/schema/spring">

    <threadPool id="lowPool"
                poolSize="1" maxPoolSize="5" threadName="LowPool"/>

    <route>
        <from uri="direct:start"/>
        <log message="Incoming message ${body}"/>
        <wireTap uri="direct:tap" executorServiceRef="lowPool"/>
        <to uri="mock:result"/>
    </route>

    <route>
```

```
         <from uri="direct:tap"/>
         <log message="Tapped message ${body}"/>
         <to uri="mock:tap"/>
    </route>

</camelContext>
```

The source code for the book contains this example in the chapter10/eip directory. You can run the example using the following Maven goals:

```
mvn test -Dtest=WireTapTest
mvn test -Dtest=SpringWireTapTest
```

When you run the example, the console output should indicate that the tapped message is being processed by a thread from the LowPool thread pool.

```
[main]                      INFO route1 - Incoming message Hello Camel
[Camel Thread 0 - LowPool] INFO route2 - Tapped message Hello Camel
```

You now have a better understanding of the overall concept of using thread pools for concurrency in Java. We'll next look at how the synchronicity of messages impacts the way thread pools are leveraged.

10.4   *Synchronicity and threading*

A caller can invoke a service either synchronously or asynchronously. If the caller has to wait until all the processing steps are complete before it can continue, it's a synchronous process. If the caller can continue before the processing has been completed, it's an asynchronous process.

The service being invoked can leverage as many threads as it wants to complete the message. The number of threads doesn't affect whether or not the caller is considered synchronous or asynchronous.

Now imagine from this point forward that the service being invoked is a Camel route. As just mentioned, the service can use multiple threads to process the message. In this section, we'll focus on which factors affect how many threads are involved in processing messages in Camel.

These factors may affect the threading model:

- *Component*—The Camel component that originates the exchange is either based on a fire-and-forget or a request-response messaging style.
- *EIPs*—As you saw in section 10.3, some EIPs support concurrency.
- *Configured synchronicity*—Some components can be configured to be either synchronous or asynchronous.
- *Transactions*—If the route is transacted, the transactional context is limited to run within one thread only.
- *Message exchange pattern (MEP)*—MEP is information stored on the exchange that tells Camel whether the message is using a fire-and-forget or request-response messaging style. Camel uses the terminology from the Java Business Integration (JBI) specification (http://en.wikipedia.org/wiki/JBI): InOnly means fire-and-forget, and InOut means request-response.

In the next four sections (10.4.1 through 10.4.4), we'll cover four different scenarios showing how synchronicity and MEP affect the threading model:

- Asynchronous caller, and Camel uses one thread to process the message
- Synchronous caller, and Camel uses one thread to process the message
- Asynchronous caller, and Camel uses multiple threads to process the message
- Synchronous caller, and Camel uses multiple threads to process the message

We'll discuss the pros and cons of each scenario and give an example of where it may be used in a real-life situation.

The source code for the book contains these examples in the chapter10/synchronicity directory. You can use these Maven goals to run the examples:

```
mvn test -Dtest=AsyncOneThreadTest
mvn test -Dtest=SyncOneThreadTest
mvn test -Dtest=AsyncMultipleThreadsTest
mvn test -Dtest=SyncMultipleThreadsTest
```

10.4.1 Asynchronous caller using one thread

In figure 10.8, you'll see that Camel uses the consumer thread all along the processing of the message. In this figure, an arrow represents a thread, and the consumer thread is shown as one long arrow.

This scenario can be implemented in a simple Camel route:

```
from("seda:start")
    .to("log:A")
    .to("log:B");
```

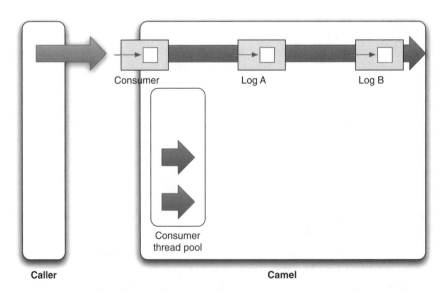

Figure 10.8 In asynchronous InOnly mode, the caller doesn't wait for a reply. On the Camel side, only one thread is used for all the processing of the message.

You can try the route from a unit test by sending an InOnly message using the send-Body method from ProducerTemplate:

```
public void testSyncInOnly() throws Exception {
    String body = "Hello Camel";
    LOG.info("Caller calling Camel with message: " + body);
    template.sendBody("seda:start", body);
    LOG.info("Caller finished calling Camel");
}
```

If you run this example, you should see output to the console that shows the threads in use during routing:

```
[main] INFO Caller - Caller calling Camel with message: Hello Camel
[main] INFO Caller - Caller finished calling Camel
[Camel Thread 0 - seda://start] INFO A - InOnly, Hello Camel
[Camel Thread 0 - seda://start] INFO B - InOnly, Hello Camel
```

The first two log lines are the caller sending the message to Camel. The last two show that the consumer thread [Camel Thread 0 - seda://start] is used to process the message in the entire route.

The caller is sending in a fire-and-forget message (InOnly), which means the caller doesn't expect a reply (and it doesn't wait for a reply). As a result, the caller can continue while the message is being processed. We view the caller's synchronicity as asynchronous.

From the Camel perspective, only one thread is involved in processing the message, which simplifies things. Table 10.5 outlines the pros and cons of this approach from the Camel perspective.

Table 10.5 Pros and cons of using one thread from the Camel perspective

Pros	Cons
■ Simple and easy ■ Supports transactional propagation	■ All the load is handled by the Camel consumer threads. ■ The consumer can be overloaded by the number of received messages.

The asynchronous InOnly scenario is often used with JMS messaging, where it's common to use Camel to route messages from JMS queues to other destinations. Real-world systems might use this scenario when routing messages between JMS destinations, such as a new order queue that's routed to a validated order queue if the order passes a sanity check. Orders that are invalid would be routed to an invalid order queue for further manual inspection.

In this example, the caller didn't expect a reply because it sent an InOnly message. The next scenario shows what happens when the caller sends an InOut (request-response) message.

10.4.2 *Synchronous caller using one thread*

This scenario is only slightly different from the previous one. In figure 10.9 you can see that Camel is still only using one thread (represented as one arrow). The difference is

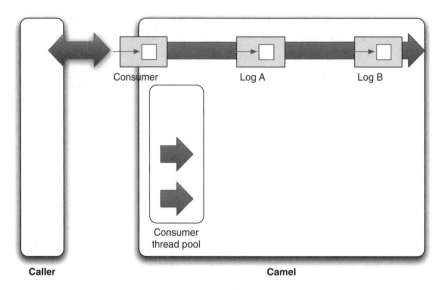

Figure 10.9   In synchronous `InOut` **mode, the caller waits for a reply. In Camel, the consumer thread is used for all the processing of the message, and it delivers the reply to the waiting caller.**

that this time the caller expects a reply, which the consumer thread in Camel has to deliver back to the waiting caller.

The route in Camel is also a bit different, because you want to transform the message to return a reply to the caller: `"Bye Camel"`.

```
from("seda:start")
    .to("log:A")
    .transform(constant("Bye Camel"))
    .to("log:B");
```

You can test this by using the `requestBody` method from `ProducerTemplate`, which sends an InOut message:

```
public void testSyncInOut() throws Exception {
    String body = "Hello Camel";
    LOG.info("Caller calling Camel with message: " + body);
    Object reply = template.requestBody("seda:start", body);
    LOG.info("Caller received reply: " + reply);
}
```

If you run this example, you should see output to the console showing the threads in use during routing.

```
[main] INFO Caller - Caller calling Camel with message: Hello Camel
[Camel Thread 0 - seda://start] INFO A - InOut, Hello Camel
[Camel Thread 0 - seda://start] INFO B - InOut, Bye Camel
[main] INFO Caller - Caller received reply: Bye Camel
```

Notice how the caller waits for the reply while the consumer thread [Camel Thread 0 - seda://start] is used to process the message for the entire route. You can see that the caller is waiting—it will log to the console after Camel has processed the message. Because the caller waits for a reply, we consider it synchronous.

The pros and cons of this configuration from the Camel perspective are the same as in the previous section and are listed in table 10.5.

The synchronous InOut scenario can be used with JMS messaging because you can return replies if the JMSReply JMS property is provided on the incoming message. Real-world systems may want to use this approach with components that natively support request-response messaging, such as web services. A system could expose a web service that clients can call to query order status.

The next two scenarios we'll cover show what happens when Camel uses multiple threads to process the messages.

10.4.3 Asynchronous caller using multiple threads

The asynchronous InOnly scenario is illustrated in figure 10.10. This time you're leveraging two threads in Camel to process the messages (represented by the two arrows).

This time there are two thread pools involved in Camel. The consumer thread will process the first part of the routing, and then the message is transferred to another thread pool, which continues routing the message.

The Camel route is yet again different. You use the Threads EIP to add the asynchronous behavior to the route:

```
from("seda:start")
    .to("log:A")
    .threads(5, 10)
    .to("log:B");
```

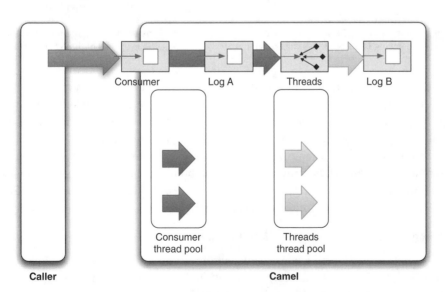

Figure 10.10 In asynchronous InOnly mode, the caller doesn't wait for a reply. On the Camel side, multiple threads are involved during the routing of the message.

By using threads(5, 10), you create a thread pool with a pool size of 5 and a maximum size of 10.

To test this scenario, you can use the following unit test:

```
public void testAsyncInOnly() throws Exception {
    String body = "Hello Camel";
    LOG.info("Caller calling Camel with message: " + body);
    template.sendBody("seda:start", body);
    LOG.info("Caller finished calling Camel");
}
```

If you run this example, you should see output to the console that shows the threads in use during routing:

```
[main] INFO Caller - Caller calling Camel with message: Hello Camel
[main] INFO Caller - Caller finished calling Camel
[Camel Thread 0 - seda://start] INFO A - InOnly, Hello Camel
[Camel Thread 1 - Threads] INFO B - InOnly, Hello Camel
```

The first two log lines indicate the caller sending the message to Camel. The last two lines show the other two threads involved in routing the message inside Camel.

In this scenario, the caller is asynchronous because it can continue without waiting for a reply.

This model has a different set of pros and cons from the Camel perspective, as listed in table 10.6.

Table 10.6   Pros and cons of using an asynchronous caller and having multiple threads, from the Camel perspective

Pros	Cons
■ Leverages the SEDA principle of decoupled stages ■ Dispatching is decoupled from consuming	■ Transaction propagation isn't supported ■ Little overhead of thread-context switching

In a real-world situation, you might want to use this scenario when consuming files, as we did in section 10.1. By not having the consumer thread process the file, it's free to pick up new files. And by using multiple threads in Camel, you can maximize throughput as multiple threads can work simultaneously on multiple files.

Another use case when multiple threads can be an advantage is when you process big messages that can be split into smaller submessages for further processing. This is what we did in section 10.1 using the parallelProcessing option on the Splitter EIP.

The next scenario is similar to this one, but it uses a request-response messaging style.

10.4.4 Synchronous caller using multiple threads

The synchronous InOut scenario involving multiple threads inside Camel is illustrated in figure 10.11. In this scenario, the situation is a bit more complex because the caller is waiting for a reply and Camel is using multiple threads to process the message. This means the consumer thread that received the request must block until the routing is

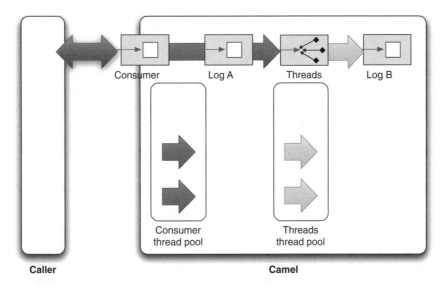

Figure 10.11 In synchronous mode, the caller waits for a reply. On the Camel side, multiple threads are involved during the routing of the message. The consumer thread has to block, waiting for the reply, which it must send back to the waiting caller.

complete, so it can deliver the reply back to the waiting caller. If this sounds a bit confusing, don't be alarmed. We'll unlock how this works when we look at the asynchronous client API in section 10.5.

The route you use for testing this scenario is as follows:

```
from("seda:start")
    .to("log:A")
    .threads(5, 10)
    .transform(constant("Bye Camel"))
    .to("log:B");
```

The unit test uses the requestBody method to send an InOut message to Camel:

```
public void testAsyncInOut() throws Exception {
    String body = "Hello Camel";
    LOG.info("Caller calling Camel with message: " + body);
    Object reply = template.requestBody("seda:start", body);
    LOG.info("Caller received reply: " + reply);
}
```

If you run this example, you should see output to the console that shows the threads in use during routing:

```
[main] INFO Caller - Caller calling Camel with message: Hello Camel
[Camel Thread 0 - seda://start] INFO A - InOut, Hello Camel
[Camel Thread 1 - Threads] INFO B - InOut, Bye Camel
[main] INFO Caller - Caller received reply: Bye Camel
```

These lines reveal that the caller waits for the reply and that two threads are involved during the routing of the message in Camel.

What the lines also reveal is that the caller received `"Bye Camel"` as the reply. This may seem a bit like magic, as the `"Bye Camel"` message was constructed in the last part of the route. That means the consumer thread somehow knew that it had to block until the reply message was ready.

Although this might seem like magic, there is no such magic in Camel or the Java language. It's the Java concurrency API that allows you to wait for an asynchronous task to complete, using what is called a `Future` handle. We'll cover this in more detail in section 10.5.

Table 10.7 presents the pros and cons of this scenario.

Table 10.7   Pros and cons of using a synchronous caller and having multiple threads, from the Camel perspective

Pros	Cons
■ Leverages the SEDA principle of decoupled stages ■ Dispatching is decoupled from consuming ■ Allows consumer to return early reply	■ Transaction propagation isn't supported ■ Minor overhead of thread-context switching ■ The consumer thread has to block while waiting for the reply to be ready

This scenario can be used when you want to return an early reply to the waiting caller. Suppose you expose a web service and want to return an OK reply as quickly as possible. By dispatching the received messages asynchronously, you allow the consumer thread to continue and return the early reply to the caller. This may sound easy, but the MEP impacts how this can be done correctly. Let's take a moment to map out the pitfalls.

10.4.5   *Returning an early reply to a caller*

Consider an example in which a caller invokes a Camel service in a synchronous manner—the caller is blocked while waiting for a reply. In the Camel service, you want to send a reply back to the waiting caller as soon as possible; the reply is an acknowledgement that the input has been received, so `"OK"` is returned to the caller. In the meantime, Camel continues processing the received message in another thread.

Figure 10.12 illustrates this example in a sequence diagram.

Implementing this example as a Camel route with the Java DSL can be done as follows:

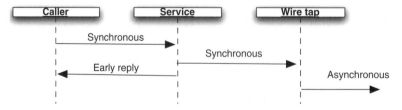

Figure 10.12   A synchronous caller invokes a Camel service. The service lets the wire tap continue processing the message asynchronously while the service returns an early reply to the waiting caller.

```
from("jetty:http://localhost:8080/early").routeId("input")
    .wireTap("direct:incoming")
    .transform().constant("OK");

    from("direct:incoming").routeId("process")
        .convertBodyTo(String.class)
        .log("Incoming ${body}")
        .delay(3000)
        .log("Processing done for ${body}")
        .to("mock:result");
}
```

❷ Return early reply

❶ Tap incoming message

You leverage the Wire Tap EIP ❶ to continue routing the incoming message in a separate thread. This gives room for the consumer to immediately reply ❷ to the waiting caller.

Here's an equivalent example using Spring XML:

```
<camelContext xmlns="http://camel.apache.org/schema/spring">

    <route routeId="input">
        <from uri="jetty:http://localhost:8080/early"/>
        <wireTap uri="direct:incoming"/>
        <transform>
            <constant>OK</constant>
        </transform>
    </route>

    <route routeId="process">
        <from uri="direct:incoming"/>
        <convertBodyTo type="String"/>
        <log message="Incoming ${body}"/>
        <delay>
            <constant>3000</constant>
        </delay>
        <log message="Processing done for ${body}"/>
        <to uri="mock:result"/>
    </route>

</camelContext>
```

❶ Tap incoming message

❷ Return early reply

The source code for the book contains this example in the chapter8/synchronicity directory. You can run the example using the following Maven goals:

```
mvn test -Dtest=EarlyReplyTest
mvn test -Dtest=SpringEarlyReplyTest
```

When you run the example, you should see the console output showing how the message is processed:

```
11:18:15 [main] INFO - Caller calling Camel with message: Hello Camel
11:18:15 [Camel Thread 0 - WireTap] INFO - Incoming Hello Camel
11:18:15 [main] INFO - Caller finished calling Camel and received reply: OK
11:18:18 [Camel Thread 0 - WireTap] INFO - Processing done for Hello Camel
```

Notice in the console output how the caller immediately receives a reply within the same second it sent the request. The last log line shows that the Wire Tap EIP finished processing the message 3 seconds after the caller received the reply.

> **NOTE**   In the preceding example, the route with ID `"process"`, you need to convert the body to a `String` type to ensure that you can read the message multiple times. This is necessary because Jetty is stream-based, which causes it to only be able to read the message once. Or, instead of converting the body, you could enable stream caching—we'll cover stream caching in chapter 13.

So far in this chapter, you've seen concurrency used in Camel routes by the various EIPs that support them. But Camel also has a strong client API, manifested in the `Pro-ducerTemplate` and `ConsumerTemplate` classes (see appendix C). These classes have easy-to-use methods for sending messages to any endpoint you choose. In the next section, you'll learn what those classes have to offer when it comes to concurrency.

10.5   *The concurrency client API*

You can use the concurrency client API directly from Java code, which means you're in full control of what should happen. You don't have to use Camel routes and EIPs to achieve concurrency.

To fully understand the concurrency API from the client point of view, we'll look at how you can achieve concurrency with pure Java. Then we'll look at the same example using Camel's `ProducerTemplate`. We'll end this section by looking at how the Camel client API allows you to easily submit concurrent messages to different endpoints and leverage a callback mechanism to gather the replies when they come back.

10.5.1   *The concurrency client API in Java*

The concurrency API in Java is located in the `java.util.concurrent` package, and it was introduced in Java 5 (aka JDK 1.5). All the concurrency behavior in Camel is built on top of this API. For example, the Camel thread pools are all `ExecutorService` instances, which are capable of executing tasks concurrently and asynchronously.

Java's concurrency API includes the following classes that are interesting to learn about and understand from a developer's point of view:

- `ExecutorService`—This is the foundation for executing tasks in an asynchronous manner.
- `Callable`—This represents an asynchronous task. Think of it as an improved `Runnable` that can return a result or throw an exception.
- `Future`—This represents the lifecycle of an asynchronous task and provides methods to test whether the task has completed or been cancelled, to retrieve its result, and to cancel the task.

Figure 10.13 is a sequence diagram that depicts how these three concepts are related and how they're involved in a typical use case where an asynchronous task is being executed.

Figure 10.13 shows how a client creates a new `Callable`, which represents the tasks (the code) you want to be executed asynchronously. The task is then submitted to an `ExecutorService`, which is responsible for further processing the task. Before the task

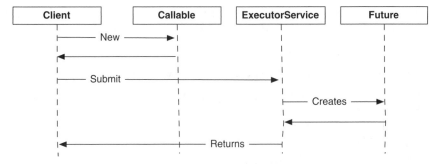

Figure 10.13 The client submits tasks (`Callable`) to be executed asynchronously by `ExecutorService`, which returns a `Future` handle to the client.

is executed, a Future is returned to the client. The Future is a handle that the client can use at any point later on to retrieve the result of the task.

Listing 10.4 shows how this works in Java code.

Listing 10.4 Asynchronous task execution using the Java API

```
public void testFutureWithDone() throws Exception {
    Callable<String> task = new Callable<String>() {          Creates
        public String call() throws Exception {          ❶ task
            Thread.sleep(5000);
            return "Camel rocks";
        }
    };

    ExecutorService executor = Executors.newCachedThreadPool();
    Future<String> future = executor.submit(task);          Submits
                                                            ❷ task
    boolean done = false;
    while (!done) {
        done = future.isDone();          Waits until
        LOG.info("Is the task done? " + done);          ❸ task is done
        if (!done) {
            Thread.sleep(2000);
        }
    }
                                        ❹ Gets task
    String answer = future.get();          result
    LOG.info("The answer is: " + answer);
}
```

The task to be executed is located within the call method of the `Callable` ❶. Note that you can use generics to specify the result type as a `String`. The task is then submitted to the `ExecutorService` ❷, which returns a `Future<String>` handle; the generic type matches the type from the task. While the task is being processed, you can do other computations, but in this example you just loop and wait for the task to be done ❸. At the end, you can retrieve the result using the get method ❹.

The source code for the book contains this example in the chapter10/client directory. You can use the following Maven goal to run the example:

```
mvn test -Dtest=CamelFutureDoneTest
```

When you run the example, the console should output what's happening:

```
07:29:30 [main] - Submitting task to ExecutorService
07:29:30 [main] - Task submitted and we got a Future handle
07:29:30 [pool-1-thread-1] - Starting to process task
07:29:30 [main] - Is the task done? false
07:29:32 [main] - Is the task done? false
07:29:34 [main] - Is the task done? false
07:29:35 [pool-1-thread-1] - Task is now done
07:29:36 [main] - Is the task done? true
07:29:36 [main] - The answer is: Camel rocks
```

As you can see from the console output, the task executes in a thread named "pool-1-thread-1" while the caller executes in the main thread. This output also proves that the client waits until the task is done.

There's a smarter way to retrieve the result than by looping and testing whether the task is done—you can use the get method on the Future handle which will automatically wait until the task is done. Removing the while loop from the code in listing 10.4 and running the example will output the following:

```
07:37:20 [main] - Submitting task to ExecutorService
07:37:20 [main] - Task submitted and we got a Future handle
07:37:20 [pool-1-thread-1] - Starting to process task
07:37:25 [pool-1-thread-1] - Task is now done
07:37:25 [main] - The answer is: Camel rocks
```

As you can see, this time you don't have to test whether the task is done. Invoking the get method on Future causes it to wait until the task is done and to react promptly when it is done.

The source code for the book contains this example in the chapter10/client directory. You can use the following Maven goal to run the example:

```
mvn test -Dtest=CamelFutureGetTest
```

You've seen how clients leverage Future to retrieve the result of tasks that have been submitted for asynchronous execution. Table 10.8 lists the most commonly used methods provided by Future.

Table 10.8 Commonly used methods in the `java.util.concurrent.Future` class

Method	Description
get()	Waits, if necessary, for tasks to complete, and then returns the result. Will throw an ExecutionException if the tasks throw an exception.
get(timeout, TimeUnit)	Waits, if necessary, for at most the specified time for the task to complete, and then returns the result if available. Will throw an ExecutionException if the tasks throw an exception. TimeoutException is thrown if timed out.
isDone()	Returns true if the task is done; otherwise false is returned.

Understanding the principle of `Future` is important because it's the same mechanism Camel leverages internally when it processes messages asynchronously. `Future` also plays a role in the concurrency client API provided by Camel, which we're going to take a look at now.

10.5.2 The concurrency client API in Camel

The client concurrency API in Camel is provided in the `ProducerTemplate` class. It offers a range of methods that Camel end users can leverage to submit messages to Camel to be further processed asynchronously.

Consider the following route:

```
from("seda:quote")
    .log("Starting to route ${body}")
    .delay(5000)
    .transform().constant("Camel rocks")
    .log("Route is now done");
```

You can see that this route will delay processing the message for 5 seconds, which means it will take at least 5 seconds for the reply to be returned. This is the same situation as in the previous example (section 10.5.1), where the `Callable` tasks also took 5 seconds to complete. This allows us to compare this example with the previous one to see how easy it is in Camel to use the concurrency client API.

Sending a message asynchronously to the `"seda:quote"` endpoint is easy to do in Camel by using the `asyncRequestBody` method as shown here:

```
public void testFutureWithoutDone() throws Exception {
    LOG.info("Submitting task to Camel");
    Future<String> future = template.asyncRequestBody("seda:quote",
                              "Hello Camel", String.class);
    LOG.info("Task submitted and we got a Future handle");

    String answer = future.get();
    LOG.info("The answer is: " + answer);
}
```

The source code for the book contains this example in the chapter10/client directory. You can use the following Maven goal to run the example:

```
mvn test -Dtest=CamelFutureTest
```

If you run this example, the console should output something like the following:

```
11:02:49 [main] - Submitting task to Camel
11:02:49 [main] - Task submitted and we got a Future handle
11:02:49 [Camel Thread 0 - seda://quote] - Starting to route Hello Camel
11:02:54 [Camel Thread 0 - seda://quote] - Route is now done
11:02:54 [main] - The answer is: Camel rocks
```

What you should notice in this example is that the Camel concurrency client API also uses the `Future` handle to retrieve the result. This allows Camel end users to more easily learn and use the Camel concurrency API, as it's based on and similar to the Java concurrency API.

Table 10.9 lists the most commonly used methods, provided by `ProducerTemplate`. All the methods listed will return a `Future` handle.

Table 10.9   Commonly used asynchronous methods in the `ProducerTemplate` class

Method	Description
asyncSend(endpoint, exchange)	Sends the exchange to the given endpoint
asyncSendBody(endpoint, body)	Sends the body to the given endpoint using InOnly as the exchange pattern
asyncSendBodyAndHeader (endpoint, body, header)	Sends the body and header to the given endpoint using InOnly as the exchange pattern
asyncRequestBody(endpoint, body)	Sends the body to the given endpoint using InOut as the exchange pattern
asyncRequestBodyAndHeader (endpoint, body, header)	Sends the body and header to the given endpoint using InOut as the exchange pattern
asyncCallback (endpoint, exchange, callback)	Sends the exchange to the given endpoint and invokes the callback when the task is done
asyncCallbackSendBody (endpoint, body, callback)	Sends the body to the given endpoint using InOnly as the exchange pattern, and invokes the callback when the task is done
asyncCallbackRequestBody (endpoint, body, callback)	Sends the body to the given endpoint using InOut as the exchange pattern, and invokes the callback when the task is done

Notice that all the methods listed in table 10.9 start with `async` in their method name. This makes them easy to remember when you need to send a message asynchronously.

The last three methods in table 10.9 support a callback mechanism, which makes sense in situations where you may need to use the same callback for several tasks. Let's look at an example now, to make this all a bit clearer.

USING ASYNCCALLBACK

Rider Auto Parts has a selected number of premium partners who are promoted exclusively on the Rider Auto Parts web store. Whenever a customer browses the items catalog, the partners are listening and can provide feedback about related items. For example, if you browse for bumper parts, the partners can suggest related items, such as bumper extensions or other car parts. The partners have to return their feedback within a given time period, so the user experience of browsing the website isn't slowed down noticeably.

Implementing such a use case is possible using the Camel concurrency client API. You can use a callback to gather the partner feedback within the given time period.

The callback is defined in Camel as the `org.apache.camel.spi.Synchronization` interface:

```
public interface Synchronization {
    void onComplete(Exchange exchange);
    void onFailure(Exchange exchange);
}
```

The callback has two methods: the first is invoked when the Exchange is processed successfully, and the second is invoked if the Exchange fails.

Listing 10.5 shows how this can be implemented in Camel.

Listing 10.5 Using a callback to gather replies asynchronously

```
public void testCallback() throws Exception {
    final List<String> relates = new ArrayList<String>();      ❶ Counts replies
    final CountDownLatch latch = new CountDownLatch(5);            received

    Synchronization callback =                                 ❷ Gathers
            new SynchronizationAdapter() {                        replies
        public void onComplete(Exchange exchange) {
            relates.add(exchange.getOut().getBody(String.class));
            latch.countDown();
        }

        public void onFailure(Exchange exchange) {
            latch.countDown();
        }
    };

    String body = "bumper";
    for (int i = 0; i < 5; i++) {                              ❸ Invokes
        template.asyncCallbackRequestBody(                        partners
            "seda:partner:" + i, body, callback);
    }
    LOG.info("Send " + 5 + " messages to partners.");

    boolean all = latch.await(1500,                            ❹ Waits for replies
                    TimeUnit.MILLISECONDS);                       with timeout

    LOG.info("Got " + relates.size() + " replies, is all? " + all);
    for (String related : relates) {
        LOG.info("Related item category is: " + related);
    }
}
```

You use a CountDownLatch ❶ to let you know when you've received all the replies or the given time period is up. The callback is used to gather the replies in the relates list.

You use the org.apache.camel.impl.SynchronizationAdapter class to implement the callback logic ❷. It allows you to override the onComplete and onFailure methods. The onComplete method is invoked when the message is routed successfully, so we get a valid reply for the business partner. The onFailure method is invoked if the routing fails. In both situations, you need to count down the latch to keep track of the number of replies coming back.

Now you're ready to send messages to the partners about which category the user is browsing. In this test, the category is set to "bumper". You use the asyncCallback-RequestBody method ❸, listed in table 10.9, to send the "bumper" message to the partners and have their replies gathered by the callback. This is done asynchronously, so you need to wait until the replies are gathered or the time period is up. For that, you use the countdown latch ❹. In this example, you wait until all five replies have been gathered or the timeout is triggered.

The source code for the book includes this example in the chapter10/client directory. You can run it by invoking the following Maven goal:

```
mvn test -Dtest=RiderAutoPartsCallbackTest
```

If you run this example, you should get the following output on the console:

```
11:03:23,078 [main] INFO - Send 5 messages to partners.
11:03:24,629 [main] INFO - Got 3 replies, is all? false
11:03:24,629 [main] INFO - Related item category is: bumper extension
11:03:24,630 [main] INFO - Related item category is: bumper filter
11:03:24,630 [main] INFO - Related item category is: bumper cover
```

In this example, you send to five different partners but only three respond within the time period.

As you've seen, the Camel concurrency client API is powerful, as it combines the power from Camel with an API resembling the equivalent concurrency API in Java. That's all we have to say about the asynchronous client API. The next section covers what you can do in Camel to improve scalability.

10.6   *The asynchronous routing engine*

Camel uses its routing engine to route messages either synchronously or asynchronously. In this section we focus on scalability and learn that higher scalability can be achieved with the help of the asynchronous routing engine.

For a system, scalability is the desirable property of being capable of handling a growing amount of work gracefully. In section 10.1, we covered the Rider Auto Parts inventory application, and you saw you could increase throughput by leveraging concurrent processing. In that sense, the application was scalable, as it could handle a growing amount of work in a graceful manner. That application could scale because it had a mix of CPU-bound and IO-bound processes, and because it could leverage thread pools to distribute work.

In this section, we'll look at scalability from a different angle. We'll look at what happens when messages are processed asynchronously.

10.6.1   *Hitting the scalability limit*

Rider Auto Parts uses a Camel application to service its web store, as illustrated in figure 10.14.

A Jetty consumer handles all requests from the customers. There are a variety of requests to handle, such as updating shopping carts, performing searches, gathering production information, and so on—the usual functions you expect from a web store. But there's one function that involves calculating pricing information for customers. The pricing model is complex and individual for each customer—only the ERP system

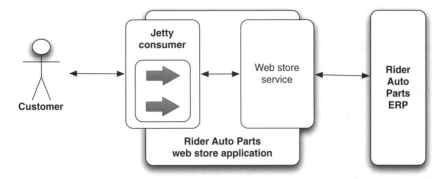

Figure 10.14   The Rider Auto Parts web store communicates with the ERP system to gather pricing information.

can calculate the pricing. As a result, the Camel application communicates with the ERP system to gather the prices. While the prices are being calculated by the ERP system, the web store has to wait until the reply comes back, before it returns its response to the customer.

The business is doing well for the company, and an increasing number of customers are using the web store, which puts more load on the system. Lately there have been problems during peak hours, with customers reporting that they can't access the web store or that it's generally responding slowly.

The root cause has been identified: the communication with the ERP system is fully synchronous, and the ERP system takes an average of 5 seconds to compute the pricing. This means each request that gathers pricing information has to wait (the thread is blocked) an average of 5 seconds for the reply to come back. This puts a burden on the Jetty thread pool, as there are fewer free threads to service new requests.

Figure 10.15 illustrates this problem. You can see that the thread is blocked (the white boxes) while waiting for the ERP system to return a reply.

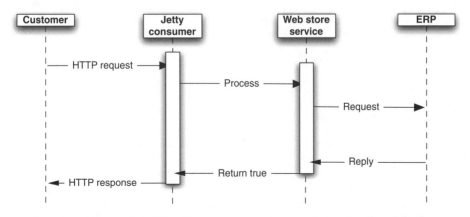

Figure 10.15   A scalability problem illustrated by the thread being blocked (represented as white boxes) while waiting for the ERP system to return a the reply.

Figure 10.15 reveals that the Jetty consumer is using one thread per request. This leads to a situation where you run out of threads as traffic increases. You've hit a scalability limit. Let's look into why, and look at what Camel has under the hood to help mitigate such problems.

10.6.2 Scalability in Camel

It would be much better if the Jetty consumer could somehow *borrow* the thread while it waits for the ERP system to return the reply, and use the thread in the meantime to service new requests. This can be done by using an asynchronous processing model. Figure 10.16 shows the principle.

If you compare figures 10.15 and 10.16, you can see that the threads are much less blocked in the latter (the white boxes are smaller). In fact, there are no threads blocked while the ERP system is processing the request. This is a huge scalability improvement because the system is much less affected by the processing speed of the ERP system. If it takes 1, 2, 5, or 30 seconds to reply, it doesn't affect the web store's resource utilization as much as it would otherwise do. The threads in the web store are much less IO-bound and are put to better use doing actual work.

Figure 10.17 shows a situation in which two customer requests are served by the same thread without impacting response times.

In this situation, customer 1 sends a request that requires a price calculation, so the ERP system is invoked asynchronously. A short while thereafter, customer 2 sends a request that can be serviced directly by the web shop service, so it doesn't leverage the

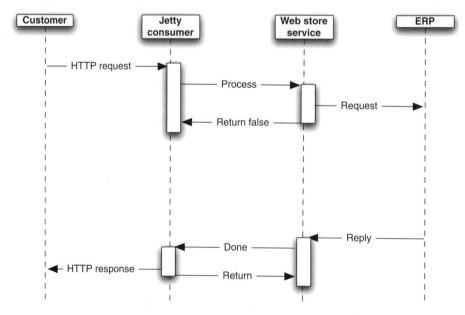

Figure 10.16   The scalability problem is greatly improved. Threads are much less blocked (represented by white boxes) when you leverage asynchronous communication between the systems.

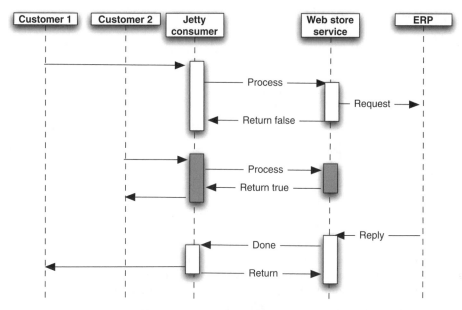

Figure 10.17 The same thread services multiple customers without blocking (white and grey boxes) and without impacting response times, resulting in much higher scalability.

asynchronous processing model (it's synchronous). The response is sent directly back to customer 2. Later, the ERP system returns the reply, which is sent back to the waiting customer 1.

In this example, you can successfully process two customers without any impact on their response time. You've achieved higher scalability.

Apache ServiceMix supports high scalability

Apache ServiceMix (http://servicemix.apache.org/) is an enterprise service bus (ESB) that can host your Camel application. In terms of high scalability, ServiceMix offers a message bus (the JBI and NMR components) for passing messages inside your application or between applications. The message bus supports the asynchronous processing model described in this chapter, which means it's highly scalable.

In the next section, we'll look under the hood to see how this is possible in Camel using the asynchronous processing model.

10.6.3 Components supporting asynchronous processing

The routing engine in Camel is capable of routing messages either synchronously or asynchronously. The latter requires the Camel component to support asynchronous processing, which in turn depends on the underlying transport supporting asynchronous communication. Table 10.10 lists the components in Camel 2.5 that support asynchronous communication.

Table 10.10   Components that support asynchronous processing

Component	Description
camel-cxf	Supports asynchronous routing at both the consumer and producer levels.
camel-jbi	Supports asynchronous routing at both the consumer and producer levels. Requires Apache ServiceMix.
camel-jetty	Supports asynchronous routing at both the consumer and producer levels.
camel-jms	Supports asynchronous routing at the producer level when using request-response over JMS queues.
camel-netty	Supports asynchronous routing at the producer level.
camel-nmr	Supports asynchronous routing at both the consumer and producer levels. Requires Apache ServiceMix.

NOTE   The Camel team will add support for additional components in the future. You can check the online documentation for an updated list of supported components: http://camel.apache.org/asynchronous-routing-engine.html.

In order to achieve high scalability in the Rider Auto Parts web store, you need to use asynchronous routing at two points. The communication with the ERP system and with the Jetty consumer must both happen asynchronously. The `camel-jetty` component already supports this.

Jetty and continuations

The Jetty servlet engine uses continuations to achieve high scalability. It allows Camel to park a request and later retrieve the request and continue processing it. You can read more about continuations at the Jetty website: http://wiki.eclipse.org/Jetty/Feature/Continuations.

Communication with the ERP system must happen asynchronously too. To understand how this is possible with Camel, we'll take a closer look at figure 10.16. The figure reveals that after the request has been submitted to the ERP system, the thread won't block but will return to the Jetty consumer. It's then up to the ERP transport to notify Camel when the reply is ready. When Camel is notified, it will be able to continue routing and let the Jetty consumer return the HTTP response to the waiting customer. To enable all this to work together, Camel provides an asynchronous API that the components must use. In the next section, we'll walk through this API.

10.6.4 *Asynchronous API*

Camel supports an asynchronous processing model, which we refer to as the *asynchronous routing engine*. There are advantages and disadvantages of using asynchronous processing, compared to using the standard synchronous processing model. They're listed in table 10.11.

Table 10.11 Advantages and disadvantages of using the asynchronous processing model

Advantages	Disadvantage
■ Processing messages asynchronously doesn't use up threads, forcing them to wait for processors to complete on blocking calls. ■ It increases the scalability of the system by reducing the number of threads needed to manage the same workload.	■ Implementing asynchronous processing is more complex.

The asynchronous processing model is manifested by an API that must be implemented to leverage asynchronous processing. You've already seen a glimpse of this API in figure 10.16; the arrow between the Jetty consumer and the web store service has the labels *Return false* and *Done*. Let's see the connection that those labels have with the asynchronous API.

ASYNCPROCESSOR

The `AsyncProcessor` is an extension of the synchronous `Processor` API:

```
public interface AsyncProcessor extends Processor {
    boolean process(Exchange exchange, AsyncCallback callback);
}
```

The `AsyncProcessor` defines a single `process` method that's similar to its synchronous `Processor.process` sibling.

Here are the rules that apply when using `AsyncProcessor`:

- A non-null `AsyncCallback` *must* be supplied; it will be notified when the exchange processing is completed.
- The `process` method *must not* throw any exceptions that occur while processing the exchange. Any such exceptions must be stored on the exchange's exception property.
- The `process` method *must* know whether it will complete the processing synchronously or asynchronously. The method will return `true` if it completes synchronously; otherwise it returns `false`.
- When the processor has completed processing the exchange, it must call the `callback.done(boolean doneSync)` method. The `doneSync` parameter *must* match the value returned by the `process` method.

The preceding rules may seem a bit confusing at first. Don't worry, the asynchronous API isn't targeted at Camel end users but at Camel component writers.

In the next section, we'll cover an example of how to implement a custom component that acts asynchronously. You'll be able to use this example as a reference if you need to implement a custom component.

NOTE You can read more about the asynchronous processing model at the Camel website: http://camel.apache.org/asynchronous-processing.html.

The `AsyncCallback` API is a simple interface with one method:

```
public interface AsyncCallback {
    void done(boolean doneSync);
}
```

It's this callback that's invoked when the ERP system returns the reply. This notifies the asynchronous routing engine in Camel that the exchange is ready to be continued, and the engine can then continue routing it.

Let's see how this all fits together by digging into the example and looking at some source code.

10.6.5   *Writing a custom asynchronous component*

The source code for the book contains the web store example in the chapter10/scalability directory. This example contains a custom ERP component that simulates asynchronous communication with an ERP system. Listing 10.6 shows how the `ErpProducer` is implemented.

> **Listing 10.6   `ErpProducer` using the asynchronous processing model**

```
import java.util.concurrent.ExecutorService;

import org.apache.camel.AsyncCallback;
import org.apache.camel.Endpoint;
import org.apache.camel.Exchange;
import org.apache.camel.impl.DefaultAsyncProducer;          ❶ Extends
                                                               DefaultAsyncProducer
public class ErpProducer extends DefaultAsyncProducer {
    private ExecutorService executor;

    public ErpProducer(Endpoint endpoint) {
        super(endpoint);
        executor = endpoint.getCamelContext()
                    .getExecutorServiceStrategy()
                    .newFixedThreadPool(this, "ERP", 10);    ❷ Implements
    }                                                           asynchronous
    public boolean process(final Exchange exchange,          ❷ process method
                    final AsyncCallback callback) {
        executor.submit(new ERPTask(exchange, callback));

        log.info("Returning false");
        return false;                                        ❸ Returns false to
    }                                                           use asynchronous
    private class ERPTask implements Runnable {              ❸ processing

        private final Exchange exchange;
        private final AsyncCallback callback;

        private ERPTask(Exchange exchange, AsyncCallback callback) {
            this.exchange = exchange;
            this.callback = callback;
        }

        public void run() {
```

```
        log.info("Calling ERP");
        try {
            Thread.sleep(5000);
        } catch (InterruptedException e) {
            // ignore
        }
        log.info("ERP reply received");

        String in = exchange.getIn().getBody(String.class);
        exchange.getOut().setBody(in + ";516");                    Sets reply
                                                              4   on exchange
        log.info("Continue routing");
        callback.done(false);                Notifies callback
    }                                    5   reply is ready
  }
}
```

When implementing a custom asynchronous component, it's most often the Producer that leverages asynchronous communication, and a good starting point is to extend the DefaultAsyncProducer ❶.

To simulate asynchronous communication, you use a thread pool to execute tasks asynchronously; this means you need to create a thread pool in the constructor. To support the asynchronous processing model, the ErpProducer must also implement the asynchronous process method ❷.

To simulate the communication, which takes 5 seconds to reply, you submit ERPTask to the thread pool. When the 5 seconds are up, the reply is ready, and it's set on the exchange ❹.

According to the rules, when you're using AsyncProcessor the callback must be notified when you're done with a matching synchronous parameter ❺. In this example, false is used as the synchronous parameter because the process method returned false ❸. By returning false, you instruct the Camel routing engine to leverage asynchronous routing from this point forward for the given exchange.

You can try this example by running the following Maven goal from the chapter10/scalability directory:

```
mvn test -Dtest=ScalabilityTest
```

This runs two test methods: one request is processed fully synchronously (not using the ERP component), and the other is processed asynchronously (by invoking the ERP component).

When running the test, pay attention to the console output. The synchronous test will log input and output as follows:

```
2010-07-16 11:41:42 [    qtp1444378545-11] INFO  input
 - Exchange[ExchangePattern:InOut, Body:1234;4;1719;bumper]
2010-07-16 11:41:42 [    qtp1444378545-11] INFO  output
 - Exchange[ExchangePattern:InOut, Body:Some other action here]
```

Notice that both the input and output are being processed by the same thread.

The asynchronous example is different, as the console output reveals:

```
2010-07-16 11:49:48 [      qtp515060127-11] INFO  input
 - Exchange[ExchangePattern:InOut, Body:1234;4;1719;bumper]
2010-07-16 11:49:48 [      qtp515060127-11] INFO  ErpProducer
 - Returning false (processing will continue asynchronously)
2010-07-16 11:49:48 [Camel Thread 0 - ERP] INFO  ErpProducer
 - Calling ERP
2010-07-16 11:49:53 [Camel Thread 0 - ERP] INFO  ErpProducer
 - ERP reply received
2010-07-16 11:49:53 [Camel Thread 0 - ERP] INFO  ErpProducer
- Continue routing
2010-07-16 11:49:53 [Camel Thread 0 - ERP] INFO  output
- Exchange[ExchangePattern:InOut, Body:1234;4;1719;bumper;516]
```

This time there are two threads used during the routing. The first is the thread from
Jetty, which received the HTTP request. As you can see, this thread was used to route the
message to the `ErpProducer`. The other thread takes over communication with the ERP
system. When the reply is received from the ERP system, the callback is notified, which
lets Camel highjack the thread and use it to continue routing the exchange. You can see
this from the last line, which shows the exchange routed to the log component.

This concludes our coverage of scalability with Camel.

10.7 *Summary and best practices*

In this chapter, we looked at thread pools, which are the foundation for concurrency
in Java. We saw how concurrency greatly improves performance and we looked at all
the possible ways to create, define, and use thread pools in Camel. You saw how easy it
was to use concurrency with the numerous EIPs in Camel, and you also saw how synchronicity affects the way threading occurs in Camel.

Java provides a concurrency API, which we compared to the Camel concurrency API.
Both APIs offer you full control over submitting and executing asynchronous tasks.

Here are some best practices related to concurrency:

- *Leverage concurrency if possible.* Concurrency can greatly speed up your applications. Note that using concurrency requires business logic that can be invoked
  in a concurrent manner.
- *Tweak thread pools judiciously.* Only tweak the thread pools when you have a
  means of measuring the changes. It's often better to rely on the default settings.
- *Know the JDK API.* Understand the asynchronous API from Java, such as `Callable`
  and the `Future` handle.
- *Use asynchronous processing for high scalability.* If you require high scalability, try
  using the Camel components that support the asynchronous processing model
  (listed in table 10.10).

In the next chapter we get more practical and learn how to develop with Camel. You
will learn, among other things, how to start a new Camel project from scratch.

11

Developing Camel projects

This chapter covers

- Creating Camel projects with Maven
- Creating Camel projects in the Eclipse IDE
- Creating custom components
- Creating custom interceptors
- Using Camel in alternative languages

At this point you should know a thing or two about how to develop Camel routes and how to take advantage of many Camel features. But do you know how to best start a Camel project from scratch? You could take an existing example and modify it to fit your use case, but that's not always ideal. And what if you need to integrate with a system that isn't supported out of the box by Camel?

In this chapter, we'll show you how to build your own Camel applications. We'll go over the Maven archetype tooling that'll allow you to skip the boring boilerplate project setup and create new Camel projects with a single command. We'll also show you how to start a Camel project from Eclipse, when you need the extra power that an IDE provides.

After that, we'll show you how to extend Camel by creating custom components and custom interceptors. Finally, we'll wrap up by showing you how Camel projects can be created in languages other than Java, like Scala.

11.1 Managing projects with Maven

Camel was built using Apache Maven right from the start, so it makes sense that creating new Camel projects is easiest when using Maven. In this section, we'll show you Camel's Maven archetypes, which are preconfigured templates for creating various types of Camel projects. After that, we'll talk about using Maven dependencies to load Camel modules and their third-party dependencies into your project.

Section 1.2 of chapter 1 has an overview of Apache Maven. If you need a Maven refresher, you might want to review that section before continuing on here.

11.1.1 Using Camel Maven archetypes

Creating Maven-based projects is a pretty simple task. You mainly have to worry about creating a POM file and the various standard directories that you'll be using in your project. But if you're creating many projects, this can get pretty repetitive because there's a lot of boilerplate setup required for new projects.

Archetypes in Maven provide a means to define project templates and generate new projects based on those templates. They make creating new Maven-based projects easy because they create all the boilerplate POM elements, as well as key source and configuration files useful for particular situations.

> **NOTE** For more information on Maven archetypes, see the guide on the official Maven website: http://maven.apache.org/guides/introduction/introduction-to-archetypes.html. Sonatype also provides a chapter on archetypes in the freely available *Maven: The Complete Reference* book: http://www.sonatype.com/books/mvnref-book/reference/archetypes.html.

As illustrated in figure 11.1, this is all coordinated by the Maven archetype plugin. This plugin accepts user input and replaces portions of the archetype to form a new project.

To demonstrate how this works, let's look at the Maven quickstart archetype, which will generate a plain Java application (no Camel dependencies). It's the default option when you run this command:

```
mvn archetype:generate
```

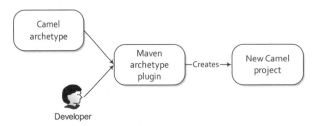

Figure 11.1   A Camel archetype and user input are processed by the Maven archetype plugin, which then creates a new Camel project.

The archetype plugin will ask you various questions, like what `groupId` and `artifactId` to use for the generated project. When it's complete, you'll have a directory structure similar to this:

```
myApp
|-- pom.xml
`-- src
    |-- main
    |   `-- java
    |        `-- camelinaction
    |             `-- App.java
    `-- test
         `-- java
              `-- camelinaction
                   `-- AppTest.java
```

In this structure, `myApp` is the `artifactId` and `camelinaction` is the `groupId`. The archetype plugin created a pom.xml file, a Java source file, and a unit test, all in the proper locations.

> **NOTE** Maven follows the convention over configuration paradigm, so locations are very important.

Without any additional configuration, Maven knows that it should compile the Java source under the src/main/java directory and run all unit tests under the src/test/java directory. To kick off this process, you just need to run the following Maven command:

```
mvn test
```

If you want to take it a step further, you could tell Maven to create a JAR file after compiling and testing by replacing the `test` goal with `package`.

You could start using Camel right from this example project, but it would involve adding Camel dependencies like camel-core, starting up the `CamelContext`, and creating the routes. Although this wouldn't take that long, there's a much quicker solution: you can use one of the six archetypes provided by Camel to generate all this boilerplate Camel stuff for you. Table 11.1 lists these archetypes and their main use cases.

Table 11.1 Camel's Maven archetypes

Archetype name	Description
camel-archetype-activemq	Creates a Camel project that has an embedded Apache ActiveMQ broker.
camel-archetype-component	Creates a new Camel component.
camel-archetype-java	Creates a Camel project that loads up a `CamelContext` in Spring and defines a sample route in Java.
camel-archetype-scala	Creates a Camel project with a sample route in the Scala DSL. In section 11.5, we'll talk more about the Scala DSL.

Table 11.1   Camel's Maven archetypes *(continued)*

Archetype name	Description
camel-archetype-spring	Creates a Camel project that loads up a `CamelContext` in Spring and defines a sample route in the Spring DSL (similar to camel-archetype-java, but with the route transposed to the Spring DSL).
camel-archetype-war	Creates a Camel project that includes the Camel web console, REST API, and a few sample routes as a WAR file.

Out of these six archetypes, the most commonly used one is probably the camel-archetype-java archetype. We'll try this out next.

USING THE CAMEL-ARCHETYPE-JAVA ARCHETYPE

The camel-archetype-java archetype listed in table 11.1 boots up a Spring-based CamelContext and a Java DSL route. With this, we'll show you how to re-create the order-routing service for Rider Auto Parts as described in chapter 2. The project will be named `order-router` and the package name in the source will be `camelinaction`.

To create the skeleton project for this service, run the following Maven command:

```
mvn archetype:create \
  -DarchetypeGroupId=org.apache.camel.archetypes \
  -DarchetypeArtifactId=camel-archetype-java \
  -DarchetypeVersion=2.5.0 \
  -DgroupId=camelinaction \
  -DartifactId=order-router
```

You specify the archetype to use by setting the `archetypeArtifactId` property to `camel-archetype-java`. You could replace this with any of the archetype names listed in table 11.1. The `archetypeVersion` property is set to the version of Camel that you want to use.

Create versus generate

The Maven archetype plugin has two main goals: `archetype:generate` and `archetype:create`. The `generate` goal is used when you need an interactive shell, prompting you through what you want to create. You can select the Camel archetypes through this interactive shell as well, so it's a useful option for developers new to Camel. The `create` goal is useful when you know what you want to create up front and can enter it all on one command line.

After a few seconds of activity, Maven will have created an order-router subdirectory in the current directory. The order-router directory layout is shown in the following listing.

Listing 11.1   Layout of the project created by camel-archetype-java

```
order-router
|-- ReadMe.txt
|-- pom.xml
```

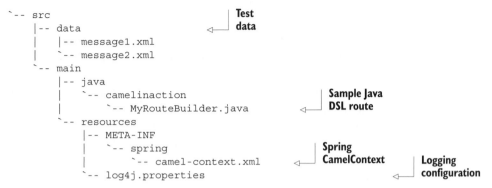

The archetype gives you a runnable Camel project, with a sample route and test data to drive it. The Readme.txt file tells you how to run this sample project: run `mvn camel:run`. Camel will continue to run until you press Ctrl-C, which causes the context to stop.

While running, the sample route will consume files in the src/data directory and, based on the content, will route them to one of two directories. If you look in the target/messages directory, you should see something like this:

```
target/messages
|-- others
|    `-- message2.xml
`-- uk
     `-- message1.xml
```

Now you know that Camel is working on your system, so you can start editing MyRouteBuilder.java to look like the order-router application. You can start by setting up FTP and web service endpoints that route to a JMS queue for incoming orders:

```
from("ftp://rider@localhost:21000/order?password=secret&delete=true")
  .to("jms:incomingOrders");
from("cxf:bean:orderEndpoint")
  .inOnly("jms:incomingOrders")
  .transform(constant("OK"));
```

At this point, if you try to run the application again using `mvn camel:run`, you'll get the following error message:

```
Failed to resolve endpoint: ftp://rider@localhost:21000/order?password=secret
    due to: No component found with scheme: ftp
```

Camel couldn't find the FTP component because it isn't on the classpath. You'd get the same error message for the CXF and JMS endpoints. There are, of course, other bits you have to add to your project to make this a runnable application: a test FTP server running on localhost, a CXF configuration, a JMS connection factory, and so on. A complete project is available in the book's source under chapter11/order-router-full.

For now, we'll focus on adding component dependencies using Maven.

11.1.2 Camel Maven dependencies

Technically, Camel is just a Java application. To use it, you just need to add its JARs to your project's classpath. But using Maven to access these JARs will make your life a whole lot easier. Camel itself was developed using Maven for this very reason.

In the previous section, you saw that using an FTP endpoint with only the camel-core module as a dependency won't work. You need to add the camel-ftp module as a dependency to your project. Back in chapter 7 you saw that this was accomplished by adding the following to the dependencies section of the POM file:

```
<dependency>
  <groupId>org.apache.camel</groupId>
  <artifactId>camel-ftp</artifactId>
  <version>2.5.0</version>
</dependency>
```

This dependency element will tell Maven to download the camel-ftp JAR from Maven's central repository at http://repo2.maven.org/maven2/org/apache/camel/camel-ftp/2.5.0/camel-ftp-2.5.0.jar. This download URL is built up from Maven's central repository URL (http://repo2.maven.org/maven2) and Maven coordinates (groupId, artifactId, and so on) specified in the dependency element. After the download is complete, Maven will add the JAR to the project's classpath.

One detail that may not be obvious at first is that this dependency also has *transitive dependencies*. What are transitive dependencies? Well, in this case you have a project called order-router and you've added a dependency on camel-ftp. The camel-ftp module also has a dependency on commons-net, among others. So you can say that commons-net is a transitive dependency of order-router. Transitive dependencies are dependencies that a dependency has—the dependencies of the camel-ftp module, in this case.

When you add camel-ftp as a dependency, Maven will look up camel-ftp's POM file from the central Maven repository and look at the dependencies it has. Maven will then download and add those dependencies to this project's classpath.

The camel-ftp module adds a whopping 24 transitive dependencies to our project! Luckily only 5 of them are needed at runtime; the other 19 are used during testing. The 5 transitive runtime dependencies can be viewed as a tree, as shown in figure 11.2.

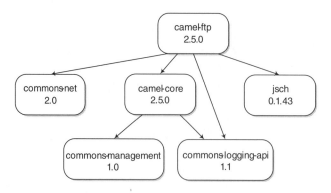

Figure 11.2 Transitive runtime dependencies of the camel-ftp module. When you add a dependency on camel-ftp to your project, you'll also get its transitive dependencies added to your classpath. In this case, commons-net, camel-core, commons-logging-api, and jsch are added. Additionally, camel-core has a dependency on commons-management, so that's added to the classpath as well.

You're already depending on camel-core in the order-router project, so only two dependencies—commons-net and jsch—are brought in by camel-ftp.

This is a view of only a small number of dependencies, but you can recognize that the dependency tree can get quite complex. Fortunately, Maven finds these dependencies for you and resolves any duplicate dependencies. The bottom line is that when you're using Maven, you don't need to worry much about your project's dependencies.

If you want to know what your project's dependencies are (including transitive ones), Maven offers the `dependency:tree` command. To see the dependencies in your project, run the following command:

```
mvn dependency:tree
```

After a few seconds of work, Maven will print out a listing like this:

```
+- org.apache.camel:camel-core:jar:2.5.0:compile
|  +- commons-logging:commons-logging-api:jar:1.1:compile
|  +- org.fusesource.commonman:commons-management:jar:1.0:compile
|  \- com.sun:tools:jar:1.5.0:system
+- org.apache.camel:camel-spring:jar:2.5.0:compile
|  +- org.springframework:spring-context:jar:3.0.4.RELEASE:compile
|  |  +- org.springframework:spring-beans:jar:3.0.4.RELEASE:compile
|  |  +- org.springframework:spring-core:jar:3.0.4.RELEASE:compile
|  |  |  \- commons-logging:commons-logging:jar:1.1.1:compile
|  |  +- org.springframework:spring-expression:jar:3.0.4.RELEASE:compile
|  |  \- org.springframework:spring-asm:jar:3.0.4.RELEASE:compile
|  +- org.springframework:spring-aop:jar:3.0.4.RELEASE:compile
|  |  \- aopalliance:aopalliance:jar:1.0:compile
|  \- org.springframework:spring-tx:jar:3.0.4.RELEASE:compile
+- org.apache.camel:camel-ftp:jar:2.5.0:compile
|  +- com.jcraft:jsch:jar:0.1.43:compile
|  \- commons-net:commons-net:jar:2.0:compile
\- log4j:log4j:jar:1.2.16:compile
```

Here, you can see that Maven is adding 18 JARs to your project's compile-time classpath, even though you only added camel-core, camel-spring, camel-ftp, and log4j. Some dependencies are coming from several levels deep in the dependency tree.

Surviving without Maven

As you can imagine, adding all these dependencies to your project without the help of Maven would be a bit tedious. If you absolutely must use an alternative build system, you can still use Maven to get the required dependencies for you by following these steps:

1 Download the POM file of the artifact you want. For camel-ftp, this would be http://repo2.maven.org/maven2/org/apache/camel/camel-ftp/2.5.0/camel-ftp-2.5.0.pom.
2 Run mvn -f camel-ftp-2.5.0.pom dependency:copy-dependencies
3 The dependencies for camel-ftp will be located in the target/dependency directory. You can now use these in whatever build system you're using.

> **(continued)**
>
> If you absolutely can't use Maven but would still like to use Maven repos, Apache Ivy (http://ant.apache.org/ivy) is a great dependency management framework for Apache Ant that can download from Maven repos. Other than that, you will have to download the JARs yourself from the Maven central repo.

You now know all you need to develop Camel projects using Maven. To make you an even more productive Camel developer, let's now look at how you can develop Camel applications inside an IDE, like Eclipse.

11.2 Using Camel in Eclipse

We haven't mentioned IDEs much so far, mostly because you don't need an IDE to use Camel. Certainly, though, you can't match the power and ease of use an IDE gives you. From a Camel point of view, having the Java or Spring DSLs autocomplete for you makes route development a whole lot easier. The common Java debugging facilities and other tools will further improve your experience.

Because Maven is used as the primary build tool for Camel projects, we'll show you how to use Maven tools to load up your Camel project in Eclipse. In this section, we'll demonstrate two ways of getting Camel projects into Eclipse: by using the Maven Eclipse plugin and by using the m2eclipse plugin for Eclipse.

11.2.1 Using the Maven Eclipse plugin

The Maven Eclipse plugin can take any Maven-based project and generate an Eclipse project. It allows you to get a Camel project into Eclipse as a plain Java project. It offers a quick way to start Camel development, but you don't get any frills beyond what a regular Java project would give you.

You can run this plugin on a project by executing the following command in the project's root directory:

```
mvn eclipse:eclipse
```

After this command completes, an Eclipse project will be available, having all the dependencies you listed in your POM as entries in the project's build path.

If you run this command on the order-router project you created in the previous section, a directory listing will show that you now have three extra files and an additional directory:

```
order-router/
|-- .classpath
|-- .project
|-- .settings
|    `-- org.eclipse.jdt.core.prefs
|-- ReadMe.txt
|-- pom.xml
|-- src
```

These are files that Eclipse interprets as a Java project. The next step after this is to import the project into Eclipse. This is an easy task in Eclipse:

1 Select File > Import > General > Existing Projects into Workspace.
2 In the wizard, select the directory where the project is located, and then select the project name (chapter11-order-router, in this case) from the list. The wizard dialog box should look something like what's shown in figure 11.3.
3 Click Finish, and your project will be imported into your Eclipse workspace.

If you take a look at the Package Explorer view now, you should see the chapter11-order-router project listed. Figure 11.4 shows an expanded view of what is inside the project. It looks mostly like what you saw from the previous directory listing, but now it includes a list of project dependencies.

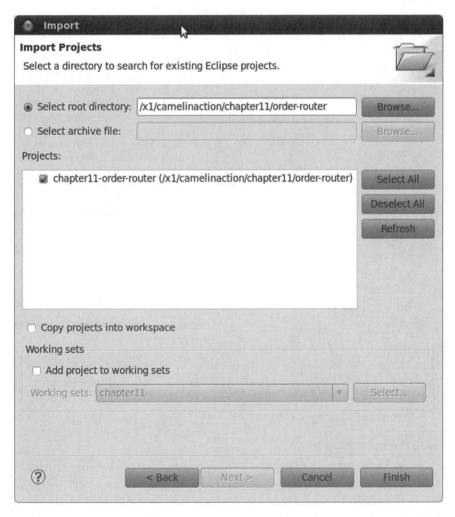

Figure 11.3 Final screen of wizard to import the chapter11-order-router project into Eclipse

Listed to the right of each project dependency in figure 11.4 are details of where the artifact exists on your local disk. This information contains a variable named M2_REPO, which points to your local Maven repository. This is the area where Maven caches downloaded dependencies so you don't download these things for every build. This variable needs to be defined for Eclipse to access your project's dependencies. To specify this, follow these steps:

1 Open up the Preferences dialog box by selecting Window > Preferences.

2 Go to Java > Build Path > Classpath Variables.

3 In the Classpath Variables pane, you need to add a variable named M2_REPO with a path pointing to the directory of your local Maven repo (recall that this is Maven's local cache of downloaded artifacts). For example, this could be something like /home/janstey/.m2/repository on Linux, C:\Documents and Settings\janstey\.m2\repository on Windows XP, or C:\Users\janstey\.m2\repository on Windows Vista/7.

Figure 11.4   Package Explorer view of the order-router project

From this point on, you can develop as if this project were a regular Java project in Eclipse. But keep in mind when adding new dependencies to your Maven POM that they won't be automatically added to the Eclipse project. The mvn eclipse:eclipse command will have to be run again and the project will have to be refreshed in the Package Explorer view.

11.2.2   *Using the m2eclipse plugin*

When using the Maven Eclipse plugin, you'll find yourself often darting back and forth between Eclipse and the command line. Eclipse will be where you develop, and the command line will be where you build. If you decide instead to use the m2eclipse plugin to develop your Camel project, you'll experience a much nicer integration with Maven and never have to leave the IDE.

When to use m2eclipse

The m2eclipse plugin does add a bit of complexity to development, so in some cases the simpler Maven Eclipse plugin is a better choice. For instance, if you already have a Maven project created, and you know you probably won't be adding new dependencies, it's much quicker to use the Maven Eclipse plugin. It will also require a lot less system resources to develop the project in Eclipse.

M2eclipse has had performance issues in the past when you have many projects open at the same time. The recommendation is to turn off automatic building for all projects. This way you can control when builds get kicked off. New versions of the plugin are improving performance all the time, so this may not be an issue in future builds.

To install m2eclipse into your Eclipse runtime, follow the latest instructions at http://m2eclipse.sonatype.org. During the writing of this book, we used m2eclipse version 0.10.2.

One thing that some developers will like right away is that you don't have to leave the IDE to run Maven command-line tools during development. You can even access the Camel archetypes right from Eclipse. To demonstrate this feature, let's recreate the chapter11-order-router example we looked at previously.

Click File > New > Maven Project to start up the New Maven Project wizard. Click Next on the first screen, and you'll be presented with a list of available archetypes, as shown in figure 11.5. This list includes the Camel archetypes.

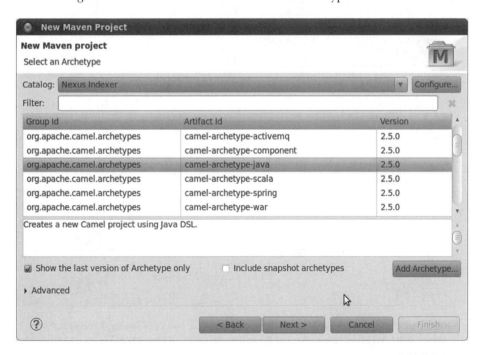

Figure 11.5   The New Maven Project wizard allows you to generate a new Camel project right in Eclipse.

Using Camel archetypes in this way is equivalent to the technique you used back in section 11.1.1. The m2eclipse plugin will also allow you to add Maven dependencies without having to regenerate your project every time, which can be forgotten if you use the Maven Eclipse plugin.

> **NOTE** If you can only see version 2.2.0 of the Camel archetypes, you'll need to perform a few additional steps. At the time of writing, an error at Maven's central repository was preventing newer Camel archetypes from being shown in m2eclipse. To get around this you'll need to do the following:
>
> 1 Click the menu item Window > Preferences and drill down to Maven > Archetypes.
> 2 Click Add Remote Catalog and enter http://camelinaction.googlecode. com/svn/trunk/misc/archetype-catalog.xml as the catalog file. Click OK and close out the Preferences dialog box.
> 3 When creating a new project as in figure 11.5, make sure to select the catalog you just added.

To run the order-router project with m2eclipse, right-click on the project in the Package Explorer and click Run As > Maven Build. This will bring up an Edit Configuration dialog box where you can specify the Maven goals to use as well as any parameters. For the order-router project, use the `camel:run` goal, as shown in figure 11.6.

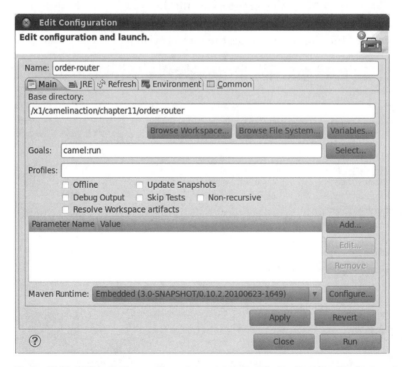

Figure 11.6 Right-clicking on the order-router project in the Package Explorer and clicking Run As > Maven Build will bring up the Edit Configuration dialog box shown here. The `camel:run` Maven goal has been entered.

Clicking Run in this dialog box will execute the `mvn camel:run` command in Eclipse, with console output showing in the Eclipse Console view.

Now you can say that you know how to create Camel projects from the command line and from Eclipse. You've also seen the two ways you can develop Camel applications in Eclipse, and the pitfalls of each. These projects only leverage what is built into Camel itself. We'll now move on to the more advanced topic of extending Camel itself, by developing custom components.

11.3 *Developing custom components*

For most integration scenarios, there's a Camel component available to help. Sometimes, though, there's no Camel component available, and you need to bridge Camel to another transport, API, data format, and so on. You can do this by creating your own custom component.

Creating a Camel component is relatively easy, which may be one of the reasons that custom Camel components frequently show up on other community sites, in addition to the official Camel distribution. In this section, we'll look at how you can create your own custom component for Camel.

11.3.1 *Setting up a new Camel component*

Just like a regular Camel project, you can start creating a new component by using a Maven archetype to generate a skeleton project. To create a new Camel component with `camelinaction.component` as the package name and `custom` as the `artifactId`, run the following Maven command:

```
mvn archetype:create \
  -DarchetypeGroupId=org.apache.camel.archetypes \
  -DarchetypeArtifactId=camel-archetype-component \
  -DarchetypeVersion=2.5.0 \
  -DgroupId=camelinaction.component \
  -DartifactId=custom
```

This will generate a project structure like that shown here.

Listing 11.2   Layout of a project created by camel-archetype-component

```
custom
|-- pom.xml
|-- ReadMe.txt
`-- src
|-- main
    |   |-- java
    |   |    `-- camelinaction
    |   |         `-- component
    |   |              |-- HelloWorldComponent.java
    |   |              |-- HelloWorldConsumer.java
    |   |              |-- HelloWorldEndpoint.java
    |   |              `-- HelloWorldProducer.java
    |   `-- resources
    |        |-- log4j.properties
```

❶ Component implementation

```
|          `-- META-INF
|              `-- services
|                  `-- org
|                      `-- apache
|                          `-- camel
|                              `-- component
|                                  `-- helloworld
`-- test
    `-- java
        `-- camelinaction
            `-- component
                `-- HelloWorldComponentTest.java
```

❷ File that maps
URI scheme to
component class

Test case for
component

This is a fully functional "Hello World" demo component containing a simple consumer that generates dummy messages at regular intervals, and a producer that prints a message to the console. You can run the test case included with this sample component by running the following Maven command:

```
mvn test
```

One of the first things to do when developing a custom component is to decide what endpoint name to use. This name is what will be used to reference the custom component in an endpoint URI. You need to make sure this name doesn't conflict with a component that already exists by checking the online component list (http://camel.apache.org/components.html). For instance, to use mycomponent as the endpoint name, you need to rename the helloworld file ❷ to mycomponent. For an explanation on how this file is used to load Camel components, see section 7.1 in chapter 7.

You should also rename the skeleton implementation classes ❶ to better match your new component name. The src directory now looks like this:

```
src
`-- main
    |-- java
    |   `-- camelinaction
    |       `-- component
    |           |-- MyComponent.java
    |           |-- MyConsumer.java
    |           |-- MyEndpoint.java
    |           `-- MyProducer.java
    |   `-- resources
    |       |-- log4j.properties
    |       `-- META-INF
    |           `-- services
    |               `-- org
    |                   `-- apache
    |                       `-- camel
    |                           `-- component
    |                               `-- mycomponent
    `-- test
        `-- java
            `-- camelinaction
                `-- component
                    `-- MyComponentTest.java
```

This project, with the appropriate renaming, is available in the chapter11/custom directory of the book's source.

When you change the component class name, to MyComponent, for example, you also need to modify the mycomponent file to point to this new class. It should now contain a line like this:

```
class=camelinaction.component.MyComponent
```

Your component can now be used in a Camel endpoint URI. But you shouldn't stop here. To understand how these classes make up a functioning component, you need to understand the implementation details of each.

11.3.2 Diving into the implementation

The four classes that make up a component in Camel have been mentioned several times before. To recap, it all starts with the Component class, which then creates an Endpoint. An Endpoint, in turn, can create Producers and Consumers. This is illustrated in figure 11.7.

We'll first look into the Component and Endpoint implementations of the custom MyComponent component.

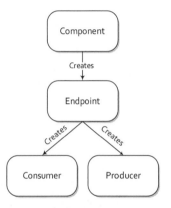

Figure 11.7 A Component
creates an Endpoint, **which**
then creates Producers **and**
Consumers.

COMPONENT AND ENDPOINT CLASSES

The first entry point into a Camel component is the class implementing the Component interface. A component's main job is to be a factory of new endpoints. It does a bit more than this under the hood, but typically you don't have to worry about these details because they're contained in the DefaultComponent class.

The component class generated by the camel-archetype-component archetype extends this default class and forms a pretty simple and typical component class structure, as shown here:

```
public class MyComponent extends DefaultComponent {

    protected Endpoint createEndpoint(
            String uri, String remaining,
            Map<String, Object> parameters) throws Exception {
        Endpoint endpoint = new MyEndpoint(uri, this);
        setProperties(endpoint, parameters);
        return endpoint;
    }
}
```

This class is pretty straightforward, except perhaps for the way in which properties are set with the setProperties method. This method takes in the properties set in the endpoint URI string, and for each will invoke a setter method on the endpoint through reflection. For instance, say you used the following endpoint URI:

```
mycomponent:endpointName?prop1=value1&prop2=value2
```

The `setProperties` method, in this case, would try to invoke `setProp1("value1")` and `setProp2("value2")` on the endpoint. Camel will take care of converting those values to the appropriate type.

The endpoint, itself, is also a relatively simple class, as shown here.

Listing 11.3 Custom Camel endpoint—`MyEndpoint`

```
public class MyEndpoint extends DefaultEndpoint {          ◁─┐   Extends from
    public MyEndpoint() {                                    ❶  default endpoint class
    }

    public MyEndpoint(String uri, MyComponent component) {
        super(uri, component);
    }

    public MyEndpoint(String endpointUri) {
        super(endpointUri);
    }

    public Producer createProducer() throws Exception {     ❷  Creates new
        return new MyProducer(this);                       ◁─┘  producer
    }

    public Consumer createConsumer(Processor processor) throws Exception {
        return new MyConsumer(this, processor);    ◁─┐
    }                                                 │   Creates new event-
                                                     ❸  driven consumer
    public boolean isSingleton() {
        return true;
    }
}
```

The first thing you'll notice is that you're deriving from another default implementation class from camel-core ❶. In this case, you're extending the `DefaultEndpoint` class. It's very common when creating a new Camel component to have the `Component`, `Endpoint`, `Consumer`, and `Producer` all derive from default implementations in camel-core. This isn't necessary, but it makes new component development much easier, and you always benefit from the latest improvements to the default implementations without having to code them yourself.

As we mentioned in chapter 7, the `Endpoint` class acts as a factory for both consumers and producers. In this example, you're creating both producers ❷ and consumers ❸, which means that this endpoint can be used in a `to` or `from` Java DSL method. Sometimes you may need to create a component that only has a producer or consumer, not both. In that case, it's recommended that you throw an exception, so users know that it isn't supported:

```
public Producer createProducer() throws Exception {
    throw new UnsupportedOperationException(
      "You cannot send messages to this endpoint:" + getEndpointUri());
}
```

The real bulk of most components is in the producer and consumer. The Component and Endpoint classes are mostly designed to fit the component into Camel. In the producers and consumers, which we'll look at next, you have to interface with the remote APIs or marshal data to a particular transport.

PRODUCERS AND CONSUMERS

The producer and consumer are where you get to implement how messages will get on or off a particular transport—in effect, bridging Camel to something else. This is illustrated in figure 11.8.

In your skeleton component project that was generated from an archetype, a producer and consumer are implemented and ready to go. These were instantiated by the MyEndpoint class in listing 11.3. The producer, named MyProducer, is shown in this listing.

Listing 11.4 Custom Camel producer—MyProducer

```
public class MyProducer extends DefaultProducer {      ◁——  Extends from
    private static final transient Log LOG =                  default producer
        ⮡LogFactory.getLog(MyProducer.class);          ❶  class
    private MyEndpoint endpoint;

    public MyProducer(MyEndpoint endpoint) {
        super(endpoint);
        this.endpoint = endpoint;
    }
                                                        ❷  Serves as
    public void process(Exchange exchange)                    entry point
        ⮡throws Exception {                                   to producer
        System.out.println(exchange.getIn().getBody());  ◁——  Prints
    }                                                   ❸  message body
}
```

Like the component and endpoint classes, the producer also extends from a default implementation class from camel-core called DefaultProducer ❶. The Producer interface extends from the Processor interface, so you use a process method ❷. As you can probably guess, a producer is called in the same way a processor is, so the entry point into the producer is the process method.

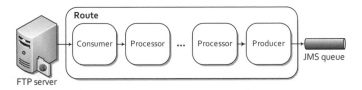

Figure 11.8 A simplified view of a route where the consumer and producer handle interfacing with external systems. Consumers take messages from an external system into Camel, and producers send messages to external systems.

The sample component that was created automatically has a very basic producer—it just prints the body of the incoming message to the screen ❸. If you were sending to an external system instead of the screen, you'd have to handle a lot more here, such as connecting to a remote system and marshaling data. In the case of data marshaling, it's often a good idea to implement this using a custom `TypeConverter`, as described in chapter 3, which makes the converters available to other parts of your Camel application.

You can see how messages could be sent out of a route, but how do they get into a route? Consumers, like the `MyConsumer` class generated in your custom component project, get the messages into a route. The `MyConsumer` class is shown in listing 11.5.

Listing 11.5   Custom Camel consumer—`MyConsumer`

```
public class MyConsumer extends ScheduledPollConsumer {          Extends from
    private final MyEndpoint endpoint;                     ❶  built-in consumer

    public MyConsumer(MyEndpoint endpoint, Processor processor) {
        super(endpoint, processor);
        this.endpoint = endpoint;
    }

    @Override                                              ❷ Is called every
    protected void poll() throws Exception {                  500 ms
        Exchange exchange = endpoint.createExchange();

        Date now = new Date();
        exchange.getIn().setBody("Hello World! The time is " + now);

        try {
            getProcessor().process(exchange);              Sends to next
        } finally {                                        processor in route
            if (exchange.getException() != null) {
                getExceptionHandler().handleException(
                    "Error processing exchange", exchange,
                    exchange.getException());
            }
        }
    }
}
```

The `Consumer` interface, itself, doesn't impose many restrictions or give any guidelines as to how a consumer should behave, but the `DefaultConsumer` class does, so it's helpful to extend from this class when implementing your own consumer. In listing 11.5, you extend from a subclass of `DefaultConsumer`, the `ScheduledPollConsumer` ❶. This consumer has a timer thread that will invoke the poll method every 500 milliseconds ❷.

> **TIP**   See the discussion of the Timer and Quartz components in chapter 7 for more information on creating routes that need to operate on a schedule.

Typically, a consumer will either poll a resource for a message or set up an event-driven structure for accepting messages from remote sources. In this example, you have no remote resource, so you can create an empty exchange and populate it with a "Hello World" message. A real consumer still would need to do this.

A common pattern for consumers is something like this:

```
Exchange exchange = endpoint.createExchange();
// populate exchange with data
getProcessor().process(exchange);
```

Here you create an empty exchange, populate it with data, and send it to the next processor in the route.

At this point, you should have a good understanding of what is required to create a new Camel component. You may even have a few ideas about what you'd like to bridge Camel to next! Another useful way of extending Camel is by writing custom interceptors. Let's look at this next.

11.4   Developing interceptors

Interceptors in Camel are used to perform some action on a message as it goes in and out of a processor. Features like the tracer discussed in chapter 12 use a custom interceptor to trace each message going in and out of processors. We also talked about interceptors back in chapter 6, where you used them to simulate errors occurring on a particular endpoint. Convenience methods built into Camel's DSL were used in that case.

In this section, we'll look at how you can create your own custom interceptor.

11.4.1 Creating an InterceptStrategy

To create a new interceptor, you need to use the `InterceptStrategy` interface. By implementing a custom `InterceptStrategy`, you gain complete control over what the interceptor does.

The `InterceptStrategy` interface only has a single method:

```
Processor wrapProcessorInInterceptors(
    CamelContext context,
    ProcessorDefinition<?> definition,
    Processor target,
    Processor nextTarget) throws Exception;
```

This method essentially wraps each processor within a route with another processor. This wrapper processor will contain the logic you want for your interceptor.

In Camel, `InterceptStrategy` classes are used to implement a delay after each node in a route, to trace messages as they flow through a route, and to record performance metrics. Figure 11.9 shows a conceptual view of how an `InterceptStrategy` modifies a route.

Every processor in the route shown in figure 11.9 is wrapped by an interceptor processor. This work of modifying the route is done automatically when you add the

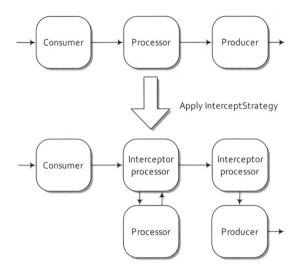

Figure 11.9 Applying an InterceptStrategy to a route essentially wraps each processor with an interceptor processor.

InterceptStrategy to the CamelContext. You can add an InterceptStrategy directly to the CamelContext with a single method call:

```
context.addInterceptStrategy(new MyInterceptor());
```

Adding an InterceptStrategy in Spring is also easy. You just add one as a bean, and Camel will automatically find it on startup and add it to the CamelContext. This is all you would need to write:

```
<bean id="myInterceptor" class="camelinaction.MyInterceptor"/>
```

What happens if you define more than one strategy? Figure 11.10 shows that in this case Camel will stack the interceptors used for each real processor.

You may be wondering what an actual interceptor looks like. In the simplest case, you could just log an entry message before the processor and an exit message after the processor has completed. This is demonstrated in listing 11.6.

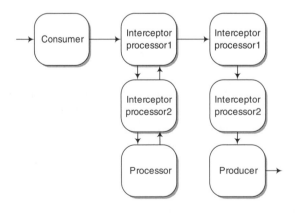

Figure 11.10 Interceptors are stackable, meaning the more InterceptStrategy classes you add to the CamelContext, the more interceptor processors will be added before each real processor is executed.

Listing 11.6 A custom interceptor

```
public class MyInterceptor implements InterceptStrategy {
    private static final transient Log log
        = LogFactory.getLog(MyInterceptor.class);

    public Processor wrapProcessorInInterceptors(
        CamelContext context,                          ❶ The target
        ProcessorDefinition<?> definition,                processor model
        final Processor target,              The target
        Processor nextTarget)              ❷ processor
        throws Exception {
        return new DelegateAsyncProcessor(new Processor() {

            public void process(Exchange exchange) throws Exception {
                log.info("Entering the processor...");
                target.process(exchange);              Call into the
                log.info("Exiting the processor...");  ❸ target processor
            }
        });
    }
}
```

The wrapProcessorInInterceptors method gives the interceptor developer plenty of information to help create a custom interceptor. First off, you have access to the entire CamelContext, which lets you access many different services, like the bean registry or the many type converters. Next, and most importantly, you have access to the target processor ❷ that you need to call, and its DSL object equivalent ❶. Why was the DSL object provided? The DSL object provides richer description details than the runtime processor, so if your interceptor is, for example, graphically reporting the structure of a Camel route as it's being used, more detailed descriptions of each node may be helpful.

It isn't enforced by the interface, but interceptors are supposed to call the target processor ❸ when they have done their work. After the target processor is finished, the interceptor can do some more work before returning to the next node in the route. In this way, an interceptor allows you to do operations before and after each processor in a route.

Sometimes, you don't want to attach an interceptor to a particular processor. In this case, instead of always returning a wrapped processor, you could return the target processor. This would leave the target processor out of the interceptor scheme.

For example, you could ignore wireTap nodes from the interceptor scheme by using information from the processor's model class:

```
if ("wireTap".equals(definition.getShortName())) {
    return target;
} else {
    return new Processor() {
        ...
    };
}
```

This checks the name of the processor through its DSL object, and if it's a wire tap, it doesn't wrap it with an interceptor.

You've now seen how to develop custom Camel components and interceptors. Let's step outside the Java world and see how Camel can be used from other languages.

11.5   *Using alternative languages*

Throughout this book, we've focused on Camel's two main methods of specifying routing rules: the Java DSL and Spring XML configuration. We did this to focus on the concepts themselves, rather than how they end up being implemented, but Camel does provide advanced users with a number of options for creating routes in other JVM languages. For instance, you can create routes in the Groovy, Scala, and Ruby languages.

The Scala DSL is probably the most mature of the three, having a custom DSL created to take advantage of language features in Scala. The Groovy DSL is well-used too. In fact, another open source project called the Open eHealth Integration Platform (IPF) is a Groovy-based project built on top of Apache Camel.

In this section, we'll take a look at how you can create Camel applications using Scala. We'll first look at some of the constructs you can use to create a route in Scala, and then we'll see how to add these routes to a `CamelContext`.

11.5.1   *The Scala DSL*

As you may have assumed, when using the Scala DSL you're coding in a real programming language—Scala. In this way it's more comparable to the Java DSL than Spring XML configuration.

Recall the following route from section 11.1.1:

```
from("ftp://rider@localhost:21000/order?password=secret")
  .to("jms:incomingOrders");
```

Because this is the Java DSL, it also must be enclosed within a `RouteBuilder` class as follows:

```
class MyRouteBuilder extends RouteBuilder {
    public void configure() throws Exception {
        from("ftp://rider@localhost:21000/order?password=secret")
          .to("jms:incomingOrders");
    }
}
```

This should look pretty familiar to you now—it's about the simplest Camel route you can get: consuming messages from one endpoint and producing them into another endpoint.

Now let's see what the Scala version of this route looks like:

```
class MyRouteBuilder extends RouteBuilder {
    "ftp://rider@localhost:21000/order?password=secret"
  ➥to "jms:incomingOrders"
}
```

It starts off mostly the same as the Java DSL version, with a `MyRouteBuilder` class extending from `RouteBuilder`. In this case, `RouteBuilder` is in the org.apache.camel. scala.builder package.

Learn more about Scala

This isn't a book about Scala, so many assumptions are made in this section about your knowledge of Scala. Because Scala is quite different from Java, it's recommended that you learn about the language fundamentals before trying to use the Scala DSL in Camel. Otherwise, you may get frustrated by language features that are very different from Java.

The main online resource for Scala is http://www.scala-lang.org, and if you want in-depth information about Scala, we recommend the book coauthored by the language's creator, *Programming in Scala* by Martin Odersky, Lex Spoon, and Bill Venners.

Another must-have for Scala DSL development is a plugin for your IDE so you can avail yourself of code completion. The Scala IDE for Eclipse is available at http://www.scala-ide.org.

You may notice that the Scala DSL route is a lot less verbose. One of the aims of the Scala DSL was to eliminate text that didn't add anything to the function of a route. In the Java DSL, there's a lot of text used to conform to the Java language. Scala gives you a lot more freedom in creating your own operators and relaxes requirements for parentheses, dots, and semicolons.

In the previous one-line route, you have very few extraneous characters: there are two endpoint URI strings and a `to` operator. The `from` method used in other Camel DSLs isn't needed here; simply specifying an endpoint URI is enough to start a route. The `to` operator can also be replaced with `-->` which may be more aesthetically pleasing to you, but it has exactly the same function as `to`. There's also no need to specify a configure method as there is in the Java DSL. Route statements are entered directly into the class body.

Note that in order to break this simple route into several lines of code, you would need to introduce a code block, as follows:

```
class MyRouteBuilder extends RouteBuilder {
    "ftp://rider@localhost:21000/order?password=secret" ==> {
        to("jms:incomingOrders")
    }
}
```

The `==>` operator is used to start the code block, and the braces indicate the start and end of the block. These code blocks can be nested arbitrarily. In this way, Camel will know how to end a route's construction and add it into the `CamelContext`. In the Scala DSL, a route ends after either a code line ends in the simple case, or when the code block ends if you're using code blocks.

> **The Scala DSL and EIPs**
> The Scala DSL doesn't support all the EIPs that are available in the Java and Spring DSLs, but it does support most of them. EIPs that don't have a Scala DSL equivalent can be accessed from the Java DSL. You can find examples of what the EIPs look like in Scala at the Apache Camel website: http://camel.apache.org/scala-dsl-eip.html.

11.5.2 *Adding Scala routes to the CamelContext*

Scala routes are added to the `CamelContext` in much the same way as Java DSL routes are. We discussed the different approaches to this in chapter 2. The reason you can use the same approach is that Scala ultimately compiles down to Java bytecode, so when the `CamelContext` is searching for a `RoutesBuilder` in a package you specified, it doesn't care whether it originated from Java or Scala. For example, to load a Scala-based route into a Spring `CamelContext`, you would just define the `CamelContext` like this:

```
<camelContext xmlns="http://camel.apache.org/schema/spring">
  <package>camelinaction</package>
</camelContext>
```

This will pick up all Scala routes in the `camelinaction` package—exactly the same as for Java routes. An example of this is provided in the chapter11/scala-router directory of the book's source. To run this example, execute the following Maven command:

```
mvn camel:run
```

There may be times when you want to mix Java and Scala within a single project. For instance, you may already have a working Java-based system using Camel, and you want to add a new route using the Scala DSL. What do you do in this case?

11.5.3 *Mixing Java and Scala*

As we've said before, both Java and Scala compile down to Java bytecode, so it should be easy to mix the two. It mostly involves setting up your Maven project to compile both types of sources and put the resultant bytecode class files in the same location.

Suppose you have a project that has Java and Scala source files as follows:

```
scala-router-javacontext
|-- pom.xml
`-- src
    `-- main
        |-- java
        |   `-- camelinaction
        |       `-- Main.java
        `-- scala
            `-- camelinaction
                `-- MyRouteBuilder.scala
```

The `Main` class creates a new `CamelContext` and adds the Scala `RouteBuilder` `MyRouteBuilder` to the context as follows:

```
public class Main {
    public static void main(String args[]) throws Exception {
        CamelContext context = new DefaultCamelContext();
        context.addRoutes(new MyRouteBuilder());
        ...
```

Both `Main` and `MyRouteBuilder` are in the same package, so this should all work nicely, except that it doesn't. If you try to run the `Main` class now, you'll get a compilation error saying `MyRouteBuilder` can't be found. It can't be found because it hasn't been compiled yet!

By default, Maven will compile all Java sources in src/main/java, but it has no such settings in place for Scala. You can get around this by configuring the maven-scala-plugin as shown here.

Listing 11.7   Configuring compilation of both Java and Scala sources

```
<plugin>
  <groupId>org.scala-tools</groupId>
  <artifactId>maven-scala-plugin</artifactId>
  <version>2.9.1</version>
  <executions>
    <execution>
      <id>scala-compile-first</id>                    ◁─┐  Compiles Scala
      <phase>process-resources</phase>                 ❶  source
      <goals>
        <goal>add-source</goal>
        <goal>compile</goal>
      </goals>
    </execution>
  </executions>
</plugin>
<plugin>
  <groupId>org.apache.maven.plugins</groupId>
  <artifactId>maven-compiler-plugin</artifactId>
  <executions>
    <execution>                                        ◁─┐  Compiles Java
      <phase>compile</phase>                            ❷  source
      <goals>
        <goal>compile</goal>
      </goals>
    </execution>
  </executions>
</plugin>
```

You can configure the maven-scala-plugin to compile the Scala source in the process-resources phase of your Maven build ❶. The process-resources phase happens just before the compile phase ❷, which is where the Java source is compiled. You didn't specify where your Scala source was, so the maven-scala-plugin used the default location of src/main/scala. Now all class files are saved into the target/classes folder and so will be on the same classpath when you run your application.

The source for this example is in chapter11/scala-router-javacontext of the book's source. To run the example, use the following Maven command:

```
mvn compile exec:java
```

You should now know some of the concepts needed to create routes in the Scala DSL. The next step would be to try out your own Scala route by either copying the example from this book, or by using the camel-archetype-scala archetype to create your own Scala DSL project. This archetype was mentioned in table 11.1, earlier in the chapter.

11.6 *Summary and best practices*

Knowing how to create Camel projects is very important, and you may have wondered why we chose to discuss this so late in the book. We felt it was best to focus on the core concepts first and worry about project setup details later. Also, you should now have a better idea of what cool Camel applications you can create, having read about the features first. At this point, though, you should be well-equipped to start your own Camel application and make it do useful work.

Before we move on, there are a few key ideas that you should take away from this chapter:

- *The easiest way to create Camel applications is with Maven archetypes.* Nothing is worse than having to type out a bunch of boilerplate code for new projects. The Maven archetypes that are provided by Camel will get you started much faster.
- *The easiest way to manage Camel library dependencies is with Maven.* Camel is just a Java framework, so you can use whatever build system you like to develop your Camel projects. Using Maven will eliminate many of the hassles of tracking down JAR files from remote repos, letting you focus more on your business code than the library dependencies.
- *It's easy to load up a Maven-based Camel project in Eclipse.* Whether you use the maven-eclipse-plugin or m2eclipse, importing Camel projects is easy.
- *If you find no component in Camel for your use case, create your own.* Camel allows you to write and load up your own custom components easily. There's even a Maven archetype for starting a custom component project.
- *Use interceptors to inject processing around nodes in a route.* It's true, Camel interceptors are an advanced topic. They give you the additional power to control or monitor what's happening inside a route.
- *You don't have to write routes in Java or Spring if you don't want to.* Camel also provides DSLs in Scala and Groovy.

Next on the agenda is how to monitor and manage your Camel application. Then we'll look at how to deploy to a production environment.

*Management
and monitoring*

12

This chapter covers

- Monitoring Camel instances
- Tracking application activities
- Using notifications
- Managing Camel applications
- Managing custom components

Applications in production are often critical for businesses. That's especially true for applications that sit at an intermediate tier and integrate all the business applications and partners—Camel is often in this role.

To help ensure high availability, your organization must monitor its production applications. By doing so, you can gain important insight into the applications and foresee trends that otherwise could cause business processes to suffer. In addition, monitoring also helps with related issues, such as operations reporting, service level agreement (SLA) enforcement, and audit trails.

It's also vital for the operations staff to be able to fully manage the applications. For example, if an incident occurs, staff may need to stop parts of the application from running while the incident investigations occur. You'll also need management capabilities to carry out scheduled maintenance or upgrades of your applications.

Management and monitoring are often two sides of the same coin. For example, management tooling includes monitoring capabilities in a single coherent dashboard, allowing a full overview for the operations staff.

In this chapter, we'll review different strategies for monitoring your Camel applications. We'll first cover the most common approach, which is to check on the health of those applications. Then we'll look at the options for tracking activity and managing those Camel applications.

12.1   *Monitoring Camel*

It's standard practice to monitor systems with periodic health checks.

For people, checking one's health involves measuring parameters at regular intervals, such as pulse, temperature, and blood pressure. By checking over a period of time, you not only know the current values but also trends, such as whether the temperature is rising. All together, these data give insight into the health of the person.

For a software system, you can gather system-level data such as CPU load, memory usage, and disk usage. You can also collect application-level data, such as message load, response time, and many other parameters. This data tells you about the health of the system.

Checks on the health of Camel applications can occur at three levels:

- *Network level*—This is the most basic level, where you check that the network connectivity is working.
- *JVM level*—At this level, you check the JVM that hosts the Camel application. The JVM exposes a standard set of data using the JMX technology.
- *Application level*—Here you check the Camel application using JMX or other techniques.

To perform these checks, you need different tools and technologies. The Simple Network Management Protocol (SNMP) enables both JVM and system-level checks. Java Management Extensions (JMX) is another technology that offers similar capabilities to SNMP. You might use a mix of both: SNMP is older and more mature and is often used in large system-management tools such as IBM Tivoli, HP OpenView, and Nagios. JMX, on the other hand, is a pure Java standard and is used by Fuse HQ and Hyperic.

In the following sections, we'll go over the three levels and look at some approaches you can use for performing automatic and periodic health checks on your Camel applications.

12.1.1 *Checking health at the network level*

The most basic health check you can do is to check whether a system is alive. You may be familiar with the ping command, which you use to send a ping request to a remote host. Camel doesn't provide a ping service out of the box, but creating such a service is easy. The ping service only reveals whether Camel is running or not, but that will do for a basic check.

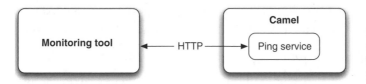

Figure 12.1   A monitoring tool monitors Camel with a ping service by sending periodic HTTP GET requests.

Suppose you have been asked to create such a ping service for Rider Auto Parts. The service is to be integrated with the existing management tools. You choose to expose the ping service over HTTP, which is a universal protocol that the management tool easily can leverage. The scenario is illustrated in figure 12.1.

Implementing the service in Camel is easy using the Jetty component. All you have to do is expose a route that returns the response, as follows:

```
from("jetty:http//0.0.0.0:8080/ping").transform(constant("PONG\n"));
```

When the service is running, you can invoke an HTTP GET, which should return the PONG response.

You can try this on your own with the book's source code. In the chapter12/health directory, invoke this Maven goal:

```
mvn compile exec:java -PPingService
```

Then invoke the HTTP GET using either a web browser or the curl command:

```
curl http://0.0.0.0:8080/ping
PONG
```

The ping service can be enhanced to leverage the JVM and Camel APIs to gather additional data about the state of the internals of your application.

Another use for the ping service is when using a load balancer in front of multiple instances of Camel applications. This is often done to address high availability, as shown in figure 12.2. The load balancer will call the ping service to assess whether the particular Camel instance is ready for regular service calls.

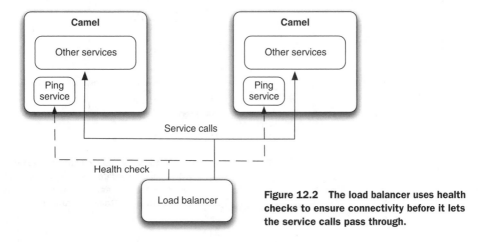

Figure 12.2   The load balancer uses health checks to ensure connectivity before it lets the service calls pass through.

Network-level checks offer a quick and coarse assessment of the system's state of health. Let's move on to the JVM level, where you monitor Camel using JMX.

12.1.2 Checking health at the JVM level

The Simple Network Management Protocol (SNMP) is a standard for monitoring network-attached devices. It's traditionally used to monitor the health of servers at the OS level by checking parameters such as CPU load, disk space, memory usage, and network traffic, but it can also be used to check parameters at the application level, such as the JVM.

Java has a built-in SNMP agent that exposes general information, such as memory and thread usage, and that issues notifications on low memory conditions. This allows you to use existing SNMP-aware tooling to monitor the JVM where Camel is running.

There is also a wide range of commercial and open source monitoring tools that use SNMP. Some are simpler and have a shell interface, and others have a powerful GUI. You may work in an organization that already uses a few selected monitoring tools, so make sure these tools can be used to monitor your Camel applications as well.

The SNMP agent in the JVM is limited to only exposing data at the JVM level; it can't be used to gather information about the Java applications that are running. JMX, in contrast, is capable of monitoring and managing both the JVM and the applications running on it.

In the next section, we'll look at how you can use JMX to monitor Camel at the JVM and application levels.

12.1.3 Checking health at the application level

Camel provides JMX monitoring and management out of the box in the form of an agent that leverages the JMX technology. This is illustrated in figure 12.3.

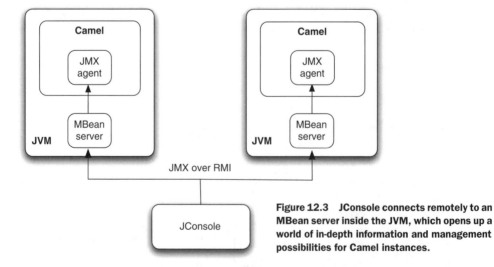

Figure 12.3   JConsole connects remotely to an MBean server inside the JVM, which opens up a world of in-depth information and management possibilities for Camel instances.

The JMX agent exposes remotely (over Remote Method Invocation) a wealth of standard details about the JVM, and some Camel information as well. The former is standard in the JDK, and the latter is provided by Camel. The most prominent feature the Camel JMX agent offers is the ability to remotely control the lifecycle of any service in Camel. For example, you can stop routes and later bring those routes into action again. You can even shut down Camel itself.

So how do you use JMX with Camel? Camel comes preconfigured with JMX enabled at the *developer level*, by which we mean that Camel allows you to connect to the JVM from the same localhost where the JVM is running. If you need to manage Camel from a remote host, you'll need to explicitly enable this in Camel.

We think this is important to cover thoroughly, so we've devoted the next section to this topic.

12.2 *Using JMX with Camel*

To use JMX with Camel, you need the following four Spring JAR files on the classpath:

- spring-core.jar
- spring-beans.jar
- spring-context.jar
- spring-aop.jar

These JARs are needed because Camel uses Spring JMX to expose its managed beans to the JMX server. Using Spring JMX is much easier than using the low-level clumsy JMX API. With Spring JMX, you can add a few JMX annotations in the Camel codebase to expose the information you want to manage from JMX.

When Camel starts, it logs at INFO level whether JMX is enabled or not:

```
2010-01-09 11:15:23,520 [viceMain.main()] INFO  DefaultCamelContext
- JMX enabled. Using DefaultManagedLifecycleStrategy.
```

If those four Spring JARs are missing, Camel will report it as follows:

```
2010-01-09 11:44:07,960 [viceMain.main()] WARN  DefaultCamelContext
- Could not find needed classes for JMX lifecycle strategy. Needed
class is in spring-context.jar using Spring 2.5 or newer
(spring-jmx.jar using Spring 2.0.x). NoClassDefFoundError:
org/springframework/jmx/export/metadata/JmxAttributeSource
2010-01-09 11:44:07,960 [viceMain.main()] WARN  DefaultCamelContext
- Cannot use JMX. Fallback to using DefaultManagementStrategy.
```

With Maven, it's easy to ensure that the JARs are included in the classpath—you just add a dependency for the camel-spring component:

```
<dependency>
    <groupId>org.apache.camel</groupId>
    <artifactId>camel-spring</artifactId>
    <version>2.5.0</version>
</dependency>
```

If you don't want to use `camel-spring`, you can add the aforementioned four JAR files individually.

Now let's look at how to use a simple management tool with Camel.

12.2.1 Using JConsole to manage Camel

Java provides a JMX tool named *JConsole*. You'll use it to connect to a Camel instance and see what information is available.

First, you need to start a Camel instance. You can do this from the chapter12/ health directory using this Maven command:

```
mvn compile exec:java -PPingService
```

Then, from another shell, you can start JConsole by invoking `jconsole`.

When JConsole starts, it displays a window with two radio buttons. The Local radio button is used to connect to existing JVMs running on the same host. The Remote radio button is used for remote management, which we'll cover shortly. The Local should already list a process, and you can click the Connect button to connect JConsole to the Camel instance. Figure 12.4 shows the Camel MBeans (Management Beans) that are visible from JConsole.

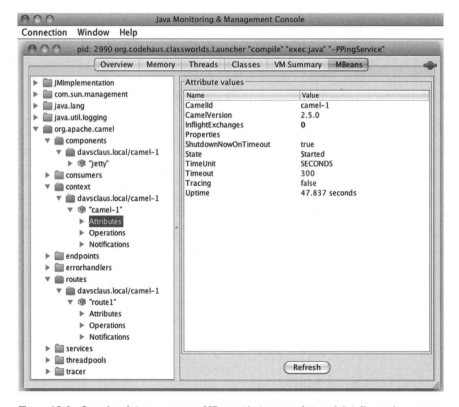

Figure 12.4   Camel registers numerous MBeans that expose internal details, such as usage statistics and management operations.

Camel registers many MBeans that expose statistics and operations for management. Those MBeans are divided into nine categories, which are listed in table 12.1. Most MBeans expose a set of standard information and operations, concerning things such as lifecycle. We encourage you to spend a moment browsing the MBeans in JConsole to see what information they provide.

Table 12.1 Categories of exposed Camel MBeans

Category	Description
Components	Lists the components in use.
Consumers	Lists all the input consumers for the Camel routes. Some consumers have additional information and operations, such as the JMS, Timer, and File/FTP consumers.
Context	Identifies the `CamelContext` itself. This is the MBean you need if you want to shut down Camel.
Endpoints	Lists the endpoints in use.
Errorhandlers	Lists the error handlers in use. You can manage error handling at runtime, such as by changing the number of redelivery attempts or the delay between redeliveries.
Routes	Lists all the routes in use. Here you can obtain route statistics, such as the number of messages completed, failed, and so on.
Services	Lists miscellaneous services in use.
Threadpools	Lists all the thread pools in use. Here you can obtain statistics about the number of threads currently active and the maximum number of threads that have been active. You can also adjust the core and maximum pool size of the thread pool.
Tracer	Allows you to manage the Tracer service. The Tracer is a Camel-specific service that's used for tracing how messages are routed at runtime. We'll cover the use of the Tracer in detail in section 12.3.4.

When you need to monitor and manage a Camel instance from a remote computer, you must enable remote management in Camel.

12.2.2 Using JConsole to remotely manage Camel

To be able to remotely manage Camel, you need to instruct Camel to register a JMX connector. That can be done in the following three ways:

- Using JVM properties
- Configuring the `ManagementAgent` from Java
- Configuring the JMX agent from Spring XML

We'll go over each of these three methods in the following sections.

USING JVM PROPERTIES

By specifying the following JVM property on JVM startup, you can tell Camel to create a JMX connector for remote management:

```
-Dorg.apache.camel.jmx.createRmiConnector=true
```

If you do this, Camel will log, at INFO level on startup, the JMX service URL that's needed to connect. It will look something like this:

```
2010-01-09 13:28:32,216 [main            ] INFO  DefaultManagementAgent
- JMX Connector thread started and listening at:
service:jmx:rmi:///jndi/rmi://davsclaus.local:1099/jmxrmi/camel
```

To connect to a remote JMX agent, you can use the Remote radio button from JConsole and enter the service URL listed in the log. By default, port 1099 is used, but this can be configured using the org.apache.camel.jmx.rmiConnector.registryPort JVM property.

CONFIGURING THE MANAGEMENTAGENT FROM JAVA

The org.apache.camel.management.DefaultManagementAgent class is provided by Camel as the default JMX agent. You can configure it to allow remote connections as shown here:

```
public class PingServiceMain {
    public static void main(String[] args) throws Exception {
        CamelContext context = new DefaultCamelContext();

        DefaultManagementAgent agent = new DefaultManagementAgent(context);
        agent.setCreateConnector(true);
        context.getManagementStrategy().setManagementAgent(agent);

        context.addRoutes(new PingService());
        context.start();
    }
}
```

All you need to do is create an instance of DefaultManagementAgent, configure it to create a connector, and tell Camel to use it. The agent can also configure the registry port by using the setRegistryPort method.

But there is a simpler way: you can configure the settings directly using the ManagementAgent, as follows:

```
public class PingServiceMain {
    public static void main(String[] args) throws Exception {
        CamelContext context = new DefaultCamelContext();

        context.getManagementStrategy().getManagementAgent()
            .setCreateConnector(true);

        context.addRoutes(new PingService());
        context.start();
    }
}
```

CONFIGURING A JMX AGENT FROM SPRING XML

If you use Spring XML with Camel, configuring a JMX connector is even easier. All you have to do is add <jmxAgent> in the <camelContext>, as shown here:

```
<camelContext id="camel" xmlns="http://camel.apache.org/schema/spring">
    <jmxAgent id="agent" createConnector="true"/>
    ...
</camelContext>
```

The `<jmxAgent>` also offers a `registryPort` attribute that you can use to set a specific port number if the default port 1099 isn't suitable.

You may have noticed that this example doesn't provide any credentials when connecting to a JMX agent. This may not be appropriate in production environments, so you can enable authentication with JMX. The JMX documentation explains how to use security with JMX: http://download.oracle.com/javase/6/docs/technotes/guides/management/agent.html.

Now that you've seen how to check the health of your applications, it's time to learn how to keep an eye on what your applications are doing.

12.3 *Tracking application activity*

Beyond monitoring an application's health, you need to ensure it operates as expected. For example, if an application starts malfunctioning or has stopped entirely, it may harm business. There may also be business or security requirements to track particular services for compliance and auditing.

A Camel application used to integrate numerous systems may often be difficult to track because of its complexity. It may have inputs using a wide range of transports, and schedules that trigger more inputs as well. Routes may be dynamic if you're using content-based routing to direct messages to different destinations. And there are errors occurring at all levels related to validation, security, and transport. Confronted with such complexity, how can you keep track of the behavior of your Camel applications?

You do this by tracking the traces that various activities leave behind. By configuring Camel to leave traces, you can get a fairly good insight into what's going on, both in real time and after the fact. Activity can be tracked using logs, whose verbosity can be configured to your needs. Camel also offers a notification system that you can leverage.

Let's look at how you can use log files and notifications to track activities.

12.3.1 *Using log files*

Monitoring tools can be tailored to look for patterns, such as error messages in logs, and they can use pattern matching to react appropriately, such as by raising an alert. Log files have been around for decades, so any monitoring tool should have good support for efficient log file scanning. Even if this solution sounds basic, it's a solution used extensively in today's IT world.

Log files are read not only by monitoring tools but also by people, such as operations, support, or engineering staff. That puts a burden on both Camel and your applications to produce enough evidence so that both humans and machines can diagnose the issues reported.

Camel offers four options for producing logs to track activities:

- *Using core logs*—Camel logs various types of information in its core logs. Major events and errors are reported by default.
- *Using custom logging*—You can leverage Camel's logging infrastructure to output your own log entries. You can do this from different places, such as from the

route using the log EIP or log component. You can also use regular logging from Java code to output logs from your custom beans.

- *Using Tracer*—Tracer is used for tracing how and when a message is routed in Camel. Camel logs, at INFO level, each and every step a message takes. Tracer offers a wealth of configuration options and features.
- *Using notifications*—Camel emits notifications that you can use to track activities in real time.

Let's look at these options in more detail.

12.3.2 *Using core logs*

Camel emits a lot of information at DEBUG logging level and an incredible amount at TRACE logging level. These levels are only appropriate for development, where the core logs provide great details for the developers.

In production, you'll want to use INFO logging level, which generates a limited amount of data. At this level, you won't find information about activity for individual messages—for that you need to use notifications or the Tracer, which we'll cover in section 12.3.4.

The core logs in production usage usually only provide limited details for tracking activity. Important lifecycle events such as the application being started or stopped are logged, as are any errors that occur during routing.

12.3.3 *Using custom logging*

Custom logging is useful if you're required to keep an audit log. With custom logging, you're in full control of what gets logged.

In EIP terms, it's the Wire Tap pattern that describes this problem. By tapping into an existing route, you can tap messages to an audit channel. This audit channel, which is often an internal queue (SEDA or VM transport), is then consumed by a dedicated audit service, which takes care of logging the messages.

USING WIRE TAP FOR CUSTOM LOGGING

Let's look at an example. At Rider Auto Parts, you're required to log any incoming orders. Figure 12.5 shows the situation where orders flowing in from CSV files are wire-tapped to an audit service before moving on for further processing.

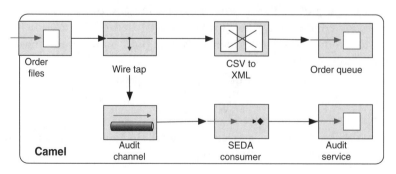

Figure 12.5 Using a wire tap to tap incoming files to an audit service before the file is translated to XML and sent to an order queue for further processing

Implementing the routes outlined in figure 12.5 in Camel is fairly straightforward:

```
public void configure() throws Exception {
    from("file://rider/orders")
        .wireTap("seda:audit")
        .bean(OrderCsvToXmlBean.class)
        .to("jms:queue:orders");

    from("seda:audit")
        .bean(AuditService.class, "auditFile");
}
```

The first route is routing incoming order files. These are wire-tapped to an internal SEDA queue ("`seda:audit`") for further processing. The messages are then transformed from CSV to XML using the `OrderCsvToXmlBean` bean before being sent to a JMS queue.

The second route is used for auditing. It consumes the tapped messages and processes them with an `AuditService` bean, which follows:

```
public class AuditService {
    private Log LOG = LogFactory.getLog(AuditService.class);

    public void auditFile(String body) {
        String[] parts = body.split(",");
        String id = parts[0];
        String customerId = parts[1];
        String msg = "Customer " + customerId + " send order id " + id;
        LOG.info(msg);
    }
}
```

This implementation of the `AuditService` bean has been kept simple by logging the audit messages using the Apache Commons Logging log kit. The actual logging is done in the `auditFile` method.

The source code for the book contains this example in the chapter12/logging directory, which you can try using the following Maven goal:

```
mvn test -Dtest=AuditTest
```

USING THE CAMEL LOG COMPONENT

Camel provides a Log component that's capable of logging the Camel `Message` using a standard format at certain interesting points. To leverage the Log component, you simply route a message to it, as follows:

```
public void configure() throws Exception {
    from("file://rider/orders")
        .to("log:input)
        .bean(OrderCsvToXmlBean.class)
        .to("log:asXml)
        .to("jms:queue:orders");
}
```

In this route, you use the Log component in two places. The first is to log the incoming file, and the second is after the transformation.

You can try this example using the following Maven goal from the chapter12/ logging directory:

```
mvn test -Dtest=LogComponentTest
```

If you run the example, it will log the following:

```
2010-01-10 14:00:23,389 [: FileComponent] INFO  incoming
- Exchange[BodyType:org.apache.camel.component.file.GenericFile,
Body:123,4444,20100110,222,1]
2010-01-10 14:00:23,399 [: FileComponent] INFO  asXml
- Exchange[BodyType:String,
Body:<order><id>123/id><customerId>4444/customerId><date>20100110
</date><item><id>222</id><amount>1</amount></itemn></order>]
```

By default, the Log component will log the message body and its type at INFO logging level. Notice that in the first log line, the type is GenericFile, which represents a java.io.File in Camel. In the second log line, the type has been changed to String, because the message was transformed to a String using the OrderCsvToXmlBean bean.

You can customize what the Log component should log by using the many options it supports. Consult the Camel Log documentation for the options (http:// camel.apache.org/log.html). For example, to make the messages less verbose, you can disable showing the body type and limit the length of the message body being logged by using the following configuration:

```
log:incoming?showBodyType=false&maxChars=40
```

That results in the following output:

```
2010-01-10 14:06:10,187 [: FileComponent] INFO  incoming
- Exchange[Body:123,4444,20100110,222,1]
2010-01-10 14:06:10,197 [: FileComponent] INFO  asXml
- Exchange[Body:<order><id>123/id><customerId>444...]
```

> **TIP** The Log component has a showAll option to log everything from the Exchange.

The Log component is used to log information from the Exchange, but what if you want to log a message in a custom way? What you need is something like System. out.println, so you can input whatever String message you like into the log. That's where the Log EIP comes in.

USING THE LOG EIP

The Log EIP is built into the Camel DSL. It allows you to log a human-readable message from anywhere in a route, as if you were using System.out.println. It's primarily meant for developers, so they can quickly output a message to the log console. But that doesn't mean you can't use it for other purposes as well.

Suppose you want to log the filename you received as input. This is easy with the Log EIP—all you have to do is pass in the message as a String:

```
public void configure() throws Exception {
    from("file://riders/orders")
        .log("We got incoming file ${file:name} containing: ${body}")
        .bean(OrderCsvToXmlBean.class)
```

```
        .to("jms:queue:orders");
}
```

The `String` is based on Camel's Simple expression language, which supports the use of placeholders that are evaluated at runtime. In this example, the filename is represented by `${file:name}` and the message body by `${body}`. If you want to know more about the Simple expression language, refer to appendix A.

You can run this example using the following Maven goal from the chapter12/logging directory:

```
mvn test -Dtest=LogEIPTest
```

If you run this example, it will log the following:

```
2010-01-10 15:11:18,001 [: FileComponent] INFO  route1
- We got incoming file someorder.csv containing: 123,4444,20100110
```

The Log EIP will, by default, log at `INFO` level using the route ID as the logger name. In this example, the route was not explicitly named, so Camel assigned it the name `route1`.

Using the Log EIP from Spring XML is also easy, as shown here:

```
<camelContext id="camel" xmlns="http://camel.apache.org/schema/spring">
  <route>
    <from uri="file://target/rider/orders"/>
    <log message="Incoming file ${file:name} containing: ${body}"/>
    <bean beanType="camelinaction.OrderCsvToXmlBean"/>
    <to uri="jms:queue:orders"/>
  </route>
</camelContext>
```

The Spring example is also provided in the source code for the book, which you can try using the following Maven goal:

```
mvn test -Dtest=LogEIPSpringTest
```

The Log EIP also offers options to configure the logging level and log name, in case you want to customize those as well, as shown below in Spring XML:

```
<log message="Incoming file ${file:name} containing: ${body}"
    logName="Incoming" loggingLevel="DEBUG"/>
```

In the Java DSL, the logging level and log name are the first two parameters. The third parameter is the log message:

```
.log(LoggingLevel.DEBUG, "Incoming",
    "Incoming file ${file:name} containing: ${body}")
```

Anyone who has had to browse millions of log lines to investigate an incident knows it can be hard to correlate messages.

USING CORRELATION IDS

When logging messages in a system, the messages being processed can easily get interleaved, which means the log lines will be interleaved as well. What you need is a way to correlate those log messages so you can tell which log lines are from which messages.

You do this by assigning a unique ID to each created message. In Camel, this ID is the `ExchangeId`, which you can grab from the `Exchange` using the `exchange.get-ExchangeId()` method.

TIP You can tell the Log component to log the ExchangeId by using the following option: showExchangeId=true. When using the Log EIP, you can use ${id} from the Simple expression language to grab the ID.

To help understand how and when messages are being routed, Camel offers Tracer, which logs message activity as it occurs.

12.3.4 Using Tracer

Tracer's role is to trace how and when messages are routed in Camel. It does this by intercepting each message being passed from one node to another during routing. Figure 12.6 illustrates this principle.

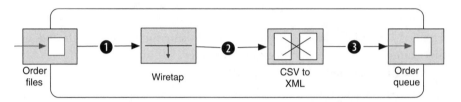

Figure 12.6   Tracer sits between each node in the route (at ❶, ❷, and ❸) and traces the message flow.

You may remember being told that Camel has a Channel sitting between each node in a route—at points ❶, ❷, and ❸ in figure 12.6. The Channel has multiple purposes, such as error handling, security, and interception. Because the Tracer is implemented as an interceptor, it falls under the control of the Channel, which at runtime will invoke it.

To use the Tracer, you need to enable it, which is easily done in either the Java DSL or Spring XML. In the Java DSL, you enable it by calling context.setTracing(true) from within the RouteBuilder class:

```
public void configure() throws Exception {
    context.setTracing(true);
    ...
}
```

In Spring XML, you enable the Tracer from <camelContext> as follows:

```
<camelContext id="camel" trace="true"
            xmlns="http://camel.apache.org/schema/spring">
```

When running with Tracer enabled, Camel will record trace logs at INFO level, which at first may seem a bit verbose. To reduce the verbosity, we have configured the Tracer to not show properties and headers. Here is an example of Tracer output:

```
2010-01-10 16:40:58,229 [: FileComponent] INFO  Tracer
- ca18a05b-a7a6-401b-8f83-e97ba35df87e >>> (route1)
from(file://target/rider/orders) --> wireTap(seda://audit) <<<
Pattern:InOnly, BodyType:org.apache.camel.component.file.GenericFile,
Body:123,4444,20100110,222,1
```

```
2010-01-10 16:40:58,241 [: FileComponent] INFO  Tracer
- ca18a05b-a7a6-401b-8f83-e97ba35df87e >>> (route1) wireTap
(seda://audit) --> camelinaction.OrderCsvToXmlBean@129103 <<<
Pattern:InOnly, BodyType:org.apache.camel.component.file.GenericFile,
Body:123,4444,20100110,222,1
2010-01-10 16:40:58,241 [1: seda://audit] INFO  Tracer
- b4d4c842-3884-41aa-a216-d230a6661a9e >>> (route2)
from(seda://audit) --> camelinaction.AuditService@5db23e <<<
Pattern:InOnly, BodyType:org.apache.camel.component.file.GenericFile,
Body:123,4444,20100110,222,1
2010-01-10 16:40:58,251 [: FileComponent] INFO  Tracer
- ca18a05b-a7a6-401b-8f83-e97ba35df87e >>> (route1)
camelinaction.OrderCsvToXmlBean@129103 --> seda://queue:orders <<<
Pattern:InOnly, BodyType:String,
Body:<order><id>123/id><customerId>4444/customerId><date>20100110
</date><item><id>222</id><amount>1</amount></item></order>
```

The interesting thing to note from the trace logs is that the log starts with the exchange ID, which you can use to correlate messages. In this example, there are two different IDs in play: `ca18a05b-a7a6-401b-8f83-e97ba35df87e` and `b4d4c842-3884-41aa-a216-d230a6661a9e`. You may wonder why we have two IDs when there is only one incoming message. That's because the wire tap creates a copy of the incoming message, and the copied message will use a new exchange ID because it's being routed as a separate process.

Next, the Tracer outputs which route the message is currently at, followed by the `from --> to` nodes. This is probably the key information when using Tracer, because you can see each individual step the message takes in Camel.

Then the Tracer logs the message exchange pattern, which is either `InOnly` or `InOut`. Finally, it logs the information from the `Message`, just as the Log component would do.

> **TIP** You can use the Delay interceptor to slow processing down to a pace we humans can follow. For example, you could delay and tail the log file, watching what happens in the log file while the message is being routed, to get a better understanding of what's going on. You can learn more about the Delay interceptor in the Camel documentation: http://camel.apache.org/delay-interceptor.html.

CUSTOMIZING THE TRACER

We just said that we had customized the Tracer to be less verbose. This can be done by defining a bean in the `Registry` with the bean ID `traceFormatter`. In Spring XML this is easy—all you do is this:

```
<bean id="traceFormatter"
      class="org.apache.camel.processor.interceptor.DefaultTraceFormatter">
   <property name="showProperties" value="false"/>
   <property name="showHeaders" value="false"/>
</bean>
```

The formatter has many other options that you can read about in its online documentation (http://camel.apache.org/tracer). One of the options is `maxChars`, which can limit the message body being logged. For example, setting it to a value of 200 will limit the Tracer to only output at most 200 characters.

If you have many routes, the Tracer will output a lot of logs. Fortunately, you can customize the Tracer to only trace certain routes. You can even do this at runtime using JMX, but we'll get to that a bit later.

ENABLING OR DISABLING TRACER FOR SPECIFIC ROUTES

Remember that you can enable the Tracer from the `<camelContext>` tag? You can do the same with the `<route>` tag.

Suppose you only wanted to trace the first route—you could enable the Tracer on that particular route, as shown here:

```
<camelContext id="camel" xmlns="http://camel.apache.org/schema/spring">
    <route trace="true">
        <from uri="file://rider/orders"/>
        <wireTap uri="seda:audit"/>
        <bean beanType="camelinaction.OrderCsvToXmlBean"/>
        <to uri="jms:queue:orders"/>
    </route>

    <route>
        <from uri="seda:audit"/>
        <bean beanType="camelinaction.AuditService"/>
    </route>
</camelContext>
```

Doing this from the Java DSL is a bit different. You need to do it using the fluent builder syntax by using either `tracing()` or `noTracing()`, as follows:

```
public void configure() throws Exception {
    from("file://target/rider/orders")
        .tracing()
        .wireTap("seda:audit")
        .bean(OrderCsvToXmlBean.class)
        .to("jms:queue:orders");

    from("seda:audit")
        .bean(AuditService.class, "auditFile");
}
```

If a route isn't explicitly configured with a Tracer, it will fall back and leverage the configuration from the `CamelContext`. This allows you to quickly turn tracing on and off from the `CamelContext` but still have some special routes with their own settings.

The Tracer can also be managed using JMX. This allows you to enable tracing for a while to see what happens and identify issues.

MANAGING TRACER USING JMX

The Tracer can be managed from the JMX console in two places. You can enable or disable tracing at either the context or at routes. For example, to enable tracing globally, you could change the tracing attribute to `true` at the `CamelContext` MBean. You could do the same on a per route basis using the `Routes` MBeans.

You can configure what the Tracer logs from the `Tracer` MBean, as shown in figure 12.7.

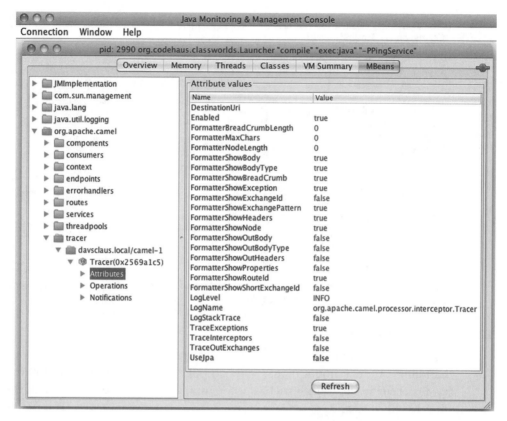

Figure 12.7 Managing the Tracer from JMX allows you to customize the trace logging and change many attributes at runtime.

We've prepared an example for you to try in the source code for the book. First, run this Maven goal in the chapter12/tracer directory:

```
mvn compile exec:java -PManageTracer
```

This will start an application that will run for a while.

Then start jconsole and connect to the application. Click on the MBeans tab and expand the org.apache.camel node in the tree. Figure 12.8 shows where you're going.

Click on the value for the Tracing attribute, which should be editable. Change the value from false to true, and press Enter to confirm. You should be able to see the changes in the console logged by the application.

Spend some time playing with this. For example, change some of the other options on the Tracer.

Monitoring applications via the core logs, custom logging, and Tracer is like looking into Camel's internal journal after the fact. If the log files get very big, it may feel like you're looking for a needle in a haystack. Sometimes you might prefer to have Camel call you when particular events occur. This is where the notification mechanism comes into play.

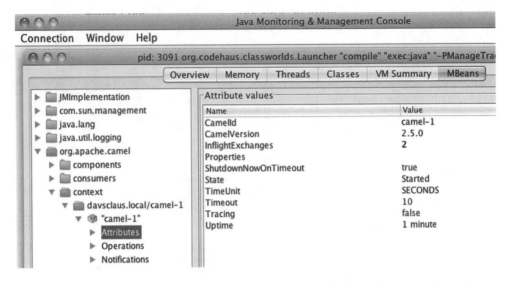

Figure 12.8   To enable tracing, select the `CamelContext` under the Context node and change the `Tracing` attribute from `false` to `true`.

12.3.5 *Using notifications*

For fine-grained tracking of activity, Camel's management module offers notifiers for handling internal notifications. These notifications are generated when specific events occur inside Camel, such as when an instance starts or stops, when an exception has been caught, or when a message is created or completed. The notifiers subscribe to these events as listeners, and they react when an event is received.

Camel uses a pluggable architecture, allowing you to plug in and use your own notifier, which we'll cover later in this section. Camel provides the following notifiers out of the box:

- `LoggingEventNotifier`—A notifier for logging a text representation of the event using the Apache Commons Logging framework. This means you can use log4j, which has a broad range of appenders that can dispatch log messages to remote servers using UDP, TCP, JMS, SNMP, email, and so on.
- `PublishEventNotifier`—A notifier for dispatching the event to any kind of Camel endpoint. This allows you to leverage Camel transports to broadcast the message any way you want.
- `JmxNotificationEventNotifier`—A notifier for broadcasting the events as JMX notifications. For example, management and monitoring tooling can be used to subscribe to the notifications.

You'll learn in the following sections how to set up and use an event notifier and how to build and use a custom notifier.

WARNING   Because routing each exchange produces at least two notifications, you can be overloaded with thousands of notifications. That's why you should always filter out unwanted notifications. The `PublishEventNotifier` will leverage Camel to route the event message, which will potentially induce a second load on your system. That's why the notifier is configured by default to not generate new events during processing of events.

CONFIGURING AN EVENT NOTIFIER

Camel doesn't use event notifiers by default, so to use a notifier you must configure it. This is done by setting the notifier instance you wish to use on the `ManagementStrategy`. When using the Java DSL, this is done as shown here:

```
LoggingEventNotifier notifier = new LoggingEventNotifier();
notifier.setLogName("rider.EventLog");
notifier.setIgnoreCamelContextEvents(true);
notifier.setIgnoreRouteEvents(true);
notifier.setIgnoreServiceEvents(true);
context.getManagementStrategy().setEventNotifier(notifier);
```

First you create an instance of `LoggingEventNotifier`, because you're going to log the events using log4j. Then you set the log name you wish to use. In this case, you're only interested in some of the events, so you ignore the ones you aren't interested in.

The configuration when using Spring XML is a bit different, because Camel will pick up the notifier automatically when it scans the registry for beans of type `EventNotifier` on startup. This means you just have to declare a Spring bean, like this:

```
<bean id="eventLogger"
      class="org.apache.camel.management.LoggingEventNotifier">
    <property name="logName" value="rider.EventLog"/>
    <property name="ignoreCamelContextEvents" value="true"/>
    <property name="ignoreRouteEvents" value="true"/>
    <property name="ignoreServiceEvents" value="true"/>
</bean>
```

You can also write your custom `EventNotifier` instead of using the built-in notifiers.

USING A CUSTOM EVENT NOTIFIER

Rider Auto Parts wants to integrate an existing Camel application with the company's centralized error log database. They already have a Java library that's capable of publishing to the database, and this makes the task much easier. Figure 12.9 illustrates the situation.

They decide to implement a custom event notifier named `RiderEventNotifier`, which uses their own Java code, allowing ultimate flexibility. The following listing shows the important snippets of how to implement this.

In listing 12.1, you extend the `EventNotifierSupport` class, which is an abstract class meant to be extended by custom notifiers. If you don't want to extend this class, you can implement the `EventNotifier` interface instead. The `RiderFailurePublisher` class is the existing Java library for publishing failure events to the database.

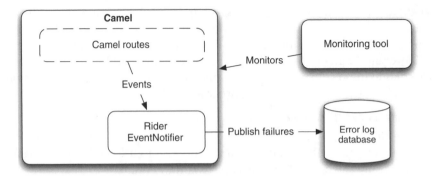

Figure 12.9   Failure events must be published into the centralized error log database using the custom `RiderEventNotifier`.

Listing 12.1   A custom event notifier publishes failure events to a central log database

```
public class RiderEventNotifier extends EventNotifierSupport {

    private RiderFailurePublisher publisher;

    public void notify(EventObject eventObject) throws Exception {       ❶ Filters
        if (eventObject instanceof ExchangeFailedEvent)                     failure
            notifyFailure((ExchangeFailedEvent) eventObject);               events
        }
    }

    protected void notifyFailure(ExchangeFailedEvent event) {
        String id = event.getExchange().getExchangeId();
        Exception cause = event.getExchange().getException();
        Date now = new Date();

        publisher.publish(appId, id, now,              ❷ Publishes
                    cause.getMessage());                 failure events
    }

    public boolean isEnabled(EventObject eventObject) {
        return true;
    }

    protected void doStart() throws Exception {}

    protected void doStop() throws Exception {}
}
```

The `notify` method is invoked by Camel with the event being passed in as a `java.util.EventObject` instance. You use an `instanceof` test to filter for the events you're interested in, which are failure events ❶. Then information is extracted from the event, such as the unique exchange ID and the exception message to be published. This information is then published using the existing Java library ❷.

   TIP   If you have any resources that must be initialized, Camel offers `doStart` and `doStop` methods for this kind of work, as shown in listing 12.1.

The source code for the book contains this example in the chapter12/notifier directory, which you can try using the following Maven goal:

```
mvn test -Dtest=RiderEventNotifierTest
```

We've now reviewed four ways to monitor Camel applications. You learned to use Camel's standard logging capabilities and to roll a custom solution when needed. In the next section, we'll take a further look at how to manage both Camel and your custom Camel components.

12.4 Managing Camel applications

We already touched on how to manage Camel in section 12.2, where we covered how to use JMX with Camel. In this section, we'll take a deeper dive into management-related use cases and show how you can management-enable your custom Camel components and services.

We'll start by looking at how you can manage the lifecycles of your Camel applications.

12.4.1 Managing Camel application lifecycles

It's essential to be able to manage the lifecycles of your Camel applications. You should be able to stop and start Camel in a reliable manner, and you should be able to pause or stop a Camel route temporarily, to avoid taking in new messages while an incident is being mitigated. Camel offers you full lifecycle management on all levels.

Suppose you want to stop an existing Camel route. To do this, you connect to the application with JMX as you learned in section 12.2. Figure 12.10 shows JConsole with the route in question selected.

As you can see in figure 12.10, route1 has been selected from the MBeans tree. You can view its attributes, which reveal various stats such as the number of exchanges completed and failed, its performance, and so on. The `State` attribute displays information about the lifecycle—whether it's started or stopped.

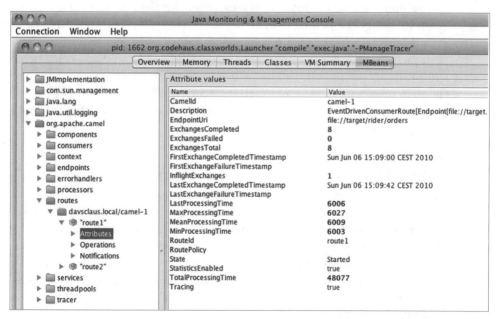

Figure 12.10 Selecting the route to manage in JConsole

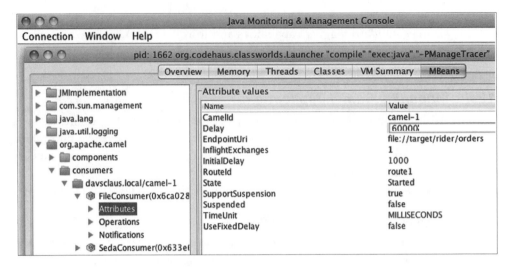

Figure 12.11   Adjusting a file consumer at runtime by changing the `Delay` attribute

To stop the route, select the Operations entry and click the `stop` operation. Then return to the Attributes entry and click the Refresh button to update the attributes. You should see the `State` attribute's value change to Stopped.

MANAGING CONSUMERS

Starting and stopping routes is a common thing to do, but what if you want to adjust how the routes behave at runtime? Camel allows you to manage the consumers, and you can adjust them at runtime.

Imagine you have a route that uses a file consumer to pick up new files, and you want to change the polling interval for the file consumer. Figure 12.11 shows how you can do this by selecting the file consumer under consumers in the MBean tree. You can then change the `Delay` attribute by clicking on it and editing it. The changes to the attributes aren't enforced immediately. You have to restart the consumer, which is done by invoking the `stop` and then the `start` operation.

You may have built some Camel components of your own that you would like to manage. This can also be done.

12.4.2 *Managing custom Camel components*

Suppose Rider Auto Parts has developed a Camel ERP component to integrate with their ERP system, and the operations staff has requested that the component be managed. The component has a verbosity switch that should be exposed for management. Running with verbosity enabled allows the operations staff to retrieve additional information from the logs, which is needed when some sort of issue has occurred.

Listing 12.2 shows how you can implement this on the `ERPEndpoint` class, which is part of the ERP component. This code listing has been abbreviated to show only the relevant parts of the listing—the full example is in the source code for the book in the chapter12/custom directory.

Listing 12.2 Management-enabling a custom endpoint

```
import org.apache.camel.spi.ManagementAware;
import org.springframework.jmx.export.annotation.ManagedAttribute;
import org.springframework.jmx.export.annotation.ManagedResource;

@ManagedResource(description = "Managed ERPEndpoint")              Exposes class
public class ERPEndpoint extends DefaultEndpoint          ❶ as MBean
        implements ManagementAware<ERPEndpoint> {

    private boolean verbose;

    public ERPEndpoint(String endpointUri, Component component) {
        super(endpointUri, component);
    }

    @ManagedAttribute
    public boolean isVerbose() {
        return verbose;
    }
                                                        Exposes attributes
                                                     ❷ for management
    @ManagedAttribute
    public void setVerbose(boolean verbose) {
        this.verbose = verbose;
    }                                                   Tells Camel
                                                     ❸ to use this
    public Object getManagedObject(ERPEndpoint object) {   MBean
        return this;
    }
}
```

If you've ever tried using the JMX API to expose the management capabilities of your custom beans, you'll know it's a painful API to leverage. It's better to go for the easy solution and leverage Spring JMX. You'll notice, in the source code from listing 12.2, that it uses the Spring @ManagedResource annotation ❶ to expose this class as an MBean. In the same way, you can expose the verbose property as a managed attribute by using the @ManagedAttribute ❷ annotation on the getter and setter methods.

What remains is to tell Camel to enlist this MBean for management, which is done by implementing the ManagementAware interface. This interface brings in the get-ManagedObject method ❸, where you simply return this.

You can run the following Maven goal from chapter12/custom directory to try out this example:

```
mvn compile exec:java -Pcustom
```

When you do, the console will output a log line every 5 seconds, as the route below illustrates:

```
from("timer:foo?period=5000")
    .setBody().simple("Hello ERP calling at ${date:now:HH:mm:ss}")
    .to("erp:foo")
    .to("log:reply");
```

What you want to do now is turn on the verbose switch from your custom ERP component. Figure 12.12 shows how this is done from JConsole.

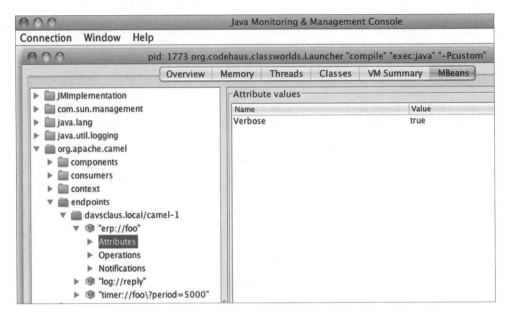

Figure 12.12   Enabling the Verbose attribute at runtime using JConsole

As you can see in figure 12.12, your custom component is listed under endpoints as erp://foo, which was the URI used in the route. The figure also shows the Verbose attribute. If you change this value to true, the console should immediately reflect this change. The first two of the following lines are from before the verbose switch was enabled. When the switch is enabled, it starts to output Calling ERP..., as shown below:

```
2010-01-30 15:09:49,118 [foo            ] INFO  reply
- Exchange[BodyType:String, Body:Simulated response from ERP]
2010-01-30 15:09:54,118 [foo            ] INFO  reply
- Exchange[BodyType:String, Body:Simulated response from ERP]
Calling ERP with: Hello ERP calling at 15:09:59
2010-01-30 15:09:59,118 [foo            ] INFO  reply
- Exchange[BodyType:String, Body:Simulated response from ERP]
Calling ERP with: Hello ERP calling at 15:10:04
2010-01-30 15:10:04,118 [foo            ] INFO  reply
- Exchange[BodyType:String, Body:Simulated response from ERP]
```

What you have just learned about management-enabling a custom component is in fact the same principle Camel uses for its components. A Camel component consists of several classes, such as Component, Endpoint, Producer, and Consumer, and you can management-enable any of those. For example, the schedule-based components, such as the Timer, allow you to manage the consumers to adjust how often they should trigger.

Congratulations! You have now learned all there is to managing Camel applications and enlisting your custom components for management.

12.5 *Summary and best practices*

A sound strategy for monitoring your applications is necessary when you take them into production. Your organization may already have strategies that must be followed for running and monitoring applications.

In this chapter, we looked at how you can monitor your Camel applications using health-level checks. You learned that existing monitoring tools could be used via SNMP or JMX protocols. Using JMX allows you to manage Camel at the application level, which is essential for lifecycle management, and performing functions such as stopping a route.

We also looked at what Camel has to offer in terms of logging. You learned about the Camel logs and how you can use custom logging. We also covered the Camel notification system, which is pluggable, allowing you to hook in your own notification adapter and send notifications to a third party.

Here are a few simple guidelines:

- *Involve the operations team.* Monitoring and management isn't an afterthought. You should involve the operations team early in the project's lifecycle. Your organization likely already has procedures for managing applications, which must be followed.
- *Use health checks.* For example, develop a *happy page* that does an internal health check and reports back on the status. A happy page can then easily be accessed from a web browser and monitoring tools.
- *Provide informative error messages.* When something goes wrong, you want the operations staff receiving the alert to be able to understand what the error is all about. If you throw exceptions from business logic, include descriptive information about what's wrong.
- *Use the Tracer.* If messages aren't being routed as expected, you can enable the Tracer to see how they're actually being routed. But beware; the Tracer can be very verbose and your logs can quickly fill up with lines if your application processes a lot of messages.
- *Read log files from testing.* Have developers read the log files to see which exceptions have been logged. This can help them preemptively fix issues that otherwise could slip into production.

Management and monitoring aren't the sole tasks the operations staff plays with regards to your Camel applications. The staff is also very much involved in the deployment process, taking your applications into production. The next chapter covers this topic, walking through the various deployment strategies.

Running and deploying Camel

This chapter covers

- Starting Camel
- Starting and stopping routes at runtime
- Shutting down Camel
- Deploying Camel

In the previous chapter, you learned all about monitoring and managing Camel. We'll now shift focus to another topic that's important to master: running and deploying Camel applications.

We'll start with the topic of running Camel—you'll need to fully understand how to start, run, and shut down Camel reliably and safely, which is imperative in a production environment. We'll also review various options you can use to tweak how Camel and routes are started. We'll continue on this path, looking at how you can dynamically start and stop routes at runtime. Your applications won't run forever, so we'll spend some time focusing on how to shut down Camel in a safe manner.

The other part of the chapter covers various strategies for deploying Camel. We'll take a look at four common runtime environments supported by Camel.

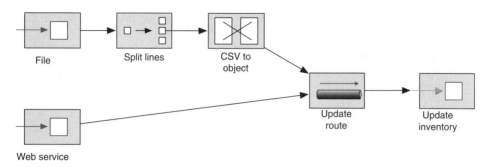

Figure 13.1   A Rider Auto Parts application accepting incoming inventory updates from either files or a web service

As we discuss these topics, we'll work through an example involving Rider Auto Parts. You've been asked to help move a recently developed application safely into production. The application receives inventory updates from suppliers, provided via a web service or files. Figure 13.1 shows a high-level diagram of the application.

13.1   Starting Camel

In chapter 1, you learned how to download, install, and run Camel. That works well in development, but the game plan changes when you take an application into production.

Starting up a Camel application in production is harder than you might think, because the order in which the routes are started may have to be arranged in a certain way to ensure a reliable startup. It's critical that the operations staff can safely manage the application in their production environment.

Let's look now at how Camel starts.

13.1.1   How Camel starts

Camel doesn't start magically by itself. Often it's the server (container) that Camel is running inside that invokes the `start` method on `CamelContext`, starting up Camel. This is also what you saw in chapter 1, where you used Camel inside a standalone Java application. A standalone Java application isn't the only deployment choice—you can also run Camel inside a container such as Spring or OSGi.

Regardless of which container you use, the same principle applies. The container must prepare and create an instance of `CamelContext` up front, before Camel can be started, as illustrated in figure 13.2.

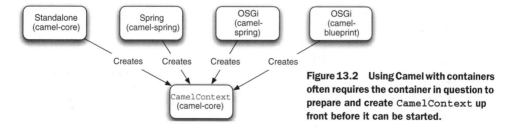

Figure 13.2   Using Camel with containers often requires the container in question to prepare and create `CamelContext` up front before it can be started.

Because Spring is a common container, we'll outline how Spring and Camel work together to prepare a `CamelContext`.

PREPARING CAMELCONTEXT IN A SPRING CONTAINER

Spring allows third-party frameworks to integrate seamlessly with Spring. To do this, the third-party frameworks must provide a `org.springframework.beans.factory.xml.NamespaceHandler`, which is the extension point for using custom namespaces in Spring XML files. Camel provides the `CamelNamespaceHandler`.

When using Camel in the Spring XML file, you would define the `<camelContext>` tag as follows:

```
<camelContext xmlns="http://camel.apache.org/schema/spring">
```

The `http://camel.apache.org/schema/spring` namespace is the Camel custom namespace. To let Spring know about this custom namespace, it must be identified in the `META-INF/spring.handlers`, where you map the namespace to the class implementation:

```
http\://camel.apache.org/schema/spring=
        org.apache.camel.spring.handler.CamelNamespaceHandler
```

The `CamelNamespaceHandler` is then responsible for parsing the XML and delegating to other factories for further processing. One of these factories is the `CamelContextFactoryBean`, which is responsible for creating the `CamelContext` that essentially is your Camel application.

When Spring is finished initializing, it signals to third-party frameworks that they can start by broadcasting the `ContextRefreshedEvent` event.

STARTING CAMELCONTEXT

At this point, `CamelContext` is ready to be started. What happens next is the same regardless of which container or deployment option you're using with Camel. Figure 13.3 shows a flow diagram of the startup process.

`CamelContext` is started by invoking its `start` method. The first step in figure 13.3 determines whether or not autostartup is enabled for Camel. If it's disabled, the entire startup process is skipped. By default, Camel is set to autostart, which involves the following four steps.

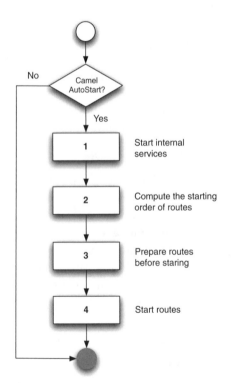

Figure 13.3   Flow diagram showing how Camel starts by starting internal services, computing the starting order of routes, and preparing and starting the routes.

1 *Start internal services*—Prepares and starts internal services used by Camel, such as the type-converter mechanism.

2 *Compute starting order*—Computes the order in which the routes should be started. By default, Camel will start up all the routes in the order they are defined in the Spring XML files or the `RouteBuilder` classes. We'll cover how to configure the order of routes in section 13.1.3.

3 *Prepare routes*—Prepares the routes before they're started.

4 *Start routes*—Starts the routes by starting the consumers, which essentially opens the gates to Camel and lets the messages start to flow in.

After step 4, Camel writes a message to the log indicating that it has been started and that the startup process is complete.

In some cases, you may need to influence how Camel is started, and we'll look at that now.

13.1.2 *Camel startup options*

Camel offers various options when it comes to starting Camel. For example, you may have a maintenance route that should not be autostarted on startup. You may also want to enable tracing on startup to let Camel log traces of messages being routed. Table 13.1 lists all the options that influence startup.

The options from table 13.1 can be divided into two kinds. The first four options are related to startup and shutdown, and the remainder are miscellaneous options. We'll look at how to use the miscellaneous options first, and then we'll turn our attention to the startup and shutdown options.

Table 13.1 Camel startup options

Option	Description
AutoStartup	This option is used to indicate whether or not the route should be started automatically when Camel starts. This option is enabled by default.
StartupOrder	This option dictates the order in which the routes should be started when Camel starts. We'll cover this in section 13.1.3.
ShutdownRoute	This option is used to configure whether or not the route in question should stop immediately or defer while Camel is shutting down. We'll cover shutdown in section 13.3.
ShutdownRunningTask	This option is used to control whether Camel should continue to complete pending running tasks at shutdown or stop immediately after the current task is complete. We'll cover shutdown in section 13.3.
Tracing	This option is used to trace how an exchange is being routed within that particular route. This option is disabled by default.
Delayer	This option is used to set a delay in milliseconds that slows down the processing of a message. You can use this during debugging to reduce how quickly Camel routes messages, which may help you track what happens when you watch the logs. This option is disabled by default.

Table 13.1   Camel startup options *(continued)*

Option	Description
HandleFault	This option is used to turn fault messages into exceptions. This is not a typical thing to do in a pure Camel application, but when deployed into a JBI container like Apache ServiceMix, you'll need to set this option to let the Camel error handler react to faults. This option is disabled by default. We'll cover this in more detail shortly.
StreamCaching	This option is used to cache streams that otherwise couldn't be accessed multiple times. You may want to use this when you use redelivery during error handling, which requires being able to read the stream multiple times. This option is disabled by default. We'll cover this in more detail shortly.

CONFIGURING STREAMCACHING

The miscellaneous options are often used during development to turn on additional logging, such as the `Tracing` option, which we covered in the last chapter. Or you may need to turn on stream caching if you use Camel with other stream-centric systems. For example, to enable stream caching, you can do the following with the Java DSL:

```
public class MyRoute extends RouteBuilder {
    public void configure() throws Exception {
        context.setStreamCaching(true);

        from("jbi:service:http://rider.com/AutoPartService")
            .to("xslt:html-parts.xsl")
            .to("jbi:service:http://rider.com/HtmlService");
    }
}
```

The same example using Spring XML would look like this:

```
<camelContext streamCache="true"
              xmlns="http://camel.apache.org/schema/spring">
    <route>
        <from uri="jbi:service:http://rider.com/AutoPartService"/>
        <to uri="xslt:html-parts.xsl"/>
        <to uri="jbi:service:http://rider.com/HtmlService"/>
    </route>
</camelContext>
```

All the options from table 13.1 can be scoped at either context or route level. The preceding stream cache example was scoped at context level. You could also configure it on a particular route:

```
public class MyRoute extends RouteBuilder {
    public void configure() throws Exception {
        from("jbi:service:http://rider.com/AutoPartService")
            .streamCaching()
            .to("xslt:html-parts.xsl")
            .to("jbi:service:http://rider.com/HtmlService");
    }
}
```

You can configure route-scoped stream caching in Spring XML as follows:

```
<camelContext xmlns="http://camel.apache.org/schema/spring">
    <route streamCache="true">
        <from uri="jbi:service:http://rider.com/AutoPartService"/>
        <to uri="xslt:html-parts.xsl"/>
        <to uri="jbi:service:http://rider.com/HtmlService"/>
    </route>
</camelContext>
```

NOTE Java DSL uses the syntax noXXX to disable an option, such as noStream-Caching or noTracing.

There is one last detail to know about the context and route scopes. The context scope is used as a fallback if a route doesn't have a specific configuration. The idea is that you can configure the default setting on the context scope and then override when needed at the route scope. For example, you could enable tracing on the context scope and then disable it on the routes you don't want traced.

CONFIGURING HANDLEFAULT

In the preceding example, you route messages using the JBI component. The Handle-Fault option is used to control whether or not Camel error handling should react to faults.

Suppose sending to the jbi:service:http://rider.com/HtmlService endpoint fails with a fault. Without HandleFault enabled, the fault would be propagated back to the consumer. By enabling HandleFault, you can let the Camel error handler react when faults occur.

The following code shows how you can let the DeadLetterChannel error handler save failed messages to files in the error directory:

```
public class MyRoute extends RouteBuilder {
    public void configure() throws Exception {
        errorHandler(deadLetterChannel("file:errors"));

        from("jbi:service:http://rider.com/AutoPartService")
            .streamCaching().handleFault()
            .to("xslt:html-parts.xsl")
            .to("jbi:service:http://rider.com/HtmlService");
    }
}
```

The equivalent example in Spring XML is as follows:

```
<camelContext xmlns="http://camel.apache.org/schema/spring">
    <errorHandler id="EH" type="DeadLetterChannel"
                  deadLetterUri="file:errors"/>

    <route streamCache="true" errorHandlerRef="EH" handleFault="true">
        <from uri="jbi:service:http://rider.com/AutoPartService"/>
        <to uri="xslt:html-parts.xsl"/>
        <to uri="jbi:service:http://rider.com/HtmlService"/>
    </route>
</camelContext>
```

We'll now look at how to control the ordering of routes.

13.1.3 Ordering routes

The order in which routes are started and stopped becomes more and more important the more interdependent the routes are. For example, you may have reusable routes that must be started before being leveraged by other routes. Also, routes that immediately consume messages that are bound for other routes may have to be started later to ensure that the other routes are ready in time.

To control the startup order of routes, Camel provides two options: `AutoStartup` and `StartupOrder`. The former dictates whether the routes should be started or not. The latter is a number that dictates the order in which the routes should be started.

USING STARTUPORDER TO CONTROL ORDERING OF ROUTES

Let's return to our Rider Auto Parts example, outlined at the beginning of the chapter. Figure 13.4 shows the high-level diagram again, this time numbering the three routes in use, ❶, ❷, and ❸.

❶ The file-based route will poll incoming files and split each line in the file. The lines are then converted to an internal `camelinaction.inventory.UpdateInventoryInput` object, which is sent to the ❸ route.

❷ The web service route is much simpler because incoming messages are automatically converted to the `UpdateInventoryInput` object. The web service endpoint is configured to do this.

❸ This route is a common route that's reused by the first two routes.

You now have a dependency among the three routes. Routes ❶ and ❷ depend upon route ❸, and that's why you need to use `StartupOrder` to ensure that the routes are started in correct order.

The following listing shows the Camel routes with the `StartupOrder` options in boldface.

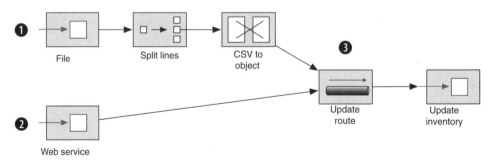

Figure 13.4   Camel application with two input routes ❶ and ❷ which depend on a common route ❸

Listing 13.1 Starting routes in a specific order

```
public class InventoryRoute extends RouteBuilder {

    @Override
    public void configure() throws Exception {
        from("cxf:bean:inventoryEndpoint")
            .routeId("webservice").startupOrder(3)
            .to("direct:update")
            .transform().method("inventoryService", "replyOk");

        from("file://target/inventory/updates")
            .routeId("file").startupOrder(2)
            .split(body().tokenize("\n"))
                .convertBodyTo(UpdateInventoryInput.class)
                .to("direct:update")
            .end();

        from("direct:update")
            .routeId("update").startupOrder(1)
            .to("bean:inventoryService?method=updateInventory");
    }
}
```

Listing 13.1 shows how easy it is in the Java DSL to configure the order of the routes using StartupOrder. Listing 13.2 shows the same example using Spring XML.

NOTE In listing 13.1, routeId is used to assign each route a meaningful name, which will then show up in the management console or in the logs. If you don't assign an ID, Camel will auto-assign an ID using the scheme route1, route2, and so forth.

Listing 13.2 Spring XML version of listing 13.1

```
<camelContext xmlns="http://camel.apache.org/schema/spring">

    <route id="webservice" startupOrder="3">
        <from uri="cxf:bean:inventoryEndpoint"/>
        <to uri="direct:update"/>
        <transform>
            <method bean="inventoryService" method="replyOk"/>
        </transform>
    </route>

    <route id="file" startupOrder="2">
        <from uri="file://target/inventory/updates"/>
        <split>
            <tokenize token="\n"/>
            <convertBodyTo
                type="camelinaction.inventory.UpdateInventoryInput"/>
            <to uri="direct:update"/>
        </split>
    </route>

    <route id="update" startupOrder="1">
        <from uri="direct:update"/>
```

```
        <to uri="bean:inventoryService?method=updateInventory"/>
    </route>

</camelContext>
```

You should notice that the numbers 1, 2 and 3 are used to dictate the order of the routes. Let's take a moment to see how this works in Camel.

HOW STARTUPORDER WORKS

The `StartupOrder` option in Camel works much like the `load-on-startup` option for Java servlets. As with servlets, you can specify a positive number to indicate the order in which the routes should be started.

The numbers don't have to be consecutive. For example, you could have used the numbers 5, 20, and 87 instead of 1, 2, and 3. All that matters is that the numbers must be unique.

You can also omit assigning a `StartupOrder` to some of the routes. In that case, Camel will assign these routes a unique number starting with 1,000 upwards. This means that the numbers from 1 to 999 are free for Camel users, and the numbers from 1,000 upward are reserved by Camel.

> **TIP**   The routes are stopped in the reverse order in which they were started.

In practice, you may not need to use `StartupOrder` often. It's only important when you have route dependencies, as in the previous example.

The source code for the book contains this example in the chapter13/startup directory. You can try it out using the following Maven goals:

```
mvn test -Dtest=InventoryJavaDSLTest
mvn test -Dtest=InventorySpringXMLTest
```

You've now learned to control the order in which routes are started. Let's move on and take a look at how you can omit starting certain routes and start them on demand later, at runtime.

13.1.4   *Disabling autostartup*

Table 13.1 listed the `AutoStartup` option, which is used to specify whether or not a given route should be automatically started when Camel starts. Sometimes you may not want to start a route automatically—you may want to start it on demand at runtime to support business cases involving human intervention.

At Rider Auto Parts, there has been a demand to implement a manual process for updating the inventory based on files. As usual, you've been asked to implement this in the existing application depicted in figure 13.4.

You come up with the following solution: add a new route to the existing routes in listing 13.1. The new route listens for files being dropped in the manual directory, and uses these files to update the inventory.

```
from("file://target/inventory/manual")
    .routeId("manual")
    .log("Doing manual update with file ${file:name}")
```

```
    .split(body().tokenize("\n"))
       .convertBodyTo(UpdateInventoryInput.class)
       .to("direct:update")
    .end();
```

As you can see, the route is merely a copy of the file-based route in listing 13.1. Unfortunately, your boss isn't satisfied with the solution. The route is always active, so if someone accidentally drops a file into the manual folder, it would be picked up.

To solve this problem, you use the `AutoStartup` option to disable the route from being activated on startup:

```
from("file://target/inventory/manual")
    .routeId("manual").noAutoStartup()
    .log("Doing manual update with file ${file:name}")
    .split(body().tokenize("\n"))
       .convertBodyTo(UpdateInventoryInput.class)
       .to("direct:update")
    .end();
```

You can start the route when a manual file is meant to be picked up. This can be done by using a management console, such as JConsole, to manually start the route, waiting until the file has been processed, and manually stopping the route again.

> **TIP** There is a subtle difference between using Boolean-based options in the Java DSL and Spring XML. For example, `AutoStartup` is implemented as `autoStartup="false"` in Spring XML and as `noAutoStartup()` in the Java DSL.

You've now learned how to configure Camel with various options that influence how it starts up. In the next section, we'll look at various ways of programmatically controlling the lifecycle of routes at runtime.

13.2 *Starting and stopping routes at runtime*

In chapter 12, you learned how to use management tooling, designed for operations staff, to start and stop routes at runtime. Being able to programmatically control routes at runtime is also desirable. For example, you might want business logic to automatically turn routes on or off at runtime. In this section, we'll look at how to do this.

You can start and stop routes at runtime in several ways, including these:

- *Using* `CamelContext`—By invoking the `startRoute` and `stopRoute` methods.
- *Using* `RoutePolicy`—By applying a policy to routes that Camel enforces automatically at runtime.
- *Using JMX*—By obtaining the `ManagedRoute` MBean for the particular routes and invoking its `start` or `stop` methods. If you have remote management enabled, you can control the routes from another machine.

The use of JMX was covered in the previous chapter, so we'll discuss using `CamelContext` and `RoutePolicy` in this chapter.

13.2.1 Using CamelContext to start and stop routes at runtime

The CamelContext provides methods to easily start and stop routes.

To illustrates this, we'll continue with the Rider Auto Parts example from section 13.1.4. About a month into production with the new route, one of the operations staff forgot to manually stop the route after use, as he was supposed to. Not stopping the route leads to a potential risk because files accidentally dropped into the manual directory will be picked up by the route.

You are again summoned to remedy this problem, and you quickly improve the route with the two changes shown in bold in the following listing.

Listing 13.3   After a file has been processed, the route is stopped

```
from("file://target/inventory/manual?maxMessagesPerPoll=1")
    .routeId("manual").noAutoStartup()
    .log("Doing manual update with file ${file:name}")
    .split(body().tokenize("\n"))
        .convertBodyTo(UpdateInventoryInput.class)
        .to("direct:update")
    .end()
    .process(new Processor() {
        public void process(Exchange exchange) throws Exception {
            exchange.getContext().getInflightRepository().remove(exchange);
            exchange.getContext().stopRoute("manual");
        }
    });
```

The first change uses the maxMessagesPerPoll option to tell the file consumer to only pick up one file at a time. The second change stops the route after that one file has been processed. This is done with the help of the inlined Processor, which can access the CamelContext and tell it to stop the route by name. (CamelContext also provides a startRoute method for starting a route.) Before you stop the route, you must unregister the current exchange from the in-flight registry, which otherwise would prevent Camel from stopping the route, because it detects there is an exchange in progress.

The source code for the book contains this example, which you can try from the chapter13/startup directory using the following Maven goal:

```
mvn test -Dtest=ManualRouteWithStopTest
```

Even though the fix to stop the route was simple, using the inlined processor at the end of the route isn't an optimal solution. It would be better to keep the business logic separated from the stopping logic. This can be done with a feature called OnCompletion.

USING ONCOMPLETION

OnCompletion is a feature that allows you to do *additional* routing after the original route is done. The classic example would be to send an email alert if a route fails, but it has a broad range of uses.

Instead of using the inlined processor to stop the route, you can use OnCompletion in the RouteBuilder to process the StopRouteProcessor class containing the logic to stop the route. This is shown in bold in the following code:

```
public void configure() throws Exception {
    onCompletion().process(new StopRouteProcessor("manual"));

    from("file://target/inventory/manual?maxMessagesPerPoll=1")
        .routeId("manual").noAutoStartup()
        .log("Doing manual update with file ${file:name}")
        .split(body().tokenize("\n"))
        .convertBodyTo(UpdateInventoryInput.class)
        .to("direct:update");
}
```

The implementation of the StopRouteProcessor is simple, as shown here:

```
public class StopRouteProcessor implements Processor {
    private final String name;

    public StopRouteProcessor(String name) {
        this.name = name;
    }

    public void process(Exchange exchange) throws Exception {
        exchange.getContext().getInflightRepository().remove(exchange);
        exchange.getContext().stopRoute(name);
    }
}
```

This improves the readability of the route, as it's shorter and doesn't mix high-level routing logic with low-level implementation logic. By using OnCompletion, the stopping logic has been separated from the original route.

Scopes can be used to define OnCompletions at different levels. Camel supports two scopes: context scope (high level) and route scope (low level). In the preceding example, you used context scope. If you wanted to use route scope, you'd have to define it within the route as follows:

```
from("file://target/inventory/manual?maxMessagesPerPoll=1")
    .onCompletion().process(new StopRouteProcessor("manual")).end()
    .routeId("manual").noAutoStartup()
    .log("Doing manual update with file ${file:name}")
    .split(body().tokenize("\n"))
        .convertBodyTo(UpdateInventoryInput.class)
        .to("direct:update")
    .end;
```

Notice the use of .end() to indicate where the OnCompletion route ends. You have to do this when using route scope so Camel knows which pieces belong to the *additional* route and which to the original route. This is the same principle as when you use OnException at route scope.

TIP   OnCompletion also supports filtering using the OnWhen predicate so that you can trigger the additional route only if the predicate is true. In addition, OnCompletion can be configured to only trigger when the route completes successfully or when it fails by using the OnCompleteOnly or OnFailureOnly options. For example, you can use OnFailureOnly to build a route that sends an alert email to support personnel when a route fails.

The source code for the book contains this example in the chapter13/startup directory. You can try it using the following Maven goal:

```
mvn test -Dtest=ManualRouteWithOnCompletionTest
```

We've now covered how to stop a route at runtime using the CamelContext API. We'll now look at another feature called RoutePolicy, which can also be used to control the lifecycle of routes at runtime.

13.2.2 *Using RoutePolicy to start and stop routes at runtime*

A RoutePolicy is a policy that can control routes at runtime. For example, a Route-Policy can control whether or not a route should be active. But you aren't limited to such scenarios—you can implement any kind of logic you wish.

The org.apache.camel.spi.RoutePolicy is an interface that defines two callback methods Camel will automatically invoke at runtime:

```
void onExchangeBegin(Route route, Exchange exchange);
void onExchangeDone(Route route, Exchange exchange);
```

The idea is that you implement this interface, and Camel will invoke the callbacks when a route has just begun and when it's done. You're free to implement whatever logic you want in these callbacks. For convenience, Camel provides the org.apache. camel.impl.RoutePolicySupport class, which you can use as a base class to extend when implementing your custom policies.

Let's build a simple example using RoutePolicy to demonstrate how to flip between two routes, so only one route is active at any time. Figure 13.5 shows this principle.

As you can see in this figure, the RoutePolicy is being used to control the two routes, starting and stopping them so only one is active at a time. The following listing shows how this can be implemented.

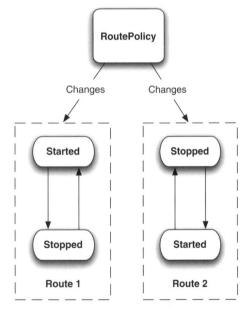

Figure 13.5 RoutePolicy changes the active state between the two routes so only one route is active at any time.

Listing 13.4 A `RoutePolicy` that flips two routes being active at runtime

```
public class FlipRoutePolicy extends RoutePolicySupport {
    private final String name1;
    private final String name2;                          ❶ Identifies
                                                            routes to flip
    public FlipRoutePolicy(String name1, String name2) {  ◁
        this.name1 = name1;
        this.name2 = name2;
    }

    @Override
    public void onExchangeDone(Route route, Exchange exchange) {
        String stop = route.getId().equals(name1) ? name1 : name2;
        String start = route.getId().equals(name1) ? name2 : name1;

        CamelContext context = exchange.getContext();
        try {
            exchange.getContext().getInflightRepository().remove(exchange);
            context.stopRoute(stop);
            context.startRoute(start);              ❷ Flips the two routes
        } catch (Exception e) {
            getExceptionHandler().handleException(e);
        }
    }
}
```

In the constructor, you identify the names of the two routes to flip ❶. As you extend the `RoutePolicySupport` class, you only override the `onExchangeDone` method, as the flipping logic should be invoked when the route is done. You then compute which of the two routes to stop and start with the help of the `route` parameter, which denotes the current active route. Having computed that, you then use `CamelContext` to flip the routes ❷. If an exception is thrown, you let the `ExceptionHandler` take care of it, which by default will log the exception.

To use `FlipRoutePolicy`, you must assign it to the two routes. In the Java DSL, this is done using the `RoutePolicy` method, as shown in the following `RouteBuilder`:

```
public void configure() throws Exception {
    RoutePolicy policy = new FlipRoutePolicy("foo", "bar");

    from("timer://foo")
        .routeId("foo").routePolicy(policy)
        .setBody().constant("Foo message")
        .to("log:foo").to("mock:foo");

    from("timer://bar")
        .routeId("bar").routePolicy(policy).noAutoStartup()
        .setBody().constant("Bar message")
        .to("log:bar").to("mock:bar");
}
```

If you're using Spring XML, you can use `RoutePolicy` as shown here:

```
<bean id="flipPolicy" class="camelinaction.FlipRoutePolicy">
    <constructor-arg index="0" value="foo"/>
    <constructor-arg index="1" value="bar"/>
</bean>
```

```
<camelContext xmlns="http://camel.apache.org/schema/spring">
    <route id="foo" routePolicyRef="flipPolicy">
        <from uri="timer://foo"/>
        <setBody><constant>Foo message</constant></setBody>
        <to uri="log:foo"/>
        <to uri="mock:foo"/>
    </route>

    <route id="bar" routePolicyRef="flipPolicy" autoStartup="false">
        <from uri="timer://bar"/>
        <setBody><constant>Bar message</constant></setBody>
        <to uri="log:bar"/>
        <to uri="mock:bar"/>
    </route>
</camelContext>
```

As you can see, you use the `routePolicyRef` attribute on the `<route>` tag to reference the `flipPolicy` bean defined in the top of the XML file.

The source code for the book contains this example in the chapter13/routepolicy directory. You can try it using the following Maven goals:

```
mvn test -Dtest=FlipRoutePolicyJavaDSLTest
mvn test -Dtest=FlipRoutePolicySpringXMLTest
```

When running either of the examples, you should see the two routes being logged interchangeably (`foo` and `bar`).

```
INFO  foo - Exchange[BodyType:String, Body:Foo message]
INFO  bar - Exchange[BodyType:String, Body:Bar message]
INFO  foo - Exchange[BodyType:String, Body:Foo message]
INFO  bar - Exchange[BodyType:String, Body:Bar message]
INFO  foo - Exchange[BodyType:String, Body:Foo message]
INFO  bar - Exchange[BodyType:String, Body:Bar message]
```

We've now covered both starting and controlling routes at runtime. It's time to learn about shutting down Camel, which is more complex than it sounds.

13.3   *Shutting down Camel*

The new inventory application at Rider Auto Parts is scheduled to be in production at the end of the month. You're on the team to ensure its success and help run the final tests before it's handed over to production. These tests also cover reliably shutting down the application.

Shutting down the Camel application is complex because there may be numerous in-flight messages being processed. Shutting down while messages are in flight may harm your business because those messages could potentially be lost. So the goal of shutting down a Camel application reliably is to shut it down when its *quiet*—when there are no in-flight messages. All you have to do is find this quiet moment.

This is hard to do because while you wait for the current messages to complete, the application may take in new messages. You have to stop taking in new messages while the current messages are given time to complete. This process is known as *graceful shutdown*, which means shutting down in a reliable and controlled manner.

13.3.1 *Graceful shutdown*

When `CamelContext` is being stopped, which happens when its `stop()` method is invoked, it uses a strategy to shut down. This strategy is defined in the `Shutdown-Strategy` interface. The default implementation of this `ShutdownStrategy` interface uses the graceful shutdown technique.

For example, when you stop the Rider Auto Parts example, you'll see these log lines:

```
DefaultCamelContext         - Apache Camel 2.5.0 is shutting down
DefaultShutdownStrategy     - Starting to graceful shutdown routes
                              (timeout 300 seconds)
DefaultShutdownStrategy     - Route: update shutdown complete.
DefaultShutdownStrategy     - Route: file suspended and shutdown deferred.
DefaultShutdownStrategy     - Route: webservice shutdown complete.
DefaultShutdownStrategy     - Route: file shutdown complete.
DefaultShutdownStrategy     - Graceful shutdown of routes completed in
                              0 seconds
DefaultInflightRepository   - Shutting down with no inflight exchanges.
DefaultCamelContext         - Uptime: 7.422 seconds
DefaultCamelContext         - Apache Camel 2.5.0 is shutdown
```

This tells you a few things. You can see the graceful shutdown is using a 300-second timeout. This is the maximum time Camel allows for shutting down gracefully before it starts to shut down more aggressively by forcing routes to stop immediately. The default value is 300 seconds, which you can configure on the `CamelContext`. For example, to use 20 seconds as the default timeout value, you can do as follows:

```
camelContext.getShutdownStrategy().setTimeout(20);
```

Doing this in Spring XML requires a bit more work, because you have to define a Spring bean to set the timeout value:

```
<bean id="shutdown" class="org.apache.camel.impl.DefaultShutdownStrategy">
    <property name="timeout" value="20"/>
</bean>
```

Notice that the timeout value is in seconds.

Then Camel logs the progress of the routes as they shut down, one by one, according to the order in which they were started. Notice that the `file` route is suspended and deferred, and then later is shut down.

This is a little glimpse of the complex logic the graceful shutdown process uses to shut down Camel in a reliable manner. We'll cover what *suspension* and *defer* mean in a moment.

At the end, Camel logs the completion of the graceful shutdown, which in this case was really fast and completed in less than one second. Camel also logs whether there were any in-flight messages just before it stops completely.

If Camel did not complete the graceful shutdown, it would log at `WARN` level how many in-flight messages were still in progress:

```
WARN - DefaultInflightRepository - Shutting down while there are still
                                   5 inflight exchanges.
```

SHUTTING DOWN THE RIDER AUTO PARTS APPLICATION

At Rider Auto Parts, you're in the final testing of the application before it's handed over to production. One of the tests is based on processing a big inventory file, and you wanted to test what happens if you shut down Camel while it was working on the big file. You expected Camel would continue processing the big file and only shut down when the file was completed. But the log shows something else.

At first, you see the usual logging about the shutdown in progress:

```
DefaultShutdownStrategy - Starting to graceful shutdown routes
                        (timeout 300 seconds)
DefaultShutdownStrategy - Route: update shutdown complete.
DefaultShutdownStrategy - Route: file suspended and shutdown deferred.
DefaultShutdownStrategy - Route: webservice shutdown complete.
```

Then there is a log line indicating that Camel has noticed the one in-flight exchange, which is the big file. This is expected behavior:

```
DefaultShutdownStrategy - Waiting as there are still 1 inflight and
                pending exchanges to complete before we can shutdown
```

Then the application logs the progress of the inventory update, which should happen for each line in the big file:

```
Inventory 58004 updated
```

Next come a lot of WARN logs about there being no consumers to process the Exchange:

```
WARN - DirectProducer - No consumers available on endpoint:
Endpoint[direct://update] to process: Exchange[Message:
camelinaction.inventory.UpdateInventoryInput@e9d110]
WARN - DirectProducer - No consumers available on endpoint:
Endpoint[direct://update] to process: Exchange[Message:
camelinaction.inventory.UpdateInventoryInput@5735c4]
```

Finally, you see the last log lines, which report the end of the shutdown.

```
DefaultShutdownStrategy    - Route: file shutdown complete.
DefaultShutdownStrategy    - Graceful shutdown of routes completed in
                             13 seconds
DefaultInflightRepository  - Shutting down with no inflight exchanges.
DefaultCamelContext        - Uptime: 18.742 seconds
DefaultCamelContext        - Apache Camel 2.5.0 is shutdown
```

So what went wrong? The clues have been shown in the logs. First, you noticed the WARN logs, which indicated that the direct:update consumer had been stopped. This consumer is from the first route, which has startup order 1:

```
from("direct:update")
    .routeId("update").startupOrder(1)
    .to("bean:inventoryService?method=updateInventory");
```

You then noticed that Camel stops this route as the first route during the shutdown process:

```
DefaultShutdownStrategy - Route: update shutdown complete.
```

This is a shared route that the other routes depend upon, as illustrated in figure 13.4. That's why it needed to be started before the other routes. Now the problem is that this route is also stopped before the other routes. You've got a catch-22 situation.

The good news is that it's possible to remedy this in Camel. What you need to do is somehow tell Camel to defer shutting down this shared route. This is done using the ShutdownRoute option, which was listed in table 13.1. All you have to do is add the option in the route as shown in bold here:

```
from("direct:update")
    .routeId("update").startupOrder(1)
    .shutdownRoute(ShutdownRoute.Defer)
    .to("bean:inventoryService?method=updateInventory");
```

The same route in Spring XML is as follows:

```
<route id="update" startupOrder="1" shutdownRoute="Defer">
    <from uri="direct:update"/>
    <to uri="bean:inventoryService?method=updateInventory"/>
</route>
```

Now when you run the test, the application shuts down in a reliable manner. The log shows that Camel detects that the big file is still in progress and patiently waits:

```
DefaultShutdownStrategy - Waiting as there are still 1 inflight
        and pending exchanges to complete before we can shutdown
Inventory 58026 updated
Inventory 58027 updated
DefaultShutdownStrategy - Waiting as there are still 1 inflight
        and pending exchanges to complete before we can shutdown
Inventory 58028 updated
Inventory 58029 updated
Inventory 58030 updated
DefaultShutdownStrategy - Waiting as there are still 1 inflight
        and pending exchanges to complete before we can shutdown
```

The application is now ready to be handed over to operations for deployment.

> **NOTE** Apache Camel 2.5 has been improved to handle the example we've just covered. Camel now always defers direct endpoints, which means you no longer have to configure this manually. The example illustrates the principle of how to shut down a Camel application in a reliable manner.

The source code for the book contains this example in the chapter13/shutdown directory. You can try it by using the following Maven goals:

```
mvn test -Dtest=GracefulShutdownBigFileTest
mvn test -Dtest=GracefulShutdownBigFileXmlTest
```

As you've just learned, Camel end users are responsible for configuring routes correctly to support reliable shutdown. Some may say this is a trade-off, but we, the Camel team, think of it as flexibility and don't believe computer logic can substitute for human logic in ensuring a reliable shutdown. We think it's best to give Camel users the power to configure their routes to support their use cases.

ABOUT STOPPING AND SHUTTING DOWN

Camel will leverage the graceful shutdown mechanism when it stops or shuts down routes. That means the example in listing 13.3 will stop the route in a graceful manner. As a result, you can reliably stop routes at runtime, without the risk of losing in-flight messages.

The difference between using the `stopRoute` and `shutdownRoute` methods is that the latter will also unregister the route from management (JMX). Use `stopRoute` when you want to be able to start the route again. Only use `shutdownRoute` if the route should be permanently removed.

That's all there is to shutting down Camel. It's now time to review some of the deployment strategies that are possible.

13.4   *Deploying Camel*

Camel is described as a lightweight and embeddable integration framework. This means that it supports more deployment strategies and flexibility than traditional ESBs and application servers. Camel can be used in a wide range of runtime environments, from standalone Java applications, to web containers, to the cloud.

In this section, we'll look at four different deployment strategies that are possible with Camel and present their strengths and weaknesses.

- Embedding Camel in a Java application
- Running Camel in a web environment on Apache Tomcat
- Running Camel inside JBoss Application Server
- Running Camel in an OSGi container such as Apache Karaf

These four deployment strategies are the common ways of deploying Camel.

13.4.1 *Embedded in a Java application*

It's appealing to embed Camel in a Java application if you need to communicate with the outside world. By bringing Camel into your application, you can benefit from all the transports, routes, EIPs, and so on, that Camel offers. Figure 13.6 shows Camel embedded in a standard Java application.

In the embedded mode, you must add to the classpath all the necessary Camel and third-party JARs needed by the underlying transports. Because Camel is built with Maven, you can use Maven for your own project and benefit from its dependency-management system. We discussed building Camel projects with Maven in chapter 11.

Bootstrapping Camel for your code is easy. In fact, you did that in your first ride on the Camel in chapter 1. All you need to do is create a `CamelContext` and start it, as shown in the following listing.

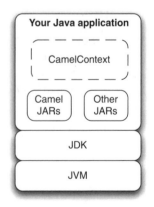

Figure 13.6   Camel embedded in a standalone Java application

Listing 13.5 Bootstrapping Camel in your Java application

```
public class FileCopierWithCamel {

    public static void main(String args...) throws Exception {
        CamelContext context = new DefaultCamelContext();
        context.addRoutes(new RouteBuilder() {
            public void configure() {
                from("file:data/inbox").to("file:data/outbox");
            }
        });
        context.start();

        Thread.sleep(10000);

        context.stop();
    }
}
```

It's important to keep a reference to `CamelContext` for the lifetime of your application, because you'll need to perform a shutdown of Camel. As you may have noticed in listing 13.5, the code execution continues after starting the `CamelContext`. To avoid shutting down your application immediately, the listing includes code to sleep for 10 seconds. In your application, you'll need to use a different means to let your application continue and only shut down when requested to do so.

Let's look at the Rider Auto Parts application illustrated in figure 13.1, and embed it in a Java application.

EMBEDDING THE RIDER AUTO PARTS EXAMPLE IN A JAVA APPLICATION

The Rider Auto Parts Camel application can be run as a standalone Java application. Because the application is using Spring XML files to set up Camel, you just need to start Spring to start the application.

Starting Spring from a main class can be done as follows:

```
public class InventoryMain {
    public static void main(String[] args) throws Exception {
        String filename = "META-INF/spring/camel-context.xml";
        AbstractXmlApplicationContext spring =
                new ClassPathXmlApplicationContext(filename);
        spring.start();

        Thread.sleep(10000);

        spring.stop();
        spring.destroy();
    }
}
```

To start Spring, you create an `ApplicationContext`, which in the preceding example means loading the Spring XML file from the classpath. This code also reveals the problem of having the main method wait until you terminate the application. The preceding code uses `Thread.sleep` to wait 10 seconds before terminating the application.

To remedy this, Camel provides a `Main` class that you can leverage instead of writing your own class. You can change the previous `InventoryMain` class to leverage this `Main` class as follows:

```
import org.apache.camel.spring.Main;

public class InventoryMain {
    public static void main(String[] args) throws Exception {
        Main main = new Main();
        main.setApplicationContextUri("META-INF/spring/camel-context.xml");
        main.enableHangupSupport();
        main.start();
    }
}
```

This approach also solves the issue of handling the lifecycle of the application. By enabling hang-up support, you tell Camel to shut down gracefully when the JVM is being terminated, such as when the Ctrl-C key combination is pressed. You can obviously also stop the Camel application by invoking the stop method on the main instance.

The source code for the book contains this example in the chapter13/standalone directory. You can try it out using the following Maven goal:

```
mvn compile exec:java
```

> **TIP** You may not need to write your own main class. For example, the
> org.apache.camel.spring.Main class can be used directly. It has parameters
> to dictate which Spring XML file it should load. By default, it loads all XML
> files from the classpath in the META-INF/spring location, so by dropping your
> Spring XML file in there, you don't even have to pass any arguments to the
> Main class. You can start it directly.

Table 13.2 summarizes the pros and cons of embedding Camel in a standalone Java application.

Table 13.2   Pros and cons of embedding Camel in a standalone Java application

Pros	Cons
■ Gives flexibility to deploy just what's needed ■ Allows you to embed Camel in any standard Java application ■ Works well with thick client applications, such as a Swing or Eclipse rich client GUI	■ Requires deploying all needed JARs ■ Requires manually managing Camel's lifecycle (starting and stopping) on your own

You now know how to make your standalone application leverage Camel. Let's look at what you can do for your web applications.

13.4.2 *Embedded in a web application*

Embedding Camel in a web application brings the same benefits as were mentioned in section 13.4.1. Camel provides all you need to connect to your favorite web container. If you work in an organization, you may have existing infrastructure to be used for deploying your Camel applications. Deploying Camel in such a well-known environment gives you immediate support for installing, managing, and monitoring your applications.

When Camel is embedded in a web application, as shown in figure 13.7, you need to make sure all JARs are packaged in the WAR file. If you use Maven, this will be done automatically.

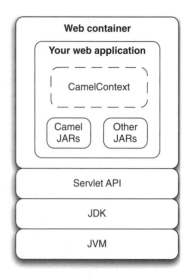

The Camel instance embedded in your web application is bootstrapped by Spring. By leveraging Spring, which is such a ubiquitous framework, you let end users use well-known approaches for deployment. This also conveniently ties Camel's lifecycle with Spring's lifecycle management and ensures that the Camel instance is properly started and stopped in the web container.

The following code demonstrates that you only need a standard Spring context listener in the web.xml file to bootstrap Spring and thereby Camel.

Figure 13.7   Camel embedded in a web application

```xml
<?xml version="1.0" encoding="UTF-8"?>
<web-app xmlns="http://java.sun.com/xml/ns/javaee"
        xmlns:xsi="http://www.w3.org/2001/XMLSchema-instance"
        xsi:schemaLocation="
          http://java.sun.com/xml/ns/javaee
          http://java.sun.com/xml/ns/javaee/web-app_2_5.xsd"
          version="2.5">

    <listener>
        <listener-class>
            org.springframework.web.context.ContextLoaderListener
        </listener-class>
    </listener>
</web-app>
```

This context listener also takes care of shutting down Camel properly when the web application is stopped. Spring will, by default, load the Spring XML file from the WEB-INF folder using the name applicationContext.xml. In this file, you can embed Camel, as shown in listing 13.6.

Specifying the location of your Spring XML file

If you want to use another name for your Spring XML file, you'll need to add a context parameter which specifies the filename as follows:

```xml
<context-param>
    <param-name>contextConfigLocation</param-name>
    <param-value>/WEB-INF/camel-context.xml</param-value>
</context-param>
```

Listing 13.6   The Spring applicationContext.xml file with Camel embedded

```
<?xml version="1.0" encoding="UTF-8"?>
<beans xmlns="http://www.springframework.org/schema/beans"
       xmlns:xsi="http://www.w3.org/2001/XMLSchema-instance"
       xmlns:camel="http://camel.apache.org/schema/spring"
       xsi:schemaLocation="
         http://www.springframework.org/schema/beans
         http://www.springframework.org/schema/beans/spring-beans.xsd
         http://camel.apache.org/schema/spring
         http://camel.apache.org/schema/spring/camel-spring.xsd">

    <import resource="camel-cxf.xml"/>

    <bean id="inventoryService" class="camelinaction.InventoryService"/>
    <bean id="inventoryRoute" class="camelinaction.InventoryRoute"/>

    <camelContext xmlns="http://camel.apache.org/schema/spring">
        <routeBuilder ref="inventoryRoute"/>
    </camelContext>
</beans>
```

Imports CXF from another XML file ❶

Listing 13.6 is a regular Spring XML file in which you can use the `<import>` tag to import other XML files. For example, this is done by having CXF defined in the camel-cxf.xml file ❶. Camel, itself, is embedded using the `<camelContext>` tag.

The source code for the book contains this example in the chapter13/war directory. You can try it out by using the following Maven goal:

```
mvn jetty:run
```

If you run this Maven goal, a Jetty plugin is used to quickly boot up a Jetty web container running the web application. To use the Jetty plugin in your projects, you must remember to add it to your pom.xml file in the `<build><plugins>` section:

```
<plugin>
    <groupId>org.mortbay.jetty</groupId>
    <artifactId>maven-jetty-plugin</artifactId>
    <version>7.1.6.v20100715</version>
</plugin>
```

If you run this goal, you should notice in the console that Jetty has been started:

```
2010-05-28 [main] INFO  DefaultCamelContext
- Apache Camel 2.5.0 (CamelContext: camelContext) started
2010-05-28 [main] INFO  ContextLoader
- Root WebApplicationContext: initialization completed in 3198 ms
2010-05-28 INFO::Started SelectChannelConnector@0.0.0.0:8080
[INFO] Started Jetty Server
```

Let's look at how you can run Camel as a web application in Apache Tomcat.

DEPLOYING TO APACHE TOMCAT

To package the application as a WAR file, you can run the `mvn package` command, which creates the WAR file in the target directory. Yes, it's that easy with Maven.

You want to leverage the hot deployment of Apache Tomcat, so you must first start it. Here's how you can start it on a Unix-based system, such as our Mac OS X laptop, using the bin/startup.sh script:

```
davsclaus:~/apache-tomcat-6.0.26$ bin/startup.sh
Using CATALINA_BASE:    /Users/davsclaus/apache-tomcat-6.0.26
Using CATALINA_HOME:    /Users/davsclaus/apache-tomcat-6.0.26
Using CATALINA_TMPDIR:  /Users/davsclaus/apache-tomcat-6.0.26/temp
Using JRE_HOME:         /System/Library/Frameworks/JavaVM.framework/Versions/
    1.5/Home
Using CLASSPATH:        /Users/davsclaus/apache-tomcat-6.0.26
/bin/bootstrap.jar
```

This will start Tomcat in the background, so you need to tail the log file to see what happens:

```
davsclaus:~/apache-tomcat-6.0.26$ tail -f logs/catalina.out
May 28, 2010 5:37:53 PM org.apache.catalina.startup.HostConfig
deployDirectory
INFO: Deploying web application directory ROOT
May 28, 2010 5:37:53 PM org.apache.coyote.http11.Http11Protocol start
INFO: Starting Coyote HTTP/1.1 on http-8080
May 28, 2010 5:37:53 PM org.apache.jk.common.ChannelSocket init
INFO: JK: ajp13 listening on /0.0.0.0:8009
May 28, 2010 5:37:53 PM org.apache.jk.server.JkMain start
INFO: Jk running ID=0 time=0/17  config=null
May 28, 2010 5:37:53 PM org.apache.catalina.startup.Catalina start
INFO: Server startup in 4351 ms
```

To deploy the application, you need to copy the WAR file to the Apache Tomcat webapps directory:

```
cp target/riderautoparts-war-1.0.war ~/apache-tomcat-6.0.26/webapps/
```

Then Apache Tomcat should show the application being started in the log file. You should see the familiar logging of Camel being started:

```
2010-05-28 [gine[Catalina]]] INFO DefaultCamelContext - Started 3 routes
2010-05-28 [gine[Catalina]]] INFO DefaultCamelContext
- Apache Camel 2.5.0 (CamelContext: camelContext) started
2010-05-28 [gine[Catalina]]] INFO ContextLoader
- Root WebApplicationContext: initialization completed in 2812 ms
```

Now you need to test that the deployed application runs as expected. This can be done by sending a web service request using SoapUI, as shown in figure 13.8. Doing this requires you to know the URL to the WSDL the web service runs at, which is http://localhost:9000/inventory?wsdl.

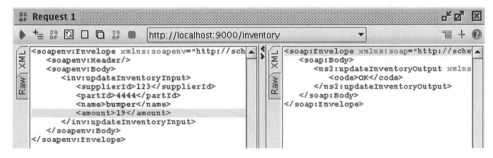

Figure 13.8 Using SoapUI testing the web service from the deployed application in Apache Tomcat

The web service returns "OK" as its reply, and you can also see from the log file that the application works as expected, outputting the inventory being updated:

```
Inventory 4444 updated
```

There's another great benefit of this deployment model, which is that you can tap the servlet container directly for HTTP endpoints. In a standalone Java deployment scenario, you have to rely on the Jetty transport, but in the web deployment scenario, the container already has its socket management, thread pools, tuning, and monitoring facilities. Camel can leverage this if you use the servlet transport for your inbound HTTP endpoints.

In the previously deployed application, you let Apache CXF rely on the Jetty transport. Let's change this to leverage the existing servlet transports provided by Apache Tomcat.

USING APACHE TOMCAT FOR HTTP INBOUND ENDPOINTS

When using Camel in an existing servlet container, such as Apache Tomcat, you may have to adjust Camel components in your application to tap into the servlet container. In the Rider Auto Parts application, it's the CXF component you must adjust.

First, you have to add `CXFServlet` to the web.xml file.

Listing 13.7   The web.xml file with `CXFServlet` to tap into Apache Tomcat

```xml
<?xml version="1.0" encoding="UTF-8"?>
<web-app xmlns="http://java.sun.com/xml/ns/javaee"
         xmlns:xsi="http://www.w3.org/2001/XMLSchema-instance"
         xsi:schemaLocation="
           http://java.sun.com/xml/ns/javaee
           http://java.sun.com/xml/ns/javaee/web-app_2_5.xsd"
           version="2.5">

    <listener>
        <listener-class>
            org.springframework.web.context.ContextLoaderListener
        </listener-class>
    </listener>

    <servlet>
        <servlet-name>CXFServlet</servlet-name>
        <servlet-class>
            org.apache.cxf.transport.servlet.CXFServlet
        </servlet-class>
    </servlet>
    <servlet-mapping>
        <servlet-name>CXFServlet</servlet-name>
        <url-pattern>/services/*</url-pattern>
    </servlet-mapping>
</web-app>
```

Maven users need to adjust the pom.xml file to depend upon the HTTP transport instead of Jetty, as follows:

```
<dependency>
    <groupId>org.apache.cxf</groupId>
    <artifactId>cxf-rt-transports-http</artifactId>
    <version>2.2.11</version>
</dependency>
```

Next, you must adjust the camel-cxf.xml file, as shown in the following listing.

Listing 13.8 Setting up the Camel CXF component to tap into Apache Tomcat

```
<beans xmlns="http://www.springframework.org/schema/beans"
       xmlns:xsi="http://www.w3.org/2001/XMLSchema-instance"
       xmlns:cxf="http://camel.apache.org/schema/cxf"
       xsi:schemaLocation="
         http://www.springframework.org/schema/beans
         http://www.springframework.org/schema/beans/spring-beans.xsd
         http://camel.apache.org/schema/cxf                          Required ①
         http://camel.apache.org/schema/cxf/camel-cxf.xsd">       import when
                                                                  using servlet
    <import resource="classpath:META-INF/cxf/cxf.xml"/>
    <import resource="classpath:META-INF/cxf/cxf-extension-soap.xml"/>
    <import resource=
        "classpath:META-INF/cxf/cxf-servlet.xml"/>
                                                   ② Web service
    <cxf:cxfEndpoint id="inventoryEndpoint"           endpoint address
        address="/inventory"
        serviceClass="camelinaction.inventory.InventoryEndpoint"/>
</beans>
```

To use Apache CXF in a servlet container, you have to import the cxf-servlet.xml resource ①. This exposes the web service via the servlet container, which means the endpoint address has to be adjusted to a relative context path ②.

In the previous example, the web service was available at http://localhost:9000/inventory?wsdl. By using Apache Tomcat, the web service is now exposed at this address:

```
http://localhost:8080/context/services/inventory?wsdl
```

Notice that the TCP port is 8080, which is the default Apache Tomcat setting.

The source code for the book contains this example in the chapter13/war-servlet directory. You can package the application using `mvn package` and then copy the riderautoparts-war-servlet-1.0.war file to the webapps directory of Apache Tomcat to hot-deploy the application. Then the web service should be available at this address: http://localhost:8080/riderautoparts-war-servlet-1.0/services/inventory?wsdl.

NOTE   Camel also provides a lightweight alternative to using CXF in the servlet container. The Servlet component that we discussed in section 7.4.2 of chapter 7 allows you to consume HTTP requests coming into the Servlet container in much the same way as you saw here with CXF. You can find more information on the Apache Camel website at http://camel.apache.org/servlet.html.

Table 13.3 lists the pros and cons of the web application deployment model of Camel.

Table 13.3   Pros and cons of embedding Camel in a web application

Pros	Cons
■ Taps into the servlet container ■ Lets the container manage the Camel lifecycle ■ Benefits the management and monitoring capabilities of the servlet container ■ Provides familiar runtime platform for operations	■ Can create annoying classloading issues on some web containers

Embedding Camel in a web application is a popular, proven, and powerful way to deploy Camel. Another choice for running Camel applications is using an application server such as JBoss Application Server.

13.4.3 *Embedded in JBoss Application Server*

A common way of deploying Camel applications in JBoss Application Server (JBoss AS) is using the web deployment model we discussed in the previous section. But JBoss AS has a pesky classloading mechanism, so you need to leverage a special Camel JBoss component to remedy this. This component isn't provided out of the box at the Apache Camel distribution, because of license implications with JBoss AS's LGPL license. This component is hosted at Camel Extra (http://code.google.com/p/camel-extra/), which is a project site for additional Camel components that can't be shipped from Apache.

In the true open source spirit, you can download the source code and build the component yourself, but the source code for the book also contains this component in the example located in the chapter13/war-jboss directory.

This example is based on the previous example with two minor additions. First, the camel-jboss-2.5.0.jar is added to the src/main/webapp/WEB-INF/lib directory, which ensures that this JAR is included when you package the application using mvn package.

The second change is to leverage the JBoss-specific classloader, which is done by adding the following bean definition in the applicationContext.xml file:

```
<bean id="jbossResolver"
      class="org.apache.camel.jboss.JBossPackageScanClassResolver"/>
```

That's all there is to it.

To deploy the application to JBoss, you start it and copy the WAR file into the server/default/deploy directory. For example, on our laptop, JBoss AS 5.1 is started as follows:

```
davsclaus:~/jboss$ bin/run.sh
```

After a while, JBoss AS is ready, and this is logged to the console:

```
15:16:43,882 INFO [ServerImpl] JBoss (Microcontainer) [5.1.0.GA (build:
    SVNTag=JBoss_5_1_0_GA date=200905221053)] Started in 27s:452ms
```

Then the WAR file is copied:

```
cp target/riderautoparts-war-jboss-1.0.war
 ~/jboss/server/default/deploy
```

You can then keep an eye on the JBoss console as it outputs the progress of the deployment. For example, Camel reports that it has picked up the JBoss classloader, as shown here:

```
15:18:42,636 INFO [STDOUT] 2010-05-30 15:18:42,636 [main] INFO
CamelContextFactoryBean - Using custom PackageScanClassResolver:
org.apache.camel.jboss.JBossPackageScanClassResolver@75d8af
```

JBoss AS uses an embedded Apache Tomcat as the servlet container, which means the web service of the application is available in a familiar location:

```
http://localhost:8080/riderautoparts-war-jboss-1.0/services/inventory?wsdl
```

Table 13.4 lists the pros and cons of deploying Camel in JBoss Application Server.

Table 13.4 Pros and cons of embedding Camel in JBoss AS

Pros	Cons
■ Taps into the JBoss AS container ■ Allows your application to leverage the facilities provided by the Java EE application server ■ Lets the JBoss AS container manage Camel's lifecycle ■ Benefits the management and monitoring capabilities of the application server ■ Provides a familiar runtime platform for operations	■ Requires a special Camel JBoss component to remedy classloading issues on JBoss

Deploying Camel as a web application in JBoss AS is a fairly easy solution. All you have to remember is to use the special Camel JBoss component to let the classloading work.

The last strategy we'll cover is in a totally different ballpark: using OSGi. OSGi is a fairly new deployment model in the Java enterprise space and brings promises of modularity to the extreme.

13.5 Camel and OSGi

OSGi is a layered module system for the Java platform that offers a complete dynamic component model. It's a truly dynamic environment where components can come and go without requiring a reboot (hot deployment). Apache Camel is OSGi-ready, in the sense that all the Camel JAR files are OSGi-compliant and are deployable in OSGi containers.

This section will show you how to prepare and deploy the Rider Auto Parts application in the Apache Karaf OSGi runtime. Karaf provides functionality on top of the

OSGi container, such as hot deployment, provisioning, local and remote shells, and many other goodies. You can choose between Apache Felix or Eclipse Equinox for the actual OSGi container. The example presented here is included with the source code for the book in the chapter13/osgi directory.

> **NOTE** In this book, we won't go deep into the details of OSGi, which is a complex topic. The basics are covered on Wikipedia (http://en.wikipedia.org/wiki/OSGi), and if you're interested in more information, we highly recommend *OSGi in Action*, by Richard S. Hall, Karl Pauls, Stuart McCulloch, and David Savage (Manning). For more information on the Apache Karaf OSGi runtime, see the Karaf website: http://karaf.apache.org.

The first thing you need to do with the Rider Auto Parts application is make it OSGi-compliant. This involves setting up Maven to help prepare the packaged JAR file so it includes OSGi metadata in the MANIFEST.MF entry.

13.5.1 *Setting up Maven to generate an OSGi bundle*

In the pom.xml file, you have to set the packaging element to bundle, which means the JAR file will be packaged as an OSGi bundle:

```
<packaging>bundle</packaging>
```

To generate the MANIFEST.MF entry in the JAR file, you can use the Apache Felix Maven Bundle plugin, which is added to the pom.xml file under the <build> section:

```
<build>
  <plugin>
    <groupId>org.apache.felix</groupId>
    <artifactId>maven-bundle-plugin</artifactId>
    <version>2.1.0</version>
    <extensions>true</extensions>
    <configuration>
      <instructions>
        <Bundle-Name>${project.artifactId}</Bundle-Name>
        <Bundle-SymbolicName>riderautoparts-osgi</Bundle-SymbolicName>
        <Export-Package>
            camelinaction,
            camelinaction.inventory
        </Export-Package>
        <Import-Package>*</Import-Package>
        <DynamicImport-Package>*</DynamicImport-Package>
        <Implementation-Title>Rider Auto Parts OSGi</Implementation-Title>
        <Implementation-Version>${project.version}</Implementation-Version>
      </instructions>
    </configuration>
  </plugin>
</build>
```

The interesting part of the maven-bundle-plugin is its ability to set the packages to be imported and exported. The plugin is set to export two packages: camelinaction and camelinaction.inventory. The camelinaction package contains the InventoryRoute

Camel route, and it needs to be accessible by Camel so it can load the routes when the application is started. The `camelinaction.inventory` package contains the generated source files needed by Apache CXF when it exposes the web service.

In terms of imports, the preceding code defines it as dynamic by using an asterisk, which means the OSGi container will figure it out. When needed, you can specify the imports by package name.

The source code for the book contains this example in the chapter13/osgi directory. If you run the `mvn package` goal, you can see the `MANIFEST.MF` entry being generated in the target/classes/META-INF directory.

You have now set up Maven to build the JAR file as an OSGi bundle, which can be deployed to the container. The next step is to download and install Apache Karaf.

13.5.2 *Installing and running Apache Karaf*

For this example, you can download and install the latest version of Apache Karaf from http://karaf.apache.org. (At the time of writing, this was Apache Karaf 2.1.2.) Installing is just a matter of unzipping the zip file.

Apache Karaf 2.1 issue when using Apache CXF

Apache Karaf version 2.1 has an issue that requires you to adjust its configuration in order to use Apache CXF. You need to download a file and save it in the etc directory with the name custom.properties.

From a Unix shell, you can do this as follows:

```
curl http://svn.apache.org/repos/asf/servicemix/smx4/features/trunk/
    assembly/src/main/filtered-resources/etc/jre.properties > etc/
    custom.properties
```

This command will download and save the file as etc/custom.properties. The Apache Karaf team will fix this problem in the 2.2 release.

To run Apache Karaf, start it from the command line using one of these two commands:

```
bin/karaf         (Unix)
bin/karaf.bat     (Windows)
```

This should start up Karaf and display a logo when it's ready. This will run in a shell mode, which means you can enter commands to manage the container.

Now you need to install Camel and Apache CXF before you install the Rider Auto Parts application. Karaf makes installing easier by using *features,* which are like *super bundles* that contain a set of bundles installed as a group. Installing features requires you to add the Camel feature descriptions to Karaf, which you do by typing the following command in the shell:

```
features:addUrl mvn:org.apache.camel.karaf/apache-camel/2.5.0/xml/features
```

You can then type `features:list` to see all the features that are available to be installed. Among these should be several Camel-related features.

The example application requires the `http`, `camel`, and `camel-cxf` features. Type these commands in the shell:

```
features:install http
features:install camel
features:install camel-cxf
```

And then wait a bit.

> **TIP**   You can type `osgi:list` to see which bundles have already been installed and their status. The shell has autocompletion, so you can press Tab to see the possible choices. For example, type `osgi` and then press Tab to see the choices.

You're now ready to deploy the Rider Auto Parts application.

13.5.3   *Deploying the example*

Karaf can install OSGi bundles from various sources, such as the filesystem or the local Maven repository.

To install using Maven, you first need to install the application in the local Maven repository, which can easily be done by running `mvn install` from the chapter13/ osgi directory. After the JAR file has been copied to the local Maven repository, you can deploy it to Apache Karaf using the following command from the shell:

```
osgi:install mvn:com.camelinaction/riderautoparts-osgi/1.0
```

Upon installing any JAR to Karaf (a JAR file is known as a *bundle* in OSGi terms), Karaf will output on the console the bundle ID it has assigned to the installed bundle, as shown:

```
Bundle ID: 98
```

You can then type `osgi:list` to see the application being installed:

```
[98] [Installed] [] [] [60] riderautoparts-osgi (1.0.0)
```

Notice that the application isn't started. You can start it by entering `osgi:start 98`, which changes the application's status when you do an `osgi:list` again:

```
[98] [Installed] [] [Started] [60] riderautoparts-osgi (1.0.0)
```

The application is now running in the OSGi container.

> **TIP**   You can install and start the bundle in a single command using the `-s` option on the `osgi:install` command, like this: `osgi:install -s mvn:com.camelinaction/riderautoparts-osgi/1.0`.

So how can you test that it works? You can start by checking the log with the `log:display` command. Among other things, it should indicate that Apache Camel has been started:

```
15:46:32,396 | INFO  | ExtenderThread-6 | DefaultCamelContext |
e.camel.impl.DefaultCamelContext 1025 | Apache Camel 2.5.0 (CamelContext:
myCamelContext) started
```

You can then use SoapUI to send a test request. The WSDL file is available at http://localhost:9000/inventory?wsdl.

When you're done testing the application, you may want to stop the OSGi container, which you can do by executing the `osgi:shutdown` command from the shell.

> **TIP**　You can tail the Apache Karaf log file using `tail -f log/karaf.log`. Note that this isn't done from within the Karaf shell but from the regular shell on your operating system.

You've now seen how to deploy the example into an OSGi container, which marks the end of our practical coverage of OSGi in this book.

Table 13.5 lists the pros and cons of deploying Camel in an OSGi container.

Table 13.5　Pros and cons of using OSGi as a deployment strategy

Pros	Cons
▪ Leverages OSGi for modularity ▪ Provides classloader isolation and hot deployment ▪ Commitment in the open source community and from big vendors endorsing OSGi	▪ Involves a learning curve for OSGi ▪ Unsupported third-party frameworks; many frameworks have yet to become OSGi compliant ▪ Requires extra effort to decide what package imports and exports to use for your module

You've now seen the most popular deployment strategies for Camel and other products.

We've only scratched the surface of OSGi in this chapter. If you go down that path, you'll need to pick up some other books, because OSGi is a big concept to grasp and master. The path of the web application is the beaten track, and there are plenty of materials and people who can help you if you come up against any problems.

13.6　*Summary and best practices*

In this chapter, we explored the internal details of how Camel starts up. You learned which options you can control and whether routes should be autostarted. You also learned how to dictate the order in which routes should be started.

More important, you learned how to shut down a running application in a reliable way without compromising the business. You learned about Camel's graceful shutdown procedures and what you can do to reorder your routes to ensure a better shutdown process.

You also learned how to stop and shut down routes at runtime. You can do this programmatically, which allows you to fully control when routes are operating and when they are not.

In the second part of this chapter, we explored the art of deploying Camel applications as standalone Java applications, as web applications, and by running Camel in an OSGi container. Remember that the deployment strategies covered in this book aren't all of your options. For example, Camel can also be deployed in the cloud, or they can be started using Java Web Start.

Here are some pointers to help you out with running and deployment:

- *Ensure reliable shutdown.* Take the time to configure and test that your application can be shut down in a reliable manner. You application is bound to be shut down at some point, whether for planned maintenance, upgrades, or unforeseen problems. In those situations, you want the application to shut down in a controlled manner without negatively affecting your business.
- *Use an existing runtime environment.* Camel is agile, flexible, and can be embedded in whatever production setup you may want to use. Don't introduce a new production environment just for the sake of using Camel. Use what's already working for you, and test early on in the project that your application can be deployed and run in the environment.

In the next (and final) chapter, we'll revisit Camel's routing capabilities, but we'll focus on the power of using annotations on beans. We'll also see how you can hide the Camel API from clients but still let clients interact with Camel by hiding the middleware layer.

14

Bean routing
and remoting

This chapter covers
- Routing using annotations on beans
- Using remoting and hiding middleware

In this chapter, we'll show you a couple of extra features in Camel that allow you to hide Camel APIs from users and developers. Hiding these APIs is sometimes necessary when you want to limit dependence on Camel. These techniques also provide approaches to solving integration problems that complement approaches we've discussed throughout this book.

First, you'll learn to use Camel's annotation-based routing, which allows regular Java beans to be used for routing. This allows you to access all of Camel's components and not write a single line of DSL code. You sacrifice many of the routing abilities that are provided in Camel's DSLs, but this isn't a problem for simple use cases.

When using the routing annotations, you still have to code against Camel APIs, just not the Camel DSL. We'll take this a step further in the last part of the chapter and discuss the art of hiding middleware. By hiding middleware, you allow users of your Camel application to only see the business interfaces; the complexity of remote transports and Camel APIs are hidden behind a clean client API.

Let's get started by looking at how to route messages using Camel's messaging annotations.

14.1   *Using beans for routing*

Throughout this book, you've seen how Camel's unique and powerful DSLs can be used to easily create complex integration applications. But in order to take advantage of this power, you need to learn a Camel DSL and its intricacies. Using a DSL also means that your application—at least the integration and routing portion—is tied to Camel. An alternative approach is to create simple integration applications. By using annotations, you can produce and consume (send and receive) messages to and from Camel endpoints by using a regular Java bean.

In this way, you don't need to learn much about Camel at all. You can write your application as you normally would in plain Java, and when you want to connect it to an external service, you can use an annotation from Camel. It sounds pretty simple because it is.

This approach of using Camel is only recommended for simple integration scenarios or when you can't invest the time to learn the Camel DSLs. We'll discuss when to use this approach in more detail in section 14.1.4.

First, let's see where this approach would be useful, and then we'll dive into the details of the messaging annotations.

14.1.1   *Inventory update at Rider Auto Parts*

Back in chapter 10, we looked at how Rider Auto Parts keeps an inventory of all the parts its suppliers currently have in stock. It was kept up to date by the suppliers periodically sending updates to Rider Auto Parts. Storing this information locally within Rider Auto Parts means the business can operate without being dependent on expensive online integrations with all the suppliers.

Suppose that you want this automated update to happen over JMS, because it has built-in reliable messaging, among other things. The updates will come in from multiple suppliers and enter through a single queue named `partnerInventoryUpdate`. Messages on this queue are then used to update the inventoryDB database. Figure 14.1 illustrates this flow.

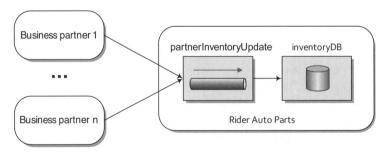

Figure 14.1   Business partners send inventory updates to the `partnerInventoryUpdate` queue. These updates are then used to update the internal inventory database.

Let's also suppose you have a Java class already available that can write this inventory update into a database. Here's the class.

Listing 14.1   A Java class that can update the inventory database

```
import javax.sql.DataSource;
import org.springframework.jdbc.core.JdbcTemplate;

public class InventoryUpdater {

    private JdbcTemplate jdbc;

    public InventoryUpdater(DataSource ds) {
        jdbc = new JdbcTemplate(ds);
    }

    public void updateInventory(Inventory inventory) {          Updates database
        jdbc.execute(toSql(inventory));                     ◁── with Spring JDBC
    }

    private String toSql(Inventory inventory) {
        Object[] args = new Object[] {
            inventory.getSupplierId(), inventory.getPartId(),
            inventory.getName(), inventory.getAmount() };
        return String.format("insert into partner_inventory " +
            "(supplier_id, part_id, name, amount) values " +
            "('%s', '%s', '%s', '%s')", args);
    }
}
```

This class has an `updateInventory` method that accepts a single parameter, an `Inventory` object, which contains details about the partner and the inventory that's being updated. This data is then fed into the inventory database.

We'll look at how the business partner sends to Rider Auto Parts in section 14.2, but for now we'll look at how this inventory service will be implemented on the Rider Auto Parts side.

14.1.2   Receiving messages with @Consume

Inventory messages are arriving at the JMS `partnerInventoryUpdate` queue, so you need to figure out how to consume them and feed them into the database. You also want to reuse the `InventoryUpdater` class shown in listing 14.1 as much as possible.

If you know how to create a route in one of Camel's DSLs, a solution may seem pretty obvious. You could set up a JMS consumer, as discussed in chapter 7, and then call the `InventoryUpdater` class using the bean component, as shown in chapter 4. Omitting the JMS component and bean setup, the route builder would look something like this:

```
public class InventoryUpdaterRoute extends RouteBuilder {
    @Override
    public void configure() throws Exception {
        from("jms:partnerInventoryUpdate")
            .to("bean:inventoryHelperInstance");
    }
}
```

To seasoned Camel users this will be simple to understand. But how can we do this without using Camel's DSLs?

The answer is, "through the `@Consume` annotation." By using the `@Consume` annotation in the `InventoryUpdater` bean, you can hook the `partnerInventoryUpdate` queue directly to the `updateInventory` method. Here's how this is done.

Listing 14.2 `InventoryUpdater` class connected to JMS queue by `@Consume`

```
import javax.sql.DataSource;

import org.apache.camel.Consume;
import org.springframework.jdbc.core.JdbcTemplate;

public class InventoryUpdater {

    ...
    @Consume(uri = "jms:partnerInventoryUpdate")
    public void updateInventory(Inventory inventory) {
        jdbc.execute(toSql(inventory));
    }
...
}
```

Connects method
to JMS queue

Adding this simple annotation tells Camel to consume messages from the `partnerInventoryUpdate` queue and invoke the `updateInventory` method with the contents. The `@Consume` annotation accepts any Camel endpoint URI, so you can easily hook up a method to anything that Camel supports!

To see this example in action, go to the chapter14/pojo-messaging directory in the book's source and run this Maven command:

```
mvn clean test
```

The test case will send a message to the `partnerInventoryUpdate` queue and check that the update makes it into the database.

You may be wondering how you get from a JMS message to an `Inventory` object. Just because you aren't using a `RouteBuilder` doesn't mean that automatic type conversion won't take place. In this case, Camel's type converters automatically convert the body of the JMS message to an `Inventory` object, which is the parameter of the invoked method. You may recall from chapter 4 that, by default, Camel assumes that if there is a single parameter in a method being called on a bean, the body of the message needs to be converted to match that type. You can also use any of the parameter-binding annotations mentioned in section 4.5.3 to define more precisely what data to map from the incoming message.

LOADING ANNOTATED CLASSES INTO CAMEL

Getting access to all of Camel's components through a simple annotation may seem like a bit of magic. As you may have guessed, there's a little more setup required to use these annotations.

The first thing you'll need to set up are the required dependencies: camel-core and camel-spring. You'll also need to use a `SpringCamelContext` as the base application—

a plain `DefaultCamelContext` from camel-core won't do. That's because when you create a `SpringCamelContext` in your Spring XML file, like so,

```
<camelContext id="camel" xmlns="http://camel.apache.org/schema/spring" />
```

it also registers a `CamelBeanPostProcessor` with the Spring application context. The `CamelBeanPostProcessor` is a Spring `BeanPostProcessor` that checks each new bean registered in the Spring application context for the `@Consume` and `@Produce` annotations. If it finds these annotations, it connects the bean to the specified Camel endpoints for you.

> **NOTE** We'll be discussing the `@Produce` annotation, which is used to send messages to a Camel endpoint, in section 14.1.3.

So all you have to do to use these annotations is create a `SpringCamelContext` and then create your bean within the Spring XML file, as follows:

```
<bean class="camelinaction.InventoryUpdater"/>
```

REFERENCING A SHARED ENDPOINT

If you have multiple beans consuming from the same endpoint URI, you may find it useful to define the endpoint once and reference it from each bean. This way, if the URI changes, you only have to change it in one place.

For example, you can set up a Camel endpoint in the context so it can be accessed from any bean:

```
<camelContext id="camel" xmlns="http://camel.apache.org/schema/spring">
  <endpoint id="inventoryQueue" uri="jms:partnerInventoryUpdate"/>
</camelContext>
```

Now you can reference the `inventoryQueue` endpoint within the `@Consume` annotation as follows:

```
@Consume(ref = "inventoryQueue")
public void updateInventory(Inventory inventory) {
    jdbc.execute(toSql(inventory));
}
```

This will have the same end result as if you were specifying the endpoint URI in the annotation. The only difference is that Camel won't have to resolve the endpoint instance (or create a new instance on the fly) because it's referencing an available instance.

SPECIFYING WHAT CAMELCONTEXT TO USE

If you have two `CamelContext` elements defined within one Spring XML file, you'll need to take extra care in making sure the `@Consume` annotation specifies which `CamelContext` it should apply to. Why is this? When you create a `SpringCamelContext`, a `BeanPostProcessor` is used to inspect each newly created bean and create consumers on the fly for the specified Camel endpoint. The problem with this is that you'll get a new consumer for each `CamelContext` defined! This may not be what you want to happen.

To get around this, you can specify the `CamelContext` id in the annotation definition. Suppose you have two `CamelContext` elements defined as follows:

```
<camelContext id="camel-1" xmlns="http://camel.apache.org/schema/spring" />
<camelContext id="camel-2" xmlns="http://camel.apache.org/schema/spring" />
```

When you use the `@Consume` annotation in your bean, you can specify the context by using the `context` attribute. For example, to reference the context with ID equal to `camel-1`, you could do the following:

```
@Consume(uri = "jms:partnerInventoryUpdate", context = "camel-1")
public void updateInventory(Inventory inventory) {
    jdbc.execute(toSql(inventory));
}
```

You now know all the details necessary for consuming messages from Camel endpoints using the `@Consume` annotation. We mentioned before that you can similarly use annotations for producing messages to Camel endpoints. We'll look at the `@Produce` annotation that does this next.

14.1.3　Sending messages with @Produce

You now have a new requirement for the `InventoryUpdater` bean. When you receive an inventory update from a partner, in addition to updating the database, you must send the update to the JMS `partnerAudit` queue for processing. Rider Auto Parts has added a new system that keeps track of how often partners send updates, whether updates had errors, and so on. Figure 14.2 illustrates this process.

This addition would be dead simple if you were using a Camel DSL route already, but you need to add this to your existing `InventoryUpdater` bean. You can do this by using the `@Produce` annotation.

Like the `@Consume` annotation described in the previous section, the `@Produce` annotation allows you to access any Camel endpoint without using one of Camel's DSLs. The difference is that the `@Produce` annotation doesn't attach to a method within a class; it attaches to a field or property setter within a class. This field can be either a `ProducerTemplate` or an interface you use in your business logic. In the case of a `ProducerTemplate`, Camel will simply inject a new `ProducerTemplate` that points to the URI you specify. If a plain interface is supplied, Camel has to do some extra work by injecting a proxy object. We'll look at both approaches next.

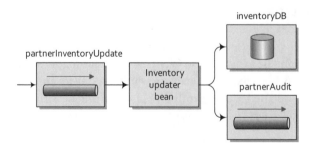

Figure 14.2　When an inventory update comes in, it's used to update the inventory database and it's also sent to the `partnerAudit` queue for auditing.

INJECTING A PRODUCERTEMPLATE

The `ProducerTemplate` class is a natural way of sending messages to Camel endpoints. You've seen it used in previous chapters, so its use should be familiar. A complete discussion of the `ProducerTemplate` is given in appendix C.

You can use the `@Produce` annotation to set up a `ProducerTemplate` for a particular endpoint URI.

Listing 14.3 Using the `@Produce` annotation to set up a `ProducerTemplate`

```
import javax.sql.DataSource;

import org.apache.camel.Consume;
import org.apache.camel.Produce;
import org.apache.camel.ProducerTemplate;
import org.springframework.jdbc.core.JdbcTemplate;

public class InventoryUpdaterAnnotatedWithProduce {         ❶ Sets up
                                                              ProducerTemplate
    @Produce(uri = "jms:partnerAudit")                        for URI
    ProducerTemplate partnerAudit;

    private JdbcTemplate jdbc;

    public InventoryUpdaterAnnotatedWithProduce(DataSource ds) {
        jdbc = new JdbcTemplate(ds);
    }

    @Consume(uri = "jms:partnerInventoryUpdate")
    public void updateInventory(Inventory inventory) {       ❷ Sends message using
        jdbc.execute(toSql(inventory));                         ProducerTemplate
        partnerAudit.sendBody(inventory);
    }

    ...

}
```

The `@Produce` annotation ❶ takes the endpoint URI `jms:partnerAudit` and creates a new `ProducerTemplate` for that URI. At any other point in the bean's use, you can then send messages to that endpoint using the `ProducerTemplate` that was created ❷.

You can also specify an endpoint reference or `CamelContext` to use for the `@Produce` annotation, as was described in the previous section for the `@Consume` annotation.

INJECTING A PROXY PRODUCER

It's also possible to send messages without using the `ProducerTemplate` at all. Camel allows you to specify an interface as the frontend for the endpoint specified. This approach allows you to eliminate the dependence on more Camel APIs, like the `ProducerTemplate`.

> **TIP** If you don't care about depending on Camel APIs, we recommend using the `ProducerTemplate` described in the previous section because it has less overhead than the solution we'll be describing next.

So how can you use a plain interface as the frontend for an endpoint? The short answer is that Camel creates an instance of the interface—a smart proxy object. This proxy object converts method calls into objects to be passed to the Camel endpoint. The whole process is described in more detail in section 14.2.2.

Suppose you define an interface for your backend audit processing systems as follows:

```
public interface PartnerAudit {
    public void audit(Inventory inventory);
}
```

The single `audit` method is intended to mean that the `Inventory` object passed in should be audited. The interface can then replace the `ProducerTemplate`, as shown here.

Listing 14.4   Using the `@Produce` annotation to set up a producer on an interface

```
import javax.sql.DataSource;

import org.apache.camel.Consume;
import org.apache.camel.Produce;
import org.springframework.jdbc.core.JdbcTemplate;

public class InventoryUpdaterAnnotatedWithProduceInterface {       ❶ Injects smart
                                                                       proxy
    @Produce(uri = "jms:partnerAudit")
    PartnerAudit partnerAudit;

    private JdbcTemplate jdbc;

    public InventoryUpdaterAnnotatedWithProduce(DataSource ds) {
        jdbc = new JdbcTemplate(ds);
    }

    @Consume(uri = "jms:partnerInventoryUpdate")
    public void updateInventory(Inventory inventory) {
        jdbc.execute(toSql(inventory));                            ❷ Sends message
        partnerAudit.audit(inventory);                                using interface
    }

    ...
}
```

The bean looks much like before, except that now there's no use of `Producer-Template`. Instead, you use the `PartnerAudit` interface as the binding point for the `@Produce` annotation ❶. This annotation will now tell Camel that a smart proxy object must be created that extends from `PartnerAudit` and passes on a message to the partnerAudit JMS queue. Then, when you call the `audit` method on the interface ❷, Camel sends a message to the endpoint specified in the `@Produce` annotation.

14.1.4 *When to use beans for routing*

You may be wondering when you should use the messaging annotations rather than one of Camel's DSLs. There's no clear-cut answer to the question, but we can give you some guidelines to make your decision easier.

In general, we recommend that you use one of Camel's DSLs if at all possible. They have built-in functionality for setting up common integration scenarios and will most likely make your life a lot easier. But they involve the added burden of learning more concepts.

You may want to use the messaging annotations in the following situations:

- You have a simple message flow where there is a single well-defined input or output URI. If you require a more dynamic bean when using annotations, see the `@RecipientList` annotation discussed in section 2.5.4.
- You would rather not learn about Camel's DSLs.
- You have a use case so simple that you have no need for EIPs.
- You just want to access Camel's library of components.

We want to stress that for complex integration scenarios, you should use one of Camel's DSLs. Trying to design a complex integration with the messaging annotations could lead to a messy solution—they were not designed for complex routings.

You've seen how you can reduce your dependence on Camel's DSLs with these annotations. Let's now take a look at how you can take that a step further and completely hide Camel from users of your application.

14.2 Hiding middleware

Middleware is defined as the software layer that lies between an operating system and an application. Middleware is used for interoperability among applications that are running in a coherent distributed system. Examples include Enterprise Application Integration (EAI), enterprise service buses (ESBs), and message queuing software (such as Apache ActiveMQ).

Camel is also used for integrating and providing interoperability among applications that may run in a coherent distributed system. You could potentially view Camel as middleware software, but that isn't entirely accurate, because Camel leverages third-party software where appropriate. For example, you can have Camel sitting on top of Apache ActiveMQ, and together they're middleware software.

An important aspect of writing software these days is trying to write business logic that focuses on the domain concepts as much as possible. You want your business logic to deal with the business domain rather than with the myriad of technology stacks out there, such as SOAP, REST, JMS, FTP, and XMPP.

One way to avoid this situation is to decouple as much middleware from your business logic as possible—to hide the middleware. By keeping your business logic hidden from the middleware, your application will be much more flexible and easy to change. This also makes the lives of clients who access the business logic easier, because they only have to deal with the business domain.

To demonstrate this, we'll cover a use case from Rider Auto Parts. You and your team have developed a *starter kit*, which is a piece of software new business partners can use to more easily integrate with Rider Auto Parts.

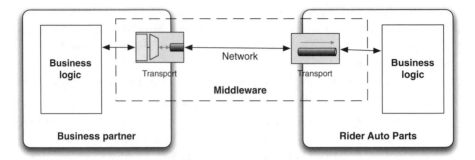

Figure 14.3   Each part of the business logic leverages middleware when communicating with the other parts.

The situation without the starter kit is two businesses needing to integrate their business logic. Because the business logic is distributed, the logic of one partner needs to communicate over the network in order to interact with the other partner's logic. That means the business logic needs to know about and use the transport. You want to hide the complexity of transports, which you can depict by labeling it as middleware, as shown in figure 14.3.

The starter kit is middleware software based on Camel and a selected third-party technology for the transport. The transport must support networking to transfer data from one machine to another. Such a transport could, for example, be HTTP- or messaging-based. The transport technology that best fits the situation should be chosen. For this example, the transport technology is messaging using Apache ActiveMQ.

The business partner deploys the starter kit in their infrastructure and uses it to communicate with Rider Auto Parts, as shown in figure 14.4.

In this example, the starter kit takes care of all the complexity involved in sending messages over the network using Apache ActiveMQ. All the business partner should focus on is a single client interface that defines the API they need to use.

In this section, you'll learn how to develop such a starter kit. We'll start by defining the client API and creating a simple test that runs in a single JVM. Then you'll learn how

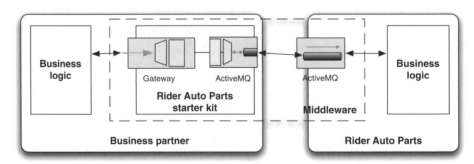

Figure 14.4   The starter kit is used by business partners to hide the middleware and easily communicate with Rider Auto Parts.

to change the middleware to switch transports without requiring any changes in the client. In section 14.2.2, we'll let the communication happen remotely between two JVMs using JMS as the transport, which is what you might use in a real-life situation.

14.2.1 *Introducing the starter kit*

The starter kit is a Camel application that defines a single interface for business partners to use when integrating their businesses with Rider Auto Parts. To keep the use case simple, the interface will provide the following two methods:

```
public interface RiderService {
    void updateInventory(Inventory inventory);
    List<ShippingDetail> shipInventory(String supplierId, String partId);
}
```

The first method is used by clients to send updated inventory information to Rider Auto Parts. This allows Rider Auto Parts to maintain current information about its suppliers' inventory situation, with all data being stored in a datastore within Rider Auto Parts. The second method is used by suppliers to find out which of the many Rider Auto Parts retail stores inventory should be shipped to.

THE DOMAIN

In this example, the information on the domain objects is kept simple and limited, as the following code snippets show (we've omitted the getters and setters):

```
public class Inventory implements Serializable {
    private String supplierId;
    private String partId;
    private String name;
    private String amount;
    ...
}
```

Here's the `ShippingDetail` domain object:

```
public class ShippingDetail implements Serializable {
    private String address;
    private String zip;
    private String country;
    private String amount;
    ...
}
```

Using the `RiderService` interface, it should be easy for business partners to send inventory information to Rider Auto Parts, as the following code example shows:

```
private void updateInventory(RiderService rider) {
    Inventory inventory = new Inventory("1234", "4444");
    inventory.setName("Bumper");
    inventory.setAmount("57");

    rider.updateInventory(inventory);
}
```

This example demonstrates the concept of decoupling business logic from the middleware. The example is pure business logic, focusing on assembling inventory information and sending it to Rider Auto Parts using the `RiderService` API. The example has no middleware logic; there's no logic present to indicate how the data is actually sent. In this case, Camel is the middleware, and the example doesn't use any Camel APIs at all. You've fully decoupled your business logic from the integration logic.

With the domain in place, let's turn our attention to setting up Camel. First you'll want to create a test that runs on a single JVM.

SETTING UP CAMEL

In Camel, you need to set up two things to implement your first test. You need a mocked `RiderService` that can act as Rider Auto Parts and return dummy data. This is easy to do—all it involves is implementing the `RiderService` interface.

Listing 14.5   Simulating Rider Auto Parts

```java
public class RiderAutoPartsMock implements RiderService {
    private static Log LOG = LogFactory.getLog(RiderAutoPartsMock.class);

    public void updateInventory(Inventory inventory) {
        LOG.info("Updating inventory " + inventory);
    }

    public List<ShippingDetail> shipInventory(String supplierId,
                                              String partId) {
        LOG.info("Shipping to Rider Road 66 and Ocean View 123");

        ShippingDetail detail = new ShippingDetail();
        detail.setAddress("Rider Road 66");
        detail.setCountry("USA");
        detail.setZip("90210");
        detail.setAmount("89");

        ShippingDetail detail2 = new ShippingDetail();
        detail2.setAddress("Ocean View 123");
        detail2.setCountry("USA");
        detail2.setZip("89103");
        detail2.setAmount("45");

        List<ShippingDetail> answer = new ArrayList<ShippingDetail>();
        answer.add(detail);
        answer.add(detail2);
        return answer;
    }
}
```

You then need to create a Spring XML file.

Listing 14.6   Spring XML setting up Camel

```xml
<beans xmlns="http://www.springframework.org/schema/beans"
       xmlns:xsi="http://www.w3.org/2001/XMLSchema-instance"
       xmlns:camel="http://camel.apache.org/schema/spring"
       xsi:schemaLocation="
         http://www.springframework.org/schema/beans
```

```
            http://www.springframework.org/schema/beans/spring-beans-3.0.xsd
            http://camel.apache.org/schema/spring
            http://camel.apache.org/schema/spring/camel-spring.xsd">

    <bean id="riderMocked"                                      ◁───  Simulates Rider
          class="camelinaction.RiderAutoPartsMock"/>            ❶    Auto Parts

    <camelContext xmlns="http://camel.apache.org/schema/spring">
        <proxy id="rider"                                       ◁───  Proxies
                serviceInterface="camelinaction.RiderService"         Camel route
                serviceUrl="direct:rider"/>                     ❷    as interface

        <route>
            <from uri="direct:rider"/>              ❸  Specifies route
            <to uri="bean:riderMocked"/>               to be invoked
        </route>
    </camelContext>
</beans>
```

First you have to define a Spring bean, `riderMocked` ❶ (the class from listing 14.5), which is used to simulate the Rider Auto Parts business.

The next part is the interesting part—it's the mechanism that decouples the business logic from the middleware. This is done by proxying ❷ the `RiderService` interface and having its method invocations proxied by sending a message to the given endpoint. We'll cover this in much more detail in section 14.2.2.

What remains is to define a route ❸ that sends the messages to Rider Auto Parts. In this example, you route the message to the mocked bean that simulates Rider Auto Parts.

The source code for the book contains this example in the chapter14/starterkit directory. You can run this example by using the following Maven goal:

```
mvn test -Dtest=StarterKitMockedTest
```

When you run the example, you should see the following lines, among others, on the console:

```
[main] INFO - Sending inventory
[main] INFO - Updating inventory 1234, 4444, Bumper, 57
[main] INFO - Shipping to Rider Road 66 and Ocean View 123
[main] INFO - Received shipping details
```

If you check the source code for the `camelinaction.StarterKitMockedTest` class, you should notice that it's not using any Camel code to execute the business logic.

In the introduction to this section, we said that Camel can hide the middleware, allowing you to decouple your business logic from the transport. You'll now see this in action as you change the transport from direct to the SEDA component without requiring any changes in the business logic.

CHANGING THE TRANSPORT TO SEDA

Changing the transport to SEDA is easily done in the Spring XML file, as follows:

```
<camelContext xmlns="http://camel.apache.org/schema/spring">
    <proxy id="rider"
            serviceInterface="camelinaction.RiderService"
```

```
            serviceUrl="seda:rider"/>

    <route>
        <from uri="seda:rider"/>
        <to uri="bean:riderMocked"/>
    </route>
</camelContext>
```

You can run this example using the following Maven goal:

```
mvn test -Dtest=StarterKitMockedSedaTest
```

When you run the example, you should see the following lines on the console:

```
[         main] INFO - Sending inventory
[seda://rider] INFO - Updating inventory 1234, 4444, Bumper, 57
[seda://rider] INFO - Shipping to Rider Road 66 and Ocean View 123
[         main] INFO - Received shipping details
```

The difference between this example and the previous one is that by using SEDA you let another thread process the route (indicated by the [seda://rider] in the console output).

Listing 14.6 uses a Camel proxy to hide the middleware, by using the <proxy/> tag. We'll now look at how this works.

14.2.2 *Using Spring remoting and Camel proxies*

Using a Camel proxy is similar to using Spring remoting, which is a feature in the Spring Framework that offers remoting support for various technologies, making it easier to remote-enable services. Spring has a limited set of technologies that can be used. Camel takes this a big step forward by remote-enabling all of the Camel components.

To understand how a Camel proxy works, let's start by adding a log in the route from listing 14.6 that will output information about the actual messages sent by the Camel proxy:

```
<route>
    <from uri="direct:rider"/>
    <to uri="log:rider"/>
    <to uri="bean:riderMocked"/>
</route>
```

The console outputs the following:

```
[main] INFO rider - Exchange[ExchangePattern:InOut,
BodyType:org.apache.camel.component.bean.BeanInvocation,
Body:BeanInvocation public abstract void
  camelinaction.RiderService.updateInventory(camelinaction.Inventory)
  with [1234, 4444, Bumper, 57]]]
```

As you can see from the output, Camel uses a BeanInvocation type in the message body. The purpose of the BeanInvocation is to hold information about a bean invocation. It indicates that the updateInventory method is to be invoked with these parameters.

Because BeanInvocation is serializable, it's possible to send it over a remote network and have it invoked on the remote side. Let's try this using JMS as the transport and using two JVMs.

USING JMS AS THE TRANSPORT

Next, we'll look at a client and server each in separate JVMs, using JMS as the transport. First we'll discuss the server and how to start it. Then we'll look at the client and run it to see it in action.

Here's the Spring XML file you use to define the server.

Listing 14.7 Server with ActiveMQ broker

```
<broker:broker persistent="false" brokerName="localhost">
    <broker:transportConnectors>
        <broker:transportConnector name="tcp" uri="tcp://localhost:61616"/>
    </broker:transportConnectors>
</broker:broker>

<bean id="riderMocked" class="camelinaction.RiderAutoPartsMock"/>

<camelContext xmlns="http://camel.apache.org/schema/spring">
    <route>
        <from uri="activemq:queue:rider"/>
        <to uri="log:server"/>
        <to uri="bean:riderMocked"/>
    </route>
</camelContext>
```

❶ ActiveMQ broker

❷ Route with service

On the server you embed an Apache ActiveMQ broker that uses TCP as the transport on port 61616 ❶. As you have two JVMs, you need a remote protocol, which in this case is TCP. In the route, you consume messages from the ActiveMQ `rider` queue ❷, which is the destination where the client will send the messages. Because you use an embedded ActiveMQ broker, you don't need to define an ActiveMQ component because Camel can leverage an intra-VM connection.

You can start the server using the following Maven command in the chapter14/starterkit directory:

```
mvn compile exec:java -PServer
```

The client is simple. All you need to do is define the proxy and configure the ActiveMQ transport, as follows:

```
<bean id="activemq"
      class="org.apache.activemq.camel.component.ActiveMQComponent">
    <property name="brokerURL" value="tcp://localhost:61616"/>
</bean>

<camelContext xmlns="http://camel.apache.org/schema/spring">
    <proxy id="rider"
           serviceInterface="camelinaction.RiderService"
           serviceUrl="activemq:queue:rider"/>
</camelContext>
```

You can run the client using the following Maven command in the chapter14/starterkit directory:

```
mvn test -Dtest=StarterKitClientTest
```

When the client is run, you should see activity in both the client and server consoles. The server should log the message received, which is similar to what you saw previously when JMS wasn't used as the transport:

```
12:34:07 - Exchange[ExchangePattern:InOut,
➥BodyType:org.apache.camel.component.bean.BeanInvocation,
➥Body:BeanInvocation public abstract void
➥camelinaction.RiderService.updateInventory(camelinaction.Inventory)
 ➥with [1234, 4444, Bumper, 57]]]
12:34:07 - Updating inventory 1234, 4444, Bumper, 57
```

Now you've seen how to decouple your business logic from the middleware and change the transport without any code changes to the business logic. With that, it's time to look under the hood at how this works.

HOW CAMEL PROXIES WORK

The code for creating Camel proxies is located in camel-core as the `org.apache.camel.component.bean.ProxyHelper` class, and it has various methods for proxying an interface with a Camel endpoint. In fact the `<proxy/>` tag you used in Spring XML is a facade that leverages the `ProxyHelper` class.

Figure 14.5 is a sequence diagram that depicts what happens at runtime when a client invokes the `shipInventory` method on a proxied `RiderService` interface.

In this figure, a client invokes the `shipInventory` method on `RiderService`. This is proxied with the help of `java.lang.reflect.Proxy`, which invokes the `CamelInvocationHandler`. This handler creates a `BeanInvocation` that contains information about the method (and its parameters) invoked on the proxy. Then the `BeanInvocation` is sent to the endpoint using a Camel `Producer`, which waits for the response to

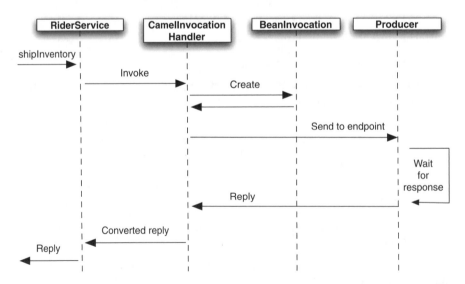

Figure 14.5   A sequence diagram showing how a Camel proxy works under the covers, sending a `BeanInvocation` message to a remote endpoint and waiting for the reply, which eventually is returned to the caller

come back. The response is then adapted to the RiderService by converting it to the same type as the return type on the method.

> **NOTE** Camel proxies will, by default, always use request-response messaging style (InOut) when a proxied method is invoked. This also applies to methods that don't return a value (whose return type is void). You can enforce a method to use the fire-and-forget messaging style (InOnly) by adding the @InOnly annotation to the method definition in the interface. But keep in mind that when using @InOnly, the method call will be fully asynchronous, so you won't know if the receiver processed the message successfully. For example, exceptions thrown by the receiver won't be propagated back to the method call.

When using a Camel proxy, there's a single rule that must be adhered to.

RULE WHEN USING A CAMEL PROXY

Camel proxies use a BeanInvocation as the message body sent to the endpoint. If the endpoint is representing a remote destination, the message body must be serialized so it can be sent over the wire. This is why the information stored in BeanInvocation must be serializable. For Camel end users, that means the parameters you pass to the proxied interface must be serializable.

For example, if you look at the updateInventory method in the RiderService interface, you can see that it uses an Inventory object as a parameter.

```
public interface RiderService {
    void updateInventory(Inventory inventory);
    List<ShippingDetail> shipInventory(String supplierId, String partId);
}
```

When you invoke the updateInventory method, as shown in the following test snippet, the Inventory object must be serializable.

```
public void testStarterKitUpdateInventory() throws Exception {
    RiderService rider = context.getRegistry().lookup("rider",
                              RiderService.class);

    Inventory inventory = new Inventory("1234", "4444");
    inventory.setName("Bumper");
    inventory.setAmount("57");

    rider.updateInventory(inventory);
}
```

This is done by implementing the java.io.Serializable interface on the Inventory class:

```
public class Inventory implements Serializable {
    ...
}
```

The same rule applies to data being returned, so the shipInventory method must also return serializable data, which is ensured by letting the ShippingDetail class implement java.io.Serializable.

USING A CAMEL PROXY FROM THE JAVA DSL

You can also create a proxy in Java code. For example, the following example from Spring XML,

```
<camelContext xmlns="http://camel.apache.org/schema/spring">
    <proxy id="rider"
           serviceInterface="camelinaction.RiderService"
           serviceUrl="activemq:queue:rider"/>
</camelContext>
```

can be rewritten in Java code using `org.apache.camel.builder.ProxyBuilder` as follows:

```
RiderService rider = new ProxyBuilder(context).endpoint("seda:rider")
                                .build(RiderService.class);
```

The source code for the book contains an example in the chapter14/starterkit directory. You can try it with the following Maven goal:

```
mvn test -Dtest=StarterKitJavaProxyBuilderTest
```

You've now learned how to decouple your business logic from the integration logic by hiding the middleware with help from Camel proxies.

14.3   *Summary and best practices*

In this last chapter of *Camel in Action*, we've shown you ways of using Camel that minimize your dependence on Camel APIs and completely hide Camel from your application's users. These abilities are considered extra features of Camel, rather than core pieces. They add functionality that experienced Camel users, which you now are, can appreciate.

There are a few things you should take away from this chapter:

- *The messaging annotations are great for simple use cases.* When all you want to do is hook up a bean to a transport supported by Camel, the messaging annotations are an easy way to go. There is little learning overhead with these, compared to using the Camel DSLs. We still recommend the Camel DSLs for more complex scenarios.
- *Use hiding middleware principles when you don't want to expose your transports.* In some cases, you may not want clients of your service to know what transport you're using to communicate with the backend. For instance, you may want to change the transport in the future without changing the client's code.

You've now made it through many Camel and general enterprise integration concepts; you have the knowledge to tackle complex integration problems with Camel.

As a final suggestion, try to keep in touch with the Camel community. It's a busy and exciting place, and we'd love to hear from you there. Hope you've enjoyed the ride!

appendix A
Simple,
the expression language

Camel offers a powerful expression language, which back in the earlier days wasn't as powerful and was labeled *Simple*. It has evolved to become much more since then, but don't worry: it's still simple to use.

The Simple language is provided out of the box in the camel-core JAR file, which means you don't have to add any JARs on the classpath to use it.

A.1 Introducing Simple

In a nutshell, the Simple expression language evaluates an expression on the current instance of Exchange that is under processing. The Simple language can be used for both expressions and predicates, which makes it a perfect match to be used in your Camel routes.

For example, the Content-Based Router EIP can leverage the Simple language to define predicates in the when clauses, as shown here:

```
from("activemq:queue:quotes")
    .choice()
        .when(simple("${body} contains 'Camel'")).to("activemq:camel")
        .when(simple("${header.amount} > 1000")).to("activemq:bigspender")
        .otherwise().to("activemq:queue:other");
```

The equivalent Spring XML example would be as follows:

```
<route>
    <from uri="activemq:queue:quotes"/>
    <choice>
        <when>
            <simple>${body} contains 'Camel'</simple>
            <to uri="activemq:camel"/>
        </when>
```

```
        <when>
            <simple>${header.amount} > 1000</simple>
            <to uri="activemq:bigspender"/>
        </when>
        <otherwise>
            <to uri="activemq:queue:other"/>
        </otherwise>
    </choice>
</route>
```

As you can see from the preceding examples, the Simple expression is understandable and similar to other scripting languages. In these examples, Camel will evaluate the expression as a `Predicate`, which means the result is a `boolean`, which is either `true` or `false`. In the example, you use operators to determine whether the message body contains the word `Camel` or whether the message header `amount` is larger than `1000`.

That gives you a taste of the Simple language. Let's look at its syntax.

A.2   Syntax

The Simple language uses `${ }` placeholders for dynamic expressions, such as those in the previous examples. You can use multiple `${ }` placeholders in the same expression, but nested placeholders aren't supported.

The following expression *is not* valid:

```
"${header.${header.bar}}"
```

The following *is* valid:

```
"Hello ${header.name} thanks for ordering ${body}"
```

An alternative syntax was introduced in Camel 2.5 to accommodate a clash with Spring's property placeholder feature. You can now also use `$simple{ }` placeholders with Simple, such as shown in this example:

```
"Hello $simple{header.name} thanks for ordering $simple{body}"
```

These examples use variables such as `body` and `header`. The next section covers this.

A.3   Built-in variables

The Simple language provides a number of variables that bind to information in the current `Exchange`. You've already seen the `body` and `header`. Table A.1 lists all the variables available.

Table A.1   Variables in the Simple language

Variable	Type	Description
body in.body	Object	Contains the input message body
out.body	Object	Contains the output message body

Table A.1   Variables in the Simple language *(continued)*

Variable	Type	Description

`header.XXX`
`in.header.XXX`
`in.headers.XXX`
	`Object`	Contains the input message header XXX

`out.header.XXX` `out.headers.XXX`	`Object`	Contains the output message header XXX
`property.XXX`	`Object`	Contains the `Exchange` property XXX
`exchangeId`	`String`	Contains the unique ID of the `Exchange`
`sys.XXX` `sysenv.XXX`	`String`	Contains the system environment XXX
`exception`	`Object`	Contains the exception on the `Exchange`, if any exists
exception.stacktrace	`String`	Contains the exception `stacktrace` on the `Exchange`, if any exists; requires Camel 2.6 or better
`exception.message`	`String`	Contains the exception message on the `Exchange`, if any exists
`threadName`	`String`	Contains the name of the current thread; can be used for logging purposes

The variables can easily be used in a Simple expression, as you've already seen. Logging the message body can be done using ${body} as shown in the following route snippet:

```
from("activemq:queue:quotes")
    .log("We received ${body}")
    .to("activemq:queue:process");
```

The Simple language also has a set of built-in functions.

A.4   Built-in functions

The Simple language has four functions at your disposal, as listed in table A.2.

Table A.2   Functions provided in the Simple language

Function	Type	Description
`bodyAs(type)`	`type`	Converts the `body` to the given type. For example, `bodyAs(String)` or `bodyAs(com.foo.MyType)`. Will return `null` if the body could not be converted.
`mandatoryBodyAs(type)`	`type`	Converts the body to the given type. Will throw a `NoTypeConversionAvailableException` if the body could not be converted.

Table A.2   Functions provided in the Simple language *(continued)*

Function	Type	Description
headerAs(key, type)	type	Converts the header with the given key to the given type. Will return null if the header could not be converted.
bean:beanId[?method]	Object	Invokes a method on a bean. Camel will look up the bean with the given ID from the Registry and invoke the appropriate method. You can optionally explicitly specify the name of the method to invoke.
date:command:pattern	String	Formats a date. The command must be either now or header.XXX: now represents the current timestamp, whereas header.XXX will use the header with the key XXX. The pattern is based on the java.text.SimpleDataFormat format.
properties:[locations:]key	String	Resolves a property with the given key using the Camel Properties component. The Camel Properties component is covered in section 6.1.6 of chapter 6.

For example, to log a formatted date from the message header, you could do as follows:

```
<route>
    <from uri="activemq:queue:quote"/>
    <log message="Quote date ${date:header.myDate:yyyy-MM-dd HH:mm:ss}"/>
    <to uri="activemq:queue:process"/>
</route>
```

In this example, the input message is expected to contain a header with the key myDate, which should be of type java.util.Date.

Suppose you need to organize received messages into a directory structure containing the current day's date as a parent folder. The file producer has direct support for specifying the target filename using the Simple language as shown in bold:

```
from("activemq:queue:quote")
    .to("file:backup/?fileName=${date:now:yyyy-MM-dd}/${exchangeId}.txt")
    .to("activemq:queue:process");
```

Now suppose the file must use a filename generated from a bean. You can use the bean function to achieve this:

```
from("activemq:queue:quote")
    .to("file:backup/?fileName=${bean:uuidBean?method=generate}")
        .to("activemq:queue:process");
```

In this example, Camel will look up the bean with the ID uuidBean from the Registry and invoke the generate method. The output of this method invocation is returned and used as the filename.

The Camel Properties component is used for property placeholders. For example, you could store a property in a file containing a configuration for a big-spender threshold.

```
big=5000
```

Then you could refer to the `big` properties key from the Simple language:

```
from("activemq:queue:quotes")
    .choice()
        .when(simple("${header.amount} > ${properties.big}")
            .to("activemq:bigspender")
        .otherwise()
            .to("activemq:queue:other");
```

The Simple language also has built-in variables when working with the Camel File and FTP components.

A.5   *Built-in file variables*

Files consumed using the File or FTP components have file-related variables available to the Simple language. Table A.3 lists those variables.

Table A.3   File-related variables available when consuming files

Variable	Type	Description
`file:name`	`String`	Contains the filename (relative to the starting directory)
`file:name.ext`	`String`	Contains the file extension
`file:name.noext`	`String`	Contains the filename without extension (relative to the starting directory)
`file:onlyname`	`String`	Contains the filename without any leading paths
`file:onlyname.noext`	`String`	Contains the filename without extension and leading paths
`file:parent`	`String`	Contains the file parent (the paths leading to the file)
`file:path`	`String`	Contains the file path (including leading paths)
`file:absolute`	`Boolean`	Whether or not the filename is an absolute or relative file path
`file:absolute.path`	`String`	Contains the absolute file path.
`file:length` `file:size`	`Long`	Contains the file length
`file:modified`	`Date`	Contains the modification date of the file as a `java.util.Date` type

Among other things, the file variables can be used to log which file has been consumed:

```
<route>
    <from uri="file://inbox"/>
    <log message="Picked up ${file:name}"/>
    ...
</route>
```

The File and FTP endpoints have options that accept Simple language expressions. For example, the File consumer can be configured to move processed files into a folder you specify. Suppose you must move files into a directory structure organized by dates. This can be done by specifying the expression in the move option, as follows:

```
<from uri="file://inbox?move=backup/${date:now:yyyyMMdd}/${file:name}"/>
```

TIP   The FTP endpoint supports the same move option as shown here.

Another example where the file variables come in handy is if you have to process files differently based on the file extension. For example, suppose you have CSV and XML files:

```
from("file://inbox")
    .choice()
        .when(simple("${file:ext} == 'txt'")).to("direct:txt")
        .when(simple("${file.ext} == 'xml'")).to("direct:xml")
        .otherwise().to("direct:unknown");
```

NOTE   You can read more about the file variables at the Camel website: http://camel.apache.org/file-language.html.

In this appendix, we've used the Simple language for predicates. In fact, the previous example determines whether the file is a text file or not. Doing this requires operators.

A.6   *Built-in operators*

The first example in this appendix implemented the Content-Based Router EIP with the Simple expression language. It used predicates to determine where to route a message, and these predicates use operators. Table A.4 lists all the operators supported in Simple.

Table A.4   Operators provided in the Simple language

Operator	Description
==	Tests whether the left side is equal to the right side
>	Tests whether the left side is greater than the right side
>=	Tests whether the left side is greater than or equal to the right side
<	Tests whether the left side is less than the right side
<=	Tests whether the left side is less than or equal to the right side
!=	Tests whether the left side is not equal to the right side
contains	Tests whether the left side contains the String value on the right side
not contains	Tests whether the left side doesn't contain the String value on the right side
in	Tests whether the left side is in a set of values specified on the right side; the values must be separated by commas

Table A.4 Operators provided in the Simple language *(continued)*

Operator	Description
not in	Tests whether the left side is not in a set of values specified on the right side; the values must be separated by commas
range	Tests whether the left side is within a range of values defined with the following syntax: *from..to*
not range	Tests whether the left side is not within a range of values defined with the following syntax: *from..to*
regex	Tests whether the left side matches a regular expression pattern defined as a String value on the right side
not regex	Tests whether the left side doesn't match a regular expression pattern defined as a String value on the right side
is	Tests whether the left side type is an instance of the value on the right side
not is	Tests whether the left side type is not an instance of the value on the right side

The operators require the following syntax:

```
${leftValue} <OP> rightValue
```

The value on the left side must be enclosed in a ${ } placeholder. The operator must be separated with a single space on the left and right. The right value can either be a fixed value or another dynamic value enclosed using ${ }.

Let's look at some examples.

```
simple("${in.header.foo} == Camel")
```

Here you test whether the foo header is equal to the String value "Camel". If you want to test for "Camel rocks", you must enclose the String in quotes (because the value contains a space):

```
simple("${in.header.foo} == 'Camel rocks'")
```

Camel will automatically type coerce, so you can compare apples to oranges. Camel will regard both as fruit:

```
simple("${in.header.bar} < 200")
```

Suppose the bar header is a String with the value "100". Camel will convert this value to the same type as the value on the right side, which is numeric. It will therefore compute 100 < 200, which renders true.

You can use the range operator to test whether a value is in a numeric range.

```
simple("${in.header.bar} range 100..199")
```

Both the from and to range values are inclusive. You must define the range exactly as shown.

A regular expression can be used to test a variety of things, such as whether a value is a four-digit value:

```
simple("${in.header.bar} regex '\d{4}'")
```

You can also use the built-in functions with the operators. For example, to test whether a given header has today's date, you can leverage the date function:

```
simple("${in.header.myDate} == ${date:now:yyyyMMdd}")
```

> **TIP** You can see more examples in the Camel Simple online documentation: http://camel.apache.org/simple.html.

The Simple language also allows you to combine two expressions together.

A.6.1 Combining expressions

The Simple language can combine expressions using the and or or operators.

The syntax for combining two expressions is as follows:

```
${leftValue} <OP> rightValue <and|or> ${leftValue} <OP> rightValue
```

Here's an example using and to group two expressions:

```
simple("${in.header.bar} < 200 and ${body} contains 'Camel'")
```

From Camel 2.5 onwards you can combine any number of expressions. In previous releases you could only combine exactly two expressions.

The Simple language also supports an OGNL feature.

A.7 The OGNL feature

Both the Simple language and Bean component support an Object Graph Navigation Language (OGNL) feature when specifying the method name to invoke. OGNL allows you to specify a chain of methods in the expression.

Suppose the message body contains a Customer object that has a getAddress() method. To get the ZIP code of the address, you would simply type the following:

```
simple("${body.getAddress().getZip()}")
```

You can use a shorter notation, omitting the get prefix and the parentheses.

```
simple("${body.address.zip}")
```

In this example, the ZIP code will be returned. But if the getAddress method returns null, the example would cause a NoSuchMethodException to be thrown by Camel. If you want to avoid this, you can use the null-safe operator ?. as follows:

```
simple("${body?.address.zip}")
```

The methods in the OGNL expression can be any method name. For example, to invoke a sayHello method, you would do this:

```
simple("${body.sayHello}")
```

Camel uses the bean parameter binding, which we covered in chapter 4. This means that the method signature of sayHello can have parameters that are bound to the current Exchange being routed:

```
public String sayHello(String body) {
    return "Hello " + body;
}
```

The OGNL feature has specialized support for accessing Map and List types. For example, suppose the getAddress method has a getLines method that returns a List. You could access the lines by their index values, as follows:

```
simple("${body.address.lines[0]}")
simple("${body.address.lines[1]}")
simple("${body.address.lines[2]}")
```

If you try to index an element that is out of bounds, an IndexOutOfBoundsException exception is thrown. You can use the null-safe operator to suppress this exception:

```
simple("${body.address?.lines[2]}")
```

If you want to access the last element, you can use last as the index value, as shown here:

```
simple("${body.address.lines[last]}")
```

The access support for Maps is similar, but you use a key instead of a numeric value as the index. Suppose the message body contains a getType method that returns a Map instance. You could access the gold entry as follows:

```
simple("${body.type[gold]}")
```

You could even invoke a method on the gold entry like this:

```
simple("${body.type[gold].sayHello}")
```

This concludes our tour of the various features supported by the Camel Simple language. We'll now take a quick look at how to use the Simple language from custom Java code.

A.8 Using Simple from custom Java code

The Simple language is most often used directly in your Camel routes, in either the Java DSL or a Spring XML file. But it's also possible to use it from custom Java code.

Here's an example that uses the Simple language from a Camel Processor.

Listing A.1 Using the Simple language from custom Java code

```
import org.apache.camel.Exchange;
import org.apache.camel.Processor;
import org.apache.camel.builder.SimpleBuilder;

public class MyProcessor implements Processor {

    public void process(Exchange exchange) throws Exception {
        SimpleBuilder simple = new SimpleBuilder(
```

```
                                   "${body} contains 'Camel'");
        if (simple.matches(exchange) {
            System.out.println("This is a Camel message");
        } else {
            System.out.println("This is NOT a Camel message");
        }
    }
}
```

As you can see in listing A.1, all it takes is creating an instance of `SimpleBuilder`, which is capable of evaluating either a predicate or an expression. In the listing, you use the Simple language as a predicate.

To use an expression to say "Hello," you could do the following:

```
SimpleBuilder simple = new SimpleBuilder("Hello ${header.name}");
String s = simple.evaluate(exchange, String.class);
System.out.println(s);
```

Notice how you specify that you want the response back as a `String` by passing in `String.class` to the `evaluate` method.

Listing A.1 uses the Simple language from within a Camel `Processor`, but you're free to use it anywhere, such as from a custom bean. Just keep in mind that the `Exchange` must be passed into the `matches` method on the `SimpleBuilder`.

A.9   *Summary*

This appendix covered the Simple language, which is an expression language provided with Camel.

You saw how well it blends with Camel routes, which makes it easy to define predicates in routes, such as those needed when using the Content-Based Router.

We also looked at how easy it was with the Simple language to access information from the `Exchange` message by using the built-in variables. You saw that Simple provides functions, such as a date function that formats dates and a bean function that invokes methods on beans.

Finally, we covered OGNL notation, which makes it even easier to access data from nested beans.

All together, the Simple language is a great expression language that should help you with 95 percent of your use cases.

appendix B
Expressions
and predicates

Expressions and predicates are built-in types in Camel that you've seen used throughout this book. They're very versatile and are used in different places, but they're most noticeable in the Camel routes. For example, predicates are used in the Message Filter and Content-Based Router EIPs. Expressions are used for computing correlation keys for the Aggregator EIP, and appendix A covered the Simple expression language, which is another testament to the versatility of expressions.

B.1   Expressions

A Camel expression (`org.apache.camel.Expression`) is evaluated at runtime on the instance of `Exchange` that is under processing. You can use either standard or custom expressions.

B.1.1   Standard expressions

The `org.apache.camel.Expression` interface is as follows:

```
public interface Expression {
    <T> T evaluate(Exchange exchange, Class<T> type);
}
```

The `evaluate` method uses generics to specify the desired return type.

SYNTAX SUGAR

Camel provides syntax sugar for working with expressions. Suppose you want to implement a route that can return a message consisting of "Hello " plus the input message. This can be done using the Message Translator EIP, which leverages an `Expression` to transform a message. With the help of the syntax sugar, you can use the fluent builder style in the Java DSL to express that you want to prepend "Hello " to the message body:

```
from("direct:hey").transform(body().prepend("Hello "));
```

Alternatively, you could use the Simple expression language (covered in appendix A), which may be easier to understand in this example:

```
from("direct:hey").transform(simple("Hello ${body}"));
```

Simple comes in handy when using Spring XML, because it's a scripting language that can be used in XML, as opposed to the former solution, which can't easily be used in Spring XML. That's because it's based on Java code, which you can't use directly in Spring XML files.

USING EXPRESSIONS WITH SPRING XML

In the Java DSL, you have all the power of the Java language, which you don't have at your fingertips in Spring XML. The following route isn't possible in Spring XML.

```
<route>
    <from uri="direct:hey"/>
    <transform>
        <body><prepend>Hello </prepend></body>
    </transform>
</route>
```

Instead, you can leverage Simple, like this:

```
<route>
    <from uri="direct:hey"/>
    <transform>
        <simple>Hello ${body}</simple>
    </transform>
</route>
```

Although Camel provides a lot of built-in expressions to support many common use cases, there could be situations where you need to implement a custom expression.

B.1.2   Using custom expressions

Suppose you need to transform the message in a different way, and only the power of the Java programming language can perform the transformation. In this case, you can use a custom expression, as shown in listing B.1.

Listing B.1   Implementing a custom expression

```
public class MyExpression implements Expression {

    public <T> T evaluate(Exchange exchange, Class<T> type) {
        String body = exchange.getIn().getBody(String.class);
        Object answer;
        if (body.contains("Camel")) {
            answer = "Yes Camel rocks";
        } else {
            answer = "Hello " + body;
```

```
        }
        return exchange.getContext().getTypeConverter()
                .convertTo(type, answer);
    }
}
```

Using a custom expression in the Java DSL is just a matter of providing an instance in the Transform EIP, as follows:

```
from("direct:hey").transform(new MyExpression());
```

When using custom expressions in Spring XML, you have to define the expression as a bean, and then use the method call expression to invoke the expression:

```
<bean id="myExpression" class="camelinaction.MyExpression"/>

<camelContext id="camel" xmlns="http://camel.apache.org/schema/spring">
    <route>
        <from uri="direct:hey"/>
        <transform>
            <method ref="myExpression"/>
        </transform>
    </route>
</camelContext>
```

You may have noticed that listing B.1 uses the Camel type converter to convert the answer to the given type. Camel offers an `ExpressionAdapter` class that removes the need for converting. Here's the same custom expression using the adapter:

Listing B.2 Implementing custom expression by extending `ExpressionAdapter`

```
public class MyExpression extends ExpressionAdapter {

    @Override
    public Object evaluate(Exchange exchange) {
        String body = exchange.getIn().getBody(String.class);
        if (body.contains("Camel")) {
            return "Yes Camel rocks";
        } else {
            return "Hello " + body;
        }
    }
}
```

That's it for expressions. Let's look now at predicates.

B.2 Predicates

A Camel predicate (`org.apache.camel.Predicate`) is a specialized expression that always returns a `boolean` type. This makes predicates useful for yes/no kinds of expressions. For example, predicates are used with the Content-Based Router EIP. There are standard predicates and also custom and compound predicates.

B.2.1 *Standard predicates*

This is the `Predicate` interface:

```
public interface Predicate {
    boolean matches(Exchange exchange);
}
```

First we'll cover the common use cases for using predicates.

SYNTAX SUGAR

Camel provides syntax sugar for working with predicates. Suppose you want to filter messages using the Message Filter EIP and only allow "Camel" messages to pass through the filter. This can easily be defined in a Camel Java DSL route, as follows:

```
from("direct:quotes")
    .filter(body().contains("Camel")).to("direct:camelQuotes");
```

As you can see, you can define the predicate as if the body contained the word "Camel" using the fluent builder style.

Implementing this example using Spring XML requires a different approach, because Spring XML is not Java code and it doesn't provide the same level of syntax sugar.

USING PREDICATES WITH SPRING XML

When you use Spring XML, you can use expression languages such as Simple (covered in appendix A). For example, you can leverage Simple as follows:

```
<route>
    <from uri="direct:quotes"/>
    <filter>
        <simple>${body} contains 'Camel'</simple>
        <to uri="direct:camelQuotes"/>
    </filter>
</route>
```

Although Camel provides a lot of built-in predicates to support many common use case, there may be situations where you need to implement a custom predicate.

B.2.2 *Using custom predicates*

Suppose you need to filter messages using a more complex algorithm, or you just feel more comfortable using Java code to compute the predicate. In that case, you can implement a custom predicate.

Listing B.3 Implementing a custom predicate

```
public class MyPredicate implements Predicate {

    public boolean matches(Exchange exchange) {
        String body = exchange.getIn().getBody(String.class);
        if (body.contains("Camel")) {
            return true;
        } else if (body.startsWith("Secret")) {
            return true;
```

```
        }
        return false;
    }
}
```

As you can see in listing B.3, it's easy to implement a custom predicate. All you have to do is implement the `matches` method and return either `true` or `false`.

Using a custom predicate in a route is just as easy. You simply provide an instance of it to the filter EIP:

```
from("direct:quotes")
    .filter(new MyPredicate()).to("direct:camelQuotes");
```

When using custom predicates in Spring XML, you have to define the predicate as a bean, and then use the method call expression to invoke the predicate. Here's the equivalent example in Spring XML:

```
<bean id="myPredicate" class="camelinaction.MyPredicate"/>

<camelContext id="camel" xmlns="http://camel.apache.org/schema/spring">
    <route>
        <from uri="direct:quotes"/>
        <filter>
            <method ref="myPredicate"/>
            <to uri="direct:camelQuotes"/>
        <filter>
    </route>
</camelContext>
```

Before we end this appendix, we want to show you one last thing: how to combine other predicates into a compound predicate.

B.2.3 *Using compound predicates*

You may have a number of existing predicates you want to use together. For example, you may want to define a predicate as follows: *Is the message a `String` message and either a Camel or a secret quote?*

In this definition, you have three predicates:

- A Is the message a `String` type?
- B Is the message a `"Camel"` quote?
- c Is the message a `"Secret"` quote?

You just have to use these three predicates together in a compound predicate:

```
A and (B or C)
```

Implementing this in Camel can be done with the help of `PredicateBuilder`, which provides a range of predicate-related methods. The builder has methods to combine two predicates using the binary operators and and or. You can then define this in your Camel routes, like this:

```
Predicate a = body().isInstanceOf(String.class);
Predicate b = body().contains("Camel");
Predicate c = body().startsWith("Secret");

Predicate bc = PredicateBuilder.or(b, c);
Predicate compound = PredicateBuilder.and(a, bc);

from("direct:quotes")
    .filter(compound).to("direct:camelQuotes");
```

First you define the three predicates. Then, to build the compound predicate, you first combine predicates b and c together using the or operator. Then this combined predicate is combined with the a predicate using the and operator.

B.3   Summary

This appendix covered two central concepts used in Camel: expressions and predicates. Both are used throughout Camel and this book.

In many normal use cases, the built-in predicates and expressions should be sufficient. In this appendix, you learned how to use custom expressions and predicates. This should give you enough information that you'll have no trouble using predicates and expressions with Camel.

appendix C
The producer
and consumer templates

Throughout this book, you've seen the `ProducerTemplate` used as an easy way of sending messages to a Camel endpoint. While it was simple to understand in those cases, there are many more options to the `ProducerTemplate`. There is also an analog for consumers—the `ConsumerTemplate`, which makes consuming messages easy.

Both of these templates are inspired by the template utility classes in the Spring Framework that simplify access to an API. In Spring, you may have used a `JmsTemplate` or `JdbcTemplate` to simplify access to the JMS and JDBC APIs. In the case of Camel, the `ProducerTemplate` and `ConsumerTemplate` interfaces allow you to easily work with producers and consumers.

By "easily work," we mean you can send a message to any kind of Camel component in only one line of code. For example, the following code sends a JMS text message to the ActiveMQ JMS queue named `quotes`:

```
producerTemplate.sendBody("activemq:quotes", "Camel Rocks");
```

Anyone who has worked with the JMS API will know that it takes quite a bit of work to replicate what Camel does in that single line of code.

In this appendix, we'll show you how to use the `ProducerTemplate` and `Consumer-Template` in detail.

C.1   *The ProducerTemplate*

The `ProducerTemplate` has a lot of methods that at first may seem a bit overwhelming. But these methods make it powerful and flexible, which in turn makes it a time saver in many situations.

Table C.1 lists the most commonly used `ProducerTemplate` methods. Notice that the table lists two sets of methods: *send* and *request* methods. It's very important to know the difference between these two. *Send* methods are used for InOnly-style messaging, where you send a message to a given endpoint and don't expect any reply. *Request* methods are used for InOut-style messaging, where you send a message to a given endpoint and expect and wait for a reply.

Table C.1 The most commonly used `ProducerTemplate` methods

Method	MEP	Description
sendBody	InOnly	Sends a message payload to a destination.
sendBodyAndHeader	InOnly	Sends a message payload and a header to a destination.
sendBodyAndHeaders	InOnly	Sends a message payload with a map of headers to a destination.
requestBody	InOut	Sends a message payload to a destination. The reply from the destination is returned.
requestBodyAndHeader	InOut	Sends a message payload and a header to a destination. The reply from the destination is returned.
requestBodyAndHeaders	InOut	Sends a message payload with a map of headers to a destination. The reply from the destination is returned.

The `ProducerTemplate` has many variations on these methods, which you'll learn to appreciate over time. Also, for each of these methods there's a corresponding asynchronous method. If you wanted to send a message body asynchronously, you could use the `asyncSendBody` method instead of the `sendBody` method. Chapter 10 details these methods and how to use them.

C.1.1 *Using the ProducerTemplate*

Here's an example of how to use the `ProducerTemplate` to send a message to a JMS topic that's used to audit orders.

Listing C.1 Using a `ProducerTemplate` to send a message to a JMS topic

```
public class AuditOrderBean {
    private ProducerTemplate template;
    public AuditOrderBean(CamelContext context) {          ❶ Creates new
        template = context.createProducerTemplate();            template
    }
    public void auditOrder(String order) {                 ❷ Sends JMS
        template.sendBody(                                     message
            "activemq:topic:order.audit", order);             to topic
    }
}
```

In the constructor, you create a new instance of the `ProducerTemplate` ❶ by invoking `createProducerTemplate` on the `CamelContext`. This template is then used when sending the audit messages ❷.

To try this out for yourself, find the appendixC/producer directory in the book's source and run the following Maven command:

```
mvn test –Dtest=ProducerTemplateInOnlyTest
```

If you were instead accessing an HTTP service that returned a reply, you would need to use one of the request methods from table C.1. Here's how you could do this.

Listing C.2 Using a `ProducerTemplate` to get a reply from an endpoint

```
public class OrderStatusBean {
    private ProducerTemplate template;

    public OrderStatusBean() {
    }

    public OrderStatusBean(CamelContext context) {
        setTemplate(context.createProducerTemplate());
    }

    public void setTemplate(ProducerTemplate template) {
        this.template = template;
    }

    public String orderStatus(String orderId) {
        return template.requestBody(
            "http://localhost:8080/order/status?id="       ❶ Requests result
            + orderId,                                          from web service
            null, String.class);
    }
}
```

Here you use the `requestBody` method ❶ to invoke a remote HTTP service with a header `id` set to the specified order ID. You then get the order status returned as a string. Notice that you pass in `null` for the body because this particular web service only needs the `id` header. The HTTP producer will send an HTTP GET request in this case.

This example is found in the appendixC/producer directory of the book's source and can be tested using the following Maven command:

```
mvn test –Dtest=ProducerTemplateInOutTest
```

Rather than creating these templates by directly invoking the `CamelContext`, you can use features built into the Spring DSL to do this. The `template` and `consumer-Template` elements within the `camelContext` element allow you to create a template and then refer to it later by using its ID. Let's look at this in action.

Listing C.3 Declaring reusable producer and consumer templates

```
<bean id="orderStatus" class="camelinaction.OrderStatusBean">
  <property name="template" ref="producerTemplate"/>        Injects Producer-
</bean>                                                   ❶ Template bean

<camelContext xmlns="http://camel.apache.org/schema/spring">
  <template id="producerTemplate"/>                          Creates Producer-
                                                         ❷ Template bean
```

```
<consumerTemplate id="consumerTemplate"/>
<route>
  <from uri="activemq:order.status"/>
  <bean ref="orderStatus" method="orderStatus"/>
</route>
</camelContext>
```

❸ **Creates Consumer-Template bean**

Within the camelContext element, you declare reusable templates (❷ and ❸) that you can wire into the OrderStatusBean from listing C.2 by using the bean ID ❶.

NOTE   You may find the template element name a bit confusing. Why not use the name producerTemplate to align with the consumerTemplate element? At first, in Camel, there was only the producer template so the XML element was named template. When the consumer template was introduced, the template element name was kept to be backwards compatible.

You can find listing C.3 along with a test case in the appendixC/producer directory. Run the test case with the following Maven command:

```
mvn test –Dtest=ProducerTemplateDefinedInSpringTest
```

Next, we'll focus on the ConsumerTemplate, which you may not have seen much of yet.

C.2   *The ConsumerTemplate*

The ConsumerTemplate doesn't have as many methods as the ProducerTemplate. It only works using the InOnly messaging style, where you use it to poll a given endpoint for a message. Table C.2 lists the methods you're most likely to use.

Table C.2   The most commonly used ConsumerTemplate methods

Method	MEP	Description
receive	InOnly	Polls an endpoint to receive a message and will wait until a message exists. The entire message is returned.
receive(Timeout)	InOnly	Polls an endpoint to receive a message, and will wait until a timeout occurs. The entire message is returned.
receiveNoWait	InOnly	Polls an endpoint to receive a message, but will not wait if a message doesn't exist. The entire message is returned.
receiveBody	InOnly	Polls an endpoint to receive a message, and will wait until a message exists. Only the message body is returned.
receiveBody(Timeout)	InOnly	Polls an endpoint to receive a message, and will wait until a timeout occurs. Only the message body is returned.
receiveBodyNoWait	InOnly	Polls an endpoint to receive a message, but will not wait if a message doesn't exist. Only the message body is returned.

Let's take a moment to see how you could use the ConsumerTemplate to solve a problem that's been asked about again and again on the Camel mailing lists: how can you use Camel to empty a JMS queue?

C.2.1 Using the ConsumerTemplate

You can use the `ConsumerTemplate` much like the `ProducerTemplate`. For example, you can use it to empty a JMS queue containing new orders, as shown in listing C.4. Notice how easily you can use the `receiveBody` method from table C.2 to retrieve a message from a JMS queue.

Listing C.4   Using the `ConsumerTemplate` to poll a JMS queue

```
public class OrderCollectorBean {
    private ConsumerTemplate consumer;

    public void setConsumer(ConsumerTemplate consumer) {          ◁─ Sets Consumer-
        this.consumer = consumer;                                    Template on
    }                                                             ❶ bean

    public String getOrders() {
        String order = "";
        String orders = "";

        while (order != null) {
            order = consumer.receiveBody(
                "activemq:orders",                     ❷ Consumes message
                1000, String.class);                      from queue
            if (order != null) {
                orders = orders + "," + order;
            }
        }
        return orders;
    }
}
```

The `OrderCollectorBean` bean uses a setter for the `ConsumerTemplate` ❶ so you can inject it using Spring as follows:

```
<bean id="orderCollectorBean" class="camelinaction.OrderCollectorBean">
  <property name="consumer" ref="consumerTemplate"/>
</bean>
```

Of course, this requires that you already have a `consumerTemplate` element defined, as shown in listing C.3.

> **TIP**   The `template` and `consumerTemplate` elements are optional. If you have no need to refer to them by ID or configure any options on them, you can just inject them into your bean by type, using Spring's `@Autowired` annotation. This is possible because Camel creates a default instance of each on startup.

You can then empty the order queue by looping until a `null` body is returned ❷. By using the `receiveBody` method with a timeout of 1000 milliseconds, you'll wait for 1 second before returning a `null` when the queue is empty.

This example can be found in the appendixC/consumer directory of the book's source. Run the test case with the following Maven command:

```
mvn test
```

The test case essentially populates the "orders" queue in ActiveMQ with a few messages and then invokes the `OrderCollectorBean` to retrieve them.

C.3   *Summary*

In this appendix we looked at the extremely useful producer and consumer templates. These two templates give you a way of quickly accessing any Camel endpoint with one method call. In addition to the examples presented in this appendix, the `ProducerTemplate` is used throughout the book.

appendix D
The Camel community

As with any open source project, the community behind it is extremely important. We think of *community* as an all-encompassing term for the official website, mailing lists, the issue tracker, Camel users, projects based on or extending Camel, and much more. It's hard to measure how vibrant a community is when it has this many moving parts, but it's important. Having a stagnant or small community will make your (the user's) experience more difficult when things go wrong and during development in general. We think Camel's community is highly active and expanding, so you are in luck!

In this appendix we cover some main aspects of the Camel community.

D.1 Apache Camel website

The Apache Camel website, http://camel.apache.org, will be your main resource when using Camel. You may have already noticed that we reference pages from the Camel website throughout the book. That's no mistake—it's a good resource for us too.

On the Camel website, you'll find links for downloads, documentation, support, and many other topics.

D.2 FuseSource

FuseSource is a company that offers a productized version of Apache Camel, as well as training, consulting, and enterprise subscriptions to help IT organizations build mission-critical applications with Apache Camel. FuseSource does the same for other popular Apache projects, including ServiceMix, ActiveMQ, and CXF. The FuseSource team includes founders, PMC members, and many of the committers to Apache Camel, and they know the code better than anyone else does. The FuseSource website includes free downloads, documentation, training videos, webinars, and other tools to help developers get started and be successful with Apache Camel.

D.3   *Camel Tooling*

Rider is a visual designer tool from FuseSource (http://fusesource.com) for creating, editing, testing, and debugging Camel routes. Rider lets you drag and drop all the enterprise integration patterns supported by Apache Camel onto a canvas and easily wire them together and configure them. You can use Rider as a tool to visualize existing routes, modify them, or create brand new integrations.

Rider comes in two flavors: a web version which can be used with any modern web browser, or as an Eclipse plugin.

The web version is very handy for viewing and editing routing rules running inside your running application, whether it's in a standalone JVM or inside Apache Tomcat, Apache ServiceMix, or some Java EE container. Figure D.1 shows using Rider inside the Google Chrome web browser to edit routing rules from a web application running on top of Apache Tomcat.

If you use Eclipse as your IDE, using the Rider Eclipse plugin might be an easier option for you to choose, particularly if you want to design and edit your Camel routes as part of your development process. Figure D.2 shows using the Rider Eclipse plugin to edit a Spring XML containing Camel routing rules.

Visit the FuseSource Rider website (http://rider.fusesource.org) for links to all the various Rider documentation, screencasts, and download links.

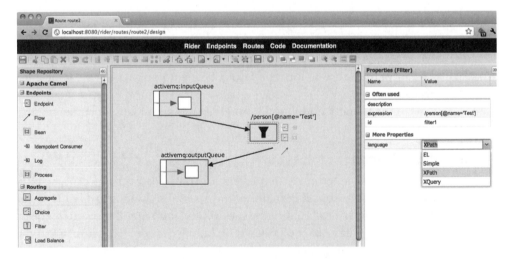

Figure D.1   Rider web tooling visualizes the route. You can drag and drop EIPs from the palette to the canvas to design the route at design time.

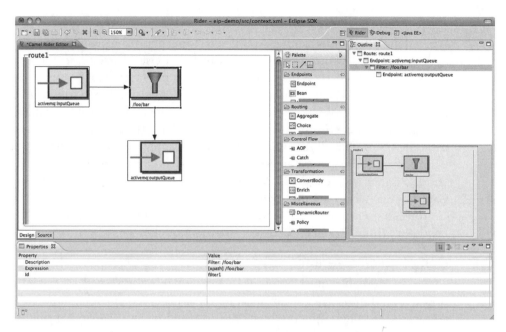

Figure D.2 Rider Eclipse tooling allows developers to design routes using the Eclipse IDE.

D.4 *Camel-extra project*

Camel ships with a large number of components, but there are also other components available separately from the camel-extra project at Google Code (http://
code.google. com/p/camel-extra). The main motivator for not including all Camel
components in the main distribution is licensing. Apache Camel is developed and
distributed under the Apache License, version 2. The camel-extra project contains
components that integrate with libraries that have GPL and LGPL licenses, which are
incompatible with Apache.

At camel-extra, you'll find components for integrating with the following, among
others:

- The Esper Event Stream Processing library
- The Hibernate ORM tool
- JBoss Application Server

The components from camel-extra are not officially affiliated with or supported by
Apache.

D.5   JIRA, mailing lists, and IRC

When things don't go as planned, you'll need to get help from people in the Camel community. If you know you have a problem with a demonstrative test case or have a feature request, you can create a ticket in Camel's JIRA instance: http://issues.apache.org/activemq/browse/CAMEL. From here, one of the Camel developers will assign the ticket to themselves and possibly commit a fix for the issue. It's also acceptable to attach a source code patch that fixes the issue directly to the JIRA ticket (http://camel.apache.org/contributing.html). This allows a Camel developer to apply your patch to the Camel source.

When you have general questions, you can send a message to the Camel user list (http://camel.apache.org/mailing-lists.html), which will be answered by one of the Camel developers or another Camel user.

You can even chat in real time with a Camel developer or user on the Camel IRC chat room (http://camel.apache.org/irc-room.html).

D.6   Camel quick reference card

There's a printable quick reference card available for several of Camel's EIPs at dzone.com (http://refcardz.dzone.com/refcardz/enterprise-integration). This card contains a short description of each EIP, followed by Java DSL and Spring XML snippets that you can reuse in your own applications.

D.7   Other resources

The Camel website has an extensive collection of links to external articles, blogs, projects, presentations, podcasts, and other sources that cover Camel (http://camel.apache.org/articles.html). There's also a link collection to other third-party Camel projects and companies who use Camel (http://camel.apache.org/user-stories.html). If you've written a blog entry or article, or your company uses Camel and wants to have a link added, please contact the Camel team on the mailing list.

appendix E
Akka and Camel

by Martin Krasser

Akka aims to be the platform for the next-generation, event-driven, scalable, and fault-tolerant architectures on the JVM. One of the core features of Akka is an implementation of the Actor model. It alleviates the developer from having to deal with explicit locking and thread management. Using the Actor model raises the abstraction level and provides a better platform for building correct concurrent and scalable applications.

Akka comes with a Camel integration module that allows Akka actors to interact with communication partners over a great variety of protocols and APIs. This appendix presents selected Akka-Camel integration features by example. In particular, it covers the following:

- An introduction to Akka's Actor API
- Implementing consumer actors for receiving messages from Camel endpoints
- Implementing producer actors for sending messages to Camel endpoints
- Using and customizing Akka's `CamelService`
- Camel's `ActorComponent` for exchanging messages with actors

We'll also look at a complete routing example that combines many of the features presented in this appendix.

The examples only scratch the surface of what can be done with Akka. Interested readers may want to refer to the Akka online documentation for details (http://akkasource.org). The Actor model is also discussed on Wikipedia: http://en.wikipedia.org/wiki/Actor_model. The code examples in this appendix are available in the source code for the book, and they include a README file that explains how to build and run them.

Akka offers both a Scala API and a Java API for actors. Here, only the Scala API will be covered. We'll assume that you already have a basic knowledge of the Scala programming language.

E.1   Introducing the Akka-Camel integration

In the Actor model, each object is an actor; an actor is an entity that has a mailbox and a behavior. Messages can be exchanged between actors, and they'll be buffered in the mailbox. Upon receiving a message, the behavior of the actor is executed. An actor's behavior can be any piece of code, such as code that changes internal state, sends a number of messages to other actors, creates a number of actors, or assumes new behavior for the next message to be received.

An important property of the Actor model is that there's no shared state between actors; all communications happen by means of messages. Messages are exchanged asynchronously, but Akka supports waiting for responses as well. Also, messages are always processed sequentially by an actor. There's no concurrent execution of a single actor instance, but different actor instances can process their messages concurrently.

Akka, itself, is written in Scala, so applications often use Akka's Scala API for exchanging messages with actors. But this is not always an option, especially in the domain of application integration. Existing applications often can't be modified to use the Scala API directly, but can use file transfer on FTP servers or low-level TCP to exchange messages with other applications. For existing applications to communicate with actors, a separate integration layer is needed, and this is where Camel fits in: Camel is designed around the messaging paradigm, and it supports asynchronous message exchanges as well.

For implementing an integration layer between Akka actors and third-party applications or components, Akka provides the akka-camel module (http://doc.akkasource. org/camel). With the akka-camel module, it's almost trivial to implement message exchanges with actors over protocols and APIs such as HTTP, SOAP, TCP, FTP, SMTP, JMS, and others. Actors can both consume messages from and produce messages for Camel endpoints.

Another important feature of the akka-camel module is that it fully supports Camel's asynchronous, nonblocking routing engine: asynchronous message exchanges with actors can be extended to a number of additional protocols and APIs. Furthermore, all Camel components are supported in a generic way: whenever a new Camel component is released by the Camel community, it can readily be used to exchange messages with Akka actors.

The following section gives a brief introduction to Akka's Actor API and shows how to create actors and exchange messages with them.

E.2   Getting started with Akka actors

Let's start with a simple example: an actor that prints any message it receives to std-out. When it receives a special stop message, the actor stops itself.

An actor implementation class must extend the `Actor` trait and implement the `receive` partial function. Incoming messages are matched against the case patterns defined in `receive`.

```
import akka.actor.Actor

class SimpleActor extends Actor {
  protected def receive = {
    case "stop" => self.stop
    case msg    => println("message = %s" format msg)
  }
}
```

If one of the patterns matches, the statement after `=>` is executed. Akka's Actor API doesn't impose any constraints on the message type and format—any Scala object can be sent to an actor.

Before sending a message to the preceding actor, clients need to create and start an instance of `SimpleActor`. This is done with the `actorOf` factory method, which returns an actor reference, and by calling the `start` method on that reference. This can be done as follows, where the client creates the actor and sends two messages to it:

```
import akka.actor.Actor._

val simpleActor = actorOf[SimpleActor].start

simpleActor ! "hello akka"
simpleActor ! "stop"
```

The actor reference, once it's created, is also used for sending messages to the actor. With the `!` (bang) operator, clients send messages with fire-and-forget semantics. The `!` operator adds the message to the actor's mailbox, and the actor processes the message asynchronously. The preceding example first sends a `"hello akka"` string that matches the second pattern in the `receive` method. The message is therefore written to `stdout`. The `"stop"` message sent afterwards is matched by the first pattern, which stops the actor. Note that sending a message to a stopped actor throws an exception.

To run the example from the appendixE directory, enter `sbt run` on the command line and select `camelinaction.SectionE2` from the list of main classes.

> **NOTE** The source code for this book contains a README file in the appendixE directory that explains how to install and set up the Simple Build Tool (sbt). All the examples in this appendix can be run by executing `sbt run` from the command line. This command displays a menu, from which you can choose the example to run by its number.

The preceding example only uses a small part of Akka's Actor API. It demonstrates how clients can send messages to actors and how actors can match and process these messages. The next step is to add an additional interface to the actor so that it can receive messages via a Camel endpoint.

E.3   *Consuming messages from Camel endpoints*

If you want to make actors accessible via Camel endpoints, actor classes need to mixin the `Consumer` trait and implement the `endpointUri` method. `Consumer` actors can be used for both one-way and request-response messaging.

E.3.1   *One-way messaging*

The following listing extends the example from the previous section and enables the actor to receive messages from a SEDA endpoint.

Listing E.1   Actor as consumer receiving messages from a SEDA endpoint

```
import akka.actor.Actor
import akka.camel.{Consumer, Message}

class SedaConsumer extends Actor with Consumer {
  def endpointUri = "seda:example"

  protected def receive = {
    case Message("stop", headers) => self.stop
    case Message(body, headers)   => println("message = %s" format body)
  }
}
```

The `endpointUri` method is implemented to return a SEDA endpoint URI. This causes the actor to consume messages from the `seda:example` queue once it is started. One important difference, compared to `SimpleActor`, is that the received messages are of type `Message`, which are immutable representations of Camel messages. A `Message` object can be used for pattern matching, and the message body and headers can be bound to variables, as shown in listing E.1.

For any consumer actor to receive messages, an application needs to start a `CamelService` before starting a consumer actor:

```
import akka.actor.Actor._
import akka.camel._

val service = CamelServiceManager.startCamelService

service.awaitEndpointActivation(1) {
  actorOf[SedaConsumer].start
}

for (template <- CamelContextManager.template) {
    template.sendBody("seda:example", "hello akka-camel")
    template.sendBody("seda:example", "stop")
}

service.stop
```

A `CamelService` can be started with `CamelServiceManager.startCamelService`. The started `CamelService` instance is returned from the `startCamelService` method call.

When a consumer actor is started, the `CamelService` is notified and it will create and start (activate) a route from the specified endpoint to the actor. This is done asynchronously, so if an application wants to wait for a certain number of endpoints to be activated, it can do so with the `awaitEndpointActivation` method. This method blocks until the expected number of endpoints have been activated in the block that follows that method.

The application is then ready to produce messages to the `seda:example` queue. A Camel `ProducerTemplate` for sending messages can be obtained via `CamelContext-Manager.template`.

This returns an instance of `Option[ProducerTemplate]` that can be used with a for comprehension. If the `CamelService` has been started, the body of the for comprehension will be executed once with the current `ProducerTemplate` bound to the `template` variable. If the `CamelService` hasn't been started, the for body won't be executed at all.

Alternatively, applications may also use `CamelContextManager.mandatory-Template` which returns the `ProducerTemplate` directly or throws an `IllegalState-Exception` if the `CamelService` hasn't been started.

The application first sends a message that will be printed to `stdout`, and then it sends a special stop message that stops the actor. Alternatively, clients can also send `Message` objects directly via the native Actor API:

```
actor ! Message("hello akka-camel")
```

Finally, the application gracefully shuts down the `CamelService`.

`SedaConsumer` is an actor that doesn't reply to the initial sender. Request-response message exchanges require a minor addition, as shown in the next section for a consumer actor with a Jetty endpoint.

E.3.2 *Request-response messaging*

Listing E.2 shows how an actor can reply to the initial sender using the `self.reply` method. In this example, the initial sender is an HTTP client that communicates with the actor over a Jetty endpoint.

Listing E.2 Actor acting as consumer which sends back replies to sender

```
class HttpConsumer1 extends Actor with Consumer {
  def endpointUri = "jetty:http://0.0.0.0:8811/consumer1"

  protected def receive = {
    case msg: Message => self.reply("received %s"
                                    format msg.bodyAs[String])
  }
}
```

NOTE Valid initial senders can either be other actors or Camel routes to that actor. This is an implementation detail: for the receiving actor, both initial sender types appear to be actor references.

When POSTing a message to http://localhost:8811/consumer1, the actor converts the received message body to a `String` and prepends `"received "` to it. The result is returned to the HTTP client with the `self.reply` method. The `self` object is the self-reference to the current actor.

The reply message is a plain `String` that's internally converted to a Camel `Message` before returning it to the Jetty endpoint. If applications additionally want to add or modify response headers, they can do so by returning a `Message` object containing the response body and headers. The next example creates an XML response and sets the `Content-Type` header to `application/xml`.

Listing E.3   An actor sending back XML messages as reply to sender

```
class HttpConsumer2 extends Actor with Consumer {
  def endpointUri = "jetty:http://0.0.0.0:8811/consumer2"

  protected def receive = {
    case msg: Message => {
      val body = "<received>%s</received>" format msg.bodyAs[String]
      val headers = Map("Content-Type" -> "application/xml")
      self.reply(Message(body, headers))
    }
  }
}
```

Consumer actors wait for their clients to initiate message exchanges. If actors themselves want to initiate a message exchange with a Camel endpoint, a different approach must be taken.

E.4   *Producing messages to Camel endpoints*

For producing messages to Camel endpoints, actors have two options. They can either use a Camel `ProducerTemplate` directly or mixin the `Producer` trait in the actor implementation class. This section will cover the use of the `Producer` trait. The use of the Camel `ProducerTemplate` is explained in appendix C.

The advantage of using the `Producer` trait is that actors fully leverage Camel's asynchronous routing engine. To produce messages to a Camel endpoint, an actor must implement the `endpointUri` method from the `Producer` trait, as follows.

Listing E.4   An actor as a producer sending messages to the defined HTTP endpoint

```
import akka.actor.Actor
import akka.camel.Producer

class HttpProducer1 extends Actor with Producer {
  def endpointUri = "http://localhost:8811/consumer2"
}
```

In this example, any message sent to an instance of `HttpProducer1` will be POSTed to http://localhost:8811/consumer2, which is the endpoint of the consumer actor in listing E.3 (these two actors are communicating over HTTP).

In the following code example, an application sends a message to the producer actor with the `!!` (bangbang) operator, which means it sends and receives eventually:

the message is sent to the actor asynchronously, but the caller also waits for a response.

```
import akka.actor.Actor._
import akka.camel.{Failure, Message}

val httpProducer1 = actorOf[HttpProducer1].start

httpProducer1 !! "Camel rocks" match {
 case Some(m: Message) => println("response = %s" format m.bodyAs[String])
 case Some(f: Failure) => println("failure = %s" format f.cause.getMessage)
 case None             => println("timeout")
}
```

The return type of !! is Option[Any]. For a producer actor at runtime, the type can be one of the following:

- Some(Message) for a normal response
- Some(Failure) if the message exchange with the endpoint failed
- None if waiting for a response timed out

The timeout for a response is defined by the timeout attribute on the actor reference (ActorRef.timeout). The default value is 5000 (ms) and it can be changed by applications.

As you've probably realized, HttpProducer1 doesn't implement a receive method. This is because the Producer trait provides a default receive implementation that's inherited by HttpProducer1. The default behavior of Producer.receive is to send messages to the specified endpoint and to return the result to the initial sender. In the preceding example, the initial sender obtains the result from the !! method call.

Actor classes can override the Producer.receiveAfterProduce method to, for example, forward the result to another actor, instead of returning it to the original sender. In this case, the original sender should use the ! operator for sending the message; otherwise it will wait for a response until timeout. In the following example, the producer actor simply writes the result to stdout instead of returning it to the sender.

```
class HttpProducer2 extends Actor with Producer {
  def endpointUri = "http://localhost:8811/consumer3"

  override protected def receiveAfterProduce = {
    case m: Message => println("response = %s" format m.bodyAs[String])
    case f: Failure => println("failure = %s" format f.cause.getMessage)
  }
}
```

A producer actor by default initiates in-out message exchanges with the specified endpoint. For initiating in-only message exchanges, producer implementations must either override the Producer.oneway method to return true or mixin the Oneway trait. The following code shows the latter approach by mixin the Oneway trait:

```
import akka.actor.Actor
import akka.camel.{Oneway, Producer}

class JmsProducer extends Actor with Producer with Oneway {
  def endpointUri = "jms:queue:test"
}
```

For producer and consumer actors to work with Camel, applications need to start the CamelService, which sets up the CamelContext for an application. The next section shows some examples of how applications can customize the process of setting up a CamelContext.

E.5   *Customizing CamelService*

When started, a CamelService creates a default CamelContext and makes it accessible via the CamelContextManager singleton. Applications can access the current Camel-Context within a for (context <- CamelContextManager.context) { … } comprehension and make any modifications they want. Alternatively, a CamelContext can also be obtained directly via CamelContextManager.mandatoryContext. This will throw an IllegalStateException if the CamelService hasn't been started.

But modifying a CamelContext after it's been started isn't always an option. For example, applications may want to use their own CamelContext implementations or to make some modifications before the CamelContext is started. This can be achieved either programmatically or declaratively, as explained in the following subsections.

E.5.1   *Programmatic customization*

If an application wants to disable JMX, for example, it should do so before the Camel-Context is started. This can be achieved by manually initializing the CamelContext-Manager and calling disableJMX on the created CamelContext:

```
import akka.camel._

CamelContextManager.init
CamelContextManager.context.disableJMX

CamelServiceManager.startCamelService
```

By default, the CamelContextManager.init method creates a DefaultCamelContext instance, but applications may also pass any other CamelContext instance as an argument to the init method:

```
import akka.camel._

val camelContext: CamelContext = ...

CamelContextManager.init(camelContext)
CamelContextManager.context.disableJMX

CamelServiceManager.startCamelService
```

When the CamelService is started, it will also start the user-defined CamelContext.

E.5.2 Declarative customization

Alternatively, a `CamelService` can be created and configured within a Spring application context. The following Spring XML configuration uses the Akka and Camel XML namespaces to set up a `CamelService` and a `CamelContext` respectively. The custom `CamelContext` is injected into the `CamelService`.

Listing E.5   Spring XML file setting up Akka and Camel

```
<beans xmlns="http://www.springframework.org/schema/beans"
       xmlns:xsi="http://www.w3.org/2001/XMLSchema-instance"
       xmlns:akka="http://www.akkasource.org/schema/akka"
       xmlns:camel="http://camel.apache.org/schema/spring"
       xsi:schemaLocation="
http://www.springframework.org/schema/beans
http://www.springframework.org/schema/beans/spring-beans-2.5.xsd
http://www.akkasource.org/schema/akka
http://scalablesolutions.se/akka/akka-1.0.xsd
http://camel.apache.org/schema/spring
http://camel.apache.org/schema/spring/camel-spring.xsd">

  <camel:camelContext id="camelContext">              Camel routes
                                                       go here
  </camel:camelContext>
                                                  ❶ Akka
  <akka:camel-service id="camelService">            CamelService
    <akka:camel-context ref="camelContext" />
  </akka:camel-service>

</beans>
```

After creating an application context from the XML configuration, a `CamelService` ❶ runs and listens for consumer actors to be started. If an application wants to interact with the `CamelService` directly, it can obtain the running `CamelService` instance either via `CamelServiceManager.service`, `CamelServiceManager.mandatoryService`, or directly from the Spring application context.

The following code shows how you can use the former approach for obtaining the `CamelService` from the `CamelServiceMananger`:

```
import org.springframework.context.support.ClassPathXmlApplicationContext
import akka.actor.Actor._
import akka.camel._

val appctx = new ClassPathXmlApplicationContext("/sample.xml")
val camelService = CamelServiceManager.mandatoryService
                                                          Do something
                                                          with CamelService
appctx.destroy
```

When the application context (`appctx`) is destroyed, the `CamelService` and the `CamelContext` are shut down as well.

In all the examples so far, routes to actors have been automatically created by the `CamelService`. Whenever a consumer actor has been started, this was detected by the `CamelService` and a route from the actor's endpoint to the actor itself was added to the current `CamelContext`. Alternatively, applications can also define custom routes to actors by using Akka's `ActorComponent`.

E.6   *The Actor component*

Accessing an actor from a Camel route is done with the Actor component, a Camel component for producing messages to actors. For example, when starting `Seda-Consumer` from listing E.1, the `CamelService` adds the following (simplified) route to the `CamelContext`:

```
from("seda:example").to("actor:uuid:<actoruuid>")
```

The route starts from `seda:example` and goes to the started `SedaConsumer` instance, where `<actoruuid>` is the consumer actor's UUID. An actor's UUID can be obtained from its reference. Endpoint URIs starting with the `actor` scheme are used to produce messages to actors.

The Actor component isn't only intended for internal use but can also be used by user-defined Camel routes to access any actor; in this case, the target actor doesn't need to implement the `Consumer` trait. The Actor component also supports Camel's asynchronous routing engine and allows asynchronous in-only and in-out message exchanges with actors.

Listing E.6 shows an example: a user-defined Camel route that sends a message to an instance of `HttpProducer1` (the producer actor from listing E.4). This producer actor sends a message to http://localhost:8811/consumer2. If the communication with the HTTP service succeeds, the producer actor returns a `Message` object containing the service response or a `Failure` object with the cause of the failure. If the producer can't connect to the service, for example, the failure cause will be a `ConnectException`. This exception can be handled in the route. Other exceptions are possible, but they aren't included here, to keep the example simple.

Listing E.6   Camel route sending message to Akka actor

```
import java.net.ConnectException
import org.apache.camel.builder.RouteBuilder
import akka.actor.Actor._
import akka.actor.Uuid
import akka.camel._

class CustomRoute(uuid: Uuid) extends RouteBuilder {
  def configure = {
    from("direct:test")
      .onException(classOf[ConnectException])
        .handled(true).transform.constant("feel bad").end        Camel route
      .to("actor:uuid:%s" format uuid)              ◁───┘ sending to actor
  }
}

val producer = actorOf[HttpProducer1].start

CamelServiceManager.startCamelService
```

```
for (context  <- CamelContextManager.context;
    template <- CamelContextManager.template) {
  context.addRoutes(new CustomRoute(producer.uuid))
  template.requestBody("direct:test", "feel good", classOf[String]) match {
    case "<received>feel good</received>" => println("communication ok")
    case "feel bad" => println("communication failed")
    case _           => println("unexpected response")
  }
}
```

After starting the target actor and a `CamelService`, the application adds the user-defined route to the current `CamelContext`. It then uses a `ProducerTemplate` to initiate an in-out exchange with the route and tries to match the response, where the response either comes from the HTTP service or from the error handler.

We'll now move on to a more advanced example that applies many of the features described so far. It combines different actor types to a simple integration solution for transforming the content of a web page.

E.7 A routing example

Camel applications usually define message-processing routes with the Camel DSL. Akka applications can alternatively define networks of interconnected actors, in combination with consumer and producer actors, to set up message-processing routes.

This section shows a simple example of how to set up a message-processing route with actors. The goal of this example is to display the Akka homepage (http://akka-source.org) in a browser, with occurrences of *Akka* in the page content replaced with an uppercase *AKKA*. The example combines a consumer and a producer actor with another actor that transforms the content of the homepage.

The setup of the example application is sketched in figure E.1; the corresponding code is shown in listing E.7.

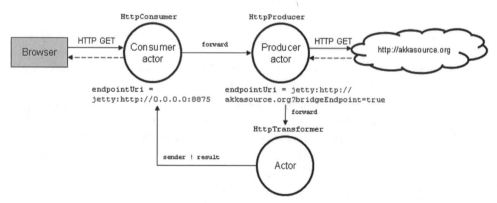

Figure E.1 The setup of the example application. A consumer and a producer actor provide connectivity to external systems. The consumer actor receives requests from a browser and forwards them to a producer actor, which fetches the HTML page. The HTML page is then forwarded to an actor that transforms the content of the page and returns the transformation result to the initial sender, so that it can be displayed in the browser.

Listing E.7 Akka consumer and producer example

```
import org.apache.camel.Exchange
import akka.actor.Actor._
import akka.actor.{Actor, ActorRef}
import akka.camel._

class HttpConsumer(producer: ActorRef) extends Actor with Consumer {
  def endpointUri = "jetty:http://0.0.0.0:8875/"
  protected def receive = {
    case msg => producer forward msg
  }
}

class HttpProducer(transformer: ActorRef) extends Actor with Producer {
  def endpointUri = "jetty:http://akkasource.org/?bridgeEndpoint=true"

  override protected def receiveBeforeProduce = {          ❶ Drops message
    case msg: Message =>                                      headers except
      msg.setHeaders(msg.headers(Set(Exchange.HTTP_PATH)))    HTTP_PATH
  }

  override protected def receiveAfterProduce = {          ❷ Forwards message
    case msg => transformer forward msg                      to transformer
  }
}
                                                         ❸ Transforms
class HttpTransformer extends Actor {                       the message
  protected def receive = {
    case msg: Failure => self.reply(msg)
    case msg: Message => self.reply(msg.transformBody[String] {
      _ replaceAll ("Akka ", "AKKA ")
    })
  }
}

CamelServiceManager.startCamelService

val httpTransformer = actorOf(new HttpTransformer).start
val httpProducer = actorOf(new HttpProducer(httpTransformer)).start
val httpConsumer = actorOf(new HttpConsumer(httpProducer)).start
```

HttpConsumer is an actor that accepts HTTP GET requests on port 8875 and is configured to forward requests to an instance of HttpProducer. When an actor forwards a message to another actor, it forwards the initial sender reference as well. This reference is needed later for returning the result to the initial sender.

A forwarded message causes the HttpProducer to send a GET request to http://akkasource.org. Before doing so, it drops all headers ❶ from the request message, except for the HTTP_PATH header, which is needed by the bridge endpoint. This preprocessing is done in the producer's receiveBeforeProduce method. The received HTML content from http://akkasource.org is then forwarded ❷ to an instance of HttpTransformer.

The HttpTransformer ❸ is an actor that replaces all occurrences of *Akka* in the message body with an uppercase *AKKA* and returns the result to the initial sender. The reference to the initial sender has been forwarded by the producer actor ❷.

After starting the `CamelService`, the actors are wired and started.

To run the example from the appendixE directory, enter `sbt run` on the command line, and select `camelinaction.SectionE7` from the list of main classes. Access http://localhost:8875 from a browser, and a transformed version of the Akka homepage should be displayed.

Finally, it should be noted that the actors and the Jetty endpoints in this example exchange messages asynchronously; no single thread is allocated or blocked for the full duration of an in-out message exchange. Although it's not critical for this example, exchanging messages asynchronously can help to save server resources, especially in applications with long-running request-response cycles and frequent client requests.

E.8 Summary

This appendix shows you how to exchange messages with Akka actors over protocols and APIs supported by the great variety of Camel components. You saw how consumer actors can receive messages from Camel endpoints and producer actors can send messages to Camel endpoints. Setting up a Camel endpoint for an actor is as easy as defining an endpoint URI for that actor.

The prerequisite for running consumer and producer actors is a started `Camel-Service` that manages an application's `CamelContext`. Applications can configure the `CamelService` either programmatically or declaratively based on custom Spring XML schemas provided by Akka and Camel.

You also saw how to use Akka's Actor component to access any actor from a user-defined Camel route. Actor endpoints are implemented by defining an `actor` endpoint URI in the route. A routing example finally demonstrated how to combine consumer and producer actors to develop a simple integration solution for transforming the content of a web page.

The features described in this appendix are those of Akka version 1.0. If you want to keep track of the latest development activities, get in touch with the Akka community via the Akka User List (http://groups.google.com/group/akka-user) and the Akka Developer List (http://groups.google.com/group/akka-dev). Your feedback is highly welcome.

index

Open Source ESBs in Action
Example Implementations in Mule
and ServiceMix
by Tijs Rademakers and Jos Dirksen

ISBN: 978-1-933988-21-4
528 pages
$44.99
September 2008

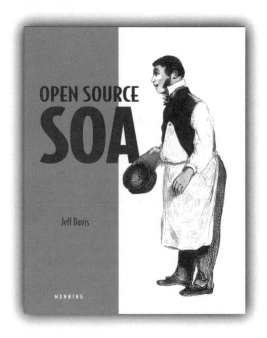

Open Source SOA
by Jeff Davis

ISBN: 978-1-933988-54-2
448 pages
$49.99
May 2009

MORE TITLES FROM MANNING

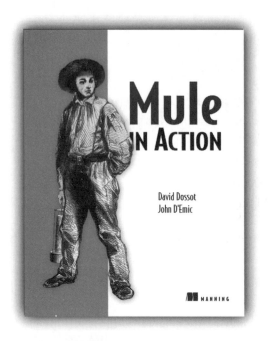

Mule in Action
by David Dossot and John D'Emic

ISBN: 978-1-933988-96-2
432 pages
$44.99
July 2009

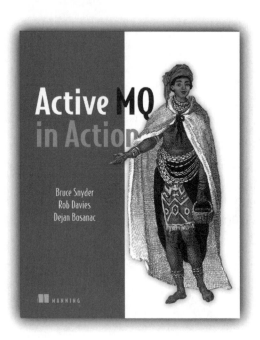

Active MQ in Action
by Bruce Snyder, Dejan Bosanac,
and Rob Davies

ISBN: 978-1-933988-94-8
375 pages
$44.99
January 2011

For ordering information go to www.manning.com

DSLs in Action
by Debasish Ghosh

ISBN: 978-1-935182-45-0
375 pages
$44.99
December 2010

Event Processing in Action
by Opher Etzion and Peter Niblett

ISBN: 978-1-935182-21-4
384 pages
$49.99
August 2010

For ordering information go to www.manning.com

MORE TITLES FROM MANNING

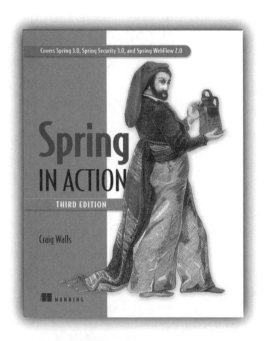

Spring in Action, Third Edition
by Craig Walls

> ISBN: 978-1-935182-35-1
> 700 pages
> $49.99
> March 2011

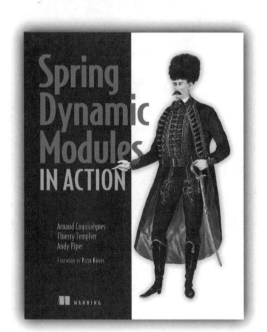

Spring Dynamic Modules in Action
by Arnaud Cogoluègnes,
   Thierry Templier, and Andy Piper

> ISBN: 978-1-935182-30-6
> 548 pages
> $59.99
> September 2010

For ordering information go to www.manning.com